MW00676483

The Gospel of The
KING
A COMMENTARY ON
MATTHEW

Stewart Custer

BJU PRESS

GREENVILLE, SOUTH CAROLINA

Library of Congress Cataloging-in-Publication Data

Custer, Stewart, 1931-
  The Gospel of the King : a commentary on Matthew / Stewart Custer.
    p. cm.
  Summary: "This is a devotional commentary on the book of Matthew"—Provided by publisher.
  Includes bibliographical references and index.
  ISBN 1-59166-464-0 (hardbound : alk. paper)
  1. Bible. N.T. Matthew—Commentaries. 2. Bible. N.T. Matthew—Devotional literature. I. Title.
  BS2575.53.C87 2005
  226.2'077 0151dc22

                                                              2005017265

The Gospel of the King: A Commentary on Matthew
Stewart Custer, PhD

© 2005 Bob Jones University Press
Greenville, South Carolina 29614

Printed in the United States of America

ISBN 1-59166-464-0

15 14 13 12 11 10 9 8 7 6 5 4 3 2 1

Dedicated to
that noble company
of those who preach
the gospel of
the Great King

TABLE OF CONTENTS

PREFACE TO THE READER

This commentary has been the intention of the author since he began teaching the Gospels in Greek in 1960. He has expounded the Gospel of Matthew to his congregation more than once over the years. He has also used the Gospel of Matthew as a springboard to texts all over the NT. It is a natural introduction to major themes throughout the NT. Its teaching is presupposed by the Epistles, which follow (Rom. 1:3; Col. 1:18; I Tim. 6:13). The key to understanding Matthew is faith in the verbally inspired text of God's holy Word. The reader should come to Scripture seeking the meaning that Matthew, the original author, had in mind, not bringing his private opinions to foist on the text. This commentary seeks to provide pastors and sincere believers in Christ help in perceiving the meaning of the great teaching of the Lord Jesus and the mighty sacrificial atonement that He made for sinful mankind. It will draw upon the reverent comments of preachers and writers of the past, but it will be very sparing in referring to critical writers who think that doubt is the key to understanding the Bible. Benedict T. Viviano may sneer at the story of the call of the tax collector and suggest instead "the possibility of a collaborative effort, in which the Gospel is the product of an early school of higher biblical studies (Stendahl), backed and accepted by a major local church" (Matthew in *The New Jerome Biblical Commentary*, Brown, Fitzmyer, and Murphy, p. 631). Such skepticism brings no spiritual benefit to the hungry-hearted believer. The reader who is interested in such comments may find a bibliography of critical interpreters beginning on page 427. Many pastors and Bible teachers who consult such skeptical works often cannot find anything that they would like to share with a congregation. The author trusts that this commentary will be a spiritual blessing to every reader. Matthew presents a wonderful picture of the Lord Jesus Christ, His birth, His teaching, His miracles, His death, and His resurrection. On every page the author has provided the lovely phraseology of the King James Bible, the beautiful precision of the Greek text (the author's own translation), and, thanks to a university library and to a computer, information from an array of commentaries and sermons on Matthew. May God bless every reader of this commentary. May each one see Jesus and confess, "Truly this was the Son of God" (Matt. 27:54b).

Special thanks go to Miss Suzette Jordan for her patient editorial wisdom and helpful suggestions and to Dr. Peter A. Steveson for checking all the Greek words and references.

INTRODUCTION

It is not by accident that the Gospel of Matthew begins the New Testament. "It would seem that the Early Church placed it in first position in the NT canon, precisely because of the profound influence of its contents on the Church and the world; so much so, that many have termed it the greatest book ever written" (ZPEB, "Matthew, Gospel of," IV, p. 120). Matthew had been a tax collector for the Roman Empire (Matt. 9:9; 10:3), but he had found the Messiah, the true Son of David prophesied by the OT (II Sam. 7:12–16). Now he was going to write the Gospel of the King, not merely of the Jews, but of all mankind. His book is not merely a biography; it is the gospel, the good news of salvation that God has brought to mankind in the person of Jesus Christ, the Savior of all who will trust in Him. He will pay careful attention to the fact that what the Lord Jesus Christ did could be found prophesied in the OT. The phrase *It is written* is a recurring theme in his Gospel (Matt. 2:5; 4:6, 7, 10; 11:10; 21:13; 26:24, 31; 27:37), making it a natural transition to the NT books. "Messianic History fulfills Messianic Prophecy; hence the frequent reference to prediction" (A. T. Pierson, *Keys to the Word*, p. 111). His presentation of the Lord's major discourses is the most complete: the Sermon on the Mount (Matt. 5–7); the instruction to the Twelve (Matt. 10:5–42); the seven parables (Matt. 13); the teaching on the church (Matt. 16:18; 18:15f.); the denunciation of the Pharisees (Matt. 23:1–36); the Olivet Discourse (Matt. 24–25). He alone gives the trinitarian baptismal formula in the Great Commission (Matt. 28:18–20). He records that no less than an angel announces that His name is "JESUS: for he shall save his people from their sins" (Matt. 1:21). The very first verse in the Gospel declares that Jesus Christ is "the son of David." It is Matthew's burden to demonstrate to his people, and to all the world, that the Lord Jesus Christ is the coming King and a perfect Savior.

Authenticity. It may be that Matthew, being a tax collector, would have been regarded by some as being something less than a patriotic Jew and that he would go out of his way to notice Jewish customs and traditions. Matthew is the only NT writer to mention specifically the two-drachma coin (διδραχμον), which was the annual temple tax (Matt. 17:24), and the larger *stater* (στατηρ), which was used to pay it (Matt, 17:27; 26:15).

Only a tax collector would think of such minute details. He is the only one to mention the really large sum of the *talent* (ταλαντον, Matt. 18:24; 25:15, 16, 20, etc.). He also has most of the references to the word *tribute* (κηνσος, Matt. 17:25; 22:17, 19; Mark 12:14). Matthew, being the only Synoptic writer present on the occasion, records the exact words of the Lord to the apostles not to take along "gold or silver or copper" (Matt. 10:9). In the same context Mark mentions only copper, and Luke only silver (Mark 6:8; Luke 9:3, both meaning *money*). Zahn observes that in the ancient world Matthew "is the only person who has ever been regarded as the writer of the Gospel which bears his name" (for the overwhelming evidence see his *Introduction*, vol. II, pp. 506–30). Matthew records that after his conversion he invited many fellow outcasts, tax collectors, and sinners to a dinner that they might hear the words of the Lord Jesus (Matt. 9:9–11). Many modern liberals have the preconceived idea that works ascribed to nonapostles (Mark, Luke) may be authentic, but works ascribed to apostles are certainly not (Matthew, John). This is mere prejudice. His fellow writers refer to him as Levi (Mark 2:14; Luke 5:27). It was common for a man to have more than one name. Simon Peter and Saul, "who also is called Paul" (Acts 13:9), are obvious examples. As a tax collector, Matthew would be used to keeping very meticulous records, so the length and fullness of detail in his Gospel is not surprising. The influence of his Gospel has been immense. The most commonly quoted chapter in the NT in the first four centuries in the writings of the Fathers was Matthew 5 (the second most quoted was Matt. 6, and the third most quoted Matt. 7). The Fathers clearly understood the staggering importance of that sermon.

It was Papias who declared, "Matthew composed the sayings [*logia*] in the Hebrew [Aramaic] tongue, and each one interpreted them as he was able." Since Matthew was a bilingual tax collector, it is logical that he collected the sayings, or sermons, of the Lord in Aramaic, as well as incorporated them into the six major discourses in his Greek Gospel. He could plainly speak or write fluently in either language. His Gospel is definitely not "translation Greek." From a legal standpoint Simon Greenleaf notes that since the men of that day were "as much disposed as those of the present time, to evade the payment of public taxes and duties, and to elude, by all possible means, the vigilance of the revenue officers,

Matthew must have been familiar with a great variety of forms of fraud, imposture, cunning, and deception, and must have become habitually distrustful, scrutinizing, and cautious; and, of course, much less likely to have been deceived in regard to many of the facts in our Lord's ministry, extraordinary as they were, which fell under his observation. This circumstance . . . adds great weight to the value of the testimony of this evangelist" (*The Testimony of the Evangelists*, pp. 14–15).

Date. Since both Irenaeus (*Against Heresies* 3.1.1) and Eusebius (*Ecclesiastical History* 5.8.2) record the tradition that Matthew wrote his Gospel "while Peter and Paul were preaching the Gospel and founding the church in Rome," it would seem that a date in the mid 60s would be a natural conclusion. Modern critical scholarship has fought against this date, largely because of unbelief in the plainly supernatural events that Matthew records in his Gospel. Blomberg sums up his position: "But perhaps a very slight preponderance of weight favors a date from ca. 58–69" (*Matt.*, p. 42). Morris suggests a date "before A.D. 70, perhaps the late 50s or early 60s" (*Matt.*, p. 11). The author agrees with these estimates from A.D. 58–69. If Matthew had written after A.D. 70, the historical events in Jerusalem would have made chapters 24–25 more spectacular. But Matthew had in mind primarily the eschatological future and not the events of his day.

Main theme. Jesus Christ, the great King, Savior of all who believe in Him

Key verses. Matt. 2:2; 27:37; 28:18

Themes.

The Kingdom of God.

The kingdom of God (or of the heavens) is a dominating theme in Matthew. The word *kingdom* (βασιλεια) occurs fifty-five times (see Matt. 3:2 note); the word *king* (βασιλευς) occurs twenty-two times (see Matt. 1:6 note). Although the theme pervades the NT (Mark 1:14–15; Luke 4:43; John 3:3; Acts 28:31; Rom. 14:17; Heb. 1:8; II Pet. 1:11; Rev. 1:9; 11:15), it is especially obvious in Matthew. John the Baptist announces it (Matt. 3:2); the Devil tempts the Lord concerning it (Matt. 4:8ff.); the Sermon on the Mount begins and ends with it (Matt. 5:3; 7:21); the Gentiles will have their place in it (Matt. 8:11); it was the usual theme of the preaching of Jesus (Matt. 9:35); Jesus commanded His disciples to preach about it (Matt. 10:7); resolute believers were pressing into it

(Matt. 11:12); the power of Jesus in casting out demons manifested the kingdom (Matt. 12:28); the Lord Jesus revealed the mysteries of the kingdom by His teaching on the parables (Matt. 13:11); Jesus delegated the keys of the kingdom to Peter (Matt. 16:19); He taught that entrance into the kingdom demanded humility (Matt. 18:3); children are prime candidates for the kingdom (Matt. 19:14); the rich shall enter the kingdom only with difficulty (Matt. 19:23); the kingdom is equally beneficial to all (Matt. 20:1–16); position in the kingdom is not given by favoritism (Matt. 20:23); open sinners enter the kingdom before the proud (Matt. 21:31); the kingdom shall be taken from the Jews and given to the Gentiles (Matt. 21:43); the kingdom is like a wedding invitation (Matt. 22:2); hypocrites will not enter the kingdom and will hinder others from entering (Matt. 23:13); the gospel of the kingdom shall be preached to all the world (Matt. 24:14); people must be constantly alert for the kingdom (Matt. 25:1ff.); the King determines who shall enter the kingdom (Matt. 25:34); there will be future celebration in the kingdom (Matt. 26:29).

The Church.

The church is the manifestation of the kingdom in the present age. The Lord Jesus chose the apostles with the clear knowledge that they would be the nucleus of the future church (Matt. 10:1–4). After His resurrection the Lord Jesus commissioned them to be His witnesses to the uttermost part of the earth (Acts 1:8). He used them to begin the church on the Day of Pentecost (Acts 2:1–42). He used them to open the door of faith to the Gentiles (Acts 10). During His earthly ministry He specifically revealed to the apostles the future existence of the church and its ultimate triumph (Matt. 16:13–19). He also gave directions for maintaining proper discipline in the church (Matt. 18:15–20). He commissioned them to make disciples of all nations and to teach them to observe all that He commanded (Matt. 28:18–20). He concluded by promising to be with His people to the consummation of the age (Matt. 28:20).

Choices in Matthew.

The Lord Jesus chose Matthew the tax collector to be His disciple; Matthew in response chose to follow the Lord from then on (Matt. 9:9–13). It was a life-transforming experience for him. Matthew organized his Gospel with a multitude of choices, divine and human, obvious in every part.

INTRODUCTION

1. God chose sinful and unlikely people for the genealogy of His Son (Matt. 1).
2. Joseph chose Mary as his bride (Matt. 1:18).
3. God chose Joseph and Mary to be the parents of His Son, the Messiah (Matt. 1:20ff.).
4. The wise men chose to seek the great King and to bring Him gifts (Matt. 2:1–12).
5. Herod chose to trick the wise men and to kill the Messiah (Matt. 2:8–18).
6. John the Baptist preached, "Repent and choose God and His Messiah" (Matt. 3:2ff.).
7. Jesus chose to identify Himself with His people in baptism (Matt. 3:13–17).
8. Jesus chose to obey His Father rather than the Devil (Matt. 4).
9. Jesus preached, "Choose God and His service" (Matt. 5–7).
   a. Choose the blessing of God rather than worldly things (5:1–12).
   b. Choose obedience to the Word of God (5:17–19).
   c. Choose purity (5:28–29).
   d. Choose kindness and well doing (5:39–44).
   e. Choose to pray to God the Father (6:6–15).
   f. Choose God, not worldly things (6:24–34).
   g. Choose life with God and thus live forever (7:13–27).
10. Jesus chose Matthew, and Matthew responded (9:9–13).
11. The ruler Jairus chose Jesus and would not be turned aside (Matt. 9:18f.).
12. The two blind men chose Jesus and would not keep silent (Matt. 9:28ff.).
13. Jesus chose the Twelve and trained them (Matt. 10:1ff.).
14. Jesus chose to denounce cities that had chosen to reject Him (Matt. 11:20).
15. Jesus taught that people should choose God's Word and were responsible (Matt. 13:1–23).
16. Jesus taught that men should be ready to sacrifice all for God (Matt. 13:44–46).
17. The Canaanite woman chose Jesus, and He gave her exactly what she asked (Matt. 15:22ff.).

18. Jesus chose to build His church on men and their confession (Matt. 16:17–18).
19. Jesus chose to pay His taxes (Matt. 17:24–27).
20. Jesus chose to save lost sheep (Matt. 18:11–14).
21. Jesus chooses to be with His people (Matt. 18:20).
22. Jesus chooses to bless little children (Matt. 19:13–15).
23. The rich young ruler chose his possessions, not Jesus (Matt. 19:21–22).
24. The disciples chose Jesus above all (Matt. 19:27–29).
25. God chooses to reward all His servants equally; salvation is free to all (Matt. 20:1–16).
26. Jesus chose to give His life a ransom for His people (Matt. 20:28).
27. Jesus chose to come as a meek King riding on a colt of an ass (Matt. 21:6–11).
28. Jesus chose to cast profiteers out of the temple (Matt. 21:12).
29. Some people choose to be pleasant while going to hell; others choose wrongly and repent (Matt. 21:28ff.).
30. The King chose to invite all to His wedding banquet (Matt. 22:9–14).
31. Jesus taught that men should choose to serve God above all (Matt. 22:36–40).
32. Jesus chose to denounce and repudiate false religious leaders (Matt. 23:13ff.).
33. Jesus chooses to return unexpectedly (Matt. 24:27–31, 37, 41; 25:6, 19, 31).
34. Judas chose to betray the Lord Jesus (Matt. 26:14ff.).
35. Jesus chose to eat the Last Supper with His disciples and sing (Matt. 26:18, 30).
36. Jesus chose to pray with His disciples and to submit to arrest (Matt. 26:36ff., 52f.).
37. Judas chose to hang himself (Matt. 27:5).
38. The people chose Barabbas, not Christ (Matt. 27:21).
39. Pilate chose to execute Christ (Matt. 27:26).
40. Joseph of Arimathaea chose to give his own tomb for Jesus (Matt. 27:57–60).
41. Jesus chose to manifest Himself to the women at the tomb (Matt. 28:9).
42. Jesus chose to manifest Himself to the eleven in Galilee (Matt. 28:16f.).

Text. Broadus has well said, "Any commentary worthy of the name must take account of the Greek text of the New Testament" (*Matt.*, p. xxxiv).

> The Nestle-Aland *Novum Testamentum Graece* lists the evidence: "a) all available Papyri, i. e.:
>
> for Matthew: $\mathfrak{P}^1$ (!), $\mathfrak{P}^{19}$, $\mathfrak{P}^{21}$, $\mathfrak{P}^{25}$, $\mathfrak{P}^{35}$ (!), $\mathfrak{P}^{37}$ (!), $\mathfrak{P}^{44}$, $\mathfrak{P}^{45}$ (!), $\mathfrak{P}^{53}$ (!), $\mathfrak{P}^{62}$, $\mathfrak{P}^{64\,(+\,67)}$ (!), $\mathfrak{P}^{70}$ (!), $\mathfrak{P}^{71}$, $\mathfrak{P}^{77}$ (!), $\mathfrak{P}^{86}$
>
> b) all the following uncials, i.e.: for Matthew: ℵ (01), A (02), B (03), C (04), D (05), L 019), W (032), Z (035), Θ (038), 058, 064, 067, 071, 073, 074, 078, 084, 085, 087, 089, 090, 092a, 094, 0104, 0106, 0107, 0118, 0119, 0128, 0133, 0135, 0136, 0137, 0138, 0148, 0160, 0161, 0164, 0170, 0197, 0200, 0204, 0231, 0234, 0237, 0242, 0249, 0250, 0255, 0271"

It then explains that the papyri that are listed with (!) beside them are "of intrinsic significance, because they were written before the III/IV century, and therefore belong to the period before the rise of the major text types" (Aland, Black, Martini, Metzger, Wikgren, *Novum Testamentum Graece*, Introduction, p. 49*). Such full and early evidence for the Gospel can be accounted for only by divine preservation.

OUTLINES OF MATTHEW

The Literary Structure. J. Alexander Findley organized the Gospel around the five major sections that conclude with the "milestone" "When Jesus had finished" (Matt. 7:28; 11:1; 13:53; 19:1; 26:1) (*Jesus in the First Gospel*, p. 15).

I. Jesus the Teacher, greater than Moses. 5:1–7:29.

II. Jesus the Captain-Saviour, greater than Joshua. 8:1–11:1.

III. Jesus the pre-existent Wisdom and Word of God, greater than Solomon. 11:2–13:53.

IV. Jesus the founder of the new Israel, rejected by the old. 13:54–19:1.

V. Jesus the world's Judge, the world's Victim, the world's Redeemer. 19:2–26:1.

Craig L. Blomberg provides a very simple outline (*Matt.*, p. 19).

I. Introduction to Jesus' Ministry (1:1–4:16).

II. The Development of Jesus' Ministry (4:17–16:20).

III. The Climax of Jesus' Ministry (16:21–28:20).

(Based on the two pivotal points [4:17; 16:21]).

The Chiastic Parallel Outline: The Great King (Matt. 27:11)

A. The Genealogy of the King. Matt. 1.

  B. *The Birth of the King. Matt. 2.*

    C. The Testing of the King.

      1. By John (Approval). Matt. 3.

      2. By the Devil (Defeat). Matt. 4.

      D. The First Sermon: Principles of the Kingdom. Matt. 5–7.

        E. The Revelation of the King's Power. Matt. 8–9.

          F. The Preaching of the Kingdom. Matt. 10–12.

            G. The Parables of the Kingdom. Matt. 13.

              H. The Revelation of the Church. Matt. 16.

                I. The Transfiguration: His True Glory. Matt. 17:1–13.

                I'. The Tribute: Temporary Submission to Human Rule. Matt. 17:14

              H'. The Discipline of the Church. Matt. 18.

G'. The Parable of the Laborers. Matt. 20.

F'. The Presentation of the King. Matt. 21.

E'. The Rebuke of the King's Enemies. Matt. 23.

D'. The Last Sermon: Prophecy of the Future Kingdom. Matt. 24–25.

C'. The Trial of the King.

1. By Caiaphas. Matt. 26.

2. By Pilate. Matt. 27:1–26.

B'. The Death of the King. Matt. 27:27–66.

A'. The Resurrection of the King. Matt. 28.

Literary Outline of Matthew

Main theme: The royal Savior, the King of the Jews

I. The Preparation of the King (Matt. 1–4)

  A. The coming of the King (1:1–25)

    1. The genealogy of the King (vv. 1–17)

    2. The Virgin Birth (vv. 18–25)

  B. The coming of the wise men (2:1–23)

    1. The wise men (vv. 1–12)

    2. The flight to Egypt (vv. 13–15)

    3. The slaying of the children (vv. 16–18)

    4. The return from Egypt (vv. 19–23)

  C. The coming of the forerunner (3:1–17)

    1. The preaching of John (vv. 1–12)

    2. The baptism of Jesus (vv. 13–17)

  D. The coming of Satan (4:1–25)

    1. The temptation of Jesus (vv. 1–11)

    2. The early Galilean ministry (vv. 12–25)

II. The Principles of the Kingdom (Matt. 5–7)

  A. The commandments (5:1–48)

    1. The Beatitudes (vv. 1–12)

    2. The Similitudes (vv. 13–16)

    3. The new law (vv. 17–48)

  B. The consecration (6:1–34)

    1. Giving (vv. 1–4)

    2. Praying (vv. 5–15)

    3. Fasting (vv. 16–18)

3. Judas's price (vv. 14–16)
4. The Last Supper (vv. 17–30)
5. Peter's denial prophesied (vv. 31–35)
6. Gethsemane (vv. 36–46)
7. The betrayal and arrest (vv. 47–56)
8. The trial (vv. 57–68)
9. Peter's denial (vv. 69–75)

B. The trial before Pilate and the Crucifixion (27:1–66)
1. The death of Judas (vv. 1–10)
2. The trial before Pilate (vv. 11–26)
3. The mocking and the Crucifixion (vv. 27–44)
4. The death of Jesus (vv. 45–56)
5. The burial of Jesus (vv. 57–66)

C. The Resurrection (28:1–20)
1. The women at the tomb (vv. 1–10)
2. The guard and their lie (vv. 11–15)
3. The Great Commission (vv. 16–20)

This outline incorporates 7 major sections, the 28 chapters, and the 109 paragraphing divisions of the Greek text of Matthew. There are, however, many other ways of organizing Matthew. Criswell and Walvoord divide it into 9 sections; C. R. Erdman into 12; Tasker into 18; Wiersbe into 26; Griffith Thomas into 60. A. T. Robertson and R. H. Mounce simply follow the 28 chapters.

The Seven Sermons

Narrative: Birth and early ministry. Matt. 1–4
 I. The Sermon on the Mount. Matt. 5–7.
Narrative: Mighty deeds. Matt. 8–9
 II. The Sermon to Disciples. Matt. 10.
Narrative: Teaching and preaching. Matt. 11:1–6.
 III. The Sermon on John the Baptist. Matt. 11:7–19.
Narrative: Rebuke and invitation. Matt. 11:20–30.
 IV. The Central Sermon: Seven Parables of the Kingdom. Matt. 13.
Narrative: Mighty deeds. Matt. 14–17.
 V. The Sermon on Children and the Church. Matt. 18.
Narrative: Miracles and teaching. Matt. 19–22.

VI. The Sermon on the Scribes and Pharisees. Matt. 23.

VII. The last Sermon: The Olivet Discourse. Matt. 24–25.

Narrative: The mighty sacrifice and triumphant resurrection.

Animals Mentioned in Matthew

Matthew mentions a great variety of animals (27 words). For first mention only:

Camel (Matt. 3:4)	Sheep (7:15)	Vultures (24:28)
Locusts (3:4)	Wolves (7:15)	Goats (25:32)
Bees implied by	Foxes (8:20)	Cock (26:34)
honey (3:4)	Sparrows (10:29)	Sponge (27:34)
Vipers (3:7)	Whale (12:40)	
Dove (3:16)	Puppies (15:26)	
Moth (6:19)	Ass (21:2)	
Birds (6:26)	Colt of an ass (21:2)	
Dogs (7:6)	Oxen (22:4)	
Pigs (7:6)	Gnat (23:24)	
Fish (7:10)	Hen (23:37)	
Snake (7:10)	Chicks (23:37)	

Numbers in Matthew

God is the Divine Mathematician. Numbers may have symbolic meaning in Scripture. The twelve apostles correspond with the twelve tribes of Israel. But that does not mean that any of the numbers in Scripture are fictitious. All biblical numbers are recorded as sober fact. The following numbers occur in Matthew (first reference).

1 (5:18) 66 times	11 (28:16) 1 time	100 (18:12, 28) 2 times
2 (4:18) 40 times	12 (9:20) 13 times	
3 (12:40) 12 times	14 (1:17) 3 times	4,000 (15:38; 16:10) 2 times
4 (24:31) 1 time	60 (13:8, 23) 2 times	
5 (14:17) 12 times		5,000 (14:21; 16:9) 2 times
6 (17:1) 1 time	70 (18:22) 1 time	
7 (12:45) 9 times	99 (18:12, 13) 2 times	10,000 (18:24) 1 time
10 (20:24) 3 times		

Old Testament Quotations and Allusions in Matthew

See Aland, Black, Martini, Metzger, and Wikgren, *The Greek New Testament*, pp. 897–918; ISBE (1988), "Quotations in the NT," IV, pp. 18–25;

ZPEB, "Quotations in the NT," V, pp. 7–11; R. H. Gundry, *The Use of the OT in St. Matthew's Gospel.*

Gen. 1:27. Matt. 19:4.
2:24. Matt. 19:5.
4:8. Matt. 23:35.
5:1. Matt. 1:1.
5:2. Matt. 19:4.
6:9–12. Matt. 24:37.
6:13–7:24. Matt. 24:38–39.
9:6. Matt. 26:52.
18:14. Matt. 19:26.
18:20–19:28. Matt. 10:15.
19:24–28. Matt. 11:23.
21:3. Matt. 1:2.
21:12. Matt. 1:2.
22:2. Matt. 3:7.
22:18. Matt. 1:1.
25:26. Matt. 1:2.
29:35. Matt. 1:2.
38:8. Matt. 22:24.
38:29–30. Matt. 1:3.
Exod. 3:6. Matt. 22:32.
3:15. Matt. 22:32.
3:16. Matt. 22:32.
4:19. Matt. 2:20.
12:1–27. Matt. 26:2.
12:14–20. Matt. 26:17.
13:9. Matt. 23:5.
16:4. Matt. 6:34.
20:10. Matt. 12:2.
20:12. Matt. 15:4.
20:12–16. Matt. 19:18–19.
20:13. Matt. 5:21.

20:14. Matt. 5:27.
21:12. Matt. 5:21.
21:17. Matt. 15:4.
21:24. Matt. 5:38.
21:32. Matt. 26:15.
23:4–5. Matt. 5:44.
23:20. Matt. 11:10.
24:8. Matt. 26:28.
26:31–35. Matt. 27:51.
29:37. Matt. 23:19.
30:13. Matt. 17:24.
34:28. Matt. 4:2.
38:26. Matt. 17:24.
Lev. 14:2. Matt. 8:4.
14:4–32. Matt. 8:4.
15:25. Matt. 9:20.
18:5. Matt. 19:17.
18:16. Matt. 14:3–4.
19:2. Matt. 5:48.
19:12. Matt. 5:33.
19:13. Matt. 20:8.
19:17. Matt. 18:15.
19:18. Matt. 5:43; 19:19; 22:39.
20:9. Matt. 15:4.
20:21. Matt. 14:3–4.
24:5–8. Matt. 12:4.
24:9. Matt. 12:4.
24:16. Matt. 26:65–66.
24:17. Matt. 5:21.
24:20. Matt. 5:38.
27:30. Matt. 23:23.
Num. 14:6. Matt. 26:65.
15:38–39. Matt. 23:5.

18:31. Matt. 10:10.
24:17. Matt. 2:2.
27:17. Matt. 9:36.
28:9–10. Matt. 12:5.
30:2. Matt. 5:33.
Deut. 5:14. Matt. 12:2.
5:16. Matt. 15:4.
5:16–20. Matt. 19:18–19.
5:17. Matt. 5:21.
5:18. Matt. 5:27.
6:5. Matt. 22:37.
6:8. Matt. 23:5.
6:13. Matt. 4:10.
6:16. Matt. 4:7.
8:3. Matt. 4:4.
13:1–3. Matt. 24:24.
15:11. Matt. 26:11.
18:13. Matt. 5:48.
18:15. Matt. 17:5.
19:15. Matt. 18:16.
19:21. Matt. 5:38.
21:6–9. Matt. 27:24.
21:22–23. Matt. 27:57–58.
23:21. Matt. 5:33.
23:24–25. Matt. 12:1.
24:1. Matt. 5:31.
24:15. Matt. 20:8.
25:5. Matt. 22:24.
30:4. Matt. 24:31.
32:5. Matt. 17:17.
32:20. Matt. 17:17.
33:2. Matt. 25:31.
33:9. Matt. 10:37.

Josh. 22:5. Matt. 22:37.
Judg. 13:5, 7. Matt. 2:23.
Ruth 4:12. Matt. 1:3.
4:13. Matt. 1:4–5.
4:17, 22. Matt. 1:6.
4:17–22. Matt. 1:4–5.
4:18–19. Matt. 1:3.
I Sam. 14:45. Matt. 10:30.
21:1–6. Matt. 12:3–4.
II Sam. 5:2. Matt. 2:6.
12:24. Matt. 1:6.
13:19. Matt. 26:65.
23:2. Matt. 22:43.
I Kings 8:13. Matt. 23:21.
9:7–8. Matt. 23:38.
10:1–10. Matt. 12:42.
17:9–24. Matt. 10:41.
17:18. Matt. 8:29.
19:20. Matt. 8:21.
22:17. Matt. 9:36.
II Kings 1:8. Matt. 3:4.
4:8–37. Matt. 10:41.
4:33. Matt. 6:6.
4:43–44. Matt. 14:20.
24:12–16. Matt. 1:11.
I Chron. 1:34. Matt. 1:2.
2:4, 5, 9. Matt. 1:3.

2:10–12. Matt. 1:4–5.
2:13–15. Matt. 1:6.
3:10–14. Matt. 1:7–10.
3:15–16. Matt. 1:11.
3:17–19. Matt. 1:12.
11:2. Matt. 2:6.
17:11. Matt. 1:1.
II Chron. 9. Matt. 6:29.
9:1–12. Matt. 12:42.
15:6. Matt. 24:7.
18:16. Matt. 9:36.
24:20–21. Matt. 23:35.
36:10. Matt. 1:11.
36:16. Matt. 5:12.
Ezra 3:2. Matt. 1:12.
9:3. Matt. 26:65.
Neh. 11:1. Matt. 4:5.
Esther 4:1. Matt. 11:21.
Job 1:20. Matt. 26:65.
2:12. Matt. 26:65.
22:29. Matt. 23:12.
38:17. Matt. 16:18.
42:2. Matt. 19:26.
Ps. 2:7. Matt. 3:17; 17:5.
6:8. Matt. 7:23.
8:3. Matt. 21:16.
22:1. Matt. 27:46.
22:7. Matt. 27:39.
22:7, 8. Matt. 26:24.
22:8. Matt. 27:43.
22:16–18. Matt. 26:24.

22:18. Matt. 27:35.
24:3–4. Matt. 5:8.
26:6. Matt. 27:24.
26:8. Matt. 23:21.
28:4. Matt. 16:27.
37:4. Matt. 6:33.
37:11. Matt. 5:5.
41:9. Matt. 26:23.
42:5, 11. Matt. 26:38.
43:5. Matt. 26:38.
48:2. Matt. 5:35.
62:10. Matt. 19:22.
62:12. Matt. 16:27.
69:21. Matt. 27:34, 48.
72:10, 11. Matt. 2:11.
72:15. Matt. 2:11.
78:2. Matt. 13:35.
91:11, 12. Matt. 4:6.
104:12. Matt. 13:32.
107:3. Matt. 8:11.
109:25. Matt. 27:39.
110:1. Matt. 22:44; 26: 64.
113–118. Matt. 26:30.
118:22–23. Matt. 21:42.
118:26. Matt. 21:9; 23:39.
Prov. 2:4. Matt. 13:44.
19:17. Matt. 25:40.
24:12. Matt. 16:27.
25:21. Matt. 5:44.
29:23. Matt. 23:12.
Isa. 5:1–2. Matt. 21:33.

6:9–10. Matt. 13:14 15.
7:14. Matt. 1:23.
8:8, 10. Matt. 1:23.
9:1–2. Matt. 4:15–16.
11:1. Matt. 2:23.
13:10. Matt. 24:29.
14:13, 15. Matt. 11:23.
19:2. Matt. 24:7.
23:1–8. Matt. 11:21–22.
26:20. Matt. 6:6.
27:13. Matt. 24:31.
29:13. Matt. 15:8–9.
34:4. Matt. 24:29.
35:5–6. Matt. 11:5.
38:10. Matt. 16:18.
40:3. Matt. 3:3.
42:1. Matt. 3:17.
42:1–4. Matt. 12:18–21.
42:18. Matt. 11:5.
49:24. Matt. 12:29.
50:6. Matt. 26:67; 27:30.
52:1. Matt. 4:5.
53:2. Matt. 2:23.
53:4. Matt. 8:17.
53:5. Matt. 26:67.
53:7. Matt. 26:63.
53:9. Matt. 26:24.
53:12. Matt. 27:38.
56:7. Matt. 21:13.
58:5. Matt. 6:16.
58:7. Matt. 25:35–36.
60:6. Matt. 2:11.
60:7. Matt. 21:13.

61:1. Matt. 11:5.
61:2–3. Matt. 5:4.
62:11. Matt. 21:5.
66:1. Matt. 5:34, 35.
Jer. 6:16. Matt. 11:29.
7:11. Matt. 21:13.
12:7. Matt. 23:38.
14:14. Matt. 7:22.
22:5. Matt. 23:38.
27:15. Matt. 7:22.
27:20. Matt. 1:11.
31:15. Matt. 2:18.
31:25. Matt. 11:28.
31:31. Matt. 26:28.
32:6–9. Matt. 27:9–10.
36:24. Matt. 26:65.
50:6. Matt. 10:6.
Lam. 2:15. Matt. 27:39.
Ezek. 13:10–12. Matt. 7:27.
17:23. Matt. 13:32.
21:26. Matt. 23:12.
22:27. Matt. 7:15.
26–28. Matt. 11:21–22.
31:6. Matt. 13:32.
32:7. Matt. 24:29.
33:5. Matt. 27:25.
34:5. Matt. 9:36.
34:17. Matt. 25:32.
36:23. Matt. 6:9.
37:12. Matt. 27:52–53.
Dan. 2:28, 29. Matt. 24:6.
2:34–35. Matt. 21:44.

2:44–45. Matt. 21:44.
3:5. Matt. 4:9.
3:10. Matt. 4:9.
3:15. Matt. 4:9.
4:12, 21. Matt. 13:32.
7:9–10. Matt. 19:28.
7:13. Matt. 26:64.
7:13–14. Matt. 24:30.
7:14. Matt. 28:18.
9:27. Matt. 24:15.
11:31. Matt. 24:15.
11:41. Matt. 24:10.
12:1. Matt. 24:21.
12:2. Matt. 25:46.
12:3. Matt. 13:43.
12:11. Matt. 24:15.
Hos. 6:6. Matt. 9:13; 12:7.
11:1. Matt. 2:15.
Joel 2:2. Matt. 24:21.
2:10. Matt. 24:29.
2:31. Matt. 24:29.
3:4–8. Matt. 11:21–22.
3:15. Matt. 24:29.
Amos 1:9–10. Matt. 11:21–22.
8:9. Matt. 27:45.
Jonah 1:17. Matt. 12:40.
3:5. Matt. 12:41.
3:6. Matt. 11:21.
3:8. Matt. 12:41.
4:9. Matt. 26:38.
Mic. 5:2. Matt. 2:6.
6:8. Matt. 23:23.

7:6. Matt. 10:21, 35–36.

Zeph. 1:3. Matt. 13:41.

Hag. 1:13. Matt. 28:20.

2:6, 21. Matt. 24:29.

Zech. 1:1. Matt. 23:35.

2:6. Matt. 24:31.

8:6. Matt. 19:26.

9:2–4. Matt. 11:21–22.

9:9. Matt. 21:5.

9:11. Matt. 26:28.

10:2. Matt. 9:36.

11:12. Matt. 26:15.

11:12–13. Matt. 27:9–10.

12:10. Matt. 24:30.

12:14. Matt. 24:30.

13:7. Matt. 26:31, 56.

14:5. Matt. 25:31.

Mal. 2:7–8. Matt. 23:3.

3:1. Matt. 11:3, 10.

4:5. Matt. 11:14.

4:5–6. Matt. 17:10–11.

Unique Elements in Matthew.

The annunciation to Joseph (Matt. 1:18–25).

The visit of the Magi (Matt. 2:1–12).

The flight to Egypt (Matt. 2:13–18).

Christ's home in Capernaum (Matt. 4:13–14).

Portions of the Sermon on the Mount (Matt. 5:13–43; 6:1–34; 7:7–11).

The instruction to the Twelve (Matt. 10:16–42).

Woe to the cities and invitation (Matt. 11:20–30).

The sign of Jonah (Matt. 12:38–45).

The parables of the tares, hid treasure, pearl, dragnet (Matt. 13:24–30; 36–53).

Paying the tax and the fish (Matt. 17:24–27).

Parable of the unmerciful servant (Matt. 18:15–35).

Parable of the householder and workers (Matt. 20:1–16).

The parable of the king and the wedding supper (Matt. 22:1–14).

The denunciation of the scribes and Pharisees (Matt. 23:1–39).

Part of the Olivet Discourse (Matt. 24:43–25:46).

The request for a guard at the tomb (Matt. 27:62–66).

Jesus' appearance to the women and the report of the guard (Matt. 28:9–15).

The appearance to the eleven and the Great Commission (Matt. 28:16–20).

The Synoptic Problem. Matthew, Mark, and Luke are called the Synoptic Gospels because they present a similar portrait of the life and teaching of the Lord Jesus. John presents a distinctive view of the Lord with 92 percent new material. He deliberately avoids repeating what he knows the others have said and records remarkable scenes such as the interview with Nicodemus (John 3) and the Upper Room Discourse (John 14–17). The problem is why these three Gospels present the life of Jesus with obvious similarities and obvious differences. The theories to account for these differences are legion.

1. The Ur-gospel theory of G. E. Lessing and J. G. Eichhorn. They held that there was an original gospel in Aramaic, later enlarged and shortened, and a version translated into Greek and later enlarged and shortened. Out of this mass of material the canonical Gospels evolved. This idea sank under its own weight.

2. The interdependence theory of Grotius. He held that the first Gospel was written from oral tradition; the second used the first; and the third used both the first and the second. Every possible order has been recommended by some critic (see Thiessen, *Introduction to the New Testament*, p. 104).

3. The written-fragments theory of Schleiermacher. He held that there were a large number of short written fragments of the gospel story that circulated independently. This theory has morphed into # 4.

4. *Formsgeschichte*, the theory of Rudolph Bultmann and Martin Dibelius. They held that there were different types of literature collected into the Gospels. The fragments were passion story tales, paradigms that were examples, tales of healings and miracles, myths, sayings of Jesus, and legends such as the Virgin Birth. Their obvious unbelief in the authenticity of the Gospel record shows the prejudice with which they wrote. In his commentary on John, Bultmann mixes the order of the paragraphs to such a degree that the publisher had to provide a chart to show the reader how to find a given paragraph (*The Gospel of John*, p. xiii).

5. The two-document theory of Bernhard Weiss. He held that one source was some form of the Gospel of Mark, and the other he called *Quelle*, German for *source*, now termed "Q." It is actually that portion of Matthew and Luke that both have in common. The major objection to the

theory is that of all the thousands of manuscripts and fragments of manuscripts that have been found, not one can be identified as "Q." Every manuscript has been clearly identified as either canonical Matthew or Luke. With such total absence of evidence the theory is a "lame duck."

6. Oral tradition. More conservative scholars such as Alford, Godet, and Westcott have favored this view, but obviously there is no documentary evidence. The most that can be said is that the book of Acts shows that the early church started and was maintained by the preaching of the apostles (Acts 2:14–40; 3:12–26; 5:42; 10:28–48). Luke gives credit to "the eyewitnesses and ministers of the word" (Luke 1:2). Paul knew a saying of the Lord Jesus that was not included in the Gospels (Acts 20:35).

The true answer to the Synoptic problem must come from the nature of the inspiration of the Scriptures. The Lord Jesus said, "For truly I say to you: Until heaven and earth pass away, one iota or one little horn shall never pass away until all things be fulfilled" (Matt. 5:18). Everything that is in Scripture must be fulfilled because God has inspired it, down to every last letter and every part of a letter. The Lord Jesus charged the Sadducees with error: "You are being led astray because you know not the Scriptures nor the power of God" (Matt. 22:29b). The apostle Peter, a recipient of the inspired Scripture, describes the process: "Knowing this first, that no prophecy of the Scripture is of any private interpretation; for prophecy was not brought by the will of man, but men being carried along by the Holy Spirit spoke from God" (II Pet. 1:20–21). The same word *being carried along* is used of the ship *being carried along* by the wind (Acts 27:15). It was the power of God that produced the holy Scriptures, not the brilliance or the ingenuity of the writers. How God imparts His holy Word is the prerogative of God alone.

All the pressure being brought to bear on conservative believers to adopt some man-made theory of Scripture production is the work of the Devil. Believers must not bow the knee to Baal (or to Bultmann either)!*

"For ever, O Lord, thy word is settled in heaven" (Ps. 119:89).

---

* C. S. Lewis writes of Bultmann and his colleagues: "These men ask me to believe they can read between the lines of the old texts; the evidence is their obvious inability to read (in any sense worth discussing) the lines themselves. They claim to see fern-seed and can't see an elephant ten yards away in broad daylight" ("Modern Theology and Biblical Criticism" in *Christian Reflections*, p. 157).

The Theology of Matthew

The Gospel of Matthew is the link between the Old Testament and the New. It is by a Jew who was a tax collector, who yet was burdened to identify himself with his people and minister to them (Matt. 10:5–6). He was also an apostle in the church, and he says more about it than any other Gospel writer (Matt. 16:18–19). He is writing the Gospel for the Hebrews, which turns out to be the same Gospel that all nations need to hear (Matt. 28:19–20). Perhaps he saw himself as that scribe instructed in the kingdom of heaven, who is like a householder, who "brings forth out of his treasure things new and old" (Matt. 13:52b). He was keenly conscious that "many shall come from the east and west, and shall sit down with Abraham, and Isaac, and Jacob, in the kingdom of heaven" (Matt. 8:11b). He recalls the declaration of the Lord Jesus that He did not come to destroy the Law or the Prophets, but to fulfill them (Matt. 5:17). He is constantly quoting the OT passages that are fulfilled in the life of the Lord Jesus (Matt. 1:22–23; 2:15, 17–18, 23; 4:14–16; 8:17; 12:17–21; 13:35; 21:4–5; 27:9–10). The Gospel of Matthew is a preaching Gospel meant to evangelize the reader. It is the divinely intended beginning of the NT.

The Doctrine of God. The reality of God fills the Gospel of Matthew. The name of the great Messiah is *God with us* (Matt. 1:23); Almighty God has the power to create people out of stones if He wishes (Matt. 3:9); the Spirit of God descended upon Christ, and a voice from heaven claimed Him as Son (Matt. 3:16–17); the Devil conceded that Christ was the Son of God (Matt. 4:3, 6); seeing God is regarded as the pinnacle of life (Matt. 5:8); to be called sons of God is the highest privilege (Matt. 5:9); God's throne is in heaven (Matt. 5:34; 23:22); God deserves single-minded obedience (Matt. 6:24); God has created the flowers (Matt. 6:28–30); the kingdom of God is characterized by righteousness (Matt. 6:33); demons recognized Jesus as the Son of God (Matt. 8:29); the miracles of healing caused men to glorify God (Matt. 9:8); the tabernacle was called the house of God (Matt. 12:4); Christ cast out demons by the Spirit of God, manifesting the kingdom of God (Matt. 12:28); the disciples worshiped Jesus as the Son of God (Matt. 14:33); Jesus repeatedly spoke of God's commands (Matt. 15:3, 4, 6); people glorified God for the miracles of Jesus (Matt. 15:31); Peter called Christ the Son of the living God (Matt. 16:16); the Devil cannot understand the things of God (Matt. 16:23); God ordained matrimonial union (Matt. 19:6); no one naturally goes into God's kingdom (Matt. 19:24); God can do the impossible (Matt. 19:26); the kingdom of God is all important (Matt. 21:31, 43); Jesus taught the way of God (Matt. 22:16); man must honor both God and government (Matt. 22:21); the Sadducees did not know the power of God (Matt. 22:29); God claimed to be the God of Abraham, Isaac, and Jacob (Matt. 22:31–32); man's duty is to love God with all his being (Matt. 22:37); the high priest put Christ under oath to the living God (Matt. 26:63); see also Matt. 27:40, 43, 46, 54.

The Lord Jesus refers to God as "the heavenly Father" (ο πατηρ ο ουρανιος) seven times in Matthew (5:48; 6:14, 26, 32; 15:13; 18:35; 23:9) and as "Father" forty-five times altogether (see text Matt. 5:16 note). The phrase *your Father who is in heaven* makes the loving care of God very real to the believer (5:16, 45; 6:1, 9; 7:11, 21, and often). The Spirit of His Father empowers witness (10:20); the righteous shall shine forth in the eschatological kingdom of their Father (13:43). In both the scene of the baptism and the Great Commission, the doctrine of the Trinity is clearly taught (Matt. 3:16–17; 28:18–20). It is confirmed by Romans 1:3–4; II Corinthians 13:14; I Peter 1:2; Revelation 1:4–6.

For a warm-hearted study see

Packer, J. I. *Knowing God.* Downers Grove, Ill.: InterVarsity Press, 1973.
Torrey, R. A. *What the Bible Teaches (About God).* New York: Revell, 1933. pp. 13–63.

For very formal theology see

Bavinck, Herman. *The Doctrine of God.* Grand Rapids: Eerdmans, 1951.

The Names and Titles of Jesus. Matthew takes pains to show the reader that Jesus is truly human and truly divine. He is born (Matt. 2) and He dies (Matt. 27) even as all human beings must. He is not, however, merely a great human being. He is the great King, the eternal Revelation of God to man, what Pelikan called *the Cosmic Christ*, the Lord of all (Pelikan Jaroslav, *The Illustrated Jesus Through the Centuries*, p. 59). All authority in heaven and earth belongs to Him (Matt. 28:18).

1. Jesus. The commonest name for Jesus in Matthew (150 times). The full name Jesus Christ occurs only three times (1:1, 18; 16:21).
2. Christ (17 times). It means the anointed one, Messiah. It seems to be used as a proper name at times (1:1, 18).
3. Lord (κυριος, 46 times in the highest sense). At the judgment people will call Him Lord (Matt. 7:21–22). One time it may mean only "sir" (Matt. 8:21).
4. Son of David (9 times). The messianic force is clear (1:1; 21:9, 15; 22:42).
5. Son of Man (29 times). This is the Lord's favorite name for Himself; no one else applies it to Him. The Son of Man has power to forgive (9:6); is lord of the Sabbath (12:8); shall send His angels (13:41); shall come again in glory (16:27–28). The title comes from Daniel 7:13 of the One Who comes to set up the kingdom of God.
6. The Coming One (3 times). Matthew 11:3; 21:9; 23:39.
7. Prophet (4 times). Matthew 13:57; 16:14; 21:11, 46.
8. Teacher (12 times). Jesus is addressed or referred to by others (8:19; 9:11; 12:38; 17:24; 19:16; 22:16, 24, 36); He implies it of Himself (10:24, 25; 23:8; 26:18).
9. Rabbi (2). Both times by Judas (26:25, 49).
10. Guide (καθηγητης). Only once in 23:10. Christ alone is the Guide.
11. Prophet (προφητης). Four times in 13:57; 16:14; 21:11, 46.
12. Master of the house (2 times, in 10:25; 13:27).
13. King of the Jews (4 times). Matthew 2:2; 27:11, 29, 37.
14. King of Israel (once in 27:42).
15. The King (3 times). Matthew quotes Zechariah 9:9 (Matt. 21:5). "The King shall say" (25:34, 40).
16. Governor (ηγουμενος), once in 2:6, quoting Micah 5:2.
17. Son of Abraham. Once in the title only (1:1).
18. Son of the carpenter (once, 13:55), by people of His own country.
19. Son of God (8 times). Satan assumes it (4:3, 6); demons call Him this (8:29); disciples in the boat claim Him (14:33); the high priest, mockers, and centurion call Him this (26:63; 27:40, 43, 54).
20. Son of the Living God (once) in Peter's confession (16:16).
21. My Son (1 time). Matthew quotes Hosea 11:1 (2:15). There is an implication of this in a parable (21:37–38).

22. My Beloved Son (2 times). God speaks at the baptism (3:17) and at the Transfiguration (17:5).

23. The Son (5 times). It occurs three times in the great "Johannine" passage (11:27), in 24:36, and in the great threefold "name" (28:19). There is another implication in the parable of the marriage feast (22:2).

24. Bridegroom (6 times). By implication Jesus refers to Himself (9:15), and in the parable of the foolish virgins, He implies Himself (25:1, 5, 6, 10).

25. Shepherd (once). Matthew quotes Zechariah 13:7, "I will smite the shepherd" (26:31).

26. Servant of the Lord (once). Matthew quotes Isaiah 42:1–4 and applies the Servant passage to Christ. (12:17–21).

27. Immanuel ("God with us") occurs once in 1:23, quoting Isaiah 7:14.

For further study see

Warfield, Benjamin B. *The Lord of Glory*. Grand Rapids: Zondervan, 1907.

Walvoord, John F. *Jesus Christ Our Lord*. Chicago: Moody Press, 1969.

Smith, Wilbur M. *The Supernaturalness of Christ*. Boston: W. A. Wilde Company, 1944.

Morgan, G. Campbell. *The Crises of the Christ*. New York: Revell, 1936.

The Mind of Christ. The Lord Jesus Christ knew the thoughts of others (Matt. 9:4). He was mentally aware of all His surroundings; He knew the characteristics of birds, animals, and flowers (6:26–30); He knew how children played in the marketplace (11:16–17); He knew about the weather predictors (16:2–3); He knew the market price of goods (five sparrows for a penny, Luke 12:6–7); He knew current events (the tower of Siloam, Luke 13:4). He was perfectly balanced in His mental power: He was moved with compassion for men (Matt. 9:36; 20:34); He had love for lost people (19:16–22; Mark 10:21); He was angry at the hardness of heart of hypocrites (Matt. 23:13), but He never lost His temper (Mark 3:5); He was indignant over the cruel treatment of the poor (23:14); on the night of His arrest He sang a hymn before going to Gethsemane (Matt. 26:30). He had no fear in a storm, only trust in His Father (Mark 4:40); He shared the sorrows of others, weeping with Mary and Martha

(John 11:35). He thought in concrete, not abstract, terms. He did not preach on the doctrine of the Trinity (three hypostases subsisting in one essence!) but rather spoke of the Father, the Son, and the Spirit (Matt. 11:27; 28:19); He anticipated the needs of men (17:25); He was always positive in His thinking: when the centurion mentioned his servant at home sick, the Lord said, "I will come and heal him" (8:7). Pilate had to say, "I find in him no fault at all" (John 18:38).

For further study see

Blaikie, William Garden. *The Inner Life of Christ*. Minneapolis: Klock and Klock, 1982.

Vos, Geerhardus. *The Self-Disclosure of Jesus*. Grand Rapids: Eerdmans, 1954.

Hastings, James, *Dictionary of Christ and the Gospels*. Grand Rapids: Baker, rpt. 1973, "The Claims of Christ," I, pp. 335–37.

The Holy Spirit. The third person of the Trinity, the Holy Spirit, is mentioned as the agent in the virgin conception of the Lord Jesus (Matt. 1:18, 20); as the source of power for the earthly ministry of the Lord (3:16); as driving the Lord to the contest with Satan (4:1); as fulfilling Isaiah 42:1–4 by empowering Christ (Matt. 12:18).

John the Baptist prophesied that the One coming after him would baptize with the Holy Spirit and fire (3:11); persecuted believers will know that the Spirit of the Father speaks in them (10:20); Isaiah (42:1–4) prophesied that God would put His Spirit on His servant (12:18); Christ cast out demons by the Spirit of God (12:28); blasphemy against the Spirit shall never be forgiven (12:31–32). Christ asked how David, empowered by the Spirit, could call his descendant Lord (22:43); in the baptismal formula the Holy Spirit is fully equal to the Father and the Son (28:19).

For further study see

Swete, Henry Barclay. *The Holy Spirit in the New Testament*. Grand Rapids: Baker Book House, rpt. 1964.

Walvoord, John F. *The Holy Spirit*. Wheaton, Ill.: Van Kampen Press, 1954.

Pache, Rene. *The Person and Work of the Holy Spirit*. Chicago: Moody Press, 1954.

Thomas, W. H. Griffith. *The Holy Spirit of God*. Grand Rapids: Eerdmans, 1964.

The Kingdom. The central theme of all of Jesus' preaching recorded by Matthew is the kingdom. The word *kingdom* (βασιλεια) occurs fifty-five times in Matthew; His customary phrase *kingdom of heaven* occurs thirty-two times in Matthew, but never elsewhere. Mark and Luke always use *kingdom of God*, but Matthew used the phrases interchangeably (Matt. 19:23–24). The Jews commonly spoke of *heaven* to avoid using the name of God (21:25). The Lord began His preaching, "Repent, for the kingdom of the heavens has drawn near" (4:17*b*). The principles of the kingdom are manifested in Christian character (5:3–10), but unless one's righteousness exceeds that of the scribes and Pharisees, he will not enter the kingdom (5:20). There is a present aspect of the kingdom in which good is mixed with evil (13:24–30); it is a period of slow growth, but it will have a cataclysmic end, which will inaugurate the future aspect of the kingdom (13:40–43). Since we are to pray for the coming of the kingdom, there is certainly an aspect that is not now present (6:10). The future aspect is called the *regeneration*, "when the Son of man shall sit on the throne of his glory" (19:28). The Lord Himself is the King (2:2), as He claimed in His teaching (13:41). The church is not identical with the kingdom; it is rather a preparatory form of the eschatological kingdom (16:18–19). OT believers as well as NT believers will participate together in the final form of the kingdom (8:11). The complete victory of the Lord is certain at the Second Coming (26:64). Both rewards and retribution will follow (16:27; 25:31–46). Compare Revelation 20:1–22:7.

For further study see

Walvoord, John F. *Major Bible Prophecies*. Grand Rapids: Zondervan, 1991, pp. 110ff, 389ff.

ZPEB, "Kingdom of God, of Heaven," III, pp. 801–9.

ISBE (1986), "Kingdom of God," III, pp. 23–29.

Elwell, Walter, ed., *Evangelical Dictionary of Biblical Theology*, "Matthew, Theology of," pp. 514–17.

Salvation. The Lord Jesus was named *Jesus* ("Jehovah is salvation") because He shall save His people from their sins (Matt. 1:21). Being in the kingdom is equivalent to being saved (19:23–26). Not every man possesses salvation: conversion is a prerequisite to entering the kingdom (18:3; 13:15). Man is naturally sinful, "an evil and adulterous generation" (12:39). Jesus preached repentance (4:17). Although the Lord pronounces "woe" on those who do not repent (11:20), He gives a most tender invitation to those who feel the burden of their sinfulness to come to Him for relief (11:28–30). A person's righteousness must exceed that of the scribes and Pharisees (5:20). Jesus clearly taught the reality of hell (5:30). If a man is to be saved, he must choose the "narrow gate" and enter it (7:13). The Lord clearly taught the necessity of His own death (16:21; 20:18–19) and that His death would provide a ransom for many (20:28), as Isaiah 53 had prophesied. Both Pilate (27:24) and Judas (27:4) recognized the Lord's sinlessness. But He took all the horror of the sin of other men upon Himself (26:39–42). He shed His blood for many for the forgiveness of sins (26:28). His earthly ministry ended not in defeat but in complete triumph in the Resurrection (28:6–10) and with the command that His salvation be proclaimed to all nations (28:18–20).

For further study see

Morris, Leon. *The Cross in the New Testament.* Grand Rapids: Eerdmans, 1965, pp. 13–62.

Guthrie, Donald. *New Testament Theology,* "The Mission of Christ." Downers Grove, Ill.: Inter-Varsity Press, 1981, pp. 408–48.

The Church. Matthew is the only Gospel writer that names the church. He records the promise of Christ, "I will build my church" (Matt. 16:18*b*). Matthew is deeply concerned to show the difference between the church and the synagogue. He had been a member of both. He spells out the necessity of church discipline to prevent the church from going down as the synagogue had (18:15–18). He records the commission of world evangelism and the promise of Christ to be with His church even to the consummation of the age (28:18–20).

For further study see

Hort, Fenton John Anthony. *The Christian Ecclesia.* London: Macmillan, 1898.

Saucy, Robert. *The Church in God's Program.* Chicago: Moody Press, 1972.

Stibbs, Alan M. *God's Church*. London: Inter-Varsity, 1959.

The Tension Between the Old and the New. The Jewish authorities resisted the teaching and authority of the Lord Jesus (Matt. 9:3, 11; 12:2–8, 14, 24, 38; 15:1–12; 16:1). The Lord Jesus gave stern warnings against the teaching of the Pharisees and Sadducees (16:6; 21:42–46; 23:1–36). The Lord revealed that He was replacing the old revelation with a new one that had higher standards (5:20–48). He did not mean to destroy the Law and the Prophets but to build upon them a higher level of devotion to God (5:17–20). The new people of God were going to be the church, not national Israel (16:18f.). In the future kingdom many from the East and the West will join the OT saints in the kingdom of heaven (8:11). The book of Acts forms a natural sequel to the Gospel records. In the book of Revelation, both the seven churches (Rev. 2–3) and the twelve tribes of Israel (Rev. 7:4–14) have their place in the world to come.

Sin. The basic meaning of the word *sin* (ἁμαρτια) is "missing the mark." The word picture is that God's standard of righteousness is the target; man has missed the whole target. The angel prophesied that Jesus would save His people from their sins (Matt. 1:21). Although the Lord attacked sinful practices (5:21–37) and demanded perfection (5:48), He recognized that even His disciples had sinful natures (7:11). He noted that all kinds of sin can be forgiven, except the unpardonable sin (12:31). Those who were not His followers He called a generation of vipers (12:34). He taught that all outward sins come from the evil nature within man (15:19). Christ had the authority to forgive sin (9:2–6), and He shed His blood to secure the forgiveness of sins for His followers (26:28). His enemies recognized Him as a friend of publicans and sinners (11:19). But on the day of judgment, Jesus will face the hypocrites and say, "Depart from me, you who are working lawlessness" (ανομια, 7:23b).

For further study see

Trench, Richard C. *Synonyms of the New Testament*, "Sin," pp. 239–49.
Elwell, Walter, ed. *Evangelical Dictionary of Biblical Theology*, "Sin," pp. 736–39.

Moses and the Law. The Lord Jesus did not come to destroy the Law but to fulfill it (Matt. 5:17). Although He attacked the oral tradition of the scribes, He defended the Law itself (15:1–6). As the Lawgiver, He was above the Law (12:5–8). It is not by accident that He goes into a mountain to proclaim the principles of the kingdom (5–7), for as the Lawgiver He pronounces the new law from the new Sinai to the new people of God. He had the authority to define or extend the Law as He wished (5:21–48). On one occasion He wiped out the ceremonial dietary regulations (15:10–20; Mark 7:19).

For further study see

Elwell, Walter, ed. *Evangelical Dictionary of Biblical Theology,* "Law," pp. 467–70.

The Fulfillment Formula in Quotations. Although there are a great many quotations and allusions to the OT in Matthew (see Introduction, pp. xxii–xxv), there are ten major quotations, each introduced by a special formula using the verb *to be fulfilled* (πληροω).

1. "But all this was done that this thing that was spoken by the Lord through the prophet might be fulfilled, saying, Behold the virgin shall be with child, and shall bring forth a son, and they shall call his name Immanuel, which is translated, God with us" (Matt. 1:22–23; Isa. 7:14).
   This is the announcement of the divine King.
2. "And he was there until the death of Herod, in order that that which was spoken by the Lord through the prophet might be fulfilled, saying, Out of Egypt I called my son" (Matt. 2:15; Hos. 11:1).
   This is the call of the King as the divine Son out of Egypt, parallel to His people (Exod. 15:1, 13).
3. "Then was fulfilled that which was spoken through Jeremiah the prophet, saying,

   In Rama a voice was heard,

   Of weeping and great lamentation;

   Rachel weeping for her children;

   And she would not be comforted,

   Because they are not" (Matt. 2:17–18; Jer. 31:15).

This is mourning for the oppression of the people of the King.

4. "And he came and dwelled in a city called Nazareth: that it might be fulfilled which was spoken through the prophets, He shall be called a Nazarene" (Matt. 2:23; Isa. 11:1).

This is the King as the Branch, Rod, out of the stem of Jesse, father of David.

5. "That it might be fulfilled which was spoken through Isaiah the prophet, saying,

> The land of Zabulon and the land of Naphthali,
>
> The way of the sea, beyond Jordan,
>
> Galilee of the nations,
>
> The people who were sitting in darkness
>
> Saw a great light,
>
> And to those who are sitting in darkness and the shadow of death
>
> Light arose upon them" (Matt. 4:14–16; Isa. 9:1–2).

This King was to be a Light to the Gentiles as well as to His people Israel.

6. "In order that it might be fulfilled which was spoken through Isaiah the prophet, saying,

> He himself took our weaknesses
>
> And bore our diseases" (Matt. 8:17; Isa. 53:4).

This King delivered His people from weakness and disease as none other could.

7. "Behold my servant whom I chose,

> My beloved, in whom my soul takes pleasure;
>
> I will put my spirit upon him
>
> And he shall proclaim justice for the Gentiles" (Matt. 12:18; Isa. 42:1).

This King shall rule the Gentiles as well as His people Israel.

8. "All these things Jesus spoke in parables to the crowds, and apart from a parable he spoke nothing to them, in order that it might be fulfilled which was spoken through the prophet, saying,

> I will open my mouth in parables;
>
> I will declare things which have been hidden from the foundation of the world" (Matt. 13:34–35; Ps. 78:2).

This King was the great Teacher of divine truth.

9. "But this was done in order that the word which was spoken through the prophet might be fulfilled, saying,

Say to the daughter of Zion;

Behold, your king comes to you,

Meek and sitting upon an ass

And upon a colt the foal of an ass" (Matt. 21:4–5; Zech. 9:9; Isa. 62:11).

This King is not afraid to come in humility and peace.

10. "Then was fulfilled that which was spoken through Jeremiah the prophet, saying,

And I took the thirty pieces of silver, the price of one who was valued by the sons of Israel, and gave them for the potter's field, even as the Lord appointed me" (Matt. 27:9–10; Zech. 11:12–13; Jer. 18:1–4).

This King knew the exact sum for which He would be betrayed. All these taken together show that the Lord Jesus had an omniscient understanding of what His life and ministry would accomplish. They also show that the prophets said far more than their contemporaries could understand. Matthew is helping us all understand.

God's Revelation. The Lord Jesus taught the verbal inspiration and inerrancy of God's written revelation, the Bible (5:18). Every letter shall be fulfilled. Matthew obviously believed this himself, for he repeatedly saw the fulfillment of the OT prophecies in the life of the Lord (1:22; 2:15, 17, 23; 4:14; 8:17; 12:17; 13:35; 21:4; 27:9). His quotations are often prefaced with the formula "that which was spoken by the Lord through the prophet" (1:22). The Lord's use of the phrase *the Scriptures* also shows His determination to honor the OT (26:53–56). The Lord's rhetorical question "Have you not read . . . " assumes the absolute infallibility of the OT text (12:3, 5; 19:4; 21:16, 42; 22:31). The way the Lord charged the Sadducees with error because they did not know the Scriptures (22:29) showed His confidence in the inspired Word of God.

For further study see

Custer, Stewart. *Does Inspiration Demand Inerrancy?* Nutley, N.J.: Craig Press, 1968.

Engelder, T. E. *Scripture Cannot Be Broken*. St. Louis: Concordia, 1944.

Geisler, Norman L., ed. *Inerrancy*. Grand Rapids: Zondervan, 1979, 1980.

Lightner, Robert. *The Saviour and the Scriptures*. Philadelphia: Presbyterian and Reformed Publishing Company, 1966.

Ryrie, Charles C. *What You Should Know About Inerrancy*. Chicago: Moody Press, 1981.

Warfield, Benjamin B. *The Inspiration and Authority of the Bible*. Philadelphia: Presbyterian and Reformed Publishing Company, 1948.

Young, Edward J. *Thy Word Is Truth*. Grand Rapids: Eerdmans, 1957.

Religious Symbols. The ancient symbols of Israel (the people of God)—the Torah (the Law), and the temple (the place of God's worship)—were replaced by the Lord Jesus Himself (Matt. 5:17–20). The church is the new people of God (16:18; 21:43). The law of Christ is the new revelation (5:22, 28, 32). The presence of Christ is the new sanctuary (28:20). Righteousness is not pharisaic deeds but the righteousness of Christ lived out (6:33). The greatest commandment is love for God and His people (22:37–40). The symbols of baptism (28:19–20) and the Lord's Supper (26:26–29) were to be the continuing symbols, ordinances, of the church (I Cor. 1:16–17; 11:23–26).

For further study see

Elwell, Walter, ed. *Evangelical Dictionary of Biblical Theology*, "Matthew, Theology of," pp. 514–17.

Ethical Conduct. Although God receives miserable sinners with compassion, He expects their conduct to change (Matt. 18:23–35). Love for God and man should characterize the believer (22:37–40). Proper ethics includes the payment of taxes (22:15–21). God rejects merely formalistic religious practices (5:20), but God cherishes the heart devotion of those who pray to Him in secret (6:6–8). Greatness in God's eyes is to be great in service for Him (20:25–28). The teaching ministry of the church should include the observance of all things that the Lord taught (Matt. 28:19–20).

For further study see

Maston, T. B. *Biblical Ethics*. Waco, Tex.: Word Books, Publishers, 1967, 1977.

ZPEB, "Ethics of Jesus," II, pp. 404–11.

ISBE (1982), "Ethics: The Ethic of Jesus," II, pp. 169–73.

Elwell, Walter, ed., *Evangelical Dictionary of Biblical Theology*, "Ethics," pp. 213–16.

Eschatology. The present age will end in an act of God by which He will remove evil from the world and will establish the righteous forever (Matt. 13:38–43). The ultimate fate of the wicked is a "furnace of fire" (13:50) or hell ("Gehenna," 5:29–30); the destiny of the righteous is glory and reward (13:43; 16:27). The coming of the Lord is imminent; all believers in every age should be watchful (24:42–44). Premillennialists have long taught that this age will end in the Tribulation period, in which the personal Antichrist will be manifested (24:15), after which the Lord will return in glory (24:29–30), will gather His elect (24:31), and will decide who will enter the millennial reign (25:31–46). They are not agreed as to whether Matthew 24:40–41 teaches the Rapture as do the Epistles (I Thess. 4:13–18), or whether it refers to the removal of the wicked before the millennial reign (Rev. 19:19–21).

For further study see

Pentecost, J. Dwight. *Things to Come*. Findlay, Ohio: Dunham, 1958.

Tan, Paul Lee. *The Interpretation of Prophecy*. Winona Lake, Ind.: BMH Books, Inc., 1974.

Walvoord, John F. *Major Bible Prophecies*. Grand Rapids: Zondervan, 1991, pp. 346–53.

Mastering the Book of Matthew

The believer in the Lord Jesus Christ must not be satisfied with a shallow knowledge of Scripture. We are commanded to "search the Scriptures" (John 5:39), meditate in them day and night (Josh. 1:8), and use them for doctrine, reproof, correction, and instruction in righteousness (II Tim. 3:16). It is a good thing for a Christian to study Scripture the way God wrote it: one book at a time. It is also good to study so as to digest and absorb that content and the great biblical truths that are in it ("Thy words were found, and I did eat them," Jer. 15:16). The reader should come to the Gospel of Matthew with the determination to learn what is in it and to apply its teaching to the life that he lives. He should know the outline of Matthew; he should have a theme to characterize each chapter; he should know each person, place, and major doctrine that is found in each chapter. He should certainly apply the teaching to his own heart relationship with his Savior. The Lord Jesus invited us, "Come unto me, all ye that labor and are heavy laden, and I will give you rest" (Matt. 11:28), but He also added, "Take my yoke upon you, and learn of me; for I am meek and lowly in heart: and ye shall find rest unto your souls" (Matt. 11:29). Let us pray the Lord that He will accomplish that in our souls.

ABBREVIATIONS

Andrews. *Life of Our Lord*—Andrews, Samuel J. *The Life of Our Lord.* Grand Rapids: Zondervan, 1862, rpt. 1954.

Arndt and Gingrich—Arndt and Gingrich. *A Greek-English Lexicon of the New Testament and Other Early Christian Literature.* Chicago: The University of Chicago Press, 1957.

ASB—The American Standard Bible, 1901.

AV—The Authorized Version (i.e., The King James Version).

Bengel, *Gnomon*—Bengel, John Albert. *Gnomon of the New Testament.* Vol. I, Matthew. Edinburgh: T. & T. Clark, 1863.

Bruce, *Expos. Greek Test.*—Bruce, A. B. *Expositor's Greek Testament.* Vol. I, "Matthew." Grand Rapids: Eerdmans, 1951.

Edersheim, *Life and Times*—Edersheim, Alfred. *The Life and Times of Jesus the Messiah.* 2 vols. Grand Rapids: Eerdmans, 1953.

Edersheim. *Sketches*—Edersheim, Alfred. *Sketches of Jewish Social Life.* Grand Rapids: Eerdmans, 1950.

ESV—The English Standard Version, 2001.

ISBE—*The International Standard Bible Encyclopedia.* 4 vols. Grand Rapids: Eerdmans, 1979-88.

KJV—The King James Version.

LXX—The Septuagint, the Greek translation of the Old Testament.

Moulton and Milligan—*The Vocabulary of the Greek Testament.* Grand Rapids: Eerdmans, 1963.

NASB—The New American Standard Bible.

NET—New English Translation (Internet). www.netbible.org

NIV—The New International Version.

NJB—The New Jerusalem Bible.

NKJV—The New King James Version.

NLT—The New Living Translation.

NRSV—The New Revised Standard Version.

NT—The New Testament.

OT—The Old Testament.

p., pp.—Page, pages.

Robertson, *Word Pictures*—Robertson, Archibald Thomas. *Word Pictures in the New Testament,* Vol. I, Matthew. Nashville: Broadman Press, 1933.

Rpt.—Reprinted.

Scroggie, *Guide to Gospels*—Scroggie, W. Graham. *A Guide to the Gospels.* London: Pickering and Inglis, 1948.

Trench, Synonyms—Trench, Richard Chenevix, *Synonyms of the New Testament.* Grand Rapids: Eerdmans, 1953.

Unger—Unger, Merrill F., *The New Unger's Bible Dictionary.* Chicago: Moody, 1988.

v., vv.—Verse, verses.

Vincent, *Word Studies*—Vincent, Marvin R., *Word Studies in the New Testament*, vol. I. Grand Rapids: Eerdmans, 1946.

ZPEB—*Zondervan Pictorial Encyclopedia of the Bible.* 5 vols. Grand Rapids: Zondervan, 1975.

All other commentaries on Matthew are referred to by the author's last name and Matt.

MATTHEW 1

THE COMING OF THE KING

Persons

Jesus Christ

Mary, His mother

Joseph

An Angel

The Holy Spirit

Persons referred to

David

Abraham

Isaac

Jacob

Judah

Phares

Zara

Thamar

Esrom

Aram

Aminadab

Naasson

Salmon

Booz

Rachab [Rahab]

Obed

Ruth

Jesse

Solomon

Wife of Urias
[Bathsheba]

Roboam
[Rehoboam]

Abia

Asa

Josaphat
[Jehoshaphat]

Joram

Ozias [Uzziah]

Joatham

Achaz

Ezekias [Hezekiah]

Manasses

Amon

Josias

Jechonias

Salathiel

Zorobabel

Abiud

Eliakim

Azor

Sadoc

Achim

Eliud

Eleazar

Matthan

Jacob

Places mentioned

Babylon

Doctrines taught

The Virgin Birth

The Holy Spirit

Salvation

Sin

Obedience

1 The book of the generation of Jesus Christ, the son of David, the son of Abraham.

Matthew 1 Exposition

I. The Genealogy of the King. vv. 1–17.

"The book of the generation of Jesus Christ, son of David, son of Abraham" (v. 1). The opening phrase, a kind of heading, refers back to the original biblical genealogy (Gen. 5:1ff.). The messianic king is the heir of Abraham, who is the first of the Hebrew people to have the promise of kings in his descendants (Gen. 17:6, 16). He is the heir of David, who had the divine promise of the messianic king (II Sam. 7:12–17; Ps. 89:27–29), who was so zealous for the honor of the Lord of hosts (I Sam. 17:45–47). To a first-century Jew, such a genealogy established beyond doubt the descent of the Lord. A. T. Robertson notes that Matthew traces the genealogy to David and Abraham to show that Christ is heir of the promises, whereas Luke traces it back to Adam to show that Christ is the second Adam, perfect man (*Word Pictures*, I, p. 4). Hengstenberg argues that the Gospel of Mark begins by calling Jesus "Son of

---

1:1. For background to the genealogy of Christ see J. Gresham Machen, *The Virgin Birth of Christ*, pp. 202–9; A. T. Robertson, *A Harmony of the Gospels*, pp. 259–62; "Genealogy of Jesus Christ," Graham Scroggie, *Guide to the Gospels*, "The Two Genealogies," pp. 505–11; Douglas and Tenney, eds., *The New International Dictionary of the Bible*, "Genealogy of Jesus Christ," p. 379; ISBE (1982), "Genealogy of Jesus," II, pp. 428–31; ZPEB, "Genealogy of Jesus Christ," II, pp. 675–77.

The name *Jesus* ('Ιησοῦς) occurs 152 times in Matt.; *Jesus* is the Greek form of the name *Joshua*, "Jehovah is salvation." There were 3 people in the OT who foreshadowed our Lord's 3 offices: Joshua was the military leader (Josh. 5:13–14); Joshua the high priest was the priestly leader (Zech. 3:1–8); and Hosea the prophet was the prophetic leader; his name was Joshua's original name (Num. 13:16). See Vincent, *Word Studies*, I, pp. 16–17.

There are many names and titles applied to the Lord Jesus in Scripture. See James Large, *Two Hundred and Eighty Titles and Symbols of Christ*; T. C. Horton, *The Wonderful Names of Our Wonderful Lord*; Philip Henry, *Christ All in All*.

Christ (Χριστός) occurs 16 times (1:1, 16, 17, 18; 2:4; 11:2; 16:16, 20; 22:42; 23:10; 24:5, 23; 26:63, 68; 27:17, 22). The word *Christ* means the *Anointed One*, the *Messiah*. For discussion see Warfield, *The Lord of Glory*, pp. 73–84; Elwell, ed. *Evangelical Dictionary of Biblical Theology*, "Jesus Christ, Name and Titles of," pp. 406–8; ZPEB, "Messiah," IV, pp. 198–207; ISBE (1986), "Messiah," III, pp. 330–38; Ryken, Wilhoit, and Longman, *Dictionary of Biblical Imagery*, "Images of Jesus" pp. 447–48. For further study see Torrey, *What the Bible Teaches*, "About Jesus Christ," pp. 63–222; Van Bruggen, *Jesus the Son of God*; Walvoord, *Jesus Christ Our Lord*; Warfield, *The Lord of Glory*; Elwell, ed., *Evangelical Dictionary of Biblical Theology*, "Jesus Christ," pp. 396–406; ZPEB, "Jesus Christ," III, pp. 497–583; ISBE (1982), "Jesus Christ," II, pp. 1034–49; Harrison, ed., *Baker's Dictionary of Theology*, "Jesus," pp. 297–98.

2 Abraham begat Isaac; and Isaac begat Jacob; and Jacob begat Judas and his brethren;

God" because Mark's Gospel starts with the baptism of John, in which the divine voice calls Jesus "my beloved Son" (Mark 1:11, *Gnomon*, I, p. 82). Matthew organized the genealogy into three groups of fourteen (the sacred number seven doubled), the Lord Jesus being the fourteenth of the third group (v. 17). God is never in a hurry; in due time He establishes His purpose. "But when the fullness of the time was come, God sent forth his Son, made of a woman, made under the law, to redeem them that were under the law, that we might receive the adoption of sons" (Gal. 4:4–5). The whole Bible is about the Savior King, Who redeems His people and makes them kings and priests unto God (Rev. 5:9–10).

"Abraham begat Isaac, and Isaac begat Jacob, and Jacob begat Judah and his brethren" (v. 2). The genealogy passes over the trials that Sarah, Rebekah, and Leah had in bearing the patriarchs (Gen. 21:1–29:35). In Hebrew thinking the descent runs through the males.

1:1, 6, 17. *David* (Δαυίδ) is named 5 times in the genealogy; 17 times in Matt. (1:1, 6 [twice], 17 [twice], 20; 9:27; 12:3, 23; 15:22; 20:30, 31; 21:9, 15; 22:42, 43, 45). In the other 3 Gospels together David is named only 22 times. Plainly the important point is that it is a royal genealogy. None of the Lord's enemies ever raised a question about His right to the throne. Pilate's question was a very serious one: "Art thou a king then?" (lit., "Are you not therefore a king?" John 18:37). For background see ZPEB, "David," II, pp. 31–43; ISBE (1979), "David," I, pp. 870–76; *Who's Who in the Bible*, "David," pp. 72–80; Alexander Whyte, *Bible Characters*, has 4 sermons: David, his virtues, his vices, his graces, his services, pp. 103–49.

The messianic title, *Son of David*, occurs 10 times in Matt. (1:1, 20; 9:27; 12:23; 15:22; 20:30, 31; 21:9, 15; 22:42).

Abraham is mentioned 7 times by Matt. (1:1, 2, 17; 3:9 [twice]; 8:11; 22:32). For background see ZPEB, "Abraham," I, pp. 21–26; ISBE (1979), "Abraham," I, pp. 15–18; Alexander Whyte, *Bible Characters*, "Abraham," I, pp. 116–28; *Who's Who in the Bible*, "Abraham," pp. 16–25.

1:2. *Isaac* is mentioned 4 times in Matt. (1:2 [twice]; 8:11; 22:32). For background see ZPEB, "Isaac," III, pp. 310–13; ISBE (1982), "Isaac," II, pp. 883–84; *Who's Who in the Bible*, "Isaac," pp. 162–65; Alexander Whyte, *Bible Characters*, "Isaac," pp. 151–61.

Jacob is mentioned 6 times in Matt. (1:2 [twice], 15, 16; 8:11; 22:32). For background see ZPEB, "Jacob," III, pp. 383–88; ISBE (1982), II, pp. 948–55; *Who's Who in the Bible*, "Jacob," pp. 173–80; Alexander Whyte, *Bible Characters*, "Jacob," I, pp. 183–93.

Judah is named twice in Matt. (1:2, 3). For background see ZPEB, "Judah," III, p. 718.

The word *brother* (ἀδελφός) occurs 39 times in Matt. (1:2, 11; 4:18 [twice], 21 [twice]; 5:22 [twice], 23, 24, 47; 7:3, 4, 5; 10:2 [twice], 21 [twice]; 12:46, 47, 48, 49, 50; 13:55; 14:3; 17:1; 18:15 [twice], 21, 35; 19:29; 20:24; 22:24 [twice], 25 [twice]; 23:8; 25:40; 28:10). For discussion see ZPEB, "Brother," I, p. 458; ISBE (1979), "Brother," p. 550; Ryken, Wilhoit, and Longman, *Dictionary of Biblical Imagery*, "Brother," pp. 125–27.

3 And Judas begat Phares and Zara of Thamar; and Phares begat Esrom; and Esrom begat Aram;

4 And Aram begat Aminadab; and Aminadab begat Naasson; and Naasson begat Salmon;

5 And Salmon begat Booz of Rachab; and Booz begat Obed of Ruth; and Obed begat Jesse;

6 And Jesse begat David the king; and David the king begat Solomon of her that had been the wife of Urias;

"And Judah begat Phares and Zara of Tamar, and Phares begat Esrom, and Esrom begat Aram" (v. 3). Here is the surprise mention of Tamar, the neglected woman who used desperate means to have children from Judah (Gen. 38:11–29). She is the first of four women referred to in the genealogy. The mention of women at all in an ancient genealogy was highly unusual.

"And Aram begat Aminadab, and Aminadab begat Naasson, and Naasson begat Salmon, and Salmon begat Boaz of Rahab, and Boaz begat Obed of Ruth, and Obed begat Jesse" (vv. 4–5). Here the genealogy mentions Rahab, the harlot and a Gentile (Josh. 2:1ff.), and Ruth, another Gentile (Ruth 4:10–13). There was plainly assimilation of Gentiles after the conquest of the land.

"And Jesse begat David the king" (v. 6a). There is a definite paragraph break at this point. The text continues with a new paragraph that emphasizes the Davidic descent. "And David begat Solomon of the [wife of] Uriah" (v. 6b). Bathsheba was the woman who flaunted her beauty at king David and got invited into the palace (II Sam. 11:2–5; 12:24). The record is stained by sin, which the coming king will atone for by His death. Contrary to customary usage, all these sinful people are mentioned with a definite purpose. God's people are not saved because they are so good; they are saved by the grace of God because He is so good and merciful. Every saint in heaven is a sinner saved by grace.

Jehovah God swore with an oath that the throne of David would endure to all generations (Ps. 89:3–4). The apostle Paul twice makes a special point of the Davidic descent of the Lord, Who "was made of the seed of

---

1:3ff. There is considerable variation in the spelling of these Hebrew names, as Broadus notes, "presenting us the English form of the common Greek form of the Hebrew words" (*Matt.*, p. 3).

7 And Solomon begat Roboam; and Roboam begat Abia; and Abia begat Asa;
8 And Asa begat Josaphat; and Josaphat begat Joram; and Joram begat Ozias;

David according to the flesh" (Rom. 1:3); "Remember . . . Jesus Christ of the seed of David" (II Tim. 2:8). He also mentioned the fact in a sermon (Acts 13:22–23), as the apostle Peter also did (Acts 2:30). The fact of the Lord's descent from David was widely known, as the intense cry of blind Bartimaeus showed: "Jesus, Son of David, have mercy on me" (Mark 10:47*b*). Matthew, however, is the only Gospel writer to record that the crowds at the Triumphal Entry were crying out, "Hosanna to the Son of David" (Matt. 21:9*b*). In the book of Revelation one of the twenty-four elders reveals to John that "the Lion of the tribe of Judah, the Root of David" prevailed to open the scroll (Rev. 5:5*b*). In the conclusion of Revelation Jesus Himself testifies, "I am the root and the offspring of David" (Rev. 22:16*b*). Thus, from the beginning of Matthew to the end of Revelation the Savior King is declared to be the Heir of David.

"And Solomon begat Rehoboam, and Rehoboam begat Abia, and Abia begat Asa, and Asa begat Jehoshaphat, and Jehoshaphat begat Joram, and Joram begat Uzziah" (vv. 7–8). Here after Joram, Matthew omits the names of three kings, Ahaziah, Joash, and Amaziah (II Kings 8:24; 11:2; 12:19–21). There is no attempt to deceive; the names of all the kings were well known. It was common practice to omit some names from a genealogy. Broadus suggests that these were omitted because they were other sons of Ahab and Jezebel rather than a new generation (*Matt.*, p. 6). A. C. Gaebelein thinks that since Ahab's daughter, Queen Athaliah, attempted to annihilate the kingly seed of the house of Judah, Ahab's descendants were omitted (*Matt.*, pp. 22–23).

1:6. The word *king* (βασιλεύς) occurs here for the first of 22 times in Matt. (1:6; 2:1, 2, 3, 9; 5:35; 10:18; 11:8; 14:9; 17:25; 18:23; 21:5; 22:2, 7, 11, 13; 25:34, 40; 27:11, 29, 37, 42). Matt. is the Gospel of the King. A king provides authority and justice for his people. In the case of the Lord Jesus, He provides eternal salvation for His people. For background see Ryken, Wilhoit, and Longman, *Dictionary of Biblical Imagery,* "King, Kingship," pp. 476–78; ZPEB, "King, Kingship," III, pp. 795–801; ISBE (1986), "King, Kingdom," III, pp. 20–23. For *kingdom* see Matt. 3:2 note.

1:7. Bengel notes, "Bad men, even though they are useless to themselves in their lifetime, do not exist in vain; since by their means the elect even are brought into the world" (*Gnomon,* I, p. 84).

9 And Ozias begat Joatham; and Joatham begat Achaz; and Achaz begat Ezekias;
10 And Ezekias begat Manasses; and Manasses begat Amon; and Amon begat Josias;
11 And Josias begat Jechonias and his brethren, about the time they were carried away to Babylon:
12 And after they were brought to Babylon, Jechonias begat Salathiel; and Salathiel begat Zorobabel;
13 And Zorobabel begat Abiud; and Abiud begat Eliakim; and Eliakim begat Azor;
14 And Azor begat Sadoc; and Sadoc begat Achim; and Achim begat Eliud;
15 And Eliud begat Eleazar; and Eleazar begat Matthan; and Matthan begat Jacob;

"And Uzziah begat Jotham, and Jotham begat Ahaz, and Ahaz begat Hezekiah, and Hezekiah begat Manassah, and Manassah begat Amon, and Amon begat Josiah, and Josiah begat Jeconiah and his brethren about the carrying away to Babylon" (vv. 9–11). Here the name of Eliakim, or Jehoiakim, is omitted (II Kings 23:34) perhaps because he was imposed on the people by Pharaoh Necho.

"And after the carrying away to Babylon, Jeconiah begat Salathiel, and Salathiel begat Zorobabel, and Zorobabel begat Abiud, and Abiud begat Eliakim, and Eliakim begat Azor, and Azor begat Sadoc, and Sadoc begat Achim, and Achim begat Eliud, and Eliud begat Eleazar, and Eleazar begat Matthan, and Matthan begat Jacob" (vv. 12–15). There is no external historical information available about this part of the genealogy. Matthew Henry observes that after all these years the messianic hope was dim: "when the house of David was buried in obscurity," Christ was "a root out of dry ground" (Isa. 53:2). "And Jacob begat Joseph the husband of Mary,

1:11. For background on the captivity see ISBE (1979) "Captivity," II, pp. 612–15; "Exile," III, pp. 221–22; ZPEB, "Exile," II, pp. 423–28; H. R. Hall, *The Ancient History of the Near East*, pp. 546–48; Herzog, Chaim, and Mordechai Gichon, *Battles of the Bible* (London: Greenhill Books, 1997), pp. 256–62.

1:16. Joseph was a quiet man who was content to work behind the scenes but who was deeply committed to obeying God at all costs. For background on Joseph see "Joseph 2," *Who's Who in the Bible*, pp. 247–48; "Joseph and Mary," Alexander Whyte, *Bible Characters*, IV, pp. 1–9; "Joseph, Husband of Mary," ISBE (1982), II, pp. 1130–31; "Joseph 2," ZPEB, III, pp. 695–96.

The word *husband, man* as distinct from *woman* (ἀνήρ) occurs 8 times in Matt. (1:16, 19; 7:24, 26; 12:41; 14:21, 35; 15:38).

Mary is named 11 times in Matt. (1:16, 18, 20; 2:11; 13:55; 27:56 [twice], 61 [twice]; 28:1 [twice]). For background see J. Gresham Machen, *The Virgin Birth of Christ*, index, p. 407;

16 And Jacob begat Joseph the husband of Mary, of whom was born Jesus, who is called Christ.
17 So all the generations from Abraham to David are fourteen generations; and from David until the carrying away into Babylon are fourteen generations; and from the carrying away into Babylon unto Christ are fourteen generations.

of whom was born Jesus, the one called Christ" (v. 16). Matthew makes it obvious that Joseph did not beget Jesus; he was an adoptive father, as the context makes clear (Matt. 1:20–23). "Therefore all the generations from Abraham to David are fourteen generations; and from David to the carrying away to Babylon fourteen generations, and from the carrying away to Babylon to the Christ fourteen generations" (v. 17). Matthew may have

---

"Mary," *Who's Who in the Bible*, pp. 283–86; ZPEB, "Mary, Mother of Jesus," IV, pp. 106–12; ISBE (1986) "Mary, 6, Mother of Jesus," III, pp. 269–73; "Mary, the Virgin," Hastings, *Dictionary of Christ and the Gospels*, II, pp. 140–42.

1:17. The 3 Hebrew letters that make up the name *David* have a numeric value of 14. The fact that the Holy Spirit is set forth under the symbol of the 7 spirits before the throne (Rev. 1:4) shows the importance of the number 7. For the significance of numbers in the Bible, see Introduction, *Numbers in the Bible*, p. xxii.

The word *generation* (γενεά) occurs 13 times in Matt. (1:17 [4 times]; 11:16; 12:39, 41, 42, 45; 16:4; 17:17; 23:36; 24:34). For a special note see Matt. 24:34.

1:18. The word *mother* (μήτηρ) occurs 26 times in Matt. (1:18; 2:11, 13, 14, 20, 21; 10:35, 37; 12:46, 47, 48, 49, 50; 13:55; 14:8, 11; 15:4 [twice], 5; 19:5, 12, 19, 29; 20:20; 27:56 [twice]. For discussion see Ryken, Wilhoit, and Longman, *Dictionary of Biblical Imagery*, "Mother, Motherhood," pp. 570–72; ISBE (1986), "Mother," III, pp. 426–27.

The *Holy Spirit* is mentioned 6 times in Matt. (1:18, 20; 3:11; 12:31, 32; 28:19), but the Spirit of God is plainly intended also in 3:16; 4:1; 10:20; 12:18, 28; 22:43. For further discussion see Swete, Henry Barclay, *The Holy Spirit in the New Testament*; John Walvoord, *The Holy Spirit*; Andrew Murray, *Spirit of Christ*; Rene Pache, *The Person and Work of the Holy Spirit*; ISBE (1982), "Holy Spirit," II, pp. 730–46; ZPEB, "Holy Spirit," III, pp. 183–96; Elwell, ed., "Holy Spirit," *Evangelical Dictionary of Biblical Theology*, pp. 344–48.

Plummer wisely observes that "it is safer to accept with reverent thankfulness what has been told us in the Gospels than to raise needless, and perhaps fruitless, questions about what has not been told" (*Matt.*, p. 7). For the doctrine of the Virgin Birth, see J. Gresham Machen, *The Virgin Birth of Christ*; Benjamin B. Warfield, "The Supernatural Birth of Jesus," *Biblical and Theological Studies*, pp. 157ff.; John F. Walvoord, "The Incarnation of the Son of God," *Jesus Christ Our Lord*, pp. 96–105; Campbell Morgan, *The Crises of the Christ*, "The Birth," pp. 63–101; Edersheim, "Virgin Birth of Jesus Christ," *Life and Times*, I, pp. 150–59; ISBE (1988), IV, pp. 990–93; "Virgin Birth," ZPEB, V, pp. 886–89; "Incarnation," ZPEB, III, pp. 267–74; "Virgin Birth of Jesus, The," *Baker's Dictionary of Theology*, pp. 543–45; Elwell, ed., "Virgin Birth," *Evangelical Dictionary of Biblical Theology*, pp. 799–802; Hastings, ed., "Incarnation," *Dictionary of Christ and the Gospels*, I, pp. 796–813; "Virgin Birth," II, pp. 804–9.

The verb *to find* (εὑρίσκω) occurs here for the first of 27 times in Matt. (1:18; 2:8; 7:7, 8, 14; 8:10; 10:39 [twice]; 11:29; 12:43, 44; 13:44, 46; 16:25; 17:27; 18:13, 28; 20:6; 21:2, 19; 22:9, 10; 24:46; 26:40, 43, 60; 27:32).

18 Now the birth of Jesus Christ was on this wise: When as his mother Mary was espoused to Joseph, before they came together, she was found with child of the Holy Ghost.
19 Then Joseph her husband, being a just man, and not willing to make her a public example, was minded to put her away privily.

been preserving the "sacred seven" in the fourteen generations of his genealogy (v. 17). Leon Morris notes that the number fourteen would have been impressive to first-century Jews (*Matt.*, p. 25). It is clear that God is working out His will in cycles of perfect symmetry.

II. The Birth of the King. vv. 18–25.

"But the birth of Jesus Christ was thus: When his mother Mary was espoused to Joseph, before they came together, she was found with child by the Holy Spirit" (v. 18). The Jewish engagement was a solemn contract that could be broken only by death or divorce. Matthew's language makes very clear that the pregnancy was a supernatural act of God and not indiscretion on the part of Mary. The doctrine of the Virgin Birth of Christ stands with transparent clarity in this passage. Those who would deny it must contradict the text. Luke supplies more details on the devout character of Mary (Luke 1:27–38, 46–55). Joseph, already regarded as her husband, jumps to very natural conclusions on hearing of this circumstance.

"But Joseph her husband, being a just man and not wishing to make her an example, desired to put her away privately" (v. 19). Joseph was known as "the carpenter" (Matt. 13:55). The fact that he was "a just man" means that he was a law-abiding, "observant" Jew. He plainly loved Mary dearly and could not stand the thought of a public trial. He did not desire to see her public shame but instead determined to dissolve the union quietly.

1:19. The word *just, righteous* (δίκαιος) occurs 19 times in Matt. (1:19; 5:45; 9:13; 10:41 [3 times]; 13:17, 43, 49; 20:4; 23:28, 29, 35 [twice]; 25:37, 46; 27:4, 19, 24). (More than any other NT book; Paul uses it 7 times in Rom.) For further study see Elwell, ed., *Evangelical Dictionary of Biblical Theology*, "Righteousness," pp. 687–89; ZPEB, "Righteousness," V, pp. 104–18; ISBE (1988), "Righteousness," IV, pp. 192–95.

The verb *to will, wish* (θέλω) occurs here for the first of 42 times in Matt. (1:19; 2:18; 5:40, 42; 7:12; 8:2, 3; 9:13; 11:14; 12:7, 38; 13:28; 14:5; 15:28, 32; 16:24, 25; 17:4, 12; 18:23, 30; 19:17, 21, and so forth).

The verb *to will, determine* (βούλομαι) occurs twice in Matt. (1:19; 11:27). For an extended comparison between these 2 verbs *to will* see Vincent, *Word Studies*, I, pp. 12–15.

The verb *to put away, release, divorce* (ἀπολύω) occurs 19 times in Matt. (1:19; 5:31, 32 [twice]; 14:15, 22, 23; 15:23, 32, 39; 18:27; 19:3, 7, 8, 9; 27:15, 17, 21, 26).

20 But while he thought on these things, behold, the angel of the Lord appeared unto him in a dream, saying, Joseph, thou son of David, fear not to take unto thee Mary thy wife: for that which is conceived in her is of the Holy Ghost.

"But while he thought on these things, behold, an angel of the Lord appeared to him in a dream, saying, Joseph, son of David, be not afraid to take Mary your wife; for that which is begotten in her is of the Holy Spirit" (v. 20). The word *angel* does not have the article with it, which denotes a regular angel. The phrase "the angel of the Lord" denoted a preincarnate appearance of the Lord Jesus, who received worship

---

1:20. This is the first of 20 times that the word *angel, messenger* (ἄγγελος) occurs in Matt. (1:20, 24; 2:13, 19; 4:6, 11; 11:10; 13:39, 41, 49; 16:27; 18:10; 22:30; 24:31, 36; 25:31, 41; 26:53; 28:2, 5). God has made His angels ministering spirits (Ps. 104:4; Heb. 1:7). Although the word can be used of a human messenger (11:10), it usually refers to a spiritual being of more than human powers. See R. K. Harrison, ed., "Angel," *The New Unger's Bible Dictionary*," pp. 61–62; Elwell, ed., "Angel," *Evangelical Dictionary of Biblical Theology*, pp. 21–23; "Angel," ZPEB, I, pp. 160–66; "Angel," ISBE (1979), I, pp. 124–27.

The word *Lord* (κύριος) occurs here for the first of 80 times in Matt. (1:20, 22, 24; 2:13, 15, 19; 3:3; 4:7, 10; 5:33; 6:24; 7:21 [twice], 22 [twice]; 8:2, 6, 8, 21, 25; 9:28, 38; 10:24, 25; 11:25; 12:8; 13:27; 14:28, 30; 15:22, 25, 27 [twice]; 16:22; 17:4, 15; 18:21, 25, 27, 31, 32, 34; 20:8, 30, 31, 33; 21:3, 9, 30, 40, 42; 22:37, 43, 44 [twice], 45; 23:39; 24:42, 45, 46, 48, 50; 25:11 [twice], 18, 19, 20, 21 [twice], 22, 23 [twice], 24, 26, 37, 44; 26:22; 27:10, 63; 28:2). Although it may be just a polite address (Matt. 21:30), it is regularly a word of divine authority. It is a parallel to the Hebrew *Adonai*, Master, One Who has the right to rule (Gen. 15:2). God is Lord of angels and prophets (Matt. 1:20, 22) and should be of every believer (Matt. 7:21). The Lord Jesus claimed the title (Matt. 21:3) and accepted it from others (Matt. 8:8). The most thorough defense of the title *Lord* as denoting the divine authority of Christ is Geerhardus Vos, *The Self-Disclosure of Jesus*, "The Lord," pp. 118–40. For further discussion see R. K. Harrison, ed., *The New Unger's Bible Dictionary*, "Lord," p. 781; ZPEB, "Lord," "Lord (Christ)," III, pp. 959–60; ISBE (1986), "Lord," III, pp. 157–58; Elwell, ed., *Evangelical Dictionary of Biblical Theology*, "Jesus Christ, Name and Titles of," "Lord," pp. 409–10.

The word *dream* (ὄναρ) occurs 6 times only in the NT in Matt. (1:20; 2:12, 13, 19, 22; 27:19). For discussion see ZPEB, "Dream," II, pp. 162–64; ISBE "Dream," I, pp. 991–92; Ryken, Wilhoit, and Longman, *Dictionary of Biblical Imagery*, "Dreams, Visions," pp. 217–19.

The verb *to appear* (φαίνω) occurs 13 times in Matt. (1:20; 2:7, 13, 19; 6:5, 16, 18; 9:33; 13:26; 23:27, 28; 24:27, 30).

The verb *to fear* (φοβέομαι) occurs 18 times in Matt. (1:20; 2:22; 9:8; 10:26, 28 [twice], 31; 14:5, 27, 30; 17:6, 7; 21:26, 46; 25:25; 27:54; 28:5, 10). Robertson notes that the verb here is an ingressive aorist, "Do not become afraid," *Word Pictures*, I, p. 9. Most reference works concentrate on fear, reverence for God: ISBE (1982), "Fear," II, pp. 289–92; Elwell, ed., *Evangelical Dictionary of Biblical Theology*, "Fear," pp. 248–49; Harrison, ed., *The New Unger's Bible Dictionary*, p. 404. Some works give a balanced survey: ZPEB, "Fear," II, pp. 518–21; Butler, ed., *Holman Bible Dictionary*, "Fear," pp. 480–82. Ryken, Wilhoit, and Longman, *Dictionary of Biblical Imagery*, provides separate articles, "Fear," pp. 275–77, and "Fear of God," pp. 277–78.

21 And she shall bring forth a son, and thou shalt call his name JESUS: for he shall save his people from their sins.

(Judg. 6:12–21). The regular angels always refuse worship (Rev. 19:10; 22:8–9). This angel addresses Joseph as "son of David" to remind him that he stands in the messianic line, and now his wife will be the mother of the great King (Isa. 32:1–2). The angel called Mary "your wife," making clear that it was the divine will that they be married. Although he was a humble carpenter, Joseph would have the privilege of being the adoptive father of the Lord of heaven. He would see to it that his home was saturated with Scripture. The Lord Jesus had a profound knowledge of Scripture at a tender age (Luke 2:46–47); His younger brother, James, quotes more Scripture in five chapters than any other NT writer. But then, Mary's prayer was filled with Scripture as well (Luke 1:46–55). "The familiarity with Scripture manifested by her song of thanksgiving (Luke 1:46ff.) shows how lovingly she had been accustomed to dwell on the word of God" (Broadus, *Matt.*, p. 8).

The angel continues, "And she shall bear a son, and you shall call his name Jesus: for he himself shall save his people from their sins" (v. 21). The name *Jesus* is the Greek form of the name *Joshua*, "Jehovah is salva-

---

The verb *to take along* (παραλαμβάνω) may imply compassionate care. It occurs 16 times in Matt. (1:20, 24; 2:13, 14, 20, 21; 4:5, 8; 12:45; 17:1; 18:16; 20:17; 24:40, 41; 26:37; 27:27).

The word *wife, woman* (γυνή) occurs 29 times in Matt. (1:20, 24; 5:28, 31, 32; 9:20, 22; 11:11; 13:33; 14:3, 21; 15:22, 28, 38; 18:25; 19:3, 5, 8, 9, 10; 22:24, 25, 27, 28; 26:7, 10; 27:19, 55; 28:5). See ZPEB, "Woman," V, pp. 950–55; ISBE (1988), "Woman," IV, pp. 1089–97; Elwell, ed., *Evangelical Dictionary of Biblical Theology*, "Woman," pp. 824–28; Ryken, Wilhoit, and Longman, *Dictionary of Biblical Imagery*, "Woman, Images of," pp. 958–62.

This is the first occurrence of one of Matthew's favorite words, *Behold!* (ἰδού). It occurs 62 times in Matt.; 200 times in the whole NT. (1:20, 23; 2:1, 9, 13, 19; 3:16, 17; 4:11; 7:4; 8:2, 24, 29, 32, 34; 9:2, 3, 10, and so forth).

1:21. The verb *to bear, bring forth* (τίκτω) occurs 4 times in Matt. (1:21, 23, 25; 2:2).

The word *name* (ὄνομα) occurs 22 times in Matt. (1:21, 23, 25; 6:9; 7:22 [3 times]; 10:2, 22, 41 [twice], 42; 12:21; 18:5, 20; 19:29; 21:9; 23:39; 24:5, 9; 27:32; 28:19). In the ancient world every Greek and Hebrew name had meaning. The name often stood for the character and authority of the person. "A name captures the essence of the person" (Ryken, Wilhoit, and Longman, *Dictionary of Biblical Imagery*, "Name," p. 583). For further discussion see ZPEB, "Name," IV, pp. 360–66; ISBE (1986), "Name," III, pp. 480–83.

The verb *to save* (σώζω) occurs here for the first of 15 times in Matt. (1:21; 8:25; 9:21, 22 [twice]; 10:22; 14:30; 16:25; 18:11; 19:25; 24:13, 22; 27:40, 42, 49). The word may mean

tion." The OT taught that only God could provide salvation. "Salvation belongeth unto the Lord [Jehovah]" (Ps. 3:8a). The angelic annunciation makes clear that the Lord did not come to earth merely to be a good example but to provide the atoning sacrifice that would save His people from sin and hell. The apostle Paul expressed this clearly, "This is a faithful saying, and worthy of all acceptation, that Christ Jesus came into the world to save sinners; of whom I am chief" (I Tim. 1:15). Spurgeon has a powerful seven-point sermon on the name *Jesus* ("Jesus," Sermon 1434, C. H. Spurgeon Collection, Metropolitan Tabernacle Pulpit, Ages Digital Library). Geerhardus Vos notes the logic of the statements, "We have, therefore, in close succession the statements, that Jehovah is salvation, and that Jesus saves, that Israel (Jehovah's people) are Jesus' people" (*Biblical Theology*, p. 332). Jesus is going to accomplish the mighty work of Jehovah God. Leon Morris notes that for Joseph to call His name meant that he was accepting Him as a son and confirming Davidic descent for Him (Isa. 43:1; *Matt.*, p. 29).

---

rescue or save from danger (Matt. 8:25), or *heal* (Matt. 9:22), as well as *save* in a religious sense (as here and in Matt. 10:22; 18:11; Rom. 10:13; I Tim. 1:15; Heb. 7:25; James 1:21). For a discussion of the religious meaning see Leon Morris, *The Cross in the New Testament*, "The Cross in Matthew and Mark," pp. 13–62; Ryken, Wilhoit, and Longman, *Dictionary of Biblical Imagery*, "Salvation," pp. 752–56; ZPEB, "Salvation," V, pp. 221–32; ISBE (1988), "Salvation," IV, pp. 287–95; Elwell, ed., *Evangelical Dictionary of Biblical Theology*, "Salvation," pp. 701–3.

This is the first of 7 times that the word *sin* (ἁμαρτία) occurs in Matt. (1:21; 3:6; 9:2, 5, 6; 12:31; 26:28). The root meaning is *to miss the mark*. "Sin is commission as well as omission" (ISBE, IV, p. 519). For a discussion of sin see Trench, *Synonyms of the New Testament*, pp. 239–49; Girdlestone, *Synonyms of the Old Testament*, pp. 76–86; ISBE (1988), "Sin," IV, pp. 518–25; Douglas and Tenney, eds., *The New International Dictionary of the Bible*, "Sin," pp. 946–47; Elwell, ed., *Evangelical Dictionary of Biblical Theology*, "Sin," pp. 736–39; ZPEB, "Sin," "Sinner," V, pp. 444–47. See also Matt. 9:11 note.

Salvation from Sin

   I. Jesus saves His people from sin. 1:21.

   II. Confessing and forsaking sin pleases God. 3:6.

   III. Jesus forgives sin. 9:2.

   IV. Jesus has divine authority to forgive sin. 9:5.

   V. Jesus proved His authority to forgive sin. 9:6.

   VI. All sin can be forgiven, except that against the Spirit. 12:31.

   VII. Jesus shed His blood to give forgiveness of sin. 26:28.

22 Now all this was done, that it might be fulfilled which was spoken of the Lord by the prophet, saying,
23 Behold, a virgin shall be with child, and shall bring forth a son, and they shall call his name Emmanuel, which being interpreted is, God with us.

"But this whole thing has happened in order that this thing that was spoken by the Lord through the prophet might be fulfilled, saying, Behold, the virgin shall be with child and shall bring forth a son, and they shall call his name Immanuel, which is translated, God with us" (vv. 22–23). This is a formal quotation of Isaiah 7:14. In context Isaiah reveals that

---

1:22. The verb *to fulfill* (πληρόω) occurs 16 times in Matt. (1:22; 2:15, 17, 23; 3:15; 4:14; 5:17; 8:17; 12:17; 13:35, 48; 21:4; 23:32; 26:54, 56; 27:9). The fulfillment of OT prophecy is a major theme in Matt. The disciples gathered together talking about it (John 1:45). The other Gospels also mention it (Mark 14:49; Luke 4:21; John 12:38). The Lord Jesus fulfilled prophecy on a number of levels, literally (as here), symbolically (Matt. 10:6), and prophetically (Matt. 26:24). See also Matt. 5:17–18. For further discussion see Fulfillment Formulas in The Theology of Matthew, pp. xxxvii–xxxix; Elwell, ed., *Evangelical Dictionary of Biblical Theology*, "Fulfillment," pp. 276–78; ZPEB, "Fulfill, Fulfillment," II, pp. 611–13; ISBE (1982), "Fulfill," II, pp. 366–69.

The word *prophet* (προήτης) occurs 37 times in Matt. (1:22; 2:5, 15, 17, 23; 3:3; 4:14; 5:12, 17; 7:12; 8:17; 10:41 [3 times]; 11:9 [twice], 13; 12:17, 39; 13:17, 35, 57; 14:5; 16:14; 21:4, 11, 26, 46; 22:40; 23:29, 30, 31, 34, 37; 24:15; 26:56; 27:9). See also *prophecy*, Matt. 7:22 note. For background see Girdlestone, *The Grammar of Prophecy*; E. J. Young, *My Servants the Prophets*; ZPEB, "Prophets and Prophecy," IV, pp. 875–903; ISBE (1986), "Prophet, Prophecy," III, pp. 986–1004; Elwell, ed., *Evangelical Dictionary of Biblical Theology*, "Prophet, Prophetess, Prophecy," pp. 641–47.

1:23. The word *God* (θεός) occurs here for the first of 51 times in Matt. See The Theology of Matthew, pp. xxix–xxx. For further discussion see ZPEB, "God," II, pp. 742–58; ISBE (1982), "God," II, pp. 493–503; Elwell, ed., *Evangelical Dictionary of Biblical Theology*, "God," pp. 288–95; Harrison, ed., Baker's *Dictionary of Theology*, "God," pp. 238–48; Ryken, Wilhoit, and Longman, *Dictionary of Biblical Imagery*, "God," pp. 332–36.

The word *virgin* (παρθένος) occurs 4 times in Matt. (1:23; 25:1, 7, 11). Liberal interpreters will claim that *'Almah* means merely *young woman*, but this contradicts uniform OT usage.

1. Gen. 24:43. KJV *virgin*. Abraham's servant was looking for a virgin who would be suitable for his master's son. Abraham's qualifications were very high.
2. Exod. 2:8. KJV *maid*. Miriam was a virgin daughter in her father's household, looking after a younger brother.
3. I Chron. 15:20. KJV *Alamoth*, virgin girls in the temple choir; impure girls were not welcome.
4. Ps. 46:1. KJV *Alamoth*, virgin girls in the temple choir.
5. Ps. 68:25. KJV *damsels*, virgin girls in the temple choir.
6. Prov. 30:19. KJV *maid*. Agur is puzzled by four things: a soaring eagle, a serpent crossing a rock, a ship at sea, and courtship. There is no puzzle about an impure relationship.
7. Song of Sol. 1:3. KJV *virgins*. Solomon's splendor caused admiration among virgins of Israel. To say that impure girls were attracted to him would have been slander.

24 Then Joseph being raised from sleep did as the angel of the Lord had bidden him, and took unto him his wife:
25 And knew her not till she had brought forth her firstborn son: and he called his name JESUS.

Jehovah has offered king Ahaz a miraculous sign "in the depth, or in the height above" (Isa. 7:11). Ahaz gives a super-pious refusal (v. 12) because he has already formed his military alliance and does not want the Lord to interfere. Isaiah then addresses the whole house of David, not just a disobedient king, and gives a supernatural sign that will remain for centuries before being fulfilled. To say as liberal interpreters do, that the word *virgin* ('Almah) means merely young woman, is to fly in the face of the context. The whole world is filled with young women who conceive; that is no supernatural sign. The son born shall be named Immanuel, "God with us," a supernatural title suitable for the great Messiah, the God-man, Who shall deliver His people from their sins. The fact that makes this interpretation mandatory is that we have a divinely inspired writer of Scripture (Matthew) who informs us that this is the correct interpretation of Isaiah. First-century Christians believed in the verbal inspiration of Scripture (II Tim. 3:15–17). Spurgeon has a beautiful sermon on "God with Us" (Sermon 1270, The C. H. Spurgeon Collection, Ages Digital Library).

"And Joseph, having been raised up from sleep, did as the angel of the Lord had commanded him, and he knew her not until she had brought forth a son; and he called his name Jesus" (vv. 24–25). The example of

---

8. Song of Sol. 6:8. KJV *virgins*. Solomon's palace had 3 categories of women: queens, daughters of kings; concubines, not royalty but full wives; and virgins, maids for the wives. To say that Solomon stocked the palace with impure girls is unthinkable in a religious poem.

9. Isa. 7:14. KJV *virgin*. God offered a supernatural sign of a virgin conceiving a child, who would be the great king.

It is significant that the LXX translates it as *virgin* (παρθένος). So do the KJV, ASB, NASB, NLT, NIV, ESV, NKJV, NRSV, *God's Word to the Nations*, and others. For examples in the papyri, see Moulton and Milligan, *Vocabulary*, p. 494.

1:24. The verb *to raise* (ἐγείρω) occurs 36 times in Matt. (1:24; 2:13, 14, 20, 21; 3:9; 8:15, 25, 26; 9:5, 6, 7, 19, 25; 10:8; 11:5, 11; 12:11, 42; 14:2; 16:21; 17:7, 9, 23; 20:19; 24:7, 11, 24; 25:7; 26:32, 46; 27:52, 63, 64; 28:6, 7).

The verb *to do* (ποιέω) occurs 86 times in Matt.

1:25. The verb *to know* (γινώσκω) occurs 20 times in Matt. (1:25; 6:3; 7:23; 9:30; 10:26; 12:7, 15, 33; 13:11; 16:3, 8; 21:45; 22:18; 24:32, 33, 39, 43, 50; 25:24; 26:10). Here it has the sense of sexual contact. For discussion see ZPEB, "Know, Knowledge," III, pp. 836–40; ISBE (1986), "Know, Knowledge," III, pp. 48–50.

Joseph's serene trust in God and heartfelt obedience to Scripture is a challenge to every believer. "One can only imagine the relief and joy of Mary when Joseph nobly rose to his high duty toward her" (A. T. Robertson, *Word Pictures*, I, p. 12). The word *until* makes clear that Joseph and Mary did have other children later in a normal fashion, as Matthew also notes (Matt. 12:46). "Whatever Jesus derived from the stock of man—of Abraham, or of David—that He derived entirely from His mother. This is the One Seed of Woman without Man" (Bengel, *Gnomon*, I, p. 91).

Practical Applications from Matthew 1

1. The NT is all about Jesus (v. 1). Our lives should center on Him as well. Paul writes, "For to me to live is Christ, and to die is gain" (Phil. 1:21).
2. Ruth, the meek and unassuming Gentile, has a place in the genealogy of the King (v. 5). Peter urges believers, "Humble yourselves therefore under the mighty hand of God, that he may exalt you in due time" (I Pet. 5:6).
3. God used wicked king Manasseh as well as good king Hezekiah to produce the Messiah (vv. 9–10). There was a place for Judas as well as John among the disciples (Matt. 10:2–4).
4. These names are totally unknown to us, but important to God (v. 14). That is a source of comfort to obscure believers everywhere. God will give a new name to the saint in glory (Rev. 2:17).
5. The Lord Jesus was born in God's perfect timing (v. 17). We should trust God for the timing of our lives. "The steps of a good man are ordered by the Lord: and he delighteth in his way" (Ps. 37:23).
6. Kindness is a great Christian virtue (v. 19). Paul urges the elect of God to put on "kindness, humbleness of mind, meekness, longsuffering" (Col. 3:12*b*).
7. Joseph received more guidance from the Lord than he expected (v. 20). God promises, "The meek will he guide in judgment: and the meek will he teach his way" (Ps. 25:9).
8. God's plan of redemption centers on saving people from sin (v. 21). David prayed, "Wash me throughly from mine iniquity, and cleanse me from my sins" (Ps. 51:2).

9. God intended all along to dwell with His people (v. 23). David prophesied, "Surely the righteous shall give thanks unto thy name: the upright
   shall dwell in thy presence" (Ps. 140:13). John saw the end: "They shall
   be his people, and God himself shall be with them, and be their God"
   (Rev. 21:3*b*).
10. Obedience is always the best way to please God (v. 24). Concerning the
    Son, it is said, "And being made perfect, he became the author of eternal
    salvation unto all them that obey him" (Heb. 5:9).

Prayer

Dear God, our heavenly Father, thank You for using not merely great and
good people, but the obscure and even the wicked, to produce the great Messiah. Have mercy upon us and use us, too, by Your grace. Hear us for Jesus'
sake. Amen.

MATTHEW 2

The Coming of the Wise Men

Persons
Jesus
Herod the king
The wise men
Chief priest and scribes
Mary

Joseph
An angel of the Lord
The children of Bethlehem
Archelaus

Persons referred to
The Jews
The prophet [Micah]
The prophet [Hosea]

The prophet Jeremiah
Rachel
The prophets

Places mentioned
Bethlehem of Judaea
Jerusalem
The land of Judah

Egypt
Galilee
Nazareth

Doctrines taught
Worship
The rule of God
Giving

Guidance
Sin
God's protection

1 Now when Jesus was born in Bethlehem of Judaea in the days of Herod the king, behold, there came wise men from the east to Jerusalem,

2 Saying, Where is he that is born King of the Jews? for we have seen his star in the east, and are come to worship him.

Matthew 2 Exposition

I. The Wise Men. vv. 1–12.

"And when Jesus was born in Bethlehem of Judea in the days of Herod the king, behold, wise men came from the east to Jerusalem" (v. 1). The Lord Jesus was born in a specific geographic location, Bethlehem, "the house of bread," well known from the days of Ruth and Boaz (Ruth 1:19), and in a specific time, the reign of Herod the Great, one of the most ruthless kings in history. The whole account is soberly factual. The wise men who came from the East were members of a priestly class in the Persian Empire who were known for their study of astrology. They were plainly acquainted with the messianic teaching of the Jews. They may have been referring to Balaam's prophecy, "There shall come a Star out of Jacob, and a Sceptre shall rise out of Israel" (Num. 24:17b). Since the deportation

---

2:1. The word *wise man* (μάγος) occurs 4 times in this chapter (2:1, 7, 16 [twice]), and twice in Acts 13:6, 8, with the more unsavory connotation of *magician*. The interpretation that the Magi were kings dates from the sixth cent. ("Magi," *Dictionary of Christ and the Gospels*, II, p. 100). There is, however, a messianic prophecy of the Redeemer coming to Zion (Isa. 59:20ff.), "And the Gentiles shall come to thy light, and kings to the brightness of thy rising" (Isa. 60:3); "they shall bring gold and incense" (v. 6). See also ISBE, "Wise Men" (1988), IV, pp. 1084f.; ZPEB, "Magi," IV, pp. 31–34.

This verb *to come* (παραγίνομαι) occurs only 3 times in Matt. (of the wise men, 2:1; of John the Baptist, 3:1; and of the Lord Jesus, 3:13).

Herod the Great is named 9 times in Matt. (2:1, 3, 7, 12, 13, 15, 16, 19, 22). The only thing he could be legitimately called *great* for was rebuilding the temple in Jerusalem. For historical background on *Herod the Great*, see Edersheim, *Life and Times*, I, pp. 123–29; "Herod," ZPEB, III, pp. 126–38; "Herod," ISBE (1982), II, pp. 688–94; see also Josephus, *Antiquities of the Jews*, Book XIV, Chap. 8–Book XVII, Chap. 8.

Bethlehem is mentioned 5 times in Matt. (2:1, 5, 6, 8, 16). It was the place in which Rachel died at the birth of Benjamin and was buried (Gen. 35:16–19); David fed the sheep at Bethlehem (I Sam. 17:15); later the Philistines had a garrison at Bethlehem (II Sam. 23:14). For color photographs of Bethlehem, the Church of the Nativity, the shepherd's fields, etc., see Custer, *Stones of Witness*, pp. 170–75. For background see ZPEB, "Bethlehem," I, pp. 538–40; ISBE (1979), "Bethlehem," I, pp. 472–74; Bourbon and Lavagno, *The Holy Land*, pp. 152–53; Giovanna Magi, *The Holy Land*, pp. 58–63; Catherine Foure, ed., *The Holy Land*, pp. 216–27.

The word *east* (ἀνατολή) occurs 5 times in Matt. (2:1, 2, 9; 8:11; 24:27).

Jerusalem is mentioned 13 times in Matt. (2:1, 3; 3:5; 4:25; 5:35; 15:1; 16:21; 20:17, 18; 21:1, 10; 23:37 [twice]). For historical background and modern images see Custer, *Stones*

there were many Jews living in the east, especially Persia. The OT prophecies made clear that a root of Jesse "shall be an ensign of the people; to
it shall the Gentiles seek" (Isa. 11:10b), and "the earth shall be full of
the knowledge of the Lord, as the waters cover the sea" (Isa. 11:9). The
Servant of Jehovah shall bring forth justice to the Gentiles (Isa. 42:1b).
Jehovah God promised concerning His Holy One, "I will also give thee
for a light to the Gentiles, that thou mayest be my salvation unto the end
of the earth" (Isa. 49:6b). In a messianic context Jehovah promised, "And
the Gentiles shall come to thy light, and kings to the brightness of thy
rising" (Isa. 60:3). These prophecies shall find their ultimate fulfillment
in the Millennium. During the Millennium Jews shall be known as the
priests of the Lord (Isa. 61:5–6). The Lord will make Jerusalem a praise in
the earth (Isa. 62:1, 7). The Gentiles will come to the Lord from the ends
of the earth (Jer. 16:19). The present worldwide evangelism springs out of
this same foundation (Acts 9:15; 11:18; 15:14–17; 22:21; 28:28). There
remains some irony in the fact that the Gentiles come to honor the king,
but Herod sent only to get rid of him.

"Saying, Where is the one who was born King of the Jews? For we saw his
star in the east, and we came in order to worship him" (v. 2). They do not
mean that the star appeared in the eastern sky but that they saw the star
while they were in the East. They may well have seen it in the direction
of the Holy Land. Although there have been many attempts to explain

---

of Witness, pp. 78–139; John Wilkinson, Jerusalem as Jesus Knew It (London: Thames and
Hudson, Ltd., 1978); Joan Comay, The Jerusalem I Love (Tel-Aviv, Israel: Leon Amiel
Publisher, 1976); Colin Thubron, Jerusalem (Amsterdam: Time-Life Books, 1976);
Jerusalem and the Holy Land (London: Dorling Kindersley Publishing, Inc., 2000); Martin
Gilbert, Jerusalem in the Twentieth Century (New York: John Wiley and Sons, 1996); John
McRay, "Herodian Jerusalem," Archaeology and the New Testament (Grand Rapids: Baker
Book House, 1991), pp. 91–127; Dan Bahat, Jerusalem [Selected Plans] (Jerusalem: Ariel
Publishing House, 1969, 1980); Ryken, Wilhoit, and Longman, Dictionary of Biblical Imagery,
"Jerusalem," pp. 436–37; Elwell, ed., Evangelical Dictionary of Biblical Theology, "Jerusalem,"
pp. 392–96; ZPEB, "Jerusalem," III, pp. 459–95; ISBE (1982), "Jerusalem," II, pp. 998–1032.
Judaea is mentioned 8 times in Matt. (2:1, 5, 22; 3:1, 5; 4:25; 19:1; 24:26). For background
see ZPEB, "Judea," III, pp. 735–38; ISBE (1982), "Judea," II, pp. 1155–56.
2:2. The word star (ἀστήρ) occurs 5 times in Matt. (2:2, 7, 9, 10; 24:29). Paul mentions
sun, moon, and stars together (I Cor. 15:41).
The verb to worship (προσκυνέω) is applied to the Lord Jesus 10 times in Matt. (2:2, 8,
11; 8:2; 9:18; 14:33; 15:25; 20:20; 28:9, 17) and once in John (9:38), but notice the words
of Thomas, "My Lord and my God" (John 20:28). Mark 5:6 notes that the Gadarene
demoniac worshiped the Lord. Luke records that the disciples worshiped Christ at the
Ascension (Luke 24:52). Worship is an attempt to honor a higher being. Traditionally,

3 When Herod the king had heard these things, he was troubled, and all Jerusalem with him.

the star as a natural physical phenomenon, none of them are satisfactory. Perhaps the most interesting suggestion was that of Kepler, who saw a conjunction of the planets Jupiter, Saturn, and Mars in A.D. 1604 and calculated that such an event could happen only once in 805 years. Thus it did occur in the spring of 6 B.C. For a discussion of the astronomical possibilities see the author's *Stars Speak*, pp. 91–98. Plummer comments, "The attempts to explain it by legendary analogies are very unsuccessful" (*Matt.*, p. 12). Broadus examines the language used of the star and concludes that we have to "regard the appearance as miraculous" (*Matt.*, p. 17). The purpose of the wise men was to worship the newborn King. This is a good indication of the deity of the Lord Jesus Christ. He will later instruct the Devil to worship God alone (Matt. 4:10). As the divine Son, however, He Himself accepted worship (Matt. 8:2; 9:18; 14:33). It is often thought that John's Gospel is the Gospel of the divine Son (which it is, John 9:38), but Matthew presents the doctrine just as surely. It was appropriate for wise men to come from Gentile nations because the salvation that the Lord Jesus would provide was for "all nations" (Matt. 28:19–20).

"And when Herod the king had heard [these things], he was troubled, and all Jerusalem with him" (v. 3). Herod was an Edomite, not a Jew, and held the throne only by military power. There has been no king in history more determined than Herod the Great to keep his crown at all costs. He did not hesitate to have his own sons killed, and even his favorite wife, Mariamne, for political reasons. All Jerusalem was troubled about the desperate means he might use to get rid of a possible successor.

---

worship is the "worth-ship" of God, the recognition of His supreme divine nature, attributes, and glory. Curiously, it is not applied to God in this sense in Matt. For other objects of worship see Matt. 4:9, 10; 18:26. For further study see ISBE (1988), "Worship," IV, pp. 1117–33; ZPEB, "Worship," V, pp. 969–90; Elwell, ed., *Evangelical Dictionary of Biblical Theology*, "Worship," pp. 837–45; Ryken, Wilhoit, and Longman, *Dictionary of Biblical Imagery*, "Worship," pp. 969–73. See also Matt. 15:9 note.

2:3. The regular verb *to hear* (ἀκούω) occurs 63 times in Matt. (2:3, 9, 18, 22, and so forth). For a variety of meanings this verb may convey see ISBE (1982), "Hear; Hearken; Listen; Obey, etc.," II, pp. 649–50; Ryken, Wilhoit, and Longman, *Dictionary of Biblical Imagery*, "Ear, Hearing," pp. 223–24.

The verb *to trouble, terrify* (ταράσσω) occurs twice in Matt. (2:3; 14:26), the latter reference to the disciples who *were terrified* at what they thought was a ghost.

4 *And when he had gathered all the chief priests and scribes of the people together, he demanded of them where Christ should be born.*
5 *And they said unto him, In Bethlehem of Judaea: for thus it is written by the prophet,*
6 *And thou Bethlehem, in the land of Juda, art not the least among the princes of Juda: for out of thee shall come a Governor, that shall rule my people Israel.*

"And when he had gathered together all the chief priests and scribes of the people, he was demanding of them where the Christ should be born" (v. 4). Here the phrase *the Christ* obviously means *the Messiah*. There is no debate among the religious leaders. They give Herod a clear answer and a Scripture passage to back it up. "And they said to him, In Bethlehem of Judaea; for thus it has been written through the prophet:

And you, Bethlehem, in the land of Judah,

By no means are you least among the rulers of Judah;

For out of you shall come forth a Ruler,

Who shall shepherd my people Israel" (vv. 5–6; Mic. 5:2).

The phrase *through the prophet* plainly assumes that God is the author of

---

2:4. The verb *to gather together* (συνάγω) occurs 24 times in Matt. (2:4; 3:12; 6:26; 12:30; 13:2, 30, 47, and so forth).

The verb *to inquire, demand* (πυνθάνομαι), only here in Matt., is clearly used in the sense of a judicial inquiry, as it is in Acts 21:33. The imperfect tense implies a persistent ferreting out of information.

The word *high priest*, in the plural *chief priests* (ἀρχιερεύς), occurs 25 times in Matt. (2:4; 16:21; 20:18; 21:15, 23, 45; 26:3 [twice], 14, 47, 51, 57, 58, 59, 62, 63, 65; 27:1, 3, 6, 12, 20, 41, 62; 28:11). There was not only a high priest but also former high priests, heads of the 24 courses of priests, temple overseers, and others. For discussion see ZPEB, "Priest in the NT," "Priests and Levites," IV, pp. 849–67; ISBE (1986), "Priest, High," "Priesthood in the NT," "Priests and Levites," III, pp. 960–70.

The word *scribe* (γραμματεύς) occurs 22 times in Matt. (2:4; 5:20; 7:29; 8:19; 9:3; 12:38; 13:52; 15:1; 16:21; 17:10; 20:18; 21:15; 23:2, 13, 15, 23, 25, 27, 29, 34; 26:57; 27:41). It is also in the *Textus Receptus* in 23:14; 26:3. Scribes were copyists of Scripture and knew every last letter, but spiritual perception was not always theirs. For background see ZPEB, "Scribe," V, pp. 298–302; ISBE (1988), "Scribes," IV, pp. 359–61.

2:5. The verb form *It has been written* (γέγραπται) occurs 9 times in Matt., referring to OT prophecy (2:5 [Mic. 5:2]; 4:4 [Deut. 8:3]; 4:6 [Ps. 91:11]; 4:7 [Deut. 6:16]; 4:10 [Deut. 6:13]; 11:10 [Mal. 3:1]; 21:13 [Isa. 56:7]; 26:24 [Isa. 53:7–8]; 26:31 [Zech. 13:7]), and once concerning the inscription on the cross (27:37). It is the usual phrase for referring to an authoritative source "which is not to be altered." See ZPEB, "Writing," V, pp. 995–1015; ISBE (1988), "Writing," IV, pp. 1136–1160.

2:6. The word *land, earth* (γῆ) occurs 43 times in Matt. (2:6, 20, 21; 4:15 [twice]; 5:5, 13, 18, 35; 6:10, 19; 9:6, 26, 31; 10:15, 29, 34; 11:24, 25, and so forth).

7 Then Herod, when he had privily called the wise men, enquired of them diligently what time the star appeared.

Scripture. The Hebrew context in Micah identifies the Ruler as an eternal being, "whose goings forth have been from of old, from everlasting" (5:2*b*). Isaiah prophesied that the Lord God "shall feed his flock like a shepherd: he shall gather the lambs with his arm, and carry them in his bosom, and shall gently lead those that are with young" (Isa. 40:11). The great Messiah will accomplish the will of God for His people perfectly. The book of Revelation prophesies the fulfillment of this prophecy: "For the lamb which is in the midst of the throne shall shepherd them and lead them unto springs of living waters" (Rev. 7:17*a*). There could not be a greater contrast than that between Herod, who treated his people as a wolf would the flock, and the Lord Jesus, who cared for His people with loving kindness. He did refer to Himself as *the good shepherd* (John 10:11).

"Then Herod, having secretly called the wise men, ascertained exactly from them the time that the star appeared" (v. 7). Herod did not want the council to know of his plans. There was no religious interest in his inquiry. He cared nothing for Scripture; he just wanted to be sure that his orders of execution would be effective in eliminating this possible rival to the throne. But he masked his venomous plans with pious words of concern for the success of the wise men's quest. Plummer notes that the religious leaders show no interest in searching out this messianic claim, and Herod's interest is solely destructive (*Matt.*, p. 13). Therefore, it is Gentiles who search out the Messiah and honor Him.

The word *least* (ἐλάχιστος) occurs 5 times in Matt. (2:6; 5:19 [twice]; 25:40, 45).

The word *governor* (ἡγεμών) occurs 10 times in Matt. (2:6; 10:18; 27:2, 11 [twice], 14, 15, 21, 27; 28:14). See Matt. 27:2 note for distinctions. It also occurs in the *Textus Receptus* in 27:23.

The verb *to shepherd* (ποιμαίνω) occurs only here in Matt. The noun *shepherd* (ποίμην) occurs 3 times in Matt. (9:36; 25:32; 26:31).

The word *Israel* (Ἰσραήλ) occurs 12 times in Matt. (2:6, 20, 21; 8:10; 9:33; 10:6, 23; 15:24, 31; 19:28; 27:9, 42). The word can refer to the nation or the people. For background see ZPEB, "Israel, History of," III, pp. 335–54; ISBE (1982), "Israel," "Israel, History of the People of," II, pp. 907–24.

2:7. The verb *to ascertain accurately* (ἀκριβόω) occurs only in this context in the NT (2:7, 16). Moulton and Milligan give an example from Vettius Valens, p. 265, *Vocabulary*, p. 19.

Matt. regularly uses *then* (τότε); he has it 90 times out of its 160 NT occurrences.

8 *And he sent them to Bethlehem, and said, Go and search diligently for the young child; and when ye have found him, bring me word again, that I may come and worship him also.*

9 *When they had heard the king, they departed; and, lo, the star, which they saw in the east, went before them, till it came and stood over where the young child was.*

"And he sent them to Bethlehem and said, Go and search carefully for the little child, and whenever you find him, report to me, in order that I also may come and worship him" (v. 8). A. T. Robertson noted that "the deceit of Herod seemed plausible enough" (*Word Pictures*, I, p. 19). Herod was skillful in using others for his own purposes. He was determined to dispose of this "little child." It never occurred to Herod that the wise men might disobey a royal command.

"And when they had heard the king, they departed, and behold, the star, which they had seen in the east, was going before them, until it came and stood over where the little child was" (v. 9). The imperfect tense of the verb, "the star . . . was going before them," makes very clear that it was not some sign high in the heavens but a light low enough to give them directional guidance from Jerusalem to Bethlehem, five miles to the south. Any astronomical star that was overhead at Bethlehem would also have been overhead at Jerusalem. This star, however, led them to the very house in which the young King was to be found. Luke tells us that on the day of His birth the holy family could find no lodging except in a cattle barn (Luke 2:6–7). But Matthew's account is sometime later, when Joseph was able to get a house for his family (v. 11).

2:8. The verb *to inquire* (ἐξετάζω) occurs twice in Matt. (2:8; 10:11).

The verb *to report, announce* (ἀπαγγέλλω) occurs 8 times in Matt. (2:8; 8:33; 11:4; 12:18; 14:12; 28:8, 10, 11). It is also used of the disciples of John the Baptist reporting his death to Jesus (Matt. 14:12).

The word *little child* (παιδίον) occurs 9 times in this context (2:8, 9, 11, 13 [twice], 14, 20 [twice], 21) and 9 times elsewhere in Matt. (11:16; 14:21; 15:38; 18:2, 3, 4, 5; 19:13, 14). See also 2:18 note, "Child."

2:9. The verb *to go before* (προάγω) occurs 6 times in Matt. (2:9; 14:22; 21:9, 31; 26:32; 28:7).

The verb *to stand* (ἵστημι) occurs 21 times in Matt. (2:9; 4:5; 6:5; 12:25, 26, 46, 47; 13:2; 16:28; 18:2, 16; 20:3, 6, 32; 24:15; 25:33; 26:15, 73; 27:11, 47).

10 When they saw the star, they rejoiced with exceeding great joy.
11 And when they were come into the house, they saw the young child with
Mary his mother, and fell down, and worshipped him: and when they had
opened their treasures, they presented unto him gifts; gold, and frankincense
and myrrh.

"And when they saw the star, they rejoiced with exceeding great joy"
(v. 10). The hearts of these wise men were very tender to the leading of
God, and God blessed their long journey with success. They were good
examples of "righteous gentiles" in the OT.

"And when they had come into the house, they saw the little child with
Mary his mother, and fell down and worshiped him, and when they had
opened their treasures, they gave to him gifts, gold, and frankincense, and
myrrh" (v. 11). These were royal gifts fit for a king. No doubt they were a
great help to the family in the coming exile in Egypt. Broadus notes that no
one in the ancient world would have visited a king without bringing a gift
(*Matt.*, p. 20).

2:10. The verb *to rejoice* (χαίρω) occurs 6 times in Matt. (2:10; 5:12; 18:13; 26:49; 27:29;
28:9).

Rejoice in the Lord
   I. Wise men rejoiced in God's guidance. 2:10.
   II. Believers should rejoice in persecution. 5:12.
   III. Shepherds rejoice in finding lost sheep. 18:13.
   IV. There can be a hypocritical rejoicing [Hail, rejoice]. 26:49.
   V. There can be a mocking rejoicing [Hail, rejoice]. 27:29.
   VI. Jesus brings a true rejoicing [Hail, rejoice]. 28:9.

The word *joy* (χαρά) occurs 6 times in Matt. (2:10; 13:20, 44; 25:21, 23; 28:8). It is a
characteristic of the believer in Christ that is produced by the Holy Spirit (Gal. 5:22). For
discussion see ISBE (1982), "Joy," II, pp. 1140–42; ZPEB, "Joy," III, pp. 714–15; Ryken,
Wilhoit, and Longman, *Dictionary of Biblical Imagery*, "Joy," pp. 464–66.

The word *great* (μέγας) occurs 30 times in Matt. (2:10; 4:16; 5:19, 35; 7:27; 8:24, 26;
11:11 [twice]; 12:6; 13:32; 15:28, and so forth).

2:11. The word *house* (οἰκία) occurs 26 times in Matt. (2:11; 5:15; 7:24, 25, 26, 27; 8:6,
14; 9:10, 23, 28; 10:12, 13, 14; 12:25, 29 [twice]; 13:1, 36, 57; 17:25; 19:29; 23:14; 24:17,
43; 26:6). For background see ZPEB, "House," III, pp. 217–21; ISBE (1982), "House," II,
pp. 770–72; Reader's Digest Association, *Great People of the Bible and How They Lived*, pp.
140, 158–59, 306–7.

The word *treasure* (θησαυρός) occurs 9 times in Matt. (2:11; 6:19, 20, 21; 12:35 [twice];
13:44, 52; 19:21). Robertson suggests that the word means "caskets" here (*Word Pictures*,
I, p. 19).

The verb *to open* (ἀνοίγω) occurs 11 times in Matt. (2:11; 3:16; 5:2; 7:7, 8; 9:30; 13:35;
17:27; 20:33; 25:11; 27:52).

12 And being warned of God in a dream that they should not return to Herod, they departed into their own country another way.
13 And when they were departed, behold, the angel of the Lord appeareth to Joseph in a dream, saying, Arise, and take the young child and his mother, and flee into Egypt, and be thou there until I bring thee word: for Herod will seek the young child to destroy him.

"And having been divinely warned in a dream not to return to Herod, they withdrew to their own country through another way" (v. 12). The Via Maris was the normal trade route from Judah to Persia, but the wise men could have cut across the Jordan and taken the Way of the Kings northward to Damascus and beyond. Note that there is no mention of camels in the narrative. We must also note that Luke's account of the presentation in the temple forty days after Jesus' birth (Luke 2:21–39) has already occurred, for now there must be a sojourn in Egypt for some time until Herod dies.

II. The Flight to Egypt. vv. 13–15.

"And when they had departed, behold, an angel of the Lord appeared in a dream to Joseph, saying, Arise and take the little child and his mother,

The verb *to bring to* (προσφέρω) occurs 15 times in Matt. (2:11; 4:24; 5:23, 24; 8:4, 15; 9:2, 32; 12:22; 14:35; 17:16; 18:24; 19:13; 22:19; 25:20).

The word *gift* (δῶρον) occurs 9 times in Matt. (2:11; 5:23, 24 [twice]; 8:4; 15:5; 23:18, 19 [twice]).

The word *gold* (χρυσός) occurs 5 times in Matt. (2:11; 10:9; 23:16, 17 [twice]. For background see ISBE (1982), "Gold," II, pp. 520–22; ZPEB, "Gold," II, pp. 771–72; Frederick Pough, *A Field Guide to Rocks and Minerals*, pp. 79, 82; Charles Chesterman, *Audubon Society Field Guide to North American Rocks and Minerals*, pp. 346–47.

The word *frankincense* (λίβανος) occurs only here in Matt. For further details see ZPEB, "Frankincense," II, pp. 606–7; ISBE (1982), "Frankincense," II, p. 360; Zohary, *Plants of the Bible*, "Ladanum," p. 194.

The word *myrrh* (σμύρνα) occurs only here in Matt. For details see ZPEB, "Myrrh," IV, p. 326; ISBE (1986), "Myrrh," III, pp. 450–51; Zohary, *Plants of the Bible*, "Myrrh" (*Commiphora abyssinica*), p. 200.

The verb *to fall* (πίπτω) occurs 19 times in Matt. (2:11; 4:9; 7:25, 27; 10:29; 13:4, 5, 7, 8, and so forth).

2:12. The verb *to divinely warn* (χρηματίζω) occurs twice in this context only in Matt. (2:12, 22). It is used of a divine revelation to Moses (Heb. 8:5).

For the word *dream* see Matt. 1:20 note.

The verb *to withdraw, make room* (ἀναχωρέω) occurs 10 times in Matt. (2:12, 13, 14, 22; 4:12; 9:24; 12:15; 14:13; 15:21; 27:5).

2:13. The verb *to seek* (ζητέω) occurs 14 times in Matt. (2:13, 20; 6:33; 7:7, 8; 12:43, 46, 47; 13:45; 18:12; 21:46; 26:16, 59; 28:5). It may be used with a bad connotation (Matt. 2:13) or with a good one (Matt. 28:5). For discussion see ISBE (1988), "Seek," IV, pp. 381–82.

14 When he arose, he took the young child and his mother by night, and departed into Egypt:
15 And was there until the death of Herod: that it might be fulfilled which was spoken of the Lord by the prophet, saying, Out of Egypt have I called my son.
16 Then Herod, when he saw that he was mocked of the wise men, was exceeding wroth, and sent forth, and slew all the children that were in Bethlehem, and in all the coasts thereof, from two years old and under, according to the time which he had diligently inquired of the wise men.

and flee into Egypt, and be there until I speak to you; for Herod is about to seek the little child in order to destroy him" (v. 13). To go to Egypt, with all its pagan idolatry, was almost unthinkable to devout Palestinian Jews. But there is no hesitation on Joseph's part; he is prepared for instant obedience.

"And he arose and took the little child and his mother by night and departed to Egypt" (v. 14). The decision to leave in the middle of the night was a wise one. No one would know which direction they took. The normal guess would have been that they had returned to Galilee.

"And he was there until the death of Herod, in order that that which was spoken by the Lord through the prophet might be fulfilled, saying, Out of Egypt I called my son" (v. 15; Hos. 11:1). In the context, Hosea is referring to God calling Israel out of Egypt in the Exodus, but Matthew correctly perceived that God was giving a prophecy that could be applied to the Messiah returning from Egypt for His ministry. The fullness

---

The verb *to destroy* (ἀπόλλυμι) occurs 19 times in Matt. (2:13; 5:29, 30; 8:25; 9:17; 10:6, 28, 39 [twice], 42; 12:14; 15:24; 16:25 [twice]; 18:14; 21:41; 22:7; 26:52; 27:20). It was the Devil's purpose all the way to the end to destroy the Lord Jesus (Matt. 27:20). In reference to people the word does not mean merely *to cause to disappear* but *to lose all that makes life worth living.*

The verb *to flee* (φεύγω) occurs 7 times in Matt. (2:13; 3:7; 8:33; 10:23; 23:33; 24:16; 26:56). For discussion see ISBE (1982), "Flee," II, p. 313; Ryken, Wilhoit, and Longman, *Dictionary of Biblical Imagery*, "Flee, Flight," p. 291.

Egypt is mentioned only 4 times in this context in the Gospels (2:13, 14, 15, 19); for historical background, see ZPEB, "Egypt," II, pp. 225–58; ISBE (1982), "Egypt," II, pp. 29–47.

2:14. This is the first of 9 times that *night* (νύξ) is mentioned in Matt. (2:14; 4:2; 12:40 [twice]; 14:25; 25:6; 26:31, 34; 28:13).

2:15. A rare word for *death* (τελευτή) occurs only here in the NT. Herod came to his "end." A verb form appears in 2:19.

17 Then was fulfilled that which was spoken by Jeremy the prophet, saying,
18 In Rama was there a voice heard, lamentation, and weeping, and great
mourning, Rachel weeping for her children, and would not be comforted, be-
cause they are not.

of meaning in Scripture at times extends to different contexts. Blomberg
argues that "this is the first of several instances in Matthew in which Jesus
recapitulates the role of Israel as a whole" (*Matt.*, p. 67).

III. The Slaying of the Children. vv. 16–18.

"Then Herod, when he saw that he was tricked by the wise men, was
exceedingly angry, and sent and slew all the children who were in Bethlehem and in all the regions around it, from two years old and under,
according to the time which he had accurately ascertained from the wise
men" (v. 16). The word *children* is masculine; Herod ordered the "boy
babies" killed because they might become rivals to his throne. This truly
exhibits the cruel and vicious nature of Herod. His only concern was to
keep his royal power. He did not care how many people he had to destroy
to do so.

"Then was fulfilled that which was spoken through Jeremiah the prophet,
saying,

> In Rama a voice was heard,
>> Of weeping and great lamentation;
> Rachel weeping for her children;
> And she would not be comforted,
> Because they are not" (vv. 17–18; Jer. 31:15).

In context Jeremiah is mourning the deportation of the Jews from Rama,
five miles north of Jerusalem, into captivity. But Matthew knows that the
Holy Spirit inspired the Scripture for our admonition and applies it to

---

2:16. The verb *to ridicule* or *trick* (ἐμπαίζω) occurs 5 times in Matt. (2:16; 20:19; 27:29, 31, 41).

The verb *to be angry* or *furious* (θυμόω) occurs only here in the NT.

The word *boy, child, servant* (παῖς) occurs 8 times in Matt. (2:16; 8:6, 8, 13; 12:18; 14:2; 17:18; 21:15).

The word *region, territory* (ὅριον) occurs 6 times in Matt. (2:16; 4:13; 8:34; 15:22, 39; 19:1).

2:17. Matt. refers to *Jeremiah* 3 times (2:17; 16:14; 27:9). For background see ZPEB, "Jeremiah (the Prophet)," III, pp. 434–40; Butler, ed., *Holman Bible Dictionary*, "Jeremiah," pp. 756–57.

19 But when Herod was dead, behold, an angel of the Lord appeareth in a dream to Joseph in Egypt,
20 Saying, Arise, and take the young child and his mother, and go into the land of Israel: for they are dead which sought the young child's life.

this context with divine approval. There is often much more involved in OT prophecy than just surface meaning. There are passages that need to be revisited again and again to determine the depth of meaning that is there. It is interesting to note that the tomb of Rachel is still in Bethlehem, and women who are childless come there to weep.

IV. *The Return from Egypt. vv. 19–23.*

"But when Herod died, behold an angel of the Lord appears in a dream to Joseph in Egypt, saying, Arise and take the little child and his mother and go into the land of Israel; for the ones who were seeking the life of the little child have died" (vv. 19–20). Again the Lord gives exact guidance

---

2:18. Rachel died in the birth of her son Benjamin (Gen. 35:16–19).

The word *weeping, bitter crying,* (κλαυθμός) occurs 7 times in Matt. (2:18; 8:12; 13:42, 50; 22:13; 24:51; 25:30). For discussion see ISBE (1988), "Weep, Weeping," IV, p. 1046; Ryken, Wilhoit, and Longman, *Dictionary of Biblical Imagery*, "Weeping," pp. 939–40.

The word *child* (τέκνον) occurs 14 times in Matt. (2:18; 3:9; 7:11; 9:2; 10:21 [twice]; 15:26; 18:25; 19:29; 21:28 [twice]; 22:24; 23:37; 27:25). It is a tender term, lit. "born one." See also ISBE (1979), "Child," I, pp. 644–46; ZPEB, "Child," I, pp. 793–94; Elwell, ed., *Evangelical Dictionary of Biblical Theology*, "Family Life and Relations," pp. 243–45; Ryken, Wilhoit, and Longman, *Dictionary of Biblical Imagery*, "Child, Children," pp. 141–43.

The verb *to comfort, beseech* (παρακαλέω) occurs 9 times in Matt. (2:18; 5:4; 8:5, 31, 34; 14:36; 18:29, 32; 26:53).

2:19. Herod the Great died in 4 B.C. Since the Lord was about 2 years old here, we may estimate that the Lord Jesus was born in 6 B.C. The present numbering system in our calendar was established by a Roman monk, Dionysius Exiguus, in A.D. 533. He did not have all the historical facts available to him that we have today. The Gospel of Luke adds one more fact, that when Jesus was born, shepherds were watching their flocks by night (Luke 2:8). Shepherds do not always do this, but in the spring, when the lambs are being born, they certainly do watch at night to drive away jackals and other predators that might try to seize the newborn lambs. Thus the spring of 6 B.C. is the probable time of the birth of the Lord. For a discussion of these dates and the calendar, see the author's *Stars Speak* (pp. 92ff.).

The verb *to die* (τελευτάω) occurs 4 times in Matt. (2:19; 9:18; 15:4; 22:25).

2:20. The word *soul, life* (ψυχή) occurs 16 times in Matt. (2:20; 6:25 [twice]; 10:28 [twice], 39 [twice]; 11:29; 12:18; 16:25 [twice], 26 [twice]; 20:28; 22:37; 26:38). It refers to the mental and spiritual powers of man that are immortal (Matt. 10:28). For further discussion see ZPEB, "Soul," V, pp. 496–98; ISBE (1988), "Soul," IV, pp. 587–89; Elwell, ed., *Evangelical Dictionary of Biblical Theology*, "Soul," pp. 743–44.

2:21. The verb *to enter in* (εἰσέρχομαι) occurs 36 times in Matt. (2:21; 5:20; 6:6; 7:13 [twice], 21; 8:5, 8; 9:25; 10:5, 11, 12, and so forth).

21 And he arose, and took the young child and his mother, and came into the land of Israel.
22 But when he heard that Archelaus did reign in Judaea in the room of his father Herod, he was afraid to go thither: notwithstanding, being warned of God in a dream, he turned aside into the parts of Galilee:
23 And he came and dwelt in a city called Nazareth: that it might be fulfilled which was spoken by the prophets, He shall be called a Nazarene.

to Joseph when he needs it. He plainly had a very close walk with the Lord. He stayed where the Lord put him and moved when the Lord told him to.

"And he arose, and took the little child and his mother and came into the land of Israel" (v. 21). This meant another trip of a hundred miles or more, depending on how far into Egypt he had gone.

"But when he heard that Archelaus was reigning in Judaea in the place of his father Herod, he was afraid to go there; but having been divinely warned in a dream, he withdrew into the regions of Galilee" (v. 22). Once again God guided the steps of Joseph to the right place so that the Lord could grow up without the notice of oppressive governmental authorities.

"And he came and dwelled in a city called Nazareth: that it might be fulfilled which was spoken through the prophets, He shall be called a

2:22. Robertson calls Herod's son Archelaus "the worst of his living sons" (*Word Pictures*, p. 21). For a summary of his brutality, see "Herod," ZPEB, III, pp. 138–40; "Herod," ISBE (1982), II, p. 694. He was finally deposed in A.D. 6 after delegations of both Jews and Samaritans begged Augustus for relief.

The word *father* (πατήρ) occurs 63 times in Matt. (2:22; 3:9; 4:21, 22; 5:16, 45, 48; 6:1, 4, 6 [twice], 8, 9, 14, 15, 18 [twice], 26, 32; 7:11, 21; 8:21; 10:20, 21, 29, 32, 33, 35, 37; 11:25, 26, 27 [3 times]; 12:50; 13:43, and so forth). For background see ZPEB, "Father," II, pp. 504–6; ISBE (1982), "Father," II, pp. 284–86. For God the *Father* see Matt. 5:16 note.

For historical background on Galilee see ZPEB, "Galilee," II, pp. 638–43; ISBE (1982), "Galilee," II, pp. 386–91; for color photographs of the region see the author's *Stones of Witness*, pp. 20–51.

2:23. The verb *to dwell, live* (κατοικέω) occurs 4 times in Matt. (2:23; 4:13; 12:45; 23:21).

This is the first of 27 times that the word *city* (πόλις) occurs in Matt. (2:23; 4:5; 5:14, 35; 8:33, 34; 9:1, 35; 10:5, 11, 14, 15, 23 [twice]; 11:1, 20; 12:25; 14:13; 21:10, 17, 18; 22:7; 23:34 [twice]; 26:18; 27:53; 28:11).

Nazareth is named 3 times in Matt. (2:23; 4:13; 21:11). For historical background on Nazareth, see ZPEB, "Nazareth," IV, pp. 388–90; ISBE, "Nazareth," (1986), III, pp. 500–501; Charles Pfeiffer, *The Biblical World*, "Nazareth," pp. 410–12; Edersheim, *Life and Times*, "The Child Life in Nazareth," I, pp. 217–34. For color photographs of Nazareth and the Mount of Precipitation, see the author's *Stones of Witness*, pp. 66–68.

Nazarene" (v. 23). The plural *prophets* is probably a reference to the whole of messianic prophecy, but it may have reference especially to Isaiah 11:1, that He shall be "a rod (*netzer*) out of the stem of Jesse." Morris does not think it refers to any OT prophecy, but only to the town of Nazareth (*Matt.*, p. 49). The multitude would know Him as "Jesus the prophet of Nazareth of Galilee" (Matt. 21:11). The location of Nazareth is beyond doubt. The spring that flows at the Greek Orthodox Church of St. Gabriel, "the church of Mary's Well," is still the only water source for the city of Nazareth. The Roman Catholic Church of the Annunciation is the largest church in the Holy Land. But Nathanael's candid exclamation, "Can any good thing come out of Nazareth?" is a clear recognition that Nazareth had no illustrious religious heritage in the first century. It was a bustling commercial town on the Via Maris, the great trade route from Damascus to Egypt. From the top of the Mount of Precipitation there is a grand panorama of the valley of Esdraelon stretching all the way to the mount of Megiddo thirty miles to the south.

Practical Applications from Matthew 2

1. The goal of every believer ought to be to worship the great King (v. 2). "Worship the Lord in the beauty of holiness" (Ps. 29:2*b*).
2. Scripture always has an answer to religious questions (v. 5). "But sanctify the Lord God in your hearts: and be ready always to give an answer to every man that asketh you a reason of the hope that is in you with meekness and fear" (I Pet. 3:15).
3. Obscure places are important to God (v. 6). "The eyes of the Lord are in every place, beholding the evil and the good" (Prov. 15:3).
4. God leads men to Christ (v. 9). "Lead me in thy truth, and teach me: for thou art the God of my salvation; on thee do I wait all the day" (Ps. 25:5).
5. God's providence brings joy (v. 10). "And he brought forth his people with joy, and his chosen with gladness" (Ps. 105:43).
6. Worship of the Lord Jesus Christ honors God (v. 11). "And again, when he bringeth in the firstbegotten into the world, he saith, And let all the angels of God worship him" (Heb. 1:6).
7. At times flight from oppressors is proper (v. 14). "But when they persecute you in this city, flee ye into another" (Matt. 10:23*a*).

8. The violence of wicked men is all recorded and waiting for them (v. 16). "And the books were opened . . . and the dead were judged out of those things which were written in the books" (Rev. 20:12b).
9. Wicked men will all go down in defeat (v. 20). "Evil shall slay the wicked: and they that hate the righteous shall be desolate" (Ps. 34:21).
10. It is well to avoid some places because of wicked rulers (v. 22). "The wicked in his pride doth persecute the poor" (Ps. 10:2a).

Prayer

Thank You, Lord God, for keeping Your promise in sending the great Messiah, Jesus Christ, into the world to save sinners like me. Help me to follow Your leading and to obey Your Word. Guide our steps for Jesus' sake. Amen.

MATTHEW 3

THE COMING OF THE FORERUNNER

Persons
John the Baptist
People of Jerusalem and Judaea
Pharisees
Sadducees

Jesus
The Spirit of God
The voice of the Father

Persons referred to
Isaiah
Abraham

Places mentioned
The wilderness of Judaea
Jerusalem
Judaea

The region of the Jordan
Galilee
Heaven

Doctrines taught
Repentance
Baptism
Confession of sin
Wrath to come
The Holy Spirit

Fire upon the wicked
Righteousness
The pleasure of the Father in the
    Son
The Trinity

1 In those days came John the Baptist, preaching in the wilderness of Judaea,
2 And saying, Repent ye: for the kingdom of heaven is at hand.

Matthew 3 Exposition

I. The Preaching of John. vv. 1–12 [Mark 1:2–8; Luke 3:3–18].

"But in those days John the Baptizer comes, preaching in the wilderness of Judaea, and saying, Be repenting: for the kingdom of the heavens has drawn near" (vv. 1–2). The phrase *in those days* refers to the time that the Lord was still living in Nazareth. John was a stern and fiery preacher in the tradition of the OT prophets. *Repent* means to change the way you think enough to change the way you act. When the prodigal son repented, he went back to his father (Luke 15:17–20). The present tense imperative emphasizes the continuous nature of the repentance. All men must continue changing for the better. The OT prophets had cried out against the sinfulness of all mankind: "Ah sinful nation, a people laden with iniquity, a seed of evildoers, children that are corrupters: they have forsaken the Lord, they have provoked the Holy One of Israel unto anger, they are gone away backward" (Isa. 1:4). "But your iniquities have sepa-

---

3:1. *John the Baptist* is mentioned in 6 main contexts in Matt. (3:1–15; 11:2–19; 14:2–10; 16:14; 17:10–13; 21:25–32). Luke has some important parallels (Luke 1:5–80; 3:1–20; 7:29–30; 11:1). For historical background see ZPEB, "John the Baptist," III, pp. 641–47; ISBE (1982), "John the Baptist," II, 1108–11; *Who's Who in the Bible*, "John the Baptist," pp. 233–36; Edersheim, *Life and Times*, I, pp. 255–84; Alexander Whyte, *Bible Characters*, "John the Baptist," IV, pp. 26–35; J. R. Porter, *The Illustrated Guide to the Bible*, pp. 160–61.

The historical present, *comes*, makes the scene a dramatic entrance for John.

The verb *to preach* (κηρύσσω) occurs 9 times in Matt. (3:1; 4:17, 23; 9:35; 10:7, 27; 11:1; 24:14; 26:13). It is one of the great words in Acts for preaching the gospel (Acts 8:5; 9:20, and so forth). For background see ZPEB, "Preacher, Preaching," IV, pp. 844–45; ISBE (1986), "Preach," III, pp. 940–43.

The word *wilderness, desert* (ἔρημος) occurs 8 times in Matt. (3:1, 3; 4:1; 11:7; 14:13, 15; 23:38; 24:26). It did not denote the sandy Sahara, but merely bone-dry earth. After the latter rains in spring, it does not rain until late fall or winter.

3:2. The apostle Paul will point out the sinfulness of mankind in greater detail (Rom. 1:18–32; 3:9–20; Gal. 5:19–21; II Tim. 3:1–7).

The verb *to repent* (μετανοέω) occurs 5 times in Matt. (3:2; 4:17; 11:20, 21; 12:41). It does not denote merely a passing change of mind but a permanent change of thinking that transforms the manner of living as well. For further discussion see Elwell, ed., *Evangelical Dictionary of Biblical Theology*, "Repentance," pp. 671–72; ZPEB, "Repentance," pp. 62–64; ISBE (1988), "Repent," IV, pp. 135–37; *Baker's Dictionary of Theology*, E. F. Harrison, ed., "Repentance," pp. 443–45.

The word *kingdom* (βασιλεία) occurs 55 times in Matt. (3:2; 4:8, 17, 23; 5:3, 10, 19 [twice], 20; 6:10, 33; 7:21; 8:11, 12; 9:35; 10:7; 11:11, 12; 12:25, 26, 28; 13:11, 19, 24, 31,

3 For this is he that was spoken of by the prophet Esaias, saying, The voice of one crying in the wilderness, Prepare ye the way of the Lord, make his paths straight.

rated between you and your God, and your sins have hid his face from you, that he will not hear" (Isa. 59:2). Jeremiah added his voice, "Fear ye not me? saith the Lord: will ye not tremble at my presence? . . . But this people hath a revolting and a rebellious heart" (Jer. 5:22a, 23a). John's message was so shocking and convicting that multitudes came out into the barren places where John was preaching in order to hear the authentic Word of the Lord. "For this is the one who was spoken of by Isaiah the prophet, saying:

> A voice of one crying in the desert;
>
> Prepare the way of the Lord
>
> Make straight his paths" (v. 3; Isa. 40:3).

The OT prophecy does not identify the voice or who is to do the preparing (see Steveson, *Isa.*, pp. 337f.). Under the guidance of the Spirit

---

33, 38, 41, 43, 44, 45, 47, 52; 16:19, 28; 18:1, 3, 4, 23; 19:12, 14, 23, 24; 20:1, 21; 21:31, 43; 22:2; 23:13; 24:7 [twice], 14; 25:1, 34; 26:29). The phrase *kingdom of the heavens* occurs 32 times; the *kingdom of God* 5 times. For the word *king* (βασιλεύς) see Matt. 1:6 note. The idea of the *rule of God* is a constant in Scripture (Ps. 59:13; 66:7; 89:9; 103:19; Dan. 4:17, 25, 32). *The church* is not revealed until Matt. 16:18. For further discussion see ISBE (1986), "Kingdom of God," III, pp. 23–29; ZPEB, "Kingdom of God, of Heaven," III, pp. 801–9; Elwell, ed., *Evangelical Dictionary of Biblical Theology,* "Kingdom of God," pp. 451–54; Harrison, ed., *The New Unger's Bible Dictionary,* "Kingdom of God, Kingdom of Heaven," p. 740; George Peters, *The Theocratic Kingdom,* 3 vols.

This is the first of 82 times that the word *heaven* or *sky* (οὐρανός) occurs in Matt. (3:2, 16, 17; 4:17; 5:3, 10, 12, 16, 18, 19 [twice], 20, 34, 45; 6:1, 9, 10, 20, 26; 7:11, 21 [twice]; 8:11, 20; 10:7, 32, 33; 11:11, 12, 23, 25; 12:50; 13:11, 24, 31, 32, 33, 44, 45, 47, 52; 14:19; 16:1, 2, 3 [twice], 17, 19 [3 times]; 18:1, 3, 4, 10 [twice], 14, 18 [twice], 19, 23; 19:12, 14, 21, 23; 20:1; 21:25 [twice]; 22:2, 30; 23:13, 22; 24:29 [twice], 30 [twice], 31, 35, 36; 25:1; 26:64; 28:2, 18). For comparison it occurs only 17 times in Mark and 35 times in Luke. For further discussion see W. M. Smith, *The Biblical Doctrine of Heaven;* Ryken, Wilhoit, and Longman, *Dictionary of Biblical Imagery,* "Heaven," pp. 370–72; Elwell, ed., *Evangelical Dictionary of Biblical Theology,* "Heaven," pp. 332–35; ZPEB, "Heaven," III, pp. 60–64; ISBE (1982), "Heaven," II, pp. 654–55; Harrison, ed., *Baker's Dictionary of Theology,* "Heaven," pp. 264–65.

The verb *to draw near* (ἐγγίζω) occurs 7 times in Matt. (3:2; 4:17; 10:7; 21:1, 34; 26:45, 46).

3:3. Matthew quotes Isaiah the prophet by name 6 times (3:3; 4:14; 8:17; 12:17; 13:14; 15:7). His portrait of suffering Messiah (Isa. 53) is a remarkable foretelling of the Crucifixion. For background see ZPEB, "Isaiah," III, pp. 313–31; ISBE (1982), "Isaiah," II, pp. 885–904; Elwell, ed., *Evangelical Dictionary of Biblical Theology,* "Isaiah, Theology of," pp. 375–79.

The verb *to prepare* (ἑτοιμάζω) occurs 7 times in Matt. (3:3; 20:23; 22:4; 25:34, 41; 26:17, 19).

4 And the same John had his raiment of camel's hair, and a leathern girdle about his loins; and his meat was locusts and wild honey.

5 Then went out to him Jerusalem, and all Judaea, and all the region round about Jordan,

Matthew applies it to John the Baptist and those who heard him. In the ancient world the visit of a king was a very important event. Roads were repaired and made as smooth as possible. Sometimes ornamental gates were erected in his honor. Some of those gates are still standing, as in Athens and Jerash, Jordan. This is why David cries out, "Lift up your heads, O ye gates; and be ye lift up, ye everlasting doors; and the King of glory shall come in" (Ps. 24:7).

"But the same John was having his clothing from camel hair and a leather belt about his loins, and his food was locusts and wild honey" (v. 4). John had only the roughest and most durable clothing and lived off the land on food that most people would rather avoid. (Those who eat roasted locusts say that they have a "nutty" flavor!) John's ministry made him an outsider to the religious and social powers of the day. But his preaching was so powerful that multitudes came to hear him. Luke adds the fact that people asked John how they could change for the better, and he gave them specific instructions (Luke 3:10–14). The church today needs to remember that it is by the foolishness of preaching that people are saved (I Cor. 1:21–25). Worldly methods will never save souls.

The *way* (ὁδός) of the Lord is the path of submission to God's rule and purpose (Ps. 119:3, 27, 30, 32, 33, 37; Isa. 48:17).

The adjective *straight* (εὐθύς, -εῖα, -ύ) may have an adverbial sense.

This is the first time that the title *Lord* is applied to Jesus by Matthew.

3:4. The word *clothing* (ἔνδυμα) occurs 7 times in Matt. (3:4; 6:25, 28; 7:15; 22:11, 12; 28:3).

The word *hair* (θρίξ) occurs 3 times in Matt. (3:4; 5:36; 10:30).

The word *camel* (κάμηλος) occurs 3 times in Matt. (3:4; 19:24; 23:24). For background see ZPEB, "Camel," I, pp. 695–99; ISBE (1979), "Camel," I, pp. 583–84; Azaria Alon, *The Natural History of the Land of the Bible*, p. 92.

The word *food* (τροφή) occurs 4 times in Matt. (3:4; 6:25; 10:10; 24:45).

Locusts (ἀκρίς) are mentioned only in Matt. 3:4; Mark 1:6; Rev. 9:3, 7 in the NT. For discussion and illustrations see Azaria Alon, *The Natural History of the Land of the Bible*, pp. 180–83; ISBE (1986), "Locust," III, pp. 149–50; ZPEB, "Locust," III, pp. 948–50; David Alexander, *The Lion Photoguide to the Bible*, pp. 32–33.

6 And were baptized of him in Jordan, confessing their sins.
7 But when he saw many of the Pharisees and Sadducees come to his bap-
tism, he said unto them, O generation of vipers, who hath warned you to flee
from the wrath to come?

"Then Jerusalem, and all Judaea, and all the region around the Jordan, were going out to him, and were being baptized in the Jordan river by him, confessing their sins" (vv. 5–6). Multitudes went out to hear the first true prophet in four centuries. The Jews performed proselyte baptism upon the Gentile converts who wished to identify themselves with synagogue worship. They would have understood John's message very clearly: he was excommunicating the entire nation for its sins. The Jews who accepted John's message were confessing their sins and begging God for forgiveness just as the miserable Gentiles had to. Morris notes that "baptism signifies death to a whole way of life (cf. Rom. 6:3)" (*Matt.*, p. 56). Christian workers still need to confront people with the fact of their sins and show them that God can forgive their sins through Christ. But the Pharisees and Sadducees who came out of curiosity to hear him would never admit that they were sinners.

"But when he saw many of the Pharisees and Sadducees coming to his baptism, he said to them: Offspring of vipers, who warned you to flee from the coming wrath?" (v. 7). Like many people of today, they wanted

---

The word *honey* (μέλι) occurs only here in Matt. For discussion see ZPEB, "Honey," III, pp. 196–97; ISBE (1982), "Honey," II, pp. 749–50. Bees are assumed.

3:5. For *Jerusalem* see Matt. 2:1 note.

The river *Jordan* (Ἰορδάνης) is named 6 times in Matt. (3:5, 6, 13; 4:15, 25; 19:1). For background see ISBE (1982), "Jordan," II, pp. 1119–25; ZPEB, "Jordan," III, pp. 684–92; for color photographs see Custer, *Stones of Witness* (p. 55); Barbara Ball, ed., *The River Jordan: An Illustrated Guide from Bible Days to the Present*, Carta.

3:6. The verb *to baptize* (βαπτίζω) occurs 7 times in Matt. (3:6, 11 [twice], 13, 14, 16; 28:19). See the noun *baptism* in Matt. 3:7 note.

The word *river* (ποταμός) occurs 3 times in Matt. (3:6; 7:25, 27).

The verb *to confess, promise, praise* (ἐξομολογέω) occurs only twice in Matt. (3:6; 11:25). For the word *sin* see Matt. 1:21 note.

3:7. This is the first of 29 times that *Pharisees* are mentioned in Matt. (3:7; 5:20; 9:11, 14, 34; 12:2, 14, 24, 38; 15:1, 12; 16:1, 6, 11, 12; 19:3; 21:45; 22:15, 34, 41; 23:2, 13, 15, 23, 25, 26, 27, 29; 27:62). The Pharisees were the party of strictest observance of the OT law. They had a multitude of minute rules by which they sought to keep every regulation of the law. For background see ZPEB, "Pharisees," IV, pp. 745–52; ISBE, (1986), "Pharisees," III, pp. 822–29; Elwell, ed., *Evangelical Dictionary of Biblical Theology*, "Pharisees," pp. 607–9;

8 *Bring forth therefore fruits meet for repentance:*
9 *And think not to say within yourselves, We have Abraham to our father: for I say unto you, that God is able of these stones to raise up children unto Abraham.*

religious benefits without the repentance and forsaking of sin. John gave them no comfort at all but denounced them as snakes rather than pious religious leaders they thought they were. John's voice "is a new one that strikes terror to the perfunctory theologians of the temple and of the synagogue" (Robertson, *Word Pictures*, I, p. 25).

"Therefore bring forth fruit worthy of repentance and think not to say in yourselves: We have Abraham as our father. For I say to you that God is able to raise up out of these stones children to Abraham" (vv. 8–9). The

Edersheim, *Life and Times*, I, pp. 96–97; II, pp. 52–62; Jacob Van Bruggen, *Jesus as the Son of God*, Appendix 1 "The Pharisees," pp. 236–72.

The *Sadducees* are mentioned 7 times in Matt. (3:7; 16:1, 6, 11, 12; 22:23, 34). They were the "liberal" party that had the closest ties with the Roman authorities. Josephus noted that the Sadducees were not popular with the people, who, instead, favored the Pharisees (*Antiquities*, XVIII, 1, 4). For further background see ZPEB, "Sadducees," V, pp. 211–16; ISBE (1988), "Sadducees," IV, pp. 278–81; Elwell, ed., *Evangelical Dictionary of Biblical Theology*, "Sadducees," pp. 699–700.

The word *baptism* (βάπτισμα) occurs only twice in Matt. (3:7; 21:25). For discussion and theological comparisons see ISBE (1979), "Baptism," I, pp. 410–26; ZPEB, "Baptism," I, pp. 464–69; Elwell, ed., *Evangelical Dictionary of Biblical Theology*, "Baptize, Baptism," pp. 50–53; Ryken, Wilhoit, and Longman, *Dictionary of Biblical Imagery*, "Baptism," pp. 72–74.

The phrase *offspring of vipers* (γεννήματα ἐχιδνῶν) occurs 3 times in Matt. (3:7; 12:34; 23:33), once by John, and twice by the Lord, applied to these false teachers. For background see ZPEB, "Viper," V, p. 885; ISBE (1988), "Viper," IV, pp. 988–89; for color photographs see Azaria Alon, *The Natural History of the Land of the Bible*, p. 203.

The word *wrath* (ὀργή) occurs only here in Matt. The principle of divine retribution upon sin is found throughout the Bible. Man provokes God to wrath (Deut. 9:7). Vengeance belongs to God (Ps. 94:1). For discussion see ZPEB, "Wrath," V, pp. 990–95; ISBE (1988), "Wrath," IV, pp. 1134–35; Elwell, ed., *Evangelical Dictionary of Biblical Theology*, "Wrath of God," pp. 845–46; R. V. G. Tasker, *The Biblical Doctrine of the Wrath of God*.

3:8. The word *repentance* (μετάνοια) occurs only twice in Matt. (3:8, 11). It denotes a profound change in thinking and living for the believer. See *repent*, Matt. 3:2 note.

The word *worthy* (ἄξιος), KJV *meet*, occurs 9 times in Matt. (3:8; 10:10–38 [which see]; 22:8). For discussion see ISBE (1988), "Worth," IV, pp. 1133–34.

The word *fruit* (καρπός) occurs 19 times in Matt. (3:8, 10; 7:16, 17 [twice], 18 [twice], 19, 20; 12:33 [3 times]; 13:8, 26; 21:19, 34 [twice], 41, 43).

3:9. The verb *to think, suppose* (δοκέω) occurs 10 times in Matt. (3:9; 6:7; 17:25; 18:12; 21:28; 22:17, 42; 24:44; 26:53, 66).

The popular idiom *in yourselves* is literally *in themselves*. See Moulton's *Grammar*, Nigel Turner, III, *Syntax*, p. 42.

10 And now also the axe is laid unto the root of the trees: therefore every tree which bringeth not forth good fruit is hewn down, and cast into the fire.
11 I indeed baptize you with water unto repentance. but he that cometh after me is mightier than I, whose shoes I am not worthy to bear: he shall baptize you with the Holy Ghost, and with fire:

stones were natural outcroppings in the wilderness in which John was preaching. There are rocks everywhere in the southern part of the land. Every convert to the Lord is a supernatural miracle. No one is naturally God's child. It takes a new birth, as Nicodemus had to learn (John 3:5–8).

"But now the ax is laid to the root of the tree; therefore every tree which is not bringing forth good fruit is being cut down and cast into the fire" (v. 10). The ax was ready for use in cutting down the worthless tree. But note that it is laid at the root: the Lord was not going to just cut it off but was ready to root it out. The ministry of John, as well as of the Lord Jesus, was in part a ministry of judgment pronounced against the false religious leaders of the day. The Light must reveal the darkness in all its squalor (John 3:19–21).

"I, on the one hand, am baptizing you with water unto repentance, but the one who is coming after me is stronger than I, of whom I am not worthy to bear his sandals; he himself shall baptize you with the Holy Spirit and with fire" (v. 11). The reference here is probably both to the Day of

---

The word *stone* (λίθος) occurs 11 times in Matt. (3:9; 4:3, 6; 7:9; 21:42, 44; 24:2 [twice]; 27:60, 66; 28:2). The Jews thought of Gentiles as lifeless stones, but God was able to impart life to them also. See Matt. 21:42 for messianic meaning.

The word *child* (τέκνον) means *born one*, most fitting because each needs to be "born again" (John 3:3, 6–8). For a summary of the word see Matt. 2:18 note.

3:10. The word *axe* (ἀξίνη) occurs only here and in the parallel Luke 3:9 in the NT.

The word *tree* (δένδρον) occurs 12 times in Matt. (3:10 [twice]; 7:17 [twice]; 7:18 [twice], 19; 12:33 [3 times]; 13:32; 21:8) and only 25 times in the whole NT. For further study see Ryken, Wilhoit, and Longman, *Dictionary of Biblical Imagery*, "Tree," pp. 890–92; Michale Zohary, *Plants of the Bible*.

The word *root* (ῥίζα) occurs 3 times in Matt. (3:10; 13:6, 21).

The word *fire* (πῦρ) occurs here for the first of 12 times in Matt. (3:10, 11, 12; 5:22; 7:19; 13:40, 42, 50; 17:15; 18:8, 9; 25:41). For further study see Ryken, Wilhoit, and Longman, *Dictionary of Biblical Imagery*, "Fire," pp. 286–89; Elwell, ed., *Evangelical Dictionary of Biblical Theology*, "Fire," pp. 256–57; ZPEB, "Fire," II, pp. 538–39; ISBE (1982), "Fire," II, pp. 305–6.

The verb *to cut off, cut down* (ἐκκόπτω) occurs 4 times in Matt. (3:10; 5:30; 7:19; 18:8).

The verb *to cast* (βάλλω) occurs 34 times in Matt. (3:10; 4:6, 18, and so forth).

12 Whose fan is in his hand, and he will throughly purge his floor, and gather his wheat into the garner; but he will burn up the chaff with unquenchable fire. 13 Then cometh Jesus from Galilee to Jordan unto John, to be baptized of him.

Pentecost (Acts 2:1–4) and the Day of Judgment (Rev. 19:11–20). In the ancient world the task of carrying the master's sandals was the job of the lowliest slave in the household. John says that he is not worthy even of that.

"Whose winnowing shovel is in his hand and he shall thoroughly cleanse his threshing floor, and shall gather his wheat into the barn [granary], but the chaff shall be burned up with unquenchable fire" (v. 12). The wheat is a symbol for the righteous; the chaff represents the wicked. The apostle John reveals that the place prepared for the good grain is the heavenly city, New Jerusalem (Rev. 21:1–5), but the place for the chaff is the lake of fire (Rev. 19:11–15). The symbol will show up again in Matthew 13:25–30, when the enemy sows weeds among the wheat. The ministry of the Lord Jesus is going to separate the wheat from the chaff. His hand is going to exercise divine power.

II. The Baptism of Jesus. vv. 13–17 [Mark 1:9–11; Luke 3:21–23] .

"Then comes Jesus from Galilee unto the Jordan to John in order to be baptized by him" (v. 13). The infinitive *in order to be baptized* is plainly a purpose construction. The Lord Jesus was deliberately putting Himself in the place of the obedient believer, submitting to the preached Word of God and seeking to honor His Father above all.

3:11. The word *worthy* (ἱκανός) occurs 3 times in Matt. (3:11; 8:8; 28:12).

The word *sandal* (ὑπόδημα) occurs only here and in Matt. 10:10.

For the *Holy Spirit* see Matt. 1:18 note.

3:12. The word *winnowing shovel* (πτύον) occurs only here in Matt.

The verb *to thoroughly cleanse* (διακαθαρίζω) occurs only here in the NT.

The word *hand* (χείρ) occurs 24 times in Matt. (3:12; 4:6; 5:30; 8:3, 15; 9:18, 25; 12:10, 13, 49; 14:31; 15:2, 20; 17:22; 18:8 [twice]; 19:13, 15; 22:13; 26:23, 45, 50, 51; 27:24). For discussion see ZPEB, "Hand," III, pp. 28–29; ISBE (1982), "Hand," II, p. 610; Ryken, Wilhoit, and Longman, *Dictionary of Biblical Imagery*, "Hand," pp. 360–62.

The word *wheat* (σῖτος) occurs 4 times in Matt. (3:12; 13:25, 29, 30). It is an important symbol of the righteous. Compare the image applied to Peter (Luke 22:31–32). For further background see Ryken, Wilhoit, and Longman, *Dictionary of Biblical Imagery*, "Wheat,"

14 But John forbad him, saying, I have need to be baptized of thee, and comest thou to me?
15 And Jesus answering said unto him, Suffer it to be so now: for thus it becometh us to fulfil all righteousness. Then he suffered him.

"But John was seeking to prevent him, saying, I have need to be baptized by you, and you come to me?" (v. 14). John understood the majesty of the Lord Jesus and his own humble position before Him.

"But Jesus answered and said to him, permit it now, for thus it is fitting for us to fulfill all righteousness. Then he permitted him" (v. 15). Thus John fulfilled his calling, but in this case by baptizing a Person much greater than he was. Although there were no sins of His own for Jesus to confess, He put Himself in the place of His sinful people who needed to repent and thus fulfilled the place of the righteous man. Morris declares that Jesus was "dedicating himself to the task of making sinners righteous" (*Matt.*, p. 65).

---

pp. 942–43; ZPEB, "Wheat," V, pp. 925–26; ISBE (1988), "Wheat," IV, pp. 1056–57; Zohary, *Plants of the Bible*, "Wheat," pp. 74–75.

The verb *to burn up* is an intensified form (κατακαίω) that occurs 3 times in Matt. (3:12; 13:30, 40). All 3 times it underscores the fierceness of the judgment.

3:13. For this verb *to come* see Matt. 2:1 note.

3:14. The word *need* (χρεία) occurs 6 times in Matt. (3:14; 6:8; 9:12; 14:16; 21:3; 26:65).

3:15. One of the great theological words, *righteousness* (δικαιοσύνη), occurs here for the first of 7 times in Matt. (3:15; 5:6, 10, 20; 6:1, 33; 21:32). The apostle Paul will develop this doctrine fully in Rom. (1:17; 3:3, 21–26; 4:3–13; 5:17, 21; 6:13–20; 8:10; 10:3–10). For discussion see ZPEB, "Righteousness," V, pp. 104–18; ISBE (1988), "Righteousness," IV, pp. 192–95; Elwell, ed., *Evangelical Dictionary of Biblical Theology*, "Righteousness," pp. 687–89; B. Przybylski, *Righteousness in Matthew and His World of Thought*. See also *just, righteous*, Matt. 1:19 note.

Righteousness from God
  I. Jesus fulfilled all righteousness. 3:15.
  II. Believers should thirst after righteousness. 5:6.
  III. Being persecuted for righteousness is blessed. 5:10.
  IV. Believers' righteousness must exceed that of Pharisees. 5:20.
  V. Righteous deeds should be done for God alone. 6:1.
  VI. Believers should seek God's righteousness. 6:33.
  VII. John came in the way of righteousness. 21:32.

*16 And Jesus, when he was baptized, went up straightway out of the water:
and, lo, the heavens were opened unto him, and he saw the Spirit of God descending like a dove, and lighting upon him:*
*17 And lo a voice from heaven, saying, This is my beloved Son, in whom I am
well pleased.*

"And when Jesus was baptized, immediately he went up from the water,
and behold, the heavens were opened to him, and he saw the Spirit of
God descending like a dove and coming upon him" (v. 16). The Lord
Jesus not only accepts baptism, but He also receives the enduement of
the Spirit to accomplish the ministry set before Him. He thus serves in
the same manner as the regular believer must. He is not going to use His
divine nature as a "cushion" to make His ministry easier. We must depend
on the Spirit to fulfill our service; the Lord chooses to do the same.

"And behold a voice out of the heavens, saying, This is my Son, the beloved One, in whom I take pleasure" (v. 17). With the word *behold* Matthew stresses the importance of what has just happened. The divine voice
blends the words of Psalm 2:7 and Isaiah 42:1. A. M. Hunter notes, "One
is the coronation formula of the Messianic King of Israel; the other the
ordination formula of the Servant of the Lord" (*Introducing New Testament Theology*, p. 15). The Lord Jesus will perform all the will of God for

---

The verb *to answer* (ἀποκρίνομαι) occurs 55 times in Matt. (3:15; 4:4; 8:8; 11:4, 25;
12:38, 39, 48; 13:11, 37, and so forth).

The verb *to leave, release, permit, forgive* (ἀφίημι) occurs 47 times in Matt. See Matt. 6:12
note.

3:16. The verb *to go up* (ἀναβαίνω) occurs 9 times in Matt. (3:16; 5:1; 13:7; 14:23, 32;
15:29; 17:27; 20:17, 18).

For the word *spirit* see Matt. 1:18 note.

The word *dove* (περιστερά) occurs 3 times in Matt. (3:16; 10:16; 21:12).

3:17. The word *voice* (φωνή) occurs 7 times in Matt. Here it refers to the voice of God, as
it does in 17:5. The voice of the Lord is a major theme in Ps. 18:13; 29:3–9. See "voice" in
Ryken, Wilhoit, and Longman, *Dictionary of Biblical Imagery*, pp. 918f.; ISBE (1988), "Voice,"
IV, p. 997.

The verb *I take pleasure* or *I am pleased* (εὐδοκέω) occurs 3 times in Matt. (3:17; 12:18;
17:5), all of God the Father taking pleasure in His dear Son, the Lord Jesus Christ. Peter
notes this same phrase (II Pet. 1:17) as do Mark (1:11) and Luke (3:22).

The Father calls Christ *beloved* (ἀγαπητός) in the same 3 contexts only in Matt. (3:17;
12:18; 17:5).

Alexander Whyte has an interesting sermon on this verse, "Our Lord as a Believing Man,"
The Walk, Conversation and Character of Jesus Christ Our Lord, pp. 181–92.

His people that was prophesied in the OT. God takes great pleasure in the active obedience of His dear Son.

Practical Applications from Matthew 3

1. All people should repent: change for the better (v. 2). The lost need to get right with God; the saved need to improve their walk and increase their dedication to God. "The goodness of God leadeth thee to repentance" (Rom. 2:4b).
2. Remember: God's rule is coming (v. 2b). "And let the peace of God rule in your hearts" (Col. 3:15a).
3. John lived a spartan life, but it never hurt him (v. 4). Paul said, "For I have learned, in whatsoever state I am, therewith to be content" (Phil. 4:11b).
4. John never curried favor with the powerful (v. 7). "God is no respecter of persons" (Acts 10:34b). "To have respect of persons is not good" (Prov. 28:21a).
5. John stressed the need for fruit in the life (v. 8). "But the fruit of the Spirit is love, joy, peace, longsuffering, gentleness, goodness, faith, meekness, temperance" (Gal. 5:22–23a).
6. Having good ancestors cannot help you (v. 9). "We have sinned with our fathers, we have committed iniquity" (Ps. 106:6a).
7. Judgment is certain for all men (v. 10). "And thinkest thou this, O man . . . that thou shalt escape the judgment of God?" (Rom. 2:3). "How shall we escape, if we neglect so great salvation?" (Heb. 2:3a).
8. The Lord Jesus Christ will settle the destiny of every man (v. 12). "Then shall the King say unto them on his right hand, Come ye blessed of my Father. . . . Then shall he say also unto them on the left hand, Depart from me, ye cursed" (Matt. 25:34a, 41a).
9. The Lord was concerned about fulfilling all righteousness (v. 15). "Bear ye one another's burdens, and so fulfil the law of Christ" (Gal. 6:2).
10. The Spirit of God empowered the Lord Jesus (v. 16); we need His power as well. "Walk in the Spirit, and ye shall not fulfil the lust of the flesh" (Gal. 5:16b).
11. We, too, ought to live to please the Father (v. 17). "Pure religion and undefiled before God and the Father is this, To visit the fatherless

and widows in their affliction, and to keep himself unspotted from the world" (James 1:27).

Prayer

Dear heavenly Father, thank You for providing salvation from sin through Your Son, the Lord Jesus Christ. Help me to bring forth the fruit of a changed life and to walk in humble obedience to Your will for Jesus' sake. Amen.

MATTHEW 4

The Coming of Satan

Persons

Jesus

The Devil

The Lord God

Angels

John the Baptist

Isaiah

Simon Peter

Andrew

James

John

The sick

Persons referred to

People of Galilee

Zebedee

The demon possessed

Multitudes from Galilee

Places mentioned

The wilderness

The holy city

A high mountain

Galilee

Nazareth

Capernaum

Zabulon and Nephthalim

Jordan

Sea of Galilee

Syria

Decapolis

Jerusalem

Judaea

Doctrines taught

Temptation

God's sustaining power

Angels

Worship of God

Repentance

The kingdom of God

Evangelism

Miracles

1 Then was Jesus led up of the Spirit into the wilderness to be tempted of the devil.

2 And when he had fasted forty days and forty nights, he was afterward an hungred.

Matthew 4 Exposition

I. The Temptation of Jesus. vv. 1–11 [Mark 1:12–13; Luke 4:1–13].

"Then Jesus was led up into the desert by the Spirit in order to be tempted by the devil" (v. 1). The first task of the ministry was to face the old evil foe and defeat him. Man in the paradise of Eden had miserably failed (Gen. 3:1–7). Now the Spirit leads the Lord into a desert place to take him on. Up to this point the Devil had succeeded in making every human being sin (Rom. 3:23). Here he directs his temptations against Christ's human nature and obviously thinks he will succeed again.

"And when he had fasted forty days and forty nights, afterwards he was hungry" (v. 2). Christ is plainly in a position of critical physical weakness, and the Devil, as usual, comes to attack. We need to consider how weak

---

4:1. The word *devil* (διάβολος) occurs 6 times in Matt. (4:1, 5, 8, 11; 13:39; 25:41). Vincent translates it *slanderer* (*Word Studies*, I, p. 27). He is called Satan (σατανᾶς) 4 times in Matt. (4:10; 12:26 [twice]; 16:23). He was behind the serpent in the Garden of Eden (Gen. 3:1ff.), as the book of Revelation makes clear (Rev. 12:9); he provoked David to sin in numbering the people (I Chron. 21:1ff.); he tried to destroy Job (Job 1:6ff.); he stood at the right hand of the high priest Joshua to resist him (Zech. 3:1); it was the Devil who put the idea of betrayal into the heart of Judas (John 13:2); it is the Devil who sows the tares among the wheat (Matt. 13:39); the apostle Paul warns that Satan tries to deceive by transforming himself into an angel of light (II Cor. 11:14); the Lord declared that everlasting fire is prepared for the Devil and his angels (Matt. 25:41). For further background see ZPEB, "Satan," V, pp. 282–86; ISBE (1988), "Satan," IV, pp. 340–44; Elwell, ed., *Evangelical Dictionary of Biblical Theology*, "Satan," pp. 714–15; Ryken, Wilhoit, and Longman, *Dictionary of Biblical Imagery*, "Satan," pp. 759–61; Louis Sperry Chafer, *Satan*; Reuben Archer Torrey, *What the Bible Teaches*, pp. 513ff.; Van der Toorn, Becking, and Vander Horst, *Dictionary of Deities and Demons in the Bible*, "Satan," pp. 726–32.

The verb *to tempt* (πειράζω) occurs 6 times in Matt. (4:1, 3; 16:1; 19:3; 22:18, 35). The 3 kinds of temptation are still prime tools of the Devil:

1. Use things for your own benefit (stones to bread). v. 3.
2. Get good things by wrong methods (cast yourself down). vv. 5–6.
3. Put something ahead of God (worship me). vv. 8–9.

For further discussion see G. Campbell Morgan, *The Crises of the Christ*, "The Temptation," pp. 149–210; ISBE (1988), "Tempt," "Temptation of Jesus," IV, pp. 784–86; ZPEB, "Temptation," "Temptation of Christ," V, pp. 669–72; Elwell, ed., *Evangelical Dictionary of Biblical Theology*, "Temptation, Test," pp. 761–63; Ryken, Wilhoit, and Longman, *Dictionary of Biblical Imagery*, "Tempter, Temptation," pp. 851–54.

For the *Holy Spirit* see Matt. 1:18 note.

3 And when the tempter came to him, he said, If thou be the Son of God, command that these stones be made bread.
4 But he answered and said, It is written, Man shall not live by bread alone, but by every word that proceedeth out of the mouth of God.

we would be after a forty-day fast. There are significant parallels between the Devil's attack in the Garden of Eden (Gen 3:1–5), the temptations of the Lord here, and the warnings against lust (I John 2:15–17).

"And the tempter came and said to him: If you are the Son of God, say that these stones become bread" (v. 3). The Devil's logic is "Since You are the Son of God, perform a miracle." In the garden the serpent suggested that the fruit was good for food and for wisdom (Gen. 3:4–6). John warns against the lust of the flesh (I John 2:15–16). Eating is normally a morally neutral action, but when it is done by a supernatural miracle for selfish purposes, it is no longer neutral. The Devil was suggesting that Jesus stay alive by His supernatural power apart from the provision of His Father. Morris notes that "turning stones into bread is not a temptation to us; it is a temptation only to someone who knows he can do it" (*Matt.*, p. 70, n. 1). But the Lord faced the attack of the Devil in the same way that every saint must: He quoted the holy Scriptures, "the sword of the Spirit" (Eph. 6:17).

"But he answered and said, It has been written: Man shall not live by

---

4:2. The verb *to fast* (νηστεύω) occurs 8 times in Matt. (4:2; 6:16 [twice], 17, 18; 9:14 [twice], 15). It is an optional method of self-discipline by abstaining from food. For background see ZPEB, "Fast, Fasting," II, pp. 501–4; ISBE (1982), "Fast," II, p. 284.

This is the first of 9 times that the verb *to be hungry* (πεινάω) occurs in Matt. (4:2; 5:6; 12:1, 3; 21:18; 25:35, 37, 42, 44).

4:3. The verb *to come to* (προσέρχομαι) occurs 51 times in Matt. (4:3, 11; 5:1; 8:2, 5, 19, 25; 9:14, 20, 28; 13:10, 27, 36; 14:12, 15, and so forth).

This is the first of 8 times that the title *Son of God* is applied to the Lord Jesus in Matt. (4:3, 6; 8:29; 14:33; 26:63; 27:40, 43, 54). The apostle Peter confesses this as well (Matt. 16:16). The Lord usually refers to Himself as the *Son of man* (Matt. 8:20; 9:6; 10:23; 11:19; 12:8, and frequently). God the Father claims Him as *my beloved Son* (Matt. 3:17; 17:5). Liddon stresses that Christ "is the Only, the Well-beloved Son of the Father" (*The Divinity of our Lord and Savior Jesus Christ*, p. 249). The rest of the NT uses the title in the same exalted sense (Mark 3:11; Luke 1:35; John 1:49; 3:18; Acts 9:20; Rom. 1:4; Heb. 4:14; I John 5:5; Rev. 2:18). For further discussion of the title see Warfield, *The Lord of Glory*, pp. 78ff.; Guthrie, *New Testament Theology*, pp. 301–21; ZPEB, "Son of God," V, pp. 480–85; ISBE (1988), "Son of God," IV, pp. 571–74; Elwell, ed., *Evangelical Dictionary of Biblical Theology*, "Jesus Christ, Name and Titles of," p. 411.

The word *bread* (ἄρτος) occurs 21 times in Matt. (4:3, 4; 6:11; 7:9; 12:4; 14:17, 19 [twice]; 15:2, 26, 33, 34, 36; 16:5, 7, 8, 9, 10, 11, 12; 26:26).

5 *Then the devil taketh him up into the holy city, and setteth him on a pin-*
nacle of the temple,
6 *And saith unto him, If thou be the Son of God, cast thyself down: for it is*
written, He shall give his angels charge concerning thee: and in their hands they
shall bear thee up, lest at any time thou dash thy foot against a stone.

bread alone, but by every word that proceeds through the mouth of God"
(v. 4; Deut. 8:3). He demonstrated that their resource was already in their
hand. The psalmist refers to God's Word by different titles and concludes,
"Moreover by them is thy servant warned: and in keeping of them there
is great reward" (Ps. 19:11). Eating, drinking, and marrying are all morally neutral, but they can become means of drawing one away from God
(Matt. 24:38).

"Then the devil takes him into the holy city and stands him on the pinnacle of the temple, and says to him, If you are the Son of God, cast yourself down; for it has been written that

He shall give his angels command concerning you

And they shall bear you up on their hands

Lest you strike your foot against a stone" (vv. 5–6; Ps. 91:11–12).

The Devil can quote Scripture to suit his purpose, but he omits a significant portion of the psalm. The psalmist had said, "For he shall give his
angels charge over thee, to keep thee in all thy ways" (Ps. 91:11). The

---

4:4. The word *man* (ἄνθρωπος) occurs 115 times in Matt. (4:4, 19; 5:13, 16, 19; 6:1, 2,
5, 14, 15, 16, 18; 7:9, 12, and so forth). For discussion see ZPEB, "Man, Nature of," IV, pp.
48–58; ISBE (1979), I, "Anthropology," pp. 131–36; Gresham Machen, *Christian View of*
Man.

The verb *to live* (ζάω) occurs 6 times in Matt. (4:4; 9:18; 16:16; 22:32; 26:63; 27:63). For
the noun form *life* (ζωή) see Matt. 7:14, note.

The word *alone, only* (μόνος) occurs 14 times in Matt. (4:4, 10; 5:47; 8:8; 9:21; 10:42;
12:4; 14:23, 36; 17:8; 18:15; 21:19, 21; 24:36).

The word *word* (ῥῆμα) occurs 5 times in Matt. (4:4; 12:36; 18:16; 26:75; 27:14).

4:5. *The holy city* is plainly Jerusalem; see Matt. 2:1, note.

The word *pinnacle* (πτερύγιον) occurs only here in Matt. It means a *little wing*, referring
to the highest point of the temple.

The *temple* (ἱερόν) is mentioned 11 times in Matt: (4:5; 12:5, 6; 21:12 [twice], 14, 15,
23; 24:1 [twice]; 26:55). The word included the whole temple area, not just the sanctuary
building. Compare *sanctuary*, Matt. 23:16 note. For background see Jacob van Bruggen,
Jesus the Son of God, pp. 38–39; ZPEB, "Temple, Jerusalem," V, pp. 622–56; ISBE (1988),
"Temple," IV, pp. 759–76; Elwell, ed., *Evangelical Dictionary of Biblical Theology*, "Temple,"
pp. 759–61; Ryken, Wilhoit, and Longman, *Dictionary of Biblical Imagery*, "Temple," pp.
849–51; Smith, ed., *Holman Book of Biblical Charts, Maps, and Reconstructions*, "Herod's
Temple," p. 153; Robert Backhouse, *The Kregel Pictorial Guide to the Temple*, 32 pp.

7 Jesus said unto him, It is written again, Thou shalt not tempt the Lord thy God.

8 Again, the devil taketh him up into an exceeding high mountain, and sheweth him all the kingdoms of the world, and the glory of them;

9 And saith unto him, All these things will I give thee, if thou wilt fall down and worship me.

angels protect God's man only as he walks humbly in God's pathway. The Devil is suggesting an arrogant presumption: a spectacular miracle only to attract followers. If the Lord Jesus leaped from the pinnacle and came floating down before the crowd, they would surely worship Him. "What Satan is suggesting is that Jesus should needlessly thrust himself into danger; he would be creating a hazard where none previously existed. And for what? To compel God to save him miraculously" (Morris, *Matt.*, p. 76). In the garden the woman saw that the tree "was pleasant to the eyes" (Gen. 3:6*b*). John warns of the lust of the eyes (I John 2:16*b*). The eyes of man are never satisfied. If one has seen the Rocky Mountains, there are always the Alps, Mount Fuji, Mount Kilimanjaro, and more. The Lord Jesus answers again by quoting Scripture.

"Jesus said to him: Again it has been written: You shall not tempt the Lord your God" (v. 7; Deut. 6:16). The pathway is always walking humbly according to God's Word. "Blessed are the undefiled in the way, who walk in the law of the Lord" (Ps. 119:1). *Again it has been written* is a very important teaching. The Lord is showing that Scripture must not be taken out of context but compared with other Scripture. The apostle Paul stressed that he was teaching what the Holy Spirit taught "comparing spiritual things with spiritual" (I Cor. 2:13*b*).

4:6. For a summary of *it has been written* see Matt. 2:5

The verb *to command, give charge* (ἐντέλλομαι) occurs 4 times in Matt. (4:6; 17:9; 19:7; 28:20).

The verb *to take, take up* (αἴρω) occurs 19 times in Matt. (4:6; 9:6, 16; 11:29; 13:12; 14:12, 20; 15:37; 16:24, and so forth).

4:7. This verb *to tempt* (ἐκπειράζω) occurs only here in Matt. and only in Luke 4:12; 10:25; I Cor. 10:9 in the rest of the NT. For the root verb see Matt. 4:1 note.

4:8. The word *mountain* (ὄρος) occurs 16 times in Matt. (4:8; 5:1, 14; 8:1; 14:23; 15:29; 17:1, 9, 20; 18:12; 21:1, 21; 24:3, 16; 26:30; 28:16). For discussion see Ryken, Wilhoit, and Longman, *Dictionary of Biblical Imagery*, "Mountain," pp. 572–74.

The verb *to show* (δείκνυμι) occurs 3 times in Matt. (4:8; 8:4; 16:21).

The word *world* (κόσμος) occurs 9 times in Matt. (4:8; 5:14; 13:35, 38; 16:26; 18:7; 24:21; 25:34; 26:13). It refers to the beautiful order and arrangement of the world and the

10 Then saith Jesus unto him, Get thee hence, Satan: for it is written, Thou shalt worship the Lord thy God, and him only shalt thou serve.

"Again the devil takes him up into an exceedingly high mountain and shows him all the kingdoms of the world and their glory, and says to him: All these things I will give to you, if you will fall down and worship me" (vv. 8–9). Here is the expression of the Devil's supreme goal: he wanted the place of God. The prophet had described his sin already (Isa. 14:12–14). In the garden the Devil had tempted Eve with the prospect of being like God, knowing good and evil (Gen. 3:5). John solemnly warns against the pride of life (I John 2:16b). Luke's account notes that the Devil showed Him the kingdoms "in a moment of time" (Luke 4:5). It was a mental viewing and not a transportation. The Lord Jesus dismisses the Devil and quotes Scripture to him again.

"Then Jesus says to him, Be gone, Satan: for it has been written: You shall worship the Lord your God and him only shall you serve" (v. 10; Deut. 6:13). Worship and worship service are the supreme goals of mankind as well as of all creation (Rev. 6:5–14). It is striking that the Lord Jesus used the book of Deuteronomy three times over to defeat the Devil. It is not the usual book that believers turn to in temptation. However, "all scripture is God-breathed and profitable for teaching, for reproof, for correction, for child training in righteousness, that the man of God may be complete,

whole creation, but it may also refer to the world system that is opposed to God (I John 2:15–17). Believers should keep themselves "unspotted from the world" (James 1:27). For further discussion see Ryken, Wilhoit, and Longman, *Dictionary of Biblical Imagery*, "World," pp. 967–69; ZPEB, "World." V, pp. 963–68; ISBE (1988), "World," IV, pp. 1112–16; Elwell, ed., *Evangelical Dictionary of Biblical Theology*, "World," pp. 836–37; Harrison, ed., *Baker's Dictionary of Theology*, "World," p. 560.

The word *glory* (δόξα) occurs 7 times in Matt. (4:8; 6:29; 16:27; 19:28; 24:30; 25:31 [twice]). Here it refers to the outward glory of the world. For discussion of the many connotations it may have see ZPEB, "Glory," II, pp. 730–35; ISBE (1982), "Glory," II, pp. 477–83; Elwell, ed., *Evangelical Dictionary of Biblical Theology*, "Glory," pp. 287–88; Ryken, Wilhoit, and Longman, *Dictionary of Biblical Imagery*, "Glory," pp. 330–31. See also the verb *to glorify*, Matt. 5:16 note.

4:9. The verb *to give* (δίδωμι) occurs 56 times in Matt. (4:9; 5:31, 42; 6:11; 7:6, 7, 11 [twice]; 9:8; 10:1, 8, 19; 12:39; 13:8, 11 [twice], 12; 14:7, 8, 9, 11, 16, 19, and so forth). For discussion see ISBE (1982), "Give," II, pp. 473–74.

For a summary of the verb *to worship* see Matt. 2:2 note.

4:10. For the word *Satan* see Matt. 4:1 note.

The verb *to serve* [with worship] (λατρεύω) occurs only here in Matt., but 21 times in the whole NT.

11 Then the devil leaveth him, and, behold, angels came and ministered unto him.
12 Now when Jesus had heard that John was cast into prison, he departed into Galilee;

thoroughly equipped for every good work" (II Tim. 3:16–17). In the light of this paragraph every believer should saturate himself with God's holy Word. The psalmist well said, "Thy word have I hid in mine heart, that I might not sin against thee" (Ps. 119:11). The more believers saturate themselves with Scripture, the safer they are. The psalmist exclaims, "O how love I thy law! it is my meditation all the day" (Ps. 119:97).

"Then the devil leaves him, and behold angels came and were ministering to him" (v. 11). No doubt they supplied strength to His human nature as they had to Elijah when he fled to the desert (I Kings 19:5–8). The Devil had totally failed in his crafty attempts to ensnare the Lord. Every believer should echo David's prayer: "Let the words of my mouth, and the meditation of my heart, be acceptable in thy sight, O Lord, my strength, and my redeemer" (Ps. 19:14).

II. The Early Ministry. vv. 12–25 [Mark 1:14–15; Luke 4:14–15].

"But when he heard that John was given up, he withdrew into Galilee" (v. 12). The ministry of John the Baptist had been fulfilled. He had faithfully prepared the way for the Lord Jesus and now was imprisoned. The Lord Jesus now went to Galilee to begin His public ministry away from the places of power in Jerusalem. John had ministered in the desert, but the Lord Jesus did the unexpected. He was going to minister in the highly populated Galilee region.

4:11. The verb *to serve, minister to* (διακονέω) occurs 6 times in Matt. (4:11; 8:15; 20:28 [twice]; 25:44; 27:55). Here the imperfect tense implies continuing service. For discussion see Ryken, Wilhoit, and Longman, *Dictionary of Biblical Imagery*, "Servant," p. 774; Butler, ed., *Holman Bible Dictionary*, "Service," pp. 1249–50.

Serving like a Deacon

   I. Angels served the Lord. 4:11.

   II. Peter's mother-in-law served. 8:15.

   III. Jesus came, not to be served, but to serve. 20:28.

   IV. The wicked say, "When did we not serve you?" 25:44.

   V. Women from Galilee served the Lord. 27:55.

4:12. This is the first of 31 times that the verb *to betray, deliver over* [to authorities] (παραδίδωμι) occurs in Matt. (4:12; 5:25; 10:4, 17, 19, 21; 11:27; 17:22; 18:34; 20:18, 19; 24:9, 10; 25:14, 20, 22; 26:2, 15, 16, 21, 23, 24, 25, 45, 46, 48; 27:2, 3, 4, 18, 26).

13 And leaving Nazareth, he came and dwelt in Capernaum, which is upon the sea coast, in the borders of Zabulon and Nephthalim:
14 That it might be fulfilled which was spoken by Esaias the prophet, saying,
15 The land of Zabulon, and the land of Nephthalim, by the way of the sea, beyond Jordan, Galilee of the Gentiles;
16 The people which sat in darkness saw great light; and to them which sat in the region and shadow of death light is sprung up.

"And having left Nazareth, he came and dwelled in Capernaum by the seaside in the regions of Zabulon and Nephthali" (v. 13). The people of Nazareth were not friendly toward the Lord (as Luke 4:16–30 makes clear), so He "came down to Capernaum, a city of Galilee, and taught them on the sabbath days" (Luke 4:31). Matthew picks up his fulfillment theme again. "That it might be fulfilled which was spoken through Isaiah the prophet saying:

The land of Zabulon and the land of Nephthali,

the way of the sea, beyond Jordan,

Galilee of the nations,

The people who were sitting in darkness

Saw a great light,

And to those who are sitting in darkness and the shadow of death

Light arose upon them" (vv. 14–16; Isa. 9:1–2).

Vincent notes that it means *to hand over*, "often with the accompanying notion of treachery" (*Word Studies*, I, p. 30). For an analysis of the term see ISBE (1979), "Betray," I, pp. 480–81; Elwell, ed., *Evangelical Dictionary of Biblical Theology*, "Deliver," pp. 162–63.

4:13. *Capernaum* ("the village of Nahum") was a small town on the shore of Galilee, mentioned 4 times in Matt. (4:13; 8:5; 11:23; 17:24). For historical background on Capernaum see "Capernaum," ZPEB, I, pp. 746–48; "Capernaum," ISBE (1979), I, pp. 609–10. For color photographs of Capernaum today see Custer, *Stones of Witness*, pp. 41–43.

The verb *dwelled* (κατῴκησεν) has the sense in the aorist of "lived, settled down" in Capernaum.

4:14. For a summary of the verb *to fulfill*, see Matt. 1:22 note.

4:15. The word *sea, lake* (θάλασσα) occurs 17 times in Matt. (4:15, 18 [twice]; 8:24, 26, 27, 32; 13:1, 47; 14:24, 25, 26; 15:29; 17:27; 18:6; 21:21; 23:15). The reference here is to the Sea of Galilee, or Gennesaret, a small lake 13 miles north and south by 8 miles east and west. It is 608 feet below sea level (and falling). The reference in 21:21 and 23:15 is indeterminate. For background see ZPEB, "Galilee, Sea of," II, pp. 643–48; ISBE (1982), "Galilee, Sea of," II, pp. 391–93; Pfeiffer and Vos, *Wycliffe Historical Geography of Bible Lands*, pp. 126–29; for color photographs see Custer, *Stones of Witness*, pp. 38–55.

The word *Gentile, nation*, occurs 15 times in Matt. (4:15; 6:32; 10:5, 18; 12:18, 21; 20:19, 25; 21:43; 24:7 [twice], 9, 14; 25:32; 28:19). The word refers to all non-Jews. For discussion see ZPEB, "Gentiles," II, pp. 696–97; ISBE (1982), "Gentile," II, pp. 443–44; Ryken, Wilhoit, and Longman, *Dictionary of Biblical Imagery*, "Gentile," pp. 324–25.

17 From that time Jesus began to preach, and to say, Repent: for the kingdom of heaven is at hand.

Thus, Matthew quotes the preamble to the great messianic prophecy of the child born who shall be called

"Wonder of a Counselor,

God of might,

Father of eternity,

Prince of peace" (Isa. 9:6, Hebrew). ·

Steveson comments, "This is a prophecy of Christ, who grew up in Nazareth, a city in Zebulon, darkened because of its lack of spiritual light" (*Isa.*, p. 81). He holds that "the way of the sea" refers to the western side of Galilee and that "beyond Jordan" refers to the eastern shore. Galilee was surrounded by heathen nations (pp. 80–81).

"And from that time Jesus began to be preaching and saying: Repent; for the kingdom of the heavens has drawn near" (v. 17). The present imperative stresses continuous action, *Be repenting*. He was summoning the people to change the way they were thinking and living. He, the King, was near.

4:16. This word *light* ($\varphi\tilde{\omega}\varsigma$) occurs 7 times in Matt. (4:16 [twice]; 5:14, 16; 6:23; 10:27; 17:2). It is a regular word for spiritual illumination (I Thess. 5:5; I John 1:7). For discussion see Ryken, Wilhoit, and Longman, *Dictionary of Biblical Imagery*, "Light," pp. 509–12; ZPEB, "Light," III, pp. 932–34; ISBE (1986), "Light," III, pp. 134–36; Elwell, ed., *Evangelical Dictionary of Biblical Theology*, "Light," pp. 486–87.

The word *darkness* ($\sigma\kappa\acute{o}\tau o\varsigma$) occurs 7 times in Matt. (4:16; 6:23 [twice]; 8:12; 22:13; 25:30; 27:45). Physically it is merely the absence of light, but religiously it denotes spiritual blindness (John 1:5). The wicked walk in darkness (Ps. 82:5). For further discussion see ZPEB, "Dark, Darkness," II, pp. 29–30; ISBE (1979), "Dark, Darkness," I, pp. 868–69; Elwell, ed., *Evangelical Dictionary of Biblical Theology*, "Darkness," pp. 142–43; Ryken, Wilhoit, and Longman, *Dictionary of Biblical Imagery*, "Darkness," pp. 191–93.

The word *death* ($\theta\acute{a}\nu\alpha\tau o\varsigma$) occurs 7 times in Matt. (4:16; 10:21; 15:4; 16:28; 20:18; 26:38, 66). Death is the penalty for sin (Gen. 2:17; 3:3). For discussion see ZPEB, "Death," II, pp. 70–72; ISBE (1979), "Death," I, pp. 898–901; Elwell, ed., *Evangelical Dictionary of Biblical Theology*, "Death, Mortality," pp. 154–56; Ryken, Wilhoit, and Longman, *Dictionary of Biblical Imagery*, "Death," pp. 198–99.

4:17. For a summary of the verb *to repent* see Matt. 3:2 note.

For the verb *to draw near* see Matt. 3:2 note.

18 And Jesus, walking by the sea of Galilee, saw two brethren, Simon called Peter, and Andrew his brother, casting a net into the sea: for they were fishers. 19 And he saith unto them, Follow me, and I will make you fishers of men. 20 And they straightway left their nets, and followed him.

"And walking alongside the sea of Galilee, he saw two brothers, Simon, the one called Peter, and Andrew his brother, casting a net into the sea; for they were fishermen" (v. 18). Such a sight can be seen even to the present day, for the Sea of Galilee is filled with tilapia, a fine-tasting fish (still called "St. Peter's fish"). "And he said to them, Come after me, and I will make you fishermen of men" (v. 19). The apostle Paul writes familiarly to the Corinthians of his evangelization of them, "Being crafty, I caught you with guile" (II Cor. 12:16b). The Lord obviously had touched the hearts of these two brothers.

"And immediately they left their nets and followed him" (v. 20). Thus the Lord Jesus began calling the Twelve to follow Him. Those who follow the Lamb are a very select company in heaven (Rev. 14:4), probably martyrs of the Tribulation period.

4:18. Peter (Πέτρος) is named 23 times in Matt. (4:18; 8:14; 10:2; 14:28, 29; 15:15; 16:16, 18, 22, 23; 17:1, 4, 24; 18:21; 19:27; 26:33, 35, 37, 40, 58, 69, 73, 75). For historical background on Peter, see F. F. Bruce, Peter, Stephen, James, and John; Kenneth Frederick, The Making of a Disciple; Oscar Cullmann, Peter: Disciple—Apostle—Martyr; Who's Who in the Bible, "Peter," pp. 348–55; Douglas and Tenney, eds., The New International Dictionary of the Bible, "Peter," pp. 771–73; "Peter, Simon," ZPEB, IV, pp. 733–39; "Peter," ISBE (1986), III, pp. 802–7.

Andrew is mentioned twice in Matt. (4:18; 10:2). For historical background on Andrew, see Who's Who in the Bible, "Andrew," pp. 43–44; ZPEB, "Andrew," I, pp. 156–58; ISBE (1979), "Andrew," I, pp. 122–23.

The number two (δύο) occurs 40 times in Matt. (4:18, 21; 5:41; 6:24; 8:28; 9:27; 10:10, 29; 14:17, 19; 18:8 [twice], 9, 16, 19, 20, and so forth). See Introduction, "Numbers," p. xxii.

The verb to walk (περιπατέω) occurs 7 times in Matt. (4:18; 9:5; 11:5; 14:25, 26, 29; 15:31).

The word casting net (ἀμφίβληστρον) occurs only here in the NT. It is to be distinguished from the dragnet (σαγήνη), found only in Matt. 13:47 in the NT. For distinctions see Trench, Synonyms of the New Testament, pp. 236f.; ZPEB, "Net," IV, pp. 412–13; ISBE (1986), "Net, Seine," III, pp. 523–24. For illustrations of fishnets see V. Gilbert Beers, The Victor Book of Bible Knowledge, pp. 362–65.

The word fisherman (ἁλιεύς) occurs only in this context in Matt. (4:18, 19).

4:19. The word come! (δεῦτε) occurs 6 times in Matt. (4:19; 11:28; 21:38; 22:4; 25:34; 28:6). Here it is closely linked in thought to the verb follow in v. 20.

4:20. This word immediately (εὐθέως) occurs 13 times in Matt. (4:20, 22; 8:3; 13:5; 14:22, 31; 20:34; 21:2; 24:29; 25:15; 26:49, 74; 27:48).

21 And going on from thence, he saw other two brethren, James the son of Zebedee, and John his brother, in a ship with Zebedee their father, mending their nets; and he called them.
22 And they immediately left the ship and their father, and followed him.
23 And Jesus went about all Galilee, teaching in their synagogues, and preaching the gospel of the kingdom, and healing all manner of sickness and all manner of disease among the people.

"And going on from there, he saw two other brothers, James, the one of Zebedee, and John his brother, in the boat with Zebedee their father, mending their nets; and he called them" (v. 21). Their response was unquestioning obedience.

"And immediately they left the boat and their father and followed him" (v. 22). The Lord later commented, "The one that loves father or mother more than me is not worthy of me" (Matt. 10:37a). It is interesting that a third of the apostolic company were fishermen. John describes seven of them as going fishing (John 21:2–3). Matthew Henry observes that all the men the Lord Jesus called were diligent, hard-working men. "Those who have learned to bear hardships, and to run hazards, are best prepared for the fellowship and discipleship of Jesus Christ."

"And he went about all Galilee, teaching in their synagogues and preaching the gospel of the kingdom, and healing every disease and every weakness among the people" (v. 23). The word *their* indicated the sharp divi-

---

The verb *to follow* (ἀκολουθέω) occurs 25 times in Matt. (4:20, 22, 25; 8:1, 10, 19, 22, 23; 9:9 [twice], 19, 27; 10:38; 12:15; 14:13; 16:24; 19:2, 21, 27, 28; 20:29, 34; 21:9; 26:58; 27:55). It means much more than merely walking along behind someone. It refers to the moral adherence and devotion to the cause of the Master. The Lord Jesus gave an uncompromising command to *follow* Him (Matt. 8:22). John conveys the seriousness of following (John 1:40–43). For further discussion see ISBE (1982), "Follow," II, pp. 326–27; Elwell, ed., *Evangelical Dictionary of Biblical Theology*, "Follow, Follower," pp. 263–64.

4:21. For historical background on James, son of Zebedee, see *Who's Who in the Bible*, "James," pp. 182–83; ZPEB, "James," III, pp. 391–93; "James," ISBE (1982), II, p. 958.

For background on John his brother, see ZPEB, "John, the Apostle," III, pp. 637–41; "Johannine Theology, III, pp. 623–36; ISBE (1982), "John the Apostle," II, pp. 1107–8; see also ISBE, "Johannine Theology," II, pp. 1081–91.

The word *boat* (πλοῖον) occurs 13 times in Matt. (4:21, 22; 8:23, 24; 9:1; 13:2; 14:13, 22, 24, 29, 32, 33; 15:39). For background see ISBE (1988), "Ships, Boats," IV, pp. 482–89; ZPEB, "Boat," I, p. 631; Shelley Wachsmann, "The Galilee Boat," *Biblical Archaeology Review*, Sept./Oct., 1988, Vol. XIV, No. 5, pp. 18–33.

The verb *to prepare, mend* (καταρτίοω) occurs twice in Matt. (4:21; 21:16).

4:23. The word *gospel, good news* (εὐαγγέλιον) occurs 4 times in Matt. (4:23; 9:35; 24:14; 26:13). The verb form *to preach the gospel* (εὐαγγελίζω) occurs once (11:5); it is the

24 And his fame went throughout all Syria: and they brought unto him all sick people that were taken with divers diseases and torments, and those which were possessed with devils, and those which were lunatick, and those that had the palsy; and he healed them.

sion that had occurred in Matthew's lifetime. At one time he could have said *our*. *The gospel of the kingdom* is the good news of salvation provided by the great King. Matthew is the only one to use the phrase in the NT (4:23; 9:35; 24:14). It was the heart of the message on the day of Pentecost (Acts 2:36–38). It will be the message during the Tribulation period (24:14). It is clear that the Lord Jesus had the power to heal every form of disease (Matt. 8:16; 9:35) and every type of bodily infirmity known (Matt. 9:27–30; 12:22).

"And his fame went into the whole of Syria; and they brought to him all those who were sick with various diseases and torments and those who were possessed with demons and the insane and paralyzed, and he healed them" (v. 24). A. T. Robertson notes that these were cases "that the doc-

---

great verb in Acts, occurring 15 times. For further discussion see Elwell, ed., *Evangelical Dictionary of Biblical Theology*, "Gospel," pp. 305–8; ZPEB, "Gospel (Message)," II, pp. 779–84; ISBE (1982), "Gospel," II, pp. 529–32.

The verb *to go around* (περιάγω) occurs 3 times in Matt. (4:23; 9:35; 23:15). Here it refers to the first tour of Galilee by the Lord and some of His disciples (Matt. 9:9).

The verb *to teach* (διδάσκω) occurs 14 times in Matt. (4:23; 5:2, 19 [twice]; 7:29; 9:35; 11:1; 13:54; 15:9; 21:23; 22:16; 26:55; 28:15, 20). For background see ISBE (1988), "Teach," IV, pp. 743–45; ZPEB, "Teacher," V, pp. 606–7; Elwell, ed., *Evangelical Dictionary of Biblical Theology*, "Teach, Teacher," pp. 757–59.

For the verb *to preach* see Matt. 3:1 note.

The word *synagogue* (συναγωγή) occurs 9 times in Matt. (4:23; 6:2, 5; 9:35; 10:17; 12:9; 13:54; 23:6, 34). For background see ZPEB, "Synagogue," V, pp. 554–67; ISBE (1988), "Synagogue," IV, pp. 676–84; Elwell, ed., *Evangelical Dictionary of Biblical Theology*, "Synagogue," pp. 752–54; for color photographs of ancient synagogues see Custer, *Stones of Witness*, pp. 24–25, 42–43, 49.

The verb *to heal* (θεραπεύω) occurs 16 times in Matt. (4:23, 24; 8:7, 16; 9:35; 10:1, 8; 12:10, 15, 22; 14:14; 15:30; 17:16, 18; 19:2; 21:14). The Lord Jesus was a miraculous healer as Ps. 103:3 predicted of Jehovah. For further discussion see ISBE (1982), "Heal," II, pp. 640–47; ZPEB, "Healing, Health," III, pp. 54–58; Elwell, ed., *Evangelical Dictionary of Biblical Theology*, "Heal, Health," pp. 328–30.

The word *disease* (νόσος) occurs 5 times in Matt. (4:23, 24; 8:17; 9:35; 10:1). For descriptions see ZPEB, "Diseases of the Bible," II, pp. 132–42; ISBE (1979), "Disease," I, pp. 953–60.

The word *weakness* (μαλακία) occurs 3 times in Matt. only in the NT (4:23; 9:35; 10:1). Isaiah prophesied that Messiah would bear our weakness (Isa. 53:4; 53:3 LXX).

4:24. The word *report, fame* (ἀκοή) occurs 4 times in Matt. (4:24; 13:14; 14:1; 24:6).

25   And there followed him great multitudes of people from Galilee, and from Decapolis, and from Jerusalem, and from Judaea, and from beyond Jordan.

tors could not cure" (*Word Pictures*, I, p. 36). The Lord Jesus was a great healer, and hence multitudes came to Him, but His great purpose was to heal the souls of men, as the three following chapters demonstrate.

"And many crowds followed him from Galilee, and Decapolis, and Jerusalem, and Judaea, and from beyond the Jordan" (v. 25). Many people who were desperately ill and afflicted came to Him from regions all around. The Lord Jesus not only met their needs but also provided spiritual help by His sermons. God may still use afflictions to draw people to Himself. The Lord Jesus is the Great Physician who can heal the sin-sick soul.

Practical Applications from Matthew 4

1. God does bring everyone into testing (v. 1). "There hath no temptation taken you but such as is common to man: but God is faithful, who will not suffer you to be tempted above that ye are able; but will with the temptation also make a way to escape, that ye may be able to bear it" (I Cor. 10:13).

2. The Devil tempts us to get a good thing in the wrong way (v. 3). Bread is normal food, but not by capricious miracles. "The steps of a good man are ordered by the Lord: and he delighteth in his way" (Ps. 37:23). "I have been young, and now am old; yet have I not seen the righteous forsaken, nor his seed begging bread" (Ps. 37:25).

3. The Lord Jesus taught conformity to God's Word (v. 4). "Thy word is a lamp unto my feet, and a light unto my path" (Ps. 119:105). The psalmist prayed, "Order my steps in thy word: and let not any iniquity have dominion over me" (Ps. 119:133).

Syria is mentioned only here in Matt. and in Luke 2:2 in the Gospels. For background see ISBE (1988), "Syria," IV, pp. 686–94; ZPEB, "Aram," I, pp. 246–49.

The verb *to be demon possessed* (δαιμονίζομαι) occurs 7 times in Matt. (4:24; 8:16, 28, 33; 9:32; 12:22; 15:22). The reality of demons is a clear Bible doctrine. See *demon*, Matt. 7:22 note.

The verb *to be moonstruck, insane* (σεληνιάζομαι) occurs only here and in 17:15 in Matt.

The word *paralytic* (παραλυτικός) occurs 5 times in Matt. (4:24; 8:6; 9:2 [twice], 6).

4:25. *Decapolis* is mentioned only here in Matt. It was a region of originally 10 major cities east of the Jordan. For historical background see ZPEB, "Decapolis," II, pp. 81–84; ISBE (1979), "Decapolis," I, pp. 906–8.

4. The Devil tempts us to do dangerous things to gain good ends (vv. 5–6). "One thing have I desired of the Lord, that will I seek after; that I may dwell in the house of the Lord all the days of my life, to behold the beauty of the Lord, and to enquire in his temple" (Ps. 27:4).

5. The Lord Jesus put God above all human desires (v. 7). "Exalt ye the Lord our God, and worship at his footstool; for he is holy" (Ps. 99:5).

6. The Devil tempts us with worldly power and glory (v. 8). "And the world passeth away, and the lust thereof: but he that doeth the will of God abideth for ever" (I John 2:17).

7. The Lord Jesus put God and His service above all (v. 10). "Serve the Lord with gladness: come before his presence with singing" (Ps. 100:2). "Let us have grace, whereby we may serve God acceptably with reverence and godly fear" (Heb. 12:28b).

8. God's Word is a light to those in darkness (v. 16). God has called believers "out of darkness into his marvellous light" (I Pet. 2:9). We need to "walk in the light, as he is in the light" (I John1:7).

9. We must all recognize that God's kingdom is near (v. 17). "We are confident, I say, and willing rather to be absent from the body, and to be present with the Lord" (II Cor. 5:8).

10. God desires that believers "fish" for souls (v. 19). "For we preach not ourselves, but Christ Jesus the Lord; and ourselves your servants for Jesus' sake" (II Cor. 4:5).

11. The Lord Jesus has the power to meet every human need (v. 23). He is "our Lord Jesus, that great shepherd of the sheep" (Heb. 13:20b).

12. There is nothing too hard for the Lord Jesus to do (v. 24). Paul declared, "He said unto me, My grace is sufficient for thee: for my strength is made perfect in weakness. Most gladly therefore will I rather glory in my infirmities, that the power of Christ may rest upon me" (II Cor. 12:9).

Prayer

Dear heavenly Father, protect me from the assaults of the Devil. Help me to think of the power and protection of Your Son, the Lord Jesus Christ. Defeat the Devil again by the grace of the Lord Jesus. Call to my mind the Scripture I need. Amen.

THE COMMANDS OF THE KING

Persons
Jesus
The multitudes

His disciples
God (your Father)

Persons referred to
The poor in spirit
Those who mourn
The meek
Those who hunger and thirst
The merciful
The pure in heart
The peacemakers
The persecuted
The prophets

Those who break these
  commands
Scribes
Pharisees
The brother
The adversary
The neighbor
The enemy
Publicans

Places mentioned
A mountain
Hell [gehenna]
Heaven

Earth
Jerusalem

Doctrines taught
The kingdom of heaven
Righteousness
Purity
Joy
The Law and the Prophets
Judgment

Reconciliation
Lust
Adultery
Oaths
Perfection

1 And seeing the multitudes, he went up into a mountain: and when he was set, his disciples came unto him:

Matthew 5 Exposition

I. The Beatitudes. vv. 1–12 [Luke 6:20–26].

"And when he saw the crowds, he went up into the mountain, and when he was seated, his disciples came to him" (v. 1). The Sermon on the Mount is the world's most famous sermon. In it the Lord Jesus expresses the will of His Father most perfectly. He shows the true pathway to God and the meaning of life. F. B. Meyer called it *The Directory of the Devout Life* (Grand Rapids: Baker, 1954). C. K. Lehman called it "the Magna Charta of the kingdom" (*Biblical Theology*, Scottdale, Pa.: Herald Press, 1974, II, p.51). The principles of the kingdom turn out to be a shocking reversal of all the world desires and grasps for. The Lord here takes the OT teaching, fills it with new meaning, and elevates it to a staggering height for believers. It leaves unbelievers convicted and believers illuminated for new levels of devotion to God. It is addressed to disciples, not the world. Walvoord argues that the sermon gives the principles of the millennial kingdom but notes that there are present applications of them ("The Sermon on the Mount," *Major Bible Prophecies*, pp. 192–204).

In this exposition we will pay no attention to those interpreters who refuse to submit to the authority of the Lord Jesus Christ but still try to use the sermon for their own purposes. Those who teach a social gospel of reform and are not "born again" believers have nothing to help understand this message. Karl Marx was fascinated by this sermon but used it for armed rebellion; Gandhi tried to practice it and still remain a Hindu, worshiping the god Ram. Submission to Christ is the first essential in understanding the sermon.

We must also note that standard harmonies of the Gospels place the interview with Nicodemus before this sermon (Robertson, *A Harmony of the Gospels*, pp. 25f. and 48ff.). The idea of the necessity of the new birth is presupposed by the sermon but expressed by other images.

5:1. The verb *to sit down* (καθίζω) occurs 8 times in Matt. (5:1; 13:48; 19:28; 20:21, 23; 23:2; 25:31; 26:36). Rabbis in the synagogue always taught sitting down.

The word *disciple* (μαθητής) occurs 72 times in Matt. (5:1; 8:21, 23; 9:10, 11, 14 [twice], 19, 37; 10:1, 24, 25, 42; 11:1, 2; 12:1, 2, 49; 13:10, 36; 14:12, 15, 19 [twice], 22, 26;

2 And he opened his mouth, and taught them, saying,
3 Blessed are the poor in spirit: for theirs is the kingdom of heaven.

The psalmist expresses the proper attitude for the believer in coming to this sermon: "With my whole heart have I sought thee: O let me not wander from thy commandments" (Ps. 119:10).

"And he opened his mouth and was teaching them, saying" (v. 2). The sermon, which follows, is a revolutionary challenge to every reader and hearer. The divine Son of God shows us that His word is the truth (John 17:17). It grips the soul of man like no other words in the history of religious thought.

"Blessed are the beggars in spirit,

because theirs is the kingdom of the heavens" (v. 3).

15:2, 12, 23, 32, 33, 36 [twice]; 16:5, 13, 20, 21, 24; 17:6, 10, 13, 16, 19; 18:1; 19:10, 13, 23, 25; 20:17; 21:1, 6, 20; 22:16; 23:1; 24:1, 3; 26:1, 8, 17, 18, 19, 26, 35, 36, 40, 45, 56; 27:64; 28:7, 8, 13, 16). The disciples were the true believers in Christ, who left all to follow Him and became the nucleus of the church that would arise (Acts 1:15; 6:1). Judas was the shocking exception. For the verb form *to make disciples*, see Matt. 13:52. For discussion see ZPEB, "Disciple," II, pp. 129–31; ISBE (1979), "Disciple," I, pp. 947–48; Elwell, ed., *Evangelical Dictionary of Biblical Theology*, "Disciple, Discipleship," pp. 175–77; A. B. Bruce, *The Training of the Twelve*; for a liberal appraisal, E. Schweizer, *Lordship and Discipleship*.

The mountain has been traditionally regarded as the Mount of the Beatitudes on the shores of the Sea of Galilee (for color photographs of the site, see the author's *Stones of Witness*, pp. 38–39, 44–45). The "Sermon on the Plain" (Luke 6:17–49) is at times suggested as a different redaction of this same sermon, but these truths are timeless, and it would not be strange if the Lord repeated portions of this sermon on different occasions to different audiences. Blomberg notes, "Luke arranges much of his material thematically, and many of the shorter sayings common to Matthew and Luke could well have been repeated by Jesus on many different occasions" (*Matt.*, p. 96). Good teachers know that "repetition aids learning."

For the verb *to come to* (προσέρχομαι) see Matt. 4:3 note. The writer to the Hebrews urges believers "to come boldly to the throne of grace, that we may obtain mercy, and find grace to help in time of need" (Heb. 4:16). He also promises that "he is able also to save them to the uttermost that come unto God by him, seeing he ever lives to make intercession for them" (Heb. 7:25).

5:2. The imperfect tense of the verb, *was teaching*, implies continued action. The sermon that follows is an abridgement, not an exhaustive record. For a summary of the verb *to teach* (διδάσκω), see Matt. 4:23 note.

Harvey K. McArthur lists a dozen interpretations of the sermon: Understanding the Sermon on the Mount (New York: Harper, 1960). Setting aside the Roman Catholic view and those of individuals Tolstoi, Albert Schweitzer, Martin, and Dibelius, there remain some important principles to consider:

1. Common sense modification view: Calvin suggested Matt. 5:40 for this view.

2. Hyperbole view: gouging out an eye is not to be taken literally, Matt. 5:29.

Luther notes that the Lord Jesus does not begin with stern pronouncements of the Mosaic law but with "pleasant promises" (*Luther's Works: The Sermon on the Mount*, p. 10). The *beggars* are not merely poor; they are totally dependent on others for survival. The people who think that God owes them life are self deceived; the people who perceive that they are without hope unless God has mercy upon them have taken the first step to getting right with God. Literal beggars are not under discussion here. Beggars in the realm of the spirit are those who plead with God for grace. It is not an accident that the apostle Paul called himself a blasphemer, a persecutor, and chief of sinners (I Tim. 1:13, 15). He had obtained undeserved mercy from Jesus Christ (I Tim. 1:16). People in the world think that arrogant, commanding persons are the happy ones. In reality they are not happy for they are always fearing what they might lose. God's kingdom is made up of people who have bowed the knee to Him and are prepared to walk humbly in His pathway (Mic. 6:8). God promises to "cause the arrogancy of the proud to cease" (Isa. 13:11b). People who are proud and think that they are spiritually rich are beggars in the sight of God (Rev. 3:17). The Lord Jesus is restating one of the great OT promises: "For thus saith the high and lofty One that inhabiteth eternity, whose name is Holy; I dwell in the high and holy place, with him also that is of a contrite and humble spirit, to revive the spirit of the humble, and to revive the heart

---

3. General principles view: the right cheek is not important, Matt. 5:39b.

4. Attitudes, not acts, view: praying standing on the street corner is not the only way of being ostentatious, Matt. 6:5.

5. Analogy of Scripture view: finding other passages to explain a command, Matt. 5:22c; compare Gal. 3:1.

6. The dispensational view: Scofield notes a literal fulfillment in the future Millennium and a moral application to believers today, Matt. 5:2 note.

7. The repentance view: It is designed to convict and bring one to repentance.

Many expositors have recognized such principles in their comments. The sermon is so complex and comprehensive that more than one of these principles may well apply. Yet there is a striking, serene simplicity to the sermon as well. We must remember that it is by the foolishness of preaching that God brings His salvation to people (I Cor. 1:18–24).

5:3. The word *blessed* (μακάριος) occurs 13 times in Matt. (5:3, 4, 5, 6, 7, 8, 9, 10, 11; 11:6; 13:16; 16:17; 24:46). It denotes *spiritual happiness* and *well-being*. God delights in blessing His people (Gen. 1:28; 22:16–18; Ps. 1:1–3). William Fitch, *The Beatitudes of Jesus*; Maclaren, *A Garland of Gladness*; Elwell, ed., *Evangelical Dictionary of Biblical Theology*, "Beatitudes," pp. 53–55; ZPEB, "The Beatitudes," I, pp. 497–501; "Bless, Blessing," I, pp. 625–26; ISBE (1979), "Beatitudes," I, pp. 443–44. See also Bibliography, pp. 441–42.

The word *beggar, poor* (πτωχός) occurs 5 times in Matt. (5:3; 11:5; 19:21; 26:9, 11), all except here referring to financial poverty. A. W. Tozer warns against the "tyranny of

4 Blessed are they that mourn: for they shall be comforted.

of the contrite ones" (Isa. 57:15). Paul expressed it theologically by say-ing, "For I know that in me (that is, in my flesh,) dwells no good thing" (Rom. 7:18a). The true believer must turn away from himself and put the kingdom of God first in his life (Matt. 6:33). That act is called conver-sion (Acts 3:19). These beatitudes show how that occurs in the life of a believer. The first step is recognition of spiritual need. The apostle Paul expressed that when he said, "O wretched man that I am! who shall deliver me from the body of this death?" (Rom. 7:24). The cry of the pub-lican was dramatic: "God be merciful to me, the sinner" (Luke 18:13b). He used the article, *the* sinner. He was the worst sinner he could think of. God knows the heart. The Pharisee could not think of a thing he needed; he was proud of himself (Luke 18:11–12), but the Lord Jesus pronounced *woe* upon the hypocritical Pharisees (Matt. 23:13ff.).

"Blessed are the ones who mourn,

because they themselves shall be comforted" (v. 4).

things" (*The Pursuit of God*, pp. 21ff.). For discussion see ZPEB, "Poor," IV, pp. 819–21; ISBE (1986), "Poor," III, pp. 905–8; Ryken, Wilhoit, and Longman, *Dictionary of Biblical Imagery*, "Poverty," pp. 657–58.

For a statistical summary of the word *kingdom* (βασιλεία), see Matt. 3:2 note. The phrase *kingdom of God* occurs 5 times in Matt. (6:33; 12:28; 19:24; 21:31, 43); the usual phrase in Matt. is *kingdom of the heavens* (Matt. 3:2; 4:17; 5:3, 10, 19, 20; 7:21; 8:11; 10:7; 11:11, 12; 13:11, 24, 31, 33, 44, 45, 47, 52; 16:19; 18:1, 3, 4, 23; 19:12, 14, 23; 20:1; 22:2; 23:13; 25:1). The word *kingdom* has a number of levels of meaning in Scripture. In the broadest sense His kingdom rules over all; nothing exists without His permission (Ps. 103:19). But more specifically it refers to all men and angels who submit to His rule and worship Him (Rev. 5:7–14). Many specific aspects of the kingdom can be seen. It sometimes refers to the coming millennial reign (Rev. 20:1–6); it can refer to the eternal rule of God (Rev. 22:3–5). Believers are in the present aspect of the kingdom now (Rom. 14:17). Edersheim gives a famous composite definition: "It means the rule of God; which was manifested in and through Christ; is apparent in the church; gradually develops amidst hindrances; is triumphant at the second coming of Christ (the end); and, finally, perfected in the world to come" (*The Life and Times of Jesus the Messiah*, I, p. 270). See George N. H. Peters, *The Theocratic Kingdom of our Lord Jesus, the Christ*, 3 vols.; Alva J. McClain, *The Greatness of the Kingdom*; John F. Walvoord, *The Millennial Kingdom*; Elwell, ed., *Evangelical Dictionary of Biblical Theology*, "Kingdom of God," pp. 451–54; E. F. Harrison, ed., *Baker's Dictionary of Theology*, "Kingdom of God," pp. 309–14; ZPEB, "Kingdom of God, of Heaven," III, pp. 801–9; ISBE (1986), "Kingdom of God," III, pp. 23–29.

5:4. The verb *to mourn* (πενθέω) occurs twice in Matt. (5:4; 9:15).

For the verb *to comfort* see Matt. 2:18 note. The noun form, *comforter, paraclete* (παράκλητος) occurs 4 times in John (14:16, 26; 15:26; 16:7).

The *they themselves* (αὐτοί) is an intensive pronoun; *they* is already in the verb ending.

5 Blessed are the meek: for they shall inherit the earth.

God is listening to such heartfelt cries of repentance. David cried out, "The sacrifices of God are a broken spirit: a broken and a contrite heart, O God, thou wilt not despise" (Ps. 51:17). As Paul expresses it, in the Lord Jesus Christ "we are having redemption through his blood, the forgiveness of sins, according to the riches of his grace" (Eph. 1:7). John declares that "the blood of Jesus, his Son, is cleansing us from all sin" (I John 1:7*b*). To worldly people, mourning, especially before God, is one of the last things they want to think of. But God has promised, "To this man will I look, even to him that is poor and of a contrite spirit, and trembleth at my word" (Isa. 66:2*b*). It is God's purpose "to comfort all that mourn; to appoint unto them that mourn in Zion, to give unto them beauty for ashes, the oil of joy for mourning" (Isa. 61:2*b*–3*a*). The apostle Paul prays that the Lord Jesus Christ will "comfort your hearts, and establish you in every good word and work" (II Thess. 2:17). The Holy Spirit comforts God's people now, but the vision of Revelation assures God's people that God "shall wipe away every tear from their eyes, and death shall not be; neither sorrow nor crying nor toil shall be any more, because the first things passed away" (Rev. 21:4). The second step in salvation is heart repentance for sin.

"Blessed are the meek,

because they themselves shall inherit the earth" (v. 5).

The Lord Jesus is referring to the promise "The meek shall inherit the earth" (Ps. 37:11). People who are meek and humble are regularly trampled upon by the arrogant and the forceful. The world is filled with people who live in pride and pretense. But God is watching, and He will even everything out. "Meekness is therefore an active and deliberate

---

5:5. The word *meek* (πραΰς) occurs 3 times in Matt. (5:5; 11:29; 21:5) and in I Pet. 3:4 only in the NT. Meekness is not weakness. The Lord Himself is the example of meekness (11:29; 21:5). For the idea of *meekness* see A. W. Tozer, *The Pursuit of God*, pp. 109ff.; Elwell, ed., *Evangelical Dictionary of Biblical Theology*, "Meekness," p. 519; ZPEB, "Meekness," IV, pp. 163–64; ISBE (1986), "Meek, Meekness," III, pp. 307–8.

The verb *to inherit* (κληρονομέω) occurs 3 times in Matt. (5:5; 19:29; 25:34). The believer will inherit the earth, everlasting life, and the kingdom! How wonderful to have an inheritance that cannot be corrupted or defiled, and will not fade away (I Pet. 1:4). It is strong motivation to serve the Lord Christ heartily (Col. 3:24). For further discussion see ZPEB, "Inheritance," III, pp. 277–79; ISBE (1982), "Inherit," II, pp. 823–25; Elwell, ed., *Evangelical Dictionary of Biblical Theology*, "Inheritance," pp. 374–75; Ryken, Wilhoit, and Longman, *Dictionary of Biblical Imagery*, "Inheritance," pp. 420–21.

6 *Blessed are they which do hunger and thirst after righteousness: for they shall be filled.*

acceptance of undesirable circumstances that are wisely seen by the individual as only part of a larger picture" (S. A. Meier, *Evangelical Dictionary of Biblical Theology*, p. 519). David assures believers that evildoers shall be cut off (Ps. 37:9). The meek hear the stern condemnation of sin in Scripture and bow in humble penitence before God. "For all have sinned and are coming short of the glory of God" (Rom. 3:23). "If we say that we have not sinned, we are making him a liar, and his word is not in us" (I John 1:10). The humble man begs God for forgiveness as the publican did (Luke 18:13*b*). The arrogant man hardens his heart and turns away from God. Scripture warns, "Behold, ye have sinned against the Lord: and be sure your sin will find you out" (Num. 32:23*b*). The meek will discover that God will sustain them in this life until their tasks are done, but in the long view, God will give them heaven and earth in the world to come (Rev. 21:1–3). David had said the same thing: "The Lord knoweth the days of the upright: and their inheritance shall be for ever" (Ps. 37:18). The Lord Jesus is not just being innovative; He is reading the OT carefully and interpreting it properly. But no one else has said it so clearly and succinctly as He. But He also gave us the perfect example: "Take my yoke upon you and learn from me, because I am meek and lowly in heart, and you shall find rest in your souls" (Matt. 11:29). The third step in salvation is fervent submission to the will of God.

> "Blessed are the ones who are hungering and thirsting for
> righteousness,
> because they themselves shall be filled" (v. 6).

The psalmist cried out, "As the hart panteth after the water brooks, so panteth my soul after thee, O God. My soul thirsteth for God, for the living God: when shall I come and appear before God?" (Ps. 42:1–2). The promises in the prophets are very clear. "Ho, every one that thirsteth, come ye to the waters, and he that hath no money; come ye, buy, and eat; yea, come, buy wine and milk without money and without price . . .

5:6. For the verb *to hunger* (πεινάω) see Matt. 4:2 note.

The verb *to be thirsty* (διψάω) occurs 5 times in Matt. (5:6; 25:35, 37, 42, 44).

For the word *righteousness* (δικαιοσύνη) see Matt. 3:15 note.

The verb *to be filled* [with food](χορτάζω) occurs 4 times in Matt. (5:6; 14:20; 15:33, 37).

7 Blessed are the merciful: for they shall obtain mercy.
8 Blessed are the pure in heart: for they shall see God.

Incline your ear, and come unto me: hear, and your soul shall live; and I will make an everlasting covenant with you" (Isa. 55:1, 3). The psalmist exclaimed, "How sweet are thy words unto my taste! yea, sweeter than honey to my mouth!" (Ps. 119:103). The seeking soul comes to know that the great King Himself is "THE LORD OUR RIGHTEOUSNESS" (Jer. 23:6b). The apostle Paul spoke of "the righteousness of God which is by faith in Jesus Christ" (Rom. 3:22, Greek text). John Stott notes the "progression of relentless logic" in the first four beatitudes (*The Message of the Sermon on the Mount*, p. 46). The fourth step in salvation is the heartfelt desire for God and His righteousness.

"Blessed are the merciful,

because they themselves shall receive mercy" (v. 7).

The prophet promised, "And if thou draw out thy soul to the hungry, and satisfy the afflicted soul; then shall thy light rise in obscurity, and thy darkness be as the noonday; and the Lord shall guide thee continually, and satisfy thy soul in drought, and make fat thy bones: and thou shalt be like a watered garden, and like a spring of water, whose waters fail not" (Isa. 58:10–11). Mercy is an attribute of God (Ps. 5:7; 6:4; 13:5; 21:7; 23:6; 25:7, 10; 31:7, and often). One who has received the love of God in salvation should allow that love to flow through him to the lives of others. The apostle Paul notes, "Even as we received mercy, we faint not" (II Cor. 4:1b). He also exhorts, "And be walking in love, even as Christ loved us and gave himself in behalf of us an offering and a sacrifice to God for a sweet smelling savour" (Eph. 5:2). The fifth step in salvation is allowing God to change the life of selfishness to one of service and benefit to others.

5:7. The word *merciful* (ἐλεήμων) occurs only here in Matt.

The verb *to be merciful, have mercy on* (ἐλεέω) occurs here for the first of 8 times in Matt. (5:7; 9:27; 15:22; 17:15; 18:33 [twice]; 20:30, 31). The prayer "Have mercy upon me" is one of the great refrains of the Psalms (4:1; 6:2; 9:13; 25:16; 27:7; 30:10; 31:9; 37:21; 51:1, and often). For further discussion see Elwell, ed., *Evangelical Dictionary of Biblical Theology*, "Mercy," pp. 520–23; ZPEB, "Mercy, Merciful," IV, pp. 188–90; ISBE (1986), "Mercy, Merciful," III, pp. 322–23.

5:8. The word *pure* (καθαρός) occurs 3 times in Matt. (5:8; 23:26; 27:59), of the heart, the inside of the cup, and the linen grave cloth. For discussion see ZPEB, "Purity," IV, pp.

9 *Blessed are the peacemakers: for they shall be called the children of God.*

"Blessed are the pure in heart,

because they themselves shall see God" (v. 8).

Many people need to echo David's prayer: "Create in me a clean heart, O God; and renew a right spirit within me" (Ps. 51:10). We all need to remember the warning "Keep thy heart with all diligence; for out of it are the issues of life" (Prov. 4:23). A walk with God is always a matter of heart dedication. God can always see what is in a person's heart. We need to pray with David, "Let the words of my mouth, and the meditation of my heart, be acceptable in thy sight, O Lord, my strength, and my redeemer" (Ps. 19:14). Habakkuk revealed the purity of God: "Art thou not from everlasting, O Lord my God, mine Holy One? . . . Thou art of purer eyes than to behold evil, and canst not look on iniquity" (Hab. 1:12*a*, 13*a*). When the psalmist asks, "Who shall ascend into the hill of the Lord? or who shall stand in his holy place?" the answer is "He that hath clean hands, and a pure heart; who hath not lifted up his soul unto vanity, nor sworn deceitfully" (Ps. 24:3–4). It was Job's faith that "though after my skin worms destroy this body, yet in my flesh shall I see God" (Job 19:26). David longed "to see thy power and thy glory" (Ps. 63:2*a*). To those who walk righteously the promise is "Thine eyes shall see the king in his beauty: they shall behold the land that is very far off" (Isa. 33:17). God's command was "Be ye holy; for I am holy" (Lev. 11:44; I Pet.1:16). The writer to the Hebrews urges, "Follow peace with all men, and holiness, without which no man shall see the Lord" (Heb. 12:14). The sixth step in salvation is purity of heart so that we may see God and not be consumed.

"Blessed are the peacemakers,

because they themselves shall be called sons of God" (v. 9).

958–60; ISBE (1986), "Pure, Purification, Purity," III, pp. 1054–56; Elwell, ed., *Evangelical Dictionary of Biblical Theology*, "Purity," pp. 660–61.

The word *heart* (καρδία) occurs 16 times in Matt. (5:8, 28; 6:21; 9:4; 11:29; 12:34, 40; 13:15 [twice], 19; 15:8, 18, 19; 18:35; 22:37; 24:48). It regularly refers to the person's inmost being, his soul, his inner man. The Lord Jesus classed heart, soul, and mind together (Matt. 22:37). For discussion see ZPEB, "Heart," III, pp. 58–60; ISBE (1982), "Heart," II, pp. 650–53; Elwell, ed., *Evangelical Dictionary of Biblical Theology*, "Heart," pp. 331–32; Ryken, Wilhoit, and Longman, *Dictionary of Biblical Imagery*, "Heart," pp. 368–69.

5:9. The word *peacemaker* (εἰρηνοποιός) occurs only here in the Bible. For background see ISBE (1986), "Peacemaker," III, p. 733; ZPEB, "Peacemaker," IV, p. 668.

10 Blessed are they which are persecuted for righteousness' sake: for theirs is the kingdom of heaven.

We must remember that in the ancient world women did not have independence and the right to vote. The reference to *sons* here means that all believers, whether men or women, are children of God, citizens of the kingdom. That was a revolutionary idea to the ancients. The psalmist said, "Great peace have they which love thy law" (Ps. 119:165a). Isaiah declared, "There is no peace, saith the Lord, unto the wicked" (Isa. 48:22). The word *son* emphasizes the fact that the believer is an heir, a representative of the Father. The person who follows the way of the Lord must reach out and be a blessing to others. The apostle Paul gives a striking illustration of this. He likens the Christian life to a Roman triumph, the parade of victory (II Cor. 2:14ff.). When an army returned to Rome after a victory, they would open vials of perfume that would waft across the crowds as they marched in. To the victorious troops the aroma was celebration, but to the condemned prisoners, it was an anticipation of death (II Cor. 2:16). Thus the Christian's life should be an aroma of victory that attracts others to the Savior; those who turn away are doomed to the second death. The seventh step in salvation is a public testimony that attracts people to the Savior.

> "Blessed are the ones who have been persecuted on account of righteousness,
>
> because theirs is the kingdom of the heavens" (v. 10).

The consequence of choosing God's way and walking with Him is that the world will hate you. The Lord Jesus warned the disciples, "Woe unto you, when all men shall speak well of you! For so did their fathers to the false prophets" (Luke 6:26). Persecution may take many different forms. Sometimes it may be merely sneering pity directed to those who take the Bible seriously; at times it may be jeering and mockery; other times it may be hateful deeds, and even violence and martyrdom. From the days of Cain and Abel (Gen. 4) it has been the lot of God's people. The early

---

5:10. The verb *to persecute, pursue* (διώκω) occurs 6 times in Matt. (5:10, 11, 12, 44; 10:23; 23:34). For background on persecution see Elwell, ed., *Evangelical Dictionary of Biblical Theology*, "Persecution," pp. 599–600; ZPEB, IV, pp. 704–7; ISBE (1986), "Persecute, Persecution," III, pp. 771–74.

Note that the phrase *the kingdom of the heavens* begins and ends these 8 beatitudes (vv. 3, 10). These 8 steps are the heart of God's kingdom.

11 Blessed are ye, when men shall revile you, and persecute you, and shall say all manner of evil against you falsely, for my sake.
12 Rejoice, and be exceeding glad: for great is your reward in heaven: for so persecuted they the prophets which were before you.

church had to endure it (Acts 4:1ff.; 5:17–18; 7:1–8:4; 9:1–2). The Lord's word to His suffering church is "Be faithful unto death, and I will give you the crown of life" (Rev. 2:10c). The compensation for faithfulness is immense (Rev. 7:9–17). The eighth step in salvation is faithfulness in the face of opposition and persecution.

> "Blessed are you,
>
> whenever they reproach and persecute you, and say all evil
>   against you, falsely, on account of me" (v. 11).

The world will attack believers for no other reason than that they try to obey the Lord Jesus Christ. The world heaps contempt on those who believe the Bible and desire to please Christ. Other religions must be treated with respect, but Christ must not be mentioned at all! The Lord assured the disciples, "If the world hates you, know that it has hated me first" (John 15:18). Peter exclaims, "If you are being reproached for the name of Christ, blessed [are you]! because the Spirit of glory and of God is resting upon you" (I Pet. 4:14). To stand among the heroes of the faith is a great honor.

> "Keep on rejoicing and exulting, because great is your reward
>   in the heavens; for so they persecuted the prophets who were
>   before you" (v. 12).

The believer who is persecuted for his faith is standing in a glorious company. Going all the way back to Cain, who slew Abel (Gen. 4:8), wicked people persecuted the righteous, as Jezebel did Elijah (I Kings 19:2–3) and Jehoiakim did Urijah (Jer. 26:21–23). The psalmist complained,

---

5:11. The verb *to reproach* (ὀνειδίζω) occurs 3 times in Matt. (5:11; 11:20; 27:44). For discussion see ISBE (1988), "Reproach," IV, p. 139. Peter reminds us that if we are reproached for Christ, we should be happy (I Pet. 4:14).

For *evil, the evil one* see Matt. 5:37 note.

5:12. The word *reward, pay* (μισθός) occurs 10 times in Matt. (5:12, 46; 6:1, 2, 5, 16; 10:41 [twice], 42; 20:8). Paul wrote of the trying of the believer's works at the judgment seat of Christ: "If any man's work abide which he has built, he shall receive a reward" (I Cor. 3:14). Rewards are an important theme all the way to the end: "Behold, I am coming quickly, and my reward is with me" (Rev. 22:12a). For discussion see Ryken, Wilhoit, and Longman, *Dictionary of Biblical Imagery*, "Reward," pp. 719–20; ISBE (1988),

13 Ye are the salt of the earth: but if the salt have lost his savour, wherewith shall it be salted? it is thenceforth good for nothing, but to be cast out, and to be trodden under foot of men.

"Many are my persecutors and mine enemies; yet do I not decline from thy testimonies" (Ps. 119:157). David mentioned the statutes of the Lord and said, "In keeping of them there is great reward" (Ps. 19:8, 11b). The ultimate reward awaits the saints in heaven (Rev. 21:7).

Walvoord interpreted the Sermon on the Mount as the principles of the millennial kingdom that yet have practical applications to the present age ("The Sermon on the Mount," *Major Bible Prophecies*, pp 192–204). In part he is correct, but he fails to see the absolutely timeless quality of these ethical principles. They are all found in the OT, they apply to believers today, and they will apply during the Millennium. His argument that this sermon does not mention the "cross, crucifixion, death" (p. 194) is not convincing because when Jesus did mention them to His closest followers, they did not understand but were deeply disturbed and distressed (Matt. 16:21–23). However, the argument that it cannot apply to the Millennium because persecution will not exist then is short-sighted. Millions of unconverted people are being born all over the world. Until they are converted, they will persecute God's people. This is true today and will be true in the Millennium. But the rate of conversion will be much higher in the Millennium.

II. The Similitudes. vv. 13–16.

"You are the salt of the earth; but if the salt be made tasteless, by what shall it be salted? It is good for nothing but to be cast out and trampled upon by men" (v. 13). This is a beautiful picture of God's people, who add flavor and tastefulness to life in this world. In contrast to the money-grubbing hatefulness of the world, believers add the flavor of kindness, helpfulness, and intercessory prayer to the world. When the men of Sodom tried to

"Reward," IV, pp. 179–80; ZPEB, "Reward," V, p. 99; Elwell, ed., *Evangelical Dictionary of Biblical Theology*, "Reward," pp. 685–87.

5:13. The word *salt* (ἅλας) occurs only here, twice, in Matt. For the imagery see "Salt," Ryken, Wilhoit, and Longman, *Dictionary of Biblical Imagery*, p. 752; ZPEB, "Salt," V, p. 220.

The verb *to make tasteless or foolish* (μωραίνω) occurs only here in Matt.

The verb *to be strong, useful* (ἰσχύω) occurs 4 times in Matt. (5:13; 8:28; 9:12; 26:40).

The verb *to trample upon* (καταπατέω) occurs only twice in Matt. (5:13; 7:6).

14 Ye are the light of the world. A city that is set on an hill cannot be hid.
15 Neither do men light a candle, and put it under a bushel, but on a candle-
stick; and it giveth light unto all that are in the house.

destroy Lot and his family, they found out that he was the only thing that
kept them from disaster (Gen. 19:1–25). Morris observes that believers "act
as a kind of moral antiseptic. And they give a tang to life like salt to a dish
of food" (Morris, *Matt.*, p. 104). But if the believer loses his testimony and
fails to be salt, he must be put in a place where he cannot do damage to the
testimony of Christ. If salt loses its quality of flavor, it cannot be thrown
into the yard; it will kill the plants. The street would be the ancient place
of disposal. There everyone could tread upon it without damage. That is a
fearful picture of the believer put in the place of chastisement.

"You are the light of the world. A city that is set on a hill cannot be hidden" (v. 14). The apostle Paul picks up this image and writes to the Ephe-
sians, "For you were once darkness, but now you are light in the Lord;
keep walking as children of light" (Eph. 5:8). In the ancient world cities
were regularly built on hills for defensive reasons. They could be seen
from a long way off. Even at night the oil lamps and torches would be
easily seen in the total darkness of the countryside. That is a striking way
of setting forth the responsibility, and obligation, of the believer to let his
Christian testimony shine before his neighbors and fellow workers.

"Neither do they light a lamp and place it under a peck measure, but upon
the lampstand, and it lights all who are in the house" (v. 15). The Lord

---

5:14. For a summary of the word *light*, see Matt. 4:16 note; for the symbolism see "Light,"
Ryken, Wilhoit, and Longman, *Dictionary of Biblical Imagery*, pp. 509–12; ZPEB, "Light,"
III, pp. 932–34; ISBE (1986), "Light," III, pp. 134–36.

The verb *to hide* (κρύπτω) occurs 5 times in Matt. (5:14; 13:35, 44 [twice]; 25:25).
Compare a related verb (Matt. 11:25; 25:18).

5:15. The word *lamp* (λύχνος) occurs twice in Matt. (5:15; 6:22). It refers to a small oil
lamp.

The verb *to put, appoint* (τίθημι) occurs 5 times in Matt. (5:15; 12:18; 22:44; 24:51;
27:60).

The word *peck measure* (μόδιος) occurs only here and in the Synoptic parallels in the NT
(Mark 4:21; Luke 11:33). It was a basket smaller than a bushel.

The verb *to shine* (λάμπω) occurs 3 times in Matt. (5:15, 16; 17:2).

16 Let your light so shine before men, that they may see your good works, and glorify your Father which is in heaven.
17 Think not that I am come to destroy the law, or the prophets: I am not come to destroy, but to fulfil.

thus teaches that He puts the believer in a definite place of service and testimony. Every believer has a place that needs the illumination of the Lord.

"Let your light so shine before men, that they may see your good works and may glorify your Father who is in the heavens" (v. 16). The good works here are not done in order to earn salvation, but rather to give evidence of God's salvation already received. Good works honor and glorify the heavenly Father.

III. The New Law vv. 17–48 [Luke 6:27–36].

"Do not suppose that I came in order to destroy the law or the prophets; I came not to destroy, but to fulfill" (v. 17). The reference to "the law and the prophets" is plainly intended to denote the whole OT revelation. When Jesus mentions "the law and the prophets" again in 7:12, He is bringing the sermon to its conclusion. The ministry of the Lord Jesus Christ was fulfilling and expanding all that the OT prophets had seen. Aside from a denunciation of hypocrisy (Matt. 23), the ministry of the Lord Jesus was entirely positive.

5:16. The Lord Jesus refers to God as *Father* (πατήρ) 44 times in Matt. (5:16, 45, 48; 6:1, 4, 6 [twice], 8, 9, 14, 15, 18 [twice], 26, 32; 7:11, 21; 10:20, 29, 32, 33; 11:25, 26, 27 [3 times]; 12:50; 13:43; 15:13; 16:17, 27; 18:10, 14, 19, 35; 20:23; 23:9; 24:36; 25:34; 26:29, 39, 42, 53; 28:19). Only He does so. The doctrine of the "new birth" comes naturally from this idea. "God is love" (I John 4:8, 16) is a natural explanation. By His teaching the Lord enlarged the whole concept of God and laid the foundation for a huge body of teaching on God. For further study of God the Father see Bavinck, *The Doctrine of God*, pp. 266ff.; Elwell, ed., *Evangelical Dictionary of Biblical Theology*, "Fatherhood of God," pp. 247–48; ZPEB, "Fatherhood of God," II, pp. 505–6; ISBE (1982), "Father," II, pp. 285–86.

The word *work* (ἔργον) occurs here for the first of five times in Matt. (5:16; 11:2; 23:3, 5; 26:10). Works are not the basis of salvation, but the manifestation of obedience to God's will. For further discussion see ISBE (1988), "Work," IV, pp. 1107–11; Elwell, ed., *Evangelical Dictionary of Biblical Theology*, "Work," pp. 831–35.

The verb *to glorify* (δοξάζω) occurs 4 times in Matt. (5:16; 6:2; 9:8; 15:31). For discussion see ISBE (1982), "Glory," II, pp. 477–83. See also the word *glory*, Matt. 4:8 note.

5:17. The verb *to think that, suppose* (νομίζω) occurs 3 times in Matt. (5:17; 10:34; 20:10).

Mistaken Suppositions

   I. Do not suppose I came to destroy the law. 5:17.

   II. Do not suppose I came to send peace on earth. 10:34.

   III. Christian workers should not suppose they are "more saved" than others. 20:10.

The word *destroy* (καταλύω) occurs 5 times in Matt. (5:17 [twice]; 24:2; 26:61; 27:40).

18 For verily I say unto you, Till heaven and earth pass, one jot or one tittle shall in no wise pass from the law, till all be fulfilled.
19 Whosoever therefore shall break one of these least commandments, and shall teach men so, he shall be called the least in the kingdom of heaven: but whosoever shall do and teach them, the same shall be called great in the kingdom of heaven.

"For truly I say to you, Until heaven and earth pass away, an iota or one horn shall never pass away until all things are fulfilled" (v. 18). The prophets and Scripture writers regularly use the idiom "the Lord says," "God says," "Scripture says"; but in this context the Lord Jesus uses the term "I say" (5:18, 20, 22, 26, 28, 32, 34, 39, 44). He was plainly emphasizing His divine authority (see Jacob van Bruggen, *Jesus the Son of God*, pp. 93–94). The *iota* was the smallest letter of the Greek alphabet; the *horn* was a small projection on a letter that distinguished it from another (such as O and Q). This certainly teaches the doctrine of the verbal inspiration of the Scriptures. For a list of books that defend verbal inerrancy see The Theology of Matthew, pp. xxxix–xl. God's revelation of the OT and NT was intended to last to the end of time.

"Whoever therefore shall break one of the least of these commandments and shall teach men thus, shall be called least in the kingdom of the heavens; but whoever shall do and teach them, this one shall be called great in the kingdom of the heavens" (v. 19). The persons who most honor God's

---

The word *law* (νόμος) occurs 8 times in Matt. (5:17, 18; 7:12; 11:13; 12:5; 22:36, 40; 23:23); it does not occur at all in Mark, but it is a major part of Paul's argument in Rom. 2:12–27; 3:19–31; 7:1–25. The phrase *the law and the prophets* denoted the whole OT revelation. For further study see ZPEB, "Law in the OT," III, pp. 883–94; "Law in the NT," III, pp. 894–96; ISBE (1986), "Law in the OT," III, pp. 76–85; "Law in the NT," III, pp. 85–91; Elwell, ed., *Evangelical Dictionary of Biblical Theology*, "Law," pp. 467–71; E. F. Harrison, *Baker's Dictionary of Theology*, "Law," pp. 317–19.

For the verb *to fulfill* (πληρόω) see Matt. 1:22 note.

5:18. The word *amen, truly* (ἀμήν) occurs here for the first of 30 times in Matt. (5:18, 26; 6:2, 5, 16; 8:10; 10:15, 23, 42; 11:11; 13:17; 16:28; 17:20; 18:3, 13, 18; 19:23, 28; 21:21, 31; 23:36; 24:2, 34, 47; 25:12, 40, 45; 26:13, 21, 34). It is a word of divine approval. See ZPEB, "Amen," I, pp. 127–28; ISBE (1979), "Amen," I, p. 110; Arndt and Gingrich, p. 45.

The number *one* (εἰς) occurs here for the first of 66 times in Matt. (5:18 [twice], 19, 29, 30, 36, 41; 6:24 [twice], 27, 29; 8:19; 9:18; 10:29, 42; 12:11; 13:46; 16:14; 17:4 [3 times]; 18:5, 6, 10, 12, 14, 16, 24, 28; 19:5, 6, 16, 17; 20:12, 13, 21 [twice]; 21:19, 24; 22:35; 23:8, 9, 10, 15; 24:40 [twice], 41 [twice]; 25:15, 18, 24, 40, 45; 26:14, 21, 22, 40, 47, 51, 69; 27:14, 15, 38 [twice], 48; 28:1). For the significance of biblical numbers see Introduction, pp. xxii, and ZPEB, "Number," IV, pp. 452–61; ISBE (1986), "Number," III, pp. 556–61; Ryken, Wilhoit, and Longman, *Dictionary of Biblical Imagery*, "Numbers in the Bible," pp. 599–600.

20 For I say unto you, That except your righteousness shall exceed the right-eousness of the scribes and Pharisees, ye shall in no case enter into the kingdom of heaven.

Word in this life shall be most honored in the coming kingdom. Those who detract from God's revelation shall be considered least. The question of the person's salvation is not really settled by this statement.

"For I say to you that except your righteousness exceed that of the scribes and Pharisees, you will never enter into the kingdom of the heavens" (v. 20). The phrase *I say unto you* assumes divine authority. Geerhardus Vos declares, "The solemn manner in which Jesus puts his 'I say unto you' by the side of, or even apparently over against, the commandment of God, goes far beyond the highest that is conceivable in the line of prophetic authority" (*The Self-Disclosure of Jesus*, p. 18). The *never* (a double negative) is most emphatic. "The righteousness demanded by Jesus surpasses anything imagined by the Pharisees" (D. A. Carson, *The Sermon on the Mount*, p. 41). Doing the righteous deeds of the Pharisees is not at all as important as doing the will of the Father (Matt. 7:21; see Przybylski, *Righteousness in Matthew and His World of Thought*, p. 114). This declaration of the Lord cannot be limited to segments of Jewish re-ligion. It clearly means that there are famous preachers of large churches and theologians in prestigious chairs of learning that will be turned into hell. They have dared to twist God's Word from its true meaning and force it into their private interpretations. Some may even be surprised at their final destination. Lest any one think that I have overstated this betrayal, let me give concrete examples. The famous theologian Rudolf Bultmann wrote, "I must say bluntly: it is impossible to see what more was done by the historical Jesus who goes to his death in obedient love than by all those who, for example, in the World War took the same road, also in obedient love. . . . Jesus Christ who has the full power to forgive sin is not to be found in this fashion. I have done him no wrong and he has nothing to forgive me. And since the forgiveness cannot be verified as a discernible objective event, I am not at all helped by reading touching stories of how Jesus forgave the sinful woman or Zacchaeus" (*Faith and*

5:19. The verb *to loose* (λύω) occurs 6 times in Matt. (5:19; 16:19 [twice]; 18:18 [twice]; 21:2). The word *commandment* (ἐντολή) occurs 6 times in Matt. (5:19; 15:3; 19:17; 22:36, 38, 40). The commandments were the specific provisions of the law. For further discussion see ISBE (1979), "Command, Commandment," I, p. 736; ZPEB, "Commandment," I, p. 919.

21 Ye have heard that it was said of them of old time, Thou shalt not kill; and whosoever shall kill shall be in danger of the judgment:
22 But I say unto you, That whosoever is angry with his brother without a cause shall be in danger of the judgment: and whosoever shall say to his brother, Raca, shall be in danger of the council: but whosoever shall say, Thou fool, shall be in danger of hell fire.

Understanding, New York: Harper, 1969, pp. 127–28). A more arrogant repudiation of Scripture can hardly be imagined. Yet one of Bultmann's radical followers, Schubert Miles Ogden, wrote, "If the corpse of a man was actually resuscitated, this would be just as relevant to my salvation as an existing self or person as that the carpenter next door just drove a nail in a two-by-four" (*Christ Without Myth*, New York: Harper, 1961, p. 136). God's Word is very clear on this point. "To this man will I look, even to him that is poor and of a contrite spirit, and trembleth at my word" (Isa. 66:2*b*). Thomas may have had his doubts, but he resolved them. His words of confession before the Lord Jesus demonstrate the depth of his trust: "My Lord and my God" (John 20:28*b*).

"You heard that it was said by the ancients: You shall not murder, and whoever murders shall be guilty in the judgment" (v. 21). The custom of the Jews was always to quote the rabbis of the past for authority, but the Lord Jesus never did. As the omniscient Son of God, He could declare the whole counsel of God with divine authority.

"But I say to you that the one who is angry with his brother shall be liable to the judgment; but whoever shall say to his brother, Blockhead, shall be

5:20. The verb *to have more than enough, to abound* (περισσεύω) occurs 5 times in Matt. (5:20; 13:12; 14:20; 15:37; 25:29). Paul prayed that "your love may abound yet more and more in full knowledge and all discernment" (Phil. 1:9*b*).

5:21. The verb *to murder* (φονεύω) occurs 5 times in Matt. (5:21 [twice]; 19:18; 23:31, 35).

The word *guilty, liable* (ἔνοχος) occurs 5 times in Matt. (5:21, 22 [3 times]; 26:66). It is "the legal and moral condition that results from a violation of God's law" (ZPEB, "Guilt," II, p. 852). See also ISBE (1982), "Guilt; Guilty," II, pp. 580–81; Elwell, ed., *Evangelical Dictionary of Biblical Theology*, "Guilt," p. 319.

The word *judgment* (κρίσις) occurs 12 times in Matt. (5:21, 22; 10:15; 11:22, 24; 12:18, 20, 36, 41, 42; 23:23, 33). Couch, *Dictionary of Premillennial Theology*, "Judgments, Various," pp. 225–27; Harrison, ed., *The New Unger's Bible Dictionary*, "Judgments," p. 727; ISBE (1982), "Judging, Judge," II, pp. 1161–62; ZPEB, "Judging," III, pp. 758–60.

5:22. The verb *to be angry* (ὀργίζω) occurs 3 times in Matt. (5:22; 18:34; 22:7), the last two in parables representing God. Judicial anger is proper only for God.

The word *blockhead* (ῥακά) comes from an Aramaic word meaning *empty* (Arndt and Gingrich, p. 741).

23 Therefore if thou bring thy gift to the altar, and there rememberest that thy brother hath ought against thee;
24 Leave there thy gift before the altar, and go thy way; first be reconciled to thy brother, and then come and offer thy gift.

liable to the Sanhedrin; but whoever shall say, Fool, shall be liable to the Gehenna of fire" (v. 22). The contrast is striking. The Pharisees counsel, *Avoid murder*, but the Lord Jesus commands, *Avoid anger*. That simple command condemns the race. Who among us can say that he has never been angry? Again, the *I say unto you* assumes vastly greater authority than the ancients had. Bitter anger against a brother is far more damaging to the one who has it than to the object of the anger. The believer should commit all anger to the Lord; He can deal with offenders far better than we can. Paul warns, "Beloved, avenge not yourselves, but give place to [divine] wrath, for it has been written, Vengeance is mine; I will repay, says the Lord" (Rom. 12:19). As Lord of all, it is His prerogative to repay,

The word *Sanhedrin* (συνέδριον) occurs 3 times in Matt. (5:22; 10:17; 26:59). It was (and is) the highest court of law in Judaism. For background see Edersheim, *Life and Times*, II, pp. 553–57; ZPEB, "Sanhedrin," V, pp. 268–73; ISBE (1988), "Sanhedrin," IV, pp. 331–34; Harrison, ed., *The New Unger's Bible Dictionary*, "Sanhedrin," pp. 1126–28.

The word *fool* (μωρός) occurs 6 times in Matt. (5:22; 7:26; 23:17; 25:2, 3, 8). The word not only means *stupid* but also may bear the idea of atheism and arrogant rebellion against God (Ps. 14:1; 53:1; Prov. 14:9; 26:11). For further discussion see ISBE (1982), "Fool, Foolish," II, p. 331; ZPEB, "Folly," II, p. 581; Elwell, ed., *Evangelical Dictionary of Biblical Theology*, "Fool, Foolishness," pp. 264–65; Ryken, Wilhoit, and Longman, *Dictionary of Biblical Imagery*, "Folly," pp. 296–97.

The word *hell, Gehenna* (γέεννα) occurs 7 times in Matt. (5:22, 29, 30; 10:28; 18:9; 23:15, 33). Note the parallel passages (Mark 9:43, 45, 47; Luke 12:5). It denotes the final abode of the wicked dead. The only other NT occurrence is James 3:6. The word comes from "the valley of Hinnom," which was a place of idolatrous worship and human sacrifice south of Jerusalem (Jer. 7:31–32). It became the garbage dump of Jerusalem. John calls this place "the lake of fire" (Rev. 19:20; 20:10, 14–15). People should note that it is the loving Savior Who warns so solemnly about this place of eternal punishment. For further discussion see W. G. T. Shedd, *The Doctrine of Endless Punishment*; John Blanchard, *What Ever Happened to Hell?*; D. G. Moore, *The Battle for Hell*; R. A. Peterson, *Hell on Trial*; Robert Govette, *Eternal Suffering of the Wicked*; Mark Minnick, *The Doctrine of Eternal Punishment*; Elwell, ed., *Evangelical Dictionary of Biblical Theology*, "Hell," pp. 338–40; ZPEB, "Hell," III, pp. 114–17; ISBE (1982), "Hell, History of," II, pp. 677–79. See also Matt. 18:9.

5:23. For the word *gift*, see Matt. 2:11 note.

The word *altar* (θυσιαστήριον) occurs 6 times in Matt. (5:23, 24; 23:18, 19, 20, 35). The altar was the place of sacrifice and communion with God. For background see ZPEB, "Altar," I, pp. 118–22; ISBE (1979), "Altar," I, pp. 100–104; Elwell, ed., *Evangelical Dictionary of Biblical Theology*, "Altar," pp. 15–16; Ryken, Wilhoit, and Longman, *Dictionary of Biblical Imagery*, "Altar," pp. 20–21.

The verb *to remember* (μιμνήσκομαι) occurs 3 times in Matt. (5:23; 26:75; 27:63).

25 Agree with thine adversary quickly, whiles thou art in the way with him; lest at any time the adversary deliver thee to the judge, and the judge deliver thee to the officer, and thou be cast into prison.
26 Verily I say unto thee, Thou shalt by no means come out thence, till thou hast paid the uttermost farthing.

not ours. Blomberg calls attention to the fact that when the epithet is accurate, it is not wrong to apply it, as the Lord Jesus did to the scribes and Pharisees who had spurned His teaching (Matt. 23:17, 19; *Matt.*, p. 107).

"Therefore if you bring your gift to the altar, and there remember that your brother has something against you, leave your gift there before the altar, and go; first be reconciled to your brother, and then, having come back, continue offering your gift" (vv. 23–24). The contrast between the aorist and present tenses is instructive. Plainly, God will not accept a gift from someone with a guilty conscience. Offering a gift to God is not a substitute for making things right with a brother.

"Be making friends with your adversary quickly, while you are in the way with him, lest the adversary deliver you to the judge, and the judge deliver you to the officer, and you be cast into prison" (v. 25). The present periphrastic imperative shows the necessity of constantly making friends with adversaries. The believer should live his life "aboveboard." There should be no question about his integrity.

"Truly I say to you, you shall not come out from there until you have paid the last cent" (v. 26). The word *not* is an emphatic double negative. In

5:24. The verb *to be reconciled* (διαλλάσσομαι) occurs only here in Matt.

The word *first* (πρῶτος) occurs 25 times in Matt. (5:24; 6:33; 7:5; 8:21; 10:2; 12:29, 45; 13:30; 17:10, 27; 19:30 [twice]; 20:8, 10, 16 [twice], 27; 21:28, and so forth).

5:25. The verb *to make friends* (εὐνοέω) occurs only here in Matt.

The word *adversary, opponent at law* (ἀντίδικης) occurs only here [twice] in Matt.

The word *officer* (ὑπηρέτης) occurs only twice in Matt. (5:25; 26:58). In both cases it refers to an officer of the court. Moulton and Milligan provide a variety of examples of this word (*Vocabulary*, p. 655). See also ZPEB, "Officer," IV, pp. 504–5; ISBE (1986), "Officer," III, pp. 582–83.

The word *prison* (φυλακή) occurs 10 times in Matt. (5:25; 14:3, 10, 25; 18:30; 24:43; 25:36, 39, 43, 44). For background see ZPEB, "Prison," IV, pp. 869–70; ISBE (1986), "Prison," III, pp. 973–75; Ryken, Wilhoit, and Longman, *Dictionary of Biblical Imagery*, "Prison," pp. 663–64.

5:26. The verb *to repay, reward* (ἀποδίδωμι) occurs 18 times in Matt. (5:26, 33; 6:4, 6, 18; 12:36; 16:27; 18:25 [twice], 26, 28, 29, 30, 34; 20:8; 21:41; 22:21; 27:58).

The word *last* (ἔσχατος) occurs 10 times in Matt. (5:26; 12:45; 19:30 [twice]; 20:8, 12, 14, 16 [twice]; 27:64).

27 Ye have heard that it was said by them of old time, Thou shalt not commit adultery:
28 But I say unto you, That whosoever looketh on a woman to lust after her hath committed adultery with her already in his heart.
29 And if thy right eye offend thee, pluck it out, and cast it from thee: for it is profitable for thee that one of thy members should perish, and not that thy whole body should be cast into hell.

the ancient world the prison was often a debtor's prison.

"You have heard that it was said, You shall not commit adultery" (v. 27). The command comes from Exodus 20:14; Deuteronomy 5:18. The violation of the marriage bond is always condemned in Scripture. Modern society tries to manipulate this as a social contract, but marriage was ordained by God, not society (Gen. 2:22–25). The prophet warns against forgetting "the Lord thy maker" (Isa. 51:13). But here the Lord Jesus raises the responsibility from the outward act to the inward desire.

"But I say unto you, that every one who is looking at a woman in order to lust after her has already committed adultery with her in his heart" (v. 28). Again the contrast is clear. The Pharisees would counsel, *Avoid*

The word *cent, quadrans* (κοδράντης) denoted a small copper coin worth 2 mites (Mark 12:42), actually a fourth of a cent. It occurs only here in Matt.

5:27. The verb *to commit adultery* (μοιχεύω) occurs 4 times in Matt. (5:27, 28, 32; 19:18).

5:28. The verb *to see, look at, take heed* (βλέπω) occurs 20 times in Matt. (5:28; 6:4, 6, 18; 7:3; 11:4; 12:22; 13:13 [twice], 14 [twice], 16, 17; 14:30; 15:31 [twice]; 18:10; 22:16; 24:2, 4). For the diverse meanings of this word see ISBE (1988), "See," IV, pp. 379–80.

The verb *to lust after, long for* (ἐπιθυμέω) occurs twice in Matt. (5:28; 13:17).

5:29. The word *eye* (ὀφθαλμός) occurs 24 times in Matt. (5:29, 38 [twice]; 6:22 [twice], 23; 7:3 [twice], 4 [twice], 5 [twice]; 9:29, 30; 13:15 [twice], 16; 17:8; 18:9 [twice]; 20:15, 33; 21:42; 26:43).

The word *right* (δεξιός) occurs 12 times in Matt. (5:29, 30, 39; 6:3; 20:21, 23; 22:44; 25:33, 34; 26:64; 27:29, 38). For further discussion see Ryken, Wilhoit, and Longman, *Dictionary of Biblical Imagery*, "Right, Right Hand," pp. 727–28.

The verb *to cause to stumble* (σκανδαλίζω) occurs 14 times in Matt. (5:29, 30; 11:6; 13:21, 57; 15:12; 17:27; 18:6, 8, 9; 24:10; 26:31, 33 [twice]). The image of the godly life being a walk with God (Ps. 1:1–2) naturally lends itself to sin being a cause of stumbling. The rough roads of the ancient world made it a vivid image. For a discussion see Ryken, Wilhoit, and Longman, *Dictionary of Biblical Imagery*, "Stumble, Stumbling block," pp. 822–24.

The verb *to gouge out* (ἐξαιρέω) occurs twice in Matt. (5:29; 18:9), both the same command.

The word *body* (σῶμα) occurs 14 times in Matt. (5:29, 30; 6:22 [twice], 23, 25 [twice]; 10:28 [twice]; 26:12, 26; 27:52, 58, 59).

30 And if thy right hand offend thee, cut it off, and cast it from thee: for it is profitable for thee that one of thy members should perish, and not that thy whole body should be cast into hell.
31 It hath been said, Whosoever shall put away his wife, let him give her a writing of divorcement:
32 But I say unto you, That whosoever shall put away his wife, saving for the cause of fornication, causeth her to commit adultery: and whosoever shall marry her that is divorced committeth adultery.

adultery; the Lord Jesus commands, *Avoid the lustful look.* In God's sight the inward desire is just as much sin as the outward act. Putting on a nice façade does not fool God. That certainly means that the believer's relationship with God must be real, heartfelt, not just something "put on."

"But if your right eye cause you to stumble, gouge it out and cast it from you; for it is profitable for you that one of your members perish and not your whole body be cast into hell" (v. 29). This is hyperbole; self-mutilation does no spiritual good. The believer must not allow anything to stand between himself and supreme spiritual devotion to God. An eye is a small thing to lose in comparison with the spiritual blessing of God.

"And if your right hand cause you to stumble, cut it off and cast it from you; for it is profitable for you that one of your members perish, and not that your whole body be cast into hell" (v. 30). Here Jesus changes the illustration but repeats the spiritual principle. Material and physical losses are not at all as important as the loss of God's approval. The danger of being cast into an eternal lake of fire outweighs all other considerations. It is inconceivable that the Lord Jesus Christ would scare people with a myth. He is speaking soberly about eternal realities. The people who leave this realm in death go to one of two places: either to the heaven prepared by the Father (Matt. 25:34) or to the hell prepared for the Devil and his angels (Matt. 25:41). People may desire to repress the idea of hell, but no one can deny that the Lord Jesus taught it.

"And it was said, Whoever will put away his wife, let him give her a certificate of divorce" (v. 31). Such a document was for her protection.

"But I say to you that everyone who puts away his wife, except for the

5:30. For the word *hand* see Matt. 3:12 note.
5:31. The word *certificate of divorce* (ἀποστάσιον), Arndt and Gingrich, p. 97, occurs twice in Matt. (5:31; 19:7). It was a legal document. See ISBE (1979), "Divorce," I, pp. 974–79; ZPEB, "Divorce," II, pp. 149–51; Elwell, ed., *Evangelical Dictionary of Biblical Theology,* "Divorce," pp. 183–85 ("God ordained marriage as a monogamous, permanent, and exclusive union," p. 185).

33 Again, ye have heard that it hath been said by them of old time, Thou shalt not forswear thyself, but shalt perform unto the Lord thine oaths:

cause of fornication, causes her to commit adultery, and whoever shall marry one who has been put away, commits adultery" (v. 32). This is a plain declaration that a government document cannot overturn the law of God. The exceptive clause makes clear that if there has already been fornication, the guilty party has already broken the union, and the innocent party is free to get a divorce. Broadus observes, "It is not said that in such a case the husband *must* put away the offending wife, but in saying that he must not except in that case, it is implied that then he *may*" (*Matt.*, p. 112). Leon Morris adds, "Divorce might happen, but it was not meant to be. Marriage is for life" (*Matt.*, p. 122). The Pharisees would counsel, *Divorce a wife with a proper document.* The Lord declares, *Whoever puts away his wife causes her to commit adultery.* In the ancient world the average woman had no means of support except marriage. Without a husband she could be reduced to begging or prostitution.

"Again you heard that it was said by the ancients: You shall not break an oath, but you shall repay to the Lord your oaths" (v. 33). In the ancient world the Jews had multiplied oaths beyond reason. Everything that they said was "by the Holy City" or "by the beard of the prophet." It did not ensure the truth of what followed. The only exclamation that Scripture encourages is "Praise the Lord!" (Ps. 33:2; 104:35; 105:45; 106:1, 48; 111:1; 112:1; 113:1, 9; 115:18; 116:19; 117:1, 2; 135:1, 3, 21; 146:1; 147:12, 20; 148:1, 14; 149:1, 9; 150:1, 6; Isa. 12:4; Jer. 20:13; Rom. 15:11).

5:32. The word *fornication, sexual immorality* (πορνεία) occurs 3 times in Matt, (5:32; 15:19; 19:9). The apostle Paul often gives a list of sins the believer should avoid: *fornication* leads the list every time it is mentioned (I Cor. 5:11; 6:9; Gal. 5:19; Eph. 5:3; Col. 3:5). For further discussion see Elwell, ed., *Evangelical Dictionary of Biblical Theology*, "Immorality, Sexual," p. 367; ZPEB, "Fornication," II, p. 601.

The verb *to marry* (γαμέω) occurs 6 times in Matt. (5:32; 19:9, 10; 22:25, 30; 24:38). For background see ISBE (1986), "Marriage," III, pp. 261–66; ZPEB, "Marriage," IV, pp. 92–102; Elwell, ed., *Evangelical Dictionary of Biblical Theology*, "Marriage," pp. 510–13; Ryken, Wilhoit, and Longman, *Dictionary of Biblical Imagery*, 'Marriage," pp. 537–39.

The verb *to commit adultery* (μοιχάω) occurs twice in Matt. (5:32; 19:9).

5:33. The verb *to break an oath* (ἐπιορκέω) occurs only here in the NT.

The word *oath* (ὅρκος) occurs 4 times in Matt. (5:33; 14:7, 9; 26:72). For background see ZPEB, "Oath," IV, pp. 476–79; ISBE (1986), "Oath," III, pp. 572–74.

34 But I say unto you, Swear not at all; neither by heaven; for it is God's throne:
35 Nor by the earth; for it is his footstool: neither by Jerusalem; for it is the city of the great King.
36 Neither shalt thou swear by thy head, because thou canst not make one hair white or black.

"But I say to you, Swear not at all; neither by heaven, because it is the throne of God; nor by the earth, because it is the footstool of his feet; nor by Jerusalem, because it is the city of the great King" (vv. 34–35). Just as the Lord forbad murder and immorality, He forbids making vain oaths. The believer should review his exclamations very critically. Even such mild exclamations as *Gosh!* (a slight modification of *God*) and *Gee!* (the first syllable of *Jesus*) have very dangerous origins. The believer is surrounded by the curses and exclamations of a very wicked world. Our conversation must be different. By right of creation the whole world belongs to God and should be treated with respect. On the day of judgment the wicked will not only have to face charges of murder and adultery but also answer why they defaced rocks in a public park and threw garbage into freshwater streams. It is all recorded and waiting for them, including every idle word (Matt. 12:36). The phrase *the great King* is a reference to Himself, for He is the prophesied Messiah, rightful King of the city of God (II Sam. 7:12–29; Ps. 2:1–12; Isa. 9:6–7; 32:1–17).

"Neither should you swear by your head, because you are not able to make one hair white or black" (v. 36). A person may dye his hair, but it will grow back the color it is. Our bodies are simply on loan to us for a while; the time will come when God will take them back. The believer in Christ has the hope of a resurrection body (I Cor. 15:51–57; II Cor. 5:1–3).

5:34. The verb *to swear* (ὀμνύω) occurs 13 times in Matt. (5:34, 36; 23:16 [twice], 18 [twice], 20 [twice], 21 [twice], 22 [twice]; 26:74).

The word *throne* (θρόνος) occurs 5 times in Matt. (5:34; 19:28 [twice]; 23:22; 25:31), in every case referring to the throne of God or Christ. The throne is a symbol of royal authority. God's throne is above all. For discussion see ZPEB, "Throne," V, pp. 740–41; ISBE (1988), "Throne," IV, pp. 844–45; Ryken, Wilhoit, and Longman, *Dictionary of Biblical Imagery*, "Throne," pp. 868–69.

5:35. For the word *earth* see Matt. 2:6 note.

The word *footstool* (ὑποπόδιον) occurs only here in Matt.

For the word *king* see Matt. 1:6 note.

5:36. The word *head* (κεφαλή) occurs 12 times in Matt. (5:36; 6:17; 8:20; 10:30; 14:8, 11; 21:42; 26:7; 27:29, 30, 37, 39). Jesus has nowhere to lay His head (Matt. 8:20); it was

37 But let your communication be, Yea, yea; Nay, nay: for whatsoever is more than these cometh of evil.
38 Ye have heard that it hath been said, An eye for an eye, and a tooth for a tooth:
39 But I say unto you, That ye resist not evil: but whosoever shall smite thee on thy right cheek, turn to him the other also.

"Jesus is clearly refuting both Jewish casuistry and superficial swearing. People were using oaths not in a spiritual way, but in a clever way" (Douma, *The Ten Commandments*, p. 92).

"But let your word be, Yes, yes; no, no; but whatever is more than these is of the evil one" (v. 37). The Devil may provoke the believer to push his position more than the facts deserve. But so may the sinful nature of the believer. In either case, the believer must be honest and restrained in advocating his position. The modern media tend to "hype" or "demonize" the truth according to their prejudices. James repeats this teaching and emphasizes it (James 5:12).

"You heard that it was said: An eye for an eye, and a tooth for a tooth" (v. 38). This was an often-repeated provision of mercy that the punishment not exceed the crime (Exod. 21:24; Lev. 24:20; Deut. 19:21).

"But I say to you that you resist not evil, but whoever hits you on the right cheek, turn to him the other also" (v. 39). The slap on the cheek

anointed (26:7); a crown of thorns was thrust upon it (27:29); blows were rained upon it (27:30); the charge was put over it (27:37). For discussion see ISBE (1982), "Head," II, pp. 639–40; ZPEB, "Head," III, pp. 52–53; Ryken, Wilhoit, and Longman, *Dictionary of Biblical Imagery*, "Head," pp. 367–68.

5:37. The word *evil* (πονηρός) occurs 26 times in Matt. (5:11, 37, 39, 45; 6:13, 23; 7:11, 17, 18; 9:4; 12:34, 35 [3 times], 39, 45 [twice]; 13:19, 38, 49; 15:19; 16:4; 18:32; 20:15; 22:10; 25:26). An abstract noun such as *evil* (πονηρός) may have the article or not, and still mean *evil*. The phrase *the evil one* (ὁ πονηρός) is one of the titles for the Devil. The idea is *one who causes evil in others*. It may have that meaning here, but in view of the abstract usage in v. 39, it might not. The biblical idea is not that it is a social wrong but that it is something that God declares is sin, something contrary to His will. The evil one deliberately disobeys God's will. The evil depravity of man's nature is a clear Bible doctrine (Gen. 6:5; Ps. 51:4–5; Rom. 1:18–32; II Tim. 3:1–5). For a discussion of evil and sin, see Elwell, ed., *Evangelical Dictionary of Biblical Theology*, "Evil," pp. 221–25; ISBE (1982), "Evil," II, pp. 206–10; E. F. Harrison, *Baker's Dictionary of Theology*, "Evil," pp. 201–2; ZPEB, "Evil," II, p. 420; Butler, ed., *Holman Bible Dictionary*, "Evil," pp. 447–48.

5:38. The word *tooth* (ὀδούς) occurs 8 times in Matt. (5:38 [twice]; 8:12; 13:42, 50; 22:13; 24:51; 25:30).

5:39. The verb *to resist* (ἀνθίστημι) occurs only here in Matt.

The verb *to hit* (ῥαπίζω) occurs only twice in the NT (5:39; 26:67).

40 And if any man will sue thee at the law, and take away thy coat, let him have thy cloak also.
41 And whosoever shall compel thee to go a mile, go with him twain.
42 Give to him that asketh thee, and from him that would borrow of thee turn not thou away.

was a public rebuke. We are commanded to resist the Devil: "Resist the devil and he will flee from you" (James 4:7b). But we are not to repay persecution or insult, but we are to persevere in testimony and accept opposition with steadfastness.

"And to the one who wishes to go to law with you and to take your tunic, let him have your cloke also" (v. 40). The tunic was an inner garment, similar to a nightshirt that extended to the knees. The cloak was the heavier outer garment. By law a creditor could take the tunic, but not the cloke (Exod. 22:26–27). The Lord is saying, Let them have even more than the law allows.

"And whoever shall force you to go one mile, go with him two" (v. 41). One of the most hated laws of the Romans was the one that allowed a soldier to commandeer a citizen to carry a burden for a mile. It would be a shock for the man to carry it a second mile. That would provoke a discussion that could lead to a testimony for Christ.

"Give to the one who asks you, and from the one who wishes to borrow from you, turn not away" (v. 42). The believer should maintain a generous spirit toward those in need. *Giving* is one of the great characteristics

---

The word *cheek* (σιαγών) occurs only here and in Luke 6:29 in the NT.

The verb *to turn* (στρέφω) occurs 6 times in Matt. (5:39; 7:6; 9:22; 16:23; 18:3; 27:3).

5:40. The verb *to judge* (κρίνω) occurs 6 times in Matt. (5:40; 7:1 [twice], 2 [twice]; 19:28). See Elwell, ed., *Evangelical Dictionary of Biblical Theology*, "Judgment; Judgment, Day of," pp. 436–39; ZPEB, "Judging, Judgment," III, pp. 758–60; ISBE (1982), "Judging, Judge," II, pp. 1161–62; E. F. Harrison, *Baker's Dictionary of Theology*, "Judge, Judgment," p. 303. See also related terms, *to discern* (διακρίνω), Matt. 16:3; 21:21; *to condemn* (κατακρινω) Matt. 12:41 note.

The word *tunic* (χιτών) occurs only twice in Matt. (5:40; 10:10). It was a knee-length shirt.

The word *robe, garment* (ἱμάτιον) occurs 13 times in Matt. (5:40; 9:16 [twice], 20, 21; 14:36; 17:2; 21:7, 8; 24:18; 26:65; 27:31, 35). For discussion see ZPEB, "Robe," V, pp. 130–31; ISBE (1988), "Robe," IV, pp. 204–5.

5:41. The verb *to force one to go* (ἀγγαρεύω) occurs only twice in Matt. (5:41; 27:32) and in Mark 15:21 in the NT.

5:42. The verb *to ask* (αἰτέω) occurs 14 times in Matt. (5:42; 6:8; 7:7, 8, 9, 10, 11; 14:7; 18:19; 20:20, 22; 21:22; 27:20, 58).

43 Ye have heard that it hath been said, Thou shalt love thy neighbour, and hate thine enemy.
44 But I say unto you, Love your enemies, bless them that curse you, do good to them that hate you, and pray for them which despitefully use you, and persecute you;
45 That ye may be the children of your Father which is in heaven: for he maketh his sun to rise on the evil and on the good, and sendeth rain on the just and on the unjust.

of God. He promises, "A new heart also will I give you, and a new spirit will I put within you" (Ezek. 36:26a).

"You have heard that it was said: You shall love your neighbor, and hate your enemy" (v. 43). The maxim to love your neighbor comes from Leviticus 19:18.

"But I say to you, Love your enemies and pray in behalf of the ones who are persecuting you, in order that you may be sons of your Father who is in heaven, because he causes his sun to rise upon the evil and the good, and he causes it to rain upon the righteous and the unrighteous" (vv. 44–45). God

The command *to give* (aorist of δίδωμι) reflects the nature of God, for God loves to give to His people strength (Ps. 29:11), their heart desires (Ps. 37:4), power (Ps. 68:35), grace and glory (Ps. 84:11), sleep (Ps. 127:2), wisdom (Prov. 2:6), and much more. For discussion see Matt. 4:9 note.

The verb *to lend*, or in the middle, *borrow* (δανείζω) occurs only here in Matt.

The verb *to turn away* (ἀποστρέφω) occurs only twice in Matt. (5:42; 26:52).

5:43. The great verb *to love* (ἀγαπάω) occurs 8 times in Matt. (5:43, 44, 46 [twice]; 6:24; 19:19; 22:37, 39). It is *the love that gives*, a high and holy love, a major theme in John's Gospel (37 times, John 3:16, and so forth). For further discussion see ISBE (1986), "Love," III, pp. 173–76; ZPEB, "Love," III, pp. 989–96; Trench, *Synonyms of the New Testament*, pp. 41–44.

The verb *to hate* (μισέω) occurs 5 times in Matt. (5:43; 6:24; 10:22; 24:9, 10). For discussion see ISBE (1982), "Hate, Hatred," II, pp. 629–33; ZPEB, "Hate," III, pp. 46–47; Elwell, ed., *Evangelical Dictionary of Biblical Theology*, "Hate, Hatred," p. 326.

The command, *You shall love your neighbor*, is cited 3 times in Matt. (5:43; 19:19; 22:39).

The word *enemy* (ἐχθρός) occurs 7 times in Matt. (5:43, 44; 10:36; 13:25, 28, 39; 22:44). For discussion see ZPEB, "Enemy," II, pp. 305–7; ISBE (1982), "Enemy," II, p. 81. All believers were at one time enemies until "we were reconciled to God by the death of his Son" (Rom. 5:10b).

5:44. The verb *to pray* (προσεύχομαι) occurs 15 times in Matt. (5:44; 6:5 [twice], 6 [twice], 7, 9; 14:23; 19:13; 24:20; 26:36, 39, 41, 42, 44). The noun form *prayer* (προσευχή) occurs twice (21:13, 22). For further study see Andrew Murray, *With Christ in the School of Prayer*; *The Ministry of Intercessory Prayer*; E. M. Bounds, *The Necessity of Prayer*; Matthew Henry, *The Quest for Communion with God*; Elwell, ed., *Evangelical Dictionary of Biblical Theology*, "Prayer," pp. 621–26; ZPEB, "Prayer," IV, pp. 835–44; ISBE (1986), "Prayer," III, pp. 931–39.

46 For if ye love them which love you, what reward have ye? do not even the publicans the same?
47 And if ye salute your brethren only, what do ye more than others? do not even the publicans so?
48 Be ye therefore perfect, even as your Father which is in heaven is perfect.

manifests universal goodwill toward all mankind. His sun and the rain cause the crops to grow for both the righteous and the wicked. If we are true children of the heavenly Father, we will manifest such goodwill as well.

"For if you love [only] the ones who love you, what reward do you have? Do not even the tax collectors the same thing?" (v. 46). Tax collectors and other despised people have their friends.

"And if you love only your brethren, what are you doing more? Do not even the Gentiles do the same thing?" (v. 47). That was a humiliating comparison, for the Jews prided themselves on being superior to the pagan Gentiles.

"Therefore be perfect as your heavenly Father is perfect" (v. 48). This is plainly impossible and is one of the most convicting statements in Scripture. "As applied to God perfection indicates the possession of every affirmative quality in superlative degree so that He is above all comparison, admitting of no deviation from absolute completeness in the embodiment

5:45. The word *sun* (ἥλιος) occurs 5 times in Matt. (5:45; 13:6, 43; 17:2; 24:29). For discussion see ZPEB, "Sun," V, pp. 540–42; ISBE (1988), "Sun," IV, pp. 662–63; Ryken, Wilhoit, and Longman, *Dictionary of Biblical Imagery*, "Sun," pp. 827–28.

The word *good* (ἀγαθός) occurs 16 times in Matt. (5:45; 7:11 [twice], 17, 18; 12:34, 35 [3 times]; 19:16, 17 [twice]; 20:15; 22:10; 25:21, 23). Good is the pinnacle of ethical virtue. God alone is absolutely good. For further discussion see Elwell, ed., *Evangelical Dictionary of Biblical Theology*, "Good," p. 305; ZPEB, "Good," II, pp. 775–76; ISBE (1982), "Good," II, pp. 525–27; E. F. Harrison, ed., *Baker's Dictionary of Theology*, "Good," pp. 252–53.

The verb *to rain* (βρέχω) occurs only here in Matt.

For the word *righteous* see Matt. 1:19 note.

5:46. The word *tax collector* (τελώνης) occurs 8 times in Matt. (5:46; 9:10, 11; 10:3; 11:19; 18:17; 21:31, 32).

5:47. The verb *to salute, greet* (ἀσπάζομαι) occurs twice in Matt. (5:47; 10:12).

The word *Gentile* (ἐθνικός) occurs 3 times in Matt. (5:47; 6:7; 18:17).

5:48. The word *perfect* (τέλειος) occurs 3 times in Matt. (5:48 [twice]; 19:21). As it applies to God it refers to absolute perfection, but as it applies to all other beings it can mean only relative perfection. Blomberg suggests that *mature* is a better translation in this context (*Matt.*, p. 115), but it is difficult to see how that characterizes God. Paul exhorts believers, "Be therefore followers of God, as dear children, and keep walking in love" (Eph. 5:1–2a). For explanations see Elwell, ed., *Evangelical Dictionary of Biblical Theology*, "Perfect," pp. 598–99; ISBE (1986), "Perfect," III, pp. 764–65; E. F. Harrison, ed., *Baker's Dictionary of Theology*, "Perfect, Perfection," pp. 401–2.

of every excellence" (ZPEB, "Perfect," IV, p. 697). The psalmist has well said, "As for God, his way is perfect" (Ps. 18:30a); "Great is the Lord, and greatly to be praised; and his greatness is unsearchable" (Ps. 145:3). The "perfecting of the saints" (Eph. 4:12a) is obviously a work in progress, but He will continue the work until we all come in the unity of the faith unto a perfect man, unto the measure of the stature of the fullness of Christ (Eph. 4:13). "But the path of the just is as the shining light, that shineth more and more unto the perfect day" (Prov. 4:18).

Practical Applications from Matthew 5

1. True disciples always seek the Lord and His teaching (v. 1). "Blessed are they that keep his testimonies, and that seek him with the whole heart" (Ps. 119:2).
2. God always blesses those who beg Him for help (v. 3). "You have not, because you ask not" (James 4:2b).
3. God is the Comforter of those who mourn (v. 4). "Thou hast turned for me my mourning into dancing" (Ps. 30:11a).
4. God exalts the meek who trust Him (v. 5). "The meek will he guide in judgment: and the meek will he teach his way" (Ps. 25:9).
5. God satisfies those who hunger for Him (v. 6). "For he satisfies the longing soul, and fills the hungry soul with goodness" (Ps. 107:9).
6. God rewards the merciful (v. 7). "With the merciful thou wilt show thyself merciful" (Ps. 18:25a).
7. God draws the pure in heart to Himself (v. 8). "Every word of God is pure: he is a shield unto them that put their trust in him" (Prov. 30:5).
8. God blesses the peacemakers because He is for peace (v. 9). "But the meek shall inherit the earth; and shall delight themselves in the abundance of peace" (Ps. 37:11).
9. God blesses those who suffer for His sake (v. 10). "For unto you it is given in the behalf of Christ, not only to believe on him, but also to suffer for his sake" (Phil. 1:29).
10. When men make life miserable here, rejoice, for God will make it blessed in heaven (vv. 11–12). "Blessed is the man that endureth temptation: for when he is tried, he shall receive the crown of life, which the Lord hath promised to them that love him" (James 1:12).

11. Believers need to think of being salt for others (v. 13). "Let your speech be always with grace, seasoned with salt, that you may know how you ought to answer every man" (Col. 4:6).
12. Believers need to let their light shine before others (vv. 14–15). "For you were sometimes darkness, but now are you light in the Lord: walk as children of light" (Eph. 5:8).
13. Believers need a heart relationship with God, not merely outward show (v. 20). "With my whole heart have I sought thee: O let me not wander from thy commandments" (Ps. 119:10).
14. Anger can hurt as surely as murder (v. 22). "He that is slow to anger is better than the mighty; and he that ruleth his spirit than he that taketh a city" (Prov. 16:32).
15. A guilty conscience hurts one's relationship with God (vv. 23–24). "Whoso is partner with a thief hateth his own soul" (Prov. 29:24a).
16. Wicked thoughts can harm as surely as wicked deeds (v. 28). "For as he thinketh in his heart, so is he" (Prov. 23:7a).
17. Believers should use respectful speech (v. 34). "Being reviled, we bless; being persecuted, we suffer it" (I Cor. 4:12b).
18. Vengeful retaliation harms the one who does it (vv. 38–39). Only God can say, "Vengeance is mine; I will repay, saith the Lord" (Rom. 12:19b).
19. Believers should be generous (pp. 40–42). "Cast thy bread upon the waters: for thou shalt find it after many days" (Eccles. 11:1).
20. Believers should love people however they are treated (v. 44). "With good will doing service, as to the Lord, and not to men" (Eph. 6:7).

Prayer

Lord Jesus, help me to seek Your blessing above all. Enable me to shine with Your light in this dark, wicked world. Enable me to live day by day with Your grace, wisdom, and strength. Make us what we ought to be to honor Your Father. Amen.

MATTHEW 6

The Consecration to God

Persons
Jesus
Your Father
God

Persons referred to
Men
Hypocrites
The heathen
Thieves

Masters
Solomon
The Gentiles

Places referred to
Heaven
Synagogues
Your closet

Earth
The field

Doctrines taught
Reward
Prayer
The kingdom of God
Forgiveness
Temptation
Evil

Fasting
Singleness of purpose
Faith
Righteousness
Worry

1 Take heed that ye do not your alms before men, to be seen of them: otherwise ye have no reward of your Father which is in heaven.

Matthew 6 Exposition

I. Giving. vv. 1–4.

It is not an accident that consecration to God begins with giving. If the believer's relation to God centers on *getting*, he is not as consecrated to God as he thinks. Consecration is giving, devoting, oneself to God. To be devoted to God is a high and holy privilege. Our thoughts should center on how great He is and how privileged we are to have communion with the Lord of the universe. The believer should read Alexander Whyte's *Lancelot Andrewes and His Private Devotions* (Edinburgh: Oliphant, Anderson and Ferrier, 1896). Andrews, a translator of the King James Bible, was one of the most devout believers in all of British history. The believer's walk with God is vastly more important than any other category in the Christian life. Giving, praying, and serving are important to the believer, but God Himself must be supreme.

"Pay close attention that you do not your righteous charity before men in order to be seen by them; otherwise you are not having a reward before your Father who is in heaven" (v. 1). Charity is highly pleasing to God, but not if it is a grandstand play intended to attract the praise of men. This is a sobering thought: God is watching every deed and the heart motive behind it. Our purpose ought always to be to please God, not just to look good before men. F. B. Meyer had profound insight when he characterized this paragraph "The Inwardness of True Religion" (*The Directory of the Devout Life*, p. 100). The Lord Jesus always portrays God as a loving Father Who is constantly caring for His children. A. T. Robertson argues that the Lord is addressing the three categories of righteous deeds that the Pharisees were very proud of: alms, prayer, and fasting (*Word Pictures*, I, p. 50).

6:1. The verb *to pay close attention to, beware of* (προσέχω) occurs 6 times in Matt. (6:1; 7:15; 10:17; 16:6, 11, 12).

The word *righteous charity* (δικαιοσύνη) normally means *righteousness*, but here it plainly refers to a gift (alms). For the word see Matt. 3:15 note.

This verb *to see, observe* (θεάομαι) occurs 4 times in Matt. (6:1; 11:7; 22:11; 23:5).

For God as *Father*, see Matt. 5:16 note. The greatest concentration of uses (12 times) occurs in Matt. 6.

For the word *reward* see Matt. 5:12 note.

2 Therefore when thou doest thine alms, do not sound a trumpet before thee, as the hypocrites do in the synagogues and in the streets, that they may have glory of men. Verily I say unto you, They have their reward.

3 But when thou doest alms, let not thy left hand know what thy right hand doeth:

4 That thine alms may be in secret: and thy Father which seeth in secret himself shall reward thee openly.

"Therefore whenever you give a gift to the needy, do not sound a trumpet before you, as the hypocrites do in the synagogues and the streets, in order that they may be seen of men; truly I say to you, they have received their reward" (v. 2). The book of Job points clearly to the hypocrite's sin: he forgets that God is watching (Job 8:13). The believer who walks with the Lord may give his gifts quietly, in serene confidence that his heavenly Father knows and is pleased. No one else needs to know. Morris gives examples of those who take the sounding of the trumpet literally, but he takes it as figurative (*Matt.*, p. 137 n. 7).

"But when you give a gift for the needy, let not your left hand know what your right hand is doing, in order that your gift to the needy may be in secret; and your Father who sees in secret shall reward you" (vv. 3–4). This is encouragement to give gifts in deepest secrecy. If your heavenly Father is the only One Who knows, He will reward you richly. The more a person tries to "advertise" his good deeds, the less God is interested.

6:2. The word *gift to the needy* (ἐλεημοσύνη) occurs 3 times in Matt. (6:2, 3, 4).

The verb *to sound a trumpet* (σαλπίζω) occurs only here in Matt.

The word *hypocrite* (ὑποκριτής) occurs 13 times in Matt. (6:2, 5, 6; 7:5; 15:7; 22:18; 23:13, 15, 23, 25, 27, 29; 24:51), elsewhere Mark 7:6; Luke 6:42; and so forth. It was the classical Greek word for a *play actor* or *pretender*. In the Greek plays the actors wore masks to help identify themselves with the role they performed. See also *hypocrisy* (Matt. 23:28; Gal. 2:13; I Pet. 2:1). "The sacrifice of the wicked is abomination: how much more, when he bringeth it with a wicked mind?" (Prov. 21:27). For further study see R. K. Harrison, ed., *The New Unger's Bible Dictionary*, "Hypocrisy," "Hypocrite," p. 599; E. F. Harrison, ed., *Baker's Dictionary of Theology*, "Hypocrisy, Hypocrite," pp. 274–75; Elwell, ed., *Evangelical Dictionary of Biblical Theology*, "Hypocrisy," p. 362; ZPEB, "Hypocrisy," III, pp. 234–35; ISBE (1982), "Hypocrisy," II, p. 790.

The word *street* (ῥύμη) occurs only here in Matt., and in Luke 14:21; Acts 9:11; 12:10 in the rest of the NT.

For the verb *to glorify* see Matt. 5:16 note.

6:3. The word *left hand* (ἀριστερός) occurs only here in Matt.; the word *right* (δεξιος) occurs 12 times in Matt.; see Matt. 5:29 note.

6:4. The word *secret* (κρυπτός) occurs 5 times in Matt. (6:4 [twice], 6 [twice]; 10:26).

5 And when thou prayest, thou shalt not be as the hypocrites are: for they love to pray standing in the synagogues and in the corners of the streets, that they may be seen of men. Verily I say unto you, They have their reward.

6 But thou, when thou prayest, enter into thy closet, and when thou hast shut thy door, pray to thy Father which is in secret; and thy Father which seeth in secret shall reward thee openly.

7 But when ye pray, use not vain repetitions, as the heathen do: for they think that they shall be heard for their much speaking.

II. Praying. vv. 5–15.

"And whenever you are praying, be not as the hypocrites, because they love to pray standing in the synagogues and in the corners of the wide streets, in order to be seen by men; truly I say to you, they have their reward" (v. 5). The perfect tense, *having taken their stand*, implies a public pose in view of people in order to impress them. They pray to gain the admiration of men; God looks away. The Lord is not outlawing public prayer, but ostentatious prayer. Whenever a person prays in order to enhance his own reputation, God is not listening.

"But you, whenever you pray, enter into your private place and shut the door in order to pray to your Father in secret; and your Father, who sees in secret, shall reward you" (v. 6). The Lord emphasizes the *you*. Be sure *you* pray in a way that pleases God. Sometimes the reward may be in the sense of the nearness of God's presence, rather than an outward manifestation. The nearer God's child draws to the heavenly Father, the more blessed are the times of prayer.

"But when you pray, do not babble, even as the gentiles, for they think that they shall be heard by their many words" (v. 7). The poor Tibetan monks who have a prayer written in a prayer wheel and whirl it around

6:5. For a summary of the verb *to pray* see Matt. 5:44 note.

The word *wide street* (πλατεῖα) occurs twice in Matt. (6:5; 12:19).

For a summary of the word *reward* (μισθός) see Matt. 5:12 note.

6:6. The word *private place, inner room* (ταμεῖον) occurs only twice in Matt. (6:6; 24:26).

The verb *to shut* (κλείω) occurs 3 times in Matt. (6:6; 23:13; 25:10).

The word *door* (θύρα) occurs 4 times in Matt. (6:6; 24:33; 25:10; 27:60).

6:7. The verb *to babble, to speak without thinking* (βατταλογέω) occurs only here in the NT. Arndt and Gingrich suggest that it may be a hybrid form, rendering an Aramaic idiom (p. 137). See also Moulton and Milligan, *Vocabulary*, p. 107. Vincent suggests the parallels of the worshipers of Baal (I Kings 18:26) "and the Romanists with their paternosters and aves" (*Word Studies*, I, p. 43).

The word *many words* (πολυλογία) occurs only here in the NT.

8 Be not ye therefore like unto them: for your Father knoweth what things ye have need of, before ye ask him.

9 After this manner therefore pray ye: Our Father which art in heaven, Hallowed be thy name.

hour after hour are a sad example of such superstitious practice. God is never impressed by the quantity of deeds or words. Broadus warns against the endless repetitions of the rosary by Roman Catholics (*Matt.*, p. 130). The heart devotion is everything before God.

"Therefore be not like them; for your Father knows the things you need before you ask him" (v. 8). God is omniscient; He knows all things. He knows what we are going to ask for, and He knows what we really need, which are sometimes very different things. God knows the secrets of the heart (Ps. 44:21*b*). The prayer begins with God, not our needs. The first three petitions have to do with God, His name, His kingdom, His will. The fourth petition is for our physical needs; petitions five through seven deal with our spiritual needs. Blomberg correctly notes that this prayer can be more accurately called "The Disciples' Prayer" (*Matt.*, p. 118).

"Thus therefore be praying:

Our Father who is in the heavens;

May your name be hallowed" (v. 9).

The present tense imperative means *continue praying*. This prayer is not just for church services; it is a prayer believers ought to be praying

6:8. The verb *to be like* (ὁμοιόω) occurs 8 times in Matt. (6:8; 7:24, 26; 11:16; 13:24; 18:23; 22:2; 25:1).

This verb *to know* (οἶδα) occurs 24 times in Matt. See Matt. 6:32 note.

For the word *need* see Matt. 3:14 note.

For the verb *to ask* see Matt. 5:42 note.

6:9. The verb *to pray* (προσεύχομαι) occurs 15 times in Matt. (5:44; 6:5 [twice], 6 [twice], 7, 9; 14:23; 19:13; 24:20; 26:36, 39, 41, 42, 44).

For this prayer as such see Marcus Dods, *The Prayer That Teaches to Pray*; ZPEB, III, "Lord's Prayer, the," pp. 972–78; ISBE (1986), "Lord's Prayer," III, pp. 160–64; Elwell, ed., *Evangelical Dictionary of Biblical Theology*, "Lord's Prayer, the," pp. 489–91; A. B. Bruce, *The Training of the Twelve*, pp. 52–68. See also Bibliography, pp. 442–44.

For the Fatherhood of God see Matt. 5:16 note.

For the word *name* see Matt. 1:21 note.

The verb *to hallow, sanctify, set apart for God* (ἁγιάζω) occurs 3 times in Matt. (6:9; 23:17, 19). For the doctrine of sanctification see ZPEB, "Sanctification," V, pp. 264–67; ISBE (1988), "Sanctification," IV, pp. 321–31; Elwell, ed., *Evangelical Dictionary of Biblical Theology*, "Sanctification," pp. 708–13.

10 Thy kingdom come, Thy will be done in earth, as it is in heaven.

constantly. Does not Paul command, "Pray without ceasing" (I Thess. 5:17)? This is not a liturgical prayer; it is a guide for all our praying. The word *Father* makes clear that it is for born-again believers, who know God as their heavenly Father (John 3:3–16). When we consider the divine majesty of God, we may feel that the address should be *Sovereign Lord, Ruler of the universe*, but the Lord Jesus portrays God as a loving heavenly Father Who delights in hearing His children pray to Him. Because of the atoning sacrifice of the Lord Jesus upon the cross, we may come boldly before the throne of grace (Heb. 4:16). If the word *Father* makes Him near and dear to us, the phrase *who is in the heavens* makes clear the exalted majesty of His Person. When we finally come to that celestial city He has prepared for us, we will find that there is still a throne there (Rev. 22:1). The word *our* reminds us that we do not pray as isolated individuals but as members of the family of God, all of whom need grace and help from the Father. When we pray that God's name be made holy, we are praying that God will enable us to revere and glorify His Person as we ought. As obedient children we need to remember His command, "Be holy for I am holy" (I Pet. 1:16*b*). Our character needs to be conformed to His holy will.

"Let your kingdom come" (v. 10*a*).

This is a prayer for the glorious eschatological kingdom that the Lord Jesus will establish when He returns. Some will argue that it refers to a spiritual kingdom, but it would be strange to pray for what we already have. This petition envisions a day in which "the earth shall be full of the knowledge of the Lord, as the waters cover the sea" (Isa. 11:9*b*). The book of Revelation tells us that the Lord Jesus will return and establish a thousand-year millennial reign on the earth (Rev. 20:1–7), and after that an eternal kingdom that embraces the whole universe (Rev. 21–22).

6:10. For the word *kingdom* see Matt. 3:2 note. See also Custer, *From Patmos to Paradise*, Rev. 21, 22.

The word *will* (θέλημα) occurs 6 times in Matt. (6:10; 7:21; 12:50; 18:14; 21:31; 26:42). The will of God is a major theme in Scripture. The ideas of the kingdom and the will of God are intertwined in Scripture. The Lord Jesus devoted Himself to the will of His Father (Matt. 26:39, 42). For further discussion see Elwell, ed., *Evangelical Dictionary of Biblical Theology*, "Will of God," pp. 820–22; ZPEB, "Will," V, pp. 931–33; ISBE (1988), "Will of God." IV, pp. 1064–67; Harrison, ed., *Baker's Dictionary of Theology*, "Will," "Will of God," pp. 552–53.

For the word *heaven* see Matt. 3:2 note.

11 Give us this day our daily bread.

If the believer truly desires that future kingdom, his present life should reflect submission to the will of the Lord even now. The present wicked world needs to see people who can walk with God now (Heb. 11).

"Let your will come to pass,

as in heaven, also upon earth" (v. 10b).

The psalmist refers to the Lord's throne in heaven and the angels that do His commandments and adds, "Bless ye the Lord, all ye his hosts; ye ministers of his, that do his pleasure" (Ps. 103:21). But in praying that God's will be done on earth, we are also praying that we will do His will even now. We confess that we do not do His will perfectly now, but we should desire to do so. As far as His grace enables us, we should seek to do His will now. The believer should never seek to pull God's will over to his, but rather to conform his will to the Lord's. This does not mean just passive submission, but active, joyful obedience. The phrase *upon earth* is our assurance that God intends to win even here. Glasscock observes, "One important lesson to be learned about prayer is that petitioning God is not to be self-focused but God-honoring and God-centered" (*Matt.*, p. 147). We are also praying that God's kingdom rule come to earth. We pray for a future, universal obedience to God's will.

"Give us today our daily bread" (v. 11).

6:11. For the word *bread* see Matt. 4:3 note.

The word *daily* (ἐπιούσιος) occurs only here and in the parallel in Luke 11:3 in the NT.

This is a good verse to note the power of Matthew Henry's exposition:

"Every word here has a lesson in it: (1) We ask for *bread*; that teaches us sobriety and temperance; we ask for *bread*, not dainties, not superfluities; that which is wholesome, though it be not nice. (2) We ask for *our* bread; that teaches us honesty and industry: we do not ask for the bread out of other people's mouths, not the bread of deceit (Prov. 20:17), not the bread of idleness (Prov. 31:27), but the bread honestly gotten. (3) We ask for our *daily* bread; which teaches us not to take thought for the morrow (v. 34), but constantly to depend upon divine Providence, as those that live from hand to mouth. (4) We beg of God to *give* it us, not to sell it us, nor lend it us, but *give* it. The greatest of men must be beholden to the mercy of God for their daily bread. (5) We pray, 'Give it to *us*; not to me only, but to others in common with me.' This teaches us charity, and a compassionate concern for the poor and needy. It intimates also, that we ought to pray with our families; we and our households eat together, and therefore ought to pray together. (6) We pray that God would give it us *this day*; which teaches us to renew the desire of our souls toward God, as the wants of our bodies are renewed; as duly as the day comes, we must pray to our heavenly Father, and reckon we could as well go a day without meat [food], as without prayer."

95

12 And forgive us our debts, as we forgive our debtors.
13 And lead us not into temptation, but deliver us from evil: for thine is the kingdom, and the power, and the glory, for ever. Amen.

This is the sole petition for the physical needs of the believer. The verb *give* is an aorist tense, implying one time, "give today." Modern life thinks of continuous action, retirement plans, extended benefits. But this is a simple prayer, Give us what we need today. The illustration is bread, the staff of life. The average Israelite did not have meat daily; bread was the regular fare (Ruth 2:14). The fatted calf was killed only on very special occasions (Luke 15:27). Needless to say, a great percentage of praying today centers on the physical well-being of believers. This prayer puts the emphasis elsewhere. The believer may well ignore the fads and luxuries of modern life. Now the Lord turns His attention to the three petitions that address the spiritual well-being of the believer:

"And forgive us our debts, even as we forgave our debtors" (v. 12). The aorist, *forgave*, assumes it is our past practice. Some have claimed that this is legal ground (*Scofield Study Bible*, p. 1002). But this has nothing to do with salvation; it is the daily practice of the believer that is here under discussion. If the believer is going to get hardhearted, the Lord will start collecting debts too. We must all learn to have the gracious spirit that the Lord Jesus manifested. This is perhaps the hardest petition to pray sincerely; hence the Lord Jesus reinforces it (vv. 14–15). Believers do not reach perfection in this life. We all have much to ask forgiveness for: sins of omission and sins of commission. We should remember the cry of Isaiah when he saw the holiness of the Lord: "Woe is me! for I am undone" (Isa. 6:5*a*).

"And lead us not into temptation [testing]" (v. 13*a*). The aorist imperative seeks to avert what has not yet happened. God does not tempt anyone (James 1:13), but He does test people (James 1:3). The

---

6:12. This is the first time that the verb *to leave, forgive* (ἀφίημι) has the meaning *to forgive* in Matt. See also 6:14, 15; 9:2, 5, 6; 12:31, 32; 18:21, 27, 32, 35. For a discussion of the doctrine see Leon Morris, *The Cross in the New Testament*, pp. 49–59; ZPEB, "Forgiveness," II, pp. 596–600; ISBE (1982), "Forgiveness, II, pp. 340–44; Elwell, ed., *Evangelical Dictionary of Biblical Theology*, "Forgiveness," pp. 267–70.

The word *debt* (ὀφειλή) occurs only here in Matt.; the word *debtor* (ὀφειλέτης) occurs only twice in Matt. (6:12; 18:24). Deissmann comments on the large number of debt documents that have been found in the papyri (*Light from the Ancient East*, p. 331). But the meaning of *debt* in this context is plainly *sin*, as the parallel in Luke 11:4 demonstrates.

6:13. The verb *to lead in* (εἰσφέρω) occurs only here in Matt.

14 For if ye forgive men their trespasses, your heavenly Father will also forgive you:
15 But if ye forgive not men their trespasses, neither will your Father forgive your trespasses.

believer should never seek temptation, but in this world we never reach a place where there are no tests. We must learn how to walk humbly with God and seek sustaining grace from Him. The psalmist assures us, "Under his wings shalt thou trust" (Ps. 91:4b). The arrogant and self-confident are soon defeated.

"But deliver us from the evil one" (v. 13b).
The evil one is the personal devil, Satan (Matt. 4:1–11; 13:19, 38; John 17:15; Rev. 12:9). He is a roaring lion seeking to devour us (I Pet. 5:8). The Lord Jesus Christ is the Victor and our Deliverer. God will crush Satan under the believers' feet (Rom. 16:20). One day we shall see him cast into the lake of fire and sulfur (Rev. 20:10). Some expositors prefer making evil refer to abstract evil rather than the Devil (Leon Morris). It may well refer to both ideas.

Some manuscripts add the following:

"For yours is the kingdom and the power and the glory forever"
    (v. 13c).
It is drawn from David's prayer of dedication for the temple (I Chron. 29:11–13), a very appropriate conclusion for a public prayer. In the ancient world prayers were often ended by a "seal," an impromptu sentence of praise. Believers can learn much from the Lord's Prayer. We need to pray more for the things of God and His service, more for the spiritual battle in which we are engaged, and not solely for the financial and material concerns of life.

"For if you forgive men their false steps, your heavenly Father will also forgive you; but if you will not forgive men, neither will your Father forgive your false steps" (vv. 14–15). Forgiving others is difficult enough

The word *testing, temptation* (πειρασμός) occurs twice in Matt. (6:13; 26:41).

The verb *to deliver, rescue* (ῥύομαι) occurs only twice in Matt. (6:13; 27:43). For discussion see ISBE (1979), "Deliver," I, pp. 915–16; ZPEB, "Deliver," II, pp. 89–90; Elwell, ed., *Evangelical Dictionary of Biblical Theology*, "Deliver," pp. 162–63.

For the phrase *the evil one* (ὁ πονηρός) see Matt. 5:37 note.

6:14, 15. The word *false step* (παράπτωμα), "a step alongside the path," occurs only in these 2 verses in Matt., but it is an important word in Paul's argument (Rom. 4:25; 5:16, 20;

16 Moreover when ye fast, be not, as the hypocrites, of a sad countenance: for they disfigure their faces, that they may appear unto men to fast. Verily I say unto you, They have their reward.
17 But thou, when thou fastest, anoint thine head, and wash thy face;
18 That thou appear not unto men to fast, but unto thy Father which is in secret: and thy Father, which seeth in secret, shall reward thee openly.
19 Lay not up for yourselves treasures upon earth, where moth and rust doth corrupt, and where thieves break through and steal:

that the Lord gives additional encouragement for believers to be forgiving. God graciously overlooks a multitude of "missteps" in the life of the believer. We all need to learn to be considerate and gracious toward our fellow believers. God is supremely gracious toward us.

III. Fasting. vv. 16–18.

"But whenever you fast, be not gloomy as the hypocrites, for they disfigure their faces in order that they may appear to men to be fasting; truly I say to you, they have their reward" (v. 16). Note that this word about fasting is not a command but an assumption. Once the believer has told someone about his fasting, God is looking the other way. "But you, when you fast, anoint your head and wash your face, in order that you may not appear to men to be fasting, but to your Father who is in secret; and your Father who sees in secret shall reward you" (vv. 17–18). God is conscious of all forms of self-denial for His sake and is pleased with His faithful servants. The author has seen some believers who will forgo vacations in order to have more to give to missions. God is watching.

IV. Treasures. vv. 19–24.

"Stop treasuring up for yourselves treasures on the earth, where moth and rust ruin, and where thieves dig through and steal" (v. 19). The present tense verbs stress the constant process of destruction and loss that man's

---

II Cor. 5:19; Eph. 1:7; 2:5; Col. 2:13). See Trench, *Synonyms*, pp. 245–46; ZPEB, "Trespass," V, pp. 811–12; ISBE (1988), "Trespass," IV, pp. 903–4.

6:16. The word *sad, gloomy* (σκυθρωπός) occurs only here and in Luke 24:17 in the NT.

For the verb *to appear* see Matt. 1:20 note.

For the verb *to fast, abstain from food* (νηστεύω) see Matt. 4:2 note.

6:17. The verb *to wash* (νίπτω) occurs twice in Matt. (6:17; 15:2). See Trench, *Synonyms*, pp. 160–63. See Matt. 15:2 note for ceremonial sense.

6:19. The verb *to treasure up* (θησαυρίζω) occurs twice in Matt. (vv. 19, 20).

For the noun *treasure* (θησαυρός) see Matt. 2:11 note.

20 But lay up for yourselves treasures in heaven, where neither moth nor rust doth corrupt, and where thieves do not break through nor steal:
21 For where your treasure is, there will your heart be also.
22 The light of the body is the eye: if therefore thine eye be single, thy whole body shall be full of light.
23 But if thine eye be evil, thy whole body shall be full of darkness. If therefore the light that is in thee be darkness, how great is that darkness!

earthly treasures endure. The only real treasure that the believer has is what is laid up in heaven for him.

"But keep treasuring up for yourselves treasures in heaven, where neither moth nor rust ruins, and where thieves do not dig through and steal; for where your treasure is, there your heart shall be also" (vv. 20–21). The present tense verb, *keep treasuring*, shows that the believer should make it a continuing practice to lay up treasures and rewards in heaven and not here in this life. Our heart should be with the Lord. He will take care of any rewards.

"The lamp of the body is the eye. If therefore your eye be sound, your whole body shall be full of light" (v. 22). If you have a sound, healthy eye, you have a good perception of light. Significantly, the only other use of the word *full of light* is to the transfiguration vision of Christ (Matt. 17:5). If our eyes are spiritually healthy, we will see the spiritual glory of Christ and walk in His light.

"But if your eye be evil, your whole body shall be filled with darkness. If therefore the light that is in you is darkness, how great is the darkness"

The verb *to ruin* (ἀφανίζω) occurs 3 times in Matt., all in this context (vv. 16, 19, 20).

The word *moth* (σής) occurs only in vv. 19, 20, and in Luke 12:33 in the NT.

The word *rust* (βρῶσις) occurs twice in this context only in Matt. (vv. 19, 20). The word means lit. *eating*, but that easily extends to *corrosion* and *rust*.

The verb *to dig through* (διορύσσω) occurs 3 times in Matt. (6:19, 20; 24:43).

The word *thief* (κλέπτης) occurs 3 times in Matt. (6:19, 20; 24:43).

The verb *to steal* (κλέπτω) occurs 5 times in Matt. (6:19, 20; 19:18; 27:64; 28:13). See ISBE (1988), "Steal," IV, pp. 614–15.

6:22. The word *lamp* (λύχνος) occurs twice in Matt. (5:15; 6:22). It denotes a small oil lamp. For background and illustrations see ZPEB, "Lamp," III, pp. 865–66; ISBE (1986), "Lamp," III, pp. 68–69.

For the word *eye* see Matt. 5:29 note.

The word *sound, single* (ἁπλοῦς) occurs only here in Matt. It denotes a well-focused eye.

The word *full of light* (φωτεινός) occurs twice in Matt. (6:22; 17:5).

6:23. For the word *evil* (πονηρός) see Matt. 5:37 note.

For the word *darkness* (σκότος) see Matt. 4:16 note.

24 No man can serve two masters: for either he will hate the one, and love the other; or else he will hold to the one, and despise the other. Ye cannot serve God and mammon.
25 Therefore I say unto you, Take no thought for your life, what ye shall eat, or what ye shall drink; nor yet for your body, what ye shall put on. Is not the life more than meat, and the body than raiment?

(v. 23). Spiritual darkness is the deepest darkness, abysmal darkness. When rich men who know not God die, they can carry away nothing with them (Ps. 49:16–17); "they shall never see light" (Ps. 49:19b).

"No one is able to be slaving for two masters; for either he will hate the one and love the other, or he will be devoted to one and will despise the other. You are not able to be slaving for God and Mammon" (v. 24). One or the other will be supreme. Modern man is still torn between religious aspirations and materialism. William Tyndale wrote in *The Parable of the Wicked Mammon*, "The love that God hath to Christ is infinite, and Christ died and suffered all things not for Himself, to obtain favour or ought else; for He had ever the full favour of God, and was Lord over all things; but to reconcile us to God, and to make us heirs with Him of His Father's kingdom" (quoted in Philip Hughes, *The Theology of the English Reformers*, p. 48). How ridiculous to substitute things for the worship of the Lord of the universe.

V. Anxiety. vv. 25–34.

"On account of this I say to you: Stop being anxious for your life, what you shall eat, or what you shall drink, or for your body, what you shall wear. Is not the soul more important than food and the body than clothing?" (v. 25). Amid the uncertainties of modern life anxiety seems to

---

6:24. The verb *to slave for* (δουλεύω) occurs only here in Matt.

For the verb *to hate* see Matt. 5:43 note.

For the verb *to love* see Matt. 5:43 note.

The word *other* (ἕτερος) denotes *another of a different kind*. It occurs 10 times in Matt. (6:24 [twice]; 8:21; 10:23; 11:3, 16; 12:45; 15:30; 16:14; 21:30).

The verb *to be devoted to* (ἀντέχομαι) occurs only here in Matt.

The verb *to despise* (καταφρονέω) occurs only in 6:24; 18:10 in Matt.

The word *mammon* (μαμωνᾶς) is an Aramaic word transliterated into Greek, personifying *wealth, property* (Arndt and Gingrich, p. 491). It occurs only here in Matt. and in Luke 16:9, 11, 13 in the NT. See also ZPEB, "Mammon," IV, p. 48; ISBE (1986), "Mammon," III, p. 232.

26 Behold the fowls of the air: for they sow not, neither do they reap, nor gather into barns; yet your heavenly Father feedeth them. Are ye not much better than they?
27 Which of you by taking thought can add one cubit unto his stature?

be almost a normal response. But it should have no place in the life of a believer. The Lord Jesus commands us to stop being anxious. God will providentially care for His people.

"Look at the birds of the sky, because they do not sow or reap or gather into barns, but your heavenly Father feeds them; are you not worth more than they?" (v. 26). This is an argument from the less to the greater. If God cares for small creatures, will He not care more for you? As Henry Scudder phrased it, "It is altogether needless to take thought about the success of your actions, for success is cared for already by God, Matt. 6:26, 30, 32" (*The Christian's Daily Walk,* p. 190, 1673).

"But who of you by being anxious is able to add to his stature one cubit?" (v. 27). This is obviously an impossibility and not worth the time worrying about. Everyone can live his life in the fear of God, whatever

6:25. The verb *to be anxious* (μεριμνάω) occurs 7 times in Matt. (6:25, 27, 28, 31, 34 [twice]; 10:19).

Be Not Anxious

   I. Be not anxious for life, drink. 6:25.
   II. Be not anxious for stature. 6:27.
   III. Be not anxious for clothes. 6:28.
   IV. Be not anxious for food. 6:31.
   V. Be not anxious for tomorrow. 6:34.
   VI. Be not anxious for testimony in persecution. 10:19.

For the word *soul, life,* see Matt. 2:20 note.

For the word *body* see Matt. 5:29 note.

The verb *to eat* (ἐσθίω) occurs 24 times in Matt. (6:25, 31; 9:11; 11:18, 19; 12:1, and so forth).

The verb *to drink* (πίνω) occurs 15 times in Matt. (6:25, 31; 11:18, 19, and so forth).

The verb *to clothe* (ἐνδύω) occurs 3 times in Matt. (6:25; 22:11; 27:31).

6:26. The verb *to look at, behold, pay special attention to* (ἐμβλέπω) occurs twice in Matt. (6:26; 19:26).

The word *bird* (πετεινόν) occurs 4 times in Matt. (6:26; 8:20; 13:4, 32). Both Paul (Rom. 1:23) and James (3:7) use birds as illustrations.

For the word *sky, heaven,* see Matt. 3:2 note.

The verb *to sow* (σπείρω) occurs 17 times in Matt. (6:26; 13:3 [twice], 4, 18, 19 [twice], 20, 22, 23, 24, 27, 31, 37, 39; 25:24, 26).

The verb *to reap* (θερίζω) occurs 3 times in Matt. (6:26; 25:24, 26).

28 And why take ye thought for raiment? Consider the lilies of the field, how they grow; they toil not, neither do they spin:
29 And yet I say unto you, That even Solomon in all his glory was not arrayed like one of these.
30 Wherefore, if God so clothe the grass of the field, which to day is, and to morrow is cast into the oven, shall he not much more clothe you, O ye of little faith?
31 Therefore take no thought, saying, What shall we eat? or, What shall we drink? or, Wherewithal shall we be clothed?
32 (For after all these things do the Gentiles seek:) for your heavenly Father knoweth that ye have need of all these things.

his height. To think of David and Goliath is to think of God's enabling power (I Sam. 17:32–50).

"And why are you anxious concerning clothing? Consider the lilies of the field, how they grow; they labor not, neither do they spin" (v. 28). Wildflowers are a great example of God's abundant provision for small things. "But I say to you that not even Solomon in all his glory was arrayed like one of these" (v. 29). The wealth and splendor of King Solomon was great indeed (I Kings 10:1–23). His portico in the temple was famous (John 10:23; Acts 3:11; 5:12).

"But if God so clothes the grass of the field, which today is, and tomorrow is cast into the oven, shall he not much rather clothe you, O you of little faith?" (v. 30). God is much more interested in people than in flowers. But those people who belong to Him are assured of eternal provisions (Rev. 21:1–3). "Therefore be not anxious, saying, What shall we eat? or

The verb *to feed* (τρέφω) occurs twice in Matt. (6:26; 25:37).

The verb *to be worth more than* (διαφέρω) occurs 3 times in Matt. (6:26; 10:31; 12:12).

6:27. The verb *to add* (προστίθημι) occurs twice in Matt. (6:27, 33).

The word *stature, height* (ἡλικία) may also refer to *length of life, age*. See Arndt and Gingrich, pp. 345–46.

The word *cubit* (πῆχυς) occurs only here in Matt.

6:28. For the word *clothing* (ἔνδυμα) see Matt. 3:4 note.

The verb *to consider* (καταμανθάνω) occurs only here in the NT.

The word *lily* (κρίνον) occurs only here and in the parallel (Luke 12:27) in the NT. The madonna lily (*Lilium candidum* L.) and the crown anemone (*Anemone coronaria* L.) have been suggested as growing in the area. See Zohary, *Plants of the Bible*, pp. 170–71, 176–77; Moldenke, *Plants of the Bible*; ZPEB, "Lily," III, p. 936; ISBE (1986), "Lily," III, p. 137.

The word *field* (ἀγρός) occurs 17 times in Matt. (6:28, 30; 13:24, 27, 31, 36, 38, 44 [twice]; 19:29; 22:5; 24:18, 40; 27:7, 8 [twice], 10).

The verb *to grow* (αὐξάνω) occurs twice in Matt. (6:28; 13:32).

33 But seek ye first the kingdom of God, and his righteousness; and all these things shall be added unto you.
34 Take therefore no thought for the morrow: for the morrow shall take thought for the things of itself. Sufficient unto the day is the evil thereof.

What shall we drink? Or With what shall we be clothed? For all these things the Gentiles are seeking; for your heavenly Father knows that you are having need of all these things" (vv. 31–32). This thought of the Father's knowledge and care is repeated from Matthew 6:8 to emphasize the importance of this truth. The apostle Paul calls the Father of the Lord Jesus "the Father of mercies, and the God of all comfort" (II Cor. 1:3b). James notes that "every good gift and every perfect gift is from above, and comes down from the Father of lights" (James 1:17a).

The Lord Jesus now sums up this teaching in a major principle: "But be seeking first the kingdom of God and his righteousness, and all these things shall be added to you" (v. 33). The believers' priorities must be correct. God is vastly more important than any of His gifts. If the believer makes God supreme in his life, the rest will fall into proper place. The present tense imperative (*be seeking*) stresses the continuing nature of the responsibility.

"Therefore be not anxious for tomorrow, for tomorrow shall be anxious for itself; sufficient for the day is its evil" (v. 34). Don't borrow trouble from tomorrow. The believer must learn to trust God every day.

The verb *to labor, toil* (κοπάω) occurs only twice in Matt. (6:28; 11:28). It implies hard work.

The verb *to spin* (νήθω) occurs only here in Matt.

6:29. *Solomon* is named 5 times in Matt. (1:6, 7; 6:29; 12:42 [twice]).

The verb *to clothe, array* (περιβάλλω) occurs 5 times in Matt. (6:29, 31; 25:36, 38, 43).

6:30. The verb *to clothe* (ἀμφιέννυμι) occurs twice in Matt. (6:30; 11:8).

The word *grass, greenery for cattle* (χόρτος) occurs 3 times in Matt. (6:30; 13:26; 14:19).

The word *oven* (κλίβανος) occurs only here and in the parallel, Luke 12:28, in the NT. Weeds and brush were often used to heat ovens; wood was scarce (I Kings 17:10, 12).

The word *little faith* (ὀλιγόπιστος) occurs 4 times in Matt. (6:30; 8:26; 14:31; 16:8) and in Luke 12:28 only in the NT.

6:32. This verb *to know* (οἶδα) is the word for absolute, intuitive knowledge, not for learned information (γινώσκω). See Custer, *Treasury of New Testament Synonyms*, pp. 106–16.

6:33. For the verb *to seek* see Matt. 2:13 note.

For the word *righteousness* see Matt. 3:15 note.

6:34. This word *evil* (κακία) occurs only here in Matt. See Paul's usage: Rom. 1:29; I Cor. 5:8; Eph. 4:31; Col. 3:8, and more. For the more frequent word for *evil* (πονηρός) see Matt. 5:37 note.

Practical Applications from Matthew 6

1. Impressing people is not the believer's business; pleasing God is his life work (v. 1). It was Paul's trust to so speak "not as pleasing men, but God, who tries our hearts" (I Thess. 2:4b).
2. The best praying is secret prayer (v. 6). Moses left the tabernacle to direct the people, "but his servant Joshua, the son of Nun, a young man, departed not out of the tabernacle" (Exod. 33:11b).
3. Vain repetition is not true prayer (v. 7). The priests of Baal cried "from morning until noon, saying, O Baal, hear us" (II Kings 18:26), but Elijah said, "Lord God of Abraham, Isaac, and of Israel, let it be known this day that thou art God in Israel," and the fire fell (I Kings 18:36b).
4. Believers pray to a loving heavenly Father (v. 9). Jesus prayed, "that the world may know that thou hast sent me, and hast loved them, as thou hast loved me" (John 17:23b).
5. The will of the Father is the most important thing to believers (v. 10). Epaphras was "always laboring fervently for you in prayers, that you may stand perfect and complete in all the will of God" (Col. 4:12b).
6. Believers need to seek deliverance from evil from the Father, not devices (v. 13). Paul prayed, "God, even our Father, who has loved us, and has given us everlasting consolation and good hope through grace, comfort your hearts, and establish you in every good word and work" (II Thess. 2:16b–17).
7. The believer should not have his heart set on earthly treasures (v. 19). "For the fashion of this world passes away" (I Cor. 7:31b).   .
8. The believer should lay up treasures in heaven—things God can reward (v. 20). "And whoever shall give to one of these little ones a cup of cold water in the name of a disciple, truly I say to you, he shall never lose his reward" (Matt. 10:42).
9. The believer should choose the right Master—God alone (v. 24). "For the earth is the Lord's, and the fullness thereof" (I Cor. 10:28b).
10. The believer should not live with worries (v. 25). "Be anxious for nothing; but in everything by prayer and supplication with thanksgiving let your requests be made known to God" (Phil. 4:6).
11. The believer can take birds as examples of God's care (v. 26). "Who giveth food to all flesh: for his mercy endureth forever" (Ps. 136:25).

12. The believer can take flowers as examples of God's love of beauty (v. 30). "And the earth brought forth grass, and herb yielding seed after his kind, and the tree yielding fruit, whose seed was in itself, after his kind: and God saw that it was good" (Gen. 1:12).
13. Believers should remember that God already knows about everything they need (v. 32). "For he knoweth our frame; he remembereth that we are dust" (Ps. 103:14).
14. Every believer should make God first in his life (v. 33). "Be still, and know that I am God: I will be exalted among the heathen, I will be exalted in the earth" (Ps. 46:10).
15. The believer should never worry about tomorrow (v. 34). "For my God shall supply all your need according to his riches in glory by Christ Jesus" (Phil. 4:19).

Prayer

Heavenly Father, enable me to live for Your kingdom. Provide for us today what we need. Help me to set my heart on heaven, not the things of this earth. Deliver me from the attacks of the Devil and help me to live for You for Jesus' sake. Amen.

MATTHEW 7

Character

Persons
Jesus
The people

Persons referred to
Your brother
A man and his son
Your Father
False prophets
Many who profess

A wise man
A foolish man
Demons
The scribes

Places referred to
Heaven

Doctrines
Judgment
Hypocrisy
Holiness
Prayer
Evil
Goodness
The Law and the Prophets
Destruction

Life
Fruitfulness
Retribution
Iniquity
Wisdom
Foolishness
Authority

1 Judge not, that ye be not judged.
2 For with what judgment ye judge, ye shall be judged: and with what measure ye mete, it shall be measured to you again.
3 And why beholdest thou the mote that is in thy brother's eye, but considerest not the beam that is in thine own eye?

Matthew 7 Exposition

I. Crises in Character. vv. 1–12 [Luke 6:31, 37–42].

"Stop judging, in order that you be not judged" (v. 1). This is a warning as well as a command. It is easy for the believer to develop a censorious attitude toward the sinners around him. The Pharisees certainly did that. But the Lord Jesus always manifested a kindly and compassionate attitude toward people that He knew were dark-dyed sinners. This is a command not to be gullible, but to avoid looking down on others. Believers need discernment of other people's character, but they must not develop a superiority complex.

"For with the judgment you are judging, you shall be judged; and with the measure you are measuring, it shall be measured to you" (v. 2). The picture is of a person who fills a measure of grain precisely to the top and levels it off; nothing heaped up or running over. If that is the way he treats others, the Lord will treat him that way too. The Lord, instead, wishes to fill our cup until it runs over (Ps. 23:5).

"But why do you look at the speck in the eye of your brother, but the beam in your own eye you do not notice?" (v. 3). The Lord uses striking hyperbole to call attention to the way people overlook the grossest faults in themselves but are quick to pounce upon the slightest fault in others. All mankind stands convicted here.

7:1. For the verb *to judge* see Matt. 5:40 note.

7:2. The word *judgment* (κρίμα) occurs only here in Matt.

The verb *to measure* (μετρέω) occurs only here, twice, in Matt.

The noun *measure* (μέτρον) occurs twice in Matt. (7:2; 23:32).

7:3. For the verb *to see* (βλέπω) see Matt. 5:28 note.

The word *speck, mote* (κάρφος) occurs 3 times in Matt. (7:3, 4, 5).

The word *beam, log* (δοκός) occurs 3 times in Matt. (7:3, 4, 5). For comment see Douglas, ed., *The New International Dictionary of the Bible*, "Beam," p. 129.

The verb *to notice, consider* (κατανοέω) occurs only here in Matt.

4 Or how wilt thou say to thy brother, Let me pull out the mote out of thine eye; and, behold, a beam is in thine own eye?

5 Thou hypocrite, first cast out the beam out of thine own eye; and then shalt thou see clearly to cast out the mote out of thy brother's eye.

6 Give not that which is holy unto the dogs, neither cast ye your pearls before swine, lest they trample them under their feet, and turn again and rend you.

"Or how shall you say to your brother: Permit me to pull the speck out of your eye, and behold the beam is in your own eye?" (v. 4). The Lord emphasizes this quirk of human nature.

"Hypocrite, first cast out the beam out of your own eye, and then you will see clearly to cast the speck out of the eye of your brother" (v. 5). This is a grand spiritual principle: deal with the faults in your own life first; then you will be able to help others overcome theirs.

"Do not give what is holy to dogs, neither cast your pearls before pigs, lest they trample them under their feet and turn again and tear you in pieces" (v. 6). In the ancient world dogs were considered unclean animals, wild scavengers, that ran in packs. In today's terms *strays*. Dogs ate the corpse of Jezebel (I Kings 21:23; II Kings 9:35–37). A. M. Hunter notes that the style of the Lord's teaching here is that of the OT prophet: poetic parallelism (*A Pattern for Life*, p. 16). The Lord gives the same warning for dogs, and then for pigs, and then gives the consequences.

"Keep on asking and it shall be given to you; keep on seeking and you

---

7:4. The verb *to cast out* (ἐκβάλλω) occurs 28 times in Matt. (7:4, 5 [twice], 22; 8:12, 16, 31; 9:25, 33, 34, 38; 10:1, 8; 12:20, 24, 26, 27 [twice], 28, 35 [twice]; 13:52; 15:17; 17:19; 21:12, 39; 22:13; 25:30).

7:5. The verb *to see clearly* (διαβλέπω) occurs only here in Matt.

7:6. For the verb *to give* (δίδωμι) see Matt. 4:9 note.

The word *dog* (κύων) occurs only here in Matt. and in Luke 16:21; Phil. 3:2; II Pet. 2:22; and Rev. 22:15 in the rest of the NT. For discussion see Ryken, Wilhoit, and Longman, *Dictionary of Biblical Imagery*, "Dogs," pp. 213–14; ISBE (1979), "Dog," I, pp. 980–81; ZPEB, "Dog," II, pp. 153–54; A. Gondrexon-Ives Browne, *Guide to the Dogs of the World*, "Canaan Dog," pp. 82–83; "Pharaoh Hound," pp. 180–81. Compare the diminutive, *little dog*, Matt. 15:26–27.

The word *pearl* (μαργαρίτης) occurs 3 times in Matt. (7:6; 13:45, 46). Pearls may still be found in the Red Sea, but the finest come from the Persian Gulf. For background see ISBE (1986), "Pearl," III, p. 734; ZPEB, "Pearl," IV, pp. 668–69.

The word *pig* (χοῖρος) occurs 4 times in Matt. (7:6; 8:30, 31, 32).

The verb *to tear in pieces* (ῥήγνυμι) occurs only here and in 9:17 in Matt.

For the verb *to trample upon* see Matt. 5:13 note.

7 Ask, and it shall be given you; seek, and ye shall find; knock, and it shall
be opened unto you:
8 For every one that asketh receiveth; and he that seeketh findeth; and to him
that knocketh it shall be opened.
9 Or what man is there of you, whom if his son ask bread, will he give him a
stone?

shall find; keep on knocking and it shall be opened to you" (v. 7). The
Lord now gives a threefold parallelism on prayer. The trio of present
tense verbs strongly emphasizes the necessity of persistence in prayer. The
greatest blessing of prayer is not the answer; it is the time of fellowship
with the Almighty. The answers will come in God's perfect timing.

"For everyone who keeps on asking continues receiving, and everyone
who keeps on seeking continues finding, and to the one who keeps on
knocking, it shall be opened" (v. 8). Again the present tense verbs underscore the need for persevering prayer. Believers tend to be content with
a little prayer, but God desires constant communication with His people.
The apostle Paul commands believers, "Keep on rejoicing; keep on
praying without ceasing; in everything keep on giving thanks" (I Thess.
5:17–18a). Again the present tense verbs are important. For the believer,
the conversation with the Lord should never cease. It is not that the
believer should become a solitary hermit but that he should be constantly
praying to the Lord whatever is going on around him. It is a mindset, not
a location that is important.

"Or who is the man among you, who, if his son shall ask bread, will he
give him a stone?" (v. 9). The answer is obvious. Every normal father will
provide food for his hungry children. Is God something less than a good
father? No, He is a supremely great heavenly Father, Who can provide
all things for His dear children. But the timing and the nature of the gifts
must be left in His hands. Sometimes His children ask for cake when they
really need spinach! The vitamins are more important than the flavor.

7:7. For the verb *to ask*, see Matt. 5:42 note. See also D. E. Hiebert, *Working with God
Through Prayer*, pp. 4ff.

For the verb *to seek* see Matt. 2:13 note.

7:8 For the verb *to find* see Matt. 1:18 note.

The verb *to knock* (κρούω) occurs twice in Matt. (7:7, 8).

7:9. For the word *bread* see Matt. 4:3 note.

For the word *stone* see Matt. 3:9 note.

10 Or if he ask a fish, will he give him a serpent?
11 If ye then, being evil, know how to give good gifts unto your children, how much more shall your Father which is in heaven give good things to them that ask him?
12 Therefore all things whatsoever ye would that men should do to you, do ye even so to them: for this is the law and the prophets.
13 Enter ye in at the strait gate: for wide is the gate, and broad is the way, that leadeth to destruction, and many there be which go in thereat:

"Or if he ask for a fish, will he give him a snake?" (v. 10). With the fishing community of the Sea of Galilee nearby, this was an illustration that would be very apt. If children ask for something wholesome, like a fish, will a father give them something disgusting, like a snake? We may be sure that our heavenly Father will provide very wholesome sustenance for His children.

"Therefore if you, being evil, know how to be giving good gifts to your children, how much rather will your Father who is in the heavens give good things to those who keep on asking him?" (v. 11). The Lord clearly teaches the sinful depravity of mankind and God's continuing love toward people. Fatherly love is a humble illustration of the love of God. The necessity of continuing prayer is clear.

"Therefore all things whatever you are wishing that men do for you, thus also keep doing for them; for this is the law and the prophets" (v. 12). The believer should treat others in just the same way that he wishes to be treated. This is the general principle that should guide the life of every believer. This is the fulfillment of the OT revelation and the keynote for the NT revelation that will follow. The life and death of the Lord Jesus secures this salvation for the believer and enables him to live to the glory of God.

II. Contrasts in Character. vv. 13–27 [Luke 6:43–49].

"Enter in through the narrow gate; because wide is the gate that leads into destruction and many are the ones going in through it" (v. 13). The Lord

---

7:10. The word *fish* (ἰχθύς) occurs 5 times in Matt. (7:10; 14:17, 19; 15:36; 17:27).

The word *snake, serpent* (ὄφις) occurs 3 times in Matt. (7:10; 10:16; 23:33). For comment on the nature of snakes see Ryken, Wilhoit, and Longman, *Dictionary of Biblical Imagery,* "Serpent," pp. 773–74; ISBE (1988), "Serpent," IV, pp. 417–18; ZPEB, "Serpent," V, pp. 356–58. For description and color photos see Azaria Alon, *The Natural History of the Land of the Bible,* pp. 195–210.

7:11. For the word *evil* see Matt. 5:37 note.

7:13. The word *gate* (πύλη) occurs 3 times in this context (7:13 [twice], 14), and once for the gates of Hades (Matt. 16:18) in Matt. In the ancient world gates were absolutely

14 Because strait is the gate, and narrow is the way, which leadeth unto life, and few there be that find it.

Jesus Himself is that narrow gate. He will give the invitation later, "Come unto me, all you who are laboring and are heavy laden, and I will give you rest" (Matt. 11:28). In the Upper Room He said, "I am the way, the truth, and the life: no man comes to the Father, but by me" (John 14:6b). The same image is seen in the Lord's claim to be the door of the sheep and the door of salvation (John 10:7, 9). The Lord is the fulfillment of the type of the gate of the tabernacle court (Exod. 27:16), the one way to God's presence. Luther speaks of the solitary believer before the narrow gate and says, "When I am alone, therefore, I am not alone . . . I have Christ with me" (*Luther's Works*, vol. 21, *The Sermon on the Mount*, p. 242).

"Because narrow is the gate and hard pressing is the way that leads unto life, and few are the ones who are finding it" (v. 14). Philip Mauro was correct in claiming that to call the present world "the land of the living" is a mistake; it is really "the land of the dying" (Feinberg, *The Fundamentals for Today*, I, p. 192). The true land of the living is the realm of God in heaven, with the good angels and the redeemed saints (Rev. 21:1–6). Here Matthew portrays the Lord Jesus as introducing the doctrine of

necessary for a city's defense (Neh. 2:3, 13). City gates were unusually large and heavy (Judg. 16:2–3). The idea of a broad gate and a narrow gate seems odd to modern thinking, but the Greek city of Mycenae is a classical example of such gates. The famous "Lion Gate" is a broad gate for triumphal approaches. On the other side of the city the only other gate was one so narrow that a single soldier could keep the enemy out. See Branigan and Vickers, *Hellas*, pp. 74–75. For further discussion see Ryken, Wilhoit, and Longman, *Dictionary of Biblical Imagery*, "Gate," pp. 321–22; ZPEB, "Gate," II, pp. 655–57; ISBE (1982), "Gate," II, p. 408.

The word *narrow* (στενός) occurs only here and in v. 14 in Matt.

The word *wide, broad* (εὐρύχωρος) occurs only here in the NT.

The word *broad* (πλατύς) occurs only here in Matt.

The verb *to lead away* (ἀπάγω) occurs 5 times in Matt. (7:13, 14; 26:57; 27:2, 31).

For the verb *to find* see Matt. 1:18 note.

The word *destruction* (ἀπώλεια) occurs twice in Matt. (7:13; 26:8). For discussion see ISBE (1979), "Destruction," I, pp. 932–34; Harrison, ed., *Baker's Dictionary of Theology*, "Destruction," p. 165.

For the verb *to enter in* see Matt. 2:21 note.

7:14. The verb *to press hard* (θλίβω) occurs only here in Matt.

The word *life* (ζωή) occurs 7 times in Matt. (7:14; 18:8, 9; 19:16, 17, 29; 25:46). Guthrie notes that "eternal life is clearly not life as we now know it made endless, but a different

15 Beware of false prophets, which come to you in sheep's clothing, but inwardly they are ravening wolves.

eternal life to the multitudes (Broadus, *Matt.*, p. 164). But He has already talked to individuals about it (John 3:1–16). Paul desired that "mortality might be swallowed up of life" (II Cor. 5:4b) and also argues, "For if by the trespass of the one death reigned through the one, by much more the ones who are receiving the abundance of grace and of the gift of righteousness shall reign in life through the one, Jesus Christ" (Rom. 5:17). The Lord Jesus Christ is "the Author of life" (Acts 3:15), and the "Lord of both the dead and the living" (Rom. 14:9b). Paul also makes clear that God is perfectly just in sending wrath upon "the vessels of wrath fitted to destruction" (Rom. 9:22b).

"Beware of false prophets, who come to you in sheep's clothing, but within are ravenous wolves" (v. 15). False religious teachers may look respectable

kind of life which no enemy can destroy" (*New Testament Theology*, p. 877). "Life is a central motif of the four Gospels" (Elwell, ed., *Evangelical Dictionary of Biblical Theology*, "Life," p. 485). For further study see Butler, ed., *Holman Bible Dictionary*, "Life," pp. 881–83; ZPEB, "Life," III, pp. 927–32; ISBE (1986), "Life," III, pp. 129–34.

Eternal Life

    I. Narrow is the way that leads to life. 7:14.

    II. Better is loss of livelihood than everlasting fire. 18:8.

    III. Better is physical affliction than everlasting hell. 18:9.

    IV. Doing good works is not the path to life. 19:16.

    V. Keeping God's commands brings life. 19:17 (Acts 16:31).

    VI. Putting God ahead of all others brings life. 19:29.

    VII. Living for God's people pleases God. 25:40, 46.

7:15. The word *false prophet* (ψευδοπροφήτης) occurs 3 times in Matt. (7:15; 24:11, 24). The word *sheep* (πρόβατον) occurs 11 times in Matt. (7:15; 9:36; 10:6, 16; 12:11, 12; 15:24; 18:12; 25:32, 33; 26:31). Sheep are mentioned more often than any other animal in Scripture. They are often a symbol for God's obedient people (Ps. 23; John 10; Isa. 53:6; Mic. 2:12). For further discussion see Ryken, Wilhoit, and Longman, *Dictionary of Biblical Imagery*, "Sheep," pp. 782–85; ZPEB, "Sheep," V, pp. 385–88; ISBE (1988), "Sheep," IV, pp. 463–65; Butler, ed., *Holman Bible Dictionary*, "Sheep," p. 1259.

Sheep

    I. False prophets try to deceive the sheep of God. 7:15.

    II. The unsaved are as sheep without a Shepherd. 9:36.

    III. Believers should go to seek lost sheep. 10:6, 16.

    IV. Believers should rescue the fallen sheep. 12:11–12.

    V. The Lord went to the lost sheep. 15:24.

    VI. The Lord seeks even one lost sheep. 18:12.

    VII. The Lord shall gather His sheep in glory. 25:32–33.

16 Ye shall know them by their fruits. Do men gather grapes of thorns, or figs of thistles?
17 Even so every good tree bringeth forth good fruit; but a corrupt tree bringeth forth evil fruit.

and sound good to the world, but Christ regards them as dangerous animals. Peter warned against false teachers coming in to bring heresies (II Pet. 2:1). Paul also warned against false teachers as wolves coming to destroy (Acts 20:29). False teachers may look like sheep, but they intend to eat you! It is not surprising that Satan tries to transform himself into an angel of light to deceive (II Cor. 11:14).

"You shall fully know them by their fruits. Do men gather a bunch of grapes from thorns, or figs from thistles?" (v. 16). The believer must look at the life of the teacher and not just listen to his words. The Lord uses a rhetorical question to drive home the truth that what is in the heart of man will be manifest in the life.

"Thus every good tree produces good fruit, but the bad tree produces evil fruit" (v. 17). The *evil* fruit is plainly *rotten* fruit, disgusting to all. Corruption in the heart of man is the real meaning. The present tense verbs emphasize the constant production of fruit, for good or for evil.

The word *ravenous, grasping* (ἅρπαξ) occurs only here in Matt.

The word *wolf* (λύκος) occurs only here and in 10:16 in Matt. Wolves hunt at night so the Scriptures warn against the fierce evening wolves (Hab. 1:8; Zeph. 3:3). For further discussion see Ryken, Wilhoit, and Longman, *Dictionary of Biblical Imagery*, "Wolf," p. 958; ZPEB, "Wolf," V, p. 950; ISBE (1988), "Wolf," IV, pp. 1088–89. For a photograph see Azaria Alon, *The Natural History of the Land of the Bible*, p. 239.

For the word *beware* see Matt. 6:1 note.

7:16. This verb *to know* (ἐπιγινώσκω) occurs 6 times in Matt. (7:16, 20; 11:27 [twice]; 14:35; 17:12). It is an intensified form that may imply full or accurate knowledge. Note Paul's emphasis in Rom. 1:32, "who have fully known the righteous ordinance of God."

The verb *to gather* (συλλέγω) occurs 7 times in Matt. (7:16; 13:28, 29, 30, 40, 41, 48).

The word *a bunch of grapes* (σταφυλή) occurs only here in Matt.

The word *thorn* (ἄκανθα) occurs 5 times in Matt. (7:16; 13:7 [twice], 22; 27:29). ISBE (1988), "Thorn," refers to "the enormous number of prickly plants in Palestine" (IV, p. 842); see also ZPEB, "Thorns," V, pp. 736–37. Zohary, *Plants of the Bible*, suggests a number of examples: "Christ Thorn," pp. 154–55; "Thorny Burnet," p. 156; and a number of others, pp. 157–60, with color photos.

The word *fig* (σῦκον) occurs only here in Matt.

The word *thistle* (τρίβολος) occurs only in Matt. 7:16; Heb. 6:8 in the NT.

7:17. For the word *tree* see Matt. 3:10 note.

For the word *fruit* see Matt. 3:8 note.

*18 A good tree cannot bring forth evil fruit, neither can a corrupt tree bring
forth good fruit.*
*19 Every tree that bringeth not forth good fruit is hewn down, and cast into the
fire.*
20 Wherefore by their fruits ye shall know them.
*21 Not every one that saith unto me, Lord, Lord, shall enter into the kingdom
of heaven; but he that doeth the will of my Father which is in heaven.*

"A good tree is not able to keep bearing bad fruit; neither is a bad tree
able to keep bearing good fruit" (v. 18). There will be a consistency of
practice, for good or for ill, in opposite directions.

"Every tree that is not producing good fruit is cut down and cast into the
fire" (v. 19). Every orchardist knows that if the fruit of a tree is mealy and
tasteless, much less rotten, there is nothing to do but to cut it down and replace it with a good tree. The whole direction of the paragraph is not about
trees, but about people. The Lord Jesus is dividing the whole world into
two groups: people who bear fruit for God and those who bear rotten fruit.
The psalmist taught the same thing: "Blessed is the man . . . his delight is
in the law of the Lord . . . and he shall be like a tree planted by the rivers
of waters, that bringeth forth his fruit in his season" (Ps. 1:1–3). He gives
the contrast also: "The ungodly are not so: but are like the chaff which the
wind driveth away" (Ps. 1:4). Fire is a major symbol of divine wrath, both
in the OT (Num. 11:1; Ps. 89:46; Isa. 66:15; Jer. 4:4; Ezek. 22:21) and in
the NT (Matt. 3:10; II Thess. 1:8; II Pet. 3:7; Jude 7; Rev. 20:14–15).

"Therefore by their fruits you shall know them" (v. 20). The believer is
authorized to be a fruit inspector. We should not judge the eternal destiny of
any person, but we can see whether the conduct matches the biblical teaching. Again the intensified verb implies, *you shall know them accurately.*

"Not everyone who says to me: Lord, Lord, shall enter into the kingdom
of the heavens, but the one who does the will of my Father who is in
the heavens" (v. 21). Empty profession counts for nothing with God. He

The word *bad* (σαπρός) occurs 5 times in Matt. (7:17, 18; 12:33 [twice]; 13:48).

For the word *evil* see Matt. 5:37 note.

7:19. For the verb *to cut down, cut off* see Matt. 3:10 note.

7:21. For the *kingdom of the heavens* see Matt. 3:2 note.

For the word *will* see Matt. 6:10 note.

For the word *Lord* (κύριος) see Matt. 1:20 note.

22 Many will say to me in that day, Lord, Lord, have we not prophesied in thy name? and in thy name have cast out devils? and in thy name done many wonderful works?
23 And then will I profess unto them, I never knew you: depart from me, ye that work iniquity.

looks upon the heart and desires to see the life changed to devotion. The Lord later illustrated this teaching by the parable of the two sons (Matt. 21:28–31). The one son said he would serve but never did. "Matthew's religious self-understanding is that of a disciple doing the will of God as distinct from that of a righteous person doing righteousness" (B. Przybylski, *Righteousness in Matthew and His World of Thought*, p.115). The latter phrase was the Pharisees' interpretation.

"Many will say to me in that day: Lord, Lord, did we not prophesy in your name, and in your name cast out demons, and in your name did many mighty works?" (v. 22). The phrase *in that day* certainly refers to the Day of Judgment. Liberal preachers can preach polished sermons as surely as Bible-believing preachers can. But God sees the heart and the motive. There is no reward for a preacher who preaches for his own reputation instead of the glory of God. The Lord Jesus will be the Judge in all future judgments (John 5:22–23). The Father will compel all mankind to recognize the authority of His Son. The Lamb is in the midst of the throne of God (Rev. 7:17).

"And then I will confess to them: I never knew you; depart from me, you who are working lawlessness" (v. 23). The expression *I never knew you* is very emphatic (ουδεποτε εγνων υμας), "I never at any time knew you."

7:22. The verb *to prophesy* (προφητεύω) occurs 4 times in Matt. (7:22; 11:13; 15:7; 26:68). For more information see ZPEB, "Prophets and Prophecy," IV, pp. 875–903; ISBE (1986), "Prophet; Prophecy," III, pp. 986–1004; Elwell, ed., *Evangelical Dictionary of Biblical Theology*, "Prophet, Prophetess, Prophecy," pp. 641–47.

The word *demon* (δαιμόνιον) occurs 11 times in Matt. (7:22; 9:33, 34 [twice]; 10:8; 11:18; 12:24 [twice], 27, 28; 17:18). The reality of demonic beings is a clear Bible doctrine: Eph. 6:11–12; I Tim. 4:1–2; Rev. 12:9; 18:2. They are called *unclean spirits* (Matt. 10:1; 12:43; Acts 5:16; 8:7; Rev. 16:13). For further study see Merrill Unger, *Biblical Demonology*; Elwell, ed., *Evangelical Dictionary of Biblical Theology*, "Demon," pp. 163–65; ISBE (1979), "Demon," I, pp. 919–23; Ryken, Wilhoit, and Longman, *Dictionary of Biblical Imagery*, "Demons," pp. 202–3. See also the verb *to be demon possessed*, Matt. 4:24 note. See also Matt. 8:31 note.

The word *mighty work, power* (δύναμις) occurs 12 times in Matt. (7:22; 11:20, 21, 23; 13:54, 58; 14:2; 22:29; 24:29, 30; 25:15; 26:64).

7:23. The verb *to confess* (ὁμολογέω) occurs 4 times in Matt. (7:23; 10:32 [twice]; 14:7).

The verb *to work* (ἐργάζομαι) occurs 4 times in Matt. (7:23; 21:28; 25:16; 26:10).

24 Therefore whosoever heareth these sayings of mine, and doeth them, I will liken him unto a wise man, which built his house upon a rock:
25 And the rain descended, and the floods came, and the winds blew, and beat upon that house; and it fell not: for it was founded upon a rock.

This is a sharp contrast with the present tense participle, "You who are constantly working." The whole direction of their lives was away from Him. The psalmist expresses this revulsion, "Depart from me, all ye workers of iniquity" (Ps. 6:8a). The Lord Jesus gave a contrast: "But the one who is doing the truth comes to the light, in order that his works may be made manifest that they have been worked in God" (John 3:21).

"Therefore everyone who is hearing these my words and is doing them, I will liken him to a wise man, who built his house upon the bedrock" (v. 24). We must all note the present tense verbs, *who keeps on hearing and doing.* It is a universal obligation for all believers. This double illustration is a powerful conclusion to this unique sermon. It assumes the Negev Desert conditions in the south of the Holy Land. (For color photographs of the Negev Desert, see the author's *Stones of Witness,* pp. 182–83.) In the south a level stretch of ground may look like a good place to build a house, but it may be a dry streambed. When the spring rains come, there may be a cataract of raging floodwater flowing over it.

"And the rain came down, and the rivers came, and the winds blew and beat upon that house, and it did not fall, for it had been founded upon the bedrock" (v. 25). The floodwaters could not overwhelm the solid stone walls built upon bedrock. "The Lord is my rock" is a constant theme

---

The word *lawlessness* (ἀνομία) occurs 4 times in Matt. (7:23; 13:41; 23:28; 24:12). For discussion see Trench, *Synonyms,* pp. 243–44; ISBE (1986), "Lawless," III, pp. 92–93; ZPEB, "Law in the NT," III, pp. 894–96.

For the verb *to know* see Matt. 1:25 note.

7:24. The word *wise, thoughtful* (φρόνιμος) occurs 7 times in Matt. (7:24; 10:16; 24:45; 25:2, 4, 8, 9). It refers to using the mind or understanding (φρήν) properly. For further discussion see Matt. 11:19 note.

The word *rock* (πέτρα) occurs 5 times in Matt. (7:24, 25; 16:18; 27:51, 60). It does not denote merely a *stone,* but *bedrock* upon which one could build a house or a church. See also Matt. 16:18 note.

7:25. The word *rain* (βροχή) occurs only in this context in the NT (Matt. 7:25, 27). For discussion see Ryken, Wilhoit, and Longman, *Dictionary of Biblical Imagery,* "Rain," pp. 694–95; ZPEB, "Rain," V, pp. 27–28; ISBE (1988), "Rain," IV, pp. 35–36.

For the word *river* see Matt. 3:6 note.

26 And every one that heareth these sayings of mine, and doeth them not, shall be likened unto a foolish man, which built his house upon the sand:
27 And the rain descended, and the floods came, and the winds blew, and beat upon that house; and it fell: and great was the fall of it.
28 And it came to pass, when Jesus had ended these sayings, the people were astonished at his doctrine:

in Psalms (18:2, 31, 46; 28:1; 31:2, 3; 42:9; 61:2; 62:2, 7; 71:3; 89:26; 92:15; 94:22; 95:1).

"And everyone who is hearing these my words and is not doing them shall be likened to a foolish man, who built his house upon the sand" (v. 26). The sand denotes anything other than the Lord. It is easy for floodwaters to wash away sand and undermine walls until the house collapses in a pile of rubble. It is a graphic illustration of the destruction of the life that is not built upon the Lord's teaching. It may look like a rich life here, but it leads to abject misery in the life to come (Luke 16:19–23).

"And the rain came down and the rivers came and the winds blew and beat upon that house, and it fell, and the fall of it was great" (v. 27). The last word of the sermon is the word *great*, stressing the enormity of the destruction of a human life. It is terrible to see the destruction of a hollow, hypocritical life. This does not teach annihilation but accountability in the Day of Judgment. The Lord promised, "But I say to you that every idle word which men shall say they shall give an account concerning it in the Day of Judgment" (Matt. 12:36).

III. Conclusion by Matthew. vv. 28–29.

"And it came to pass when Jesus had finished these words, the crowds were

---

The word *wind* (ἄνεμος) occurs 9 times in Matt. (7:25, 27; 8:26, 27; 11:7; 14:24, 30, 32; 24:31). For discussion see Ryken, Wilhoit, and Longman, *Dictionary of Biblical Imagery*, "Wind," pp. 951–52; ZPEB, "Wind," V, p. 934; ISBE (1988), "Wind," IV, pp. 1067–68.

The verb *to fall upon* (προσπίπτω) occurs only here in Matt.

For the verb *to fall* see Matt. 2:11 note.

The verb *to be founded* (θεμελιόω) occurs only here in Matt., but it is an important word for Paul (Eph. 3:17; Col. 1:23).

7:26. For the word *foolish man* (μωρός) see Matt. 5:22 note.

The word *sand* (ἄμμος) occurs only here in Matt.

7:27. The word *fall* (πτῶσις) occurs only here and in Luke 2:34 in the NT.

7:28. The verb *to end, finish* (τελέω) occurs 7 times in Matt. (7:28; 10:23; 11:1; 13:53; 17:24; 19:1; 26:1). Each of these occurrences marks the end of a discourse or of a journey (10:23).

29 For he taught them as one having authority, and not as the scribes.

astonished at his teaching" (v. 28). And so all serious readers have been astonished at both the depth and the simplicity of these profound words.

"For he was teaching them as having authority, and not as their scribes" (v. 29). The scribes were always quoting the sayings of the fathers for authority (as modern-day rabbis do). The Riziner Rabbi said, "I dislike the man who is like snow; at first white and pure; later muddy and soiled." The Lubliner Rabbi said, "I don't like the good man who preens himself on his goodness" (Leo Rosten, *Treasury of Jewish Quotations*, p. 232). The Lord Jesus did not need to quote anyone. The Father has given the Son authority to execute judgment (John 5:27a). His words were divinely inspired truth. The audience was stunned to hear such authority. As John would record later, Jesus was "the way, the truth, and the life" (John 14:6b). His sayings were the voice of God. The discussion over this sermon has gone on for two thousand years and is still going on. The truth of this message still convicts every heart.

Practical Applications from Matthew 7

1. A judgmental, censorious attitude attracts the judgment of God (v. 1). Paul warns, "Wherefore you are inexcusable, O man who is judging, for that in which you are judging the other, you are condemning yourself, for you, the one judging, are practicing the same things" (Rom. 2:1).

The verb *to be amazed, astonished* (ἐκπλήσσω) occurs 4 times in Matt. (7:28; 13:54; 19:25; 22:33).

The word *teaching* (διδαχή) occurs 3 times in Matt. (7:28; 16:12; 22:33) but is a key word later (Acts 2:42; Rom. 6:17; II Tim. 4:2; II John 9–10).

7:29. This is the first of 10 times that the word *authority* (ἐξουσία) occurs in Matt. (7:29; 8:9; 9:6, 8; 10:1; 21:23 [twice], 24, 27; 28:18). Authority ultimately comes from God (Rom. 13:1; Ps. 29:4, 10). The Lord Jesus claimed that the Father had given Him authority over all flesh (John 17:2a) and that He had authority to forgive sin (Mark 2:10). Paul taught that Christ is the Head over all rule and authority (Col. 2:10b). Christ has the authority to make men sons of God (John 1:12). Alexander Whyte has a powerful message on this verse in *The Walk, Conversation and Character of Jesus Christ Our Lord*, pp. 134–41. For further discussion see Warfield, *The Inspiration and Authority of the Bible*; ZPEB, "Authority," I, pp. 420–21; ISBE (1979), "Authority," I, pp. 364–71; Elwell, ed., *Evangelical Dictionary of Biblical Theology*, "Authority," pp. 45–46; E. F. Harrison, ed., *Baker's Dictionary of Theology*, "Authority," pp. 80–81; J. Norval Geldenhuys, *Supreme Authority*.

For the verb *to teach* see Matt. 4:23 note.

For the word *scribe* see Matt. 2:4 note.

2. A person who judges others harshly shall receive stern judgment from the Lord (v. 2). The high priest condemned the Lord for blasphemy (Matt. 26:65), but when he faces the Lord in judgment, he shall be condemned for murder (John 5:22).

3. If a believer corrects himself first, he will see clearly how to help correct others (v. 5). "Who are you that judges another man's servant?" (Rom. 14:4a).

4. Believers should be discerning about the person to whom they witness (v. 6). Some people have no taste for spiritual things. Paul warns, "Beware of dogs, beware of evil workers" (Phil. 3:2a). He is not writing about the four-footed variety!

5. Every believer who keeps on asking will receive an answer (v. 8). Paul urges believers to be "praying always with all prayer and supplication in the Spirit, and watching thereunto with all perseverance" (Eph. 6:18a).

6. God the Father will give good gifts to those who ask Him (v. 11). Jesus said, "For the Father himself loves you, because you have loved me" (John 16:27a).

7. Whatever you want people to do for you, do also for them (v. 12). "Walk in love as, Christ also loved us" (Eph. 5:2a).

8. Believers should choose the narrow gate and the narrow path that leads to God (vv. 13–14). The psalmist could say, "With my whole heart have I sought thee: O let me not wander from thy commandments" (Ps. 119:10).

9. Believers cannot see the heart, but they must be fruit inspectors (vv. 17–20). "But the fruit of the Spirit is love, joy, peace, longsuffering, gentleness, goodness, faith, meekness, self control" (Gal. 5:22–23a).

10. Believers should do the will of their heavenly Father (v. 21). "And be not conformed to this age: but be transformed by the renewing of your mind that you may approve what is the good and well pleasing and perfect will of God" (Rom. 12:2).

11. Many have tried to earn their way to heaven (v. 22). The Pharisee boasted of his fasting and tithing (Luke 18:12), but God had respect to the penitent tax collector (Luke 18:13–14).

12. Whoever builds his life on the teachings of the Lord Jesus is secure (vv. 24–25). Jesus said, "I am the way, the truth, and the life: no man comes to the Father, but by me" (John 14:6).

13. Whoever builds his life on any other foundation will lose all (vv. 26–27). "And I will punish the world for their evil, and the wicked for their iniquity; and I will cause the arrogancy of the proud to cease" (Isa. 13:11a).

Prayer

Dear God, help me to have a forgiving attitude toward others. Enable me to pray in faith. Grant that my life may center on the gate of heaven. Provide grace that my life may rest on You as the solid Rock, for Jesus' sake. Amen.

MATTHEW 8

Miracles of Deliverance

Persons
Jesus
A leper
A centurion
A servant
Peter
His wife's mother

Those who were demon possessed
Those who were sick
A scribe
His disciples
Two who were demon possessed

Persons referred to
Moses
Abraham
Isaac
Jacob
Children of the kingdom
Isaiah

Great multitudes
My father
The dead
Pig keepers
The whole city

Places referred to
The mountain
Capernaum
A centurion's house
The kingdom
Outer darkness

Peter's house
The other side of Galilee
The sea
Country of the Gergesenes
The tombs

Doctrines
Worship
Authority
Faith
The kingdom

Outer darkness
Following Jesus
Son of God

1 When he was come down from the mountain, great multitudes followed him.
2 And, behold, there came a leper and worshipped him, saying, Lord, if thou wilt, thou canst make me clean.

Matthew 8 Exposition

I. The Leper Healed. vv. 1–4 [Mark 1:40–45; Luke 5:12–16].

"And when he came down from the mountain, great crowds followed him" (v. 1). The people had heard wonderful words, but the question was, were they the words of God? Was He just a good teacher? Can His deeds match His words? Matthew now records three miracles of healing that demonstrate how mighty the Lord's power really was.

"And behold, a leper came and worshiped him, saying, Lord, if you will, you can make me clean" (v. 2). Leprosy was the most feared disease in the ancient world. Not only did it make one an outcast but there also was no cure. The *behold* makes clear the unusual circumstance of a leper approaching anyone. The leper comes with the clear faith that the Lord Jesus has the divine power to do the impossible. There was no hesitation on the part of the Lord.

8:1. For the word *mountain* see Matt. 4:8 note.

8:2. The word *leper* (λεπρός) occurs 4 times in Matt. (8:2; 10:8; 11:5; 26:6). The disease is now called Hansen's disease. For discussion see ISBE (1986), "Leper, Leprosy," III, pp. 103–6; ZPEB, "Diseases of the Bible," Leprosy, II, pp. 138–39; Douglas and Tenney, eds., *The New International Dictionary of the Bible*, "Diseases, Leprosy," pp. 273–74.

For the verb *to worship* see Matt. 2:2 note.

For the word *Lord* see Matt. 1:20 note.

The verb *to cleanse* (καθαρίζω) occurs 7 times in Matt. (8:2, 3 [twice]; 10:8; 11:5; 23:25, 26).

8:3. For the word *hand* see Matt. 3:12 note.

The verb *to stretch out* (ἐκτείνω) occurs 6 times in Matt. (8:3; 12:13 [twice], 49; 14:31; 26:51).

The verb *to touch* (ἅπτω) occurs 9 times in Matt. (8:3, 15; 9:20, 21, 29; 14:36 [twice]; 17:7; 20:34).

The Touch of Jesus

    I. He touched a leper: leprosy gone. Matt. 8:3.

    II. He touched Peter's mother-in-law: fever gone. 8:15.

    III. He touched the eyes of 2 blind men: they saw. 9:29.

    IV. He touched Peter, James, and John: comfort and courage. 17:7.

    V. He touched the eyes of 2 blind men at Jericho: they saw and followed. 20:34.

For the verb *I will* see Matt. 1:19 note.

The word *leprosy* (λέπρα) occurs only here in Matt.

3 And Jesus put forth his hand, and touched him, saying, I will; be thou clean. And immediately his leprosy was cleansed.
4 And Jesus saith unto him, See thou tell no man; but go thy way, shew thyself to the priest, and offer the gift that Moses commanded, for a testimony unto them.

"And he stretched out his hand and touched him, saying, I will; be clean; and immediately his leprosy was cleansed" (v. 3). The Lord was certainly the first person to touch him since he had become a leper. The Lord healed him with a word, just as He had healed Moses of leprosy as a sign (Exod. 4:7). This too was a sign of divine power. Carson notes that when Jesus touched the leper "Jesus does not become unclean, but the leper becomes clean! When Jesus comes in contact with defilement, he is never defiled. Far from it: his touch has the power to cleanse defilement" (D. A. Carson, *When Jesus Confronts the World*, p. 20).

"And Jesus says to him: See that you tell no one, but go; show yourself to the priest and offer the gift which Moses commanded, for a testimony to them" (v. 4). It was a quiet thing to do, but what a staggering testimony! The priests would no doubt have to look the ceremony up in the scrolls

---

This is the first of 20 miracles that Matthew records. (Matt. alone records the *).

1. Healing the leper. Matt. 8:3.
2. Healing the centurion's servant. 8:5–13.
3. Healing Peter's mother-in-law. 8:14–15.
4. Calming the storm. 8:23–27.
5. Delivering the Gadarene demoniac. 8:28–34.
6. Healing a paralytic. 9:1–8.
7. Healing the woman with the issue of blood. 9:20–22.
8. Raising the daughter of Jairus. 9:18–26.
9. Healing the 2 blind men. 9:27–31. *
10. Healing a dumb demoniac. 9:32–33. *
11. Healing the man with the withered hand. 12:10–13.
12. Healing the blind and dumb demoniac. 12:22.
13. Feeding the 5,000. 14:15–21.
14. Walking on the sea. 14:25–33.
15. Healing the Syrophenician's daughter. 15:21–28.
16. Feeding the 4,000. 15:32–38.
17. Restoring the lunatic boy. 17:14–18.
18. Providing the stater. 17:24–27. *
19. Healing the blind man at Jericho. 20:29–34.
20. The withering of the fig tree. 21:18–22.

The miracle of Christ's resurrection is unique. God the Father is said to have raised Jesus from the dead (Rom. 8:11; I Cor. 15:15), but Jesus also "rose" from the dead (I Cor. 15:4).

5 And when Jesus was entered into Capernaum, there came unto him a centurion, beseeching him,
6 And saying, Lord, my servant lieth at home sick of the palsy, grievously tormented.
7 And Jesus saith unto him, I will come and heal him.

(see Lev. 14:1–32). No one of them had ever done it before. And all during the public ministry of the Lord the lepers would keep coming for cleansing! It is no surprise that Luke records that "a great company of the priests were obedient to the faith" (Acts 6:7).

II. The Centurion's Servant Healed. vv. 5–13 [Luke 7:1–10].

"And when he entered into Capernaum, a centurion came to him, beseeching him" (v. 5). Here was a man from outside the chosen people. Was the Messiah for Jews alone? The great Servant of Jehovah was to be "a light of the Gentiles" as well (Isa. 42:1, 6*b*).

"And saying, Lord, my servant has been laid in the house a paralytic, terribly tormented" (v. 6). The centurion obviously cared deeply for his household servant and had real faith in the Lord Jesus.

"And he says to him, I will come and heal him" (v. 7). The Lord Jesus was quick to respond to this earnest plea. Edersheim notes, "He was captain of

---

For further discussion see ZPEB, "Miracles," IV, pp. 241–50; ISBE (1986), "Miracle," III, pp. 371–81; Elwell, ed., *Evangelical Dictionary of Biblical Theology*, "Miracle," pp. 531–34; B. Gerhardsson, *Mighty Acts of Jesus According to Matthew*.

8:4. For the verb *to show* see Matt. 4:8 note.

The word *priest* (ἱερεύς) occurs 3 times in Matt. (8:4; 12:4, 5).

Moses is named 7 times in Matt. (8:4; 17:3, 4; 19:7, 8; 22:24; 23:2). For background see ZPEB, "Moses," IV, pp. 279–95; ISBE (1986), "Moses," III, pp. 415–25; Alexander Whyte, *Bible Characters*, "Moses," I, pp. 228–50; *Who's Who in the Bible*, "Moses," pp. 300–311.

The word *testimony* (μαρτύριον) occurs 3 times in Matt. (8:4; 10:18; 24:14). For background see ZPEB, "Testimony," V, p. 682; ISBE (1988), "Testimony," IV, p. 797.

8:5. For *Capernaum* see Matt. 4:13 note.

A *centurion* (ἑκατοντάρχης) is mentioned 4 times in Matt. (8:5, 8, 13; 27:54). He was the commander normally of a hundred men. Mark uses the Roman term (κεντυριων, Mark 15:39). For further discussion see ZPEB, "Centurion," I, pp. 772–73; ISBE (1979), "Centurion," I, p. 629; Douglas and Tenney, eds., *The New International Dictionary of the Bible*, "Centurion," p. 197.

8:6. For the word *servant, boy* see Matt. 2:16 note.

For the word *paralytic* see Matt. 4:24 note.

The verb *to torment* (βασανίζω) occurs 3 times in Matt. (8:6, 29; 14:24).

The adverb *terribly* (δεινῶς) occurs only here in Matt.

8 The centurion answered and said, Lord, I am not worthy that thou should-
est come under my roof: but speak the word only, and my servant shall be
healed.
9 For I am a man under authority, having soldiers under me: and I say to
this man, Go, and he goeth; and to another, Come, and he cometh; and to my
servant, Do this, and he doeth it.
10 When Jesus heard it, he marvelled, and said to them that followed, Verily I
say unto you, I have not found so great faith, no, not in Israel.

the troop quartered in Capernaum, and in the service of Herod Antipas"
(*Life and Times of Jesus the Messiah*, I, p. 546). He would have known that
the Jews regarded the houses of Gentiles as defiled, so he is quick to ex-
cuse the Lord from such a task.

"And the centurion answered and said, Lord, I am not worthy that you
should enter under my roof, but say a word only, and my servant shall be
healed" (v. 8). His words manifest an earnest and serene trust in the divine power of the Lord Jesus. He goes on to say the following.

"For I also am a man under authority, having under myself soldiers, and
I say to this one: Go, and he goes, and to another: Come, and he comes,
and to my slave: Do this, and he does it" (v. 9). He was a disciplined officer of the Roman army. He regarded the Lord Jesus as the divine Commander of all nature. Surely, if He commanded something, it would be
done.

"And when Jesus heard, he marveled and said to the ones who were following: Truly I say to you, I did not find such faith, not even in Israel"
(v. 10). The Lord Jesus was moved to see such firm trust in His word by a
Roman and seized the opportunity to teach His people something about

8:7. For the verb *to heal* see Matt. 4:23 note.

8:8. For the word *worthy* see Matt. 3:11 note.

The word *roof* (στέγη) occurs only here in Matt.

This verb *to heal* (ἰάομαι) occurs 4 times in Matt. (8:8, 13; 13:15; 15:28).

8:9. For the word *authority* see Matt. 7:29 note.

The word *slave* (δοῦλος) occurs 30 times in Matt. (8:9; 10:24, 25; 13:27, 28; 18:23, 26,
27, 28, 32; 20:27; 21:34, 35, 36; 22:3, 4, 6, 8, 10; 24:45, 46, 48, 50; 25:14, 19, 21, 23, 26,
30; 26:51). For background on the institution see ZPEB, "Slave, Slavery," V, pp. 453–60;
ISBE, (1988), "Slavery," IV, pp. 539–46; Ryken, Wilhoit, and Longman, *Dictionary of
Biblical Imagery*, "Slave, Slavery," pp. 797–99.

8:10. The verb *to marvel* (θαυμάζω) occurs 7 times in Matt. (8:10, 27; 9:33; 15:31; 21:20;
22:22; 27:14).

11 And I say unto you, That many shall come from the east and west, and shall sit down with Abraham, and Isaac, and Jacob, in the kingdom of heaven.
12 But the children of the kingdom shall be cast out into outer darkness: there shall be weeping and gnashing of teeth.
13 And Jesus said unto the centurion, Go thy way; and as thou hast believed, so be it done unto thee. And his servant was healed in the selfsame hour.

the universal nature of God's people. Israel and the church should not be confused, but in the eternity to come there will be true unity among all the redeemed (Rev. 21:23–22:5).

"And I say to you that many shall come from the east and the west and shall recline at the table with Abraham and Isaac and Jacob in the kingdom of the heavens" (v. 11). The Lord Jesus reveals that there shall be many people besides Jews in God's kingdom. The apostle Paul noted that Gentile believers used to be aliens from the commonwealth of Israel and strangers from the covenants of promise, "But now in Christ Jesus you who were once far off were made near by the blood of Christ" (Eph. 2:13).

"But the sons of the kingdom shall be cast out into outer darkness; there shall be weeping and grinding of teeth" (v. 12). These "sons of the kingdom" were those scribes and Pharisees who were so sure that they would inherit the kingdom to the exclusion of all others (Matt. 9:10–13).

Seven Marvels

    I. Jesus marveled at the centurion's faith. 8:10.

    II. The disciples marveled at Jesus calming the storm. 8:27.

    III. Multitudes marveled at the casting out of a demon. 9:33.

    IV. The multitude marveled when they saw miracles of healing. 15:31.

    V. The disciples marveled that the fig tree withered away. 21:20.

    VI. The Herodians marveled at Jesus' answer. 22:22.

    VII. Pilate marveled at the Lord's silence. 27:14.

The word *faith* (πίστις) occurs 8 times in Matt. (8:10; 9:2, 22, 29; 15:28; 17:20; 21:21; 23:23). The word denotes a trust in God and thus devotion to God. For further discussion see ZPEB, "Faith, Faithfulness," II, pp. 479–91; ISBE (1982), "Faith," II, pp. 270–73; Elwell, ed., *Evangelical Dictionary of Biblical Theology*, "Faith," pp. 236–39.

For the name *Israel* see Matt. 2:6 note.

8:11. The verb *to recline at the table* (ἀνακλίνω) occurs only twice in Matt. (8:11; 14:19).

For the word *east* see Matt. 2:1 note.

The word *west* (δυσμή) occurs twice in Matt. (8:11; 24:27).

8:12. For the verb *to cast out* see Matt. 7:4 note. Some degree of vigor is assumed.

For the word *darkness* see Matt. 4:16 note.

14 And when Jesus was come into Peter's house, he saw his wife's mother laid, and sick of a fever.

15 And he touched her hand, and the fever left her: and she arose, and ministered unto them.

16 When the even was come, they brought unto him many that were possessed with devils: and he cast out the spirits with his word, and healed all that were sick:

"And Jesus said to the centurion: Go; as you believed, let it be done to you. And his servant was healed in that hour" (v. 13). This declaration illustrates the power of faith in Jesus and the Lord's great pleasure in those who believe in Him.

III. Peter's Mother-in-law and Others Healed. vv. 14–17 [Mark 1:29–34; Luke 4:38–41].

"And when Jesus had come into the house of Peter, he saw his mother-in-law bedridden and sick with a fever" (v. 14). In the ancient world widows were completely dependent on family or charity for subsistence (I Tim. 5:3–5).

"And he touched her hand, and the fever left her, and she arose and was ministering to him" (v. 15). This was an instantaneous, miraculous healing. The aorist verbs denote point action but are followed by an imperfect tense, *was ministering*, denoting continuing service. She felt well and was able to help in preparing the evening meal.

"But when evening had come, they brought to him many who were demon possessed, and he cast out the spirits by a word and healed all who were sick" (v. 16). Mark 1:29 recounts that they had come from the synagogue, so they had waited until sundown on the Sabbath to carry the sick and the demon possessed to Jesus. In the ancient world, rituals of exorcism were

The phrase *weeping and grinding of teeth* occurs 6 times in Matt. (8:12; 13:42, 50; 22:13; 24:51; 25:30). In every case it portrays the sorrow of the wicked at receiving their just punishment.

8:13. The verb *to believe* (πιστεύω) occurs 11 times in Matt. (8:13; 9:28; 18:6; 21:22, 25, 32 [3 times]; 24:23, 26; 27:42). It is always essential for the person to believe Christ, or God, for any blessing to come to him. For further discussion see Elwell, ed., *Evangelical Dictionary of Biblical Theology*, "Faith," pp. 236–39; ZPEB, "Faith, Faithfulness," II, pp. 479–91; ISBE (1982), "Faith," II, pp. 270–73.

This verb *to heal* (ἰάομαι) occurs 4 times in Matt. (8:8, 13; 13:15; 15:28).

8:14. The word *mother-in-law* (πενθερά) occurs twice in Matt. (8:14; 10:35).

The verb βάλλω may have the sense of "having been put," that is, *laid down, bedridden*.

The verb *to be sick with a fever* (πυρέσσω) occurs only here in Matt.

8:15. The word *fever* (πυρετός) occurs only here in Matt.

For the verb *to minister* see Matt. 4:11 note.

17 That it might be fulfilled which was spoken by Esaias the prophet, saying, Himself took our infirmities, and bare our sicknesses.
18 Now when Jesus saw great multitudes about him, he gave commandment to depart unto the other side.

long and complicated things (not to mention dangerous!), but here the Lord commands the spirits to leave and they go! He was also able to heal all who came to Him for help. There was no disease or infirmity so severe that He could not heal the sufferer. There is no other "healer" in the world's history who could do that. He is "the Lord that healeth thee" (Exod. 15:26b).

"In order that it might be fulfilled which was spoken through Isaiah the prophet, saying,

> He himself took our weaknesses
>
> And bore our diseases" (v. 17, Isa. 53:4).

The Lord Jesus fulfilled the ministry of the mighty Servant of Isaiah 53. The day of His atoning sacrifice was drawing near (Isa. 53:4–5). The day will come in which He will bring every saint to perfection in glory. Walvoord argued that all these mighty miracles provided the credentials prophesied of Messiah in Isaiah 35:5–6, but many of those prophesied miracles also relate to the future millennial kingdom (*Major Bible Prophecies*, p. 205).

IV. The Disciples Tested. vv. 18–22 [Luke 9:57–60].

"And when Jesus saw a crowd around him, he commanded to go away to the other side" (v. 18). A crowd could hinder serious inquirers from coming to the Lord. He directed the disciples to take Him to the eastern side of the Sea of Galilee. Fishermen could do that easily.

8:16. The word *evening* (ὀψία) occurs 7 times in Matt. (8:16; 14:15, 23; 16:2; 20:8; 26:20; 27:57).

The word *spirit* (πνεῦμα) can refer to an evil spirit (as here) or to the Holy Spirit (Matt. 1:18).

8:17. For *Isaiah* the prophet see Matt. 3:3 note.

The word *weakness, sickness* (ἀσθένεια) occurs only here in Matt.

For the word *disease* see Matt. 4:23 note.

8:18. The verb *to command* (κελεύω) occurs 7 times in Matt. (8:18; 14:9, 19, 28; 18:25; 27:58, 64).

8:19. The title *teacher* (διδάσκαλος) occurs 12 times in Matt. (8:19; 9:11; 10:24, 25; 12:38; 17:24; 19:16; 22:16, 24, 36; 23:8; 26:18). The title was equivalent to *Rabbi* (John 1:38). It was a title the Lord expected (John 13:13). It is still an office in the church (Eph. 4:11). "Jesus is the supreme expression of the divine teacher, showing compassion

19 And a certain scribe came, and said unto him, Master, I will follow thee whithersoever thou goest.
20 And Jesus saith unto him, The foxes have holes, and the birds of the air have nests; but the Son of man hath not where to lay his head.

"And one scribe came to him and said, Teacher, I will follow you wherever you go" (v. 19). The Lord had already referred to scribes in an unfavorable way (Matt. 5:20). Most of them probably avoided Him, but the text stresses that *one* scribe came with zeal. His statement is an emotional expression of religious fervor. The Lord Jesus gives him a warning of the cost that would be demanded. Christianity is not just "happy, happy" excitement, but rather a lifelong walk through hostile and indifferent circumstances.

"And Jesus says to him: The foxes have holes and the birds of the heaven nests, but the Son of man has not where to lay his head" (v. 20). The phrase *Son of man* was the Lord's favorite expression for Himself. It could mean just *man*, for God addresses Ezekiel by that phrase (Ezek. 2:1). But Daniel sees "One like the Son of Man" coming to rule the kingdom of God (Dan. 7:13). Thus the title combines the human nature and divine authority. It is as the Son of man that the Lord sends forth His angels to establish His kingdom (Matt. 13:41–43). It is a sobering thought to

---

combined with clarity, power and authority in his instruction" (Ryken, Wilhoit, and Longman, *Dictionary of Biblical Imagery*, "Teacher, Teaching," pp. 842–44). For further discussion see ZPEB, "Teacher," V, pp. 606–7; "Teaching of Jesus," V, pp. 607–11; Alexander Whyte, *The Walk, Conversation and Character of Jesus Christ Our Lord*, "He Taught Them as One Having Authority" (pp. 134–41).

8:20. The word *fox* (ἀλώπηξ) occurs only here in Matt. and in the parallel in Luke 9:58 and in the Lord's appraisal of crafty Herod Antipas (Luke 13:32).

The word *hole* (φωλεός) occurs only here in Matt.

For the word *bird* see Matt. 6:26 note.

The word *nest* (κατασκήνωσις) occurs only here in Matt.

The phrase *the Son of man* (ὁ υἱὸς τοῦ ἀνθρώπου) occurs here for the first of 30 times in Matt. (8:20; 9:6; 10:23; 11:19; 12:8, 32, 40; 13:37, 41; 16:13, 27, 28; 17:9, 12, 22; 18:11; 19:28; 20:18, 28; 24:27, 30, 37, 39, 44; 25:13, 31; 26:2, 24, 45, 64). It is significant that the title occurs in Ps. 8:4–6 of the universal dominion of the messianic King. The writer to the Hebrews makes a point of quoting this psalm in reference to the Lord Jesus and His glory (Heb. 2:6–9). Guthrie comments, "Of all the titles appearing in the synoptic gospels 'Son of man' is both the most significant and the most enigmatic" (*New Testament Theology*, p. 270). For further discussion see Girdlestone, *Old Testament Synonyms*, p. 46; ISBE (1988), "Son of Man," IV, pp. 574–81; Warfield, *The Lord of Glory*, pp. 84–88; Elwell, ed., *Evangelical Dictionary of Biblical Theology*, "Jesus Christ, Name and Titles of," pp. 411–12; ZPEB, "Son of Man, the," V, pp. 485–86.

For the word *head* see Matt. 5:36 note.

21 And another of his disciples said unto him, Lord, suffer me first to go and bury my father.

22 But Jesus said unto him, Follow me; and let the dead bury their dead.

23 And when he was entered into a ship, his disciples followed him.

24 And, behold, there arose a great tempest in the sea, insomuch that the ship was covered with the waves: but he was asleep.

ponder that the Lord Jesus had no property or home to His name, and yet He was Lord of all. Alexander Whyte has a powerful sermon on "The Son of Man Hath Not Where to Lay His Head" (*The Walk, Conversation and Character of Jesus Christ Our Lord*," pp. 202–10).

"But another of his disciples said to him: Lord, permit me first to go and bury my father" (v. 21). If his father were in critical condition, he would have been at home with him. What he is really offering is to take care of all his responsibilities for his father for the rest of his life and then come to follow the Lord. The Lord will not take second place in any disciple's life.

"But Jesus says to him: Follow me and permit the dead to bury their own dead" (v. 22). The spiritually dead can bury the physically dead. The spiritually alive should minister to the living while they have the opportunity. The text does not tell us whether either of these two ever actually came and followed the Lord.

V. The Storm Calmed. vv. 23–27 [Mark 4:36–41; Luke 8:22–25].

"And when he entered into the boat, his disciples followed him" (v. 23). It was much easier to cross the sea in a boat than to walk all the way around it.

8:21. The verb *to permit* (ἐπιτρέπω) occurs twice in Matt. (8:21; 19:8).

The verb *to bury* (θάπτω) occurs 3 times in Matt. (8:21, 22; 14:12).

8:22. For the verb *to follow* see Matt. 4:20 note.

The word *dead* (νεκρός) occurs 12 times in Matt. (8:22 [twice]; 10:8; 11:5; 14:2; 17:9; 22:31, 32; 23:27; 27:64; 28:4, 7).

The phrase "let the dead bury the dead" was a proverb known to Euripides (*Alcest*, line 894).

8:23. For the word *boat* see Matt. 4:21 note.

The verb *to embark, get into* (ἐμβαίνω) occurs 5 times in Matt. (8:23; 9:1; 13:2; 14:22; 15:39).

8:24. The word *shaking* (σεισμός) can refer to a *storm*, as here, or to an *earthquake*. It occurs 4 times in Matt. (8:24; 24:7; 27:54; 28:2).

The verb *to hide, cover* (καλύπτω) occurs twice in Matt. (8:24; 10:26).

The verb *to sleep* (καθεύδω) occurs 7 times in Matt. (8:24; 9:24; 13:25; 25:5; 26:40, 43, 45). For its biblical significance see ZPEB, "Sleep," V, pp. 460–61; ISBE (1988), "Sleep," IV, pp. 548–49; Ryken, Wilhoit, and Longman, *Dictionary of Biblical Imagery*, "Sleep," p. 799.

25 And his disciples came to him, and awoke him, saying, Lord, save us: we perish.

26 And he saith unto them, Why are ye fearful, O ye of little faith? Then he arose, and rebuked the winds and the sea; and there was a great calm.

27 But the men marvelled, saying, What manner of man is this, that even the winds and the sea obey him!

28 And when he was come to the other side into the country of the Gergesenes, there met him two possessed with devils, coming out of the tombs, exceeding fierce, so that no man might pass by that way.

"And, behold, a great storm arose in the sea, so that the boat was covered by the waves, but he himself was asleep" (v. 24). Storms can blow down from the Galilean hills very quickly and with surprising force.

"And they come to him and raise him up, saying: Lord, save us, we are perishing" (v. 25). They were professional fishermen, and they knew that the circumstances were out of their control. The contrast between the aorist tense *save immediately* and the present tense *we are being swamped* is striking. They were in the process of going down. The situation was very serious.

"And he says to them: Why are you cowardly, you of little faith? Then he arose and rebuked the winds and the sea, and there was a great calm" (v. 26). The Lord of the universe commanded and the elements hushed to a complete calm.

"But the disciples marveled, saying, What kind of man is this that even the winds and the sea obey him?" (v. 27). They were thoroughly convinced of His divine power. He was Lord of the winds and the sea and all else as well.

VI. The Demoniac Delivered. vv. 28–34 [Mark 5:1–20; Luke 8:26–39].

"And when he had come to the other side into the region of the Gadarenes, two who were demon possessed met him, coming out of the

8:25. For the verb *to save* see Matt. 1:21 note.

For the verb *to perish* see Matt. 2:13 note.

8:26. The word *cowardly* (δειλός) occurs only here in Matt.

For the word *little faith* see Matt. 6:30 note.

The verb *to command, rebuke* (ἐπιτιμάω) occurs 6 times in Matt. (8:26; 12:16; 16:22; 17:18; 19:13; 20:31).

The word *calm* (γαλήνη) occurs only here in Matt.

8:27. For the verb *marvel* see Matt. 8:10 note.

The verb *to obey* (ὑπακούω) occurs only here in Matt.

29 And, behold, they cried out, saying, What have we to do with thee, Jesus, thou Son of God? art thou come hither to torment us before the time? 30 And there was a good way off from them an herd of many swine feeding. 31 So the devils besought him, saying, If thou cast us out, suffer us to go away into the herd of swine.

tombs, exceedingly violent, so that no one was strong enough to pass through that way" (v. 28). These two were so feared that people avoided that road. The Lord deliberately chose that path in order to demonstrate His power over the kingdom of darkness.

"And, behold, they cried out, saying, What have we to do with you, Son of God? Did you come here to torment us before the time?" (v. 29). The demons recognize His absolute power over them and their final destination. Should He choose to visit flaming wrath on them immediately, He could. Mark calls them "unclean spirits" (Mark 5:13). The phrase *Son of God* is not merely a polite title; the demons know what it means. He will be their Judge. God has prepared everlasting fire for the Devil and his angels (Matt. 25:41).

"But there was at a distance from them a herd of pigs feeding themselves" (v. 30). The text does not say whether the herdsmen were Jews or Gentiles, but in either case they were a serious temptation to observant Jews.

"But the demons were beseeching him, saying, If you cast us out, send us into the herd of pigs" (v. 31). After the demons had possessed a human being, anything was better than to be cast out. The imperfect tense *were beseeching* implies a continuous action.

8:28. There is no good explanation for why the manuscripts have so many variations to this name. Some have Gadarenes; others have Gergesenes; others have Gerasenes. Compare Mark 5:1 and Luke 8:26. For a discussion of the manuscript evidence see Bruce M. Metzger, *A Textual Commentary on the Greek New Testament*, pp. 23–24. All these places were near one another on the east side of the Sea of Galilee. See also Broadus, *Matt.*, p. 188; Morris, *Matt.*, p. 208.

The word *grave, tomb* (μνημεῖον) occurs 7 times in Matt. (8:28; 23:29; 27:52, 53, 60 [twice]; 28:8).

The word *hard, violent* (χαλεπός) occurs only here in Matt. The word has the same sense as our phrase *a hardened or violent criminal* has.

8:29. The verb *to cry out* (κράζω) occurs 12 times in Matt. (8:29; 9:27; 14:26, 30; 15:22, 23; 20:30, 31; 21:9, 15; 27:23, 50).

For the title *Son of God* see Matt. 4:3 note.

For the verb *to torment* see Matt. 8:6 note.

8:30. For the word *pig* see Matt. 7:6 note.

The verb *to feed* (βόσκω) occurs twice in this context only in Matt. (vv. 30, 33).

32 And he said unto them, Go. And when they were come out, they went into the herd of swine: and, behold, the whole herd of swine ran violently down a steep place into the sea, and perished in the waters.
33 And they that kept them fled, and went their ways into the city, and told every thing, and what was befallen to the possessed of the devils.
34 And, behold, the whole city came out to meet Jesus: and when they saw him, they besought him that he would depart out of their coasts.

"And he said to them, Go. And they went out and entered into the pigs, and, behold, the whole herd rushed down the steep bank into the sea and died in the waters" (v. 32). This is a porcine commentary on demon possession: death is preferable.

"And the ones who were feeding them fled, and went away into the city, and reported all things, and the things of the ones who were demon possessed" (v. 33). Morris observes that they told their story so as to exonerate themselves from all blame for the loss of the pigs (*Matt.*, p. 211). It was a sensational event, an act of supernatural power. But the owners of the pigs had lost their investment.

"And, behold, all the city went out to meet Jesus, and when they had seen him, they were beseeching him that he would depart from their regions" (v. 34). There were no doubt others there who were engaged in questionable activities, and they feared His power to judge. Instead of getting right with God, they just wanted Jesus to go away and leave them alone. A. T. Robertson observes, "They cared more for hogs than for human souls, as often happens today" (*Word Pictures*, I, p. 70).

Practical Applications from Matthew 8

1. People recognized at once the divine power and authority of the Lord Jesus (v. 2). The leper asked for something that no one but God could give. When Naaman came with a letter asking for healing, the king of Israel cried out, "Am I God, to kill and to make alive, that this man doth send unto me to recover a man of his leprosy?" (II Kings 5:7*b*).

8:31. This word for *demon* (δαίμων) occurs only here in the NT. See Matt. 7:22 note.

8:32. The verb *to rush* (ὁρμάω) occurs only here in Matt.

The word *steep bank, cliff* (κρημνός) occurs only here in Matt.

2. The Lord Jesus encouraged people to be thankful to God for blessings received (v. 4). "And let the peace of God rule in your hearts, to the which also you are called in one body; and be thankful" (Col. 3:15).

3. The Lord Jesus was quick to volunteer to come and help (v. 7). The ministry of "helps" is one of the Spirit-empowered services of the church (I Cor. 12:28).

4. Trust in the Lord's power and authority pleases the Lord (vv. 9–10). "But without faith it is impossible to please him: for he that comes to God must believe that he is, and that he is a rewarder of them that diligently seek him" (Heb. 11:6).

5. "Many shall come from the east and the west, and shall sit down with Abraham, and Isaac, and Jacob, in the kingdom of heaven" (v. 11). John saw "a great multitude, which no man could number, of all nations, and kindreds, and people, and tongues, stood before the throne, and before the Lamb, clothed with white robes, and palms in their hands; and cried with a loud voice, saying, Salvation to our God who sits upon the throne, and unto the Lamb" (Rev. 7:9b–10).

6. "He cast out the spirits with his word, and healed all that were sick" (v. 16b). "Every tongue should confess that Jesus Christ is Lord, to the glory of God the Father" (Phil. 2:11b).

7. "And he said unto them, Why are you fearful, O you of little faith?" (v. 26). David could say to God, "I will fear no evil: for thou art with me" (Ps. 23:4b). The risen Lord said to John, "Fear not; I am the first and the last" (Rev. 1:17b).

8. "The whole city came out to meet Jesus: and when they saw him, they besought him that he would depart out of their regions" (v. 34b). Some people would rather be sick and demon possessed than to suffer financial loss. Paul could say, "I have suffered the loss of all things, and do count them but dung, that I may win Christ" (Phil. 3:8b).

Prayer

Lord Jesus, help me to trust in You for every need. Enable me to remember Your miracles and to be confident of Your keeping power. Guide my steps that I may arrive in Your presence by Your grace right on time. Amen.

MATTHEW 9

MIRACLES AND TEACHING

Persons
Jesus
A man paralyzed
Scribes
The multitude
Matthew
Publicans
Sinners
Pharisees

Disciples of John
A ruler [Jairus]
His daughter
A woman with an issue of blood
Two blind men
A dumb man, demon possessed
Jesus' disciples
The Lord of the harvest

Persons referred to
A physician
Children of the bride chamber
Bridegroom
Mourners

David
Ruler of demons
Laborers

Places mentioned
His own city [Capernaum]
The tax office
Matthew's house

The ruler's house
All the cities and villages

Doctrines taught
Forgiveness of sins
Blasphemy
Authority to forgive
The call to service
Repentance

Fasting
Faith
Mercy
The gospel of the kingdom
Compassion

1 And he entered into a ship, and passed over, and came into his own city.

2 And, behold, they brought to him a man sick of the palsy, lying on a bed: and Jesus seeing their faith said unto the sick of the palsy; Son, be of good cheer; thy sins be forgiven thee.

3 And, behold, certain of the scribes said within themselves, This man blasphemeth.

Matthew 9 Exposition

I. The Paralytic Healed. vv. 1–8 [Mark 2:1–12; Luke 5:17–26].

"And he embarked into a boat and passed across and came into his own city" (v. 1). The Lord Jesus crossed back to the west side of the Sea of Galilee. Capernaum was the place of His dwelling now (Matt. 4:13).

"And, behold, they were bringing to him a paralytic who was lying upon a pallet. And when Jesus saw their faith, he said to the paralytic: Have courage, child, your sins are forgiven" (v. 2). The Lord Jesus saw the assured faith of the men who carried the paralytic and encouraged the young man to trust as well. But the Lord also saw the need of forgiveness.

"And, behold, certain of the scribes said in themselves: This man blasphemes" (v. 3). The scribes spent their lives copying Scripture, but many of them had no spiritual perception. These scribes assume that Jesus is just one more religious leader. This man expresses their contempt for the Lord Jesus. James warns against those who blaspheme the worthy name of Jesus (James 2:7).

9:1. For the verb to embark see Matt. 8:23 note.

For the word boat see Matt. 4:21 note.

The verb to cross over (διαπεράω) occurs twice in Matt. (9:1; 14:34).

9:2. For the word paralytic see Matt. 4:24 note. For palsy see ZPEB, "Palsy," IV, p. 587.

The word bed, pallet (κλίνη) occurs twice in Matt. (9:2, 6). It was a thin pad that could double as a stretcher.

The verb to have courage (θαρσέω) occurs 3 times in Matt. (9:2, 22; 14:27). See ISBE (1979), "Courage," I, p. 788. It is one of the cardinal virtues.

For the word child (τέκνον) see Matt. 2:18 note.

For the word sin see Matt. 1:21 note.

For the word forgive see Matt. 6:12 note.

9:3. For the word scribe see Matt. 2:4 note.

The verb to blaspheme (βλασφημέω) occurs 3 times in Matt. (9:3; 26:65; 27:39). People who did not believe in Him thought that He claimed divine prerogatives. For discussion see ISBE (1979), "Blaspheme, Blasphemy," I, pp. 521–22. See also the noun blasphemy, Matt. 12:31 note.

4 And Jesus knowing their thoughts said, Wherefore think ye evil in your hearts?

5 For whether is easier, to say, Thy sins be forgiven thee; or to say, Arise, and walk?

6 But that ye may know that the Son of man hath power on earth to forgive sins, (then saith he to the sick of the palsy,) Arise, take up thy bed, and go unto thine house.

7 And he arose, and departed to his house.

8 But when the multitudes saw it, they marvelled, and glorified God, which had given such power unto men.

•

"But Jesus, having known their thoughts, said: Why are you thinking evil in your hearts?" (v. 4). Scripture is very clear that Jesus had the divine attribute of omniscience. He knew, just as God the Father knows, the thoughts of every person. Now He is going to give these scribes a demonstration of His divine powers.

"For what is easier, to say: Your sins are forgiven, or to say: Rise up and be walking?" (v. 5). The Lord has caught them here. On a shallow level it is easier to say, "Your sins are forgiven," for who could tell? But if you say "Rise up and walk," the person must get up to prove it. On an exalted level only God can say, "Your sins are forgiven," but Christ had that power as well.

"But in order that you may know that the Son of man has authority to forgive sins—then he says to the paralytic: Arise, take up your bed and go into your house" (v. 6). The Lord proves His divine authority by instantly healing the paralytic. His command did it all.

"And he arose, and departed to his house" (v. 7). The relief and joy of the young man can be well imagined. But the stunned scribes had no answer to this miracle.

"But when the crowds saw it, they were afraid and glorified God, who had given such authority to men" (v. 8). The crowds had no perception of the deity of Christ, but they did see that Christ had authority that other men did not. Morris suggests that the word *afraid* means "awe-struck" (*Matt.*, p. 217).

9:4. The word *thought* (ἐνθύμησις) occurs twice in Matt. (9:4; 12:25).

9:5. The word *easy* (εὔκοπος) occurs twice in Matt. (9:5; 19:24).

9:6. For the phrase *Son of Man* see Matt. 8:20 note.

For the word *authority* see Matt. 7:29 note.

9 *And as Jesus passed forth from thence, he saw a man, named Matthew, sitting at the receipt of custom: and he saith unto him, Follow me. And he arose, and followed him.*
10 *And it came to pass, as Jesus sat at meat in the house, behold, many publicans and sinners came and sat down with him and his disciples.*
11 *And when the Pharisees saw it, they said unto his disciples, Why eateth your Master with publicans and sinners?*

II. Matthew Called. vv. 9–13 [Mark 2:13–17; Luke 5:27–32].

"And when Jesus went forth from there, he saw a man sitting at the tax office, called Matthew, and says to him: Follow me. And he arose and followed him" (v. 9). The Lord's divine authority transcended political authority. Interestingly, Luke alone adds, "and he left all things" (Luke 5:28). As a tax collector, Matthew had more "things" to leave than the other disciples, but he did so cheerfully.

"And it came to pass, while he was reclining at table in the house, behold also many tax collectors and sinners came and were reclining at table with Jesus and his disciples" (v. 10). Matthew gave a farewell banquet for his friends and colleagues and gave them the opportunity to meet Jesus. It may well have been done under a grape arbor in the garden in plain view of the street.

"And when the Pharisees saw it, they were saying to his disciples: Why is your teacher eating with the tax collectors and sinners?" (v. 11). Plainly "their

9:9. The word *tax office* (τελώνιον) occurs only here in Matt. and in the parallels (Mark 2:14; Luke 5:27) in the NT. It was probably of the nature of a toll booth along the Roman road that ran by the Sea of Galilee.

9:10. The verb *to recline at table* (ἀνάκειμαι) occurs 5 times in Matt. (9:10; 22:10, 11; 26:7, 20). In Roman times at a formal meal people leaned on the left elbow and ate with the right hand. For background see ISBE (1986), "Meals," III, pp. 291–92.

The verb *to recline at the table with* (συνανάκειμαι) occurs twice in Matt. (9:10; 14:9).

For the word *tax collector* see Matt. 5:46 note.

The word *sinner* (ἁμαρτωλός) occurs 5 times in Matt. (9:10, 11, 13; 11:19; 26:45). All mankind is sinful (Rom. 3:9–23), but God has provided salvation from sin in Christ (Rom. 6:13–23); whoever trusts in Christ for salvation shall be saved (Rom. 10:9–13). For further study see ZPEB, "Sinner," V, pp. 444–47; ISBE (1988), "Sin," IV, pp. 518–25; Harrison, ed., *The New Unger's Bible Dictionary*, "Sin," pp. 1198–99; Butler, ed., *Holman Bible Dictionary*, "Sin," pp. 1281–83. See also Matt. 1:21 note.

Sinners

I. Matthew invited sinners to meet Jesus. 9:10.

II. The Pharisees sneered at sinners. 9:11.

III. The Lord came to call sinners to repentance. 9:13.

IV. The Lord was known as a Friend of sinners. 11:19.

V. The Lord died for the sinners who slew Him. 26:45.

12 But when Jesus heard that, he said unto them, They that be whole need not a physician, but they that are sick.

13 But go ye and learn what that meaneth, I will have mercy, and not sacrifice: for I am not come to call the righteous, but sinners to repentance.

14 Then came to him the disciples of John, saying, Why do we and the Pharisees fast oft, but thy disciples fast not?

15 And Jesus said unto them, Can the children of the bridechamber mourn, as long as the bridegroom is with them? but the days will come, when the bridegroom shall be taken from them, and then shall they fast.

teacher" would never sully Himself by associating with such miserable sinners. How Jesus could be a "Friend of sinners" was beyond their comprehension.

"But when Jesus heard, he said, The ones who are strong have no need of a physician, but the ones who are sick" (v. 12). *But*, in contrast to the Pharisees, the Lord Jesus is the Good Physician, Who seeks the sick and the helpless.

"But go and learn what this is: I want mercy and not sacrifice; for I came not to call righteous ones but sinners" (v. 13, Hos. 6:6a). The OT had already revealed that God was seeking sinners for reconciliation (Hos. 6:1, 6). The Lord Jesus was seeking to save the lost (Matt. 18:11). That was wholly outside the thinking of the Pharisees.

III. John's Disciples Taught. vv. 14–17 [Mark 2:18–22; Luke 5:33–39].

"Then the disciples of John come to him, saying, Why are we and the Pharisees fasting many times, but your disciples are not fasting?" (v. 14). These disciples had heard John's tribute to the Lord (Matt. 3:11–12) and were sincerely puzzled by this apparent omission of piety in Jesus' disciples. The Lord uses this question to illuminate the great change that His coming would make in practice.

"And Jesus said to them, The sons of the wedding hall are not able to be mourning as long as the bridegroom is with them [are they?], but days will come when the bridegroom will be taken from them, and then they shall

9:12. The word *physician* (ἰατρός) occurs only here in Matt.

9:13. The verb *to learn* (μανθάνω) occurs 3 times in Matt. (9:13; 11:29; 24:32).

The word *mercy* (ἔλεος) occurs 3 times in Matt. (9:13; 12:7; 23:23).

The word *sacrifice* (θυσία) occurs twice in Matt. (9:13; 12:7).

For the word *righteous* see Matt. 1:19 note.

9:14. For the verb *to fast* see Matt. 4:2 note.

9:15. The word *wedding hall* (νυμφών) occurs only here in Matt.

The word *bridegroom* (νυμφίος) occurs 6 times in Matt. (9:15 [twice]; 25:1, 5, 6, 10).

16 No man putteth a piece of new cloth unto an old garment, for that which is put in to fill it up taketh from the garment, and the rent is made worse.

17 Neither do men put new wine into old bottles: else the bottles break, and the wine runneth out, and the bottles perish: but they put new wine into new bottles, and both are preserved.

18 While he spake these things unto them, behold, there came a certain ruler, and worshipped him, saying, My daughter is even now dead: but come and lay thy hand upon her, and she shall live.

fast" (v. 15). The Lord shows that fasting is not a matter of daily ritual as the Pharisees had made it, but a focusing of spiritual attention in times of need.

"But no one puts a patch of unfulled cloth upon an old garment; for the fullness of it takes away from the garment and the rent becomes worse" (v. 16). Newly woven cloth is soft and very flexible, unsuited for patching an old garment.

"Neither do they pour new wine into old wineskins; but if otherwise, the skins are rent and the wine pours out and the wineskins are destroyed; but they pour new wine into unused wineskins, and both are preserved" (v. 17). The new wineskins are supple enough to expand with the fermentation process. The Lord is making clear the fact that the new aspect of the kingdom that He is

9:16. The word *patch* (ἐπίβλημα) occurs only here in Matt.

The word *a piece of cloth* (ῥάκος) occurs only here in Matt.

The word *unfulled, new* (ἄγναφος) occurs only here in Matt. Fuller's earth was used to give body and strength to new cloth; without it, the cloth could be easily stretched. Today it is said to be Sanforized.

The word *rent* (σχίσμα) occurs only here in Matt.

9:17. The word *wine* (οἶνος) occurs 4 times in Matt. (9:17 [3 times]; 27:34). For discussion see ZPEB, "Wine," V, pp. 935–38; ISBE (1988), "Wine," IV, pp. 1068–72.

The word *wineskin* (ἀσκός) occurs 4 times in this verse only in Matt.

The verb *to preserve* (συντηρέω) occurs here only in Matt.

9:18. The word *ruler* (ἄρχων) occurs 5 times in Matt. (9:18, 23, 34; 12:24; 20:25).

The word *daughter* (θυγάτηρ) occurs 8 times in Matt. (9:18, 22; 10:35, 37; 14:6; 15:22, 28; 21:5).

For the verb *to worship* see Matt. 2:2 note.

For the verb *to die* see Matt. 2:19 note.

The verb *to put upon* (ἐπιτίθημι) occurs 7 times in Matt. (9:18; 19:13, 15; 21:7; 23:4; 27:29, 37).

For the verb *to live* see Matt. 4:4 note.

For further discussion on Jairus see ZPEB, "Jairus," III, p. 390; ISBE (1982), "Jairus," II, p. 957; *Who's Who in the Bible*, "Jairus," p.181.

19 And Jesus arose, and followed him, and so did his disciples.
20 And, behold, a woman, which was diseased with an issue of blood twelve years, came behind him, and touched the hem of his garment:
21 For she said within herself, If I may but touch his garment, I shall be whole.
22 But Jesus turned him about, and when he saw her, he said, Daughter, be of good comfort; thy faith hath made thee whole. And the woman was made whole from that hour.

bringing in is not a mere "patch" on the old, but a new advent of power and blessing that believers will later call the church age.

IV. The Raising of Jairus's Daughter. vv. 18–26.

"While he was speaking these things, behold, a ruler came and worshiped him, saying, My daughter is at the point of death, but come, put your hand upon her, and she shall live" (v. 18). He was Jairus, a ruler of a synagogue (Mark 5:22). Luke adds the fact that the daughter was about twelve years old (Luke 8:42). The language the ruler used indicates that she was either at the point of death or already dead. It was an extreme situation.

"And Jesus arose, and his disciples, and followed him" (v. 19). The Lord Jesus was always willing to help those in need, as He still is!

"And, behold, a woman who had a hemorrhage for twelve years came behind and touched the fringe of his garment" (v. 20). She did not want to attract attention to herself, but she did believe in His healing power. Luke, the physician, noted that she had spent all her livelihood on physicians and could not be healed (Luke 8:43).

"For she was saying in herself, If I only touch his garment I shall be healed" (v. 21). She had genuine faith in the power of the Lord Jesus.

"But when Jesus turned and saw her, he said, Have courage, daughter; your faith has healed you. And the woman was healed from that hour" (v. 22). The fact that she had an issue of blood would have made her religiously unclean. She was probably used to slipping away from people lest they avoid her. The Lord deliberately encouraged her. It is moving to see

---

9:20. The word *fringe* (κράσπεδον) occurs 3 times in Matt. (9:20; 14:36; 23:5).

For the number 12 see Introduction, "Numbers," p. xxii.

9:21. For the verb *to touch* see Matt. 8:3 note.

The verb *to save* (σώζω) often has the connotation of *to heal* (Acts 4:9; 14:9).

9:22. For the verb *to have courage* see Matt. 9:2 note.

23 And when Jesus came into the ruler's house, and saw the minstrels and the people making a noise,
24 He said unto them, Give place: for the maid is not dead, but sleepeth. And they laughed him to scorn.
25 But when the people were put forth, he went in, and took her by the hand, and the maid arose.
26 And the fame hereof went abroad into all that land.
27 And when Jesus departed thence, two blind men followed him, crying, and saying, Thou son of David, have mercy on us.

Jesus helping one believer on the way to helping another. The thronging crowd was always a pressure on Him, but He was always in charge and able to help all. Edersheim notes that it was probably the fringe of the *tallith* that she touched (*Life and Times*, I, p. 626). It was a kind of prayer shawl that is still worn by Orthodox Jews.

"And when Jesus entered the house of the ruler and saw the flute players and the crowd screaming in uproar, he said, Make room, for the girl did not die, but is sleeping; and they were jeering at him" (vv. 23–24). In the East there is a much more outward manifestation of grief at funerals than people in the West would show. The shrill flutes and the screams of wailing women would let the whole neighborhood know that there had been a death in the family.

"But when the crowd was put out, he went in and grasped her hand, and the girl was raised up" (v. 25). This was an instantaneous, miraculous restoration to life. When the professional mourners saw her, they probably dropped their flutes!

"And the fame of it went forth into all that land" (v. 26). That miracle was "news" that would spread like wildfire. The family would never tire of telling people what the Lord Jesus had done.

9:23. The word *flute player* (αὐλητής) occurs only here in Matt.

The verb *to scream in uproar* (θορυβέω) occurs only here in Matt. It is regularly used for the wailing and screaming of professional mourners.

9:24. For the verb *to make room* see Matt. 2:12 note.

The word *girl* (κοράσιον) occurs 3 times in Matt. (9:24, 25; 14:11).

The verb *to jeer at, laugh at* (καταγελάω) occurs only here in Matt.

9:25. The verb *to grasp, lay hold of* (κρατέω) occurs 12 times in Matt. (9:25; 12:11; 14:3; 18:28; 21:46; 22:6; 26:4, 48, 50, 55, 57; 28:9).

9:26. The word *fame, report* (φήμη) occurs only here in Matt.

9:27. For the title *Son of David* see Matt. 1:1 note.

The word *blind* (τυφλός) occurs 17 times in Matt. (9:27, 28; 11:5; 12:22; 15:14 [4 times], 30, 31; 20:30; 21:14; 23:16, 17, 19, 24, 26).

28 And when he was come into the house, the blind men came to him: and Jesus saith unto them, Believe ye that I am able to do this? They said unto him, Yea, Lord.
29 Then touched he their eyes, saying, According to your faith be it unto you.
30 And their eyes were opened; and Jesus straitly charged them, saying, See that no man know it.
31 But they, when they were departed, spread abroad his fame in all that country.
32 As they went out, behold, they brought to him a dumb man possessed with a devil.

V. Other Miracles of Deliverance. vv. 27–34.

"And when Jesus went away from there, two blind men followed him, crying and saying, Son of David, have mercy on us" (v. 27). They called upon Him as the expected Messiah, the great Servant of the Lord, who was to open blind eyes (Isa. 35:5; 42:1–7).

"And when he came into the house, the blind men came to him, and Jesus says to them: Are you believing that I am able to do this? They say to him, Yes, Lord" (v. 28). Matthew uses the article *the house*. Morris suggests that it was "the house where people had given him lodging" (*Matt.*, p. 234). For the blind men it was a matter not of religious enthusiasm but of genuine faith in the Lord.

"Then he touched their eyes, saying, According to your faith, let it come to pass for you" (v. 29). He spoke the divine promise and they believed.

"And their eyes were opened, and Jesus sternly warned them, saying, See that no man knows" (v. 30). The Lord loved helping people, but He desired to keep the worldly excitement down.

"But they, when they had gone out, spread it abroad in that whole land" (v. 31). They meant well, but their actions raised crowds of curiosity seekers.

"But while they were going out, behold, they brought to him a dumb man who was demon possessed" (v. 32). In this case the man's malady was caused by a demon rather than a physical affliction.

9:28. For the verb *believe* see Matt. 8:13 note.

9:29. For the word *faith* see Matt. 8:10 note.

9:30. The verb *to sternly warn* (ἐμβριμάομαι) occurs only here in Matt.

9:31. The verb *to spread abroad* (διαφημίζω) occurs twice in Matt. (9:31; 28:15).

9:32. The word *dumb* (κωφός) occurs 7 times in Matt. (9:32, 33; 11:5; 12:22 [twice]; 15:30, 31).

33 And when the devil was cast out, the dumb spake: and the multitudes marvelled, saying, It was never so seen in Israel.
34 But the Pharisees said, He casteth out devils through the prince of the devils.
35 And Jesus went about all the cities and villages, teaching in their synagogues, and preaching the gospel of the kingdom, and healing every sickness and every disease among the people.

"And when the demon was cast out, the dumb man spoke. And the crowds marveled, saying, It never appeared thus in Israel" (v. 33). There was no record of such a series of miracles in the history of the people.

"But the Pharisees were saying, By the ruler of the demons he casts out demons" (v. 34). Thus, they continued attributing the work of God to the Devil.

VI. The Compassion of Jesus. vv. 35–38.

"And Jesus was going around all the cities and villages, teaching in their synagogues, and preaching the gospel of the kingdom, and healing every sickness and every weakness" (v. 35). The imperfect tense *was going* emphasizes the continuous nature of Jesus' preaching and healing. He was curing not only every disease but every disability as well. There was no sickness that He could not cure, and there was no deformity that He could not make whole.

"But when he saw the crowds, he was moved with compassion for them, because they were harassed and thrown down as sheep not having a

---

9:34. For the word *ruler* see Matt. 9:18 note.

9:35. For the verb *to go around* see Matt. 4:23 note. Robertson holds that this is the third tour of Galilee (extending to 11:1; see *A Harmony of the Gospels*, p. 78).

The word *village* (κώμη) occurs 4 times in Matt. (9:35; 10:11; 14:15; 21:2).

For the words *sickness* and *weakness* see Matt. 4:23 notes.

9:36. The verb *to be moved with compassion* (σπλαγχνίζομαι) occurs 5 times in Matt. (9:36; 14:14; 15:32; 18:27; 20:34). God is compassionate (Exod. 34:6; Deut. 30:3; Ps. 78:38; Jer. 12:15; Lam. 3:22–23); the Lord is full of compassion (James 5:11, a cognate form). Jesus manifested this attribute of God. For discussion see Elwell, ed., *Evangelical Dictionary of Biblical Theology*, "Compassion," p. 109; ZPEB, "Compassion," I, p. 932; ISBE (1979), "Compassion," I, p. 755.

The verb *to harass* (σκύλλω) occurs only here in Matt. It originally meant *to flay, skin*.

The verb *to throw down* (ῥίπτω) occurs 3 times in Matt. (9:36; 15:30; 27:5).

For the word *sheep* see Matt. 7:15 note.

The word *shepherd* (ποιμήν) occurs 3 times in Matt. (9:36; 25:32; 26:31). The image of a shepherd is a powerful picture of the loving care of God for His people (Ps. 23:1; Isa. 40:11; John 10:1–16; Heb. 13:20; I Pet. 2:25). The Lord Jesus referred to His earthly people as "the lost sheep of the house of Israel" (Matt. 15:24). It is as the slain Lamb that

36 But when he saw the multitudes, he was moved with compassion on them, because they fainted, and were scattered abroad, as sheep having no shepherd.
37 Then saith he unto his disciples, The harvest truly is plenteous, but the labourers are few;
38 Pray ye therefore the Lord of the harvest, that he will send forth labourers into his harvest.

shepherd" (v. 36). He understood the constant troubles, annoyances, and heartaches that people endure. He is the good Shepherd, Who gives His life for the sheep (John 10:11).

"Then he says to his disciples: The harvest indeed is great, but the workers are few" (v. 37). The harvest is the sum total of the world's population, divided into wheat and weeds (Matt. 13:24–30), sheep and goats (Matt. 25:31–46). The world needs to hear the message of salvation.

"Pray therefore the Lord of the harvest that he would send out workers into his harvest" (v. 38). The most important single thing for believers to do is to pray to the Lord of the harvest. Busywork does not win souls. The power of God alone can save souls. One of the characteristics of God is that He is a Worker, in Creation (Gen. 2:7ff.) and in Redemption (John 5:17). Believers are to work heartily for the Lord (Eph. 6:5; Col. 3:22–24). It is a unique responsibility to ask the Lord of all to call and send out workers for the harvest. No one can just go; the Lord must call him. No one can reap; the Lord must change the heart. But we can pray; and God is listening.

---

the great Shepherd leads His people to the celestial fountains of living water (Rev. 7:17). For further discussion see Ryken, Wilhoit, and Longman, *Dictionary of Biblical Imagery*, "Sheep, Shepherd," pp. 782–85; ZPEB, "Shepherd," V, pp. 397–98; ISBE (1988), "Sheep, Shepherd," IV, pp. 463–65.

9:37. The word *harvest* (θερισμός) occurs 6 times in Matt. (9:37, 38 [twice]; 13:20 [twice], 39).

The word *worker, laborer* (ἐργάτης) occurs 6 times in Matt. (9:37, 38; 10:10; 20:1, 2, 8). For discussion see Ryken, Wilhoit, and Longman, *Dictionary of Biblical Imagery*, "Work, Worker," pp. 965–67; ISBE (1988), "Work," IV, pp. 1107–11; ZPEB, "Works of God," V, pp. 962–63.

9:38. This verb *to ask, pray* (δέομαι) occurs only here in Matt. See Matt. 5:44 note for the more frequent verb *to pray*.

Practical Applications from Matthew 9

1. The spiritual well-being of a person is vastly more important than the physical well-being (v. 2). "The days of our years are threescore years and ten; and if by reason of strength they be fourscore years, yet is their strength labor and sorrow; for it is soon cut off, and we fly away" (Ps. 90:10).

2. The claims of Christ transcend any human occupation (v. 9). Paul could say, "I press toward the mark for the prize of the high calling of God in Christ Jesus" (Phil. 3:14).

3. The Lord Jesus deliberately associated with tax collectors and sinners (v. 11). "For the Son of man came to seek and to save that which was lost" (Luke 19:10).

4. The Lord Jesus came to call sinners to repentance (v. 13). Paul taught that "the goodness of God leads you to repentance" (Rom. 2:4b).

5. It is a good thing to rejoice in the Lord (v. 15). "Rejoice in the Lord, ye righteous; and give thanks at the remembrance of his holiness" (Ps. 97:12).

6. Faith in the Lord Jesus is a life-transforming power (v. 22). Paul prayed "that Christ may dwell in your hearts by faith; that you . . . may be able . . . to know the love of Christ" (Eph. 3:17–19).

7. It is good to seek mercy from the Lord (v. 27). David sang, "Surely goodness and mercy shall follow me all the days of my life: and I will dwell in the house of the Lord for ever" (Ps. 23:6).

8. The Lord Jesus was moved with compassion for needy people (v. 36). Believers should also show compassion for others ("Having compassion one of another," I Pet. 3:8; Jude 22).

9. Believers should pray that the Lord send forth laborers into His harvest (v. 38). Paul asked believers, "Continue in prayer . . . praying also for us, that God would open to us a door of utterance, to speak the mystery of Christ" (Col. 4:2–3).

Prayer

O Lord of the Harvest, send forth laborers to reap the harvest of souls for You. Give Your people grace to reach others with the good news of salvation in Christ. Cause Your people to pray and give and go that the harvest may be great to Your eternal glory. In Jesus' name. Amen.

MATTHEW 10

Mission of the Apostles

Persons

Jesus
Simon Peter
Andrew
James of Zebedee
John
Philip
Bartholomew
Thomas

Matthew
James son of Alphaeus
Lebbaeus [Thaddaeus]
Simon the Canaanite
Judas Iscariot
The Spirit
The Father

Persons referred to

Gentiles
Samaritans
The sick
Lepers
The dead
Workman
Governors
Kings
Brother
Father
Child

Disciples
Master
Servant
Lord
Daughter
Mother
Daughter-in-law
Mother-in-law
Prophet
A righteous man
Little ones

Places mentioned

Sodom
Gomorrha

Cities of Israel
Hell

Doctrines taught

Lost sheep
The kingdom of heaven
Peace

Day of Judgment
Wisdom

1 *And when he had called unto him his twelve disciples, he gave them power against unclean spirits, to cast them out, and to heal all manner of sickness and all manner of disease.*

2 *Now the names of the twelve apostles are these; The first, Simon, who is called Peter, and Andrew his brother; James the son of Zebedee, and John his brother;*

3 *Philip, and Bartholomew; Thomas, and Matthew the publican; James the son of Alphaeus, and Lebbaeus, whose surname was Thaddaeus;*

4 *Simon the Canaanite, and Judas Iscariot, who also betrayed him.*

Matthew 10 Exposition

I. The Choice of the Apostles. vv. 1–4 [Mark 6:7; Luke 9:1–3].

"And when he had called his twelve disciples, he gave them authority over unclean spirits so as to cast them out, and to heal every sickness and every weakness" (v. 1). The Lord Jesus delegated authority to the apostles to have a ministry of deliverance for their suffering people. This is preparation for the NT church. The Lord is training them for future service.

"But the names of the twelve apostles are these: First, Simon, the one called Peter, and Andrew his brother, and James, the one of Zebedee, and John his brother, Philip and Bartholomew, Thomas and Matthew the tax collector, James the one of Alphaeus and Thaddaeus, Simon the Canaanite, and Judas Iscariot, the one who also betrayed him" (vv. 2–4). The Lord chose ordinary men but gave them a graduate program of instruction

---

10:1. For the word *disciple* see Matt. 5:1 note.

For the word *authority* see Matt. 7:29 note.

For the verb *to heal* see Matt. 4:23 note.

10:2. The word *apostle* (ἀπόστολος) occurs only here in Matt., but 80 times in the NT. The basic meaning is *one sent with a commission* (Arndt and Gingrich, p. 99). There are only 3 others who are ranked with the Twelve: Paul (Rom. 1:1), Barnabas (Acts 14:14), and James, the Lord's brother (Gal. 1:19). Any others were probably simple messengers. Their great importance lay in the fact that they were witnesses of Christ's resurrection (Acts 1:21–22). They were the nucleus of the church (Acts 2:14; 4:33; 5:12; 6:2; Gal. 2:9). A. T. Robertson suggests that there were 3 groups of 4 apostles in each group. In the 4 lists of apostles (Matt. 10:2ff.; Mark 3:16f.; Luke 6:14f.; Acts 1:13f.) Peter is always first; Andrew, James, and John are next, but in random order; Philip is always number 5, but Bartholomew, Matthew, and Thomas are the next 3, but in random order; James the son of Alphaeus is always number 9, but Thaddaeus and Simon the Canaanite are in random order; Judas is always last (*A Harmony of the Gospels*, p. 271). For further discussion see Elwell, ed., *Evangelical Dictionary of Biblical Theology*, "Apostle," pp. 33–35; ZPEB, "Apostle," I, pp. 216–20; ISBE (1979), "Apostle," I, pp. 192–95; and each individual name; *Who's Who in the Bible*, "Peter," pp. 348–55, and so forth; Alexander Whyte, *Bible Characters*, "Peter," IV, pp. 46–56, "John," pp. 57ff., "Matthew," pp. 63ff.

5 These twelve Jesus sent forth, and commanded them, saying, Go not into the way of the Gentiles, and into any city of the Samaritans enter ye not:
6 But go rather to the lost sheep of the house of Israel.
7 And as ye go, preach, saying, The kingdom of heaven is at hand.

unparalleled in the history of education. Matthew does not hide the fact that he was "the tax collector," but now he is much more. Glasscock notes that Matthew and Simon the Zealot (Luke 6:15) would have been political enemies before this, but now they are brothers in the Lord (*Matt.*, p. 221).

II. The Charge to the Apostles. vv. 5–42 [Mark 6:7–11; Luke 9:1–5].

"These twelve Jesus sent forth, commanding them, saying, Go not into the way of Gentiles, and enter not into a city of the Samaritans, but rather go to the lost sheep of the house of Israel" (vv. 5–6). Although Mark and Luke do not present this material as a single discourse, they do provide parallels to some of the teaching. The good news had to go to Israel first because the Lord is the "Redeemer the Holy One of Israel" (Isa. 54:5). It is only after they have heard that the invitation can be given, "Ho, every one that thirsteth, come ye to the waters" (Isa. 55:1a). It is significant that even in Israel the sheep are "lost." "As it is written, There is none righteous, no, not one" (Rom. 3:10; Ps. 36:1).

"But while you are going, keep on preaching, saying, The kingdom of the heavens has drawn near" (v. 7). The King is among His people.

10:4. *Judas Iscariot* is mentioned 5 times in Matt. (10:4; 26:14, 25, 47; 27:3). For further discussion see ZPEB, "Judas Iscariot," III, p. 732; ISBE (1982), "Judas Iscariot," II, pp. 1151–53; Harrison, ed., *The New Unger's Bible Dictionary*, "Judas Iscariot," pp. 720–21; *Who's Who in the Bible*, "Judas Iscariot," pp. 258–59.

For the verb *to betray* see Matt. 4:12 note.

10:5. The verb *to send* [with a commission] (ἀποστέλλω) occurs 22 times in Matt. (2:16; 8:31; 10:5, 16, 40; 11:10; 13:41; 14:35; 15:24; 20:2; 21:1, 3, 34, 36, 37; 22:3, 4, 16; 23:34, 37; 24:31; 27:19).

For the word *Gentile* see Matt. 4:15 note.

The word *Samaritan* occurs only here in Matt.

10:6. For the word *sheep* see Matt. 7:15 note.

For the verb *to be lost, destroyed,* see Matt. 2:13 note.

10:7. For the verb *to preach* see Matt. 3:1 note.

For the word *kingdom* see Matt. 3:2 note.

For the verb *to draw near* see Matt. 3:2 note.

8 Heal the sick, cleanse the lepers, raise the dead, cast out devils: freely ye have received, freely give.
9 Provide neither gold, nor silver, nor brass in your purses,
10 Nor scrip for your journey, neither two coats, neither shoes, nor yet staves: for the workman is worthy of his meat.

"Keep on healing sick people; keep on raising dead people; keep on cleansing lepers; keep on casting out demons; freely you received; freely give" (v. 8). The present tense verbs emphasize the constant power that the Lord imparted to the apostolic ministry.

"Do not acquire gold, or silver, or copper in your belts, nor a bag for the way, neither two tunics, nor sandals, nor a staff; for the worker is worthy of his food" (vv. 9–10). In the parallel accounts Mark mentions *copper* with the plain meaning of *money* (Mark 6:8); Luke mentions *silver*, again meaning *money* (Luke 9:3), but Matthew gives the exact phrase that the Lord used. Being a tax collector, he would have an ear for precise terms of money, and he was the only Synoptic Gospel writer present on the occasion. The point that the Lord is driving home is that the work of the ministry is not accomplished by money but by the power of God. They

10:8. The verb *to be sick* (ἀσθενέω) occurs 3 times in Matt. (10:8; 25:36, 39). For discussion see ISBE (1988), "Sick," IV, pp. 498–99.

For the verb *to heal* see Matt. 4:23 note.

10:9. The verb *to acquire* (κτάομαι) occurs only here in Matt.

The word *belt, purse* (ζώνη) occurs twice in Matt. (3:4; 10:9). Belts were like sashes and could be used to hold money.

For the word *gold* see Matt. 2:11 note.

The word *silver* (ἀργύριον) occurs only here in Matt.

The word *copper* (χαλκός) occurs only here in Matt.

10:10. The word *bag* (πήρα) occurs only here in Matt. It could refer to a shepherd's bag, a traveler's bag, or even a beggar's bag (Arndt and Gingrich, p. 662).

For the word *tunic* see Matt. 5:40 note.

For the word *sandal* see Matt. 3:11 note.

The word *staff* (ῥάβδος) occurs only here in Matt.

For the word *worker* see Matt. 9:37 note.

For the word *food* see Matt. 3:4 note.

For the word *worthy* see Matt. 3:11 note.

Worthy Workmen

    I. Workman for the Lord is worthy of food. 10:10.

    II. Inquire who is worthy: seek worthy friends. 10:11.

    III. If a household is worthy, add your peace to it. 10:13.

11 And into whatsoever city or town ye shall enter, enquire who in it is worthy; and there abide till ye go thence.
12 And when ye come into an house, salute it.
13 And if the house be worthy, let your peace come upon it: but if it be not worthy, let your peace return to you.
14 And whosoever shall not receive you, nor hear your words, when ye depart out of that house or city, shake off the dust of your feet.

did not have to go out and *acquire* these things; just go, and the Lord would provide what they needed. There is no implication that they could not take a staff if they already had one. There is great stress on the word *worthy* in this context; it occurs seven times (vv. 10, 11, 13 [twice], 37 [twice], 38). To serve the Lord is a high and holy privilege.

"And into whatever city or town you enter, inquire who in it is worthy; and there abide until you go forth" (v. 11). The disciples were not to frequent the inns, which were often notorious, but rather find honest citizens and begin the testimony with them.

"But when you enter into a house, salute it; and if the house is worthy, let your peace come upon it, but if it is not worthy, let your peace return to you" (vv. 12–13). The ancient salutation was *Peace!* (*Shalom*), which is still the traditional greeting in the Middle East (*Salem* in Arabic). This is precedent for praying for a house, dedicating it to the Lord. It is the responsibility of the believer to bring peace to a place. But if the place is unworthy, you do not lose your peace. Let it abide in your heart.

"And whoever shall not receive you, nor hear your words, whenever you go out of that house or city, shake off the dust of your feet" (v. 14). The

---

IV. If it is unworthy, let your peace return [do not lose it].

V. If one loves his father more than Me, he is not worthy. 10:37.

VI. If he loves a son more than Me, he is not worthy. 10:37.

VII. He that takes not his cross is not worthy of Me. 10:38.

10:11. For the verb *to inquire* see Matt. 2:8 note.

The verb *to abide, remain* (μένω) occurs 3 times in Matt. (10:11; 11:23; 26:38). It is one of the great words in John (15:4–16).

10:12. For the verb *to salute, greet* see Matt. 5:47 note.

10:13. The word *peace* (εἰρήνη) occurs 4 times in Matt. (10:13 [twice], 34 [twice]).

The verb *to return, be converted* (ἐπιστρέφω) occurs 4 times in Matt. (10:13; 12:44; 13:15; 24:18).

10:14. The verb *to receive, take* (δέχομαι) occurs 10 times in Matt. (10:14, 40 [4 times], 41 [twice]; 11:14; 18:5 [twice]).

15 Verily I say unto you, It shall be more tolerable for the land of Sodom and Gomorrha in the day of judgment, than for that city.
16 Behold, I send you forth as sheep in the midst of wolves: be ye therefore wise as serpents, and harmless as doves.
17 But beware of men: for they will deliver you up to the councils, and they will scourge you in their synagogues;

shaking off of the dust was a "violent gesture of disfavor" (A. T. Robertson, *Word Pictures*, I, p. 80). The implication is that God's wrath will rest upon that place and the believer would not want one speck of dust from that place clinging to him!

"Truly I say to you, It shall be more tolerable for the land of Sodom and Gomorrah in the day of judgment than for that city" (v. 15). Those ancient people had less light, and hence less responsibility, than contemporary people. Yet God judged them sternly (Gen. 19:1–28).

"Behold, I am sending you as sheep in the midst of wolves; be therefore wise as snakes and innocent as doves" (v. 16). The Lord uses characteristics of well-known animals to teach spiritual truth. Believers are not to be predators, but they must be wary of those who would harm them. The phrase *in the midst* shows that they are surrounded by enemies who desire to harm them. Their only protection is the Lord. That is why David wrote, "The Lord is my shepherd; I shall not want" (Ps. 23:1). He also expanded the idea, "The Lord is my rock, and my fortress, and my deliverer;

The verb *to shake off* (ἐκτινάσσω) occurs only here in Matt.

The word *dust* (κονιορτός) occurs only here in Matt.

10:15. The word *tolerable* (ἀνέκτος) occurs 3 times in Matt. (10:15; 11:22, 24).

The phrase *day of judgment* is a recurring theme in Scripture (Matt. 10:15; 11:22, 24; 12:36; Mark 6:11; II Pet. 2:9; 3:7; I John 4:17). *Day of wrath* is a parallel phrase (Job 21:30; Prov. 11:4; Zeph. 1:15; Rom. 2:5). For further discussion see Ryken, Wilhoit, and Longman, *Dictionary of Biblical Imagery*, "Judgment," pp. 470–74; ISBE (1982), "Judgment, Last," II, pp. 1162–63; ZPEB, "Judging, Judgment," III, pp. 758–60; Douglas and Tenney, eds., *The New International Dictionary of the Bible*, "Judgment," pp. 558–59.

10:16. For the words *sheep* and *wolf* see Matt. 7:15 note.

For the word *snake* see Matt. 7:10 note.

The word *innocent* (ἀκέραιος) occurs only here in Matt. It means lit. *unmixed*. The servant of the Lord needs single-minded devotion to God.

For the word *dove* see Matt. 3:16 note.

10:17. For the verb *to beware* see Matt. 6:1 note.

For the verb *to betray, deliver up* see Matt. 4:12 note.

For the word *Sanhedrin, council* see Matt. 5:22 note.

For the word *synagogue* see Matt. 4:23 note.

18 And ye shall be brought before governors and kings for my sake, for a testimony against them and the Gentiles.
19 But when they deliver you up, take no thought how or what ye shall speak: for it shall be given you in that same hour what ye shall speak.
20 For it is not ye that speak, but the Spirit of your Father which speaketh in you.

my God, my strength, in whom I will trust; my buckler, and the horn of my salvation, and my high tower. I will call upon the Lord, who is worthy to be praised: so shall I be saved from mine enemies" (Ps. 18:2–3).

"But beware of men: for they will deliver you to councils and in their synagogues they will scourge you" (v. 17). There were local councils (courts of justice) as well as the supreme Sanhedrin. Synagogues were, and are, places of assembly as well as of worship.

"And you shall be brought before governors and kings on account of me for a testimony to them and to the Gentiles" (v. 18). This prophecy was fulfilled literally to the Twelve (Acts 4:1ff.) as well as to Paul (Acts 23:1ff.; 26:1ff.). But the warning is to all believers to the end of time.

"But whenever they deliver you up, do not be anxious about how or what you shall speak, for it shall be given to you in that hour what you should speak" (v. 19). No believer must write out a speech ahead of time. When persecution comes, the Spirit of God will impart to the believer what he needs to say for the Lord.

"For it is not you who are speaking, but the Spirit of your Father who is speaking in you" (v. 20). This is a precious promise of support in times of persecution. (It is not, however, a promise for lazy preachers about sermon

The verb *to scourge, whip* (μαστιγόω) occurs 3 times in Matt. (10:17; 20:19; 23:34). For background see ZPEB, "Scourge," V, pp. 297–98.

10:18. For the word *governor* see Matt. 2:6 note.

For the word *king* see Matt. 1:6 note.

10:19. For the verb *to be anxious* see Matt. 6:25 note.

10:20. For the word *father* see Matt. 2:22 note.

For the *Holy Spirit* see Matt. 1:18 note.

Although the word *trinity* is not found in Scripture, the teaching that there are three persons who make up the divine being is. The loving relationship between the Father, the Son, and the Spirit is the foundation for our salvation. If God were a monistic (block) being, there would be no reason for Him to change by creating other beings, but if the loving fellowship between the three Persons is eternal, then it is logical for God to create other beings to share that loving relationship. For further discussion see Packer, *Knowing God*, pp. 57ff.; Guthrie, *New Testament Theology*, pp. 111–15; Bavinck, *The Doctrine of God*, pp. 255ff.; St. Augustine, *On the Trinity*, in *The Basic Writings of St. Augustine*, II,

21 And the brother shall deliver up the brother to death, and the father the child: and the children shall rise up against their parents, and cause them to be put to death.
22 And ye shall be hated of all men for my name's sake: but he that endureth to the end shall be saved.
23 But when they persecute you in this city, flee ye into another: for verily I say unto you, Ye shall not have gone over the cities of Israel, till the Son of man be come.

preparation!) The Lord Jesus speaks of His Father and of the Spirit of God, Who empower the testimony of faithful believers. The doctrine of the Trinity is assumed here, as it is throughout the NT (Matt. 1:20; 3:16–17; 28:19; John 14:16–18; 15:26; 16:7–10; Acts 1:7–8; Rom. 1:3–4; 8:3–4; II Cor. 13:14; Gal. 4:4–6; Titus 3:4–6; I Pet. 1:2; I John 4:13–14; Jude 20–21; Rev. 3:21–22).

"And brother shall betray brother to death, and a father a child, and children shall rise up against their parents, and shall cause them to be put to death" (v. 21). Religious fanaticism against the truth will be stronger than family ties.

"And you shall be hated by all on account of my name; but the one who endures to the end shall be saved" (v. 22). Believers must learn how to endure the hatred of the world. "Whoever wishes to be a friend of the world is an enemy of God" (James 4:4b). *The end* refers to the end of the persecution, the end of the believer's life, or the end of the age.

"But whenever they persecute you in this city, flee into the other; for truly I say to you, you shall not complete the cities of Israel until the Son of

pp. 667ff.; ZPEB, "Trinity," V, pp. 822–24; ISBE (1988), "Trinity," IV, pp. 914–21; Harrison, ed., *Baker's Dictionary of Theology*, "Trinity," pp. 531–32.

10:21. The verb *to kill, cause to be put to death* (θανατόω) occurs 3 times in Matt. (10:21; 26:59; 27:1).

For the word *brother* see Matt. 1:2 note.

For the word *child* see Matt. 2:18 note.

The word *parent* (γονεύς) occurs only here in Matt.

10:22. For the verb *to hate* see Matt. 5:43 note.

The verb *to endure* (ὑπομένω) occurs twice in Matt. (10:22; 24:13).

The word *end* (τέλος) occurs 6 times in Matt. (10:22; 17:25; 24:6, 13, 14; 26:58).

For the verb *to save* see Matt. 1:21 note.

10:23. For the verb *to persecute* see Matt. 5:10 note.

For the verb *to flee* see Matt. 2:13 note.

24 The disciple is not above his master, nor the servant above his lord.
25 It is enough for the disciple that he be as his master, and the servant as his lord. If they have called the master of the house Beelzebub, how much more shall they call them of his household?

man comes" (v. 23). The word *other* implies "the other of a different kind." The believer does not have to stay and be martyred; he can flee to a different kind of place that will give better heed to the truth. "Jesus calls his followers to bravery but not foolishness" (Blomberg, *Matt.*, p. 176). The actions of the apostle Paul certainly illustrate the application of this directive (Acts 9:22–25; 14:19–20; 16:22–40; 17:10; 19:21–20:1). Expositors have seen a variety of applications in this verse. Some think it refers to the Lord rejoining the disciples at the end of the journey; others hold it refers to His coming judgment on Jerusalem; others hold that it refers to the ministry during the Tribulation period and the eschatological judgment (see Broadus, *Matt.*, pp. 227f.; Morris, *Matt.*, pp. 257f.; Walvoord, *Matt.*).

"A disciple is not above the teacher; neither is a slave above his lord" (v. 24). If the Lord Jesus is to be slain for His people, the disciples ought not think that they will have it easy. Even in the OT prophecies the Lord Jesus is called Lord (Ps. 110:1–5).

"It is enough for the disciple that he be as his teacher and the slave as his Lord. If they called the lord of the house Beelzeboul, how much rather

---

For the word *other* see Matt. 6:24 note.

10:24. For the word *disciple* see Matt. 5:1 note.

For the word *teacher* see Matt. 8:19 note.

For the word *slave* see Matt. 8:9 note.

For the word *Lord* see Matt. 1:20 note.

10:25. The word *master of the house* (οἰκοδεσπότης) occurs 7 times in Matt. (10:25; 13:27, 52; 20:1, 11; 21:33; 24:43).

The word *member of a household* (οἰκιακός) occurs only here and in v. 36 in the NT.

The name *Beelzebul* (βεελζεβούλ) occurs 3 times in Matt. (10:25; 12:24, 27). The OT identifies Baalzebub as the god of Ekron, a Philistine city (II Kings 1:2–6). For background see ZPEB, "Beelzebub," I, pp. 505–6; ISBE (1979), "Beelzebul," I, pp. 447–48; Elwell, ed., *Evangelical Dictionary of Biblical Theology*, "Gods and Goddesses," Baalzebub, p. 302; Van Der Toorn, Becking, and Van Der Horst, *Dictionary of Deities and Demons in the Bible*, "Baal Zebub," pp. 154–56.

10:26. For the verb *to hide* see Matt. 8:24 note.

The verb *to reveal* (ἀποκαλύπτω) occurs 4 times in Matt. (10:26; 11:25, 27; 16:17).

For the word *secret* see Matt. 6:4 note.

26 *Fear them not therefore: for there is nothing covered, that shall not be revealed; and hid, that shall not be known.*
27 *What I tell you in darkness, that speak ye in light: and what ye hear in the ear, that preach ye upon the housetops.*
28 *And fear not them which kill the body, but are not able to kill the soul: but rather fear him which is able to destroy both soul and body in hell.*

those of his household" (v. 25). *Beelzeboul* is Hebrew for "lord of dung." Some manuscripts have *Beelzebub*, "lord of flies." Both phrases were rabbinic terms for idols or for Satan. These adversaries were scraping the bottom of the barrel for insults to heap upon the Lord Jesus. It is no surprise that they pour contempt on His followers. The Pharisees will later charge the Lord with casting out demons by the ruler of demons (Matt. 12:24).

"Therefore fear them not; for nothing has been hidden that shall not be revealed, or secret which shall not be made known" (v. 26). In the life to come the Lord will lift the veil, and we will know the true nature of every person. The Lord's illustration of the rich man and Lazarus revealed the perception of truth in the next realm (Luke 16:22–31).

"What I say to you in the darkness, say in the light, and what you hear in the ear, preach upon the rooftops" (v. 27). The roofs in the Middle East are flat, making an ideal pulpit for proclaiming a message to those who pass by.

"And stop fearing those who kill the body, but are not able to kill the soul; but rather keep fearing the one who is able to destroy both soul and body in Gehenna" (v. 28). *Fearing God* is not terror but a holy reverence that worships and praises Him. The verb *to destroy* does not imply annihilation but rather the loss of all that makes life worth living. There is

---

10:27. The word *darkness* (σκοτία) occurs only here in Matt.

For the word *light* see Matt. 4:16 note

The word *ear* (οὖς) occurs 7 times in Matt. (10:27; 11:15; 13:9, 15 [twice], 16, 43).

For the verb *to preach* see Matt. 3:1 note.

The word *roof* (δῶμα) occurs twice in Matt. (10:27; 24:17). See ISBE (1982), "House," [III, E, roof], II, pp. 771–72; for full-color reconstructions of ancient buildings see Marsha Smith, ed., *Holman Book of Biblical Charts, Maps, and Reconstructions*, pp. 140, 157.

10:28. For the verb *to fear* see Matt. 1:20 note.

The verb *to kill* (ἀποκτείνω) occurs 13 times in Matt. (10:28 [twice]; 14:5; 16:21; 17:23; 21:35, 38, 39; 22:6; 23:34, 37; 24:9; 26:4). For discussion see ISBE (1986), "Kill," III, pp. 15–17; ZPEB, "Crimes and Punishments," (Homicide), I, pp. 1032–33.

For the verb *to destroy* see Matt. 2:13 note.

For the word *Gehenna* (γέεννα) see Matt. 5:22 note.

29 Are not two sparrows sold for a farthing? and one of them shall not fall on the ground without your Father.
30 But the very hairs of your head are all numbered.
31 Fear ye not therefore, ye are of more value than many sparrows.
32 Whosoever therefore shall confess me before men, him will I confess also before my Father which is in heaven.

no teaching in Scripture that death means the end of existence; rather it teaches that the soul is transferred to a different realm (Ps. 16:9–11; 23:6; Isa. 14:9–17; Dan. 12:2–3; Luke 16:19–31; Rom. 2:3–11; II Cor. 5:1–10; I Tim. 6:7–19; Rev. 20:12–15). For the loving Savior to give such a solemn warning should cause every lost person to consider his eternal destiny.

"Are not two sparrows sold for a penny? And one of them shall not fall upon the ground without your Father" (v. 29). A sparrow makes a very small meal, and yet God cares even for lowly creatures. This should cause every believer to have a reverence for life.

"But even the hairs of your head have been all numbered" (v. 30). This is another way of saying that God is omniscient. He perceives and understands every last thing in His universe. This is evidence that God is interested in numbers.

"Therefore, stop fearing; you are more valuable than many sparrows" (v. 31). The present tense verb implies that they were already afraid. Man should be a good custodian of animals, but he does not exist just to care for them (as in India where they are worshiped).

"Therefore, all who shall confess me before men, I also shall confess him before my Father who is in the heavens" (v. 32). The book of Acts will develop this theme in the witness of the church to all men (Acts

---

10:29. The word *sparrow* (στρουθίον) occurs twice in this context only in Matt. (10:29, 31). There are several species of sparrows in the area (see Peter C. Alden, *National Audubon Society Field Guide to African Wildlife*, pp. 875–76).

The verb *to sell, be a merchant* (πωλέω) occurs 6 times in Matt. (10:29; 13:44; 19:21; 21:12 [twice]; 25:9).

The word *penny* (ἀσσάριον) occurs only here in Matt. It was a small copper coin, actually about a half penny. See Arndt and Gingrich, p. 117; ISBE (1986), "Money," III, p. 409; Douglas and Tenney, eds., *The New International Dictionary of the Bible*, "Money," p. 669.

For the verb *to fall* see Matt. 2:11 note.

10:30. For the word *hair* see Matt. 3:4 note.

The verb *to count, number* (ἀριθμέω) occurs only here in Matt.

10:32. For the verb *to confess* see Matt. 7:23 note.

*33 But whosoever shall deny me before men, him will I also deny before my
Father which is in heaven.*
*34 Think not that I am come to send peace on earth: I came not to send
peace, but a sword.*
*35 For I am come to set a man at variance against his father, and the daughter
against her mother, and the daughter in law against her mother in law.*

1:8; 2:32–36; 8:1–4). The thought of the Lord Jesus' acknowledging the
believer as a "good and faithful servant" (Matt. 25:21) is a tremendous
impetus to fervent service.

"But whoever shall deny me before men, I will also deny him before my
Father who is in the heavens" (v. 33). The Lord's word, "I never knew
you," will settle the eternal destiny of many (Matt. 7:23b).

"Do not suppose that I came to bring peace upon the earth; I came not
to bring peace, but a sword" (v. 34). The First Advent was intended not
to bring in the age of peace but to launch an attack on the kingdom of
darkness and deliver its slaves to a future kingdom of God. Believers must
wield the sword of the Spirit to set men free from Satan's kingdom. The
future Millennium will be the kingdom of peace (Isa. 32:1, 17).

"For I came to separate a man from his father, and a daughter from her
mother, and a daughter-in-law from her mother-in-law, and the enemies of
a man shall be the ones of his own household" (vv. 35–36). "Once again
we have *I came* with its implication of a previous existence elsewhere"
(Morris, *Matt.*, p. 266). The claims of Christ transcend those of any other
relationship. He is the great King, worthy of our highest allegiance.

10:33. The verb *to deny* (ἀρνέομαι) occurs 4 times in Matt. (10:33 [twice]; 26:70, 72). For
explanation see ZPEB, "Deny," II, pp. 101–2; Elwell, ed., *Evangelical Dictionary of Biblical
Theology*, "Denial," p. 166.

10:34. For the verb *to suppose* see Matt. 5:17 note.

For the word *peace* see Matt. 10:13 note.

The word *sword* (μάχαιρα) occurs 7 times in Matt. (10:34; 26:47, 51, 52 [3 times], 55).
This word for *sword* refers to the short, heavy Roman sword. For background see ISBE
(1988), "Weapons of War," Sword, IV, pp. 1033–43; ZPEB, "Armor, Arms," I, pp. 312–20;
Ryken, Wilhoit, and Longman, *Dictionary of Biblical Imagery*, "Sword," pp. 835–36.

10:35. The verb *to separate* (διχάζω) occurs only here in the NT.

The word *daughter-in-law* is literally *bride* (νύμφη), which occurs only here in Matt.

For *mother-in-law* see Matt. 8:14 note.

10:36. For the word *enemy* see Matt. 5:43 note.

For the word *member of a household* see Matt. 10:25 note.

36 And a man's foes shall be they of his own household.
37 He that loveth father or mother more than me is not worthy of me: and he that loveth son or daughter more than me is not worthy of me.
38 And he that taketh not his cross, and followeth after me, is not worthy of me.
39 He that findeth his life shall lose it: and he that loseth his life for my sake shall find it.
40 He that receiveth you receiveth me, and he that receiveth me receiveth him that sent me.
41 He that receiveth a prophet in the name of a prophet shall receive a prophet's reward; and he that receiveth a righteous man in the name of a righteous man shall receive a righteous man's reward.

"The one who loves father or mother over me is not worthy of me, and the one who loves son or daughter over me is not worthy of me" (v. 37). The Lord Jesus deserves the supreme loyalty of His people. His claims will divide family loyalties.

"And he who does not take his cross and follow after me is not worthy of me" (v. 38). The Lord is promising to die for His people; they should be ready to die for Him. The Lord Jesus repeats the charge that He is worthy of supreme devotion, for He is the great King, God the Son. In the word *cross* He anticipates the means of His atonement. The disciples did not understand then, but afterwards they would always remember that He told them directly about His death.

"The one who finds his life shall lose it, and the one who loses his life on account of me shall find it" (v. 39). This is a true paradox. The person who centers his attention on himself shall destroy himself. The person who will sacrifice himself for the cause of the Lord Jesus will find that the Lord will preserve him unto everlasting life. He cannot lose anything that he gives to the Lord.

"The one who receives you receives me, and the one who receives me receives the one who sent me" (v. 40). The Lord is going to accept the treatment given to His disciples as done to Himself. But it was the Father Himself who sent the Son to be the propitiation for our sins (I John 4:10b).

"The one who receives a prophet in the name of a prophet shall receive a prophet's reward, and the one who receives a righteous man in the name

---

10:38. The word *cross* (σταυρός) occurs 5 times in Matt. (10:38; 16:24; 27:32, 40, 42). For discussion see *crucify*, Matt. 20:19 note.

10:39. For the word *life, soul*, see Matt. 2:20 note.

10:41. For the word *reward* see Matt. 5:12 note.

42 And whosoever shall give to drink unto one of these little ones a cup of cold water only in the name of a disciple, verily I say unto you, he shall in no wise lose his reward.

of a righteous man shall receive a righteous man's reward" (v. 41). The Lord in all of Scripture uses reward as an incentive for a righteous man to obey the truth (Ps. 19:11; Matt. 5:12; I Cor. 3:8; Rev. 22:12).

"And whoever shall give to one of these little ones a cup of cold water in the name of a disciple, truly I say to you, he shall never lose his reward" (v. 42). The double negative makes the *never* very emphatic. For endless ages the saint he helped will have a bond of appreciation for him. God is a rewarder of those who diligently seek Him (Heb. 11:6). Although Matthew has recorded more than the other Gospels about this charge to the apostles, he does not tell us anything about the actual ministry of the apostles (see Mark 6:12; Luke 9:6).

Practical Applications from Matthew 10

1. The Lord Jesus had to give the apostles their power to serve (v. 1). Paul said to the elders of Ephesus, "I commend you to God, and to the word of his grace, which is able to build you up" (Acts 20:32b). He wrote, "So that neither is the one who plants anything, nor the one who waters, but God who causes to increase" (I Cor. 3:7).
2. The Lord directed the apostles to go to the lost sheep of the house of Israel (v. 6). Paul explained that "it pleased God by the foolishness of preaching to save them that believe" (I Cor. 1:21b).
3. Financial resources cannot buy success in the ministry (v. 9). Paul's testimony was "For by the grace of God I am what I am" (I Cor. 15:10a).
4. Never let circumstances upset your peace (v. 13). Peace is part of the fruit of the Spirit (Gal. 5:22); believers should let the peace of God rule in their hearts (Col. 3:15).

10:42. The verb *to give to drink* (ποτίζω) occurs 5 times in Matt. (10:42; 25:35, 37, 42; 27:48).

The word *cup* (ποτήριον) occurs 7 times in Matt. (10:42; 20:22, 23; 23:25, 26; 26:27, 39). The contents of the cup made all the difference. For its significance see Ryken, Wilhoit, and Longman, *Dictionary of Biblical Imagery*, "Cup," p. 186; ZPEB, "Cup," I, pp. 1044–45; ISBE (1979), "Cup," I, pp. 836–37; Elwell, ed., *Evangelical Dictionary of Biblical Theology*, "Cup," pp. 138–39.

5. God's servants are sheep in the midst of wolves (v. 16). They should expect attacks and God's protection: "We are troubled on every side, yet not distressed; we are perplexed, but not in despair; persecuted, but not forsaken; cast down, but not destroyed" (II Cor. 4:8–9).

6. Pastors and Christian workers should not fear the attacks and insults that may come to them (v. 26). In the judgment all will become known, and believing servants of the Lord will be recognized for their faithfulness. "The laborer is worthy of his reward" (I Tim. 5:18b).

Prayer

Dear Lord Jesus, give us the grace to follow the example of Your apostles in seeking the lost to win them for You. Help us to look beyond the present hardships and the scorn of men to the eternal joy of the redeemed in Your presence. Cause us to remember the cup of cold water. Amen.

MATTHEW 11

JOHN'S QUESTION

Persons
- Jesus
- Disciples of Jesus
- John the Baptist
- Disciples of John
- The multitudes
- The Father
- The Son
- All who labor

Persons referred to
- The blind
- The lame
- Lepers
- The deaf
- The poor
- A prophet
- Elijah
- Children
- Publicans
- Sinners
- The wise
- The prudent
- All who labor

Places mentioned
- The prison [at Machaerus]
- The wilderness
- The marketplace [*agora*]
- Chorazin
- Bethsaida
- Tyre
- Sidon
- Capernaum
- Sodom

Doctrines taught
- Messianic signs
- The gospel
- The kingdom of heaven
- Wisdom
- Repentance
- The Day of Judgment
- Heaven
- Hell
- Revelation
- Invitation

1 And it came to pass, when Jesus had made an end of commanding his twelve disciples, he departed thence to teach and to preach in their cities.

2 Now when John had heard in the prison the works of Christ, he sent two of his disciples,

3 And said unto him, Art thou he that should come, or do we look for another?

4 Jesus answered and said unto them, Go and shew John again those things which ye do hear and see:

Matthew 11 Exposition

I. John's Question. vv. 1–6 [Luke 7:18–35].

"And it came to pass, when Jesus finished commanding his twelve disciples, he departed from there in order to be teaching and preaching in their cities" (v. 1). As soon as the Lord had finished instructing His disciples, He went back to His ministry of preaching throughout the land. The present tense infinitives emphasize His constant practice of preaching and teaching as He traveled through the cities. Matthew is the only Gospel writer to use the phrase *the twelve disciples* (Matt. 11:1; 20:17; 26:20).

"But when John had heard in the prison the works of Jesus, he sent through his disciples, and said to him: Are you the Coming One or are we waiting for another?" (vv. 2–3). There was no real doubt in John's mind as to the Lord's authority. The question was a plea for help in the midst of very discouraging circumstances. John was one step away from execution (Matt. 14:1–12). But he was to be faithful unto death, for the Lord was going to replace his ministry by His own and His messianic death.

"And he answered and said to them, Go and announce to John the things which you are hearing and seeing" (v. 4). They had seen the messianic signs (Isa. 29:18; 35:4–6), but John would not be delivered.

11:1. The verb *to command* (διατάσσω) occurs only here in Matt.

11:2. The word *prison* (δεσμωτήριον) occurs only here in Matt.

For a summary of *John the Baptist* see Matt. 3:1 note.

11:3. The title *the Coming One* (ὁ ἐρχόμενος) is a definite messianic term (Matt. 16:28; 21:9; 24:30; 26:64 all use the verb ἔρχομαι of the Lord Jesus).

For *another* [of a different kind] (ἕτερος), see Matt. 6:24 note. John was hoping for a coming king who would crush his foes and establish the final aspect of the kingdom. He was wondering why the Lord did not do that.

The verb *to wait for* (προσδοκάω) occurs only in 11:3; 24:50 in Matt.

11:4. For the verb *to announce* see Matt. 2:8 note.

5 The blind receive their sight, and the lame walk, the lepers are cleansed, and the deaf hear, the dead are raised up, and the poor have the gospel preached to them.

6 And blessed is he, whosoever shall not be offended in me.

7 And as they departed, Jesus began to say unto the multitudes concerning John, What went ye out into the wilderness to see? A reed shaken with the wind?

"Blind people receive their sight and the lame walk, lepers are being cleansed, deaf people hear, and dead people are being raised up, and the poor are being evangelized" (v. 5). Although these signs have their ultimate fulfillment in the millennial reign (Isa. 35:4–8; 61:1–3), there was a foretaste of these blessings in the ministry of the Lord. Morris notes that there is no miracle recorded in the OT of the blind receiving their sight (*Matt.*, p. 276). *The poor* have precious little given to them, but God loves to give.

"And blessed is he whoever is not caused to stumble in me" (v. 6). The Lord was constantly seeking to bless people and to protect them from spiritual harm.

II. Jesus' Answer. vv. 7–19.

"But while they were departing, Jesus began to say to the crowds concerning John: What did you go into the desert to behold? A reed being shaken by the wind?" (v. 7). A reed shaking in the wind is a striking picture. The Lord deliberately contrasts a fragile plant to the rock-solid character of the prophet John the Baptist.

11:5. The verb *to receive sight, look up* (ἀναβλέπω) occurs 3 times in Matt. (11:5; 14:19; 20:34).

For the word *blind* see Matt. 9:27 note.

The word *lame* (χωλός) occurs 5 times in Matt. (11:5; 15:30, 31; 18:8; 21:14).

For the word *leper* see Matt. 8:2 note.

For the word *deaf, dumb* see Matt. 9:32 note.

For the word *dead* see Matt. 8:22 note.

For the word *poor* see Matt. 5:3 note.

11:6. For the word *blessed* see Matt. 5:3 note.

For the verb *to cause to stumble* see Matt. 5:29 note.

11:7. The word *reed* (κάλαμος) occurs 5 times in Matt. (11:7; 12:20; 27:29, 30, 48). For background see ZPEB, "Reed," V, pp. 51–52; ISBE (1988), "Reed," IV, pp. 63–64; Zohary, *Plants of the Bible*, "Reed," p. 134, with color photos.

For the word *desert* see Matt. 3:1 note.

8 But what went ye out for to see? A man clothed in soft raiment? behold, they that wear soft clothing are in kings' houses.

9 But what went ye out for to see? A prophet? yea, I say unto you, and more than a prophet.

10 For this is he, of whom it is written, Behold, I send my messenger before thy face, which shall prepare thy way before thee.

11 Verily I say unto you, Among them that are born of women there hath not risen a greater than John the Baptist: notwithstanding he that is least in the kingdom of heaven is greater than he.

12 And from the days of John the Baptist until now the kingdom of heaven suffereth violence, and the violent take it by force.

"But what did you go out to see? A man clothed with soft clothing? Behold, the ones wearing soft things are in the houses of kings" (v. 8). The average person in the ancient world wore clothing that modern people would regard as very coarse.

"But what did you go out to see? A prophet? Yes, I say to you, and more than a prophet" (v. 9). The Lord ranks John as greater than the prophets because he had a unique task: being the forerunner of the Messiah.

"This is the one concerning whom it has been written:

"Behold I send my messenger before your face, who shall prepare
your way before you" (v. 10; Mal. 3:1).

Malachi tells us that the Lord "shall suddenly come to his temple" and "he is like a refiner's fire" (Mal. 3:1b, 3a). The Lord is a great King and will judge His foes.

"Truly I say to you, among those born of women a greater than John the Baptist has not been raised up; but the one who is least in the kingdom of the heavens is greater than he" (v. 11). This does not mean morally greater; the Lord has just expressed His approval of John in that regard. But it does mean that ordinary believers in the coming church age will have greater perception of God's providential plan than John could have. He was faithful unto death even though he did not understand the reason for what was happening to him.

11:8. The word *soft* (μαλακός) occurs only twice here in Matt.

11:9. For the word *prophet* see Matt. 1:22 note.

11:10. For the word *angel, messenger* see Matt. 1:20 note.

11:11. For the word *truly* see Matt. 5:18 note. It is strong emphasis.

13 For all the prophets and the law prophesied until John.
14 And if ye will receive it, this is Elias, which was for to come.
15 He that hath ears to hear, let him hear.
16 But whereunto shall I liken this generation? It is like unto children sitting in the markets, and calling unto their fellows,

"But from the days of John the Baptist until now the kingdom of the heavens is suffering violence, and the forcefully resolute are taking it by force" (v. 12). The meaning is that they are pressing into the kingdom of God past the opposition of the Devil, the world, the scribes and Pharisees, and others who would detract from Christ's teaching. To this day believers must often come to Christ past the opposition of relatives, friends, religious leaders, and others who desire to prevent them. Some interpret this passage as referring to violently wicked men who attack the kingdom (Morris, *Matt.*, p. 282).

"For all the prophets and the law prophesied until John" (v. 13). John's preaching was the climax and conclusion of OT prophecy. Now the Lord was going to accomplish the redemption of His people on the cross, and the gospel of salvation would flow out to all nations in the preaching of the church.

"And if you are willing to receive it, he himself is Elijah, the one about to come. Let the one who has ears continue hearing" (vv. 14–15). People should concentrate their powers of perception on the Word. The Lord did not mean that John was personally Elijah, for He will later explain that Elijah must yet come before the Second Coming (Matt. 17:11). But John was ministering in the spirit and power of Elijah as the angel told Zacharias that he would (Luke 1:17). Not everyone will understand this, so the Lord urges believers to continue hearing the Word. There is more revelation coming in the NT writers.

"But to what shall I liken this generation? It is like children sitting in the markets, calling to their friends, saying,

---

11:12. The verb *to exercise force, violence* (βιάζω) occurs only here in Matt.

The word *forceful or violent person* (βιαστής) occurs only here in the NT.

The verb *to snatch away, take* (ἁρπάζω) occurs 3 times in Matt. (11:12; 12:29; 13:19).

11:13. For the word *law* see Matt. 5:17 note.

11:14. *Elijah* is named 9 times in Matt. (11:14; 16:14; 17:3, 4, 10, 11, 12; 27:47, 49). The ministry of Elijah is found in I Kings 17:1–19:21; 21:17–28; II Kings 1:3–2:15. For background see Alexander Whyte, *Bible Characters*, "Elijah," III, pp. 93–100; ZPEB, "Elijah," II, pp. 284–87; ISBE (1982), "Elijah," II, pp. 64–68; *Who's Who in the Bible*, "Elijah," pp. 89–96.

17 And saying, We have piped unto you, and ye have not danced; we have mourned unto you, and ye have not lamented.
18 For John came neither eating nor drinking, and they say, He hath a devil.
19 The Son of man came eating and drinking, and they say, Behold a man gluttonous, and a winebibber, a friend of publicans and sinners. But wisdom is justified of her children.

We played the flute for you, and you did not dance;

We mourned and you did not beat the breast" (vv. 16–17). Everywhere children play, acting out adult activities in their games. Here they played the flute and others would not do the wedding dances; they played mournful tunes and others would not do a funeral procession. They just "wouldn't play." So there were many people in that generation who would not respond to John's stern pronouncement of coming judgment and would not respond to the Lord's gracious offer of salvation. To the present day, there are many who do not respond to any form of the gospel message.

"For John came neither eating nor drinking, and they say, He has a demon" (v. 18). John came as an ascetic and maintained a stern, unbending denunciation of evil, and people called him demon possessed.

"The Son of man came eating and drinking, and they say: Behold, a man who is a glutton and a winebibber, a friend of tax collectors and sinners. But wisdom is justified by her works" (v. 19).The phrase *eating and drinking* does not imply excess in the Lord Jesus. Morris notes that "far from being an ascetic, he ate and drank normally, as other people did" (*Matt.*, p. 285). That generation of unbelievers stands condemned, totally unre-

---

For the verb *to will* see Matt. 1:19 note.

11:16. For the word *child* see Matt. 2:8 note.

The word *marketplace, agora* (ἀγορά) occurs 3 times in Matt. (11:16; 20:3; 23:7). See ZPEB, "Market, Marketplace," IV, pp. 91–92; ISBE (1986), "Market, Marketplace," III, p. 260; Ryken, Wilhoit, and Longman, *Dictionary of Biblical Imagery*, "Marketplace," p. 537

11:17. The verb *to play the flute* (αὐλέω) occurs only here in Matt.

The verb *to mourn* (θρηνέω) occurs only here in Matt.

The verb *to lament, beat the breast in grief* (κόπτω) occurs 3 times in Matt. (11:17; 21:8; 24:30).

11:19. The word *glutton* (φάγος) occurs only here in Matt.

The word *drinker, winebibber* (οἰνοπότης) occurs only here in Matt.

The word *wisdom* (σοφία) occurs 3 times in Matt. (11:19; 12:42; 13:54). Biblically, it refers to being able to choose the highest good and being able to use all knowledge for greatest benefit to God and man. For further discussion see ZPEB, "Wisdom," V, pp. 939–

20 Then began he to upbraid the cities wherein most of his mighty works were done, because they repented not:
21 Woe unto thee, Chorazin! woe unto thee, Bethsaida! for if the mighty works, which were done in you, had been done in Tyre and Sidon, they would have repented long ago in sackcloth and ashes.
22 But I say unto you, It shall be more tolerable for Tyre and Sidon at the day of judgment, than for you.

sponsive to the Word of God, no matter how it was delivered. A remnant submits and is saved; the majority turn away to perdition.

III. Jesus' Pronouncement of Woe. vv. 20–24.

"Then he began to reproach the cities in which most of his mighty works were done, because they did not repent" (v. 20). There is always responsibility. Much light demands a great response. Luke adds, "But to everyone to whom much was given, from him much shall be required" (Luke 12:48*b*).

"Woe to you, Chorazin! woe to you, Bethsaida! because if the mighty works which have been done in you, were done in Tyre and Sidon, they would have repented long ago in dust and ashes" (v. 21). The unbelievers in these cities had hardened their hearts against scenes of great miracles and faithful preaching.

"But I say to you, it shall be more tolerable for Tyre and Sidon in the Day of Judgment, than for you" (v. 22). There are gradations of punishment as well as of reward in God's judgment (Luke 12:42–48).

45; ISBE (1988), "Wisdom," IV, pp. 1074–82; Elwell, ed., *Evangelical Dictionary of Biblical Theology*, "Wisdom," pp. 823–24; Ryken, Wilhoit, and Longman, *Dictionary of Biblical Imagery*, "Wisdom," pp. 955–57.

The verb *to justify, declare righteous* (δικαιόω) occurs only twice in Matt. (11:19; 12:37). It is one of Paul's great theological terms (Rom. 2:13; 3:4, 20, 24, 26, 28, 30; 4:2, 5; 5:1, 9; 6:7; 8:30, 33, and so forth).

11:20. For the verb *to reproach* see Matt. 5:11 note.

For the verb *to repent* see Matt. 3:2 note.

11:21. The word *Woe* (οὐαί) occurs 13 times in Matt. (11:21 [twice]; 18:7 [twice]; 23:13, 15, 16, 23, 25, 27, 29; 24:19; 26:24). It is an expression of intense lamentation. For discussion see ISBE (1988), "Woe," IV, p. 1088.

The words *Chorazin* and *Bethsaida* occur only here in Matt. For background see ZPEB, I, "Bethsaida," pp. 542–43; "Chorazin," p. 800; ISBE (1979), "Bethsaida," I, p. 475; "Chorazin," p. 652. For archaeological excavations see Rami Arav and Richard Freund, *Bethsaida*. Kirksville, Missouri: Truman State University Press, 1999. For color photographs of Chorazin see the author's *Stones of Witness*, p. 42.

For *Tyre* and *Sidon* see ZPEB, "Tyre," V, pp. 832–34; "Sidon," V, pp. 426–28; ISBE (1988), "Tyre," IV, pp. 932–34; "Sidon," IV, pp. 500–502; Pfeiffer, *The Biblical World*, "Tyre," pp. 590–91; "Sidon," p. 528.

23 And thou, Capernaum, which art exalted unto heaven, shalt be brought down to hell: for if the mighty works, which have been done in thee, had been done in Sodom, it would have remained until this day.
24 But I say unto you, That it shall be more tolerable for the land of Sodom in the day of judgment, than for thee.
25 At that time Jesus answered and said, I thank thee, O Father, Lord of heaven and earth, because thou hast hid these things from the wise and prudent, and hast revealed them unto babes.

"And you, Capernaum, exalted to heaven, to Hades shall be brought down; because if the mighty works which were done in you were done in Sodom, it would have remained until today" (v. 23). The word order emphasizes *Hades*. Granted that Sodom was a wicked city; but it had little light and so had less responsibility than Capernaum, which had been the scene of great miracles (Matt. 8:5ff.) and great sermons (John 6:35–59).

"But I say to you that it shall be more tolerable for the land of Sodom in the Day of Judgment, than for you" (v. 24). Jesus repeats the condemnation for emphasis. It should cause us all to consider how much greater light we have received. "No one ever appeared on earth with such words of tenderness, of love, and compassion, as did the Lord Jesus, and yet, again and again, in fact, more frequently than any one of the apostles, our Lord saw fit to warn men of a judgment to come" (Wilbur M. Smith, *Therefore Stand*, p. 463).

IV. The Son's Prayer and Invitation. vv. 25–30.

"At that time Jesus answered and said, I praise you, Father, Lord of heaven and earth, because you hid these things from the wise and intelligent and revealed them to children" (v. 25). It is significant that it was children who were praising the Lord Jesus in the temple (Matt. 21:15–16). The Lord Jesus expresses His close relationship to His heavenly Father. He communed with His Father on the spur of the moment, giving us an example that we should take to heart.

11:23. The verb *to exalt* (ὑψόω) occurs 3 times in Matt. (11:23; 23:12 [twice]).
The word *Hades* (ᾅδης) occurs twice in Matt. (11:23; 16:18). See 16:18 note.
For *Capernaum* see Matt. 4:13 note.
11:25. For the verb *to confess, promise, praise* (ἐξομολογέω) see Matt. 3:6 note.
The word *wise* (σοφός) occurs twice in Matt. (11:25; 23:34).
The word *child* (νήπιος) occurs twice in Matt. (11:25; 21:16).

26 Even so, Father: for so it seemed good in thy sight.
27 All things are delivered unto me of my Father: and no man knoweth the
Son, but the Father; neither knoweth any man the Father, save the Son, and he
to whomsoever the Son will reveal him.
28 Come unto me, all ye that labour and are heavy laden, and I will give you rest.

"Yea, Father, because thus it seemed good before you" (v. 26). The Lord
Jesus was always devoted to pleasing His heavenly Father.

"All things were given to me by my Father, and no one knows the Son
except the Father, nor does anyone know the Father except the Son, and
whomever the Son wishes to reveal him" (v. 27). This passage is a revelation of the serene interaction between the Persons of the Trinity. This is a
relationship infinitely above all other relationships. The Lord Jesus speaks
of Himself as "the Son," infinitely above all human relations. It expresses
the divine nature of the Lord Jesus and His love for His heavenly Father.
Liberal critics have struggled with this passage. One called it "a bolt from
the Johannine blue" (Karl von Hase, prof. of church history, Jena, 1876).
It does indeed sound like something from the Gospel of John, but it is in
Matthew, and it reveals the unity of teaching on the deity of Christ. He
is the Son of God in a sense in which no other human being ever can
be. Geerhardus Vos noted that there is no statement in the Johannine
writings with a higher Christology than this statement in Matthew (*The
Self-Disclosure of Jesus*, p. 144).

"Come unto me, all you who labor and are burdened, and I will give you
rest" (v. 28). The Son can give a universal invitation. He can meet the
need and lift the burden of everyone who comes to Him. In the OT it was
Jehovah Who invited sinners to come to Him: "Come now, and let us
reason together, saith the Lord: though your sins be as scarlet, they shall
be as white as snow; though they be red like crimson, they shall be as
wool" (Isa. 1:18). God promised the Israelites rest (Exod. 33:14), but they
were not faithful to Him.

11:27. For the verb *to know fully* (ἐπιγινώσκω) see Matt. 7:16 note. Only deity can know
deity fully.

11:28. For this word *come* (δεῦτε) see Matt. 4:19 note. The same word is used for the
invitation to the millennial kingdom (Matt. 25:34).

For the verb *to labor* see Matt. 6:28 note.

The verb *to give rest* (ἀναπαύω) occurs only here and in 26:45 in Matt. This verb denotes
the temporary rest along the pathway, not the eternal rest of heaven. See Custer, *A
Treasury of New Testament Synonyms*, pp. 40–42.

29 Take my yoke upon you, and learn of me; for I am meek and lowly in heart: and ye shall find rest unto your souls.
30 For my yoke is easy, and my burden is light.

"Take my yoke upon you and learn of me, because I am meek and lowly in heart, and you shall find rest for your souls" (v. 29). Accepting the yoke implies submission to the will of the Lord Jesus Christ. He is not an arrogant king; He is meek and humble. Believers will find rest of heart in serving Him. Alexander Whyte has an interesting sermon on "Our Lord's Favourite Graces, Meekness and Lowliness of Heart," *The Walk, Conversation and Character of Jesus Christ Our Lord,* pp. 316–23.

"For my yoke is easy and my burden is light" (v. 30). Contrary to the ruthless kings of earth, this King sustains and helps His servants.

Practical Applications from Matthew 11

1. Even great men can become discouraged (v. 3). David said, "Why art thou cast down, O my soul? and why art thou disquieted within me? hope in God: for I shall yet praise him, who is the health of my countenance, and my God" (Ps. 43:5).
2. Blessed is the person who is not offended in Jesus (v. 6). But John put it positively, "Blessed are they that do his commandments, that they may have right to the tree of life" (Rev. 22:14a).
3. John came as a stern ascetic, denouncing sin; the Lord came as a loving friend, inviting sinners to God (vv. 18–19). But the world refused both appeals. "The world by wisdom knew not God" (I Cor. 1:21b).
4. In the midst of a solemn discourse the Lord Jesus pauses to thank His heavenly Father for His wisdom and love (v. 25a). Paul urged, "Pray without ceasing" (I Thess. 5:17).

11:29. The word *yoke* (ζυγός) occurs only in this context in Matt. (11:29, 30).
For the word *meek* see Matt. 5:5 note.

The word *humble, lowly* (ταπεινός) occurs only here in Matt. Humility was a rare virtue in the ancient world (as it still is).

11:30. The word *burden* (φορτίον) occurs twice in Matt. (11:30; 23:4), contrasting the light burden of the Lord with the dreadful burdens of the Pharisees. See Custer, *A Treasury of New Testament Synonyms,* p. 3; Ryken, Wilhoit, and Longman, *Dictionary of Biblical Imagery,* "Heavy," pp. 373–74.

The word *light* (ἐλαφρός) occurs only here in Matt.

5. God hides His wisdom from the shrewd and the crafty but reveals it to the simple and trusting (v. 25). "Trust in the Lord with all thine heart; and lean not unto thine own understanding" (Prov. 3:5).

6. If the Lord Jesus invites us, *Come unto me,* will we answer Him *I'm just too busy?* (v. 28). We pray when we are in trouble; why not when He invites us?

Prayer

Lord Jesus, give us ears to hear Your precious words; give us grace to respond in obedience. We come to You for help. Lift our burdens and help us to take up Yours and to learn to serve as we should. Amen.

MATTHEW 12

LORD OF THE SABBATH

Persons
Jesus
His disciples
Pharisees
A man with a withered hand
Great multitudes

A demon-possessed man
Scribes
Mary, His mother
The brethren of the Lord

Persons referred to
David
Priests
A man with one sheep
Isaiah
Gentiles
Beelzebub
Satan
The Spirit of God

A good man
An evil man
Jonah
Men of Nineveh
Queen of the south
Solomon
Unclean spirits
God the Father

Places mentioned
Grain fields
The house of God
A synagogue

Doctrines taught
It is lawful to do well on the
  Sabbath
The Lordship of Christ
The Servant of the Lord
Demon possession
The unpardonable sin

The Day of Judgment
Repentance
Degrees of wickedness
The will of God

1 At that time Jesus went on the sabbath day through the corn; and his disciples were an hungred, and began to pluck the ears of corn and to eat.

2 But when the Pharisees saw it, they said unto him, Behold, thy disciples do that which is not lawful to do upon the sabbath day.

3 But he said unto them, Have ye not read what David did, when he was an hungred, and they that were with him;

Matthew 12 Exposition

I. Eating Grain on the Sabbath. vv. 1–8 [Mark 2:23–28; Luke 6:1–5].

"In that time Jesus went on the Sabbath through the grain fields, but his disciples were hungry and began to pluck the heads of wheat and eat" (v. 1). Jesus had already taught them about the dietary regulations and their fulfillment in the new dispensation. The relationship of the OT and the NT is like the parallelism of Hebrew poetry. The OT was a true revelation, but it was not complete; the NT added to the revelation and brought it to completion. For a poetic example:

"Some trust in chariots, and some in horses:

But we will remember the name of the Lord our God" (Ps. 20:7).

"But when the Pharisees saw it, they said to him, Behold your disciples are doing what it is not lawful to be doing on the Sabbath" (v. 2). Picking off the heads of wheat and crushing them in their hands the Pharisees classified as "harvesting" the wheat.

"But he said to them, Did you not read what David did when he was hungry and the ones with him, how he entered into the house of God and ate

12:1. The word *Sabbath* (σάββατον) occurs 11 times in Matt. (12:1, 2, 5 [twice], 8, 10, 11, 12; 24:20; 28:1 [twice]). In this context the Lord Jesus is claiming divine sovereignty over the Sabbath. In Jewish practice the holy day is observed from sundown on Friday to sundown on Saturday. For further discussion see Ryken, Wilhoit, and Longman, *Dictionary of Biblical Imagery*, "Sabbath," pp. 747–48; ZPEB, "Sabbath," V, pp. 181–89; ISBE (1988), "Sabbath," IV, pp. 247–52; Elwell, ed., *Evangelical Dictionary of Biblical Theology*, "Sabbath," pp. 697–98.

The word *grainfield* (σπόριμος) occurs only here in Matt.

For the verb *to be hungry* see Matt. 4:2 note.

The word *head of wheat* (στάχυς) occurs only here in Matt. The KJV "ear of corn" gives a different picture to Americans.

12:2. For *Pharisees* see Matt. 3:7 note.

The verb *it is lawful* (ἔξεστιν) occurs 9 times in Matt. (12:2, 4, 10, 12; 14:4; 19:3; 20:15; 22:17; 27:6).

12:3. The verb *to read* (ἀναγινώσκω) occurs 7 times in Matt. (12:3, 5; 19:4; 21:16, 42; 22:31; 24:15). For discussion see ISBE (1988), "Read," IV, pp. 49–50.

4 How he entered into the house of God, and did eat the shewbread, which was not lawful for him to eat, neither for them which were with him, but only for the priests?

5 Or have ye not read in the law, how that on the sabbath days the priests in the temple profane the sabbath, and are blameless?

6 But I say unto you, That in this place is one greater than the temple.

7 But if ye had known what this meaneth, I will have mercy, and not sacrifice, ye would not have condemned the guiltless.

the loaves of the presentation, which was not lawful for him to eat, neither for the ones who were with him, but for the priests only?" (vv. 3–4; I Sam. 21:1–7). Bengel comments, "They had read the letter, without perceiving the spirit" (*Gnomon*, I, p. 264). This passage manifests the Lord's knowledge of a minute part of a rather obscure text. But David clearly understood that the well-being of his men was more important than the ritual observance of dietary regulations. Blomberg argues that the fourth commandment itself is fulfilled in Christ "and therefore need no longer be observed literally" (*Matt.*, p. 196).

"Or did you not read in the law that on the Sabbath days the priests in the temple profane the Sabbath and are not guilty?" (v. 5). The priests had to work hard on the Sabbath to offer up all the sacrifices and offerings that the people brought.

"But I say to you that one greater than the temple is here" (v. 6). This statement can mean only that the Lord Jesus is claiming to be God, for only God is greater than the supreme place of His worship. "The temple was not only the worship center of Hebrew culture but also the art gallery, concert plaza and poetry library" (Ryken, Wilhoit, and Longman, *Dictionary of Biblical Imagery*, "Temple," p. 849).

"But if you had known what this is,

I desire mercy and not sacrifice,

you would not have condemned the innocent" (v. 7; Hos. 6:6a LXX).

God did not desire all the animal sacrifices; He desired to see man changed into His attributes of mercy and goodness. The Israelites did not

For *David* see Matt. 1:1 note.

12:4. For *loaf, bread*, see Matt. 4:3 note.

12:5. For the *law* see Matt. 5:17 note.

For the *temple* see Matt. 4:5 note.

8 For the Son of man is Lord even of the sabbath day.

9 And when he was departed thence, he went into their synagogue:

10 And, behold, there was a man which had his hand withered. And they asked him, saying, Is it lawful to heal on the sabbath days? that they might accuse him.

11 And he said unto them, What man shall there be among you, that shall have one sheep, and if it fall into a pit on the sabbath day, will he not lay hold on it, and lift it out?

12 How much then is a man better than a sheep? Wherefore it is lawful to do well on the sabbath days.

understand this and concentrated on multitudes of offerings rather than the internal devotion to God.

"For the Son of man is Lord of the Sabbath" (v. 8). The Lord Jesus could not make a more obvious claim to being God. God ordained the Sabbath (Exod. 20:8–11); only God could exercise authority over it. The Lord Jesus is greater than the Sabbath. He could give the Sabbath and He could change the Sabbath. Morris argues that the true Sabbath observance means showing mercy as the Lord does in the following paragraph (Matt., p. 304).

II. Healing on the Sabbath. vv. 9–14 [Mark 3:1–6; Luke 6:6–11].

"And he departed from there and came into their synagogue" (v. 9). The Pharisees would certainly be in "their" synagogue on the Sabbath.

"And, behold, a man who had a withered hand. And they ask him, saying, Is it lawful to heal on the Sabbath? that they might accuse him" (v. 10). They were deliberately laying a trap for Him that they might have evidence in the synagogue against Him.

"But he said to them, Who is the man among you who shall have one sheep, and if it should fall on the Sabbath into a pit, will he not lay hold on it and raise it up?" (v. 11). Every shepherd would give the same answer. Of course he would lift it out, or it could die overnight.

12:7. For the word mercy see Matt. 9:13 note.

12:8. For the word Lord see Matt. 1:20 note.

12:9. For the word synagogue see Matt. 4:23 note.

12:10. The word dry, withered (ξηρός) occurs twice in Matt. (12:10; 23:15).

For the verb to heal see Matt. 4:23 note.

The verb to accuse (κατηγορέω) occurs twice in Matt. (12:10; 27:12).

12:11. The word pit, ditch (βόθυνος) occurs twice in Matt. (12:11; 15:14).

13 Then saith he to the man, Stretch forth thine hand. And he stretched it forth; and it was restored whole, like as the other.
14 Then the Pharisees went out, and held a council against him, how they might destroy him.
15 But when Jesus knew it, he withdrew himself from thence: and great multitudes followed him, and he healed them all;
16 And charged them that they should not make him known:

"By how much more therefore is a man worth than a sheep? So that it is lawful to keep on doing well on the Sabbath days" (v. 12). Healing a handicapped person is more important than rescuing a sheep.

"Then he says to the man: Stretch out your hand. And he stretched it out and it was restored whole as the other" (v. 13). It was an instantaneous miracle that was visible to all. The Lord changed a trap into an outstanding testimony. The man would long remember that Sabbath day.

"But the Pharisees went out and took council against him in order that they might destroy him" (v. 14). They were not pleased that a handicapped person was delivered. They could think only of destroying the person who opposed them. The word *destroy* shows the mindset of fanaticism. They would not be content to merely answer Him; they wanted to annihilate Him. The cross was not an accident.

III. Jesus, the Servant of Jehovah. vv. 15–21 [Mark 3:7–12].

"But when Jesus knew it, he withdrew from there. And great crowds followed him, and he healed them all" (v. 15). This informs us clearly that Jesus knew their thoughts. He put Himself outside the range of their plans.

"And he charged them that they should not make him manifest, in order that what was spoken through Isaiah the prophet might be fulfilled, saying:" (vv. 16–17). The Lord Jesus was not seeking fame; He did His mighty deeds quietly. He was the true fulfillment of the Servant of the Lord prophesied by Isaiah.

12:12. For the verb *to be worth more than* see Matt. 6:26.

12:13. The verb *to restore* (ἀποκαθίστημι) occurs twice in Matt. (12:13; 17:11).

For the verb *to stretch out* see Matt. 8:3 note.

12:14. The word *counsel, plan* (συμβούλιον) occurs 5 times in Matt. (12:14; 22:15; 27:1, 7; 28:12).

For the verb *to destroy* see Matt. 2:13 note.

12:15. For the verb *to withdraw* see Matt. 2:12 note.

17 That it might be fulfilled which was spoken by Esaias the prophet, saying,
18 Behold my servant, whom I have chosen; my beloved, in whom my soul is
well pleased: I will put my spirit upon him, and he shall shew judgment to the
Gentiles.
19 He shall not strive, nor cry; neither shall any man hear his voice in the
streets.
20 A bruised reed shall he not break, and smoking flax shall he not quench, till
he send forth judgment unto victory.
21 And in his name shall the Gentiles trust.

> "Behold my servant whom I chose,
>
> My beloved, in whom my soul takes pleasure;
>
> I will put my spirit upon him
>
> And he shall proclaim justice for the Gentiles" (v. 18; Isa. 42:1).

Matthew begins with his favorite word, *behold*, and goes on to set forth
the great pleasure that God takes in this mighty servant. The language
parallels that of John, "The Father loves the Son" (John 3:36a). The
thought of *justice* for the Gentiles is significant. The oppressed Jews would
have thought of vengeance. "The servant will make sure that right is
done to the nations as well as to Israel" (Morris, *Matt.*, p. 310, note 48).

> "He shall not strive nor cry out,
>
> Neither shall anyone hear his voice in the wide streets" (v. 19,
>   Isa. 42:2).

He will not be a "rabble rouser," fomenting disorder. The Lord was always
a force for peace and goodwill.

> "A bruised reed shall he not break
>
> And smoking flax shall he not quench,
>
> Until he sends forth justice unto victory.
>
> And in his name shall the Gentiles hope" (vv. 20–21; Isa. 42:3–4a).

These are striking pictures of Messiah, but puzzling to Western minds.
The bruised reed refers to a "cattail," a hollow reed, which, if stepped

---

12:16. For the word *servant* (παῖς) see Matt. 2:16 note.

12:18. The verb *to choose* (αἱρετίζω) occurs only here in the NT.

For the word *beloved* see Matt. 3:17 note.

For the verb *to take pleasure* see Matt. 3:17 note.

12:19. The verb *to strive, argue* (ἐρίζω) occurs only here in the NT.

The verb *to cry out* (κραυγάζω) occurs only here in Matt.

*22 Then was brought unto him one possessed with a devil, blind, and dumb:
and he healed him, insomuch that the blind and dumb both spake and saw.
23 And all the people were amazed, and said, Is not this the son of David?
24 But when the Pharisees heard it, they said, This fellow doth not cast out
devils, but by Beelzebub the prince of the devils.*

on, has no strength to erect itself and will die. A young tree would have
strength to snap back. Reeds were common near streams, and a broken
one would be considered a small loss. But Messiah will not tear out the
broken reed but instead will prop it up and see to it that it lives. Flax
could be used as a wick in a lamp. If it was blown out, it could smoke for a
while, but people would put water on it to stop it. But Messiah would instead fan it back into flame. These images portray the gentle and compassionate nature of the great Messiah. Messiah will not give up on broken
people, poor sinners as they are. Morris observes, "Most of us regard the
world's down-and-outs as not worth troubling ourselves over; we do not
see how anything can be made of them" (*Matt.*, p. 312). But instead the
Lord Jesus is prepared to heal and restore all those who call upon Him.
The images obviously refer to lost people. The Gentiles as well as the
Jews have good reason to hope in Him.

IV. The Charge of Beelzeboul. vv. 22–37 [Mark 3:22–30].

"Then a man possessed by a demon, blind and dumb, was brought to him,
and he healed him, so that the dumb man was speaking and seeing" (v. 22).
The demon had to flee at the Lord's command, and the Lord corrected the
physical disabilities.

"And all the crowds were astonished, and were saying, Is this not the
Son of David?" (v. 23). Some would paraphrase it to say, "This is not the
Son of David, is it?" The question does express some form of doubt. The
Pharisees immediately seized on this to attack the Lord.

"But when the Pharisees heard, they said, This man is not casting out

---

For the word *wide street* see Matt. 6:5 note.

12:20. For the word *reed* see 11:7 note.

12:21. The verb *to hope* (ἐλπίζω) occurs only here in Matt. For discussion see ZPEB,
"Hope," III, pp. 198–200; ISBE (1982), "Hope," II, pp. 751–55.

12:22. For the verb *to heal* see Matt. 4:23 note.

12:23. The phrase *Son of David* is clearly a messianic title (Matt. 1:1; 9:27; 15:22; 20:30,
31; 21:9, 15).

25 And Jesus knew their thoughts, and said unto them, Every kingdom divided against itself is brought to desolation; and every city or house divided against itself shall not stand:
26 And if Satan cast out Satan, he is divided against himself; how shall then his kingdom stand?
27 And if I by Beelzebub cast out devils, by whom do your children cast them out? therefore they shall be your judges.
28 But if I cast out devils by the Spirit of God, then the kingdom of God is come unto you.

demons except by Beelzeboul the ruler of the demons" (v. 24). This is the worst form of blasphemy, to attribute the work of God to the power of the Devil and demons.

"But knowing their thoughts, he said to them, Every kingdom divided against itself is made desolate, and every city or house divided against itself shall not stand" (v. 25). The Lord Jesus had supernatural power to perceive the thoughts and intents of every person. Here He gives them a general principle that they certainly know.

"And if Satan casts out Satan, he is divided against himself; how therefore shall his kingdom stand?" (v. 26). Satan is not partly good, nor would he hinder the evil deeds of his helpers.

"And if I by Beelzeboul am casting out the demons, by whom are your sons casting them out? On account of this they shall be your judges" (v. 27). Exorcism was practiced by Jews as well as Christians (Acts 19:13).

"But if I am casting out the demons by the Spirit of God, then the kingdom of God came upon you" (v. 28). The Lord presents a contrasting thought. The kingdom was present in the person of the King, but the Pharisees did not recognize Him.

"Or how is anyone able to enter into the house of a strong man and to

---

12:24. For the word *Beelzeboul* see Matt. 10:25 note.

12:25. For the word *thought* see Matt. 9:4 note.

The verb *to divide* (μερίζω) occurs 3 times only in Matt. (12:25 [twice], 26).

The verb *to make desolate* (ἐρημόω) occurs only here in Matt.

12:26. For the word *Satan* see Matt. 4:1 note.

12:28. The verb *to come upon* (φθάνω) occurs only here in Matt.

*29 Or else how can one enter into a strong man's house, and spoil his goods,
except he first bind the strong man? and then he will spoil his house.
30 He that is not with me is against me; and he that gathereth not with me
scattereth abroad.
31 Wherefore I say unto you, All manner of sin and blasphemy shall be forgiven unto men: but the blasphemy against the Holy Ghost shall not be forgiven
unto men.
32 And whosoever speaketh a word against the Son of man, it shall be forgiven
him: but whosoever speaketh against the Holy Ghost, it shall not be forgiven
him, neither in this world, neither in the world to come.*

snatch away his goods, except he first bind the strong man? And then he
will thoroughly plunder his house" (v. 29). This is an accurate psychology
of crime.

"The one who is not with me is against me, and the one who is not gathering with me is scattering abroad" (v. 30). Animals left alone will scatter.
There is no neutral ground concerning the Lord Jesus Christ. Every person who is not a devoted follower of the Lord is an adversary who drives
people away from Christ.

"On account of this I say to you, all sin and blasphemy shall be forgiven
men, but the blasphemy against the Spirit shall not be forgiven" (v. 31).
Deliberately attributing the work of God to the Devil shows a perversity
for which there is no cure. It manifests a permanent choice of heart that
can never be changed. The blasphemy against the Holy Spirit is "overt,
verbal, and conscious repudiation of the fact that God is at work in
Jesus Christ accomplishing his designs through the power of the Holy
Spirit" (Elwell, ed., *Evangelical Dictionary of Biblical Theology*, "Blasphemy
Against the Holy Spirit," p. 67).

"And whoever says a word against the Son of man, it shall be forgiven
him; but whoever says a word against the Holy Spirit, it shall not be
forgiven him, neither in this age nor in the coming one" (v. 32). The
difference is that someone may be misinformed about the Lord or His

---

12:29. For the verb *to snatch away* see Matt. 11:12 note.

The verb *to bind* (δέω) occurs 10 times in Matt. (12:29; 13:30; 14:3; 16:19 [twice]; 18:18
[twice]; 21:2; 22:13; 27:2).

The verb *to thoroughly plunder* (διαρπάζω) occurs only here in Matt.

12:30. For the verb *to gather with* see Matt. 2:4 note.

The verb *to scatter* (σκορπίζω) occurs only here in Matt.

33 Either make the tree good, and his fruit good; or else make the tree corrupt, and his fruit corrupt: for the tree is known by his fruit.
34 O generation of vipers, how can ye, being evil, speak good things? for out of the abundance of the heart the mouth speaketh.
35 A good man out of the good treasure of the heart bringeth forth good things: and an evil man out of the evil treasure bringeth forth evil things.

ministry and can be corrected. But someone who, under the conviction of the Holy Spirit, attributes evil to God, shows a perversity that must be condemned. The poor soul who, in a fit of anger, cursed God, and now worries over having committed this sin, ought to beg God for forgiveness and let God cleanse away his sin of anger. The person who has really committed this sin is not worried about it at all.

"Either make the tree good, and its fruit good; or make the tree rotten, and its fruit rotten; for the tree is known from its fruit" (v. 33). A person should be consistent and candid before men. The life should back up the testimony.

"Offspring of vipers! How are you, being evil, able to be speaking good things? For out of the abundance of the heart the mouth is speaking" (v. 34). The Lord Jesus denounces these false religious leaders, who pose as good men but are committed to opposing the work of God and instead lead men into perdition by their sinful example. The psalmist prayed, "Let the words of my mouth, and the meditation of my heart, be acceptable in thy sight, O Lord, my strength, and my redeemer" (Ps. 19:14). He could say, "With my whole heart have I sought thee: O let me not wander from thy commandments. Thy word have I hid in mine heart, that I might not sin against thee" (Ps. 119:10–11).

"The good man out of the treasury of his heart brings forth good things, but the evil man out of the evil treasury brings forth evil things" (v. 35). The psalmist warned, "The fool hath said in his heart, There is no God. They are corrupt, they have done abominable works, there is none that doeth good" (Ps. 14:1).

12:31. The word *blasphemy* (βλασφημία) occurs 4 times in Matt. (12:31 [twice]; 15:19; 26:65). It refers to speaking evil or reviling God, Christ, the Spirit, or the things of God. For further discussion see Elwell, ed., *Evangelical Dictionary of Biblical Theology,* "Blasphemy," p. 67; ZPEB, "Blasphemy," I, p. 624; ISBE (1979), "Blaspheme, Blasphemy," I, pp. 521–22.

For *the Holy Spirit* see Matt. 1:18 note.

12:32. An unpardonable sin is always one that the person will not admit is sin and will not accept forgiveness for. For further discussion of the unpardonable sin see ZPEB,

36 But I say unto you, That every idle word that men shall speak, they shall give account thereof in the day of judgment.
37 For by thy words thou shalt be justified, and by thy words thou shalt be condemned.
38 Then certain of the scribes and of the Pharisees answered, saying, Master, we would see a sign from thee.
39 But he answered and said unto them, An evil and adulterous generation seeketh after a sign; and there shall no sign be given to it, but the sign of the prophet Jonas:

"But I say to you that every idle word that men shall speak, they shall give an account concerning it in the Day of judgment" (v. 36). If every idle word will be judged, what can we say about deliberate words? The psalmist wisely prays, "Let the words of my mouth, and the meditation of my heart, be acceptable in thy sight, O Lord, my strength, and my redeemer" (Ps. 19:14).

"For out of your words you shall be justified, and out of your words you shall be condemned" (v. 37). All believers have grounds for echoing David's prayer, "Set a watch, O Lord, before my mouth; keep the door of my lips" (Ps. 141:3).

V. The Sign of the Evil Generation. vv. 38–50 [Mark 3:31–35; Luke 8:19–21].

"Then certain of the scribes and Pharisees answered him, saying, Teacher, we wish to see a sign from you" (v. 38). God had given signs for the call of Moses (Exod. 4:8–9). But the multitudes had already seen the signs and miracles that the Lord had worked (vv. 21–22).

"But he answered and said to them: An evil and adulterous generation is seeking after a sign, and no sign shall be given to it, except the sign of the prophet Jonah" (v. 39). Jonah was sent to the most cruel and evil people that the Israelites could think of, the Assyrians (Jonah 1:1–2). But Jonah was a unique sign.

"Unpardonable Sin," V, p. 845; ISBE (1988), "Sin," Unforgivable Sin, IV, p. 524; Butler, ed., *Holman Bible Dictionary*, "Unpardonable Sin, The," p. 1383.

12:34. For *offspring of vipers* see Matt. 3:7 note.

12:35. For the word *treasure* see Matt. 2:11 note.

12:36. The word *idle* (ἀργός) occurs 3 times in Matt. (12:36; 20:3, 6).

12:37. For the verb *to justify* see Matt. 11:19 note.

12:38. The word *sign* (σημεῖον) occurs 13 times in Matt. (12:38, 39 [3 times]; 16:1, 3, 4 [3 times]; 24:3, 24, 30; 26:48) and 75 times in the entire NT. A divine sign was greatly valued in the OT (Exod. 4:8–9; Josh. 4:5–7; II Kings 20:8–11). For further study see ZPEB, "Sign," V, pp. 429–31; ISBE (1988), "Sign," IV, pp. 505–8; Butler, ed., *Holman Bible Dictionary*, "Sign," pp. 1277–79; Gerhardsson, *The Mighty Acts of Jesus According to Matthew*.

40 For as Jonas was three days and three nights in the whale's belly; so shall the Son of man be three days and three nights in the heart of the earth.
41 The men of Nineveh shall rise in judgment with this generation, and shall condemn it: because they repented at the preaching of Jonas; and, behold, a greater than Jonas is here.
42 The queen of the south shall rise up in the judgment with this generation, and shall condemn it: for she came from the uttermost parts of the earth to hear the wisdom of Solomon; and, behold, a greater than Solomon is here.

"For even as Jonah was in the belly of the whale three days and three nights, so shall the Son of man be in the heart of the earth three days and three nights" (v. 40). The account of Jonah and the whale is not just a story. The Lord Jesus puts His stamp of approval on the narrative as historic fact. There will be people in heaven because of the preaching of Jonah. The Lord is here making a claim that He will be killed, be buried in a tomb for three days, and rise again. "No one has known that about himself except One Christ, the Son of God" (Wilbur M. Smith, *Therefore Stand*, p. 364). He is staking everything on His ability to come forth from the tomb. He knows that He will conquer death. This is the first time that the Lord prophesied His own death (Matt. 12:39–40; 16:21; 17:22–23; 20:17–19).

"The men of Nineveh shall rise up in the judgment with this generation and shall condemn it, because they repented at the preaching of Jonah, and, behold, a greater than Jonah is here" (v. 41). The Lord is putting Himself above the OT prophets.

"The queen of the south shall rise up in the judgment with this generation and shall condemn it, because she came from the ends of the earth to hear the wisdom of Solomon, and, behold, a greater than Solomon is here" (v. 42). The queen was the queen of Sheba who visited Solomon to

---

12:39. The prophet *Jonah* is named 5 times in Matt. (12:39, 40, 41 [twice]; 16:4).

12:40. The word *whale, sea creature* (κῆτος) occurs only here in the NT.

The number *three* (τρεῖς) occurs 12 times in Matt. (12:40 [4 times]; 13:33; 15:32; 17:4; 18:16, 20; 26:61; 27:40, 63). See Introduction, "Numbers," p. xxii.

12:41. The word *Ninevite* (Νινευίτης) occurs only here in Matt.

The verb *to condemn* (κατακρίνω) occurs 4 times in Matt. (12:41, 42; 20:18; 27:3).

12:42. The word *queen* (βασίλισσα) occurs only here in Matt.

The word *end* (πέρας) occurs only here in Matt.

43 When the unclean spirit is gone out of a man, he walketh through dry places, seeking rest, and findeth none.
44 Then he saith, I will return into my house from whence I came out; and when he is come, he findeth it empty, swept, and garnished.
45 Then goeth he, and taketh with himself seven other spirits more wicked than himself, and they enter in and dwell there: and the last state of that man is worse than the first. Even so shall it be also unto this wicked generation.
46 While he yet talked to the people, behold, his mother and his brethren stood without, desiring to speak with him.

learn of his wisdom (I Kings. 10:1–10). The Lord is putting Himself above the wisest king in the history of Israel.

"But whenever the unclean spirit goes out from a man, he goes through dry places seeking rest and does not find it" (v. 43). An evil spirit finds it more congenial to be in a human being, controlling him.

"Then he says, I will return into my house from whence I came out; and having come, he finds it empty, having been swept, and having been adorned" (v. 44). Once a person has been demon possessed, there is no protection for him. The saved person has the Spirit of God within (I Cor. 2:12; 3:16). But self-reformation is no protection from demonic attack.

"Then he goes and takes with himself seven other spirits more evil than himself, and they enter in and continue dwelling there; and the last things of that man are worse than the first. Thus it shall be for this evil generation" (v. 45). Their rejection of the true Messiah will bring on the disasters of the conflict with Rome and their ultimate defeat and deportation. The demons love to foment disaster, and this evil generation will be easy prey. Note that just as there are degrees of holiness, there are also degrees of depravity. The Jews thought that the Roman occupation under Pilate was terrible, but it was nothing compared to the coming sacking of Jerusalem in A.D. 70.

"While he was still speaking to the crowds, behold his mother and broth-

---

12:43. The word *waterless, dry* (ἄνυδρος) occurs only here in Matt.

12:44. The verb *to be empty* (σχολάζω) occurs only here in Matt.

The verb *to sweep* (σαρόω) occurs only here in Matt.

The verb *to adorn, set in order* (κοσμέω) occurs 3 times in Matt. (12:44; 23:29; 25:7).

12:45. The number 7 (ἑπτά) occurs 9 times in Matt. (12:45; 15:34, 36, 37; 16:10; 18:22; 22:25, 26, 28). See Introduction, "Numbers," p. xxii.

For the verb *to live, dwell*, see Matt. 2:23 note.

12:46. For the word *mother* see Matt. 1:18 note.

*47 Then one said unto him, Behold, thy mother and thy brethren stand with-
out, desiring to speak with thee.*
*48 But he answered and said unto him that told him, Who is my mother? and
who are my brethren?*
*49 And he stretched forth his hand toward his disciples, and said, Behold my
mother and my brethren!*
*50 For whosoever shall do the will of my Father which is in heaven, the same
is my brother, and sister, and mother.*

ers stood outside, seeking to speak with him" (v. 46). All that the Lord
was doing was still a mystery to them.

"But a certain one said to him, Behold your mother and your brothers
stand outside, seeking to speak to you" (v. 47). One of the crowd relayed
the fact to the Lord.

"But he answered and said to the one who spoke to him, Who is my
mother, and who are my brothers?" (v. 48). The Lord took the opportunity to teach a profound truth.

"And he stretched out his hand upon his disciples and said, Behold my
mother and my brothers" (v. 49). The Lord is clearly teaching that all
true believers are brought into a close family relationship with Himself.
He was not disparaging His family but exalting believers into a place of
remarkable fellowship.

"For whoever shall do the will of my Father who is in the heavens, he
himself is my brother and sister and mother" (v. 50). The Lord makes His
followers the cherished members of His heavenly family. He has a dear,
loving relationship with every believer. The redeemed in glory are the
children of the heavenly King (Rev. 21:7).

Practical Applications from Matthew 12

1. If a human king cared for his servants, how much more does God
   care for His servants (v. 3)? "My help cometh from the Lord. . . . He
   will not suffer thy foot to be moved: he that keepeth thee will not
   slumber" (Ps. 121:2–3).
2. God prizes the showing of mercy more than sacrifices (v. 7). "Mercy
   and truth shall be to them that devise good" (Prov. 14:22b).

12:49. For the word *disciple* see Matt. 5:1 note.

3. If we should be kind to animals, we should be kind to people also (vv. 11–12). "A righteous man regardeth the life of his beast: but the tender mercies of the wicked are cruel" (Prov. 12:10). "Be kind one to another, tenderhearted" (Eph. 4:32a).

4. The servant of the Lord shall prop up a bruised reed; shall He not uphold a weak servant (vv. 18–20)? "God has chosen the weak things of the world to confound the mighty" (I Cor. 1:27b).

5. The Lord can totally break the power of the Devil (v. 22). "Submit yourselves therefore to God. Resist the devil, and he will flee from you" (James 4:7).

6. The ministry of the Lord Jesus was a manifestation of the rule of God (v. 28). "And let the peace of God rule in your hearts" (Col. 3:15a).

7. The desire of the heart to do good to others comes from God (v. 35). "But the one who looks into the perfect law of liberty and continues, not being a forgetful hearer, but a doer of work, this man shall be blessed in his doing" (James 1:25).

8. If men must give account of every idle word, what about deliberate words? (v. 36). No wonder the psalmist prayed, "Set a watch, O Lord, before my mouth; keep the door of my lips" (Ps. 141:3).

9. In spite of all his failures, Jonah became the instrument of repentance for the people of Nineveh (v. 41). "The law of the Lord is perfect, converting the soul; the testimony of the Lord is sure, making wise the simple" (Ps. 19:7).

10. Self-reformation is weak and easily undone (v. 45). Jesus promised, "If you continue in my word, then are you my disciples indeed; and you shall know the truth, and the truth shall make you free" (John 8:31b–32).

11. The Lord Jesus claimed believers as His family (vv. 49–50). "Now therefore you are no longer strangers and foreigners, but fellow citizens with the saints, and of the household of God" (Eph. 2:19).

Prayer

Lord Jesus, help us to honor and serve You above all. Protect us from uttering words that would dishonor You. Give us the grace to do the will of Your Father, even as You did. Strengthen us so that we do not become weary in well doing. Amen.

MATTHEW 13

KINGDOM PARABLES

Persons
Jesus
Great multitudes
His disciples
People in a synagogue

Persons referred to
A sower
Isaiah
The wicked one
Prophets
Righteous men
One who hears without understanding
One who hears, quickly receives, and forgets
One who hears among thorns
One who hears, understands, and is fruitful
A man who sowed good seed
An enemy
Servants
A man who sowed a mustard seed
A woman who baked bread
A man who found a treasure
A merchant seeking pearls
Angels
The wicked
The just
A householder
The carpenter [Joseph]
His mother Mary
His brothers: James
Joses
Simon
Judas
His sisters

Places mentioned
The seaside
The house
His own country

Doctrines taught
Diversity of response to the Word
A fruitful life
The kingdom of heaven
Spiritual understanding
The Devil's work
The deceitfulness of riches
Spiritual fruitfulness
Future judgment
Hell
The cost of the kingdom
Wisdom
Unbelief

1 *The same day went Jesus out of the house, and sat by the sea side.*
2 *And great multitudes were gathered together unto him, so that he went into*
a ship, and sat; and the whole multitude stood on the shore.
3 *And he spake many things unto them in parables, saying, Behold, a sower*
went forth to sow;

Matthew 13 Exposition

I. *The Sower. vv. 1–23 [Mark 4:3–25; Luke 8:5–18].*

"In that day Jesus went out of the house and was sitting alongside the
sea" (v. 1). The Sea of Galilee is a lovely place to sit alongside and talk.
The phrase *in that day* refers to the same day He preached the sermon in
the synagogue (Matt. 12:9–50). Matthew Henry notes that the Lord thus
preached two sermons on the same Sabbath day and draws the conclusion
that it is good to preach morning and evening messages in church today.
The second sermon "will be so far from driving out the morning sermon,
that it will rather clinch it, and fasten the nail in a sure place."

"And many crowds gathered together to him, so that he entered into a
boat to sit, and all the crowd stood upon the shore" (v. 2). In the boat He
could be seen easily by the multitude, and the slope of the ground coming
down to the sea would make a natural amphitheater for the crowd to see
and hear.

"And he spoke many things to them in parables, saying: Behold, the
sower went out in order to be sowing" (v. 3). The phrase *many things*
shows that Matthew is recording only a bare outline of what the Lord

---

13:1. Many consider these seven parables to be central to the teaching of the entire book.
They finally explain what the kingdom is all about. The kingdom is the whole rule of God
in the coming age. Some wonder why Jesus did not call it the church age, but that would
focus only on the *good* aspect, and the coming age was going to be *mixed* in its character
and will have several stages. He will discuss the church, but with His disciples alone
(Matt. 16:13–20). The present company was a mixed crowd of believers and unbelievers.
Morris warns against the idea that the interpretations in the Gospel are those of the early
church rather than of Jesus Himself (*Matt.*, p. 344). That view not only militates against
inspiration but also fails to perceive the divine power in the biblical text. George N. H.
Peters argued that the kingdom was offered and postponed (*The Theocratic Kingdom*, II, pp.
11ff.). It is better to think of God's kingdom as always having two stages: a slow growth
stage (that is still going on) and a triumphal manifestation in an earthly millennium (Rev.
20:1–6) and an eternal reign without foes (Rev. 21–22).

13:3. The word *parable* (παραβολή) occurs 17 times in Matt. (13:3, 10, 13, 18, 24, 31,
33, 34 [twice], 35, 36, 53; 15:15; 21:33, 45; 22:1; 24:32). A *parable* is a story, *cast alongside*,
to illuminate the subject being discussed. The Lord loved to use such parables in His
teaching. He was a grand master at using simple people and events to teach profound
spiritual truths. For added helps on interpreting parables see R. C. Trench, *The Parables;*

4 And when he sowed, some seeds fell by the way side, and the fowls came and devoured them up:

5 Some fell upon stony places, where they had not much earth: and forthwith they sprung up, because they had no deepness of earth:

6 And when the sun was up, they were scorched; and because they had no root, they withered away.

spent some time discussing. In the second parable the sower is the Son of man (v. 34), but here the sower may refer to anyone who gives out the Word of God. The emphasis here is not on the sower but on the power of the seed to bring forth fruit. The Word of God has always had this power (Isa. 55:10–11). In this scene the Lord is doing the sowing, but later His followers will be doing it (Matt. 28:19–20; Acts 1:8; Rom. 1:16–17). Every Christian worker must remember that the power does not lie in himself, but in the Word of God that he shares with people. The Lord asked Jeremiah, "Is not my word . . . like a hammer that breaketh the rock in pieces?" (Jer. 23:29).

"And while he is sowing, some fell upon the pathway, and the birds came and devoured them" (v. 4). The picture is of a path that leads from the village through the fields. All the farmers would walk out to their plot, trampling the path as hard as concrete. Any seed that accidentally fell on the path would not penetrate the hard surface. The birds would be quick to see that seed lying there and eat it up. In the second parable the seed is identified as wheat (v. 25), but here it is not identified.

"But some fell on rocky ground where it was not having much earth, and immediately it sprouted because it was not having much earth, but when the sun was risen, it was scorched, and because it was not having root, it was withered" (vv. 5–6). Normally we think of rocky ground as soil that

G. H. Lang, *The Parabolic Teaching of Scripture*; S. Kistemaker, *The Parables of Jesus*; D. Wenham, *The Parables of Jesus*; C. L. Blomberg, *Interpreting the Parables*; R. H. Stein, *An Introduction to the Parables of Jesus*; Ryken, Wilhoit, and Longman, *Dictionary of Biblical Imagery*, "Parable," pp. 623–24; ZPEB, "Parable," IV, pp. 590–97; ISBE (1986), "Parable," III, pp. 655–59; *Holman Bible Dictionary*, "Parables," pp. 1071–73. For a visual treat see *The Parables of Our Lord and Saviour Jesus Christ*, pictures by John Everett Millais, engraved by the Brothers Dalziel, New York: Dover, 1864, 1975, 76 pp.

For the verb *to sow* see Matt. 6:26 note; for help on *the sower* see Alexander Whyte, *Bible Characters*, "The Sower," VI, pp. 9–18.

13:4. For the word *bird* see Matt. 6:26 note.

13:5. The word *rocky ground* (πετρώδης) occurs only here and in v. 20 in Matt.

13:6. For the word *sun* see Matt. 5:45 note.

The verb *to wither away, dry up* (ξηραίνω) occurs 3 times in Matt. (13:6; 21:19, 20).

7 And some fell among thorns; and the thorns sprung up, and choked them:
8 But other fell into good ground, and brought forth fruit, some an hundred-fold, some sixtyfold, some thirtyfold.
9 Who hath ears to hear, let him hear.
10 And the disciples came, and said unto him, Why speakest thou unto them in parables?
11 He answered and said unto them, Because it is given unto you to know the mysteries of the kingdom of heaven, but to them it is not given.

has rocks scattered through it here and there, but that type of soil would be considered good ground in the Holy Land. Rocky ground here refers to ground that has bedrock lying just under the surface. The warmth of the rock would cause the seed to sprout quickly, but there would be no place for roots to go, and the plants would wither away.

"But other fell among the thorns, and the thorns sprang up and choked them" (v. 7). These thorns may be those called "mock orange" and often grow more than head high, with thorns four to five inches long. They are a real problem for farmers.

"But other fell upon the good ground and was giving fruit, some a hundred, some sixty, and some thirtyfold. Let the one who has ears keep on hearing" (vv. 8–9). The present imperative implies that we have not yet "heard" all the truth that is in this parable.

"And the disciples came and said to him: Why are you speaking to them in parables?" (v. 10). The disciples saw that some of the people were plainly mystified, and the disciples themselves had questions of their own. The psalmist prayed, "Open thou mine eyes, that I may behold wondrous things out of thy law" (Ps. 119:18). That is a good prayer for all believers to pray on opening Scripture.

13:7. For the word *thorn* see Matt. 7:16 note.

The verb *to choke* (πνίγω) occurs twice in Matt. (13:7; 18:28).

13:8. For the word *fruit* see Matt. 3:8 note.

13:9. For the word *ear* see Matt. 10:27 note.

The verb *to hear* (ἀκούω) occurs 17 times in this chapter alone (vv. 9, 13 [twice], 14, 15 [twice], 16, 17 [3 times], 18, 19, 20, 22, 23, 43 [twice]). There is a pressing responsibility to hear the divine revelation with understanding and submission. See Matt. 2:3 note.

13:11. The word *mystery* (μυστήριον) occurs only here in Matt. God's revelation of mysteries to mankind manifests His omniscience, sovereignty, and grace (Elwell, ed., *Evangelical Dictionary of Biblical Theology*, "Mystery," pp. 546–47). For further study see ZPEB, "Mystery," IV, pp. 327–30; ISBE (1986), "Mystery," III, pp. 451–55; Harrison, ed., *Baker's Dictionary of Theology*, "Mystery," pp. 366–67.

12 For whosoever hath, to him shall be given, and he shall have more abundance: but whosoever hath not, from him shall be taken away even that he hath.
13 Therefore speak I to them in parables: because they seeing see not; and hearing they hear not, neither do they understand.
14 And in them is fulfilled the prophecy of Esaias, which saith, By hearing ye shall hear, and shall not understand; and seeing ye shall see, and shall not perceive:

"But he answered and said to them: Because to you it has been given to know the mysteries of the kingdom of the heavens, but to them it has not been given" (v. 11). A *mystery* is a divinely revealed truth so profound that some mystery still remains about it. God gives spiritual perception to His people, but not to unbelievers. This is the reason that the saints rejoice in the truths of Scripture, but people of the world can see nothing there to interest them.

"For whoever has, to him it shall be given and he shall have abundance; but whoever has not, even that which he has shall be taken from him" (v. 12). The saints who love Scripture constantly find more truths to rejoice in. People who despise Scripture constantly lose the ability to see anything in it. The servant who used ten talents well got more; the one who got one but did not use it lost it (Matt. 25:20–28).

"On account of this I am speaking to them in parables, because seeing, they see not, and hearing, they hear not, neither do they understand, and in them the prophecy of Isaiah is fulfilled, which says:

> In hearing you hear and never understand,
> And seeing you see and never perceive.
> For the heart of this people grew dull,
> And with their ears they heard with difficulty,
> And their eyes they closed,
> Lest they should see with their eyes,
> And hear with their ears,

13:12. For the verb *to have abundance* see Matt. 5:20 note.

13:13. The verb *to understand* (συνίημι) occurs 9 times in Matt. (13:13, 14, 15, 19, 23, 51; 15:10; 16:12; 17:13). In this context the Lord stresses the need for spiritual understanding. Believers need to pray the psalmist's prayer, "Open thou mine eyes, that I may behold wondrous things out of thy law" (Ps. 119:18). Paul prayed that believers might be filled "with the knowledge of his will in all wisdom and spiritual understanding" (Col. 1:9*b*). For discussion see ISBE (1988), "Understanding," IV, p. 945.

*15 For this people's heart is waxed gross, and their ears are dull of hearing,
and their eyes they have closed; lest at any time they should see with their eyes
and hear with their ears, and should understand with their heart, and should be
converted, and I should heal them.*
16 But blessed are your eyes, for they see: and your ears, for they hear.

> And understand in their heart,
>
> And should be converted, and I should heal them" (vv. 13–15;
>   Isa. 6:9–10, LXX).

In the context Isaiah is speaking to people who had refused to hear the
word of the Lord and were under judgment. The Lord here gives a precise
quotation from the Septuagint, which would be considered normal in
the Greek- speaking Galilean region. A. T. Robertson argues, "It is clear,
therefore, that Jesus spoke both Aramaic and Greek according to the
demands of the occasion and read the Hebrew as well as the Septuagint,
if we may argue from the O. T. quotations in the Gospels which are partly
like the Hebrew text and partly like the LXX" (*A Grammar of the Greek
New Testament*, p. 29). Although the Lord was speaking very clearly,
the unbelieving people were not understanding and were not profiting
from the blessed teaching of the Lord. Hearing with submission leads to
conversion and spiritual benefit, but they did not believe. There must
be spiritual understanding in the heart, the inmost being of the believer.
The apostle Paul emphasizes that "there is none that understand; there
is none who seek God" (Rom. 3:11). But the Lord has given the Spirit to
His people that they might be "understanding what the will of the Lord
is" (Eph. 5:17*b*). Now we should be "filled with the Spirit" (Eph. 5:18*b*).
Paul prayed that believers might be filled with "all wisdom and spiritual
understanding" (Col. 1:9*b*). Every believer should echo the psalmist's zeal,
"O how love I thy law! it is my meditation all the day" (Ps. 119:97).

"But blessed are your eyes because they are seeing and your ears because
they are hearing" (v. 16). The disciples had surrendered to the Lord and
now they could see and hear Scripture accurately.

13:15. The verb *to grow dull* (παχύνω) occurs only here in Matt.

For the word *heart* see Matt. 5:8 note.

For the verb *to be converted, return* see Matt. 10:13 note.

For the verb *to heal* see Matt. 8:8 note.

13:16. For the word *blessed* see Matt. 5:3 note.

17 For verily I say unto you, That many prophets and righteous men have desired to see those things which ye see, and have not seen them; and to hear those things which ye hear, and have not heard them.
18 Hear ye therefore the parable of the sower.
19 When any one heareth the word of the kingdom, and understandeth it not, then cometh the wicked one, and catcheth away that which was sown in his heart. This is he which received seed by the way side.
20 But he that received the seed into stony places, the same is he that heareth the word, and anon with joy receiveth it;

"For truly I say to you that many prophets and righteous men passionately desired to see the things you are seeing and did not see them, and to hear the things you are hearing and did not hear" (v. 17). Consider the prayers of the psalmist: "Let my prayer come before thee . . . for my soul is full of troubles" (Ps. 88:2–3a; Ps. 102:1; 119:170).

"Therefore hear the parable of the sower" (v. 18). The Lord commands the disciples to hear with understanding. Now the Lord explains the parable so that all believers may understand. The Lord spoke in parables not to hide their meaning from His people but so that His explanations may bring them to clearer understanding of the truth. The world, without spiritual insight, gropes for meaning. Isaiah cried out to wicked rulers, "Wherefore hear the word of the Lord, ye scornful men" (Isa. 28:14a).

"If anyone hears the word of the kingdom and does not understand it, the evil one comes and snatches away what has been sown in his heart. This is the one sown alongside the path" (v. 19). The deeds of the birds are equivalent to the deeds of the Devil. Everyone has had the experience of reading a portion of Scripture and getting the idea, "You need to talk to so-and-so; you're missing a TV program; you ought to check your e-mail!" Few people recognize these thoughts as the work of the Devil. He is skillful at distracting people from the Word of God.

"But the one who was sown upon the rocky places, this is the one who hears the word and immediately with joy receives it, but he has no root in himself, but is temporary, but when tribulation or persecution on account of the word comes, immediately he is caused to stumble" (vv. 20–21). There are people who are glad to hear spiritual truth, but it does

13:17. For the word *amen, truly,* see Matt. 5:18 note.

For the word *to passionately desire* see Matt. 5:28 note.

13:19. For *the evil one* see Matt. 5:37 note.

21 Yet hath he not root in himself, but dureth for a while: for when tribulation or persecution ariseth because of the word, by and by he is offended.
22 He also that received seed among the thorns is he that heareth the word; and the care of this world, and the deceitfulness of riches, choke the word, and he becometh unfruitful.
23 But he that received seed into the good ground is he that heareth the word, and understandeth it; which also beareth fruit, and bringeth forth, some an hundredfold, some sixty, some thirty.

not change their lives. This person is quick to embrace what is new and quick to abandon it when difficulties come. The word did not take root in his heart. The bedrock of sin was in the way. There was no commitment to God in what he did. When the psalmist said, "I have chosen the way of truth: thy judgments have I laid before me" (Ps. 119:30), he was not referring to a temporary decision. He added, "I have stuck unto thy testimonies" (Ps. 119:31a).

"But the one who was sown among the thorns, this one is the one who hears the word and the cares of the age, and the deceitfulness of riches choke the word and it becomes unfruitful" (v. 22). Worldly cares weigh heavily on everyone. There is a real deception in riches. People think that because they have money and many possessions things are all right with them. The advertising world exists on the proposition that you must have this "thing," whatever it may be, to be truly happy. In fact you may be just as happy if you had never heard of that "thing." When you die, you will leave every last "thing" behind you. The only things you will have in the next realm are your relationship with God and with other people. If you are right with God, you will have everlasting joy (Rev. 21:1–4). If you are not right with God, you will have everlasting sorrow (Matt. 24:49–51). If you have helped God's people, they will be there to thank you (Heb. 12:22–23; Luke 16:22–25). If you have harmed people, they will be there to jeer at you (Isa. 14:4–11).

"But the one who was sown upon the good ground, this one is the one who hears the word and understands it, who also brings forth fruit and

13:21. For the word *root* see Matt. 3:10 note.

The word *tribulation, trouble* (θλῖψις) occurs 4 times in Matt. (13:21; 24:9, 21, 29). For *the great tribulation* see Matt. 24:21 note.

13:22. The word *care* (μέριμνα) occurs only here in Matt.

The word *deception, deceitfulness* (ἀπάτη) occurs only here in Matt.

13:23. The verb *to bear fruit* (καρποφορέω) occurs only here in Matt.

*24 Another parable put he forth unto them, saying, The kingdom of heaven is
likened unto a man which sowed good seed in his field:*
*25 But while men slept, his enemy came and sowed tares among the wheat,
and went his way.*
*26 But when the blade was sprung up, and brought forth fruit, then appeared
the tares also.*
*27 So the servants of the householder came and said unto him, Sir, didst not
thou sow good seed in thy field? from whence then hath it tares?*

produces some a hundred, some sixty, and some thirtyfold" (v. 23). The
persons who submit to God's Word will bring forth fruit, but in varying
degrees. Paul desired the Philippians to be "filled with the fruits of righteousness" (Phil. 1:11*a*).

II. The Darnel Among the Wheat. vv. 24–30.

"Another parable he put forth to them, saying, The kingdom of the
heavens is like a man who sows good seed in his field, but while men were
sleeping, his enemy came and resowed darnel in the midst of the wheat
and departed" (vv. 24–25). The parallel to this parable is plainly the enemy in the Garden of Eden (Gen. 3). The Devil loves to ruin what is good.
The whole history of mankind is that of a conflict between good and evil.
God is drawing mankind to Himself, but the Devil is dragging man down
into sin and degradation. It is morally necessary for a good person to have
enemies. His good must be tested to become strong.

"But when the stalks sprouted and produced fruit, then the darnel was
also manifest" (v. 26). The wheat would be bowed over with the heavy
weight of grain, but the darnel stalks would be straight as an arrow, with
just a few seeds.

"But the slaves of the master of the house came and said to him, Lord, did

---

13:24. For *the man who sowed good seed*, see Alexander Whyte, *Bible Characters*, VI,
pp. 19–29.

13:25. For the word *enemy* see Matt. 5:43 note.

The verb *to resow* (ἐπισπείρω) occurs only here in the NT. It is a technical term for
sowing a second crop in a field. See Moulton and Milligan, *Vocabulary*, p. 245; Arndt and
Gingrich, *Lexicon*, "to sow afterward," p. 300.

The word *darnel* (ζιζάνιον) occurs 8 times in Matt. alone in the NT (13:25, 26, 27,
29, 30, 36, 38, 40). Darnel (*Lolium temulentum* L.) is a weed that looks like wheat but
produces no edible seeds. A poisonous fungus grows in the kernels. For further discussion
see Zohary, *Plants of the Bible*, p. 161; ZPEB, "Tares," V, p. 596; ISBE (1988), "Weeds," IV,
p. 1045.

13:26. For the word *stalk, grass* see Matt. 6:30 note.

28 He said unto them, An enemy hath done this. The servants said unto him, Wilt thou then that we go and gather them up?
29 But he said, Nay; lest while ye gather up the tares, ye root up also the wheat with them.
30 Let both grow together until the harvest: and in the time of harvest I will say to the reapers, Gather ye together first the tares, and bind them in bundles to burn them: but gather the wheat into my barn.

you not sow good seed in your field? Whence does it have darnel?" (v. 27). Servants of the Lord are often puzzled by events, but the Lord always knows what is happening.

"But he said to them, An enemy did this. But the slaves say to him, Do you wish, therefore, that we go and gather them?" (v. 28). They want to help by pulling the weeds out, but they do not understand the complexity of the problem. In the religious world the *wheat* was a weed until he was converted.

"But he said, No, lest in gathering the darnel, you uproot the wheat together with them" (v. 29). To make an application: shutting out unconverted people from a church removes potential converts. But they are very different from an apostate, who has already made a final choice.

"Permit them both to grow together until the harvest, and in the time of harvest I will say to the reapers: Gather first the darnel and bind them into bundles in order to burn them up, but gather the wheat into my barn" (v. 30). This was good agricultural practice, but it is also a prophecy of the judgment (Matt. 3:12; 25:31–46). The darnel was burned so that it would not contaminate the field again; the wicked will be cast into hell so that they will never again be able to harm the righteous. The barn implies careful provision for the well-being of the harvest of grain (Matt. 25:33–34; Rev. 20:1–6). John makes clear in Revelation 20 that this is a millennial context.

13:27. For the word *master of the house* see Matt. 10:25 note.

13:28. For the verb *to gather* see Matt. 7:16 note.

13:29. The verb *to uproot* (ἐκριζόω) occurs only twice in Matt. (13:29; 15:13).

13:30. The verb *to grow together* (συναυξάνω) occurs only here in the NT.

For the word *harvest* see Matt. 9:37 note.

The word *reaper* (θεριστής) occurs only twice in this context in the NT (Matt. 13:30, 39).

For the verb *to burn up* see Matt. 3:12 note.

31 Another parable put he forth unto them, saying, The kingdom of heaven is like to a grain of mustard seed, which a man took, and sowed in his field:
32 Which indeed is the least of all seeds: but when it is grown, it is the greatest among herbs, and becometh a tree, so that the birds of the air come and lodge in the branches thereof.
33 Another parable spake he unto them; The kingdom of heaven is like unto leaven, which a woman took, and hid in three measures of meal, till the whole was leavened.

III. The Mustard Seed. vv. 31–32 [Mark 4:30–32].

"Another parable he put forth to them, saying: The kingdom of the heavens is like a seed of mustard, which a man took and sowed in his field" (v. 31). The mustard seed is a small, unremarkable seed but is a perfect sphere.

"Which is smaller, on the one hand, than all the seeds, but whenever it is grown, it is greater than all the herbs, and becomes a tree, so that the birds of the sky may come and roost in its branches" (v. 32). The seed is smaller than the usual beans, lentils, and other herb seeds. In well-watered places the plant may reach ten or twelve feet tall. Yet it is still an herb, without the strength of a small tree. It is not unusual to see a single mustard plant in a garden in Palestine. One plant can produce enough mustard seeds for any family. In the first century the Christian faith started with twelve men, but as time progresses, there is a vast company of the redeemed gathering in heaven. Their strength is not in themselves but in the Lord, Who is gathering them.

IV. The Leaven. vv. 33–35.

"Another parable he spoke to them: The kingdom of the heavens is like leaven, which a woman put in three measures of wheat flour until the whole was leavened" (v. 33). This was the very measure that Sarah used for her unexpected guests (Gen. 18:6). Leaven is an apt illustration

13:31. Both the word *seed* (**κόκκος**) and the word *mustard* (**σίναπι**) occur twice in Matt. (13:31; 17:20).

For *the man who sowed a mustard seed*, see Alexander Whyte, *Bible Characters*, VI, pp. 30–38.

13:32. The word *branch* (**κλάδος**) occurs 3 times in Matt. (13:32; 21:8; 24:32).

13:33. The word *leaven, yeast* (**ζύμη**) occurs 4 times in Matt. (13:33; 16:6, 11, 12).

For *the woman who took leaven* see Alexander Whyte, *Bible Characters*, VI, pp. 49–58. See also ZPEB, "Leaven," III, pp. 901–3; ISBE (1986), "Leaven," pp. 97–98; Ryken, Wilhoit, and Longman, *Dictionary of Biblical Imagery*, "Leaven," p. 498.

The verb *to put in, mix*, (**ἐγκρύπτω**) occurs only here in Matt.

34 All these things spake Jesus unto the multitude in parables; and without a parable spake he not unto them:
35 That it might be fulfilled which was spoken by the prophet, saying, I will open my mouth in parables; I will utter things which have been kept secret from the foundation of the world.
36 Then Jesus sent the multitude away, and went into the house: and his disciples came unto him, saying, Declare unto us the parable of the tares of the field.
37 He answered and said unto them, He that soweth the good seed is the Son of man;

of hidden, quiet, but thorough working. The spread of the gospel has followed that course to a remarkable degree. The power of God works in believers to cause them to grow in strength and testimony. The OT prophesied just such a new revelation: "I will open my mouth in a parable: I will utter dark sayings of old" (Ps. 78:2). Morris notes that the leaven was actually "a piece of fermented dough from a previous baking" (*Matt.*, p. 353, n. 83).

"All these things Jesus spoke in parables to the crowds, and apart from a parable he spoke nothing to them, in order that it might be fulfilled which was spoken through the prophet, saying,

I will open my mouth in parables;

I will declare things which have been hidden from the foundation of the world" (vv. 34–35; Ps. 78:2).

The Lord Jesus shed a flood of light on the OT prophecies.

V. The Explanation of the Darnel Among the Wheat. vv. 36–43.

"Then he sent away the crowds and went into the house, and his disciples came to him, saying: Explain to us the parable of the darnel among the wheat" (v. 36). There were puzzling and disturbing ideas in that parable for the disciples. The Lord proceeds to give a thorough explanation.

"But he answered and said, The one who sows the good seed is the Son of man" (v. 37). The Lord Himself is the major figure in this parable.

The word *measure* (σάτον), a dry measure, is equivalent to about a peck and a half (Arndt and Gingrich, p. 752).

The word *wheat flour* (ἄλευρον) occurs only here in Matt.

13:35. The verb *to declare* (ἐρεύγομαι) occurs only here in the NT.

For the verb *to hide* see Matt. 5:14 note.

13:36. The verb *to explain* (διασαφέω) occurs only twice in the NT (Matt. 13:36; 18:31). It was dropping out of usage during NT times. See Moulton and Milligan, *Vocabulary*, p. 153.

38 The field is the world; the good seed are the children of the kingdom; but the tares are the children of the wicked one;
39 The enemy that sowed them is the devil; the harvest is the end of the world; and the reapers are the angels.
40 As therefore the tares are gathered and burned in the fire; so shall it be in the end of this world.
41 The Son of man shall send forth his angels, and they shall gather out of his kingdom all things that offend, and them which do iniquity;
42 And shall cast them into a furnace of fire: there shall be wailing and gnashing of teeth.

"But the field is the world, but the good seed, these are the sons of the kingdom; but the darnel are the sons of the evil one" (v. 38). The Lord sows His good wheat in the world, but the Devil sows his evil workers among them. The religious scene has always been a mixed one. Truth and error have always been at war.

"But the enemy who sowed them is the devil, but the harvest is the consummation of the age; but the reapers are angels" (v. 39). The angels cannot make a mistake as to who belongs to God and who belongs to the Devil (Ezek. 9:1–6).

"Therefore even as the darnel is gathered up and burned in fire, thus it shall be in the consummation of the age" (v. 40). God has already decided how the age shall end. The righteous must be preserved from the harmful influence of the wicked.

"The Son of man shall send his angels, and they shall gather all the stumbling blocks and the ones who do lawlessness, and shall cast them into the furnace of fire; and there shall be weeping and grinding of teeth" (vv. 41–42). The angels will collect all sinners and will put them where they belong. The Bible clearly warns that there is a lake of fire ahead for all the wicked (Rev. 20:11–15). The sinners will grieve over being caught, but they will never change their opposition to God.

13:37. For the title *Son of man* see Matt. 8:20 note.

13:38. For the word *world* see Matt. 4:8 note.

13:39. The word *consummation, end* (συντέλεια) occurs 5 times in Matt. (13:39, 40, 49; 24:3; 28:20), each with the connotation of *the end of the age*. The subject of how the world shall come to an end is very complex. For further discussion see the Introduction, p. xli, as well as ZPEB, "End of the World," II, p. 304; "Eschatology," II, pp. 342–58; ISBE (1982), "Eschatology," pp. 130–43; Walvoord, *Major Bible Prophecies*, "Signs of the Lord's Return," pp. 249–64; Pentecost, *Things to Come*.

13:41. The word *stumbling block* (σκάνδαλον) occurs 5 times in Matt. (13:41; 16:23; 18:7 [3 times]). See also Matt. 16:23 note.

43 Then shall the righteous shine forth as the sun in the kingdom of their Father. Who hath ears to hear, let him hear.
44 Again, the kingdom of heaven is like unto treasure hid in a field; the which when a man hath found, he hideth, and for joy thereof goeth and selleth all that he hath, and buyeth that field.
45 Again, the kingdom of heaven is like unto a merchant man, seeking goodly pearls:

"Then shall the righteous shine forth as the sun in the kingdom of their Father. Let the one who has ears keep on hearing" (v. 43). God shall vindicate the righteous in the coming kingdom. He shall wipe away every tear and shall satisfy them with everlasting life and joy (Rev. 21:2–7). Now the ministry of the church is to invite men to forsake their sin and turn to God, for He is ready to forgive them (Rev. 22:17).

VI. The Hid Treasure. v. 44.

"The kingdom of the heavens is like a treasure that has been hidden in a field, which a man found and hid, and for the joy of it goes and sells all that he has and buys that field" (v. 44). The man is surprised to find it, but he does not just grab it and run. He recognizes the greatness of the treasure and is prepared to sacrifice everything to get it. This is the attitude of the believer toward God's salvation. He secures the treasure in the proper way and values it above all. In modern terms:

1. He recognizes his need of salvation Rom. 3:10, 23.
2. He trusts the grace of the Lord Jesus for redemption. Rom. 3:22, 24.
3. He calls upon the Lord Jesus Christ for salvation. Rom. 10:13.
4. Thereafter he seeks to serve Him as a redeemed believer. Rom. 12:1.

VII. The Pearl. vv. 45–46.

"Again the kingdom of the heavens is like a merchant man seeking beautiful pearls; but when he found one very valuable pearl, he sold all, as many things as he had, and bought it" (vv. 45–46). Here the merchant

---

For the word *lawlessness* see Matt. 7:23 note.

13:42. The phrase *the furnace of fire* (κάμινον τοῦ πυρός) occurs twice in Matt. (13:42, 50). The word *furnace* may also mean *oven* (Moulton and Milligan, *Vocabulary*, p. 320).

For the word *weeping, bitter crying*, see Matt. 2:18 note.

13:43. For the word *righteous* see Matt. 1:19 note.

13:44. For the word *treasure* see Matt. 2:11 note.

For *the man who finds the treasure* see Alexander Whyte, *Bible Characters*, VI, pp. 59–68.

The verb *to buy* (ἀγοράζω) occurs 7 times in Matt. (13:44, 46; 14:15; 21:12; 25:9, 10; 27:7).

46 Who, when he had found one pearl of great price, went and sold all that he had, and bought it.
47 Again, the kingdom of heaven is like unto a net, that was cast into the sea, and gathered of every kind:
48 Which, when it was full, they drew to shore, and sat down, and gathered the good into vessels, but cast the bad away.
49 So shall it be at the end of the world: the angels shall come forth, and sever the wicked from among the just,

is systematically searching for beautiful pearls. When he finds the exceptional one, he is ready to secure it. There are people who are "seekers" after God. They try one religion after another without finding peace of conscience. Then they "find" Christ and discover the peace that passes understanding. They turn away from all other religions and center their trust and hope in Christ alone. "For the word of the cross is to them that perish foolishness; but to us who are saved it is the power of God" (I Cor. 1:18). In the culture of the ancient world a man who found such a pearl would take it and present it to the king. From then on he would be known as "a friend of the king." His fortune would be made. For believers today the sacrifice of Christ on the cross is the only thing that can give them access to God.

VIII. The Dragnet. vv. 47–52.

"Again, the kingdom of the heavens is like a dragnet, which was cast into the sea and gathered of every kind; which, when it was full, they dragged to the shore and sat down and put the good into containers, but cast the rotten out" (vv. 47–48). The dragnet was shaped like a large bag and gathered things indiscriminately. Thomson has a vivid description of the use of the dragnet (*The Land and the Book*, p. 402). The implication is that the kingdom will gather many kinds of people, but not all will truly belong to God. The organized church presents the gospel to all and gathers those who

13:45. For the word *pearl* see Matt. 7:6 note.

For *the merchant who bought the pearl* see Whyte, *Bible Characters*, VI, pp. 69–77.

13:46. The word *very valuable, expensive* (πολύτιμος) occurs only here in Matt.

The verb *to sell* (πιπράσκω) occurs 3 times in Matt. (13:46; 18:25; 26:9).

13:47. The word *dragnet* (σαγήνη) occurs only here in the NT.

13:48. The verb *to drag* (ἀναβιβάζω) occurs only here in the NT.

The word *container* (ἄγγος) occurs only here in the NT.

For the word *rotten* see Matt. 7:17 note.

50 And shall cast them into the furnace of fire: there shall be wailing and gnashing of teeth.
51 Jesus saith unto them, Have ye understood all these things? They say unto him, Yea, Lord.
52 Then said he unto them, Therefore every scribe which is instructed unto the kingdom of heaven is like unto a man that is an householder, which bringeth forth out of his treasure things new and old.
53 And it came to pass, that when Jesus had finished these parables, he departed thence.

profess Christ into their fellowship. Only God knows the hearts of those who come. At the end of this life there will be an infallible separation.

"Thus it shall be in the consummation of the age; the angels shall go out and shall separate the evil ones from the midst of the righteous and shall cast them into the furnace of fire; there shall be weeping and grinding of teeth" (vv. 49–50). The Lord solemnly warns again of the separation of the wicked from the righteous. Evil people may satisfy every lust in this world, but once they are taken out of it, they will never be satisfied again (Luke 16:19–31).

Now the Lord asks a searching question. "Have you understood all these things? They say to him, Yes. But he said to them: On account of this every scribe who has been taught in the kingdom of the heavens is like a man who is master of the house, who brings out of his treasure things new and old" (vv. 51–52). It is significant that the Lord likens understanding to a treasure. Understanding is crucial for every believer (v. 13 note). Otherwise they may be troubled when they see the wicked prospering and the righteous suffering (Ps. 37). They need to remember that oceans of comfort await the righteous (Rev. 7:13–17), and a lake of fire awaits the wicked (Rev. 20:11–15). The whole passage raises the question for every reader: Have you received Christ as your Savior from your sins?

IX. *The Unbelief at Nazareth. vv. 53–58.*

"And it came to pass when Jesus ended these parables, he departed from there, and came into his own country and was teaching them in their

---

13:49. The verb *to separate* (ἀφορίζω) occurs 3 times in Matt. (13:49; 25:32 [twice]).

13:51. Solomon greatly valued understanding: "Evil men understand not judgment: but they that seek the Lord understand all things" (Prov. 28:5).

13:52. The verb *to be, or to make a disciple* (μαθητεύω) occurs 3 times in Matt. (13:52; 27:57; 28:19) and not in the other Gospels. See the noun *disciple* in Matt. 5:1 note.

54 And when he was come into his own country, he taught them in their syna-
gogue, insomuch that they were astonished, and said, Whence hath this man
this wisdom, and these mighty works?
55 Is not this the carpenter's son? is not his mother called Mary? and his breth-
ren, James, and Joses, and Simon, and Judas?
56 And his sisters, are they not all with us? Whence then hath this man all
these things?
57 And they were offended in him. But Jesus said unto them, A prophet is not
without honour, save in his own country, and in his own house.
58 And he did not many mighty works there because of their unbelief.

synagogue so that they were astonished and said, Whence is this wisdom
to this man, and these mighty powers?" (vv. 53–54). There was no trust or
submission to Him, only amazement that He knew so much. Some scholars suppose that Matthew assembled these parables from different occasions and put them together into this chapter, but Matthew's language
here teaches something different. Morris notes that verse 53 "seems to
mean that Jesus gave them as a coherent series" (*Matt.*, p. 334).

"Is not this one the son of the carpenter? Is not his mother called Mary
and his brothers James and Joseph and Simon and Judas?" (v. 55). The
sneering attitude is obvious in these words. They regarded Him as a common laborer and His family as very ordinary "poor folks." They will have
an eternity in hell to remember the marvelous opportunity they had and
threw away.

"And his sisters; are they not all with us? From whence therefore does
this man have all these things?" (v. 56). The *all* implies that there were
a number of sisters. The psalmist declared, "Lo, children are an heritage
of the Lord . . . Happy is the man that hath his quiver full of them" (Ps.
127:3, 5). The holy family was a large and happy one. The devout and
humble faith of Joseph and Mary (Matt. 1:18–25; Luke 1:26–56) was
plainly imparted to their children. "James the Lord's brother" is the only
one who went on to become influential in the early church (Acts 12:17;
15:13; 21:18; I Cor. 15:7; Gal. 1:19; James 1:1).

"And they took offense at him. But Jesus said to them, A prophet is not
without honor except in his own country and in his own house" (v. 57).
There was no faith in the hearts of His neighbors.

13:53. For the verb *to end* see Matt. 7:28 note.

"And he did not do there many mighty works on account of their un-belief" (v. 58). But even here the word is not *any*, but rather *not many*. It is ironic that in this chapter that sets forth the grand sweep of God's program for the ages, the local people manifest such stony unbelief. Throughout eternity they will remember that they had such a remarkable opportunity and passed it up.

Practical Applications from Matthew 13

1. Believers should not be discouraged because of the apparently small number of serious Christians (vv. 4–7). It is part of God's plan (I Cor. 1:27–29).
2. There is spiritual truth in Scripture for all who have ears to hear (v. 9). The psalmist prayed, "Make me to understand the way of thy precepts: so shall I talk of thy wondrous works" (Ps. 119:27).
3. God blessed the eyes and ears of believers, for they see and hear the truth (v. 16). Jesus said, "If you abide in my word, truly you are my disciples, and you shall know the truth, and the truth shall make you free" (John 8:31b–32).
4. The Devil is skillful in distracting people from the truth (v. 19). "Put on the whole armor of God, that you may be able to stand against the methods of the devil" (Eph. 6:11).
5. Trusting in yourself will always fail (v. 21). "Trust in the Lord with all thine heart; and lean not unto thine own understanding" (Prov. 3:5).
6. The deceitfulness of riches has destroyed many (v. 22). "Riches profit not in the day of wrath" (Prov. 11:4a). "He that trusteth in his riches shall fall" (Prov. 11:28a).
7. The Devil puts his followers in the Lord's field (v. 25). "In this the children of God are manifest, and the children of the devil: whoever is not doing righteousness is not of God" (I John 3:10a).
8. The Lord taught the reality of a burning hell (v. 42). "The wicked shall be turned into hell, and all the nations that forget God" (Ps. 9:17).
9. The better a Christian knows the teachings of the Scriptures, the more treasures he can show to others (v. 52). Aquila and Priscilla helped Apollos to understand the Scriptures (Acts 18:24–26).

13:54. The word *country, homeland* (πατρίς) occurs only twice in Matt. (13:54, 57). For the word *wisdom* see Matt. 11:19 note.

10. Human unbelief can hinder the work of God (v. 58). "Well, they were broken off because of unbelief, but you stand by faith" (Rom. 11:20*a*).

Prayer

Lord Jesus, give us grace to hear Your Word and to bring forth fruit for You. Help us to turn away from lesser things and to seek You and Your salvation. Enable us to share the treasures of Your Word and grace with others. Amen.

MATTHEW 14

Martyrdom and Miracles

Persons
Herod the tetrarch
Jesus
John the Baptist
Herodias
Daughter of Herodias [Salome]

John's disciples
Jesus' disciples
The multitude
Peter
Men of Gennesaret

Persons referred to
Those sitting with Herod
The diseased

Places mentioned
A prison
A desert place
Villages

Sea of Galilee
A mountain
Land of Gennesaret

Doctrines taught
Rising from the dead
Jesus' compassion
Prayer

Salvation
Faith
Worship of Jesus

1 At that time Herod the tetrarch heard of the fame of Jesus,

2 And said unto his servants, This is John the Baptist; he is risen from the dead; and therefore mighty works do shew forth themselves in him.

3 For Herod had laid hold on John, and bound him, and put him in prison for Herodias' sake, his brother Philip's wife.

4 For John said unto him, It is not lawful for thee to have her.

5 And when he would have put him to death, he feared the multitude, because they counted him as a prophet.

Matthew 14 Exposition

I. The Grasping King: Herod Orders John's Death. vv. 1–12 [Mark 6:14–29; Luke 9:7–9].

"At that time Herod the tetrarch heard of the report of Jesus, and said to his servants: This is John the Baptist; he was raised from the dead and on account of this the mighty deeds are at work in him" (vv. 1–2). This was Herod Antipas, tetrarch of Galilee (4 B.C–A.D 39), who was a son of Herod the Great, who had tried to kill Jesus in Bethlehem. The Lord Jesus characterized Herod Antipas as "that fox" (Luke 13:32), an apt title for a crafty ruler. A tetrarch ruled a fourth part of the province of Palestine. Herod the Great was the last king who ruled the whole province (Matt. 2:1). The fears of Herod Antipas arose from a guilty conscience, as Matthew now explains.

"For Herod had seized John and bound him and put him in prison on account of Herodias, the wife of Philip his brother" (v. 3). The whole Herodian dynasty lived like animals, but John the Baptist had the courage to object.

"For John was saying to him, It is not lawful for you to be having her" (v. 4). The Law was very clear on forbidding a man to marry his brother's wife (Lev. 18:16; 20:21). Morris notes that Salome was "both aunt and sister-in-law to her own mother!" (*Matt.*, p. 370, note 12).

14:1. The word *tetrarch, ruler of a fourth* (τετράρχης) occurs only here in Matt.

Herod Antipas is mentioned by name 4 times in this context (14:1, 3, 6 [twice]) in Matt. For more discussion see ZPEB, "Herod," Antipas, III, pp. 140–42; ISBE (1982), "Herod," Antipas , II, pp. 694–96; *Who's Who in the Bible*, "Herod Antipas," pp. 146–47; Edersheim, *Life and Times*, I, pp. 393f.; II, pp. 301–2; Dana, *New Testament World*, p. 98. For a hair-curling sermon, see Alexander Whyte, *Bible Characters*, "Herod That Fox," IV, pp. 142ff.

14:3. Herodias was first married to her uncle, Herod Philip; then to another uncle, Herod Antipas. For more background see ZPEB, "Herodias," III, pp. 146–47; and chart, p. 127; ISBE (1982), "Herodias," II, pp. 698–99.

14:4. For the verb *it is lawful* see Matt. 12:2 note.

14:5 For the verb *to kill* see Matt. 10:28 note.

6 But when Herod's birthday was kept, the daughter of Herodias danced before them, and pleased Herod.

7 Whereupon he promised with an oath to give her whatsoever she would ask.

8 And she, being before instructed of her mother, said, Give me here John Baptist's head in a charger.

9 And the king was sorry: nevertheless for the oath's sake, and them which sat with him at meat, he commanded it to be given her.

"And although he was desiring to kill him, he feared the crowd, because they regarded him as a prophet" (v. 5). Even Herod had to be careful of what the mob might do if he killed a prophet.

"But when Herod's birthday came, the daughter of Herodias danced in the midst and pleased Herod" (v. 6). It must have been a wild and suggestive dance; Herod was not interested in minuets. Young girls still come out and do a belly dance at wedding parties in Arab lands.

"Wherefore he swore with an oath to give her whatever she might ask" (v. 7). He was so excited by her performance that he played the part of the grand king, just as Herodias knew he would.

"But she, having been instructed beforehand by her mother, said, Give me here upon a platter the head of John the Baptist" (v. 8). The bitter request made the prophet the next course in the banquet. It was enough for her vanity to force a king to do what he did not want to. As for Herod, he was mouse-trapped, or, more accurately, rat-trapped. Now it would be added to his sins that he was one who killed the prophets.

"And although the king was grieved, on account of his oaths and the ones who were reclining with him, he commanded it to be given" (v. 9). He might have gone back on his oath, but there were important people reclining with him so that keeping up royal appearances was everything to him.

14:6. Josephus tells us that the daughter of Herodias and Herod Philip was named Salome (*Antiquities of the Jews*, XVIII, 5, 4), but the Gospels do not name her. For background on her see ZPEB, "Salome," V, pp. 219–20; ISBE (1988), "Salome," IV, p. 286; *Who's Who in the Bible*, "Salome," p. 375.

The verb *to please* (ἀρέσκω) occurs only here in Matt.

14:7. For the verb *to swear, confess* see Matt. 7:23 note.

14:8. The verb *to teach, instruct beforehand* (προβιβάζω) occurs only here in the NT. It has that precise meaning in Exod. 35:34 and Deut. 6:7 in the LXX. See Arndt and Gingrich, p. 710; Moulton and Milligan, *Vocabulary*, p. 538.

14:9. The verb *to grieve* (λυπέω) occurs 6 times in Matt. (14:9; 17:23; 18:31; 19:22; 26:22, 37).

For the verb *to recline at table with* see Matt. 9:10 note.

For the verb *to command* see Matt. 8:18 note.

10 And he sent, and beheaded John in the prison.
11 And his head was brought in a charger, and given to the damsel: and she brought it to her mother.
12 And his disciples came, and took up the body, and buried it, and went and told Jesus.
13 When Jesus heard of it, he departed thence by ship into a desert place apart: and when the people had heard thereof, they followed him on foot out of the cities.
14 And Jesus went forth, and saw a great multitude, and was moved with compassion toward them, and he healed their sick.

"And he sent and beheaded John in the prison" (v. 10). The guards were certainly used to such unjust butchery, but not to a prophet.

"And his head was brought upon a platter and was given to the girl, and she brought it to her mother" (v. 11). It was a gruesome course in the banquet. Now Herod had the crime of murdering a prophet hung around his neck. But Herodias had instigated it.

"And his disciples came and took up the body, and buried it, and came and reported it to Jesus" (v. 12). It was a sad task for John's disciples.

II. *The Gracious King: Jesus Feeds the Five Thousand. vv. 13–21 [Mark 6:30–44; Luke 9:10–17; John 6:1–13].*

"But when Jesus heard, he withdrew from there in a boat into a desert place apart, and when the crowds heard, they followed him on foot from the cities" (v. 13). In a very deliberate contrast Matthew portrays the Lord Jesus as a king who provides for the needs of his people (vv. 13–21) and who rescues his servants from harm (vv. 22–36). The place was not a sandy desert like the Sahara but merely dry ground. This scene is a very important event in the life of the Lord Jesus. It is the only miracle recorded in all four Gospels. The people felt profoundly their need of the Lord's healing power and blessing. With John gone, there was no other source for the prophetic Word except the Lord Jesus.

14:10. The verb *to behead* (ἀποκεφαλίζω) occurs only here in Matt. See ISBE (1986), "Punish," Beheading, III, p. 1053, III, D; Ryken, Wilhoit, and Longman, *Dictionary of Biblical Imagery*, "Violence, Stories of," p. 917.

14:11. The verb *to bring* (φέρω) occurs 4 times in Matt. (14:11 [twice], 18; 17:17). For the word *girl* see Matt. 9:24 note.

14:12. The word *body* (πτῶμα) occurs only twice in Matt. (14:12; 24:28).

14:13. For the word *desert* see Matt. 3:1 note.

14:14. This word for *sick* (ἄρρωστος) occurs only here in Matt.

15 And when it was evening, his disciples came to him, saying, This is a desert place, and the time is now past; send the multitude away, that they may go into the villages, and buy themselves victuals.
16 But Jesus said unto them, They need not depart; give ye them to eat.
17 And they say unto him, We have here but five loaves, and two fishes.
18 He said, Bring them hither to me.
19 And he commanded the multitude to sit down on the grass, and took the five loaves, and the two fishes, and looking up to heaven, he blessed, and brake, and gave the loaves to his disciples, and the disciples to the multitude.

"And he went out and saw a great crowd and was moved with compassion for them, and he healed their sick" (v. 14). The Lord was always ready to help those who were in need.

"But when it was evening, the disciples came to him, saying: The place is desert and the hour is already late; send away the crowds in order that they may go into the villages to buy themselves food" (v. 15). The disciples were thinking of the well-being of the multitude but not of the power of the Lord Jesus.

"But Jesus said to them, They have no need to depart; you give them to eat" (v. 16). The Lord commands the disciples to do what He knows is impossible for them.

"But they say to him, We have here nothing except five loaves and two fish" (v. 17). The thought of one loaf for a thousand people was ridiculous. They were still not thinking of the Lord at all. It is John who adds the fact that even this small amount was the gift of a lad who had "five barley loaves and two small fish" (John 6:9). Barley loaves were the food of the poor.

"But he said, Bring them here to me" (v. 18). There is profound significance to this statement by the Lord Jesus. The task of all Christian workers is not to meet the physical and social needs of people but to bring them to the Lord Jesus, who can meet all their needs. We must just get them to Jesus!

"And he commanded the crowds to recline upon the grass, and took the five loaves and the two fish, and having looked up to heaven, he blessed

14:15. For the word *village* see Matt. 9:35 note.

14:17. For the word *bread, loaf,* see Matt. 4:3 note.

For the word *fish* see Matt. 7:10 note.

The number 5 (πέντε) occurs 12 times in Matt. (14:17, 19; 16:9; 25:2 [twice], 15, 16 [twice], 20 [4 times]. See Introduction, "Numbers," p. xxii.

20 And they did all eat, and were filled: and they took up of the fragments that remained twelve baskets full.
21 And they that had eaten were about five thousand men, beside women and children.
22 And straightway Jesus constrained his disciples to get into a ship, and to go before him unto the other side, while he sent the multitudes away.

and broke and gave the loaves to the disciples, and the disciples to the crowds" (v. 19). The Lord had His disciples act as intermediaries to bring His miracle to the people. Mark recorded Peter's memory of that beautiful scene of spring greenery with companies of people reclining in colorful robes like flower beds in an oriental garden (Mark 6:39–40). John notes that the Passover was near (John 6:4).

"And they all ate and were filled, and they took up the remainder of the fragments, twelve baskets full" (v. 20). There was more left over at the end than there had been present at the beginning of the miracle. Did the young lad go home with a bigger basket of bread and fish than he came with? No one can out-give God.

"And the ones who were eating were about five thousand men, besides women and children" (v. 21). Whole family groups were present. A. B. Bruce calls this sequence of events the Galilean Crisis and argues that the Lord Jesus is presenting Himself as "the Son of God Incarnate" and "the bread of life" for the souls of men (*The Training of the Twelve*, p. 124). The miracle of the stilling of the storm that follows is another example of the complete control of the Lord over all His creation.

14:19. For the verb *to command* see Matt. 8:18 note.

For the word *grass* see Matt. 6:30 note. Mark 6:39 notes that the grass was green.

The verb *to bless* (εὐλογέω) occurs 5 times in Matt. (14:19; 21:9; 23:39; 25:34; 26:26). The word means *to invoke good from the presence of God*. For further ideas see Westcott's thoughtful discussion, "The Biblical Idea of Blessing," in *Hebrews*, pp. 203–6; ZPEB, "Bless, Blessing," I, pp. 625–26; ISBE (1979), "Bless," I, pp. 523–24; Elwell, ed., *Evangelical Dictionary of Biblical Theology*, "Blessedness," pp. 69–70; Ryken, Wilhoit, and Longman, *Dictionary of Biblical Imagery*, "Blessing, Blessedness," pp. 98–99.

14:20. The word *fragment* (κλάσμα) occurs only twice in Matt. (14:20; 15:37).

The word *basket* (κόφινος) occurs only twice in Matt. (14:20; 16:9). This word refers to a woven wicker basket. See ZPEB, "Basket," I, pp. 488–89; ISBE (1979), "Basket," I, pp. 437–38.

For the verb *to fill* see Matt. 5:6 note.

14:21. For the word *man*, as distinct from woman, see Matt. 1:16 note.

23 And when he had sent the multitudes away, he went up into a mountain apart to pray: and when the evening was come, he was there alone.
24 But the ship was now in the midst of the sea, tossed with waves: for the wind was contrary.
25 And in the fourth watch of the night Jesus went unto them, walking on the sea.

III. The Great King: Jesus Walks on the Water. vv. 22–36 [Mark 6:45–52; John 6:14–21].

"And immediately Jesus compelled the disciples to embark into the boat and to go before him to the other side, while he sent away the crowds" (v. 22). He did not allow the crowds to just wander away; He sent them home with His exhortation and blessing. He also sent the disciples across the sea into a storm that He knew would be dangerous. At the right time He would come to deliver them.

"And when he had sent the crowds away, he went up into the mountain by himself in order to pray. And when evening came, he was there alone" (v. 23). Having time to commune with His heavenly Father was the highest priority for the Lord. A sentence prayer at the end of a day was not enough.

"But the boat was already many stadia from the land, being tormented by the waves, for the wind was against them" (v. 24). The verb *to torment* is a strong term to use to portray the strain of the sea and wind on the boat. The storm was strong enough to keep them in the midst of the sea, away from their destination.

"And in the fourth watch of the night he came to them, walking upon the sea" (v. 25). The *fourth watch* refers to the Roman system of dividing the night into four three-hour watches. The fourth watch ran from 3:00 to 6:00 A.M. The Lord deliberately chose to come to their aid in a supernatural manner in order to demonstrate His divine power. Neither the storm nor the sea was a problem for Him.

14:22. The verb *to compel* (ἀναγκάζω) occurs only here in Matt.

14:23. For the verb *to pray* see Matt. 5:44 note.

14:24. The measure *stadion, stadium* (στάδιον) is mentioned only here in Matt. It was about 600 feet long.

For the verb *to torment* see Matt. 8:6 note.

For the word *wind* see Matt. 7:25 note.

26 And when the disciples saw him walking on the sea, they were troubled, saying, It is a spirit; and they cried out for fear.
27 But straightway Jesus spake unto them, saying, Be of good cheer; it is I; be not afraid.
28 And Peter answered him and said, Lord, if it be thou, bid me come unto thee on the water.
29 And he said, Come. And when Peter was come down out of the ship, he walked on the water, to go to Jesus.
30 But when he saw the wind boisterous, he was afraid; and beginning to sink, he cried, saying, Lord, save me.

"But when the disciples saw him walking upon the sea, they were terrified, saying that it is a ghost, and they cried out from fear" (v. 26). The storm was bad enough for them, but now this spectral figure approaching them in the darkness made them think the end was near.

"But immediately Jesus spoke to them, saying, Take courage, it is I; stop being afraid" (v. 27). The Lord was quick to reassure them and dispel their fears.

"But Peter answered him and said, Lord, if it is you, command me to come to you upon the waters" (v. 28). Peter was always the bold and enthusiastic one.

"And he said, Come. And Peter went down from the boat and walked on the water and came to Jesus" (v. 29). It was an impulsive act on the part of Peter, and it was not long before he looked at the ominous storm about him and realized the rashness of his actions.

"But when he saw the strong wind, he was afraid, and when he began to sink, he cried, saying, Lord, save me" (v. 30). He quickly forgot the Lord's command to stop fearing and began to sink into the waters. We may feel patronizing toward Peter's changeableness, but none of us have walked on water, even for a short time! He certainly did the right thing in begging the Lord to save him.

14:26. The word *ghost, phantom* (φάντασμα) occurs only here in Matt. In 1611 the word *spirit* (KJV) was the proper synonym, but as the centuries passed the word *spirit* became the proper theological term for the Holy Spirit, and now the word *ghost* is usually applied to phantoms.

For the verb *to terrify* see Matt. 2:3 note.

The word *fear* (φόβος) occurs 3 times in Matt. (14:26; 28:4, 8).

14:27. For the word *immediately, straight* see Matt. 3:3 note.

For the verb *to take courage* see Matt. 9:2 note.

For the verb *to fear* see Matt. 1:20 note.

*31 And immediately Jesus stretched forth his hand, and caught him, and said
unto him, O thou of little faith, wherefore didst thou doubt?*
32 And when they were come into the ship, the wind ceased.
*33 Then they that were in the ship came and worshipped him, saying, Of a
truth thou art the Son of God.*
34 And when they were gone over, they came into the land of Gennesaret.

"And immediately Jesus stretched out his hand and caught him and said
to him, O you of little faith, why did you doubt?" (v. 31). The scene is terribly real. All believers stand convicted of taking their eyes off Jesus and
sinking into doubt. We all need to refocus our eyes upon Him.

"And when they came up into the boat, the wind ceased" (v. 32). The
test was over, and the wind ceased, but they had learned something that
they would never forget.

"But the ones in the boat worshiped him, saying: Truly you are the Son
of God" (v. 33). The disciples were never tempted to worship a human
being. They worshiped the Lord Jesus Christ because they knew that He
was God in the same sense that the heavenly Father was God. He was the
Great King. The Lord had demonstrated this truth to them throughout
this chapter. They had learned the lesson well.

"And when they had gone across, they came into the land of Gennesaret"
(v. 34). Gennesaret was the coastal plain from Magdala to Capernaum on
the northwestern shore of the Sea of Galilee.

"And when the men of that place knew fully that it was he, they sent
into that whole region and brought all the sick to him" (v. 35). The Lord

14:28. For the verb *to command* see Matt. 8:18 note.

14:30. The verb *to sink, drown* (καταποντίζω) occurs only twice in Matt. (14:30; 18:6).
For the verb *to save* see Matt. 1:21 note.

14:31. For this word *immediately* see Matt. 4:20 note.

The verb *to catch* (ἐπιλαμβάνομαι) occurs only here in Matt.

The verb *to doubt* (διστάζω) occurs only twice in the NT (14:31; 28:17).

14:32. For the verb *to come up* see Matt. 3:16 note.

For the word *wind* see Matt. 7:25 note.

14:33. For the verb *to worship* see Matt. 2:2 note.

For the title *Son of God* see Matt. 4:3 note.

The word *truly* (ἀληθῶς) occurs 3 times in Matt. (14:33; 26:73; 27:54).

14:34. For more information on the region of Gennesaret see ZPEB, "Gennesaret;" II, pp.
695–96; ISBE (1982), "Gennesaret," II, p. 443; note also the map in Thomson, *The Land
and the Book*, p. 360.

35 And when the men of that place had knowledge of him, they sent out into all that country round about, and brought unto him all that were diseased; 36 And besought him that they might only touch the hem of his garment: and as many as touched were made perfectly whole.

had ministered in that region before and the men knew what power He possessed.

"And they were beseeching him that they might touch merely the fringe of his garment, and as many as touched were healed" (v. 36). They had implicit faith in Him and were thoroughly healed.

Practical Applications from Matthew 14

1. A person who rejects God easily falls into superstition (vv. 1–2). "Thou, Lord, only makest me dwell in safety" (Ps. 4:8*b*).
2. Herodias used her daughter to secure a man's death (v. 8). How much better to "train up a child in the way he should go: and when he is old, he will not depart from it" (Prov. 22:6).
3. Herod was proud to keep his word, even though it cost a man his life (vv. 9–10). How much better to be "having compassion one of another . . . being filled with pity" (I Pet. 3:8*b*).
4. The Lord Jesus was moved with compassion when He saw the multitude hungry and sick (v. 14). The Lord Jesus commanded, "Lift up your eyes, and look on the fields; for they are white already to harvest" (John 4:35*b*).
5. Bringing a person to Jesus will always meet his or her need (v. 18). "Come unto me, all you that labor and are heavy laden, and I will give you rest" (Matt. 11:28).
6. The Lord Jesus highly valued times of private prayer with His Father (v. 23). Paul urged, "Pray without ceasing" (I Thess. 5:17).
7. Peter had grand ambitions but not the power to fulfill them (v. 28). Paul could say, "I thank Christ Jesus our Lord, who has enabled me" (I Tim. 1:12*a*).

14:35. For the verb *to know fully* see Matt. 7:16 note.

The sick is an idiom, lit. "those having evilly."

14:36. The verb *to heal, save,* is an intensified form (διασώζω) that occurs only here in Matt. Compare Acts 28:4.

For the verb *to beseech* see Matt. 2:18 note.

For the verb *to touch* see Matt. 8:3 note.

8. The disciples worshiped Christ as the Son of God (v. 33). The writer of Hebrews said, "When he brings the first begotten into the world, he says, And let all the angels of God worship him" (Heb. 1:6).
9. Everyone who gets to Jesus has his needs met (vv. 35–36). The Lord invited the burdened to Himself: "Come unto me, all you who labor and are heavy laden, and I will give you rest" (Matt. 11:28).

Prayer

Lord Jesus, grant us the zeal to share Your compassion for the multitudes. Help us to bring them to You. Enable us to keep our spiritual gaze fixed upon You. Make us a blessing to others. Amen.

MATTHEW 15

Traditions and Miracles

Persons
- Jesus
- Scribes
- Pharisees
- The multitude
- Jesus' disciples
- Peter
- A woman of Canaan
- Four thousand men
- Women
- Children

Persons referred to
- The elders
- Father
- Mother
- Isaiah
- My heavenly Father
- Blind leaders of the blind
- A woman's daughter
- The lost sheep of Israel
- Children
- Great multitudes
- Lame
- Blind
- Dumb
- Maimed
- The God of Israel

Places mentioned
- Jerusalem
- Tyre
- Sidon
- Canaan
- Sea of Galilee
- Region of Magdala

Doctrines taught
- Traditions
- The commandment of God
- Honoring father and mother
- Heart worship
- Heart sins
- Demons
- Faith
- Glorifying God
- Compassion
- Giving thanks

1 Then came to Jesus scribes and Pharisees, which were of Jerusalem, saying,

2 Why do thy disciples transgress the tradition of the elders? for they wash not their hands when they eat bread.

3 But he answered and said unto them, Why do ye also transgress the commandment of God by your tradition?

4 For God commanded, saying, Honour thy father and mother: and, He that curseth father or mother, let him die the death.

Matthew 15 Exposition

I. Jesus Attacks Tradition. vv. 1–20 [Mark 7:1–23].

"Then Pharisees and scribes from Jerusalem came to Jesus, saying, Why are your disciples transgressing the tradition of the elders? For they are not washing their hands whenever they are eating bread" (vv. 1–2). The superpious traditionalists come from Jerusalem to challenge this innovative teacher. Since they were from Jerusalem, they would have more reputation than local teachers would. The washing was not a matter of cleansing; it was merely a ceremony. The Jew held out his hands and someone poured or sprinkled water from a pitcher on them. Without that ceremony they would not eat. It had become an empty ceremony with no true dedication to God. Peter warned against thinking that washing would change the nature of a sow (II Pet. 2:22).

"But he answered and said to them, Why are you also transgressing the law of God on account of your tradition?" (v. 3). The mere thought must have stunned the adversaries. They would assume that their tradition was the law. But the Lord exalted the law of God above their tradition.

15:1. For *Pharisees* see Matt. 3:7 note.

For *scribe* see Matt. 2:4 note.

15:2. The word *tradition* (παράδοσις) occurs 3 times only in Matt. (15:2, 3, 6). It referred to a body of human interpretations of Scripture and religious practice that came to usurp the actual teaching of Scripture. For background see ZPEB, "Tradition," V, pp. 792–95; ISBE (1988), "Tradition," IV, pp. 883–85; Guthrie, *New Testament Theology*, pp. 65–66.

The verb *to transgress, break* (παραβαίνω) occurs only in this context in Matt. (15:2, 3) and only of the fall of Judas elsewhere (Acts 1:25).

For the verb *to wash* see also Matt. 6:17 note. Pilate's washing of his hands was a ceremonial cleansing from the murder that was to follow (Matt. 27:24). The Pharisees would have been especially sensitive to that act. See ISBE (1988), "Wash," IV, p. 1022; Ryken, Wilhoit, and Longman, *Dictionary of Biblical Imagery*, "Wash, Washing," pp. 926–27.

15:3. For the word *law* see Matt. 5:17 note and 5:19 note.

5 But ye say, Whosoever shall say to his father or his mother, It is a gift, by whatsoever thou mightest be profited by me;
6 And honour not his father or his mother, he shall be free. Thus have ye made the commandment of God of none effect by your tradition.
7 Ye hypocrites, well did Esaias prophesy of you, saying,

"For God said, Honor your father and mother, and, Let the one who curses father or mother certainly be put to death" (v. 4; Exod. 20:12; 21:17).

The literal phrase "Let him die the death," is not just tautology, but emphasis. He must surely be executed. Note the Lord's vindication of divine inspiration: *God said.* The law was not the work of a committee of redactors; it was the revelation of the living God.

"But you say, Whoever shall say to his father or mother: It is a gift, whatever you may be profited from me, and never honor his father; so you made void the word of God because of your tradition" (vv. 5–6). The expression *a gift* meant that, whatever it was, it was devoted to God and could not be used for someone else, but it did not have to be given to God at once. It could be given on the deathbed. Thus, it was just a trick to avoid helping needy parents. In the ancient world there was no such thing as Social Security. If someone was too old or frail to work, as far as the state was concerned, he could just starve. That was why Paul urged believers to take special care of the elderly (I Tim. 5:4–8).

"Hypocrites! Well did Isaiah prophesy concerning you, saying,

> This people honors me with their lips,
>
> But their heart is far from me;
>
> But in vain are they worshiping me,

15:4. The verb *to honor* (τιμάω) occurs 6 times in Matt. (15:4, 6, 8; 19:19; 27:9 [twice]). See also ISBE (1982), "Honor," II, pp. 750–51; ZPEB, "Honorable, Honor," III, p. 197. It is proper to honor God as well (Ps. 104:1).

The verb *to curse, speak evil of* (κακολογέω) occurs only here in Matt.

For the verb *to die* see Matt. 2:19 note.

15:5. For the word *gift* see Matt. 2:11 note. The Hebrew word for it was *korban* (Mark 7:11). See ZPEB, "Corban," I, p. 959; ISBE (1979), "Corban," I, p. 772.

The verb *to profit* (ὠφελέω) occurs 3 times in Matt. (15:5; 16:26; 27:24).

15:6. The verb *to make void, cancel* (ἀκυρόω) occurs only here in Matt. Paul argued that the law could not make void the promise of God (Gal. 3:17).

15:7. For the word *hypocrite* see Matt. 6:2 note.

For the verb *to prophesy* see Matt. 7:22.

*8 This people draweth nigh unto me with their mouth, and honoureth me
with their lips; but their heart is far from me.*

*9 But in vain they do worship me, teaching for doctrines the commandments
of men.*

10 And he called the multitude, and said unto them, Hear, and understand:

*11 Not that which goeth into the mouth defileth a man; but that which cometh
out of the mouth, this defileth a man.*

*12 Then came his disciples, and said unto him, Knowest thou that the Phari-
sees were offended, after they heard this saying?*

Teaching for teachings commandments of men" (vv. 7–9; Isa. 29:13
    LXX).

Shallow religious show was common in Isaiah's time, in the Lord's time,
and in today's society as well. People talk piously, but they live for themselves, not for God. All their ceremonies are *in vain*, worthless in God's
sight and without any spiritual benefit for themselves.

"And having called the crowd, he said to them: Keep on hearing and understanding; not the thing that enters into the mouth defiles the man, but
the thing that goes out of the mouth, that thing defiles the man" (vv. 10–
11). Hearing the Word of God with submission brings understanding. The
Lord now gives a major principle that confounded the Pharisees. What a
person eats does not make him holy before God. What a person says does
indicate the condition of his heart. The disciples understood that he was
wiping out all the dietary regulations, as Mark 7:19 records ("cleansing
all foods"). The apostle Paul reinforces that same truth (I Cor. 8:8). The
dietary regulations had their place in helping the Israelites maintain their
national separation, but they are no longer binding.

"Then the disciples came and said to him: Do you know that the Pharisees, hearing this word, were offended?" (v. 12). They were concerned
that the most fanatically zealous party was now implacably against them.

15:8. For the word *heart* see Matt. 5:8 note.

15:9. This verb *to worship* (σέβω) occurs only here in Matt. Worship is homage to
celebrate the true worth of God. For background see a synonym in Matt. 2:2 note.

The word *commandment* (ἔνταλμα) occurs only here in Matt.

15:10. For the verb *to understand* see Matt. 13:13 note.

15:11. The verb *to defile* (κοινόω) occurs 5 times in this context only in Matt. (15:11
[twice], 18, 20 [twice]).

15:12. For the verb *to cause to stumble, offend*, see Matt. 5:29 note.

13 But he answered and said, Every plant, which my heavenly Father hath not planted, shall be rooted up.
14 Let them alone: they be blind leaders of the blind. And if the blind lead the blind, both shall fall into the ditch.
15 Then answered Peter and said unto him, Declare unto us this parable.
16 And Jesus said, Are ye also yet without understanding?

"But he answered and said: Every plant which my heavenly Father has not planted shall be rooted out" (v. 13). There is an eschatological connotation here for both the Millennium (Matt. 25:41–46) and the final state (Rev. 20:11–15). The application, however, is obvious to every generation. God does not need "religious" people; they need Him.

"Leave them alone; they are blind leaders of the blind; but if the blind should lead the blind, both will fall into a ditch" (v. 14). The Lord gives a terrible characterization of false religious leaders. The world seems to be overrun with them in the present day. Matthew Henry notes that they are "so proud, that they think they see better and further than any, and therefore undertake to be leaders of others, to show others the way to heaven, when they themselves know not one step of the way."

"But Peter answered and said to him: Explain to us this parable" (v. 15). Peter realized that the Lord was overturning the whole system of religious practice for His people. But the true worship of God had never been an outward show; it had always been a matter of heart devotion (Deut. 4:9; Heb. 11).

"But he said, Are you still also without understanding?" (v. 16). By now the Lord expected the disciples to perceive the direction of His teaching. Both Testaments urge the attainment of spiritual understanding (Prov. 4:1, 5, 7; Col. 1:9; 2:1–2).

15:13. The verb *to plant* (φυτεύω) occurs only twice in Matt. (15:13; 21:33).

For the verb *to uproot* see Matt. 13:29 note.

For a discussion of the eschatological judgments see the author's *From Patmos to Paradise*, pp. 212–16, 228–31.

15:14. The word *guide* (ὁδηγός) occurs 3 times in Matt. (15:14; 23:16, 24).

For the word *blind* see Matt. 9:27 note.

15:15. The verb *to explain* (φράζω) occurs only here in the NT. See Moulton and Milligan, *Vocabulary*, p. 675.

15:16. The word *still* (ἀκμήν), an adverbial accusative, occurs only here in the NT.

The word *without understanding* (ἀσύνετος) occurs only here in Matt. Spiritual understanding is vital for the believer. For discussion see ISBE (1988), "Understanding," IV, p. 945; Elwell, ed., *Evangelical Dictionary of Biblical Theology*, "Understanding," pp. 788–89.

17 Do not ye yet understand, that whatsoever entereth in at the mouth goeth into the belly, and is cast out into the draught?
18 But those things which proceed out of the mouth come forth from the heart; and they defile the man.
19 For out of the heart proceed evil thoughts, murders, adulteries, fornications, thefts, false witness, blasphemies:
20 These are the things which defile a man: but to eat with unwashen hands defileth not a man.

"Are you not understanding that everything that enters into the mouth moves into the stomach and is cast out into the latrine?" (v. 17). The ancient world understood the process of digestion of food.

"But the things which come out of the mouth come out of the heart, and these things defile the man" (v. 18). Defilement comes from a sinful heart, not from eating food. That was something the Pharisees could not understand. Solomon warned, "Keep thy heart with all diligence; for out of it are the issues of life" (Prov. 4:23). Jeremiah cried out, "The heart is deceitful above all things, and desperately wicked: who can know it?" (Jer. 17:9).

"For out of the heart come evil thoughts, murders, adulteries, fornications, thefts, false testimonies, blasphemies" (v. 19). The human heart is a well-spring of corruption. Solomon asks, "Who can say, I have made my heart clean, I am pure from my sin?" (Prov. 20:9). Paul warned of the reprobate mind that produces "unrighteousness, fornication, wickedness, covetousness, maliciousness" (Rom. 1:29b).

"These are the things that defile the man, but to eat with unwashed hands does not defile the man" (v. 20). The Lord's conclusion is that sin

---

15:17. This verb *to understand* (νοέω) occurs 4 times in Matt. (15:17; 16:9, 11; 24:15).

The verb *to move, make room for* (χωρέω) occurs 4 times in Matt. (15:17; 19:11, 12 [twice]).

The word *latrine* (ἀφεδρών) occurs only twice in the NT, here and in the parallel Mark 7:19.

15:18. For the word *heart* see Matt. 5:8 note.

15:19. The word *thought* (διαλογισμός) occurs only here in Matt.

The word *murder* (φόνος) occurs only here in Matt. See *kill* Matt. 10:28 note.

The word *adultery* (μοιχεία) occurs only here in Matt. For discussion see ZPEB, "Adultery," I, pp. 65–66; ISBE (1979), "Adultery," I, pp. 58–59; Ryken, Wilhoit, and Longman, *Dictionary of Biblical Imagery*, "Adultery," pp. 15–16.

For the word *fornication* (πορνεία) see Matt. 5:32 note.

The word *theft* (κλοπή) occurs only here in Matt. See *steal* Matt. 6:19 note.

The word *false testimony* (ψευδομαρτυρία) occurs twice only in the NT in Matt. (15:19; 26:59). See ZPEB, "False Swearing, Witness," II, p. 496.

For the word *blasphemy* see Matt. 12:31 note.

21 Then Jesus went thence, and departed into the coasts of Tyre and Sidon.
22 And, behold, a woman of Canaan came out of the same coasts, and cried
unto him, saying, Have mercy on me, O Lord, thou son of David; my daughter
is grievously vexed with a devil.
23 But he answered her not a word. And his disciples came and besought him,
saying, Send her away; for she crieth after us.

comes from evil thinking, not from external physical dirt. The farmer can
shovel manure with a pure heart, and the priest before the altar can wal-
low in sin by evil thinking.

II. Jesus Heals the Syrophenician Woman's Daughter. vv. 21–28 [Mark 7:24–30].

"And Jesus went out from there and withdrew into the regions of Tyre
and Sidon" (v. 21). This is the only recorded time that the Lord Jesus
went outside the traditional land of Israel. Tyre is about fifteen miles
north of the present Lebanon border with Israel, *Rosh ha Niqra* (the Cape
of the Grotto). The Lord took the disciples away from the harassment by
the Pharisees.

"And, behold, a Canaanite woman from those regions came out and was
crying out, saying, Have mercy on me, Lord, Son of David; my daughter
is evilly possessed by a demon" (v. 22). She had obviously heard of His
miracle-working power and came to beg for deliverance for her daughter.
But she was not a Jewess and had no claim upon Him.

"But he answered her not a word. And his disciples came to him and were
asking him, saying, Send her away, because she is crying after us" (v. 23).
They were thoroughly annoyed and wondered why he did not answer her.
He had healed everyone else who asked him. There are scholars who are
still troubled by His silence (Alexander, Rosner, Carson, Goldsworthy,

---

15:21. For *Tyre* and *Sidon* see Matt. 11:21 note. For color photographs of *Rosh ha Niqra* see
the author's *Stones of Witness*, pp. 16–19.

15:22. The word *Canaanite* (Χαναναῖος) occurs only here in the NT. For historical
background see ZPEB, "Canaan, Canaanites," I, pp. 701–8; ISBE (1979), "Canaan,
Canaanites," I, pp. 585–91.

For the verb *to cry out* see Matt. 8:29 note.

For the verb *to have mercy on* see Matt. 5:7 note.

For the verb *to be demon possessed* see Matt. 4:24 note.

15:23. For the verb *to send away, release*, see Matt. 1:19 note.

24 But he answered and said, I am not sent but unto the lost sheep of the house of Israel.

25 Then came she and worshipped him, saying, Lord, help me.

26 But he answered and said, It is not meet to take the children's bread, and to cast it to dogs.

27 And she said, Truth, Lord: yet the dogs eat of the crumbs which fall from their masters' table.

28 Then Jesus answered and said unto her, O woman, great is thy faith: be it unto thee even as thou wilt. And her daughter was made whole from that very hour.

New Dictionary of Biblical Theology, p. 262). But the Lord came to fulfill His promise to His covenant people. The time would come in which He would command the disciples to take the message to all the world (Matt. 28:18–20), but that time was not yet.

"But he answered and said, I was not sent except to the lost sheep of the house of Israel" (v. 24). During the public ministry the Lord was acting according to the covenant promises to His people (Rom. 15:8).

"But she came and worshiped him, saying, Lord, help me" (v. 25). There is no one in the history of the world who has come to the Lord and sincerely asked for His help who did not get it.

"But he answered and said, It is not good to take the bread of the children and to cast it to the puppies" (v. 26). The answer still sounds forbidding, but there is an obvious ray of hope that the woman perceives. The word *puppies* is a diminutive, *small dogs*. Then as now children tried to smuggle puppies into the house and feed them tidbits.

"But she said, Yes, Lord, for even the little dogs are eating from the little crumbs which fall from the table of their masters" (v. 27). She was prepared to classify herself as an unclean animal, begging for something it did not deserve. Her request was a small crumb that would not be missed by the Lord of heaven. Now her heart was prepared, and He could answer.

15:24. For the word *sheep* see Matt. 7:15 note.

15:25. The verb *to help* (βοηθέω) occurs only here in Matt. The idea of God as our divine helper is one of the major OT themes (II Cor. 6:2; Ps. 37:40; 46:5; 79:9; 109:26; 118:13; 119:86, 173, 175; Isa. 41:10, 13, 14; 49:8; 50:7, 9).

For the verb *to worship* see Matt. 2:2 note.

15:26. For the word *child* see Matt. 2:18 note.

The word *little dog, puppy* (κυνάριον) occurs only twice in this context in Matt. (15:26, 27). See also "Dog," Matt. 7:6 note.

15:27. The word *little crumb* (ψιχίον) occurs only here in Matt.

The word *table* (τράπεζα) occurs twice in Matt. (15:27; 21:12).

29 And Jesus departed from thence, and came nigh unto the sea of Galilee; and went up into a mountain, and sat down there.
30 And great multitudes came unto him, having with them those that were lame, blind, dumb, maimed, and many others, and cast them down at Jesus' feet; and he healed them:
31 Insomuch that the multitude wondered, when they saw the dumb to speak, the maimed to be whole, the lame to walk, and the blind to see: and they glorified the God of Israel.

"Then Jesus answered and said to her: O woman, great is your faith; let it be to you as you wish. And her daughter was healed from that hour" (v. 28). Every believer can see himself in this scene. We all tend to ask for things we are not ready to receive, and the Lord waits. He is ready to give, but we are not ready for the answer.

III. Jesus Heals Many Others. vv. 29–31.

"And Jesus went away from there and came to the Sea of Galilee, and went up into the mountain and sat there" (v. 29). "The mountain" is not identified, but sitting was the normal posture for teaching, so the crowds gathered.

"And many crowds came to him, having with them the lame, blind, crippled, dumb, and many others, and cast them alongside his feet, and he healed them" (v. 30). The word *cast* does not imply violence but merely the heaviness of the burden of carrying those who could not walk until they could put them at Jesus' feet. The Lord had promised rest to those who came to Him (Matt. 11:28).

"So that the crowd marveled, seeing the dumb speaking, the crippled whole, and the lame walking and the blind seeing; and they glorified the God of Israel" (v. 31). The crowd recognized the genuineness of the Lord's miracles.

15:28. For the word *faith* see Matt. 8:10 note.

For the verb *to heal* see Matt. 8:8 note.

15:29. For the word *mountain* see Matt. 4:8 note.

15:30. For the word *lame* see Matt. 11:5 note.

For the word *blind* see Matt. 9:27 note.

The word *crippled* (κυλλός) occurs only 3 times in Matt. (15:30, 31; 18:8). It refers to one who is deformed or paralyzed.

For the word *dumb* see Matt. 9:32 note.

15:31. For the verb *to marvel* see Matt. 8:10 note.

32 Then Jesus called his disciples unto him, and said, I have compassion on the multitude, because they continue with me now three days, and have nothing to eat: and I will not send them away fasting, lest they faint in the way.
33 And his disciples say unto him, Whence should we have so much bread in the wilderness, as to fill so great a multitude?
34 And Jesus saith unto them, How many loaves have ye? And they said, Seven, and a few little fishes.
35 And he commanded the multitude to sit down on the ground.

IV. The Feeding of the Four Thousand. vv. 32–39 [Mark 8:1–9].

"But Jesus called his disciples and said: I am moved with compassion over the crowd, because they have already spent three days with me, and they have nothing to eat; and I am not willing to send them away fasting, lest they faint in the way" (v. 32). The Lord Jesus was always keenly conscious of the needs of the people and was ready to help them.

"And the disciples say to him, Whence do we have in this desert so many loaves so as to feed so great a crowd?" (v. 33). The disciples had no resources and the place was so barren that there were no farms.

"And Jesus says to them: How many loaves do you have? And they said, Seven, and a few small fish" (v. 34). Some critical scholars think that the feeding of the five thousand and the feeding of the four thousand are simply variant accounts of the same event, but Matthew provides exact details that distinguish them. (See Plummer, pp. 218–19; Broadus, p. 346.) At the feeding of the five thousand the Lord used five loaves and two fish (Matt. 14:17); here he uses seven loaves and "a few small fish." Matthew is clearly teaching us that the Lord Jesus could do such a miracle anytime He chose.

"And he commanded the crowd to recline on the ground" (v. 35). He was preparing them to expect something to eat.

"He took the seven loaves and the fish, and having blessed them, he broke and was giving them to the disciples, and the disciples to the crowds" (v. 36). The imperfect tense, *was giving*, stresses the continuing miracle as He kept giving the food until all were satisfied. It is significant

---

For the verb *to glorify* see Matt. 5:16 note.

15:32. For the verb *to be moved with compassion* see Matt. 9:36 note.

15:33. For the verb *to feed, fill,* see Matt. 5:6 note.

15:34. For the number 7 see Matt. 12:45 note.

The word *small fish* (ἰχθύδιον) is a diminutive that occurs only here in Matt.

36 And he took the seven loaves and the fishes, and gave thanks, and brake them, and gave to his disciples, and the disciples to the multitude.
37 And they did all eat, and were filled: and they took up of the broken meat that was left seven baskets full.
38 And they that did eat were four thousand men, beside women and children.
39 And he sent away the multitude, and took ship, and came into the coasts of Magdala.

that the Lord always blessed the food before eating. How many present-day believers forget to ask the Lord's blessing on their meals?

"And all ate and were filled, and they took up the remainder of the fragments seven baskets full" (v. 37). Once again the fragments were much more than the original loaves and fish.

"But the ones who ate were four thousand men, besides women and children" (v. 38). The narrative makes clear that it was a supernatural miracle.

"And he sent away the crowds and went into the boat and came to the regions of Magadan" (v. 39). This place name is otherwise unknown. Some will argue that it should refer to Magdala, but there seems to be no proof. The parallel passage in Mark 8:10 refers to Dalmanutha. Morris suggests that they may have been two towns close together (*Matt.*, p. 411).

Practical Applications from Matthew 15

1. God's revelation is always superior to mere tradition (vv. 2–3). The psalmist prayed, "O send out thy light and thy truth: let them lead me" (Ps. 43:3*a*).

15:36. For the word *fish* see Matt. 7:10 note.

The verb *to give thanks* (εὐχαριστέω) occurs twice in Matt. (15:36; 26:27). See ISBE (1988), "Thank, Thankfulness," IV, pp. 822–24; Elwell, ed., *Evangelical Dictionary of Biblical Theology*, "Thankfulness, Thanksgiving," pp. 769–70.

15:37. The word *basket* (σπυρίς) occurs only twice in Matt. (15:37; 16:10). It refers to a larger basket with handles, a hamper. See ZPEB, "Basket," I, pp. 488–89; ISBE (1979), "Basket," I, p. 437–38.

For the word *fragment* see Matt. 14:20 note.

15:39. For further discussion see ZPEB, "Magadan," IV, pp. 29–30; "Magdala," IV, p. 30; ISBE (1986), "Magadan," III, p. 212.

2. Parents should train their children to honor God and obey His Word (v. 4). "Train up a child in the way he should go: and when he is old, he will not depart from it" (Prov. 22:6).

3. Mere lip service is dishonoring to God (v. 8). "I will keep thy precepts with my whole heart" (Ps. 119:69*b*).

4. Words come from the heart and may lead to sin (vv. 18–19). "If sinners entice thee, consent thou not. If they say, Come with us, let us lay wait for blood . . . walk not thou in the way with them" (Prov. 1:10*a*–15*a*).

5. Sin defiles a person (v. 20). "God gave them over to a reprobate mind . . . being filled with all unrighteousness, fornication, wickedness, covetousness, maliciousness; full of envy, murder, debate, deceit, malignity" (Rom. 1:28*b*–29).

6. The woman joined together worship and her request for help (v. 25). "I will praise the name of God with a song, and will magnify him with thanksgiving . . . For the Lord heareth the poor, and despiseth not his prisoners" (Ps. 69:30, 33).

7. The Lord may have sounded forbidding, but the woman knew He was not (v. 28). "Blessed be the Lord; for he hath showed me his marvelous kindness in a strong city" (Ps. 31:21).

8. The Lord Jesus had compassion on the hungry multitude (v. 32). "Finally, be all of one mind, having compassion one of another" (I Pet. 3:8*a*).

9. The Lord never forgot to give thanks for food (v. 36). Believers ought to be equally grateful (I Cor. 11:24; 14:6; Phil. 4:6).

Prayer

Lord Jesus, guard what we say, that our speech may honor You. Cleanse our hearts from evil thoughts and enable us to think of You. Give us the courage to stand for You in the midst of a wicked and perverse generation. Make us good witnesses for You. Amen.

MATTHEW 16

TEACHING AND CONFESSION

Persons
> Pharisees
> Sadducees
> Jesus

> His disciples
> Simon Peter
> The Father

Persons referred to
> A wicked generation
> Jonah
> Five thousand men
> Four thousand men
> John the Baptist
> Elijah
> Jeremiah

> The prophets
> My church
> Elders
> Chief priests
> Scribes
> Satan

Places mentioned
> The other side of Galilee
> The region of Caesarea Philippi
> Earth

> Heaven
> Jerusalem
> The whole world

Doctrines taught
> Heaven
> The reality of miracles
> The danger of false doctrine
> Confession of Christ
> The church of Christ

> The four necessities of redemption
> Self-denial
> The value of salvation
> Rewards of believers

1 *The Pharisees also with the Sadducees came, and tempting desired him that he would shew them a sign from heaven.*

2 *He answered and said unto them, When it is evening, ye say, It will be fair weather: for the sky is red.*

3 *And in the morning, It will be foul weather to day: for the sky is red and lowering. O ye hypocrites, ye can discern the face of the sky; but can ye not discern the signs of the times?*

Matthew 16 Exposition

I. The Leaven of the Pharisees. vv. 1–12 [Mark 8:13–21].

"And the Pharisees and Sadducees came to him, tempting him, and asking that he show them a sign from heaven" (v. 1). These two groups were normally at odds with one another (Acts 23:6–8), but on this occasion they were prepared to work together to ensnare the Lord. Neither group had any intention of obeying the Lord's teaching. They were asking for some spectacular miracle that would convince everyone of His divine power. The Lord Himself was the greatest sign that God could give to sinful mankind, but His adversaries were blind to His glorious revelation. Matthew Henry noted that they could have said with Jacob, "Surely the Lord is in this place; and I knew it not" (Gen. 28:16*b*).

"But he answered and said to them: When evening has come, you say, There will be fair weather, for the sky is red" (v. 2). A glorious sunset is regularly taken to mean a good day following. Morris recalls the old saying, "A red sky at night is the shepherd's delight" (*Matt.*, p. 414).

"And in the morning: It will be stormy today, for the sky is red and gloomy. On the one hand, you know the face of the sky, but on the other hand you are not able to discern the signs of the times" (v. 3). Some people pride

---

16:1. For the verb *to tempt* see Matt. 4:1 note.

For *Pharisees* and *Sadducees* see Matt. 3:7 notes.

For the word *sign* see Matt. 12:38 note.

16:2. The word *fair weather* (εὐδία) occurs only here in the NT.

The verb *to be red* (πυρράζω) occurs only in this context in the NT (16:2, 3).

16:3. The word *early morning* (πρωΐ) occurs 3 times in Matt. (16:3; 20:1; 21:18).

The word for *stormy weather, winter* (χειμών) occurs only twice in Matt. (16:3; 24:20).

The verb *to be gloomy, dark* (στυγνάζω) occurs only here in Matt.

The verb *to discern, doubt* (διακρίνω) occurs twice in Matt. (16:3; 21:21).

For the word *sign* see Matt. 12:38 note.

4 A wicked and adulterous generation seeketh after a sign; and there shall no sign be given unto it, but the sign of the prophet Jonas. And he left them, and departed.

5 And when his disciples were come to the other side, they had forgotten to take bread.

6 Then Jesus said unto them, Take heed and beware of the leaven of the Pharisees and of the Sadducees.

7 And they reasoned among themselves, saying, It is because we have taken no bread.

themselves on being good weather predictors, but even they are often wrong. The Lord, however, is charging these religious leaders with blindness as to His own kingship and the future manifestation of the kingdom of God.

"An evil and adulterous generation is seeking a sign, and no sign shall be given to it, except the sign of Jonah. And he left them and departed" (v. 4). Jonah was the prophet who disobeyed the Lord's command and fled to Tarshish, only to be swallowed by the great fish and spit out on the beach (Jon. 1–2). The present generation had no idea that the destruction of Jerusalem was drawing near. They might reject the word of the Lord as Jonah did, but they could not avert God's coming judgment. It would be a greater catastrophe than they could imagine. There is a parallel between Jonah being in the place of death, the fish's belly three days and three nights, and the Lord Jesus being in the tomb three days and three nights.

"And when the disciples came to the other side, they had forgotten to take bread" (v. 5). It is comforting to know that the disciples could forget obvious things, even as we do. The verse assumes that they left the way they came, by boat (Matt. 15:39).

"But Jesus said to them, Look out and beware of the leaven of the Pharisees and Sadducees" (v. 6). The danger of mere formalism in religious practice is always present.

"But they were reasoning in themselves, saying, It is because we did not take bread" (v. 7). They were reasoning on a mundane level, but the Lord was thinking of the spiritual condition of these religious enemies.

16:4. For the verb *to seek* see Matt. 6:33 note.

For the prophet *Jonah* see Matt. 12:39 note.

16:5. This is the only time that the verb *to forget* (ἐπιλανθάνομαι) occurs in Matt. See ISBE (1982), "Forget," II, pp. 339–40.

16:6. For the word *leaven* see Matt. 13:33 note.

For the verb *to beware* see Matt. 6:1 note.

8 Which when Jesus perceived, he said unto them, O ye of little faith, why reason ye among yourselves, because ye have brought no bread?

9 Do ye not yet understand, neither remember the five loaves of the five thousand, and how many baskets ye took up?

10 Neither the seven loaves of the four thousand, and how many baskets ye took up?

11 How is it that ye do not understand that I spake it not to you concerning bread, that ye should beware of the leaven of the Pharisees and of the Sadducees?

12 Then understood they how that he bade them not beware of the leaven of bread, but of the doctrine of the Pharisees and of the Sadducees.

"But when Jesus knew, he said: Why are you reasoning among yourselves, you of little faith, because you are not having bread?" (v. 8). When the Lord perceived the mistake in their reasoning, He immediately corrected it.

"Are you not yet understanding, neither remembering the five loaves of the five thousand and how many baskets you took up?" (v. 9). The Lord Jesus was never dependent on others for food. The phrase *not yet* indicates that the Lord was expecting better spiritual understanding from the disciples.

"Neither the seven loaves of the four thousand and how many baskets you took up?" (v. 10). The Lord preserved the different words for *basket* in each account. They were distinct, separate miracles.

"How are you not understanding that it was not concerning bread that I said to you? But beware of the leaven of the Pharisees and Sadducees" (v. 11). He corrected them so that they would fully understand that He was rebuking the error of the Pharisees and Sadducees and not their forgetfulness.

"Then they understood that he did not speak to beware of the leaven of bread, but of the teaching of the Pharisees and Sadducees" (v. 12). The two groups had many differences, but they were completely agreed in their opposition to Christ. The implacable hatred of the Pharisees and Sadducees for the Lord Jesus should have caused the disciples to understand the depth of wickedness in their hearts. Matthew recorded this

16:7. The verb *to reason, discuss* (διαλογίζομαι) occurs 3 times in Matt. (16:7, 8; 21:25).

16:8. For the word *of little faith* see Matt. 6:30 note.

16:9. The verb *to remember* (μνημονεύω) occurs only here in Matt.

For the verb *to understand* see Matt. 15:17 note.

For the word *basket* (κόφινος) see Matt. 14:20 note.

16:10. For this word *basket* (σπυρίς) see Matt. 15:37 note.

13 When Jesus came into the coasts of Caesarea Philippi, he asked his dis-
ciples, saying, Whom do men say that I the Son of man am?
14 And they said, Some say that thou art John the Baptist: some, Elias; and
others, Jeremias, or one of the prophets.
15 He saith unto them, But whom say ye that I am?

scene of slow perception by the disciples in order to set off sharply the
brilliance of Peter's perception of the nature of the Lord's Person in the
scene that follows.

II. The Confession of Peter. vv. 13–20 [Mark 8:27–30; Luke 9:18–21].

"But when Jesus came into the regions of Caesarea Philippi, he was asking his disciples, saying: Who do men say that the Son of man is?" (v.
13).The phrase *Jesus came* seems to focus attention on the Lord and His
purpose. *Son of man* was the Lord's favorite title for Himself. He is deliberately sharpening the disciples' perception of Himself. Matthew Henry
notes, "Ministers must be examined before they be sent forth, especially
what their sentiments are of Christ."

"But they said, Some say John the Baptist; but others Elijah; but others
Jeremiah or one of the prophets" (v. 14). These suggestions are very exalted ones. In the first-century world John was the greatest prophet; in the
OT Elijah was the greatest prophet. Some have wondered why Jeremiah
was suggested, but among Jews, Jeremiah was regarded as the custodian
of the ark, who hid it from the Babylonians and will bring it forth for
the messianic kingdom (II Mac. 2:4–7). That he was a prophet no one
doubted except the Pharisees and Sadducees.

"He says to them, But who do you say that I am?" (v. 15). There is a
sense in which every human being who hears this question must give an
answer. By this time all the disciples were very clear, but it was Peter who
immediately voiced the answer.

16:12. For the word *teaching* see Matt. 7:28 note.

16:13. *Caesarea Philippi* is mentioned only here in Matt. It was an important commercial
center on the Via Maris, the great trade route between Damascus and Egypt. It was within
view of Mount Hermon. For color photographs of the Banias spring at Caesarea Philippi
see the author's *Stones of Witness*, pp. 28–29. See also ZPEB, "Caesarea Philippi," I, pp.
682–83; ISBE (1979), "Caesarea Philippi," I, p. 569; Pfeiffer and Vos, *Wycliffe Historical
Geography of Bible Lands*, p. 166.

16:14. For *John the Baptist* see Matt. 3:1 note.

For *Elijah* see Matt. 11:14 note.

For *Jeremiah* see Matt. 2:17 note.

16 And Simon Peter answered and said, Thou art the Christ, the Son of the living God.
17 And Jesus answered and said unto him, Blessed art thou, Simon Barjona: for flesh and blood hath not revealed it unto thee, but my Father which is in heaven.
18 And I say also unto thee, That thou art Peter, and upon this rock I will build my church; and the gates of hell shall not prevail against it.

"But Simon Peter answered and said: You are the Christ, the Son of the living God" (v. 16). His bold, impulsive answer was certainly correct. It was not by accident that Peter was the preacher on the day of Pentecost (Acts 2:14ff.) or that he was chosen to open the door of faith to the Gentiles (Acts 10:1ff.). The scribes and Pharisees were good at shutting people out of the kingdom (Matt. 23:13), but Peter was going to be good at inviting people in.

"But Jesus answered and said to him: Blessed are you, Simon, son of Jonah, because flesh and blood did not reveal this to you, but my Father who is in the heavens" (v. 17). The Lord pronounces a benediction on him for his clear testimony. Peter's confession was not just a bright idea but a divine revelation. Peter had the privilege of expressing what all the apostles now understood and believed. Christ was the fulfillment of all the OT prophecies of a coming Redeemer (Job 19:25; Prov. 23:11; Isa. 44:6; 49:7, 26; 54:5; 59:20; 60:16).

"And I also say to you that you are Peter [a rock], and upon this bedrock I will build my church, and the gates of hades shall not be strong against it" (v. 18). This passage has been an interpretative battleground for many centuries. Roman Catholics say that Christ means that Peter is a rock and

---

16:17. For the word *blessed* see Matt. 5:3 note.

The word *flesh* (σάρξ) occurs 5 times in Matt. (16:17; 19:5, 6; 24:22; 26:41). For discussion see ISBE (1982), "Flesh," II, pp. 313–15; Ryken, Wilhoit, and Longman, *Dictionary of Biblical Imagery*, "Body," pp. 102–111.

The word *blood* (αἶμα) occurs 11 times in Matt. (16:17; 23:30, 35 [3 times]; 26:28; 27:4, 6, 8, 24, 25). For further discussion see Ryken, Wilhoit, and Longman, *Dictionary of Biblical Imagery*, "Blood," pp. 99–101; ZPEB, "Blood," I, pp. 626–27; ISBE (1979), "Blood," I, p. 526; Alexander, ed., *New Dictionary of Biblical Theology*, "Blood," pp. 402–4.

16:18. For the word *bedrock* (πέτρα) see Matt. 7:24 note.

The word *church* (ἐκκλησία) occurs 3 times in Matt. (16:18; 18:17 [twice]). This is the beginning of a major NT theme (Acts 2:47; 5:11; 8:1; I Cor. 1:2; 4:17; Eph. 1:22; 3:21; 5:23–32, and so forth). For further study see J. C. Ryle, *Holiness*, "The Church Which Christ Builds," pp. 210ff.; Elwell, ed., *Evangelical Dictionary of Biblical Theology*, "Church, the," pp. 95–98; ZPEB, "Church, the," I, pp. 845–57; ISBE (1979), "Church," I, pp.

upon this rock (Peter) He will build His church (the Catholic church). Protestants argue that the name Peter means *a stone, a handheld rock* (πέτρος, masculine gender). No large structure could be built on it. Instead the Lord said "upon this *rock*" (πέτρα, feminine gender), meaning *bedrock* upon which one could build a house (Matt. 7:24–25), or even a city (the city of *Petra* in Jordan). Notice that the Lord claims to be the Builder, not the rock itself. That leaves us with the question, What is the rock?

The Roman Catholics claim that it is Peter himself as the founder of Christianity. They of course claim that the present pope exercises the same authority. Although some Protestants will admit that Peter was the rock, they are quick to add that Peter alone did not have that authority, for the church is "built upon the foundation of the apostles and prophets" (Eph. 2:20), a much wider company. Broadus (*Matt.*, pp. 356–57) notes that to establish the Catholic claims one would have to prove the following:

1. That Peter *alone* was the founder of Christianity.
2. That Peter was not only founder but sovereign of all Christians.
3. That Peter had *transmissible* authority.
4. That Peter lived and died at Rome.
5. That Peter actually transmitted authority to the leading official at Rome.

None of these points can be proven. Some expositors say that it is Christ Himself Who is the rock, but in His teaching He is the builder ("I will build").

It is better to say that the church is built on the teaching and ministry of the apostles. Peter himself preached the gospel faithfully at Pentecost (Acts 2:14ff.) and to the household of Cornelius (Acts 10:34ff.). Paul declares that believers "are built upon the foundation of the apostles and prophets, Jesus Christ himself being the chief corner stone" (Eph. 2:20). Peter himself discouraged the idea of lordly authority but emphasized

---

693–96; Alexander, ed., *New Dictionary of Biblical Theology*, "Church," pp. 407–11; F. J. A. Hort, *Christian Ecclesia*; Paul Minear, *Images of the Church in the New Testament*.

The word *hades* (ᾅδης) occurs twice in Matt. (11:23; 16:18). It refers to the realm of the departed, the place to which the souls of lost men go after death (Luke 16:22–23). It is parallel to the OT *sheol*, the place to which all men went after death (Ps. 16:10; Prov. 15:24; Isa. 14:9–11). For further background see Elwell, ed., *Evangelical Dictionary of Biblical Theology*, "Hades," pp. 321–23; ZPEB, "Hades," III, pp. 7–8; ISBE (1982), "Hades," II, pp. 591–92; Harrison, ed., *The New Unger's Bible Dictionary*, "Hades," pp. 512–13; "Sheol," pp. 1178–79.

19 And I will give unto thee the keys of the kingdom of heaven: and whatsoever thou shalt bind on earth shall be bound in heaven: and whatsoever thou shalt loose on earth shall be loosed in heaven.
20 Then charged he his disciples that they should tell no man that he was Jesus the Christ.

instead being examples that the flock could follow (I Pet. 5:2–3). It is Christ alone Who is Lord of both the dead and the living (Rom. 14:9).

Another idea that is popular is that the gates of hades will not succeed in swallowing up the church, but that is not the figure. Gates are stationary. Christ is teaching that the gates of hades will not be strong against the attack of the church. Christ will smash the gates of hades, and multitudes will be delivered from the fear of death by the salvation that Christ will impart to them.

The church is not a denominational body but the sum total of all truly regenerated people in this dispensation. "The church of our text is made up of all true believers in the Lord Jesus Christ, of all who are really holy and converted people" (J. C. Ryle, "The Church Which Christ Builds," *Holiness*, p. 211).

"I shall give you the keys of the kingdom of the heavens, and whatever you shall bind upon the earth shall have been bound in the heavens, and whatever you shall loose upon the earth shall have been loosed in the heavens" (v. 19). Some would think that this passage gives unlimited authority to Peter, but the future perfect tense gives very carefully defined authority. Peter could bind on earth only what *shall have already been bound in heaven*; he could loose on earth only what *shall have already been loosed in heaven*. He could declare only what God had already decreed in heaven. Far from making a pope out of Peter, it made him a servant of God. It is Christ alone Who has the keys of death and of hades (Rev. 1:18).

"Then he commanded the disciples that they should say to no one that he himself was the Messiah" (v. 20). He did not wish to inflame the multitude into acts of political revolution (John 6:15).

16:19. The word *key* (κλείς) occurs only here in Matt. For background see ISBE (1986), III, "Key," pp. 10–11; "Keys, Power of the," pp. 11–12; ZPEB, "Key," III, pp. 785–86; "Keys, Power of the," pp. 786–87.

For the verb *to bind* see Matt. 12:29 note.

For the verb *to loose* see Matt. 5:19 note.

16:20. This verb *to command* (διαστέλλω) occurs only here in Matt.

21 From that time forth began Jesus to shew unto his disciples, how that he must go unto Jerusalem, and suffer many things of the elders and chief priests and scribes, and be killed, and be raised again the third day.
22 Then Peter took him, and began to rebuke him, saying, Be it far from thee, Lord: this shall not be unto thee.
23 But he turned, and said unto Peter, Get thee behind me, Satan: thou art an offence unto me: for thou savourest not the things that be of God, but those that be of men.

III. *The Necessity of Christ's Death. vv. 21–28 [Mark 8:31–37; Luke 9:22–25].*

"From that time Jesus began to show to his disciples that it was necessary for him to go to Jerusalem, and to suffer many things from the elders and chief priests and scribes, and to be killed, and on the third day to be raised up" (v. 21). Jesus began to teach them what He was about to do to save mankind. He spelled out for them what has been called the four necessities of redemption. What He was going to do was a mystery to men and angels. If the Devil had understood, he would never have had the Lord crucified (I Cor. 2:8). This is the second time that the Lord prophesied His death (see Matt. 16:21).

"And Peter took him to himself and began to rebuke him, saying, Mercy to you, Lord; this shall never be to you" (v. 22). The double negative *never* is very emphatic. Peter speaks out of simple human compassion. He plainly has no perception of the means of redemption.

"But he turned and said to Peter: Get behind me, Satan; you are a stumbling block to me, because you are not thinking of the things of God, but the things of men" (v. 23). God's plan of salvation for mankind was vastly greater than anything man could imagine. The thought of God suffering for creatures is still beyond us.

16:21. The verb *it is necessary* (δεῖ) occurs 8 times in Matt. (16:21; 17:10; 18:33; 23:23; 24:6; 25:27; 26:35, 54).

The verb *to suffer* (πάσχω) occurs 4 times in Matt. (16:21; 17:12, 15; 27:19).

16:22. For the verb *to rebuke* see Matt. 8:26 note.

The word *mercy* (ἵλεως) occurs only here in Matt.

16:23. The verb *to think, be mindful of* (φρονέω) occurs only here in Matt.

For the word *stumbling block* see Matt. 13:41 note. Moulton and Milligan note that Aristophanes used the word for "the stick of a mouse-trap" (*Vocabulary*, p. 576). Peter's suggestion was just *bait* to avoid the cross (Morris, *Matt.*, p. 430, note 49).

THE GOSPEL OF THE KING

24 Then said Jesus unto his disciples, If any man will come after me, let him deny himself, and take up his cross, and follow me.
25 For whosoever will save his life shall lose it: and whosoever will lose his life for my sake shall find it.

"Then Jesus said to his disciples: If anyone wishes to come after me, let him deny himself and take up his cross, and let him keep following me" (v. 24). Devotion to the Lord Jesus Christ requires self-denial, sacrifice, and determined persistence. That is why we need the grace of God so desperately (I Cor. 15:10; Eph. 2:8; II Tim. 2:1).

"For whoever wishes to save his life shall lose it; but whoever shall lose his life on account of me shall find it" (v. 25). Whoever is living in a shell to protect himself is destroying his character; whoever is sacrificing himself for the Lord's sake is making himself eternally valuable to God.

"For what is a man profited if he gain the whole world and lose his own soul? Or what shall a man give in exchange for his own soul?" (v. 26). All the treasures of Egypt are not to be compared with the experience of the pleasure of God (Heb. 11:24–26). The soul cannot be satisfied with "things." There is always the desire for more and more. But David expressed it well, "As for me, I will behold thy face in righteousness: I shall be satisfied, when I awake, with thy likeness" (Ps. 17:15).

"For the Son of man is about to come in the glory of his Father with his angels, and then he shall give to each one according to his deed" (v. 27). The Lord made clear that there was to be a Second Coming in glory to bring in the kingdom in power.

"Truly I say to you that there are some standing here who shall not taste of death until they see the Son of man coming in his kingdom" (v. 28). The scene of transfiguration, which follows, will be a foretaste of the coming in glory. The Second Coming itself will be the ultimate fulfillment of prophecy (Rev. 19:11–21).

16:24. The verb *to deny* (ἀπαρνέομαι) occurs 4 times in Matt. (16:24; 26:34, 35, 75). For discussion see ZPEB, "Deny," II, pp. 101–2; Trent Butler, ed., *Holman Bible Dictionary*, "Deny," 353–54.

For the word *cross* see Matt. 10:38 note.

16:25. For the word *life, soul,* see Matt. 2:20 note.

For the verb *to save* see Matt. 1:21 note.

26 For what is a man profited, if he shall gain the whole world, and lose his own soul? or what shall a man give in exchange for his soul?
27 For the Son of man shall come in the glory of his Father with his angels; and then he shall reward every man according to his works.
28 Verily I say unto you, There be some standing here, which shall not taste of death, till they see the Son of man coming in his kingdom.

Practical Applications from Matthew 16

1. All people forget some things (v. 5). Believers must not be forgetful hearers of the Word (James 1:25).
2. Believers should be on their guard against false doctrine (v. 6). "I have stuck unto thy testimonies: O Lord, put me not to shame" (Ps. 119:31).
3. Believers need spiritual understanding of the Scriptures (v. 9). "Open thou mine eyes, that I may behold wondrous things out of thy law" (Ps. 119:18).
4. The world has false opinions about Christ (v. 14). Believers need to be witnesses for Christ (Acts 1:8).
5. Believers still need to confess the Lord Jesus boldly (v. 16). "Every tongue should confess that Jesus Christ is Lord, to the glory of God the Father" (Phil. 2:11b).
6. The gates of hades shall not be strong against the church (v. 18b). "We are more than conquerors through him that loved us" (Rom. 8:37b).
7. Believers should deny themselves and follow the Lord Jesus (v. 24). "Denying ungodliness and worldly lusts, we should live soberly, righteously, and godly, in this present world" (Titus 2:12b).
8. Whoever wants to save his life shall lose it; whoever is willing to sacrifice his life for Christ's sake shall find it (v. 25). "Be faithful unto death, and I will give you a crown of life" (Rev. 2:10b).

16:26. For the verb to profit see Matt. 15:5 note.

The verb to gain (κερδαίνω) occurs 6 times in Matt. (16:26; 18:15; 25:16, 17, 20, 22).

16:27. The word deed, work (πράξις) occurs only here in Matt.

For the word glory see Matt. 4:8 note.

16:28. For the word death see Matt. 4:16 note.

For the word kingdom see Matt. 3:2 note.

9. What is a man profited, even if he gains the whole world but loses his own soul? (v. 27). "For what is the hope of the hypocrite, though he hath gained, when God taketh away his soul?" (Job 27:8).

10. The Son of man shall reward every man according to his works (v. 27). "To the righteous good shall be repaid" (Prov. 13:21b). "He will repay, fury to his adversaries, recompence to his enemies" (Isa. 59:18b).

Prayer

Lord Jesus, give us grace to confess You as the Son of the living God. Enable us to serve You well in spite of the opposition of men and the Devil. Help us to live in the light of Your coming and kingdom. Amen.

MATTHEW 17

TRANSFIGURATION

Persons

Jesus

Peter

James

John

Moses

Elijah

The Father

A man with a lunatic son

A demon

Tax collectors

Persons referred to

Scribes

John the Baptist

The multitudes

The lunatic child

Disciples

Men who will kill

Kings of earth

Places mentioned

A high mountain apart

Galilee

Capernaum

The sea [of Galilee]

Doctrines taught

The Transfiguration

The Sonship of Christ

The resurrection of Christ

The power of faith

The betrayal of Christ

The death of Christ

The payment of taxes

1 And after six days Jesus taketh Peter, James, and John his brother, and bringeth them up into an high mountain apart,

2 And was transfigured before them: and his face did shine as the sun, and his raiment was white as the light.

Matthew 17 Exposition

I. The Transfiguration. vv. 1–13 [Mark 9:2–13; Luke 9:28–36].

"And after six days Jesus takes with him Peter and James and John his brother and brings them into a high mountain apart" (v. 1). Although the identification of the "high mountain apart" is disputed, the obvious choice is Mount Hermon, the highest mountain in the country (9,232 feet high). It is the place where the borders of Syria, Lebanon, and Israel meet. The crest is 5,000 feet above the surrounding countryside and provides a magnificent view. When possible, hikers like to climb the mountain one day, camp overnight to see the beautiful sunrise, and come down the next day. Mount Hermon is a reasonable distance northeast of Caesarea Philippi. Luke tells us that Jesus went to the mount in order to pray, and the disciples fell asleep during the prayers (Luke 9:28–32). That seems to indicate a night vigil of prayer.

"And he was transfigured before them, and his face shone as the sun, and his garments became white as the light" (v. 2). This transformation was not just a stray beam of sunlight that fell upon Him; it was the shining forth of His glorious divine nature. The light radiated forth from within the Lord. Many years later, Peter testified that he had been an eyewitness of His divine majesty when he had been with Him in the holy mount

17:1. Mt. Hermon is the southernmost spur of the Anti-Lebanon mountain range. For background on Mt. Hermon see Anthony Huxley, *Standard Encyclopedia of the World's Mountains,* "Hermon, Mount," pp. 167–68; ZPEB, "Hermon," III, pp. 125–26; ISBE (1982), "Hermon, Mount," II, p. 688. For color photographs of Mt. Hermon, see the author's *Stones of Witness,* pp. 30–31. Although Mt. Tabor is suggested as the place of transfiguration, it is really a hill (1,843 feet high) in the midst of the highly populated Valley of Jezreel. There is a Roman Catholic basilica on top, and of course it has 3 chapels, one for Jesus, one for Moses, and one for Elijah!

For the word *mountain* see Matt. 4:8 note.

The number 6 (ἕξ) occurs only here in Matt. See Introduction, "Numbers," p. xxii.

17:2. The verb *to transfigure, transform* (μεταμορφόω) occurs only here in Matt. Paul reminded believers that they needed to be transformed by the renewing of their minds (Rom. 12:2). For further study of the Transfiguration see Campbell Morgan, *The Crises of the Christ,* "The Transfiguration," pp. 211–67; Wilbur M. Smith, *The Supernaturalness of Christ,* pp. 163–85; Edersheim, *Life and Times,* II, pp. 91–101; Elwell, ed., *Evangelical Dictionary of Biblical Theology,* "Transfiguration," pp. 782–83; ZPEB, "Transfiguration," V, pp. 796–97; ISBE, "Transfiguration," IV (1988), pp. 886–88.

3 And, behold, there appeared unto them Moses and Elias talking with him.
4 Then answered Peter, and said unto Jesus, Lord, it is good for us to be here: if thou wilt, let us make here three tabernacles; one for thee, and one for Moses, and one for Elias.

(II Pet. 1:16–18). Does the shining face imply that this is the new Moses (Exod. 34:29–35; II Cor. 3:13)?

"And behold, there was seen with them Moses and Elijah, speaking with him" (v. 3). The two most powerful leaders and prophets of the OT appear with Him. Luke informs us that they were talking about *the exodus*, which He was about to accomplish at Jerusalem (Luke 9:31). That refers to the redemptive deliverance of the coming cross. The saints in glory understood what He was about to do for their salvation. As Moses had led the people out of the bondage of Egypt, so the Lord Jesus is about to lead all the saints of all ages out of the bondage of sin by the sacrifice of Himself on the cross.

"But Peter answered and said to Jesus: Lord, it is good for us to be here; if you will, I shall build here three tabernacles, one for you, and one for Moses, and one for Elijah" (v. 4). Although expositors have been hard on Peter for his lack of spiritual perception here, he did have a good idea of the significance of the feast of the tabernacles (Lev. 23:33–43). The Israelites built booths (tabernacles) to celebrate the fruitful blessings of the Lord, and observant Jews still do. It was a prophetic foretaste of the coming millennial reign in which the future saints will worship the Lord in such a festival (Zech. 14:16). (For a summary of the nature of the theocratic kingdom, see Pentecost, *Things to Come*, pp. 441–45). Peter was a man who worked with his hands, and he here volunteers to make tabernacles for these three august persons. But he is quickly corrected by no less than God the Father Himself. God the Trinity alone is worthy of worship.

For the verb *to shine* see Matt. 5:15 note.

For the word *sun* see Matt. 5:45 note.

17:3. For *Moses* see Matt. 8:4 note.

For *Elijah* see Matt. 11:14 note.

The verb *to talk with* (συλλαλέω) occurs only here in Matt.

17:4. The word *tabernacle, tent* (σκηνή) occurs only here in Matt.

5 While he yet spake, behold, a bright cloud overshadowed them: and behold a voice out of the cloud, which said, This is my beloved Son, in whom I am well pleased; hear ye him.

6 And when the disciples heard it, they fell on their face, and were sore afraid.

7 And Jesus came and touched them, and said, Arise, and be not afraid.

"While he was still speaking, behold, a shining cloud overshadowed them, and behold a voice out of the cloud, saying, This is my Son, the Beloved, in whom I take pleasure; keep on hearing him" (v. 5). The Father expresses His delight in the ministry of His Son and commands all to listen to Him. Jesus is not to be put on a plane with even the greatest of men. This transfiguration account is the central theological revelation in the Gospel of Matthew. It shows us the true nature of the Lord Jesus Christ. See the chiastic outline of Matthew (Introduction, pp. xvi–xvii).

"And when the disciples heard, they fell upon their faces and were exceedingly afraid" (v. 6). The manifestation of divine glory was more than the disciples were able to bear. Matthew is the only Gospel to record that they fell on their faces.

"And Jesus came to them and touched them and said: Arise and stop fearing" (v. 7). He provided the comfort and reassurance that they needed. The present tense verb *stop fearing* assumes that they are afraid. The whole scene was an anticipation of resurrection glory, which would encourage the disciples in the days of hardship and persecution to come.

"And when they lifted up their eyes, they saw no one except Jesus himself alone" (v. 8). The Father desires all men to honor His Son, the Lord Jesus Christ, above all others. The vision was over, but the scene would be forever fixed in their memory. And all God's saints must remember that Jesus alone among men is to be revered and worshiped. This scene helps us perceive how great He is.

17:5.The word *cloud* (νεφέλη) occurs 4 times in Matt. (17:5 [twice]; 24:30; 26:64), all referring to heavenly clouds. Ryken, Wilhoit, and Longman, *Dictionary of Biblical Imagery*, "Cloud," p. 157; ZPEB, "Cloud," 5, pp. 894–95; ISBE (1979), "Cloud," I, pp. 725–26.

For the word *shining, full of light*, see Matt. 6:22 note.

The verb *to overshadow* (ἐπισκιάζω) occurs only here in Matt.

17:6. For the verb *to be afraid* see Matt. 1:20 note.

17:7. For the verb *to touch* see Matt. 8:3 note.

For the verb *to fear* see Matt. 1:20 note.

17:8. For the word *only, alone*, see Matt. 4:4 note.

8 And when they had lifted up their eyes, they saw no man, save Jesus only.

9 And as they came down from the mountain, Jesus charged them, saying, Tell the vision to no man, until the Son of man be risen again from the dead.

10 And his disciples asked him, saying, Why then say the scribes that Elias must first come?

11 And Jesus answered and said unto them, Elias truly shall first come, and restore all things.

12 But I say unto you, That Elias is come already, and they knew him not, but have done unto him whatsoever they listed. Likewise shall also the Son of man suffer of them.

13 Then the disciples understood that he spake unto them of John the Baptist.

"And while they were coming down from the mountain, Jesus commanded them, saying, Tell the vision to no man, until the Son of man be raised from the dead" (v. 9). The Lord is preparing the disciples for His coming death and resurrection, but they cannot see the connection.

"And the disciples asked him, saying: Why, therefore, are the scribes saying that it is necessary for Elijah to come first?" (v. 10). They are trying to think through all these teachings but do not see the necessity of two advents.

"But he answered and said: Elijah indeed comes, and shall restore all things" (v. 11). The OT prophecy of the coming of Elijah (Mal. 4:5–6) shall be fulfilled, but at the time of the Great Tribulation before the Second Coming (Rev. 11:3–11).

"But I say to you that Elijah came already, and they did not recognize him, but did to him as many things as they wished; thus also the Son of man is about to suffer by them" (v. 12). John the Baptist was the forerunner for the First Advent; Elijah will be the forerunner for the Second Advent.

"Then the disciples understood that he spoke to them concerning John the Baptist" (v. 13). The meaning of John's ministry finally dawned upon them.

17:9. For the verb *to command* see Matt. 4:6 note.

The word *vision* (ὅραμα) occurs only here in Matt. It is used of the vision of God in the burning bush (Acts 7:31) and of divine visions granted to Peter (Acts 10:17) and to Paul (Acts 18:9). For discussion see ZPEB, "Vision," V, pp. 889–90; ISBE (1988), "Vision," IV, pp. 993-94.

17:11. For the verb *to restore* see Matt. 12:13 note.

17:12. For the verb *to recognize, know fully,* see Matt. 7:16 note.

For the verb *to suffer* see Matt. 16:21 note.

17:13. For the verb *to understand* see Matt. 13:13 note.

14 And when they were come to the multitude, there came to him a certain man, kneeling down to him, and saying,
15 Lord, have mercy on my son: for he is lunatick, and sore vexed: for oft-times he falleth into the fire, and oft into the water.
16 And I brought him to thy disciples, and they could not cure him.
17 Then Jesus answered and said, O faithless and perverse generation, how long shall I be with you? how long shall I suffer you? bring him hither to me.
18 And Jesus rebuked the devil; and he departed out of him: and the child was cured from that very hour.
19 Then came the disciples to Jesus apart, and said, Why could not we cast him out?

II. *The Healing of a Boy.* vv. 14–21 [Mark 9:14–29; Luke 9:37–43].

"And when they had come to the crowd, a man came to him, kneeling down to him" (v. 14). They had no sooner come back to the crowd than a man came to the Lord seeking help.

"And saying: Lord, have mercy upon my son, because he is insane and suffers evilly; for he often falls into the fire and often into the water" (v. 15). There was clearly a strong self-destructive twist to his malady.

"And I brought him to your disciples, and they were not able to heal him" (v. 16). Neither the man nor the disciples had the faith to deal with this severe case.

"But Jesus answered and said: O faithless and twisted generation, how long shall I be with you? How long shall I endure you? Bring him here to me" (v. 17). The Lord was disturbed by the lack of faith of that generation and by their attempt to get along without God's help.

"And Jesus rebuked him, and the demon went out from him, and the boy was healed from that hour" (v. 18). No demon could resist His power.

"Then the disciples of Jesus came to him privately and said, Why were we not able to cast it out?" (v. 19). The disciples were chagrined that the Lord did it so easily when they had failed.

17:14. The verb *to kneel* (γονυπετέω) occurs only twice in Matt. (17:14; 27:29).

17:15. For the verb *to be insane, moonstruck,* see Matt. 4:24 note.

17:16. For the verb *to heal* see Matt. 4:23 note.

17:17. For the word *generation* see Matt. 1:17 note.

The verb *to pervert, twist* (διαστρέφω) occurs only here in Matt.

The verb *to endure* (ἀνέχομαι) occurs only here in Matt.

17:18. For the word *demon* see Matt. 7:22 note.

20 And Jesus said unto them, Because of your unbelief: for verily I say unto you, If ye have faith as a grain of mustard seed, ye shall say unto this mountain, Remove hence to yonder place; and it shall remove; and nothing shall be impossible unto you.
21 Howbeit this kind goeth not out but by prayer and fasting.
22 And while they abode in Galilee, Jesus said unto them, The Son of man shall be betrayed into the hands of men:
23 And they shall kill him, and the third day he shall be raised again. And they were exceeding sorry.

"But he says to them, On account of your lack of faith; for truly I say to you, If you shall have faith as a seed of mustard, you shall say to this mountain: Go over there, and it shall go; and nothing shall be impossible for you" (v. 20). The power of faith is not in a man, but in God. God can do the miraculous; man only believes.

"But this kind goes not forth except by prayer and fasting" (v. 21). See Mark 9:29.

III. The Prophecy of His Death. vv. 22–23 [Mark 9:30–32; Luke 9:43–45].

"But while they were gathering together in Galilee, Jesus said to them: The Son of man is about to be betrayed into the hands of men" (v. 22). The Lord Jesus prepared His disciples for the coming events by informing them ahead of time about the coming cruel deeds of men and the ultimate triumph. It is a sad commentary on the sinfulness of human nature that the only sinless person who ever lived was betrayed and killed by people He never harmed.

"And they shall kill him, and on the third day he shall be raised up. And they were exceedingly grieved" (v. 23). The disciples did not understand the reason for the death and raising up and could not think of Isaiah 53.

17:20. The word *smallness of faith, lack of faith* (ὀλιγοπιστία) occurs only here in the NT. For a cognate, *one who has little faith*, see Matt. 6:30 note.

17:21. The oldest manuscripts do not have this verse. Some suggest that copyists borrowed it from Mark 9:29, where it unquestionably belongs. For the evidence see Bruce Metzger, *A Textual Commentary on the Greek New Testament*, p. 43; Aland, Black, Martini, Metzger, and Wikgren, *The Greek New Testament*, p. 66.

17:22. The verb *to gather together* (συστρέφω) occurs only here in Matt. For the verb *to betray* see Matt. 4:12 note.

17:23. For the verb *to kill* see Matt. 10:28 note.

24 And when they were come to Capernaum, they that received tribute money came to Peter, and said, Doth not your master pay tribute?
25 He saith, Yes. And when he was come into the house, Jesus prevented him, saying, What thinkest thou, Simon? of whom do the kings of the earth take custom or tribute? of their own children, or of strangers?
26 Peter saith unto him, Of strangers. Jesus saith unto him, Then are the children free.
27 Notwithstanding, lest we should offend them, go thou to the sea, and cast an hook, and take up the fish that first cometh up; and when thou hast opened his mouth, thou shalt find a piece of money: that take, and give unto them for me and thee.

In their horror over the idea of His death, they seem to overlook the promise of the Resurrection. But the Lord prepared them so that when the time came, they would remember and understand. This is the third time that the Lord prophesied His death (see Matt. 12:39–40).

IV. The Temple Tax. vv. 24–27.

"But when they came into Capernaum, the ones who receive the two drachma [temple tax] came to Peter and said, Does not your teacher pay the two drachma [tax]?" (v. 24). The Lord paid every tax, just as Paul commands believers (Rom. 13:6–7).

"He says, Yes. And when they came into the house, Jesus anticipated him, saying, What does it seem to you, Simon? From whom do the kings of the earth receive custom or tax? From their own sons or from the others?" (v. 25). Peter no doubt was thinking that it was odd for the King to pay taxes to a government. But the Lord was a spiritual King and paid taxes just as His people should.

For the verb *to raise* see Matt. 1:24 note.

For the verb *to grieve* see Matt. 14:9 note.

17:24. The word *two drachma* [temple tax] (δίδραχμον) occurs only here in the NT. Matthew, the tax collector, would know it well. It was equivalent to 2 days wages.

17:25. Here the word *customs, tax* (τέλος) refers to a *toll* or *duty*. It regularly means *end* (Matt. 10:22).

The word *belonging to others* (ἀλλότριος) occurs only in this context in Matt. (17:25, 26).

The word *tax* (κῆνσος) occurs 3 times in Matt. (17:25; 22:17, 19) and once in Mark 12:14 in the NT. The Lord delivered both Matthew and Zacchaeus from being tax collectors. For further discussion see Edersheim, *Sketches of Jewish Social Life*, pp. 51–58; ZPEB, "Tax, Taxing," V, pp. 603–6; ISBE (1988), "Tax, Tribute," IV, pp. 739–42.

17:26. The word *free* (ἐλεύθερος) occurs only here in Matt.

"But he said, From the others; Jesus said to him, Then are the sons free" (v. 26). The Lord never used His freedom to take advantage of others.

"But in order that we not cause them to stumble, go to the sea; cast in a hook and take up the first fish that comes up, and when you open its mouth, you shall find a stater; take that and give to them for me and you" (v. 27). The Lord Jesus is the Sovereign of mankind and all nature. Here He commands the fish to take the coin and deliver it to Peter. He provides enough for Peter to pay his taxes as well.

Practical Applications from Matthew 17

1. Retreats to a quiet place often result in special blessing and illumination (v. 1). Moses in the mount was an example (Exod. 24:12–18); Elijah by the brook was another (I Kings 17:3–6).
2. Death could not harm Moses and Elijah (v. 3). Paul declared, "For to me to live is Christ, and to die is gain" (Phil. 1:21).
3. Believers should never put the Lord Jesus on the same plane as others (v. 4). Paul referred to the appearing of our Lord Jesus Christ "whom in his own times he shall show the blessed and only Potentate, the King of kings, and Lord of lords; who only has immortality" (I Tim. 6:15–16a).
4. God the Father commands the disciples to "keep on hearing" His Son, the Lord Jesus Christ (v. 5). Jesus said, "The words that I speak to you, they are spirit, and they are life" (John 6:63b).
5. When the disciples could not cure a lunatic, Jesus commanded them to bring him to Him (v. 17). Our task is still to bring the hurt and the ailing to the Lord Jesus that He might meet their needs. Paul and Silas gave the right directions: "Believe on the Lord Jesus Christ, and you shall be saved" (Acts 16:31b).
6. The disciples failed because of unbelief (v. 20). "He that comes to God must believe that he is, and that he is a rewarder of those who diligently seek him" (Heb. 11:6b).

17:27. The word *fishhook* (ἄγκιστρον) occurs only here in the NT.

The word *stater* (στατήρ) occurs only here in the NT. It was a coin worth 4 drachmas, about 4 days' wages.

7. The Lord Jesus commanded the disciples not to be disobedient to government but to obey the laws of men (v. 27). The apostle Paul wrote, "Render to all their dues: taxes to whom taxes are due; tolls to whom tolls are due; reverence to whom reverence; honor to whom honor" (Rom. 13:7).

Prayer

Heavenly Father, help us to honor and serve Your beloved Son. Center our lives in Him. Help us to bring people to Him. Provide for our needs. Enable us to obey Your Word. For Jesus' sake. Amen.

MATTHEW 18

KINGDOM TEACHING

Persons

Jesus

His disciples

A little child

Peter

Persons referred to

Little children

My Father

A shepherd

An offending brother

Guardian angels

Two or three witnesses

The church

A tax collector

Two or three believers

A sinning brother

A king

A servant

His wife

His children

A fellow servant

Tormentors

Places mentioned

Hell [Gehenna]

Heaven

The mountains

Earth

Doctrines taught

Greatness in the kingdom

Conversion

Humility

Hell fire

Salvation of the lost

Church discipline

The presence of Christ

Forgiveness

Compassion

The consequences of sin

1 At the same time came the disciples unto Jesus, saying, Who is the greatest in the kingdom of heaven?

2 And Jesus called a little child unto him, and set him in the midst of them,

3 And said, Verily I say unto you, Except ye be converted, and become as little children, ye shall not enter into the kingdom of heaven.

4 Whosoever therefore shall humble himself as this little child, the same is greatest in the kingdom of heaven.

Matthew 18 Exposition

I. The Greatest in the Kingdom. vv. 1–5 [Mark 9:33–37; Luke 9:46–48].

"In that hour the disciples came to Jesus, saying, Who then is greatest in the kingdom of the heavens?" (v. 1). In reality this was a complex question. The disciples already knew that the Pharisees considered themselves to be the greatest (Matt. 16:1). Moses and Elijah had appeared in a state of glory; were they to out rank them? What were the relative merits of the disciples themselves? Mark adds the fact that they had argued among themselves about it in the way (Mark 9:33–34). The Lord takes the opportunity to instruct the disciples on a number of points in the life and service of believers. He even discusses life in the future church and how to maintain discipline (vv. 15–19).

"And he called to himself a little child and set him in the midst of them and said, Truly I say to you, except you be converted and become as little children, you shall never enter into the kingdom of the heavens" (vv. 2–3). A little child, small and weak, is the opposite of a powerful leader. It was a shattering answer to a question that reflected some degree of pride. The double negative *never* was a most emphatic declaration. To become like a little child is not a "normal" goal for any adult. But in God's eyes the rulers of the mightiest empires on earth are "the basest of men" (Dan. 4:17b). Believers must be very different. Is this what Jesus meant when He stressed the importance of being "born again" (John 3:7)?

"Whoever therefore shall humble himself as this little child, this one is greatest in the kingdom of the heavens" (v. 4). The Lord said, Come,

18:1. For the word *great* see Matt. 2:10 note.

For the word *kingdom* see Matt. 3:2 note.

18:2. For the word *little child* see Matt. 2:8 note.

18:3. For the verb *to be converted, turned about,* see Matt. 5:39 note.

For the phrase *kingdom of the heavens* see Matt. 5:3 note.

5 And whoso shall receive one such little child in my name receiveth me.

6 But whoso shall offend one of these little ones which believe in me, it were better for him that a millstone were hanged about his neck, and that he were drowned in the depth of the sea.

and the little child came. Simple obedience to God is the greatest virtue. That is why Abraham's offering up of Isaac remains such a powerful example (Gen. 22:1–12), as does Daniel's praying when it means the lion's den (Dan. 6:10–16).

"And whoever receives one such little child in my name, receives me" (v. 5). The *me* is an emphatic form. The Lord puts Himself in the place of His obedient servant. What a privilege to receive such a servant of the Lord and thus to receive the Lord Himself!

II. The Dangers of Not Putting God First. vv. 6–9 [Mark 9:42–47].

"But whoever shall cause one of these little ones who believe in me to stumble, it is better for him that an ass-drawn millstone be hung about his neck, and he be drowned in the broad expanse of the sea" (v. 6). The language emphasizes the desperate, beyond-hope condition of those who would harm the faith of new believers. Such a warning ought to make skeptics and demagogues tremble.

"Woe to the world because of stumbling blocks; for it is a necessity that stumbling blocks come, but woe to the man through whom the stumbling

---

18:4. The verb *to humble* (ταπεινόω) occurs 3 times in Matt. (18:4; 23:12 [twice]). Humility is a very important Christian virtue. It is the first step in approaching God (Matt. 5:3). For discussion see A. B. Bruce, *The Training of the Twelve*, "Humility: Training in Temper," pp. 199–207; Elwell, ed., *Evangelical Dictionary of Biblical Theology*, "Humility," pp. 361–62; ZPEB, "Humility," III, pp. 222–24; ISBE (1982), "Humble," II, pp. 775–78.

The word *greater* is a comparative adjective but here is used as a superlative.

18:5. For the verb *to receive* see Matt. 10:14 note.

18:6. For the verb *to cause to stumble* see Matt. 5:29 note.

For the verb *to believe* see Matt. 8:13 note.

The verb *to hang* (κρεμάννυμι) occurs twice in Matt. (18:6; 22:40).

The word *millstone, mill* (μύλος) occurs twice in Matt. (18:6; 24:41).

The word *of an ass* (ὀνικός) occurs only here in Matt.

The word *neck* (τράχηλος) occurs only here in Matt.

For the verb *to sink, drown*, see Matt. 14:30 note.

The word *open, deep* (πέλαγος) occurs only here in Matt. and in Acts 27:5 in the NT. It refers to the open or deep sea (beyond hope of rescue). Trench defines it as the vast, uninterrupted expanse of open water (*Synonyms*, p. 45).

7 Woe unto the world because of offences! for it must needs be that offences come; but woe to that man by whom the offence cometh!

8 Wherefore if thy hand or thy foot offend thee, cut them off, and cast them from thee: it is better for thee to enter into life halt or maimed, rather than having two hands or two feet to be cast into everlasting fire.

9 And if thine eye offend thee, pluck it out, and cast it from thee: it is better for thee to enter into life with one eye, rather than having two eyes to be cast into hell fire.

block comes" (v. 7). The tests of life must come, but the person who causes them ought to tremble at the thought of what awaits him! The Lord Jesus now explains the doctrine of eternal retribution. It is not an interpretation of men; it is a divine revelation by the Son of God Himself.

"But if your hand or your foot causes you to stumble, cut it off and cast it from you; it is good for you to enter into life crippled or lame, rather than having two hands or two feet to be cast into the eternal fire" (v. 8). The article *the* is deliberate. It is the doctrine of *the* eternal fire prepared for the wicked that is revealed throughout Scripture (Isa. 66:15–16, 24; Rev. 20:13–15). The Lord is not minimizing the pain of crippling afflictions; He is emphasizing the terribleness of eternal punishment. Verses 8 and 9 form a doublet that is parallel to Matthew 5:29–30. The repetition is not redundant; it is great emphasis. The Lord graciously desires to save all men. He is longsuffering toward mankind, "not willing that any should perish, but that all should come to repentance" (II Pet. 3:9b). But He does not decree that all men repent, for that would reduce mankind to a race of robots. Instead He invites men to flee from the wrath to come and find their eternal salvation in Him. "Whosoever shall call on the name of the Lord shall be saved" (Acts 2:21b).

"And if your eye causes you to stumble, gouge it out and cast it from you; it is better for you to enter into life with one eye, than having two eyes to be cast into the Gehenna of fire" (v. 9). Of course the Lord is not advo-

18:7. For the word *woe* see Matt. 11:21 note.

For the word *stumbling block, offense,* see Matt. 13:41 note.

The word *necessity* (ἀνάγκη) occurs only here in Matt.

18:8. For the word *crippled* see Matt. 15:30 note.

For the word *lame* see Matt. 11:5 note.

The word *eternal* (αἰώνος) occurs 6 times in Matt. (18:8; 19:16, 29; 25:41, 46 [twice]). See ISBE (1982), "Eternal," II, pp. 160–62.

For *the eternal fire* compare the author's *From Patmos to Paradise,* p. 230, note.

10 Take heed that ye despise not one of these little ones; for I say unto you, That in heaven their angels do always behold the face of my Father which is in heaven.
11 For the Son of man is come to save that which was lost.
12 How think ye? if a man have an hundred sheep, and one of them be gone astray, doth he not leave the ninety and nine, and goeth into the mountains, and seeketh that which is gone astray?

cating self-mutilation; He is speaking earnestly about the danger of being cast into hell. No sacrifice is too great to avoid the eternal gehenna. It is the eternal lake of fire (Rev. 20:15).

III. The Sheep in the Kingdom. vv. 10–14.

"Take heed that you despise not one of these little ones, for I say to you that their angels in heaven are always beholding the face of my Father who is in the heavens" (v. 10). *These little ones* refers to children (v. 2) or simple believers who need the protection of guardian angels. These angels are constantly beholding the face of the Father, the Lord of the universe, to secure the protection of these believers. The implication is that it would be dangerous to try to harm one of these little ones whom the Father cherishes.

"For the Son of man came to seek and to save that which was lost" (v. 11). The purpose of the Incarnation was to save the lost.

"What do you think? If a certain man has a hundred sheep, and one of them is gone astray, will he not leave the ninety and nine upon the mountains and go and keep seeking the one which is gone astray?" (v. 12). The Lord Jesus reveals the heart of the true shepherd. He is more deeply concerned about the erring sheep than he is of the obedient ones. The true shepherd will risk everything to bring the lost sheep back safely.

18:9. For the verb *to gouge out* see Matt. 5:29 note.

For the word *gehenna, hell,* see Matt. 5:22 note.

18:11. The verse is identical with Luke 19:10, which is a fitting conclusion to the account of Zacchaeus. See Metzger, *A Textual Commentary of the Greek New Testament,* pp. 44–45; Aland, Black, Martini, Metzger, Wikgren, *The Greek New Testament,* p. 68.

18:12. For the word *sheep* see Matt. 7:15 note.

The verb *to deceive, lead astray* (πλανάω) occurs 8 times in Matt. (18:12 [twice], 13; 22:29; 24:4, 5, 11, 24). See ISBE (1979), "Deceit, Deceitful, Deceive," I, p. 908.

For the verb *to seek* see Matt. 2:13 note. It is here present tense, implying continued action.

13 And if so be that he find it, verily I say unto you, he rejoiceth more of that sheep, than of the ninety and nine which went not astray.
14 Even so it is not the will of your Father which is in heaven, that one of these little ones should perish.
15 Moreover if thy brother shall trespass against thee, go and tell him his fault between thee and him alone: if he shall hear thee, thou hast gained thy brother.
16 But if he will not hear thee, then take with thee one or two more, that in the mouth of two or three witnesses every word may be established.

"And if it should be that he find it, truly I say to you that he rejoices more over it, than over the ninety and nine who have not gone astray" (v. 13). The pastor who has seen the drunkard or gambler reclaimed knows exactly what the Lord means. He finds himself saying, "Praise God!" every time he sees that sheep.

"Thus it is not the will before your Father who is in the heavens that one of these little ones should perish" (v. 14). There is no stronger verse in Scripture for the eternal security of the believer than this one. This should lead not to presumption but to humble obedience.

IV. Discipline in the Church. vv. 15–20.

Matthew makes clear that the Lord Jesus prepared the way for church practice during the public ministry. This is a good answer to those skeptics who think that the Lord never intended the existence of the church that followed His life, death, and resurrection.

"But if your brother should sin against you, go and speak to him between you and him alone. If he should hear you, you gained your brother" (v. 15). This is clear guidance for church discipline. The word *go* shows that the believer is to seize the initiative and actively seek the correction and improvement of his brother.

"But if he will not listen, take with you one or two others, in order that by the mouth of two or three witnesses every word may be established"

18:13. For the verb *to rejoice* see Matt. 2:10 note.

18:14. For the word *will* see Matt. 6:10 note.

For the verb *to destroy, perish*, see Matt. 2:13 note.

18:15. The verb *to sin* (ἁμαρτάνω) occurs 3 times in Matt. (18:15, 21; 27:4).

18:16. The word *witness* (μάρτυς) occurs twice in Matt. (18:16; 26:65).

For the word *word* see Matt. 4:4 note.

For the verb *to stand, be established*, see Matt. 2:9 note.

*17 And if he shall neglect to hear them, tell it unto the church: but if he neglect
to hear the church, let him be unto thee as an heathen man and a publican.
18 Verily I say unto you, Whatsoever ye shall bind on earth shall be bound in
heaven: and whatsoever ye shall loose on earth shall be loosed in heaven.
19 Again I say unto you, That if two of you shall agree on earth as touching
any thing that they shall ask, it shall be done for them of my Father which is in
heaven.*

(v. 16). If the offender refuses the correction, another step must be taken.
The witnesses are important to avoid misunderstanding or even slander.
But another attempt must be made to rescue the offender.

"But if he will not listen to them, speak to the church; but if he refuses
to listen to the church, let him be to you even as the Gentile and the
tax collector" (v. 17). There should be definite steps of severity in dealing with violations of doctrine or practice. The church that ignores its
responsibility of discipline will sink into lukewarmness and error (Rev.
3:14–19). Blomberg notes that "to treat a person as a 'pagan or a tax collector' means to treat him or her as unredeemed and outside the Christian
community" (*Matt.*, p. 279).

"Truly I say to you, as many things as you bind upon the earth shall have
been bound in heaven, and as many things as you loose upon the earth
shall have been loosed in heaven" (v. 18). The future perfect verbs show
that the church has no independent authority. Anything that it teaches
in doctrine or practice must have been already established in heaven. It
is the Spirit of truth Who will guide the believers into all truth (John
16:13). The Spirit uses the truth of the Word to set believers apart for
God (John 17:17).

"Again, truly, I say to you that if two of you upon the earth shall agree
concerning any matter which they shall ask, it shall be done for them
by my Father who is in the heavens" (v. 19). This is a very comforting
promise concerning the power of unified prayer for the work of God. The
Father is listening.

18:17. For the word *church* see Matt. 16:18 note.

For the word *Gentile* see Matt. 5:47 note.

18:18. For the verb *to bind* see Matt. 12:29 note.

For the verb *to loose* see Matt. 5:19 note.

18:19. The verb *to agree* (συμφωνέω) occurs 3 times in Matt. (18:19; 20:2, 13). For
discussion see ISBE (1979), "Agree," I, p. 72.

20 For where two or three are gathered together in my name, there am I in the midst of them.
21 Then came Peter to him, and said, Lord, how oft shall my brother sin against me, and I forgive him? till seven times?
22 Jesus saith unto him, I say not unto thee, Until seven times: but, Until seventy times seven.
23 Therefore is the kingdom of heaven likened unto a certain king, which would take account of his servants.

"For where two or three are gathered together in my name, there am I in their midst" (v. 20). This is one of the simplest descriptions of a church meeting that is in Scripture. The size of the congregation is absolutely unimportant to God. It is their devotion to Him and to His Word that brings His attention.

V. The Unforgiving Servant. vv. 21–35.

"Then Peter came and said to him: Lord, how many times shall my brother sin against me, and I forgive him? Until seven times?" (v. 21). Peter expresses the concern that all the disciples felt and gives what he plainly thinks is a very generous estimate of patience. Many people would be ready to cut the brother off with the first failure. Seven is a sacred number; Peter felt good about his suggestion. He was unprepared for the answer of the Lord.

"Jesus says to him: I say not to you, until seven times, but until seventy-seven times" (v. 22). Who has been asked for forgiveness even seven times by anyone? The Lord means that the believer should forgive every time he is asked (even as God does).

"On account of this the kingdom of the heavens is like a man, a king, who wished to settle accounts with his servants" (v. 23). The word *servants* is literally slaves. In the ancient world the servants of kings were often slaves but men of great influence themselves.

18:20. For the verb *to gather together* see Matt. 2:4 note.

18:21. The word *seven times* (ἑπτάκις) occurs only twice in Matt. (18:21, 22).

18:22. The word *seventy* (ἑβδομηκοντάκις) occurs only here in the NT.

The idiom means *seventy-seven times* as Moulton makes clear (*A Grammar of New Testament Greek*, Vol. III, *Syntax*, pp. 187–88). A. B. Bruce notes that *70 times 7* would need to have the suffix -κις on both words (*Expos. Greek Test.*, I, pp. 241–42). For divergent views see Morris, *Matt.*, p. 472, note 65.

18:23. The verb *to settle* (συναίρω) occurs 3 times in Matt. (18:23, 24; 25:19). This verb with *account* (λόγος) is the normal idiom for settling accounts in the economic sense in the papyri. See Moulton and Milligan, *Vocabulary*, p. 601.

24 And when he had begun to reckon, one was brought unto him, which owed him ten thousand talents.
25 But forasmuch as he had not to pay, his lord commanded him to be sold, and his wife, and children, and all that he had, and payment to be made.
26 The servant therefore fell down, and worshipped him, saying, Lord, have patience with me, and I will pay thee all.
27 Then the lord of that servant was moved with compassion, and loosed him, and forgave him the debt.

"But when he began to settle [accounts], one was brought to him who owed ten thousand talents" (v. 24). Such a sum amounted to thirty million days' wages, an impossibility to pay.

"But because he had nothing with which to pay, his lord commanded that he be sold, and his wife, and the children, and all that he had, and payment to be made" (v. 25). It was a stern command to get as much as possible out of a bad situation.

"The slave therefore, fell down and worshiped him, saying, Have patience with me and I will pay you all" (v. 26). What he could do was obviously nothing compared with that immense debt. The apostle Paul takes this idea in a theological direction by saying, "But we know that as many things as the law says, it says to those who are under the law, in order that every mouth may be stopped and all the world may become guilty before God" (Rom. 3:19). The prophet Isaiah said the same thing: "All our righteousnesses are as filthy rags" (64:6*b*).

"But the lord of that slave was moved with compassion, and released him, and forgave him the debt" (v. 27). There was no ground for such a deed except the compassion of the Lord.

18:24. The word *talent* (τάλαντον) occurs 14 times in Matt. (18:24; 25:15–28) only in the NT. The talent was the largest weight in money in the ancient world. It contained 3,000 shekels. See Merrill F. Unger, *The New Unger's Bible Dictionary*, ed. R. K. Harrison, "Metrology," pp. 841–47; Douglas and Tenney, eds., *The New International Dictionary of the Bible*, "Money," pp. 667–70.

18:25. For the verb *to repay* see Matt. 5:26 note.

For the verb *to sell* see Matt. 13:46 note.

18:26. For the verb *to worship* see Matt. 2:2 note.

The verb *to be patient* (μακροθυμέω) occurs twice in Matt. (18:26, 29).

18:27. For the verb *to be moved with compassion* see Matt. 9:36 note.

For the verb *to release* see Matt. 1:19 note.

For the verb *to forgive* see Matt. 3:15 note.

The word *debt* (δάνειον) occurs only here in the NT.

28 But the same servant went out, and found one of his fellowservants, which owed him an hundred pence: and he laid hands on him, and took him by the throat, saying, Pay me that thou owest.

29 And his fellowservant fell down at his feet, and besought him, saying, Have patience with me, and I will pay thee all.

30 And he would not: but went and cast him into prison, till he should pay the debt.

31 So when his fellowservants saw what was done, they were very sorry, and came and told unto their lord all that was done.

32 Then his lord, after that he had called him, said unto him, O thou wicked servant, I forgave thee all that debt, because thou desiredst me:

"But that slave went out and found one of his fellow-slaves, who owed him a hundred denarii, and having grasped him, he choked him, saying, Pay what you owe " (v. 28). He had no thought of sharing the compassion of his lord. He wanted to wring everything he could out of his fellow slave.

"His fellow-slave therefore, fell down and was begging him, saying, Have patience with me, and I will pay you" (v. 29). That is the very language he had used with his lord. The imperfect tense *was begging* stresses continued pleading.

"But he would not, but went and cast him into prison until he should pay what was owed" (v. 30). That was a hard-hearted, letter-of-the-law attitude.

"Therefore, when his fellow servants saw the things that happened, they were exceedingly grieved, and went and explained to their lord all the things that had happened" (v. 31). His fellow servants were distressed when they saw his bitter attitude toward one who was in the same kind of trouble that he had been in. This parable is a serious warning to every believer who forgets the infinite debt that the Lord has paid for him.

"Then his lord called him to him and says to him: Evil slave, I forgave you all that debt because you asked me" (v. 32). There was no reason in the slave for mercy; it all depended on the grace of the lord. This *evil* is strong enough to work evil in others.

18:28. The word *denarius* (δηνάριον) occurs 6 times in Matt. (18:28; 20:2, 9, 10, 13; 22:19). It was a Roman coin, the day's wage, equal to the drachma, a Greek coin.

For the verb *to choke* see Matt. 13:7 note.

18:31. For the verb *to explain* see Matt. 13:36 note.

18:32. For the word *evil* see Matt. 5:37 note.

33 Shouldest not thou also have had compassion on thy fellowservant, even as I had pity on thee?
34 And his lord was wroth, and delivered him to the tormentors, till he should pay all that was due unto him.
35 So likewise shall my heavenly Father do also unto you, if ye from your hearts forgive not every one his brother their trespasses.

"Was it not necessary for you to have mercy on your fellow-slave, as I also had mercy on you?" (v. 33). An unforgiving spirit shows that he did not take his own forgiveness seriously. Paul exhorts all believers, "And be ye kind one to another, tenderhearted, forgiving one another, even as God for Christ's sake hath forgiven you" (Eph. 4:32). God's forgiving love should transform the believer as Paul goes on to exhort, "Be therefore followers of God as dear children; and walk in love, as Christ also has loved us" (Eph. 5:1–2a).

"And his lord was filled with wrath and delivered him to the tormentors until he should repay all that was owed" (v. 34). If the evil slave is going to be that kind of unforgiving person, justice demands that he be treated the same way.

"Thus also my heavenly Father shall do to you, if each one of you from your hearts forgive not his brother" (v. 35). The hard-hearted slave brings upon himself a law of retribution. The saints need a compassionate heart toward the brethren, for that is the nature of God. "But thou, O Lord, art a God full of compassion, and gracious, longsuffering, and plenteous in mercy and truth" (Ps. 86:15).

Practical Applications from Matthew 18

1. Little children trust their parents for food, clothing, shelter, and all else (v. 3). Believers need to trust God for all their needs. "But my God shall supply all your need according to his riches in glory by Christ Jesus" (Phil. 4:19).
2. Whoever will humble himself as a little child is greatest before God (v. 4). The greatest prophets trusted God for food, shelter, and all they needed: Moses (Exod. 24:18); Elijah (I Kings 17:5ff.).
3. Caring for the weak and helpless God accounts as done for Himself (v. 5). "Let us have grace, whereby we may serve God acceptably with reverence and godly fear" (Heb. 12:28b).

18:33. For the verb *to have mercy on* see Matt. 5:7 note.

18:34. For the verb *to be filled with wrath* see Matt. 5:22 note.

4. It is better to be crippled and on the way to heaven than to be strong and on the way to hell (vv. 8–9). "For Demas hath forsaken me, having loved this present world" (II Tim. 4:10a).

5. The Lord Jesus came to save those that are lost (v. 11). Believers need to share the gospel. "But if our gospel be hid, it is hid to them that are lost" (II Cor. 4:3).

6. It is not God's will that any perish (v. 14). "The Lord is not slack concerning his promise, as some men count slackness; but is long-suffering to us-ward, not willing that any should perish, but that all should come to repentance" (II Pet. 3:9).

7. Small church gatherings should never fear that God might overlook them (v. 20). "Thou shalt hide them in the secret of thy presence from the pride of man: thou shalt keep them secretly in a pavilion from the strife of tongues" (Ps. 31:20).

8. A believer should be quick to forgive others, even as God forgave him (v. 33). "And be ye kind one to another, tenderhearted, forgiving one another, even as God for Christ's sake hath forgiven you" (Eph. 4:32).

Prayer

Lord Jesus, enable us to trust and obey You with a childlike faith; give us the grace to forsake the path of wickedness and serve You alone. Move us to reach the lost, reconcile the erring, and fellowship with the saints. Amen.

MATTHEW 19

Jesus Corrects Errors

Persons
Jesus
Great multitudes
Pharisees
Disciples of Jesus

Little children
A rich young ruler
Peter

Persons referred to
A man who wants divorce
The Creator
Father
Mother
Wife
Moses

Eunuchs
The poor
The twelve tribes
Brothers
Sisters

Places mentioned
Galilee
Judea beyond Jordan

Doctrines taught
Divorce
Creation
The sanctity of marriage
Hardness of heart
Adultery
Prayer
Child evangelism
Eternal life

Goodness of God
God's commands
Love
The danger of riches
Salvation
The power of God
Rewards
Everlasting life

*1 And it came to pass, that when Jesus had finished these sayings, he depart-
ed from Galilee, and came into the coasts of Judaea beyond Jordan;*

2 And great multitudes followed him; and he healed them there.

*3 The Pharisees also came unto him, tempting him, and saying unto him, Is
it lawful for a man to put away his wife for every cause?*

*4 And he answered and said unto them, Have ye not read, that he which
made them at the beginning made them male and female,*

*5 And said, For this cause shall a man leave father and mother, and shall
cleave to his wife: and they twain shall be one flesh?*

Matthew 19 Exposition

I. Jesus Corrects the Pharisees on Divorce. vv. 1–12 [Mark 10:1–12].

"And it came to pass when Jesus finished these words, he departed from
Galilee and came into the regions of Judaea beyond the Jordan" (v. 1).
The Lord now moved south to Judaea east of the Jordan. Morris notes
that this is the final withdrawal from Galilee; Jesus will not return until
after the Resurrection (Matt. 28:16, *Matt.*, p. 479).

"And great crowds followed him, and he healed them there" (v. 2). The
Lord was always ready to help people who were in need. Helping others
was His normal way of living.

"And Pharisees came to him, tempting him and saying, Is it lawful for
a man to put away his wife for every reason?" (v. 3). This was a trap designed to alienate at least half of the audience from Him. The rabbis were
bitterly divided over this question. Shammai held that adultery alone was
the grounds for divorce; Hillel maintained that almost any grounds were
sufficient. However Jesus answered, there would be people offended.

"But he answered and said: Did you not read that from the beginning the
Creator made them male and female? And said, on account of this a man
shall leave his father and mother and shall be joined to his wife, and the
two shall be one flesh" (vv. 4–5; Gen. 1:27; 2:24). The Lord was not for
either interpretation; He was for God's original purpose: permanent unity.

19:1. For the verb *to finish, end*, see Matt. 7:28 note.

For the word *region, territory*, see Matt. 2:16 note.

19:2. For the verb *to heal* see Matt. 4:23 note.

19:3. For the verb *to tempt* see Matt. 4:1 note.

For the verb *to put away* see Matt. 1:19 note.

The word *reason, relationship, charge* (αἰτία) occurs 3 times in Matt. (19:3, 10; 27:37).

19:4. The verb *to create* (κτίζω) occurs only here in Matt.

6 *Wherefore they are no more twain, but one flesh. What therefore God hath joined together, let not man put asunder.*

7 *They say unto him, Why did Moses then command to give a writing of divorcement, and to put her away?*

8 *He saith unto them, Moses because of the hardness of your hearts suffered you to put away your wives: but from the beginning it was not so.*

9 *And I say unto you, Whosoever shall put away his wife, except it be for fornication, and shall marry another, committeth adultery: and whoso marrieth her which is put away doth commit adultery.*

"So that they are no longer two, but one flesh. Therefore that which God yoked together, let not man separate" (v. 6). The Lord draws a consequence, *so that.* The divinely intended marriage is a powerful unity. A. T. Robertson notes that "yoked together" is a timeless aorist, always true (*Word Pictures*, I, p. 154).

"They say to him: Why therefore did Moses command to give a writing of divorcement and to put her away?" (v. 7). The provision is found in Deuteronomy 24:1, 3, but it was not a command, merely permission. The Pharisees knew the letter of the law but did not understand the spirit.

"He said to them, Moses because of the hardness of your hearts permitted you to put away your wives, but from the beginning it has not been thus" (v. 8). The Lord Jesus put His finger on the "heart" of the problem. It was hardness of heart that led to divorce. The Lord God hates putting away (Mal. 2:16).

"But I say to you that whoever shall put away his wife, except for fornication, and shall marry another, commits adultery" (v. 9). This is the second teaching of this important doctrine (Matt. 5:32). The word *but* shows that the Lord Jesus is putting Himself on the side of the permanence and sanctity of the marriage relationship.

For the word *wife, woman*, see Matt. 1:20 note.

19:5. For the word *flesh* see Matt. 16:17 note.

19:6. The verb *to join, yoke together* (συζεύγνυμι) occurs only here in Matt.

The verb *to separate* (χωρίζω) occurs only here in Matt.

19:7. For *Moses* see Matt. 8:4 note.

For the word *divorcement* see Matt. 5:31 note.

19:8. The word *hardness of heart* (σκληροκαρδία) occurs only here in Matt.

For the verb *to permit* see Matt. 8:21 note.

For the verb *to put away* see Matt. 1:19 note.

19:9. For the word *fornication* see Matt. 5:32 note.

For the verb *to commit adultery* see Matt. 5:32 note.

10 His disciples say unto him, If the case of the man be so with his wife, it is not good to marry.

11 But he said unto them, All men cannot receive this saying, save they to whom it is given.

12 For there are some eunuchs, which were so born from their mother's womb: and there are some eunuchs, which were made eunuchs of men: and there be eunuchs, which have made themselves eunuchs for the kingdom of heaven's sake. He that is able to receive it, let him receive it.

"His disciples say to him, If the relationship of the man with his wife be thus, it is good not to marry" (v. 10). But there are profound biological and spiritual reasons for marriage, not the least of which is the fact that the Lord Jesus has chosen spiritual humanity as His bride (Rev. 21:3–27). Marriage reflects a divine original.

"But he said to them: All men are not able to make room for this word, but those to whom it has been given" (v. 11). It is God's will for some to marry and it is not God's will for others to marry. Each person must determine God's will for his own situation.

"For there are eunuchs who were born thus from their mother's womb; and there are eunuchs who were made eunuchs by men, and there are eunuchs who made themselves eunuchs on account of the kingdom of the heavens. Let the one who is able to make room for it, make room for it" (v. 12). Thus the Lord declares that there are people for whom it is not God's will that they marry. They should learn how to serve God in a single state to the glory of God.

II. Jesus Corrects the Disciples on Children. vv. 13–15 [Mark 10:13–16; Luke 18:15–17].

"Then little children were brought to him in order that he should put his hands on them and pray, but the disciples rebuked them" (v. 13). The disciples thought that the children were wasting the Lord's time, but the Lord revealed something different.

19:10. For the word *relationship, reason,* see Matt. 19:3 note.

19:11. For the verb *to make room for* see Matt. 15:17 note.

19:12. The word *eunuch* (εὐνοῦχος) occurs 3 times in this verse only in Matt.

The verb *to castrate, make one a eunuch* (εὐνουχίζω) occurs twice in this verse only in the NT.

19:13. For the word *little child* see Matt. 2:8 note.

For the verb *to pray* see Matt. 5:44 note.

*13 Then were there brought unto him little children, that he should put his
hands on them, and pray: and the disciples rebuked them.
14 But Jesus said, Suffer little children, and forbid them not, to come unto me:
for of such is the kingdom of heaven.
15 And he laid his hands on them, and departed thence.
16 And, behold, one came and said unto him, Good Master, what good thing
shall I do, that I may have eternal life?
17 And he said unto him, Why callest thou me good? there is none good but
one, that is, God: but if thou wilt enter into life, keep the commandments.*

"But Jesus said, Permit the little children, and stop hindering them from
coming to me, for of such is the kingdom of the heavens" (v. 14). This
passage is the foundation for all children's work, Sunday school, child
evangelism, and other efforts. It is God's will that children be reached
at an early age with the gospel and Christian teaching. Morris observes,
"It is not easy to think of Muhammad as concerned for little children, or
Gautama the Buddha. But the Gospels make it clear that there were often
children around Jesus" (*Matt.*, p. 486).

"And he laid his hands on them and departed from there" (v. 15). He
obviously prayed divine blessing upon them. We must meditate on what
early prayers can do for children. Susanna Wesley prayed for her children.

*III. Jesus Corrects the Rich Young Ruler and the Disciples. vv. 16–30 [Mark
10:17–31; Luke 18:18–30].*

"And, behold, one came to him and said: Teacher, what good thing shall
I do in order that I may have eternal life?" (v. 16). This young man comes
to the Lord with the pharisaic idea that doing something good will earn
eternal life. That is not a biblical teaching.

"But he said to him: Why are you asking me concerning the good thing?
One is the good Person; if you wish to enter into life, keep the commandments" (v. 17). The Lord is gently saying that God alone is good, and if
you want eternal life, you must align yourself with His will. The young
man does not understand at all.

19:14. The verb *to hinder* (κωλύω) occurs only here in Matt.

19:15. For the verb *to put on* see Matt. 9:18 note.

19:16. For the word *teacher* see Matt. 8:19 note.

For the word *good* see Matt. 5:45 note.

For the word *life* see Matt. 7:14 note.

19:17. The verb *to keep, watch* (τηρέω) occurs 6 times in Matt. (19:17; 23:3; 27:36, 54;
28:4, 20).

18 He saith unto him, Which? Jesus said, Thou shalt do no murder, Thou shalt not commit adultery, Thou shalt not steal, Thou shalt not bear false witness,
19 Honour thy father and thy mother: and, Thou shalt love thy neighbour as thyself.
20 The young man saith unto him, All these things have I kept from my youth up: what lack I yet?
21 Jesus said unto him, If thou wilt be perfect, go and sell that thou hast, and give to the poor, and thou shalt have treasure in heaven: and come and follow me.

"He says to him: Which? But Jesus said: You shall not murder, you shall not commit adultery, you shall not steal, you shall not bear false witness, honor your father and mother, and you shall love your neighbor as yourself" (vv. 18–19; Exod. 20:12–16; Lev. 19:18). The Lord refers him back to the basic commands of the law, which the man knew very well but did not understand.

"The young man says to him: All these things I have kept; what am I lacking yet?" (v. 20). The young man was not a liar or a hypocrite; he was just shallow. What he means is that he has never literally murdered anyone; he has never literally committed adultery with any woman; he has not literally stolen anything. He was a good, moral man. He has never had the thought that God sees hatred, lust, and covetousness in the heart as gross sin. The whole human race stands condemned before God, and the young man was included. He still had a nagging suspicion that what he had done was not enough to please God. Peter names seven Christian virtues, and then observes, "But he that lacks these things is blind, and cannot see afar off" (II Pet. 1:9a).

"Jesus said to him: If you wish to be perfect, go, sell your possessions and give to the poor, and you shall have treasure in heaven, and Come, follow me" (v. 21). The young man was expecting congratulations, but he got a

For the word *commandment* see Matt. 5:19 note.

19:18. The interrogative pronoun *which?* (ποῖος) is literally *what kind of?*

For the verb *to murder* see Matt. 5:21 note.

For the verb *to commit adultery* see Matt. 5:27 note.

For the verb *to steal* see Matt. 6:19 note.

The verb *to bear false witness* (ψευδομαρτυρέω) occurs only here in Matt.

19:19. For the verb *to honor* see Matt. 15:4 note.

For the verb *to love* see Matt. 5:43 note.

19:20. The verb *to keep, guard* (φυλάσσω) occurs only here in Matt.

The verb *to lack* (ὑστερέω) occurs only here in Matt.

22 But when the young man heard that saying, he went away sorrowful: for he had great possessions.
23 Then said Jesus unto his disciples, Verily I say unto you, That a rich man shall hardly enter into the kingdom of heaven.
24 And again I say unto you, It is easier for a camel to go through the eye of a needle, than for a rich man to enter into the kingdom of God.
25 When his disciples heard it, they were exceedingly amazed, saying, Who then can be saved?

stunning condemnation. He was a guilty sinner who did not want to get right with God. A life of poverty following the Lord Jesus was an abhorrent idea to him. "The principle involved is supreme devotion to Christ" (Broadus, *Matt.*, p. 407).

"But when the young man heard the word, he went away, being grieved, for he was having many possessions" (v. 22). The Lord Jesus had put His finger on the idol, and the young man knew he was guilty. Possessions have been the downfall of many.

"But Jesus said to his disciples: Truly I say to you that a rich man with difficulty shall enter into the kingdom of the heavens" (v. 23). Great riches are not usually a great blessing; they are more commonly a great danger. They steal away the heart of the possessor.

"But again I say to you, It is easier for a camel to go through the eye of a needle than for a rich man to enter into the kingdom of God" (v. 24). The thought is ridiculous. If you stretched the camel out a half mile, the carcass would rot before you got it through the eye of a needle! The Lord is saying that it is impossible for a man who trusts in his riches to put God first in his life.

"But when the disciples heard, they were exceedingly amazed, saying, Who then is able to be saved?" (v. 25). The disciples assume that if the

19:21. For the word *perfect* see Matt. 5:48 note.

For the verb *to sell* see Matt. 10:29 note.

19:22. For the verb *to grieve* see Matt. 14:9 note.

The word *possession* (κτῆμα) occurs only here in Matt.

19:23. The word *rich* (πλούσιος) occurs 3 times in Matt. (19:23, 24; 27:57).

The word *with difficulty* (δυσκόλως) occurs only here in Matt.

19:24. For the word *camel* see Matt. 3:4 note.

The word *needle* (ῥαφίς) occurs only here in Matt. Luke uses the word *surgical needle* (βελόνη) (Luke 18:25).

19:25. For the verb *to be amazed* see Matt. 7:28 note.

26 But Jesus beheld them, and said unto them, With men this is impossible; but with God all things are possible.
27 Then answered Peter and said unto him, Behold, we have forsaken all, and followed thee; what shall we have therefore?
28 And Jesus said unto them, Verily I say unto you, That ye which have followed me, in the regeneration when the Son of man shall sit in the throne of his glory, ye also shall sit upon twelve thrones, judging the twelve tribes of Israel.

rich, being greatly blessed of God, are not saved, what chance do the rest of men have.

"But Jesus looked straight at them and said, With men this is impossible, but with God all things are possible" (v. 26). The Lord gave them a piercing gaze because this truth is essential for spiritual understanding. No one is naturally saved; only God can save a human being. Money and possessions have nothing to do with salvation. There were rich men in the OT who were saved (Abraham, Job), but they were saved because of their right relation with God, not because they were rich.

"Then Peter answered and said to him: Behold, we have left all things and followed you; what therefore shall we have?" (v. 27). Leave it to Peter to be blunt! "What's in it for us?" However, it was strictly true that the apostles had left everything for the Lord. They will find out one day that no one can out-give the Lord.

"But Jesus said to them: Truly I say to you that you who have followed me, in the regeneration whenever the Son of man shall sit upon the throne of his glory, you also shall sit upon twelve thrones, judging the twelve tribes of Israel" (v. 28). This is a clear promise that there will be a literal millennial reign on the earth in fulfillment of the prophecies (Isa. 2:1–5; 11:1–10; 24:21–25:6; 32:1–20; 35:1–10; 65:18–25; Jer. 23:1–8; 33:14–26). The book of Revelation spells out the details and places it before the eternal kingdom (Rev. 20:4–6). Afterwards Satan must be loosed and conquered and the eternal kingdom established (Rev. 20:7–21:27).

For the verb *to save* see Matt. 1:21 note.

19:26. For the verb *to look straight at, pay special attention to*, see Matt. 6:26 note.

19:28. The word *regeneration* (παλιγγενεσία) occurs only here of the restored kingdom in Matt. and in Titus 3:5 of the regeneration of the individual believer.

The word *tribe* (φυλή) occurs twice in Matt. (19:28; 24:30). It denotes an ethnic group rather than a national one.

29 And every one that hath forsaken houses, or brethren, or sisters, or father, or mother, or wife, or children, or lands, for my name's sake, shall receive an hundredfold, and shall inherit everlasting life.
30 But many that are first shall be last; and the last shall be first.

"And everyone who left houses or brothers or sisters or father or mother or children or fields, on account of my name, shall receive a hundredfold, and shall inherit eternal life" (v. 29). It is not mere sacrifice that is involved, but sacrifice for Jesus' sake ("on account of my name"). The Lord knows every such sacrifice and will repay with vastly greater blessings.

"But many who are first shall be last, and the last first" (v. 30). On the simplest level this statement means that many who are "first" in the world's eyes will be last in God's regard, and many who are "last" in the world's estimation will have the greatest reward from God. There are people of power and influence in the world who have nothing but the wrath of God to expect in the world to come; there are others who have no recognition in this world at all but who will be renowned in heaven. But in the light of the explanatory parable in the following chapter, it may also mean that God will reward the last servants (Tribulation saints) first, and the first servants (apostles) last (Matt. 20:16). See Matt. 20:1–16.

Practical Applications from Matthew 19

1. Following Jesus always brings blessing (v. 2). Jesus promised, "I am the light of the world: he that follows me shall not walk in darkness, but shall have the light of life" (John 8:12*b*).
2. Christian marriage is a relationship blessed of God (v. 6). Love and respect should rule the home. "Let every one of you each love his own wife as himself, and the wife reverence her husband" (Eph. 5:33*b*).
3. Hardness of heart is a source of strife (v. 8). "But according to your hardness and impenitent heart are you treasuring up for yourself wrath in the day of wrath?" (Rom. 2:5*a*).

19:29. The word *a hundredfold* (ἑκατονταπλασίων) occurs only here in Matt.
19:30. For the word *first* see Matt. 5:24 note.
For the word *last* see Matt. 5:26 note.

4. Children ought to be brought to Jesus as soon as possible (vv. 13–14). "As ye know how we exhorted and comforted and charged every one of you, as a father doth his children, that ye would walk worthy of God, who hath called you unto his kingdom and glory" (I Thess. 2:11–12).

5. Pleasing God is the most important part of life (vv. 16–17). "For the rest, therefore, brethren, we exhort and beseech you in the Lord Jesus, that even as you received from us how it is necessary for you to walk and to please God, even as you walk, that you may abound more" (I Thess. 4:1).

6. Riches can become an idol in one's life (v. 23). "Charge them that are rich in this world, that they be not high minded, nor trust in uncertain riches, but in the living God, who gives us richly all things to enjoy" (I Tim. 6:17).

7. Every believer who has denied himself benefits in this life shall receive much more in the life to come (v. 29). "If any man's work abide which he has built, he shall receive a reward" (I Cor. 3:14).

Prayer

Lord Jesus, help us to obey Your Word; give us special grace and wisdom to lead children to You. Enable us to exalt You above all in our lives. Protect us from the idolatry of things and possessions. Amen.

MATTHEW 20

Teaching and Healing

Persons
Jesus
The twelve disciples
The mother of Zebedee's children
Her sons
Great multitude
Two blind men

Persons referred to
A householder
Laborers
The foreman
Chief priests
Scribes
The Gentiles
My Father
Rulers of the Gentiles

Places mentioned
A vineyard
Marketplace
Jerusalem
Jericho

Doctrines taught
Service
Divine reward
The death of Christ
Crucifixion
Resurrection
The coming kingdom
Ransom
Mercy
Compassion

1 For the kingdom of heaven is like unto a man that is an householder, which went out early in the morning to hire labourers into his vineyard.

2 And when he had agreed with the labourers for a penny a day, he sent them into his vineyard.

3 And he went out about the third hour, and saw others standing idle in the marketplace,

4 And said unto them; Go ye also into the vineyard, and whatsoever is right I will give you. And they went their way.

5 Again he went out about the sixth and ninth hour, and did likewise.

Matthew 20 Exposition

I. The Parable of the Laborers in the Vineyard. vv. 1–16.

"For the kingdom of the heavens is like a man who was master of the house, who went out early in the morning in order to hire workers for his vineyard" (v. 1). The word *for* links this chapter with the preceding teaching about those who are first or last. The master is a landowner who needs workers for his fields.

"And when he agreed with the workers for a denarius a day, he sent them into his vineyard" (v. 2). The denarius was the regular day's wage, mutually agreeable.

"And he went out about the third hour and saw others standing in the marketplace idle" (v. 3). The time of harvest is an emergency for farmers. If the crop is not harvested quickly, it will rot in the field. So farmers will often hire part-time workers to help get in the crop.

"And he said to them: Go you also into the vineyard, and whatever is just I will give you" (v. 4). The workers would calculate, three quarters of the

---

20:1. For the word *master of the house* see Matt. 10:25 note.

The verb *to hire* (μισθόω) occurs only in this context in Matt. (20:1, 7) in the NT. For the word *worker* see Matt. 9:37 note.

The word *vineyard* (ἀμπελών) occurs 10 times in Matt. (20:1, 2, 4, 7, 8; 21:28, 33, 39, 40, 41). For background see Zohary, *Plants of the Bible*, "Vine," pp. 54–55; ZPEB, "Vine, Vineyard," V, pp. 882–84; ISBE (1988), "Vine," IV, pp. 986–87; Ryken, Wilhoit, and Longman, *Dictionary of Biblical Imagery*, "Vine, Vineyard," pp. 914–17.

20:2. For the verb *to agree* see Matt. 18:19 note.

For the word *denarius* see Matt. 18:28 note.

20:3. For the word *idle* see Matt. 12:36 note.

For the word *marketplace* see Matt. 11:16 note.

20.4. For the word *just, righteous*, see Matt. 1:19 note.

*6 And about the eleventh hour he went out, and found others standing idle,
and saith unto them, Why stand ye here all the day idle?*

*7 They say unto him, Because no man hath hired us. He saith unto them,
Go ye also into the vineyard; and whatsoever is right, that shall ye receive.*

*8 So when even was come, the lord of the vineyard saith unto his steward,
Call the labourers, and give them their hire, beginning from the last unto the
first.*

*9 And when they came that were hired about the eleventh hour, they received
every man a penny.*

day, three quarters of the going wage. They would trust the master to keep
his word.

"And they went their way. And about the sixth and ninth hours he went
out and did likewise" (v. 5). He was determined to get the harvest in before it spoiled in the field. Every farmer would understand his persistence.

"And about the eleventh hour he went out and found others standing,
and says to them: Why are you standing here the whole day idle?" (v. 6).
There is only an hour left, but the crop is not in yet.

"They say to him, Because no one hired us. He says to them: Go you also
into the vineyard" (v. 7). Every time the master looked, he found workers and hired them, promising them a fair wage. Even one hour's labor
is worth it to the master. Anything left for the next day will be rotten.
These workers are thinking that the wage will be a very small coin, but
something is better than nothing.

"But when evening came, the lord of the vineyard says to his foreman:
Call the workers and pay them the wage, beginning from the last to
the first" (v. 8). This is equivalent to the rewards in heaven. We should
remember the Lord's word to the persecuted: "Rejoice, and be exceeding
glad: for great is your reward in heaven" (Matt. 5:12a).

"And when the ones about the eleventh hour came, they received each
one a denarius" (v. 9). No doubt their jaws dropped when they saw that
they were getting a day's wage for an hour's work! That was generosity
beyond all expectation.

20:6. The word *eleventh* (ἐνδέκατος) occurs only in this context in Matt. (20:6, 9).
For the word *idle* see Matt. 12:36 note.

20:8. The word *foreman, steward* (ἐπίτροπος) occurs only here in Matt.
For the word *wage, pay*, see Matt. 5:12 note.

10 But when the first came, they supposed that they should have received more; and they likewise received every man a penny.
11 And when they had received it, they murmured against the goodman of the house,
12 Saying, These last have wrought but one hour, and thou hast made them equal unto us, which have borne the burden and heat of the day.
13 But he answered one of them, and said, Friend, I do thee no wrong: didst not thou agree with me for a penny?

"And when the first ones came, they supposed that they would receive more, but they themselves also received a denarius" (v. 10). They had agreed to work for a denarius, and that was what they got. The application is clearly that no one in heaven is going to be "more saved" than others. All who are there will be there by the grace of God alone.

"But the ones who received were murmuring against the master of the house, saying: These last ones worked one hour, and you made them equal to us, who have borne the burden and heat of the day" (vv. 11–12). They wanted a bonus.

"But he answered one of them and said: Friend, I am not harming you; did you not agree with me for a denarius?" (v. 13). The lord addresses one of them (the spokesman for the grievance committee) and reminds him of the agreement. He is giving them exactly what he promised. All will get the same wage. The bandit on the cross will be just as saved as the apostle Paul (Luke 23:42–43; Rom. 1:14–15).

"Take up what is yours and go. But I will give to this last even as to you" (v. 14). The verb *to take up* implies that the worker had thrown down the coin in disappointment. Unfortunately some believers have the idea that they are far more valuable to the Lord than they really are. The Lord warns us all, "Thus also you, whenever you have done all the things that

---

20:10. For the verb *to suppose, think*, see Matt. 5:17 note.

20:11. The verb *to murmur, grumble* (γογγύζω) occurs only here in Matt.

20:12. The word *burden* (βάρος) occurs only here in Matt. It is often used of a burden that is thought to be too great to be borne. See the author's *Treasury of New Testament Synonyms*, pp. 1–4 (in the LXX, Jth. 7:4; Ecclus. 13:2).

20:13. The word *friend* (ἑταῖρος) occurs 3 times in Matt. (20:13; 22:12; 26:50) only in the NT. The title was a kindly address. For discussion see ISBE (1982), "Friend," II, pp. 361–62; ZPEB, "Friend," II, p. 608; Ryken, Wilhoit, and Longman, *Dictionary of Biblical Imagery*, "Friendship," pp. 308–9.

The verb *to do wrong, harm* (ἀδικέω) occurs only here in Matt.

For the verb *to agree with* see Matt. 18:19 note.

14 Take that thine is, and go thy way: I will give unto this last, even as unto thee.
15 Is it not lawful for me to do what I will with mine own? Is thine eye evil, because I am good?
16 So the last shall be first, and the first last: for many be called, but few chosen.
17 And Jesus going up to Jerusalem took the twelve disciples apart in the way, and said unto them,
18 Behold, we go up to Jerusalem; and the Son of man shall be betrayed unto the chief priests and unto the scribes, and they shall condemn him to death,

have been commanded you, say, We are unprofitable slaves; we have done that which we ought to do" (Luke 17:10). And what believer can say that he has done all that has been commanded him? God help us to do better!

"Is it not lawful for me to do what I wish with my own things? Or is your eye evil because I am good?" (v. 15). The believer should never allow God's blessing on others to cause him to be envious. God has already given every believer more good things than he deserves. The parable is an illustration of the undeserved grace of God for His people.

"Thus the last shall be first, and the first last" (v. 16). He thus gives a closure to his lesson by repeating it in inverse order (Matt. 19:30).

II. The Predictions of Jesus: His Death and Resurrection. vv. 17–19 [Mark 10:32–34; Luke 18:31–34].

"And while Jesus was going up to Jerusalem, he took the twelve disciples alongside privately, and in the way said to them" (v. 17). It was critical that He explain to them what was about to happen so that they would remember that He had forewarned them.

"Behold, we are going up to Jerusalem, and the Son of man shall be betrayed to the chief priests and scribes, and they shall condemn him to death" (v. 18). The chief priests had no authority to condemn Him to

---

20:14. For the verb *to take up* see Matt. 4:6 note.

20:15. For the verb *it is lawful* see Matt. 12:2 note.

20:16. Some manuscripts insert "For many are called, but few chosen," which is actually in Matt. 22:14. See Metzger, *A Textual Commentary on the Greek New Testament*, p. 51.

20:17. For the verb *to go up* see Matt. 3:16 note. Since Jerusalem was the spiritual high place of the country, whenever someone went to Jerusalem, he went *up*.

20:18. For the verb *to betray* see Matt. 4:12 note.

For the verb *to condemn* see Matt. 12:41 note.

*19 And shall deliver him to the Gentiles to mock, and to scourge, and to cru-
cify him: and the third day he shall rise again.*
*20 Then came to him the mother of Zebedees children with her sons, worship-
ping him, and desiring a certain thing of him.*
*21 And he said unto her, What wilt thou? She saith unto him, Grant that
these my two sons may sit, the one on thy right hand, and the other on the left,
in thy kingdom.*

death, but they would do it anyway and then pressure Pilate to actually
do it.

"And shall deliver him over to the Gentiles in order to mock and scourge
and crucify, and the third day he shall be raised" (v. 19). This was really
the fourth time that the Lord prophesied His death (see Matt. 12:39–40).
The words were so horrifying that the disciples seem not to have absorbed
what the Lord said. The Messiah is to live forever, is He not? Luke makes
the comment, "And they understood none of these things; and this word
had been hidden from them, and they were not knowing the things being
said" (Luke 18:34). Although all the Synoptic writers record this prophecy of the Lord, Matthew is the only one to mention death by crucifixion.
F. W. Krummacher begins his series of meditations on the last days of
Christ with this text of announcement (*The Suffering Saviour*, pp. 3ff.).

*III. The Patience of Jesus: Petition of the Mother of James and John. vv. 20–28
[Mark 10:35–45].*

"Then the mother of the sons of Zebedee came to him with her sons, worshiping, and asking something from him" (v. 20). Mothers have a habit of
seeking preferment for their children. In this case she was aiming very high.

"But he said to her: What do you wish? She says to him: Say that these
my two sons may sit, one on your right hand and one on your left, in
your kingdom" (v. 21). She is asking for the two highest honors that the
ancient world knew: to sit nearest the king. But she is thinking merely of
an earthly kingdom.

20:19. For the verb *to deliver over* see Matt. 4:12 note.

For the verb *to mock* see Matt. 2:16 note.

For the verb *to scourge* see Matt. 10:17 note.

The verb *to crucify* (σταυρόω) occurs here for the first of 10 times in Matt. (20:19; 23:34;
26:2; 27:22, 23, 26, 31, 35, 38; 28:5). For background see Leon Morris, *The Cross in the
NT*; ZPEB, "Crucifixion," I, pp. 1040–42; "Cross," I, pp. 1037–39; ISBE (1979), "Cross,
Crucify," I, pp. 825–30; Elwell, ed., *Evangelical Dictionary of Biblical Theology*, "Cross,
Crucifixion," pp. 136–37.

22 But Jesus answered and said, Ye know not what ye ask. Are ye able to drink of the cup that I shall drink of, and to be baptized with the baptism that I am baptized with? They say unto him, We are able.
23 And he saith unto them, Ye shall drink indeed of my cup, and be baptized with the baptism that I am baptized with: but to sit on my right hand, and on my left, is not mine to give, but it shall be given to them for whom it is prepared of my Father.
24 And when the ten heard it, they were moved with indignation against the two brethren.

"But Jesus answered and said: You do not know what you are asking. Are you able to drink the cup that I am about to drink? They say to him, We are able" (v. 22). The Lord speaks to the brothers, who were plainly in sympathy with their mother's request. At this stage they have the confidence of blissful ignorance.

"He says to them: You shall indeed drink of my cup, but to sit on my right hand and on my left is not mine to give, but to whom it shall be prepared by my Father" (v. 23). The Lord will grant nothing by personal favoritism; the will of His Father was everything to Him. The "cup" of suffering will be their portion, even as all the apostles found it was theirs. But this was not what the two brothers were asking for. When the "cup" was offered, the two brothers fled, just as all the apostles did (Matt. 26:56). But in fairness we must note that after the atoning death of Christ, James did drink his "cup" (Acts 12:2).

"And when the ten heard, they were angry concerning the two brothers" (v. 24). As far as the other disciples were concerned, the two brothers were guilty of seeking personal favoritism from the Lord. But the Lord Jesus is absolutely fair to all His people. Edersheim notes the "patience and tenderness" that the Lord shows toward these overambitious disciples (*Life and Times*, II, p. 346).

For the verb *to raise* see Matt. 1:24 note.

20:20. For the verb *to worship* see Matt. 2:2 note.

20:21. For the verb *to sit* see Matt. 5:1 note.

For the word *right* see Matt. 5:29 note.

20:22. For the word *cup* see Matt. 10:42 note.

20:23. For the verb *to prepare* see Matt. 3:3 note.

20:24. This verb *to be angry, indignant* (ἀγανακτέω) occurs 3 times in Matt. (20:24; 21:15; 26:8).

For the number 10 see Introduction, "Numbers," p. xxii.

25 But Jesus called them unto him, and said, Ye know that the princes of the Gentiles exercise dominion over them, and they that are great exercise authority upon them.
26 But it shall not be so among you: but whosoever will be great among you, let him be your minister;
27 And whosoever will be chief among you, let him be your servant:
28 Even as the Son of man came not to be ministered unto, but to minister, and to give his life a ransom for many.

"But Jesus called them to him and said: You know that the rulers of the Gentiles lord it over them, and their great ones exercise authority over them" (v. 25). Worldly people love to domineer over others, but God's people are fellow servants of God.

"It shall not be thus among you, but whoever wishes to be great among you shall be your servant" (v. 26). The Lord will rule His people and will prevent them from such domineering behavior. This verse is a two-edged sword. When a believer desires to have dominance over others, the Lord will make him a servant. But whoever chooses to serve others, the Lord will exalt.

"And whoever wishes to be first among you shall be your slave" (v. 27). The believer who desires to be supreme over the brethren God will make a slave to all. Such arrogance must be curbed. Believers are people who desire to serve and worship God and to be a blessing to others.

"Even as the Son of man came not to be ministered to, but to minister and to give his life a ransom in behalf of many" (v. 28). The Lord Jesus is the manifestation of the infinite love of God for man. He came to save sinners

20:25. The verb *to lord it over* (κατακυριεύω) occurs only here in Matt.

The verb *to exercise authority over* (κατεξουσιάζω) occurs only here in Matt.

20:26. The word *servant* (διάκονος) occurs 3 times in Matt. (20:26; 22:13; 23:11). Trench suggests that the word comes from the idea of one who runs for another (*Synonyms*, p. 32). The word came to refer to men who served officially in church (Acts 6:1–6; I Tim. 3:8–13). Paul had a strong sense of service for God in the ministry of the gospel (Rom. 1:9). For further discussion see Ryken, Wilhoit, and Longman, *Dictionary of Biblical Imagery*, "Servant," p. 774; ZPEB, "Servant," V, pp. 358–59; ISBE (1988), "Servant, Slave," pp. 419–21; Elwell, ed., *Evangelical Dictionary of Biblical Theology*, "Servant, Service," pp. 725–26.

20:27. For the word *first* see Matt. 5:24 note.

For the word *slave* see Matt. 8:9 note.

20:28. For the verb *to serve, minister to*, see Matt. 4:11 note.

The word *ransom* (λύτρον) occurs only here in Matt. The word means *the payment of a price* to secure the release of someone. For a comparison of a whole group of words on this theme see Trench, *Synonyms*, pp. 289–95. For further discussion see Ryken, Wilhoit, and

29 *And as they departed from Jericho, a great multitude followed him.*
30 *And, behold, two blind men sitting by the way side, when they heard that*
Jesus passed by, cried out, saying, Have mercy on us, O Lord, thou son of
David.
31 *And the multitude rebuked them, because they should hold their peace: but*
they cried the more, saying, Have mercy on us, O Lord, thou son of David.

and to redeem those who could not help themselves and did not understand what He was doing. Geerhardus Vos emphasized that Jesus was not
giving His life as a noble example for others to follow, but as a ransom, a
vicarious sacrifice for the sins of His people (*The Self-Disclosure of Jesus*,
pp. 280–81). The vicarious atonement is a major NT doctrine (Mark
10:45; Gal. 3:13; 4:5; I Tim. 2:6; Titus 2:14; I Pet. 1:18), with deep roots in
the OT (Ps. 34:22; 44:26; 103:4; 107:2; Isa. 50:2; 52:3; 62:12; 63:4).

IV. The Power of Jesus: Healing Two Blind Men. vv. 29–34 [Mark 10:46–52].

"And while they were going out from Jericho, a great crowd followed
him" (v. 29). It must have been a great burden to have such crowds constantly dogging their steps.

"And behold, two blind men sitting alongside the road, hearing that
Jesus was passing by, cried out, saying: Have mercy upon us, Lord, Son of
David" (v. 30). Vincent suggests that "they heard the crowd cry, *Jesus is
passing!*" (*Word Studies*, I, p. 112). No one ever cries to the Lord for mercy
in vain. They call for mercy from Him as Son of David, the rightful ruler
of God's kingdom. Mark notes that one of them was "blind Bartimaeus,
the son of Timaeus" (Mark 10:46), who apparently went on to become
well known among believers.

"And the crowd charged them that they keep silent, but they cried out the
more, saying, Have mercy on us, Lord, Son of David" (v. 31). They had the
boldness of true faith. The Lord Jesus was the only one Who could help them.

Longman, *Dictionary of Biblical Imagery*, "Ransom," p. 695; ISBE (1988), "Ransom," IV, pp.
44–45; ZPEB, "Ransom," V, p. 38; Elwell, ed., *Evangelical Dictionary of Biblical Theology*,
"Redeem, Redemption," pp. 664–65; Alexander, ed., *New Dictionary of Biblical Theology*,
"Redemption," pp. 716–20.

20:29. *Jericho* is mentioned only here in Matt. NT Jericho is a short distance from the
ruins of the OT city. For background see Pfeiffer and Vos, *Wycliffe Historical Geography of
Bible Lands*, pp. 169–72; ZPEB, "Jericho," III, pp. 451–55; ISBE (1982), "Jericho," II, pp.
992–96.

20:30. For the verb *to cry out* see Matt. 8:29 note.

For the verb *to have mercy on* see Matt. 5:7 note.

32 And Jesus stood still, and called them, and said, What will ye that I shall do unto you?
33 They say unto him, Lord, that our eyes may be opened.
34 So Jesus had compassion on them, and touched their eyes: and immediately their eyes received sight, and they followed him.

"And Jesus stood and called them and said, What are you wishing that I do for you?" (v. 32). The Lord knew what they wanted, but He compelled them to make their petition known to all.

"They say to him, Lord, that our eyes may be opened" (v. 33). All would know that they were hopelessly blind.

"But Jesus, being moved with compassion, touched their eyes, and immediately they received sight and followed him" (v. 34). The compassionate touch of Jesus gave them perfect vision. They followed, not merely tagging along with the crowd but rather by becoming His adherents. There is an ironic twist in this chapter. The two sons of Zebedee manifest spiritual blindness in asking for personal preferment (v. 21), and the two blind men manifest spiritual perception in asking Jesus for sight (v. 33).

Practical Applications from Matthew 20

1. The Lord always gives what is right to His followers (v. 2). Paul refers to "his own purpose and grace, which was given us in Christ Jesus" (II Tim. 1:9b).
2. Rewards are the prerogative of the Lord alone (v. 15). "The judgments of the Lord are true and righteous altogether . . . and in keeping of them there is great reward" (Ps. 19:9b, 11b).
3. The Lord prepared the disciples for what they would later have to endure (vv. 17–18). Many times believers have to suffer things they do not understand to prepare them for future service (Acts 8:1).
4. Honor does not come from God except through service and suffering (v. 21). Jesus said, "Whoever serves me, him will my Father honor" (John 12:26b).

20:31. For the verb *to command, rebuke* see Matt. 8:26 note.

The verb *to be silent* (σιωπάω) occurs only twice in Matt. (20:31; 26:63).

20:32. For the verb *to wish* see Matt. 1:19 note.

20:34. For the verb *to touch* see Matt. 8:3 note.

For the verb *to follow* see Matt. 4:20 note.

5. The world loves to exercise authority over people, but believers must not love such authority (vv. 25–26). "But love your enemies, and do good, and lend, hoping for nothing again; and your reward shall be great" (Luke 6:35a).
6. The Lord Jesus came to give away His life for others (v. 28). "Look not every man on his own things, but every man also on the things of others" (Phil. 2:4).
7. The Lord Jesus had compassion on others (v. 34). "Owe no man anything, but to love one another" (Rom. 13:8a).

Prayer

Lord Jesus, help us to serve You without thought of reward; instead, help us to remember Your great sacrifice on our behalf. Give us the grace to serve one another for Your sake. Amen.

The King Enters Jerusalem

Persons

Jesus

Two disciples

A great multitude

City people

Those who bought and sold

Moneychangers

Those who sold doves

The blind

The lame

Children who cried hosanna

Chief priests

Elders

Pharisees

Persons referred to

Owners of the ass

The prophet [Zechariah]

David

Thieves

Babes

Sucklings

The people

A man with two sons

Publicans

Harlots

Householder

Farmers

Servants

Householder's son

Builders

Places mentioned

Jerusalem

Bethphage

Mount of Olives

Zion

Nazareth

Galilee

The temple

Bethany

Heaven

A vineyard

Doctrines taught

Fulfilled prophecy

The coming King

Judgment on mercenaries

Faith

Answered prayer

Authority

Righteousness

Repentance

1 And when they drew nigh unto Jerusalem, and were come to Bethphage, unto the mount of Olives, then sent Jesus two disciples,

2 Saying unto them, Go into the village over against you, and straightway ye shall find an ass tied, and a colt with her: loose them, and bring them unto me.

3 And if any man say ought unto you, ye shall say, The Lord hath need of them; and straightway he will send them.

Matthew 21 Exposition

I. The Coming of Christ. vv. 1–11 [Mark 11:1–11; Luke 19:29–44; John 12:12–19].

"And when they drew near to Jerusalem and came into Bethphage to the Mount of Olives, then Jesus sent two disciples" (v. 1). They were on the east of Jerusalem, ready to cross the crest of the Mount of Olives and descend to the Kidron valley to enter Jerusalem at the temple area. All four Gospels record this event. The official presentation of the King was an important event, for men and for God. "Yet have I set my king upon my holy hill of Zion" (Ps. 2:6).

"Saying to them, Go into the village that is opposite you, and you will find an ass tethered and a colt with her; loose them and lead them to me" (v. 2). This is another example of the Lord's omniscience. The animals were there for Him to use. Krummacher has a message on the Triumphal Entry in *The Suffering Saviour* (pp. 20ff.).

"And if anyone should say something to you, say that the Lord has need of them, and immediately he will send them" (v. 3). The Lord was in full control of the situation. Of course the disciples would see to it that the animals got back to their owners. Matthew, always noticing numbers, is the only Gospel writer to mention that there were two animals.

21:1. The place *Bethphage* is mentioned here only in Matt. It was a small village close to the Jericho road on the Mount of Olives near Jerusalem. See ZPEB, "Bethphage," I, p. 541; ISBE (1979), "Bethphage," I, p. 474.

For *Jerusalem* see Matt. 2:1 note.

The *Mount of Olives* is mentioned 3 times in Matt. (21:1; 24:3; 26:30). It is the mountain on the east of Jerusalem, across the Kidron valley. For photographs and discussion see Custer, *Stones of Witness*, pp. 82–89, 129, 139; W. E. Pax, *In the Footsteps of Jesus*, pp. 150–55; 160–64; Pfeiffer and Vos, *Wycliffe Historical Geography of Bible Lands*, pp. 158–59; ZPEB, "Mount of Olives," IV, pp. 299–303; ISBE (1986), "Olives, Mount of," III, pp. 589–91. For the olive tree itself see Zohary, *Plants of the Bible*, "Olive," pp. 56–57.

21:2. The words *ass* (ὄνος) and *colt* (πῶλος) each occur 3 times only in this context in Matt. (21:2, 5, 7).

For the verb *to loose* see Matt. 5:19 note.

21:3. For the word *need* see Matt. 3:14 note.

4 All this was done, that it might be fulfilled which was spoken by the
prophet, saying,
5 Tell ye the daughter of Sion, Behold, thy King cometh unto thee, meek, and
sitting upon an ass, and a colt the foal of an ass.
6 And the disciples went, and did as Jesus commanded them,
7 And brought the ass, and the colt, and put on them their clothes, and they
set him thereon.

"But this was done in order that the word which was spoken through the
prophet might be fulfilled, saying:

> Say to the daughter of Zion;
>
> Behold, your king comes to you,
>
> Meek and sitting upon an ass
>
> And upon a colt the foal of an ass" (vv. 4–5; Zech. 9:9;
> Isa. 62:11).

The Lord does not come on a horse, a war charger, but on an ass, a
humble beast of burden. He is the Prince of Peace (Isa. 9:6b), not a conquering tyrant.

"And the disciples went and did just as Jesus commanded them" (v. 6).
They obeyed and discovered that everything was just as He had instructed.

"They brought the ass and the colt and set the garments upon them, and
he sat upon them" (v. 7). This was a most unusual royal entrance. There
was no brass band, no military guard, no advance publicity, but the people
understood what was happening. Most Americans have seen film clips of
the funeral cortege of a president, with the riderless horse, and the new
ruler following. The ass and the colt may be an ancient equivalent of
such symbolism. The crowds certainly responded in the manner of greeting the new king. The most spectacular part of the scene was the fact that
the Lord was the first person to ride that colt, and there was no bucking
(Mark 11:2)! The colt recognized the rider as the Lord of the universe
and carried Him with no protest.

21:5. For the word *king* see Matt. 1:6 note.

For the word *meek* see Matt. 5:5 note.

21:6. The verb *to direct, order,* (συντάσσω) occurs 3 times in Matt. (21:6; 26:19; 27:10)
only in the NT. In each case it is Jesus or God Who commands.

21:7. The verb *to sit upon* (ἐπικαθίζω) occurs only here in the NT.

8 *And a very great multitude spread their garments in the way; others cut down branches from the trees, and strawed them in the way.*

9 *And the multitudes that went before, and that followed, cried, saying, Hosanna to the son of David: Blessed is he that cometh in the name of the Lord; Hosanna in the highest.*

10 *And when he was come into Jerusalem, all the city was moved, saying, Who is this?*

11 *And the multitude said, This is Jesus the prophet of Nazareth of Galilee.*

"But a very great crowd spread their garments in the way, and others cut branches from the trees and strewed them in the way. And the crowds who went before him and the ones who followed were crying out, saying,

Hosanna to the Son of David;

Blessed is the one who comes in the name of the Lord;

Hosanna in the highest" (vv. 8–9; Ps. 118:25).

The crowd publicly recognized Him as "Son of David." This was a messianic title, even if the crowd did not realize all the significance of it. To spread garments in the way was to honor a king (II Kings 9:13). John tells us that the branches were palm branches (John 12:13). The imperfect tense *were crying out* indicates that the crowds continued crying out as the procession came into the city.

"And when he entered into Jerusalem, the whole city was shaken, saying, Who is this?" (v. 10). The religious hierarchy was always opposed to change, and the Roman occupation was sensitive to disturbances. The populace, however, wanted to know the reason for the celebration.

"But the crowd was saying, This is Jesus, the prophet, the one from Nazareth of Galilee" (v. 11). They recognize His supernatural powers, but they do not dare publicly to call Him king.

21:8. For the word *branch* see Matt. 13:32 note.

The superlative *very great* (πλεῖστος) may be thus an elative superlative (so Arndt and Gingrich, p. 696; Nigel Turner, Moulton's *Grammar*, III, *Syntax*, p. 31) or a true superlative, the *greatest* crowd of His ministry (A. T. Robertson, *Word Pictures*, I, p. 167).

21:9. The word *Hosanna* (ὡσαννά) occurs only 3 times in this context in Matt. (vv. 9 [twice], 15). The word originally meant *to save,* but it became a word for praise to God as the Hebrew text of Ps. 118:25 and the parallel in Mark 11:10 show. For further discussion see ZPEB, "Hosanna," III, p. 206; ISBE (1982), "Hosanna," II, p. 761; Arndt and Gingrich, p. 907.

For the title *Son of David* see Matt. 1:1 note.

21:10. The verb *to shake* (σείω) occurs 3 times in Matt. (21:10; 27:51; 28:4).

21:11. For the word *prophet* see Matt. 1:22 note.

12 And Jesus went into the temple of God, and cast out all them that sold and bought in the temple, and overthrew the tables of the moneychangers, and the seats of them that sold doves,
13 And said unto them, It is written, My house shall be called the house of prayer; but ye have made it a den of thieves.
14 And the blind and the lame came to him in the temple; and he healed them.

II. The Cleansing of the Temple. vv. 12–17 [Mark 11:15–18; Luke 19:45–48].

"And Jesus entered into the temple and cast out all the ones who were buying and selling in the temple, and overturned the tables of the money-changers, and the seats of the ones who sold doves" (v. 12). This was an act of stern rebuke to those who were defiling the worship of God. It is a standing warning against all who would introduce money-making schemes into the church.

"And he says to them: It has been written,

My house shall be called a house of prayer,

But you are making it a den of robbers" (v. 13, Isa. 56:7; Jer. 7:11, LXX).

A *house of prayer* is a lovely characterization for any place of worship, but the phrase *den of robbers* is a horrifying term to use for a supposedly sacred place. Both Jeremiah and the Lord intended to shock people into aware-ness of the evil deeds of the religious hierarchy. To them the worship of God took second place to their own financial benefits.

21:12. For the word *temple* see Matt. 4:5 note.

For the verb *to sell* see Matt. 10:29 note.

For the verb *to buy* see Matt. 13:44 note.

For the word *table* see Matt. 15:27 note. It is interesting that the word *table* is still the modern Greek word for *bank*.

The word *moneychanger* (κολλυβιστής) occurs only here in Matt.

21:13. For the verb *to write* see Matt. 2:5 note.

The word *prayer* (προσευχή) occurs twice in this context only in Matt. (21:13, 22).

For the verb *to pray* see Matt. 5:44 note.

The word *den* (σπήλαιον) occurs only here in Matt.

The word *robber* (λῃστής) occurs 4 times in Matt. (21:13; 26:55; 27:38, 44). For explanation see Trench, *Synonyms of the NT*, pp. 157–60; ISBE (1988), "Rob, Robbery," IV, p. 203; Butler, ed., *Holman Bible Dictionary*, "Robbery," pp. 1199–1200; ZPEB, "Crimes and Punishments" B, 3, I, p. 1033.

21:14. For the verb *to heal* see Matt. 4:23 note.

15 And when the chief priests and scribes saw the wonderful things that he did, and the children crying in the temple, and saying, Hosanna to the son of David; they were sore displeased,
16 And said unto him, Hearest thou what these say? And Jesus saith unto them, Yea; have ye never read, Out of the mouth of babes and sucklings thou hast perfected praise?

"And the blind and the lame came to him in the temple, and he healed them" (v. 14). The Lord's deeds caused people to worship God in the temple.

"But when the chief priests and the scribes saw the wonderful things which he did, and the children who were crying in the temple and saying, Hosanna to the Son of David, they were indignant" (v. 15). The miraculous deeds of the Lord caused no joy to these religious tyrants; they saw only a threat to their authority.. These young people were merely crying praises to the Lord for His mighty deeds.

"And they said to him: Are you not hearing what these are saying? But Jesus says to them, Yes. Did you never read that

> Out of the mouth of babies and sucklings you prepared praise?"
> (v. 16, Ps. 8:2, LXX 8:3).

The youngest of children can praise God from the heart. We must not miss the Lord's emphasis on the necessity and virtue of reading the Scriptures. The prophet Jeremiah well expresses the benefit of studying Scripture: "Thy words were found, and I did eat them; and thy word was unto me the joy and rejoicing of mine heart: for I am called by thy name, O Lord God of hosts" (Jer. 15:16). The Lord exhorted His enemies, "Search the scriptures; for in them you think you have eternal life: and they are they that testify of me" (John 5:39). David declared, "The law of the Lord is perfect, converting the soul: the testimony of the Lord is sure, making wise the simple. . . . The judgments of the Lord are true and righteous altogether. More to be desired are they than gold, yea, than much fine gold: sweeter also than honey and the honeycomb" (Ps. 19:7, 9b–10).

21:15. The word *wonderful* (θαυμάσιος) occurs only here in the NT. The idea is more than just miraculous deeds. There is a parallel in the titles of Messiah (Isa. 9:6). For discussion see ISBE (1988), "Wonder, Wonderful," IV, pp. 1100–1101; Moulton and Milligan, *Vocabulary*, p. 284.

For the verb *to be indignant* see Matt. 20:24 note.

21:16. For the verb *to read* see Matt. 12:3 note.

For the word *child* see Matt. 11:25 note.

17 And he left them, and went out of the city into Bethany; and he lodged there.
18 Now in the morning as he returned into the city, he hungered.
19 And when he saw a fig tree in the way, he came to it, and found nothing thereon, but leaves only, and said unto it, Let no fruit grow on thee henceforward for ever. And presently the fig tree withered away.

"And he left them and went outside the city to Bethany and spent the night there" (v. 17). Bethany was a small town with a peaceful atmosphere in contrast to the bustle (and hostility) of Jerusalem.

III. The Cursing of the Fig Tree. vv. 18–22 [Mark 11:12–14].

"And early in the morning, returning to the city, he was hungry" (v. 18). In the ancient world "breakfast" was often a very light meal. (See ZPEB, "Food," II, p. 586).

"And when he saw one fig tree on the way, he came to it and found nothing on it except leaves only, and he says to it: Let no one eat fruit from you forever. And the fig tree was withered immediately" (v. 19). The phrase *on the way* means that it was by the path, not in someone's garden. On a fig tree the fruit and the leaves sprout at the same time, so any fig tree with leaves could be assumed to have figs. But this tree had the promise of fruit without the reality. It was merciful of the Lord to pronounce His only act of judgment on a tree, rather than on a person. There were no doubt Pharisees who would have made striking illustrations! The whole account teaches believers the necessity of sincerity: they ought to be what they profess to be.

The verb *to nurse, suck* (θηλάζω) occurs twice in Matt. (21:16; 24:19).

For the verb *to prepare* see Matt. 4:21 note.

21:17. The verb *to spend the night* (αὐλίζομαι) occurs only here in Matt.

Bethany is mentioned twice in Matt. (21:17; 26:6). Bethany was a small village about 2 miles southeast of Jerusalem on the Jericho road over the Mount of Olives. For background see Pfeiffer and Vos, *Wycliffe Historical Geography of Bible Lands*, pp. 159–60; ZPEB, "Bethany," I, pp. 527–28; ISBE (1979), "Bethany," I, pp. 463–64.

21:18. For the verb *to be hungry* see Matt. 4:2 note.

21:19. The word *fig tree* (συκῆ) occurs 5 times in Matt. (21:19 [twice], 20, 21; 24:32). For discussion see Ryken, Wilhoit, and Longman, *Dictionary of Biblical Imagery*, "Fig, Fig Tree," pp. 283–84; ZPEB, "Fig Tree," II, p. 534; "Fig, Fig Tree," ISBE (1982), II, pp. 301–2; Zohary, *Plants of the Bible*, "Fig," pp. 58–59.

The word *leaf* (φύλλον) occurs twice in Matt. (21:19; 24:32).

For the verb *to wither* see Matt. 13:6 note.

The word *immediately* (παραχρῆμα) occurs twice in this context only in Matt. (21:19, 20).

20 And when the disciples saw it, they marvelled, saying, How soon is the fig tree withered away!
21 Jesus answered and said unto them, Verily I say unto you, If ye have faith, and doubt not, ye shall not only do this which is done to the fig tree, but also if ye shall say unto this mountain, Be thou removed, and be thou cast into the sea; it shall be done.
22 And all things, whatsoever ye shall ask in prayer, believing, ye shall receive.
23 And when he was come into the temple, the chief priests and the elders of the people came unto him as he was teaching, and said, By what authority doest thou these things? and who gave thee this authority?

"And when the disciples saw it, they marveled, saying: How immediately was the fig tree withered?" (v. 20). It was an instantaneous act of judgment. The disciples were surprised at how fast the tree withered. "The grass withereth, the flower fadeth: but the word of our God shall stand for ever" (Isa. 40:8).

"But Jesus answered and said to them: Truly I say to you, If you have faith and doubt not, you shall do, not only the matter of the fig tree, but you shall also say to this mountain: Be taken up and be cast into the sea, and it shall come to pass" (v. 21). They were standing on the lower slopes of the Mount of Olives. The Lord used the landscape to reinforce His teaching.

"And all things as many as you ask in prayer, believing, you shall receive" (v. 22). Faith in God is the spiritual secret to answered prayer. "And they that know thy name will put their trust in thee: for thou, Lord, hast not forsaken them that seek thee" (Ps. 9:10). "Trust in the Lord with all thine heart; and lean not unto thine own understanding. In all thy ways acknowledge him, and he shall direct thy paths" (Prov. 3:5–6).

IV. The Contest on Authority. vv. 23–27 [Mark 11:27–33; Luke 20:1–8].

"And when he came into the temple, the chief priests and the elders of the people came to him while he was teaching, saying: By what authority are you doing these things? And who gave you this authority?" (v. 23). They were acting as though the temple belonged to them, but in reality it belonged to the Lord Jesus. On another occasion the Lord Jesus had said to his foes, "I and my Father are one" (John 10:30). It was the temple of God.

21:21. For the word *faith* see Matt. 8:10 note.

For the verb *to doubt* see Matt. 16:3 note.

For the word *mountain* see Matt. 4:8 note.

21:23. For the word *authority* see Matt. 7:29 note.

*24 And Jesus answered and said unto them, I also will ask you one thing,
which if ye tell me, I in like wise will tell you by what authority I do these
things.*
*25 The baptism of John, whence was it? from heaven, or of men? And they
reasoned with themselves, saying, If we shall say, From heaven; he will say
unto us, Why did ye not then believe him?*
26 But if we shall say, Of men; we fear the people; for all hold John as a prophet.
*27 And they answered Jesus, and said, We cannot tell. And he said unto
them, Neither tell I you by what authority I do these things.*

"But Jesus answered and said to them: I also will ask you one thing,
which if you answer me, I will also say to you by what authority I do these
things" (v. 24). He knew that they were just trying to find something by
which to accuse Him.

"The baptism of John, whence was it? From heaven or from men? But
they were reasoning among themselves, saying: If we say, From heaven,
he will say to us, Why therefore did you not believe him?" (v. 25). The
phrase *from heaven* is a synonymous expression for *from God*. The Lord
refers them to His forerunner, the mighty prophet John the Baptist, who
had publicly commended the Lord Jesus (Matt. 3:11–12). They could not
recognize John without commending his message.

"But if we should say, From men, we fear the crowd, for all are holding
John as a prophet" (v. 26). They were afraid to say anything against John
because the people revered him as a true prophet of God. But these religious leaders had spurned his ministry.

"And they answered Jesus and said: We do not know. But he himself said
to them: Neither do I say to you by what authority I do these things"
(v. 27). Both in the case of John and of the Lord Jesus, the authority was
that of the one true God, Jehovah. Now the Lord Jesus gives the first of
three parables that manifest the wickedness of the priests and elders in
repudiating His authority.

21:25. For the word *baptism* see Matt. 3:7 note.

For the word *heaven* see Matt. 3:2 note.

21:26. For the verb *to fear* see Matt. 1:20 note.

21:27. The phrase *he himself* is the intensive pronoun, very emphatic.

28 But what think ye? A certain man had two sons; and he came to the first, and said, Son, go work to day in my vineyard.
29 He answered and said, I will not: but afterward he repented, and went.
30 And he came to the second, and said likewise. And he answered and said, I go, sir: and went not.
31 Whether of them twain did the will of his father? They say unto him, The first. Jesus saith unto them, Verily I say unto you, That the publicans and the harlots go into the kingdom of God before you.
32 For John came unto you in the way of righteousness, and ye believed him not: but the publicans and the harlots believed him: and ye, when ye had seen it, repented not afterward, that ye might believe him.

V. *The Contrast of the Two Sons. vv. 28–32.*

"But what do you think? A man had two sons, and he went to the first and said: Son, go today to work in the vineyard" (v. 28). Vineyards take constant attention to bring the grapes to harvest. This man thought surely his son would be eager to keep the vineyard in good condition.

"But he answered and said, I will not, but afterwards, he repented and went" (v. 29). For whatever reason, the son refused. He had other more important things to do. But as he thought about it, it weighed upon his conscience until finally he went into the fields and did his work as he knew he should.

"But he went to the other [son] and said likewise. But he answered and said: I [will go], sir, but he did not go" (v. 30). This son was just being agreeable. He had no intention of going to work, but he did not say so.

"Who of the two did the will of his father? They say, The first. Jesus says to them: Truly I say to you that the tax collectors and the harlots are going into the kingdom of God before you" (v. 31). The Lord Jesus is plainly saying that these religious leaders are worse sinners than the lowest members of society. They had more light and were less responsive to it than others. Being *religious* is not enough; there must be genuine, heartfelt devotion to the will of God.

21:28. For the address *son, child,* see Matt. 2:18 note.

For the word *vineyard* see Matt. 20:1 note.

21:29. The verb *to repent, change thinking, regret* (μεταμέλομαι) occurs 3 times in Matt. (21:29, 32; 27:3). Even Judas could change his thinking (Matt. 27:3), but this verb does not denote that sweeping change of heart that the verb μετανοέω does. See Trench, *Synonyms,* pp. 255–61.

21:30. For the word *sir, lord,* see Matt. 1:20 note.

*33 Hear another parable: There was a certain householder, which planted a
vineyard, and hedged it round about, and digged a winepress in it, and built a
tower, and let it out to husbandmen, and went into a far country:
34 And when the time of the fruit drew near, he sent his servants to the husbandmen, that they might receive the fruits of it.
35 And the husbandmen took his servants, and beat one, and killed another,
and stoned another.*

"For John came to you in the way of righteousness, and you did not believe him, but the tax collectors and harlots believed him; but when you
saw it, you did not change your thinking afterwards to believe in him"
(v. 32). The repentance of the dark-dyed sinners was a good example, but
these religious leaders would not follow it.

VI. The Cruel Farmers. vv. 33–46 [Mark 12:1–12; Luke 20:9–19].

"Hear another parable. There was a man, a house holder, who planted
a vineyard and hedged it around, and dug a winepress in it, and built a
tower, and let it out to farmers, and departed" (v. 33). This is the second
of three parables that emphasize the authority of the Lord Jesus and the
guilt of the chief priests and elders in rejecting His teaching. The man
in this parable was investing in and preparing rental property. He plainly
expected a good return on his investment.

"But when the time of the fruits drew near, he sent his slaves to the farmers in order to receive his fruits" (v. 34). There was obviously a percentage for the tenant farmers and a larger percentage for the owner.

"And the farmers took his slaves, and beat one, and killed another, and
stoned another" (v. 35). They chose violent means to keep all the fruits
for themselves, but this was how OT Israel treated the prophets of God
(I Kings 22:7–27). Jeremiah was a particularly apt example (Jer. 37:15–
21).

21:31. For the word *tax collector* see Matt. 5:46 note.

The word *harlot, prostitute* (πόρνη) occurs only twice in Matt. (21:31, 32).

21:32. For the verb *to believe* see Matt. 8:13 note.

21:33. For the word *vineyard* see Matt. 20:1 note.

The verb *to dig* (ὀρύσσω) occurs only twice in Matt. (21:33; 25:18).

The verb *to depart* (ἀποδημέω) occurs 3 times in Matt. (21:33; 25:14, 15).

21:35. The verb *to beat* (δέρω) occurs only here in Matt.

36 Again, he sent other servants more than the first: and they did unto them likewise.
37 But last of all he sent unto them his son, saying, They will reverence my son.
38 But when the husbandmen saw the son, they said among themselves, This is the heir; come, let us kill him, and let us seize on his inheritance.
39 And they caught him, and cast him out of the vineyard, and slew him.
40 When the lord therefore of the vineyard cometh, what will he do unto those husbandmen?
41 They say unto him, He will miserably destroy those wicked men, and will let out his vineyard unto other husbandmen, which shall render him the fruits in their seasons.

"Again, he sent other slaves, more than the first, and they did to them likewise" (v. 36). The most recent was John the Baptist (Matt. 14:1–12).

"But last of all he sent to them his son, saying: They will have respect for my son" (v. 37). This is a clear reference to Himself as God's Son. The farmers might treat slaves badly, but surely they would honor the rightful owner's son.

"But when the farmers saw the son, they said among themselves: This is the heir; come, let us kill him, and we shall have his inheritance" (v. 38). This was ruthless and savage conduct toward one who had done them no harm at all.

"And they took him and cast him out of the vineyard, and killed him" (v. 39). They followed through with their plan to do away with the heir. They threw the son out of the vineyard so that his death would not ceremonially defile the property.

"Whenever the lord of the vineyard should come, what will he do to those farmers?" (v. 40). Of course these priests and elders see themselves as on the side of righteousness and justice and answer accordingly.

"They say to him, He shall destroy those evil men harshly, and shall rent out the vineyard to other farmers, who shall give to him the fruits in their seasons" (v. 41). This is an accurate judgment that they are pronouncing on themselves, and they do not see it.

For the verb *to kill* see Matt. 10:28 note.

The verb *to stone* (λιθοβολέω) occurs only twice in Matt. (21:35; 23:37).

21:37. The verb *to reverence, have respect for* (ἐντρέπω) occurs only here in Matt.

21:38. The word *heir* (κληρονόμος) occurs only here in Matt.

The word *inheritance* (κληρονομία) occurs only here in Matt. The believer has an inheritance in glory (Eph. 1:18; Col. 3:24).

42 Jesus saith unto them, Did ye never read in the scriptures, The stone which the builders rejected, the same is become the head of the corner: this is the Lord's doing, and it is marvellous in our eyes?
43 Therefore say I unto you, The kingdom of God shall be taken from you, and given to a nation bringing forth the fruits thereof.

"Jesus says to them: Did you never read in the Scriptures:

The stone which the builders rejected,

This became the head of the corner;

This came from the Lord

And is marvelous in our eyes?" (v. 42; Ps. 117:22, Ps. 118:22, LXX).

The Lord Jesus identifies Himself with the Messianic Stone, Who shall deliver His people and build the kingdom, but the prophets had said all this before (Isa. 28:16–17). He is a "'valuable corner stone' that gives direction to the building" (Steveson, *Isa.*, p. 230).

"On account of this I say to you that the kingdom of God shall be taken away from you and shall be given to a nation bringing forth its fruits" (v. 43). The nation of Israel was the representative of God to the nations of the world in the old dispensation, but the Lord was going to build His church to be such a representative in the coming dispensation (Matt. 16:18ff.; Acts 2; Rom. 1:16–17). Every true believer has submitted to the rule of God in Christ, but the unconverted world is still in total rebellion against God and His Messiah.

21:41. For the verb *to destroy* see Matt. 2:13 note.

The word *bad, evil, wicked* (κακός) occurs 3 times in Matt. (21:41; 24:48; 27:23). For discussion see Trench, *Synonyms*, pp. 315–18; Ryken, Wilhoit, and Longman, *Dictionary of Biblical Imagery*, "Evil," pp. 248–50.

21:42. The term *the Scriptures* (αἱ γραφαί) occurs 4 times in Matt. (21:42; 22:29; 26:54, 56), always referring to the sacred, inspired, infallible revelation of God, which was delivered to the Jews and later to the church. For a discussion of the term see B. B. Warfield, *The Inspiration and Authority of the Bible*, pp. 229–41. For a formal defense see Custer, *Does Inspiration Demand Inerrancy?* pp. 13–60, Engelder, *Scripture Cannot Be Broken*; Stonehouse and Wolley, *The Infallible Word*; Young, *Thy Word Is Truth*; Lightner, *The Saviour and the Scriptures*; ZPEB, "Inspiration," III, pp. 286–93; ISBE (1982), "Inspiration," II, pp. 839–49; Harrison, ed., *The New Unger's Bible Dictionary*, "Inspiration," pp. 620–22.

For the word *stone* see Matt. 3:9 note. Christ is identified as the Messianic Stone or Rock in the NT (Acts 4:10–11; I Cor. 10:4; I Pet. 2:6–8). For further discussion see ISBE

44 And whosoever shall fall on this stone shall be broken: but on whomsoever it shall fall, it will grind him to powder.
45 And when the chief priests and Pharisees had heard his parables, they perceived that he spake of them.
46 But when they sought to lay hands on him, they feared the multitude, because they took him for a prophet.

"And the one falling upon this stone shall be broken to pieces, but upon whom it shall fall, it will crush" (v. 44). The Lord Jesus has all authority in heaven and earth (Matt. 28:18–20). His will shall be done, whatever men may seek to do.

"And when the chief priests and the Pharisees had heard his parables, they came to know that he spoke concerning them" (v. 45). It finally dawned on them that they were the wicked farmers in the parable. Now they hated the Lord all the more.

"But while they were seeking to seize him, they feared the crowds, because they were holding him to be a prophet" (v. 46). If they tried to seize a man viewed as a prophet, a benefactor of the people, they feared being stoned by the mob.

Practical Applications from Matthew 21

1. The Lord uses simple things, people, and even animals to accomplish His will (vv. 1–2). The Lord chose the colt of an ass, a fig tree, and fishermen to illustrate His teaching.
2. The arrogant and powerful do not make the best rulers (v. 5). The Lord chose David as king when he was a shepherd (II Sam. 7:8).

(1988), "Stone," IV, pp. 622–23; Ryken, Wilhoit, and Longman, *Dictionary of Biblical Imagery*, "Stone," pp. 815–16.

The verb *to reject* (ἀποδοκιμάζω) occurs only here in Matt.

21:43. For the word *kingdom* see Matt. 3:2 note.

21:44. The verb *to break to pieces* (συνθλάω) occurs only here in Matt.

The verb *to crush* (λικμάω) occurs only here in Matt. The KJV *grind to powder* is a graphic translation. See also Moulton and Milligan, *Vocabulary*, p. 376.

21:46. For the verb *to seize* see Matt. 9:25 note.

For the verb *to fear* see Matt. 1:20 note.

For the word *prophet* see Matt. 1:22; 7:22 note

3. The Lord Jesus drove out the irreverent and the money-hungry from the temple (v. 12). "But they that will be rich fall into temptation and a snare, and into many foolish and harmful lusts" (I Tim. 6:9a).

4. The children shouting praise to Christ in the temple did not please the chief priests, but they pleased the Lord (vv. 15–16). God accepted the service of little Samuel but not of the sons of Eli (I Sam. 2:12–26).

5. God expects fruit, not merely good appearances (v. 19). "God resists the proud, and gives grace to the humble" (I Pet. 5:5b).

6. Believing prayer is powerful (v. 22). "Through faith also Sara herself received strength to conceive seed, and was delivered of a child when she was past age, because she judged him faithful who had promised" (Heb. 11:11).

7. Wicked sinners will enter the kingdom before religious hypocrites will (v. 31). "Let the wicked forsake his way, and the unrighteous man his thoughts: and let him return unto the Lord, and he will have mercy upon him; and to our God, for he will abundantly pardon" (Isa. 55:7).

8. God has the power to give His kingdom to anyone He chooses (v. 43). "For there is no difference between the Jew and the Greek: for the same Lord over all is rich unto all that call upon him" (Rom. 10:13).

Prayer

Lord Jesus, give us the grace to exalt You above all; help us to make our churches real houses of prayer; make us fruitful believers for You. Preserve us from lip service; make us genuine servants for You. Amen.

MATTHEW 22

JESUS ANSWERS ENEMIES

Persons
Jesus
Pharisees
Herodians
Sadducees

God
Angels
A lawyer
David

Persons referred to
A king
His son
Servants
Armies
Wedding guests
Caesar
A childless man

His brothers
His wife
Abraham
Isaac
Jacob
Your neighbor
Messiah [Christ]

Places mentioned
A farm
A city
Highways
Heaven

Doctrines taught
The kingdom
The invitation
Judgment
The call
Temptation
Hypocrisy
Resurrection

The authority of Scripture
The power of God
Angels
The law
Love for God
Love for neighbor
Lordship of Christ

1 And Jesus answered and spake unto them again by parables, and said,
2 The kingdom of heaven is like unto a certain king, which made a marriage for his son,
3 And sent forth his servants to call them that were bidden to the wedding: and they would not come.
4 Again, he sent forth other servants, saying, Tell them which are bidden, Behold, I have prepared my dinner: my oxen and my fatlings are killed, and all things are ready: come unto the marriage.

Matthew 22 Exposition

I. The Parable of the Marriage Feast. vv. 1–14.

"And Jesus answered and spoke again in parables to them, saying: The kingdom of the heavens is like a man, a king, who made a marriage for his son" (vv. 1–2). This is the third of three parables that Jesus spoke to those who questioned His authority (Matt. 21:23). A parable is a story that illustrates a spiritual truth, but in this case there is a striking reality behind the story (Rev. 21:1–9). God is indeed preparing a marriage for His Son. There may even be a parallel in the many years that Jacob had to serve to secure Rachel as his bride (Gen. 29:11–20). Could there be a foreshadowing in Jacob's marrying both Leah and Rachel and the fact that the Lord has an OT bride in Israel and a NT bride in the church?

"And he sent his slaves to call the ones who were invited to the marriage, and they were not willing to come" (v. 3). In the ancient world the slaves of a king were very influential people. It takes some arrogance to turn down a royal invitation. In this case it illustrates the depth of human depravity.

"Again he sent other slaves, saying: Say to the ones who have been called, Behold, I have prepared my dinner; the bulls and the fatlings have

22:1. For the word *parable* see Matt. 13:3 note.

22:2. The word *marriage, wedding* (γάμος) occurs 9 times in Matt. (22:2, 3, 4, 8, 9, 10, 11, 12; 25:10) and 8 times in the rest of the NT (Luke 12:36; 14:8; John 2:1, 2, 3; Heb. 13:4; Rev. 19:7, 9). For discussion see ISBE (1986), "Marriage," III, pp. 261–66; ZPEB, "Marriage," IV, pp. 92–102; Elwell, ed., *Evangelical Dictionary of Biblical Theology*, "Marriage," pp. 510–13; Ryken, Wilhoit, and Longman, *Dictionary of Biblical Imagery*, "Marriage," pp. 537–39, "Marriage is a leading biblical metaphor for the relationship between God and the believer" (p. 538).

22:3. For the verb *to wish, will*, see Matt. 1:19 note. The imperfect tense emphasizes the continuing refusal of the invitation.

22:4. The word *dinner* (ἄριστον) may refer to any kind of meal, but in this context it plainly refers to a formal dinner.

The word *bull* (ταῦρος) occurs only here in Matt.

5 But they made light of it, and went their ways, one to his farm, another to his merchandise:
6 And the remnant took his servants, and entreated them spitefully, and slew them.
7 But when the king heard thereof, he was wroth: and he sent forth his armies, and destroyed those murderers, and burned up their city.

been slain and all things prepared; come to the wedding" (v. 4). The king had made rich provisions for his people. It was an elaborate banquet, prepared with great festivities.

"But they disregarded it and went away, one to his farm, another to his business" (v. 5). Worldly pursuits were more important to them than the king's invitation. It is a striking portrait of the common disregard of the world for the divine offer of salvation. "All day long I have stretched forth my hands unto a disobedient and gainsaying people" (Rom. 10:21b).

"But the rest seized his slaves and mistreated them and slew them" (v. 6). Here is another reference to the world's mistreatment of God's prophets, apostles, and preachers. They were messengers of grace and salvation but were persecuted for their faithfulness.

"But the king was angry and sent his army and destroyed those murderers and set their city on fire" (v. 7). This was a prophetic warning of the coming judgment on Jerusalem and the burning of the temple in A.D. 70.

"Then he says to his slaves: The wedding is ready, but the ones who have been called were not worthy; therefore, go to the main road of the streets

---

The word *fatling, fattened thing* (σιτιστός) occurs only here in the NT.

The verb *to slay, slaughter* (θύω) occurs only here in Matt.

The word *ready* (ἕτοιμος) occurs 4 times in Matt. (22:4, 8; 24:44; 25:10).

22:5. The verb *to disregard, neglect* (ἀμελέω) occurs only here in Matt.

For the word *field, farm*, see Matt. 6:28 note.

The word *business* (ἐμπορία) occurs only here in the NT.

22:6. The verb *to mistreat* (ὑβρίζω) occurs only here in Matt. It implies insolence and offensive action.

For the verb *to kill* see Matt. 10:28 note.

22:7. For the verb *to be angry* see Matt. 5:22 note.

The word *army, troops* (στράτευμα) occurs only here in Matt.

This word *murderer* (φονεύς) occurs only here in Matt.

The verb *to burn, set on fire* (ἐμπίμπρημι) occurs only here in the NT. It is found in the papyri (see Moulton and Milligan, *Vocabulary*, p. 207).

8 Then saith he to his servants, The wedding is ready, but they which were bidden were not worthy.
9 Go ye therefore into the highways, and as many as ye shall find, bid to the marriage.
10 So those servants went out into the highways, and gathered together all as many as they found, both bad and good: and the wedding was furnished with guests.
11 And when the king came in to see the guests, he saw there a man which had not on a wedding garment:
12 And he saith unto him, Friend, how camest thou in hither not having a wedding garment? And he was speechless.

and as many as you find call to the marriage" (vv. 8–9). They were to go to a prominent place and invite as many as possible to the wedding. This is parallel to the worldwide call of the gospel in the present age (Rom. 1:15–16).

"And those slaves went out into the roads and gathered together all that they found, both evil and good, and the wedding was filled with guests" (v. 10). Both the evil and the good could come to this marriage banquet. The King was able to transform all who came to Him. Paul applied it, "For whosoever shall call upon the name of the Lord shall be saved" (Rom. 10:13).

"But when the king came in to behold the guests, he saw there a man who had not been clothed with a wedding garment" (v. 11). In the ancient world a king would know that people would not have magnificent robes that his court had, and so there would be servants at the gate to supply each guest with a royal robe for the banquet. For one to refuse such a robe would be a royal insult. (See Esther 8:15.)

"And he says to him: Friend, how did you come in here, not having a wedding garment? But he was silent" (v. 12). The king addresses him with a kindly title, but there is no answer. He had refused the king's gift.

22:8. For the word *worthy* see Matt. 3:8 note.

22:9. The word *main road* (διέξοδος) occurs only here in the NT. It refers to a road that leads to a city gate (an important thoroughfare).

22:10. For the verb *to recline at table, be a dinner guest,* see Matt. 9:10 note.

22:11. For the verb *to see, behold,* see Matt. 6:1 note.

For the word *garment, clothing,* see Matt. 3:4 note.

22:12. The verb *to make silent* (φιμόω) occurs twice in Matt. (22:12, 34).

For the word *friend* see Matt. 20:13 note.

13 Then said the king to the servants, Bind him hand and foot, and take him away, and cast him into outer darkness, there shall be weeping and gnashing of teeth.
14 For many are called, but few are chosen.
15 Then went the Pharisees, and took counsel how they might entangle him in his talk.

"Then the king said to his servants: Bind him hand and foot, and cast him into the outer darkness; there shall be bitter weeping and grinding of teeth" (v. 13). The king is indignant and orders him bound and cast out of the brilliantly illuminated palace. The parable illustrates how God will treat the wicked who despise His offer of salvation. Jude mentions those who "have gone in the way of Cain," "to whom is reserved the blackness of darkness forever" (Jude 11, 13).

"For many are called, but few are chosen" (v. 14). The *called* refers to those who have heard God's offer of salvation but have refused to obey it; the *chosen* refers to those who have heard and responded in submission to it. This is in contrast to the usage in the Epistles, in which *called* is a synonym for true believers (Rom. 1:6–7). For a person to be saved, God must choose, but the individual must also respond. Only God knows how those two elements fit together.

II. The Answer to the Pharisees and the Herodians. vv. 15–22 [Mark 12:13–17; Luke 20:20–26].

"Then the Pharisees went and took counsel in order that they might trap him in his words" (v. 15). They lay very careful plans, including their natural enemies, the Herodians, in them. Matthew Henry observed that

---

22:13. For the verb *to bind* see Matt. 12:29 note.

For the word *darkness* see Matt. 4:16 note.

For the word *bitter weeping* see Matt. 2:18 note.

22:14. The word *called* (κλητός) occurs only here in Matt.

The word *chosen, elect* (ἐκλεκτός) occurs 4 times in Matt. (22:14; 24:22, 24, 31). It refers to God's free choice of people to dwell with Him in heaven. It is not based on merit but on His gracious choice. For theological discussion see Elwell, ed., *Evangelical Dictionary of Biblical Theology*, "Elect, Election," pp. 199–201; ZPEB, "Elect, Election," II, pp. 270–74; ISBE (1982), "Election," II, pp. 56–57.

22:15. The verb *to trap* (παγιδεύω) occurs only here in the NT.

For the word *Pharisee* see Matt. 3:7 note.

For the word *counsel, plan,* see Matt. 12:14 note.

*16 And they sent out unto him their disciples with the Herodians, saying,
Master, we know that thou art true, and teachest the way of God in truth,
neither carest thou for any man: for thou regardest not the person of men.
17 Tell us therefore, What thinkest thou? Is it lawful to give tribute unto
Caesar, or not?
18 But Jesus perceived their wickedness, and said, Why tempt ye me, ye hypocrites?
19 Shew me the tribute money. And they brought unto him a penny.*

"it was foretold concerning him, that *the rulers would take counsel against
him* (Ps. 2:2)."

"And they sent out to him their disciples with the Herodians, saying:
Teacher, we know that you are true, and you teach the way of God in
truth, and it is not a care for you concerning any man, for you respect not
the face of men" (v. 16). "He is no respecter of persons" (Morris, *Matt.*,
p. 555). These honeyed words of flattery were meant to put Him off guard
so that they could innocently spring their trap.

"Say therefore to us what you think: is it lawful to give tribute to Caesar
or not?" (v. 17). They thought that either way He answered, He would
lose part of His audience. If He said they should pay, the Pharisees would
be disappointed. If He said they should not pay, the Herodians would
report Him as disloyal to Caesar.

"But Jesus, having known their evil, said: Why are you tempting me,
hypocrites?" (v. 18). The Lord fully understood their insincerity and their
evil purpose. They were setting Him up for a trap.

"Show me the lawful coin of the tribute; and they brought him a denarius" (v. 19). The denarius was a Roman silver coin that was the day's wage.
The obverse bore the image of the Roman emperor.

22:16. The Herodians are mentioned only here in Matt. They felt that the Herodian
family was beneficial to the country, bringing stability to the political scene. They would
be in favor of paying taxes. For further discussion see ISBE (1982), "Herodians," II, p. 698;
ZPEB, "Herodians," III, p. 146.

The word *truth* (ἀλήθεια) occurs only here in Matt.

22:17. For the word *tribute, tax*, see Matt. 17:25 note.

The word *Caesar* (Καῖσαρ) occurs 4 times in Matt. (22:17, 21 [3 times]). For background
see ZPEB, "Caesar," I, p. 680; ISBE (1979), "Caesar," I, p. 567. The German word *kaiser*
and the Russian *tsar* are both derivatives from this title.

22:18. For the verb *to tempt, test*, see Matt. 4:1 note.

For the word *hypocrite* see Matt. 6:2 note.

22:19. The word *lawful coin, tribute money* (νόμισμα) occurs only here in the NT.
Matthew, the tax collector, would note such a highly specialized term. See Moulton and

20 And he saith unto them, Whose is this image and superscription? 21 They say unto him, Caesar's. Then saith he unto them, Render therefore unto Caesar the things which are Caesar's; and unto God the things that are God's. 22 When they had heard these words, they marvelled, and left him, and went their way. 23 The same day came to him the Sadducees, which say that there is no resurrection, and asked him,

"And he says to them: Whose is this image and inscription?" (v. 20). The Lord asks an obvious question that they cannot avoid. The fact that they could produce the coin showed that they themselves were using the things of Caesar.

"They say to him, Caesar. Then he says to them: Give back therefore the things of Caesar to Caesar and the things of God to God" (v. 21). Every citizen should meet his responsibilities to God and to government. The believer can be a godly person and a good citizen at the same time. The apostle Paul emphasized this truth: "Let every soul be subject to the higher powers. For there is no power but of God. . . . Render to all their dues: tribute to whom tribute is due" (Rom. 13:1–7a). But it was also true that man's responsibility to God transcended his responsibility to government (Acts 4:19–20).

"And when they had heard, they marveled, and left him and departed" (v. 22). There was nothing they could say against that divine logic.

III. The Answer to the Sadducees. vv. 23–33 [Mark 12:18–27; Luke 20:27–40].

"In the same day the Sadducees, who say there is no resurrection, came to him and asked him" (v. 23). They had watched their rivals go down in defeat and decided that they could lay a better trap.

Milligan, *Vocabulary*, p. 429. For illustrations of such coins see V. Gilbert Beers, *The Victor Book of Bible Knowledge*, pp. 480–81.

For the word *denarius* see Matt. 18:28 note.

22:20. The word *image* (εἰκών) occurs only here in Matt.

The word *inscription* (ἐπιγραφή) occurs only here in Matt. For background see ISBE (1982), "Inscriptions," II, pp. 831–39; Butler, ed., *Holman Bible Dictionary*, "Inscription," p. 699.

22:21. For the verb *to give back* see Matt. 5:26 note.

22:22. For the verb *to marvel* see Matt. 8:10 note.

22:23. The word *resurrection* (ἀνάστασις) occurs 4 times in Matt. in this context only (22:23, 28, 30, 31). The OT clearly taught the resurrection (Job 19:25–26; Ps. 73:23–26;

24 Saying, Master, Moses said, If a man die, having no children, his brother shall marry his wife, and raise up seed unto his brother.
25 Now there were with us seven brethren: and the first, when he had married a wife, deceased, and, having no issue, left his wife unto his brother:
26 Likewise the second also, and the third, unto the seventh.
27 And last of all the woman died also.
28 Therefore in the resurrection whose wife shall she be of the seven? for they all had her.
29 Jesus answered and said unto them, Ye do err, not knowing the scriptures, nor the power of God.

"Saying, Teacher, Moses said: If any man die, not having children, his brother shall marry his wife and shall raise up seed for his brother" (v. 24). The passage underlying this account is Deuteronomy 25:5–10, but what follows sounds like a "made-up" tale.

"But there were with us seven brothers: And the first, having married, died, and not having seed, left his wife to his brother; likewise the second and the third unto the seven" (v. 25–26). It looks as though someone would get suspicious after a while!

"But last of all the woman died. In the resurrection therefore, whose wife of the seven shall she be? For they all had her" (vv. 27–28). They were thinking in naturalistic terms and were prepared to argue against any one He would pick.

"But Jesus answered and said to them: You are erring, because you do not know the Scriptures, nor the power of God" (v. 29). The Lord Jesus gives two reasons that all unsaved people fail to understand the Bible. First, they have not studied the Bible enough to know what it teaches, and secondly, they have never had an experience of the power of God in their lives. The Lord Jesus commanded, "Be searching the Scriptures, because in them you think you have eternal life, and they are the ones who testify

Isa. 26:19; Dan. 12:2–3). For further discussion see Elwell, ed., *Evangelical Dictionary of Biblical Theology*, "Resurrection," pp. 676–79; ZPEB, "Resurrection," V, pp. 70–75; ISBE (1988), "Resurrection," IV, pp. 145–50; see also Ryken, Wilhoit, and Longman, *Dictionary of Biblical Imagery*, "Resurrection," pp. 711–12.

For *Sadducees* see Matt. 3:7 note.

22:24. The verb *to marry* (ἐπιγαμβρεύω) occurs only here in the NT. But see also Gen. 38:8; Deut. 25:5 (LXX).

For *Moses* see Matt. 8:4 note.

22:25. For the verb *to marry* see Matt. 5:32 note.

For the verb *to die* see Matt. 2:19 note.

30 For in the resurrection they neither marry, nor are given in marriage, but are as the angels of God in heaven.
31 But as touching the resurrection of the dead, have ye not read that which was spoken unto you by God, saying,
32 I am the God of Abraham, and the God of Isaac, and the God of Jacob? God is not the God of the dead, but of the living.
33 And when the multitude heard this, they were astonished at his doctrine.

concerning me" (John 5:39). The Bible clearly teaches the power of the great Messiah to deliver from sin. Secondly, they were not "born again" and hence had no spiritual perception. To those who believed on Him the Lord Jesus promised, "You shall know the truth, and the truth shall make you free" (John 8:32).

"For in the resurrection they neither marry nor are given in marriage, but are as angels in heaven" (v. 30). In other words, they will be spiritual, not physical, beings. There is no teaching in Scripture that people become angels in heaven, only that they will be spiritual beings as the angels are.

"But concerning the resurrection of the dead, did you not read what was said to you by God, saying, I am the God of Abraham and the God of Isaac and the God of Jacob? God is not the God of the dead, but of the living" (vv. 31–32; Exod. 3:6, 15). We must note that the Lord Jesus teaches that the Scriptures, even the narrative portions, are addressed to every human being. The prophets could cry out, "Hear, O heavens, and give ear, O earth: for the Lord hath spoken" (Isa. 1:2a). God is always portrayed as the God of living beings, whether they are in the realm of this world or the larger spiritual world.

"And when the crowds heard, they were astonished at his teaching" (v. 33). They had never heard anyone teach like this or apply the Scriptures with such dramatic force.

22:29. For the verb *to lead astray, err*, see Matt. 18:12 note.
For the verb *to know* see Matt. 6:32 note.
22:30. For the word *angel* see Matt. 1:20 note.
For the word *heaven* see Matt. 3:2 note.
22:32. For *Abraham* see Matt. 1:1 note.
For *Jacob* see Matt. 1:2 note.
22:33. For the verb *to be astonished* see Matt. 7:28 note.

34 But when the Pharisees had heard that he had put the Sadducees to silence, they were gathered together.
35 Then one of them, which was a lawyer, asked him a question, tempting him, and saying,
36 Master, which is the great commandment in the law?
37 Jesus said unto him, Thou shalt love the Lord thy God with all thy heart, and with all thy soul, and with all thy mind.
38 This is the first and great commandment.

IV. *The Answer to the Lawyer. vv. 34–40 [Mark 12:28–34].*

"But when the Pharisees heard that he had silenced the Sadducees, they were gathered together. And one of them, a lawyer, asked, tempting him" (vv. 34–35). Since the Pharisees were the strict interpreters of the law, many of them were experts in the courts and synagogues. Mark identifies him as a scribe (Mark 12:28).

"Teacher, What kind of commandment is greatest in the law?" (v. 36). He is asking about not a single command but a class of commandments. Plummer notes that "the Rabbis counted more than six hundred precepts in the Law, of which some were called 'weighty' and others 'light'; and there was much discussion as to which were which" (Plummer, *Matt.*, p. 308, note).

"And he said to him: You shall love the Lord your God with all your heart and with all your soul and with all your mind. This is the great and first commandment" (vv. 37–38). God has manifested such infinite love for man (John 3:16; I John 3:1) that wholehearted love for God is the only proper response. God is not primarily interested in the work believers can do for Him. He is looking for a loving heart. "All things work together for good to those who love God" (Rom. 8:28*b*).

22:35. The word *lawyer* (νομικός) occurs only here in Matt. It refers to an expert in Jewish law, an official interpreter of the Mosaic code. For further discussion see ZPEB, "Lawyer," III, pp. 896–97; ISBE (1986), "Lawyer," III, pp. 93–94.

22:36. For the interrogative pronoun *what kind of* see Matt. 19:18 note.

For the word *commandment* see Matt. 5:19 note.

22:37. For the verb *to love* see Matt. 5:43 note.

For the word *heart* see Matt. 5:8 note.

For the word *soul* see Matt. 2:20 note.

The word *mind, understanding* (διάνοια) occurs only here in Matt. It refers to the thinking powers of man. For further discussion see ZPEB, "Mind," IV, pp. 228–29; ISBE (1986), "Mind," III, pp. 362–63; Elwell, ed., "Mind/Reason," *Evangelical Dictionary of Biblical Theology*, pp. 527–30.

39 And the second is like unto it, Thou shalt love thy neighbour as thyself.
40 On these two commandments hang all the law and the prophets.
41 While the Pharisees were gathered together, Jesus asked them,
42 Saying, What think ye of Christ? whose son is he? They say unto him, The son of David.
43 He saith unto them, How then doth David in spirit call him Lord, saying,
44 The Lord said unto my Lord, Sit thou on my right hand, till I make thine enemies thy footstool?

"And the second is like it, You shall love your neighbor as yourself" (v. 39; Lev. 19:18). You shall desire the best interests of your neighbor just as you do yourself. "If a man loved God supremely, he would keep the first of the commandments; if he loved his neighbor as himself, he would keep the last ones: he would not kill, commit adultery, steal, bear false witness, or covet" (T. B. Maston, *Biblical Ethics*, p. 149).

"On these two commandments the whole law and the prophets hang" (v. 40). These two commandments sum up the governing principles of the kingdom of God. All the rest are merely applications and interpretations. The Lord Jesus had proved that He could use the Scriptures to thoroughly demolish all the traps of His enemies. But He was not just a great teacher. "Jesus demonstrated in His own life supreme love for God and equal love for His neighbor" (Maston, p. 150).

V. The Question of Jesus. vv. 41–46 [Mark 12:35–37; Luke 20:41–44].

"But while the Pharisees were gathered together, Jesus asked them, saying: What do you think concerning the Messiah [Christ]? Whose son is he? They say to him: Son of David" (vv. 41–42). That was the only orthodox answer possible. But now the Lord has a question for them that they had never considered.

"He says to them: How therefore does David in spirit call him Lord, saying:

"The Lord said to my Lord:

Sit on my right hand,

Until I put your enemies

Under your feet" (vv. 43–44; Ps. 110:1; 109:1, LXX).

22:39. For the word *neighbor* see Matt. 5:43 note.

22:40. For the verb *to hang* see Matt. 18:6 note.

22:42. For *David* see Matt. 1:1 note.

22:43. For the word *spirit* see Matt. 1:18 note.

45 If David then call him Lord, how is he his son?
46 And no man was able to answer him a word, neither durst any man from that day forth ask him any more questions.

David spoke under the inspiration of the Spirit of God and thus could not make a mistake. According to ancient custom all the descendents would be considered inferior to the ancestor. Thus, how could it be possible for King David to call his descendant *Lord?*

"If therefore David calls him Lord, how is he his son?" (v. 45). It was a shattering question for those "experts" in the Scriptures. The biblical answer is that David, under inspiration, knew that this Descendant would be the mighty Messiah, Who would bring in the kingdom of God with divine power (Ps. 2:6–12; 72:1–11; 110:1–7). But these biblical authorities had closed their eyes to the truth. No wonder that the Lord had called them "blind leaders of the blind" (Matt. 15:14). Just in passing we should note that the Lord here authenticates the accuracy of the title of the Psalm as "A Psalm of David." Liberal commentators may doubt the accuracy of the title, but the Lord did not. Adolf Saphir argued that "the Bible is not an aggregate of literary productions, but that it is the testimony and voice of the living One who is to come again—a book of history which is not yet completed" (*The Divine Unity of Scripture*, p. 227).

"And no one was able to answer him a word, neither did anyone dare from that day to ask him anything" (v. 46). The defeat was so thorough and so public that no one else dared to confront Him. The prophet Isaiah called Him "Wonderful Counsellor" (Isa. 9:6b). The apostle Paul called Him "Christ the power of God, and the wisdom of God" (I Cor. 1:24b).

Practical Applications from Matthew 22

1. An invitation from a king should be taken very seriously (vv. 2–3).
   "I have spread out my hands all the day unto a rebellious people, which walketh in a way that was not good, after their own thoughts; a people that provoketh me to anger continually to my face" (Isa. 65:2–3a).

22:44. The first word *Lord* is a translation of the Hebrew *Jehovah*, a primary name of God.
22:46. The verb *to dare* (τολμάω) occurs only here in Matt.
For the verb *to answer* see Matt. 3:15 note.

2. To make light of God's invitation to salvation brings judgment
(vv. 5–7). "Be not deceived; God is not mocked: for whatsoever a
man sows, that shall he also reap" (Gal. 6:7).

3. Everyone, good and bad, needs an invitation to God's banquet
(vv. 9–10). "For whosoever shall call upon the name of the Lord shall
be saved" (Rom. 10:13).

4. Outer darkness is the portion of those who reject God's light (v. 13).
Those who are gone astray are as "clouds that are carried with a tempest; to whom the mist of darkness is reserved for ever" (II Pet. 2:17).

5. A believer should be a good citizen as well as a good Christian
(v. 21). "I exhort therefore, that, . . . prayers . . . be made for all men;
for kings, and for all that are in authority; that we may lead a quiet
and peaceable life in all godliness and honesty" (I Tim. 2:1a–2).

6. Wrong attitudes should be repented of and corrected (v. 29). "Serve
the Lord with gladness: come before his presence with singing"
(Ps. 100:2).

7. God is the God of the living (v. 32). Those who died in the faith are
alive with Jesus and will be brought back with Him when He returns
(I Thess. 4:14).

8. Loving God is the most important thing in the life of a believer
(v. 37). The Lord promised a crown of life to those who love Him
(James 1:12b). "We love him, because he first loved us" (I John 4:19).

9. Believers should also love their neighbor (v. 39). "Owe no man any
thing, but to love one another: for he that loves has fulfilled the law"
(Rom. 13:8).

10. What a person thinks of Christ is the most important thing in his
life (v. 42). To Paul He was "our Lord Jesus Christ . . . the blessed
and only Potentate, the King of kings, and Lord of lords" (I Tim.
6:14b–15).

Prayer

Dear heavenly Father, Grant that we may come to You clothed in the
righteousness of Your dear Son, our Savior, the Lord Jesus Christ. Give us
grace to walk humbly in His service, never trusting in our good works, but
wholly depending on His righteousness alone for our salvation. In Jesus'
name. Amen.

MATTHEW 23

JESUS DENOUNCES PHARISEES

Persons
Jesus   The multitude
His disciples

Persons referred to

Scribes	One who humbles	The righteous
Pharisees	himself	The fathers
Moses	Widows	Those who killed the
Christ [Messiah]	One proselyte	prophets
Your Father in	Blind guides	Wise men
heaven	Fools	Abel
The greatest	God	Zachariah
One who exalts	The prophets	Barachiah
himself		

Places mentioned

Chief seats   Sepulchers of the righteous
The market   Hell
Widow's houses   Synagogues
Sea   Cities
Land   The place between the sanctuary
The temple   and the altar
The altar   Jerusalem
Tombs of the prophets

Doctrines taught

The authority of Moses   Judgment
Whoever exalts himself shall be Mercy
    abased   Faith
Prayer   Righteousness
Condemnation   He that comes in the name of the
Sanctification   Lord
The throne of God

1 Then spake Jesus to the multitude, and to his disciples,
2 Saying The scribes and the Pharisees sit in Moses' seat:
3 All therefore whatsoever they bid you observe, that observe and do; but do not ye after their works: for they say, and do not.
4 For they bind heavy burdens and grievous to be borne, and lay them on men's shoulders; but they themselves will not move them with one of their fingers.

Matthew 23 Exposition

I. His Description of the Pharisees. vv. 1–12 [Mark 12:38–40; Luke 20:45–47].

"Then Jesus spoke to the crowds and to his disciples, saying: The scribes and the Pharisees sit on Moses' seat" (vv. 1–2). They are in the position of authoritative teachers, but they are not to originate any teaching. Anytime a Bible teacher goes beyond what Scripture says and gives his own interpretation, he has lost divine authority.

"All therefore, as many things as they say to you, do and keep, but according to their works do not do, for they are saying and are not doing" (v. 3). The present tense in the final verbs seems to emphasize the persistent refusal of the Pharisees to obey what they are teaching. It is a moral shame for any teacher to refuse to obey what he teaches others. Matthew is the only Gospel that provides a full record of this message of denunciation against the scribes and Pharisees.

"But they bind heavy burdens and hard to carry, and put them upon the shoulders of men, but they themselves do not wish to move them with one

---

23:2. For the *Pharisees* see Matt. 3:7 note.

23:3. For the word *work* see Matt. 5:16 note.

23:4. The verb *to bind* (δεσμεύω) occurs only here in Matt.

The word *hard to carry* (δυσβάστακτος) occurs only here in Matt.

The word *shoulder* (ὦμος) occurs only here in Matt.

The word *finger* (δάκτυλος) occurs only here in Matt.

The verb *to move* (κινέω) occurs twice in Matt. (23:4; 27:39).

5 But all their works they do for to be seen of men: they make broad their phylacteries, and enlarge the borders of their garments,

6 And love the uppermost rooms at feasts, and the chief seats in the synagogues,

7 And greetings in the markets, and to be called of men, Rabbi, Rabbi.

8 But be not ye called Rabbi: for one is your Master, even Christ; and all ye are brethren.

of their fingers" (v. 4). The Pharisees had no compassion for the plight of common men. Lifting a burden with one finger implies a very light load, but even that they refused. "They are taskmasters, not burden-bearers, not sympathetic helpers" (A. T. Robertson, *Word Pictures*, I, p. 178).

"But all their works they are doing in order to be seen by men; for they enlarge their phylacteries and make the fringes great" (v. 5). The present tense verb *they are doing* emphasizes their constant practice of parading their piety. They were always making their boxes of verses larger and the fringes on their prayer shawls longer in order to attract attention to their religious practices. They never thought of genuine worship of God or of real help for people seeking God.

"But they are loving the first seats in the dinners, and the first seats in the synagogues, and the greetings in the market places, and being called by men Rabbi" (vv. 6–7). Their lives centered on gaining the praise of men, not on meeting the spiritual needs of men. They wanted the place of honor at dinners and in the synagogues. They wanted others to praise them and salute them everywhere.

"But you, be not called Rabbi, for one is the teacher of you, but all you are brothers" (v. 8). There is an equality in salvation. All believers are brothers; Christ alone is *The Teacher*. Denominational leaders must be careful not to put Luther, Calvin, Wesley, or others in the place of the

---

23:5. The verb *to enlarge* (πλατύνω) occurs only here in Matt.

The word *phylactery* (φυλακτήριον) occurs only here in the NT. It was a small box containing verses from the OT. Regularly one was bound on the forehead and another on the arm, especially during prayers. For explanations and illustrations see ISBE (1986), "Phylactery," III, pp. 864–65; ZPEB, "Phylactery," IV, pp. 786–88.

For the word *fringe* see Matt. 9:20 note.

23:6. The word *first seat, place of honor* (πρωτοκλισία) occurs only here in Matt. It implies reclining at a meal.

The word *place of honor, best seat* (πρωτοκαθεδρία) occurs only here in Matt. It implies a thronelike seat in the synagogue.

9 And call no man your father upon the earth: for one is your Father, which is in heaven.
10 Neither be ye called masters: for one is your Master, even Christ.
11 But he that is greatest among you shall be your servant.
12 And whosoever shall exalt himself shall be abased; and he that shall humble himself shall be exalted.
13 But woe unto you, scribes and Pharisees, hypocrites! for ye shut up the kingdom of heaven against men: for ye neither go in yourselves, neither suffer ye them that are entering to go in.

Lord Jesus Christ. They may be great men, but Christ is more than merely a great man. He is "the Lord from heaven" (I Cor. 15:47b).

"And call not any of you on earth father, for one is your Father, the heavenly one" (v. 9). The Lord's Prayer clearly teaches this (Matt. 6:9). The excess of the Roman Catholic church must be avoided.

"Neither be called teachers, because your teacher is one, the Christ" (v. 10). This is a standing warning to all church leaders not to seek fame as a teacher, but to lead men to the Lord Jesus Christ, our one great Teacher.

"But the one who is greatest among you shall be your servant" (v. 11). It is significant that one of Messiah's titles was *Servant of Jehovah* (Isa. 42:1; 52:13; 53:11–12). Paul exhorts believers, "By love serve one another" (Gal. 5:13b).

"But whoever shall exalt himself shall be humbled, and whoever shall humble himself shall be exalted" (v. 12). God is displeased with the proud and the arrogant, but He gives wonderful promises to the humble. "For thus saith the high and lofty One that inhabiteth eternity, whose name is Holy; I dwell in the high and holy place, with him also that is of a contrite and humble spirit, to revive the spirit of the humble, and to revive the heart of the contrite ones" (Isa. 57:15). "The Lord is nigh unto them that are of a broken heart; and saveth such as be of a contrite spirit" (Ps. 34:18).

23:7. The word *greeting* (ἀσπασμός) occurs only here in Matt.

The word *rabbi* (ῥαββί) occurs 4 times in Matt. (23:7, 8; 26:25, 49). For explanation see ISBE (1988), "Rabbi," IV, p. 30; ZPEB, "Rabbi," V, p. 16; Butler, ed., *Holman Bible Dictionary*, "Rabbi," p. 1162; Harrison, *The New Unger's Bible Dictionary*, "Rabbi," pp. 1058–59.

23:9. For the *Fatherhood of God* see Matt. 5:16 note.

23:10. Another word for *teacher* (καθηγητής) occurs only here in the NT. The Lord Jesus is the only true and infallible Teacher or Guide for every believer (see B. B. Warfield, *Lord of Glory*, p. 75).

*14 Woe unto you, scribes and Pharisees, hypocrites! for ye devour widows'
houses, and for a pretence make long prayer: therefore ye shall receive the
greater damnation.
15 Woe unto you, scribes and Pharisees, hypocrites! for ye compass sea and
land to make one proselyte, and when he is made, ye make him twofold more
the child of hell than yourselves.*

II. *His Woe to the Pharisees. vv. 13–36 [Mark 12:38–40; Luke 20:45–47].*

"But woe to you, scribes and Pharisees, hypocrites! Because you are shutting the kingdom of the heavens against men; for you are not entering,
neither are you permitting the ones entering to enter" (v. 13). Matthew
records the Lord's declaration of sevenfold Woe! against these hypocrites
(vv. 13, 15, 16, 23, 25, 27, 29). He is emphasizing what the prophets have
already charged the leaders of Israel: "Woe be unto the pastors that destroy and scatter the sheep of my pasture! Saith the Lord" (Jer. 23:1). The
Lord Jesus charges them with shutting the door of the kingdom against
men. Vincent translates, "in the face of" men (*Word Studies*, I, p. 124).
Their wicked actions slammed the door shut.

"But woe to you, scribes and Pharisees, hypocrites! Because you devour
the houses of widows and for a pretence are praying long; on account of
this you shall receive greater judgment" (v. 14). To take advantage of
poor people and then make long prayers in public is the height of hypocrisy. God is watching and judgment is waiting.

"Woe to you, scribes and Pharisees, hypocrites! Because you go around
the sea and the dry land to make one proselyte, and whenever he is made,
you make him twofold more a son of Gehenna than you" (v. 15). They
turn their convert into a worse fanatic than they are.

23:11. For the word *servant* see Matt. 20:26 note.

23:12. For the verb *to humble* see Matt. 18:4 note.

The verb *to exalt* (ὑψόω) occurs 3 times in Matt. (11:23; 23:12 [twice]).

23:13. For the word *Woe!* see Matt. 11:21 note.

23:14. The oldest manuscripts do not have v. 14; it was apparently borrowed from Mark
12:40 or Luke 20:47, where it does belong. For discussion see Bruce Metzger, A *Textual
Commentary on the Greek New Testament*, p. 60. The Gospels were inspired to supplement
one another, not to be identical.

23:15. The word *proselyte* (προσήλυτος) occurs only here in Matt. A proselyte is a
convert from the Gentiles to Judaism. For background see ZPEB, "Proselyte," IV, pp.
905–10; ISBE (1986), "Proselyte," III, pp. 1005–11.

16 Woe unto you, ye blind guides, which say, Whosoever shall swear by the temple, it is nothing; but whosoever shall swear by the gold of the temple, he is a debtor!
17 Ye fools and blind: for whether is greater, the gold, or the temple that sanctifieth the gold?
18 And, Whosoever shall swear by the altar, it is nothing; but whosoever sweareth by the gift that is upon it, he is guilty.
19 Ye fools and blind: for whether is greater, the gift, or the altar that sanctifieth the gift?
20 Whoso therefore shall swear by the altar, sweareth by it, and by all things thereon.
21 And whoso shall swear by the temple, sweareth by it, and by him that dwelleth therein.

"Woe to you blind guides who say: Whoever shall swear by the sanctuary, it is nothing; but whoever shall swear by the gold of the sanctuary is guilty" (v. 16). This is another example of the nit-picking traditions of the Pharisees. It was God who hallowed the temple and not the value of the decorations.

"Fools and blind, for which is greater, the gold, or the sanctuary that hallows the gold?" (v. 17). The sanctuary on earth was but a small copy of the heavenly sanctuary (Heb. 8:2). God is always more important than His surroundings.

"And, Whoever shall swear by the altar, it is nothing; but whoever shall swear by the gift upon it is guilty" (v. 18). To the Pharisees the gift was the important thing. But it was God's altar, and nothing offered on it could compare with the infinite value of God Himself.

"Blind ones, what is greater, the gift, or the altar that sanctifies the gift?" (v. 19). That it was God's altar made the things offered on it important.

"Therefore the one who swears by the altar, swears by it and by all the things on it, and the one who swears by the sanctuary, swears by it, and by

---

The word *dry* [land] occurs twice in Matt. (12:10; 23:15).

23:16. For the word *guide* see Matt. 15:14 note.

For the verb *to swear* see Matt. 5:34 note.

The word *sanctuary* (ναός) occurs 9 times in Matt. (23:16 [twice], 17, 21, 35; 26:61; 27:5, 40, 51). It refers to the temple building proper, as distinguished from the word *temple complex* (ἱερόν), which may include the courts, porticos, and other areas. See Trench, *Synonyms*, pp. 10–12.

23:17. For the verb *to hallow* see Matt. 6:9 note.

23:18. For the word *altar* see Matt. 5:23 note.

For the word *gift* see Matt. 2:11 note.

22 And he that shall swear by heaven, sweareth by the throne of God, and by him that sitteth thereon.
23 Woe unto you, scribes and Pharisees, hypocrites! for ye pay tithe of mint and anise and cummin, and have omitted the weightier matters of the law, judgment, mercy, and faith: these ought ye to have done, and not to leave the other undone.

the One who is dwelling in it" (vv. 20–21). The trouble with the Pharisees was that they had no reverence for God; they were going through only outward forms of worship. They were completely unaware that God was in His temple and that He should be the center of their attention. How many church members today sit piously in church while they think of Sunday dinner, or the afternoon ballgame, rather than joining in heartfelt worship of the God of heaven?

"And the one who swears by heaven swears by the throne of God and by the One who is sitting upon it" (v. 22). The believer should treat the subject of heaven with reverence, for that is the dwelling place of Almighty God. He knows the heart attitude of every man.

"Woe to you, scribes and Pharisees, hypocrites! Because you tithe mint and dill and cumin, and abandoned the weightier things of the law, judgment, mercy and faith; these things were necessary to do and not to abandon the other" (v. 23). They spent their time counting the minute seeds of their garden in order to say that they tithed exactly, but important matters of mercy and faith they had no time for.

23:23. The word *mint* (ἡδύοσμον) occurs only here in Matt. It is popularly called horsemint in the Near East. For discussion see ZPEB, "Mint," IV, p. 241; ISBE (1986), "Mint," III, p. 371; Zohary, *Plants of the Bible*, "Mint," pp. 88–89.

The word *dill* (ἄνηθον) occurs only here in the NT. This spice grows wild in Israel. The word *anise* (KJV) is a different spice. See ZPEB, "Dill," II, p. 126; "Anise," I, p. 169; ISBE (1979), "Dill," I, p. 943; Zohary, *Plants of the Bible*, "Dill," pp. 88–89.

The word *cumin* (κύμινον) occurs only here in the NT. See ZPEB, "Cummin," I, p. 1043; Zohary, *Plants of the Bible*, "Cummin," pp. 88–89, with color photo. It is still used as a spice for stewed meat.

23:24. For the word *guide* see Matt. 15:14 note.

The verb *to strain out* (διϋλίζω) occurs only here in the NT.

The word *gnat* (κώνωψ) occurs only here in the NT.

The verb *to swallow* (καταπίνω) occurs only here in Matt. Vincent suggests that it means *to gulp down* (*Word Studies*, I, p. 125).

For the word *camel* see Matt. 3:4 note.

24 Ye blind guides, which strain at a gnat, and swallow a camel.
25 Woe unto you, scribes and Pharisees, hypocrites! for ye make clean the outside of the cup and of the platter, but within they are full of extortion and excess.
26 Thou blind Pharisee, cleanse first that which is within the cup and platter, that the outside of them may be clean also.
27 Woe unto you, scribes and Pharisees, hypocrites! for ye are like unto whited sepulchres, which indeed appear beautiful outward, but are within full of dead men's bones, and of all uncleanness.

"Blind guides, who are straining out a gnat, but swallowing a camel" (v. 24). This is certainly a humorous contrast between a tiny insect and the largest land animal in the Near East. It was true that creeping things were not to be eaten (Lev. 11:41), but a camel! These religious leaders were overlooking the doctrine of God. For a religious leader to overlook such a major doctrine is a serious charge.

"Woe to you, scribes and Pharisees, hypocrites, because you are cleaning the outside of the cup and of the dish, but inside they are full of robbery and self-indulgence" (v. 25). The Lord Jesus charges them with robbery because they were taking the offerings of the people, but they were not true to their office as teachers of the truth of God.

"Blind Pharisee, first cleanse the inside of the cup, in order that the outside of it may become clean also" (v. 26). For simple sanitary reasons the inside of the cup was more important. But the Pharisees lived for appearances only. Their purifications were only rituals; they were lost sinners within.

"Woe to you, scribes and Pharisees, hypocrites, because you are like whitewashed tombs, which outside indeed appear beautiful, but inside are filled with the bones of the dead and all uncleanness" (v. 27). To

23:25. For the verb *to cleanse* see Matt. 8:2 note.

For the word *cup* see Matt. 10:42 note.

The word *dish* (παροψίς) occurs only here in the NT. Arndt and Gingrich define it as a side dish (*Lexicon*, p. 635). Moulton and Milligan define it as a dish on which dainties were served (*Vocabulary*, p. 497).

The word *robbery, plunder* (ἁρπαγή) occurs only here in Matt.

The word *self-indulgence* (ἀκρασία) occurs only here in Matt.

23:27. The word *tomb* (τάφος) occurs 6 times in Matt. (23:27, 29; 27:61, 64, 66; 28:1). For details see ZPEB, "Tomb," V, pp. 767–74; ISBE (1988), "Tomb," p. 870; Ryken, Wilhoit, and Longman, *Dictionary of Biblical Imagery*, "Grave," pp. 349–50.

The verb *to whitewash* (κονιάω) occurs only here in Matt.

The word *beautiful* (ὡραῖος) occurs only here in Matt.

The word *bone* (ὀστέον) occurs only here in Matt.

28 Even so ye also outwardly appear righteous unto men, but within ye are full of hypocrisy and iniquity.
29 Woe unto you, scribes and Pharisees, hypocrites! because ye build the tombs of the prophets, and garnish the sepulchres of the righteous,
30 And say, If we had been in the days of our fathers, we would not have been partakers with them in the blood of the prophets.
31 Wherefore ye be witnesses unto yourselves, that ye are the children of them which killed the prophets.

this day the tombs of famous rabbis such as Yohanan ben Zacchai and Maimonides are still whitewashed and adorned in the city of Tiberius. This protects Jews from accidentally touching a tomb and thus becoming ceremonially unclean.

"Thus also you appear righteous to men outside, but inside you are full of hypocrisy and lawlessness" (v. 28). This was a crushing charge to bring against men whose whole life was a pose of upholding every "jot and tittle" of the law. John makes a point of emphasizing that the Lord Jesus "knew what was in man" (John 2:25).

"Woe to you, scribes and Pharisees, hypocrites, because you build the tombs of the prophets and adorn the graves of the righteous, and you say: If we were in the days of our fathers, we would not have shared in the blood of the prophets" (vv. 29–30). Their prideful attitude showed that they thought they were superior to their ancestors. But in reality they were doing the same things to John the Baptist and the Lord Jesus that their ancestors had done to Jeremiah and the other prophets.

"So that you are witnessing against yourselves that you are the sons of the ones who killed the prophets" (v. 31). They were not only the physical descendants of their fathers but also the spiritual heirs of hostility against the prophets.

23:28. For the word *righteous* see Matt. 1:19 note.

The word *hypocrisy* (ὑπόκρισις) occurs only here in Matt. (but see *hypocrite*, Matt. 6:2 note).

For the word *lawlessness* see Matt. 7:23 note.

23:29. For the verb *to adorn* see Matt. 12:44 note.

For the word *grave* see Matt. 8:28 note.

23:30. For the word *blood* see Matt. 16:17 note.

23:31. The verb *to witness* (μαρτυρέω) occurs only here in Matt.

For the verb *to kill, murder,* see Matt. 5:21 note.

32 Fill ye up then the measure of your fathers.
33 Ye serpents, ye generation of vipers, how can ye escape the damnation of hell?
34 Wherefore, behold, I send unto you prophets, and wise men, and scribes:
and some of them ye shall kill and crucify; and some of them shall ye scourge in
your synagogues, and persecute them from city to city:
35 That upon you may come all the righteous blood shed upon the earth, from
the blood of righteous Abel unto the blood of Zacharias son of Barachias, whom
ye slew between the temple and the altar.

"And you, fill up the measure of your fathers" (v. 32). The *you* is emphatic. You resist the truth, persecute God's messengers, and see what God will bring upon you.

"Snakes, offspring of vipers, how will you flee from the judgment of Gehenna?" (v. 33). This strong language portrays the real nature of the Pharisees. They were poisonous snakes leading their people through religious formalism down the pathway to the flames of gehenna. How many are their successors in the present generation?

"On account of this, behold, I am sending to you prophets and wise men and scribes; from them you shall kill and crucify, and from them you shall scourge in your synagogues and persecute them from city to city" (v. 34). The Lord gave them a prophecy of the gospel ministry of the early church (Acts 3–9).

"In order that upon you may come all the righteous blood which has been shed upon the earth, from the blood of righteous Abel to the blood of Zechariah, son of Berechiah, whom you murdered between the sanctuary

---

23:33. For the word *snake* see Matt. 7:10 note.

For the word *viper* see Matt. 3:7 note.

For the word *judgment* see Matt. 5:21 note.

For *Gehenna* see Matt. 5:22 note.

23:34. For the word *prophet* see Matt. 1:22 note.

For the word *wise* see Matt. 11:25 note.

For the word *scribe* see Matt. 2:4 note.

For the verb *to persecute* see Matt. 5:10 note.

23:35. For the word *blood* see Matt. 16:17 note.

Abel is mentioned only here in Matt. For background see ZPEB, "Abel," I, p. 8; ISBE (1979), "Abel," I, p. 4.

Zachariah is mentioned only here in Matt. The name was spelled *Zechariah* in the OT. Critics have thought that there is an error in the text here because Zechariah is called the son of Jehoiada in II Chron. 24:20, but Broadus notes that "Zachariah's father,

*36 Verily I say unto you, All these things shall come upon this generation.
37 O Jerusalem, Jerusalem, thou that killest the prophets, and stonest them
which are sent unto thee, how often would I have gathered thy children together,
even as a hen gathereth her chickens under her wings, and ye would not!
38 Behold, your house is left unto you desolate.
39 For I say unto you, Ye shall not see me henceforth, till ye shall say, Blessed
is he that cometh in the name of the Lord.*

and the altar" (v. 35). The Lord here foretold the coming destruction
of Jerusalem in a.d. 70. The catastrophe would be a judgment for all
the murders of God's servants recorded in the OT, from the first (Abel,
Gen. 4:8) to the last (Zechariah, II Chron. 24:20–21; Zech. 1:1). Second
Chronicles is the last book in the Hebrew Bible.

"Amen I say to you, all these things shall come upon this generation"
(v. 36). They were destined to come within forty years.

III. His Lament over the Destruction of Jerusalem. vv. 37–39.

"O Jerusalem, Jerusalem, the one who killed the prophets and stoned the
ones who were sent to her, how often I wished to gather your children
together, even as a hen gathers her chicks under her wings, but you would
not" (v. 37). The Lord took no pleasure in destroying Jerusalem. It was a
judicial act demanded by the unrepented sins of the past.

"Behold, your house is left to you desolate" (v. 38). The house would be
desolated by war and siege, but the spiritual desolation was much greater.
They had repudiated the divine salvation offered by Messiah and would
be replaced by a church that would proclaim the gospel to all the world.

"For I say to you, you shall never see me until you say:

Blessed is the one who comes in the name of the Lord" (v. 39;
Ps. 118:26a).

Jehoiada, may have had the surname of Berechiah, 'blessed of Jehovah,' a name borne
by six or seven persons in history, and which might have been given to the great priest
for saving his country" (Broadus, *Matt.*, p. 477). There are numerous examples of people
bearing more than one name. See also ZPEB, "Zechariah," V, pp. 1041–42; ISBE (1988),
"Zechariah," IV, pp. 1182–83.

23:37. The word *hen* (ὄρνις) occurs only here in Matt.

The word *chick, young bird* (νοσσίον) occurs only here in the NT.

23:38. For the word *desolate, desert*, see Matt. 3:1 note.

23:39. For the verb *to bless* see Matt. 14:19 note.

For the word *name* see Matt. 1:21 note.

The great Messiah was prophesied to come in the name of the Lord (Isa. 9:6–7). It was left to the apostle Paul to declare the eschatological conversion of Israel and their ultimate salvation (Rom. 11:26–29). But the Lord Jesus is now, at the end of the ministry, prepared to discuss the eschatological future with the disciples, as the next two chapters will show.

Practical Applications from Matthew 23

1. Empty profession without the life to back it up is worth nothing (v. 3). It is like the son who promised to serve his father but did not (Matt. 21:29).
2. Some people do all their good works just to be seen by men (v. 5). Peter exhorted, "Sanctify the Lord God in your hearts" (I Pet. 3:15a).
3. Christ alone is our Lord and Master (v. 8). Paul referred to Him as "our Lord Jesus Christ, which in his own times he shall show the blessed and only Potentate, the King of kings, and Lord of lords" (I Tim. 6:14b–15).
4. The person who truly wants to be greatest will be the best servant of all (v. 11). "By love serve one another" (Gal. 5:13b).
5. But one who merely wants to exalt himself shall be abased (v. 12). The first of six things the Lord hates is "a proud look" (Prov. 6:17a).
6. Good things, done in pretence, bring greater condemnation (v. 14). The kiss of Judas shall burn forever (Matt. 26:49).
7. Men must beware of being blind guides (v. 16). The psalmist prayed, "Teach me, O Lord, the way of thy statutes; and I shall keep it unto the end" (Ps. 119:33).
8. Vain oaths should be avoided (v. 21). The correct answer should be Yes or No (Matt. 5:37).
9. Counting seeds in order to tithe them is a waste of time; believers should center their attention on deeds of mercy and faith (v. 23). "And whatever you do in word or in work, do all in the name of the Lord Jesus" (Col. 3:17a).
10. Outward appearances can be deceptive; believers should center attention on heart devotion to God (vv. 27–28). "Let the words of my mouth, and the meditation of my heart, be acceptable in thy sight, O Lord, my strength, and my redeemer" (Ps. 19:14).

11. The Lord Jesus desires to bless people, but they will not come to Him (v. 37). He still invites them: "Come unto me, all you who labor and are heavy laden, and I will give you rest" (Matt. 11:28).

Prayer

Lord Jesus, preserve us from hypocrisy; help us to truly pray to You and to truly serve You from the heart. Help us to do all things with the consciousness of Your presence with us. Put within our hearts a longing for Your coming again. Amen.

MATTHEW 24

The Prophecy of the King

Persons
Jesus
His disciples
The Son of man

Persons referred to

Many deceivers	False prophets	Two women at the
False prophets	Tribes of earth	mill
Those who endure to	Angels	The good man
the end	The elect	The thief
Daniel	This generation	The faithful steward
Those in Judea	Noah	His lord
Those with child	Those eating and	An evil servant
The elect	drinking	Fellow servants
False Christs	Two in the field	The hypocrites

Places mentioned

The temple	The housetop
Mount of Olives	The desert
All the world	Secret chambers
The holy place	Heaven
Judaea	The field
The mountains	

Doctrines taught

The end of the age	The abomination of desolation
Religious deception	The elect
The Tribulation	The coming of Christ
The gospel of the kingdom	Watchfulness

1 And Jesus went out, and departed from the temple: and his disciples came to him for to shew him the buildings of the temple.

2 And Jesus said unto them, See ye not all these things? verily I say unto you, There shall not be left here one stone upon another, that shall not be thrown down.

3 And as he sat upon the mount of Olives, the disciples came unto him privately, saying, Tell us, when shall these things be? and what shall be the sign of thy coming, and of the end of the world?

Matthew 24 Exposition

I. The Beginning of Sorrows. vv. 1–14 [Mark 13:1–13; Luke 21:5–19].

"And Jesus went out from the temple complex, and his disciples came to him in order to show him the buildings of the temple complex" (v. 1). After His lament, the Lord Jesus left the temple for the last time in His earthly ministry. As He was leaving, the disciples wanted to show Him the many beautiful buildings and porticoes of the temple area.

"But Jesus said to them: Are you not seeing all these things? Truly I say to you there shall not be left here a stone upon a stone that shall not be thrown down" (v. 2). Josephus mentions that the stones of the temple were twenty-five cubits long (37 feet; *Antiquities of the Jews*, XV, 11, 3). The Lord was not interested in sightseeing. He was burdened with the knowledge of the utter destruction that would come on the temple area (in the siege of Titus, A.D. 70). Although Titus gave orders that the temple not be burned, in the fierceness of the fighting it was burned and did come to utter destruction (Josephus, *Wars of the Jews*, VI, 2–4). For a modern appraisal of the siege tactics used see Paul Kern, *Ancient Siege Warfare*, pp. 314–22.

24:1. For the word *temple complex* see Matt. 4:5 note.

The word *building* (οἰκοδομή) occurs only here in Matt.

24:2. For the verb *to leave, permit*, see Matt. 3:15 note.

For the verb *to throw down, destroy*, see Matt. 5:17 note.

The Lord uses the emphatic word *truly* (ἀμήν) 6 times in His prophetic teaching on Olivet (24:2, 34, 47; 25:12, 40, 45).

24:3. For the word *sign* see Matt. 12:38 note.

The word *coming* (παρουσία) occurs 4 times only in this chapter in Matt. (24:3, 27, 37, 39). The word is a major doctrine in the Epistles: I Cor. 15:23; I Thess. 2:19; 3:13; 4:15; 5:23; II Thess. 2:1, 8; II Pet. 3:4, 12; I John 2:28. For further discussion see ZPEB, "Parousia," IV, pp. 600–602; ISBE (1986), "Parousia," III, pp. 664–70; Elwell, ed., *Evangelical Dictionary of Biblical Theology*, "Second Coming of Christ," pp. 719–23; Walvoord, *Major Bible Prophecies*, pp. 249–304.

4 *And Jesus answered and said unto them, Take heed that no man deceive you.*
5 *For many shall come in my name, saying, I am Christ; and shall deceive many.*
6 *And ye shall hear of wars and rumours of wars: see that ye be not troubled: for all these things must come to pass, but the end is not yet.*

"But while he was sitting upon the Mount of Olives, the disciples came to him privately, saying, Tell us, when these things shall be, and what is the sign of your coming, and of the consummation of the age?" (v. 3). There is a beautiful view of the temple area from all along the Mount of Olives. The disciples ask two very serious questions, and the Lord responds with His greatest discourse on the prophetic future.

"And Jesus answered and said to them: Take heed that you be not deceived" (v. 4). The Lord's warning shows that there will be false teachers who attempt to deceive God's people about the future. Believers must pay special attention to the Lord's teaching here so that they will not be open to deception. The Lord Jesus leaves it up to the apostle Paul to reveal the rapture of the church (I Thess. 4:13–18). In this Olivet Discourse the Lord reveals what shall happen to His earthly people, the Jews, during the seven-year tribulation period that will follow.

"For many shall come in my name, saying: I am the Christ, and shall deceive many" (v. 5). There have been many false messiahs; we may be sure that the Devil will raise up more in the future, especially as the circumstances of the end draw near.

"But you are about to hear of wars and rumors of war; see that you be not troubled; for it is necessary to come to pass, but the end is not yet" (v. 6). Wars are a certainty. There cannot be peace on earth until the Prince of Peace comes to reign (Luke 2:14; Isa. 32:1, 17).

For the word *consummation, end,* see Matt. 13:39 note.

For a summary of the message see Mal Couch, *Dictionary of Premillennial Theology,* "Olivet Discourse," pp. 286–89; Harrison, ed., *The New Unger's Bible Dictionary,* "Olivet Discourse," pp. 941–42; A. C. Gaebelein, *The Olivet Discourse.*

24:4. For the verb *to see, take heed,* see Matt. 5:28 note.

For the verb *to deceive, lead astray,* see Matt. 18:12 note.

24:5. For the title *Christ, Messiah,* see Matt. 1:1 note.

24:6. The word *war* (πόλεμος) occurs twice in Matt. only in this verse.

The verb *to be troubled, alarmed* (θροέω) occurs only here in Matt.

For the word *end* see Matt. 10:22 note.

7 For nation shall rise against nation, and kingdom against kingdom: and there shall be famines, and pestilences, and earthquakes, in divers places.
8 All these are the beginning of sorrows.
9 Then shall they deliver you up to be afflicted, and shall kill you: and ye shall be hated of all nations for my name's sake.
10 And then shall many be offended, and shall betray one another, and shall hate one another.
11 And many false prophets shall rise, and shall deceive many.

"For nation shall rise up against nation and kingdom against kingdom, and there shall be famines and earthquakes in many places" (v. 7). The course of the age will be violent and catastrophic with war and natural disasters.

"All these things are the beginning of birth pangs" (v. 8). The Lord will bring in the kingdom reign out of the birth pangs of the Tribulation period.

"Then they shall deliver you unto tribulation and they shall kill you, and you shall be hated by all the nations on account of my name" (v. 9). The prejudice of the world against true believers will flame forth in bitter persecution.

"And then many shall be caused to stumble, and they shall betray one another, and they shall hate one another" (v. 10). Human passions shall be inflamed and the world of men shall hate and devour one another.

"And many false prophets shall arise and shall lead astray many" (v. 11). The Devil has always used false prophets to deceive mankind. In the days of Moses Balaam rose up against Israel (Num. 23:1ff.); in the time of Elijah the prophets of Baal deceived many (I Kings 18:19ff.). Religious deception shall reach its climax during the Tribulation period.

24:7. The word *famine* (λιμός) occurs only here in Matt.

For the word *earthquake* see Matt. 8:24 note.

24:8. The word *birth pang* (ὠδίν) occurs only here in Matt.

24:9. For the verb *to deliver over, betray* see Matt. 4:12 note.

For the verb *to kill* see Matt. 10:28 note.

For the word *tribulation* see Matt. 13:21 note. The word is used to describe the whole 7-year *tribulation* period. For a thorough discussion of the Tribulation see Pentecost, *Things to Come*, pp. 259–369. See also 24:21 note.

For the verb *to hate* see Matt. 5:43 note.

24:10. For the verb *to cause to stumble* see Matt. 5:29 note.

24:11. For the word *false prophet* see Matt. 7:15 note.

12 And because iniquity shall abound, the love of many shall wax cold.
13 But he that shall endure unto the end, the same shall be saved.
14 And this gospel of the kingdom shall be preached in all the world for a wit-
ness unto all nations; and then shall the end come.
15 When ye therefore shall see the abomination of desolation, spoken of by Dan-
iel the prophet, stand in the holy place, (whoso readeth, let him understand:)
16 Then let them which be in Judaea flee into the mountains:

"And because lawlessness shall be multiplied, the love of many shall be extinguished" (v. 12). Modern man wishes to throw off every restraint and do whatever he wants regardless of how it harms others. Love withers away in such a climate.

"But the one who endures to the end, this one shall be saved" (v. 13). Perseverance is part of salvation.

"And this gospel of the kingdom shall be preached in the whole in-habited earth for a testimony to all the nations, and then the end shall come" (v. 14). These words presuppose a great evangelization ministry in the face of persecution.

II. The Great Tribulation. vv. 15–28 [Mark 13:14–23; Luke 21:21–24].

"Whenever therefore you see the abomination of desolation, spoken through Daniel the prophet, having taken his stand in the holy place, (let the one who reads understand,) then let the ones who are in Judaea flee into the mountains" (vv. 15–16). *The abomination of desolation* is a refer-ence to the future wicked ruler who shall claim to be Messiah and shall make a covenant with the Jews for a seven-year period, "the tribulation period" (Dan. 9:26–27). Paul calls him "the man of lawlessness, the son

---

24:12. The word *love* (ἀγάπη) occurs only here in Matt. (116 times in the NT).
For the word *lawlessness* see Matt. 7:23 note.
The verb *to be extinguished* (ψύχω) occurs only here in the NT.
24:13. For the verb *to endure* see Matt. 10:22 note.
For the verb *to save* see Matt. 1:21 note.
24:14. For the verb *to preach* see Matt. 3:1 note.
For the word *gospel* see Matt. 4:23 note.
For the word *testimony* see Matt. 8:4 note.
24:15. The word *abomination* (βδέλυγμα) occurs only here in Matt. It conveys a sense of revulsion at wicked practices. The phraseology comes from Daniel (8:13; 9:27; 11:31; 12:11). For further discussion see ZPEB, "Abomination of Desolation," I, p. 20; ISBE (1979), "Desolating Sacrilege," I, pp. 930–31; Elwell, ed., *Evangelical Dictionary of Biblical*

17 Let him which is on the housetop not come down to take any thing out of his house:
18 Neither let him which is in the field return back to take his clothes.
19 And woe unto them that are with child, and to them that give suck in those days!
20 But pray ye that your flight be not in the winter, neither on the sabbath day:

of destruction, who resists and exalts himself over all things called god or worshipped, so that he sits in the sanctuary of God, manifesting himself that he is god" (II Thess. 2:3b–4). He is the person John calls *the beast out of the sea* (Rev. 13:1–8). At the end of the Tribulation period the Lord Jesus shall return in power and shall cast this beast into the lake of fire (Rev. 19:19–21). The Jews who resist this monster will have to run for their lives, for he will intend to slay them all.

"Let not the one who is on the housetop come down to take any of the things out of his house, and let not the one who is in the field turn back to get his garment" (vv. 17–18). It was the custom in ancient times to build houses with flat roofs that could be used as decks. If a person stops to get something out of his house, the troops of the Antichrist will get him. The only hope is to flee to the hill country to the south. David did the same thing in fleeing from Saul (I Sam. 22:1; 23:13–14).

"But woe to the ones who are with child and the ones who give suck in those days" (v. 19). Women who are expecting or have very young children will be easily caught by the troops of Antichrist.

"But be praying that your flight be not in winter or on the Sabbath" (v. 20). In winter there is no greenery to hide in and no food in the fields.

Theology, "Abomination That Causes Desolation, the," p. 2; Walvoord, *Major Bible Prophecies*, pp. 258–61. Pentecost noted "that the Lord, in that great eschatological passage dealing with the future of Israel (Matt. 24–25), speaks of a yet future fulfillment of Daniel's prophecy (Matt. 24:15) after His death," and records a list of biblical titles for this wicked person (*Things to Come*, pp. 172, 334). See also the author's *From Patmos to Paradise*, "The beast out of the sea," pp. 146–50.

Daniel is mentioned by name only here in the NT.

24:16. For the word *mountain* see Matt. 4:8 note.

24:17. For the word *housetop*, *roof* see Matt. 10:27 note.

24:18. For the word *garment* see Matt. 5:40 note.

24:20. For the word *winter* see Matt. 16:3 note.

For the word *Sabbath* see Matt. 12:1 note.

21 For then shall be great tribulation, such as was not since the beginning of the world to this time, no, nor ever shall be.
22 And except those days should be shortened, there should no flesh be saved: but for the elect's sake those days shall be shortened.
23 Then if any man shall say unto you, Lo, here is Christ, or there; believe it not.
24 For there shall arise false Christs, and false prophets, and shall shew great signs and wonders; insomuch that, if it were possible, they shall deceive the very elect.

On the Sabbath the observant Jew would take only a Sabbath day's journey, a short walk. A long distance run on the Sabbath would be very obvious.

"For then shall be great tribulation such as has not been from the beginning of the world until now, nor will it ever be [again]" (v. 21). This is the passage that gives the name to that time of future persecution, the Great Tribulation. It will be the last half of Daniel's seventieth week (Dan. 9:27).

"And except those days should be shortened, no flesh would be saved; but on account of the elect those days shall be shortened" (v. 22). That is, the persecution shall be cut short at three and a half years. The Antichrist will not be able to kill them all during that time.

"Then if anyone should say to you, Behold, here is the Christ, do not believe him" (v. 23). There will be world deception on every hand. When Christ actually returns, no one will be left in doubt. "Behold, he comes with clouds; and every eye shall see him" (Rev. 1:7*a*).

"For false Christs and false prophets shall arise and shall give great signs and wonders, so as to deceive, if possible, even the elect" (v. 24). The implication is that, by the grace of God, it will not be possible to deceive the elect.

24:21. For the word *tribulation* see Matt. 13:21 note. The *Great Tribulation* refers to the future attempt of the Antichrist to wipe out the entire Jewish race during the last half of the Tribulation. He will not succeed; the remnant will be rescued and enter the millennial reign. See vv. 29–31.

24:22. The verb *to shorten* (κολοβόω) occurs only twice in this verse in Matt.

For the word *elect, chosen,* see Matt. 22:14 note.

24:23. For the verb *to believe* see Matt. 8:13 note.

24:24. For the word *false prophet* see Matt. 7:15 note.

The word *false Christ* (ψευδόχριστος) occurs only here in Matt.

For the verb *to deceive* see Matt. 18:12 note.

25 Behold, I have told you before.
*26 Wherefore if they shall say unto you, Behold, he is in the desert; go not
forth: behold, he is in the secret chambers; believe it not.*
*27 For as the lightning cometh out of the east, and shineth even unto the west;
so shall also the coming of the Son of man be.*
28 For wheresoever the carcase is, there will the eagles be gathered together.
"Behold, I have told you beforehand" (v. 25). And in these words He has
not only told the apostles but has left a warning for all believers to the end
of the age. Every generation must be on guard against satanic deception.

"If therefore they say to you: Behold, he is in the desert, do not go out;
behold he is in the inner rooms, do not believe it" (v. 26). When the
Lord comes again, it will be with such celestial glory that no one will be
able to ignore Him. If anyone claims that He has come and is hiding, he
is a deceiver.

"For as the lightning comes from the east and shines unto the west, thus
shall be the coming of the Son of man" (v. 27). He shall come with glory
so splendid that it cannot be ignored.

"Wherever the body is, there the eagles shall be gathered together" (v.
28). The image portrays a carcass lying in the wilderness and the birds of
prey homing in on it. These are normally vultures, but eagles may also
eat carrion. Both are very large birds and can be seen at quite a distance.
The idea of the illustration is that wherever these circumstances exist,
the players will gather to fulfill their purpose. Broadus declares, "When
Jerusalem is ready for destruction, the Roman armies will gather and
destroy it; when the world lies awaiting the final appearance of Christ to
judgment, he will come" (*Matt.*, p. 489). Plainly there is both a near and
a far application of Christ's words. Toussaint argues, "Thus the nation is
and will be in such a spiritual condition that false prophets will be able
to feast on it as vultures consume the flesh of a dead and decaying body"
(*Matt.*, p. 276).

24:25. The verb *to tell beforehand* (προλέγω) occurs only here in Matt.

24:26. For the word *desert* see Matt. 3:1 note.

For the word *inner room* see Matt. 6:6 note.

24:27. The word *lightning* (ἀστραπή) occurs twice in Matt. (24:27; 28:3). It is significant
that these passages refer to the glory of the Lord and the glory of an angel.

24:28. The word *eagle* (ἀετός) occurs only here in Matt. For further discussion see
ZPEB, "Eagle," II, pp. 175–76; ISBE (1982), "Eagle," II, pp. 1–2; Porter, Christensen,
Schiermacker-Hansen, *Field Guide to the Birds of the Middle East*, pp. 34–37.

29 Immediately after the tribulation of those days shall the sun be darkened, and the moon shall not give her light, and the stars shall fall from heaven, and the powers of the heavens shall be shaken:
30 And then shall appear the sign of the Son of man in heaven: and then shall all the tribes of the earth mourn, and they shall see the Son of man coming in the clouds of heaven with power and great glory.

III. The Second Coming in Glory. vv. 29–31 [Mark 13:24–27; Luke 21:25–27].

"But immediately after the tribulation of those days

The sun shall be darkened,

And the moon shall not give her light,

And the stars shall fall from heaven,

And the powers of the heavens shall be shaken" (v. 29; Isa. 13:10; Ezek. 32:7; Isa. 34:4; 13:13).

The Lord is here conflating prophecies of His return in glory. The powers of the universe shall be shaken at the advent of the great King.

"And then the sign of the Son of man shall appear in heaven, and then all the tribes of the earth shall mourn, and they shall see the Son of man coming upon the clouds of heaven with power and great glory" (v. 30). Some think that the sign is the sign of the cross; others hold that it is the appearing itself that is the sign. But everyone on the face of the earth shall see the return of the Lord in glory. This promise is repeated in Revelation 1:7. Walvoord suggests that "in the course of a day, the earth will rotate and the entire world will be able to see the approach of Christ accompanied by the hosts of heaven" (*Matt.*, p. 190). Will there be tears of repentance or hopeless sorrow of condemnation? The verb *mourn, lament* assumes the latter.

"And he shall send his angels with a great trumpet and they shall gather together his elect from the four winds, from one boundary of heaven to

24:29. For the word *sun* see Matt. 5:45 note.

The word *moon* (σελήνη) occurs only here in Matt.

The word *light* (φέγγος) occurs only here in Matt. but is often used in extrabiblical literature for the silvery light of the moon (see Trench, *Synonyms*, pp. 163f.).

24:30. For the word *sign* see Matt. 12:38 note.

For the word *tribe* see Matt. 19:28 note.

For the verb *to mourn, lament* see Matt. 11:17 note.

For the word *glory* see Matt. 4:8 note.

31 And he shall send his angels with a great sound of a trumpet, and they shall gather together his elect from the four winds, from one end of heaven to the other. 32 Now learn a parable of the fig tree; When his branch is yet tender, and putteth forth leaves, ye know that summer is nigh: 33 So likewise ye, when ye shall see all these things, know that it is near, even at the doors.

another" (v. 31). Not one of His chosen ones shall be left behind. The saved of all ages will be gathered to see the establishment of the great kingdom reign. The glorified saints will reign over the earth from heaven for that thousand years (Rev. 20:4). The saints on earth will rule in the fear of God while the earth is being repopulated during the thousand years (Isa. 32:1, 16–20).

IV. The Parable of the Fig Tree. vv. 32–35 [Mark 13:28–31; Luke 21:29–33].

"But from the fig tree learn this parable: Whenever its branch becomes tender and it sprouts leaves, you know that summer is near" (v. 32). Observing nature shows a definite sequence of events. The fig tree is a good example of the suddenness of the coming of spring. One day there are bare branches with buds; the next day there are leaves the size of a man's hand unfolding. Some have thought that the budding of the fig tree represents the return of Israel to the Holy Land, but there are no such prophecies concerning a fig tree in the OT.

"Thus also whenever you see all these things, know that it is near, even at the doors" (v. 33). Believers should always be ready for the imminent coming of the Lord, but during the Tribulation period, the signs will be sharp.

24:31. The word *trumpet* (σάλπιγξ) occurs only here in Matt. The trumpet was used primarily for announcements rather than musical ensembles in the ancient world. See ZPEB, "Music, Musical Instruments," IV, pp. 311–24; ISBE (1986), "Music," [II, A], III, pp. 436–49.

The number 4 (τέσσαρες) occurs only here in Matt. See Introduction, "Numbers," p. xxii.

For the word *wind* see Matt. 7:25 note.

The word *boundary, end* (ἄκρον) occurs in this verse only in Matt.

24:32. For the word *fig tree* see Matt. 21:19 note.

The word *tender, ready to sprout* (ἁπαλός) occurs only here in Matt.

For the word *leaf* see Matt. 21:19 note.

The word *summer* (θέρος) occurs only here in Matt.

24:33. For the word *door* see Matt. 6:6 note.

34 Verily I say unto you, This generation shall not pass, till all these things be fulfilled.
35 Heaven and earth shall pass away, but my words shall not pass away.
36 But of that day and hour knoweth no man, no, not the angels of heaven, but my Father only.
37 But as the days of Noe were, so shall also the coming of the Son of man be.

"Truly I say to you that this generation shall not pass away until all these things come to pass" (v. 34). Again there is a twofold application. The people that the Lord Jesus was talking to would see the destruction of Jerusalem within forty years in A.D. 70, but the people in the Tribulation period will see the end within seven years. In this second sense the word *generation* would refer to the "race" of the Jews.

"The heaven and the earth shall pass away, but these my words shall never pass away" (v. 35). The psalmist declared, "For ever, O Lord, thy word is settled in heaven" (Ps. 119:89). The words of Jesus are forever hidden and cherished in the hearts of His people. As they assemble in heaven His people expect to see His words fulfilled. He will never disappoint them. The double negative *never* is very emphatic.

V. *The Need for Watchfulness. vv. 36–51 [Mark 13:32–37; Luke 21:33–36].*

"But concerning that day and hour no one knows, not even the angels of heaven, not even the Son, except the Father only" (v. 36). The Father will bring the age to a conclusion at the moment He alone knows. This is the will of the Trinity. This is the only thing revealed to us that the Father knows that the Son does not. All men and angels must stand in awe of the wisdom of the heavenly Father.

"For even as the days of Noah, thus shall be the coming of the Son of man" (v. 37). *The days of Noah* refers to the time before the disaster of the great Flood.

24:34. For the word *generation* (γενεά) see Matt. 1:17 note. On 24:34 see *Scofield Study Bible*, p. 1034; Walvoord, *Matt.*, pp. 192–93; ZPEB, "Generation," II, p. 678; Arndt and Gingrich, *Lexicon*, p. 153.

24:35. For the word *heaven* see Matt. 3:2 note.

24:36. For God *the Father* see Matt. 5:16 note.

24:37. Noah is mentioned twice in Matt. (24:37, 38). For background see ISBE (1986), "Noah," III, pp. 543–45; *Who's Who in the Bible*, "Noah," pp. 324–28.

*38 For as in the days that were before the flood they were eating and drinking, marrying and giving in marriage, until the day that Noe entered into the ark,
39 And knew not until the flood came, and took them all away; so shall also the coming of the Son of man be.
40 Then shall two be in the field; the one shall be taken, and the other left.
41 Two women shall be grinding at the mill; the one shall be taken, and the other left.*

"For as in those days which were before the flood they were eating and drinking, marrying and giving in marriage, until the day that Noah entered into the ark" (v. 38). Not only were people living normally and satisfying the flesh, gorging themselves, but the earth was also filled with violence (Gen. 6:11–13).

"And they knew not until the flood came and took them all away, thus shall be also the coming of the Son of man" (v. 39). The Flood was without precedent and totally unexpected. The coming of the Lord will be a similar shock to an unbelieving world.

"Then two shall be in the field; one shall be taken along and one shall be left" (v. 40). Walvoord argues that the one taken is taken in judgment; the one who is left is left to enter the kingdom (*Matt.*, p. 193). This is parallel to the preceding verse in which the flood took the wicked away whereas Noah was left to repopulate the earth.

"Two women shall be grinding with a hand mill; one shall be taken and one shall be left" (v. 41). One woman poured in the grain; the other rubbed with a stone on a larger stone. Many examples of both stones have been found by archaeologists.

24:38. The word *flood* (κατακλυσμός) occurs only twice in this context in Matt. 24:38, 39.

The verb *to eat* (τρώγω) occurs only here in Matt. The verb has the connotation of *gnawing, munching* like animals (Arndt and Gingrich, *Lexicon*, p. 836).

For the verb *to marry* see Matt. 5:32 note. The present tense of γαμέω may imply the polygamous unions of the sons of God (Gen. 6:2).

24:40. For the verb *to take along* see Matt. 1:20 note.

For the verb *to be left* see Matt. 3:15 note.

24:41. The verb *to grind* (ἀλήθω) occurs only here in Matt.

The *mill* (μύλος) refers to a hand mill, usually operated by two women; the ass-drawn mill mentioned in Matt. 18:6 would be a commercial operation. For illustrations see ZPEB, "Mill, Millstone," IV, pp. 226–27; ISBE (1986), "Mill, Millstone," III, pp. 355–56.

42 Watch therefore: for ye know not what hour your Lord doth come.
43 But know this, that if the goodman of the house had known in what watch the thief would come, he would have watched, and would not have suffered his house to be broken up.
44 Therefore be ye also ready: for in such an hour as ye think not the Son of man cometh.
45 Who then is a faithful and wise servant, whom his lord hath made ruler over his household, to give them meat in due season?

"Keep on watching therefore, because you know not what day your Lord is coming" (v. 42). The present tense verbs underscore the need for constant watchfulness. We must be ready for an any-moment return of the Lord. This passage is the foundation for the doctrine of the imminent return of Christ. His return is next in the order of prophetic events.

"But know this, that if the master of the house knew what watch the thief would come, he would have watched and not permitted his house to be dug through" (v. 43). If the householder knew a thief was coming, he would be armed and ready. The Lord here warns His people that He will come unexpectedly.

"On account of this you be also ready, because the Son of man comes in an hour you think not" (v. 44). The Lord will surprise the whole world by His coming. Believers must be alert and watching for Him. The world will be taken completely by surprise (I Thess. 5:2–4).

"Who then is the faithful and thoughtful slave whom his lord shall put in charge of his household to give them their food in season?" (v. 45). In the ancient world the steward over an estate was often a slave who was very intelligent and experienced in managing property.

24:42. The verb *to watch* (γρηγορέω) occurs 6 times in Matt. (24:42, 43; 25:13; 26:38, 40, 41). The believer has an imperative need to keep spiritually alert. For discussion see ISBE (1988), "Watch," IV, pp. 1022–23; ZPEB, "Watch," V, p. 901; Ryken, Wilhoit, and Longman, *Dictionary of Biblical Imagery*, "Watch, Watchman," pp. 928–29; Blackstone, *Jesus Is Coming*, "Watching," pp. 63ff.

24:43. For the word *thief* see Matt. 6:19 note.
For the verb *to dig through* see Matt. 6:19 note.

24:45. The word *faithful* (πιστός) occurs 5 times in Matt. (24:45; 25:21 [twice], 23 [twice]). It may express loyalty to God or to man. For discussion see ZPEB, "Faith, Faithfulness," II, pp. 479–91; ISBE (1982), "Faithful, Faithfulness," II, pp. 273–75; Elwell, ed., *Evangelical Dictionary of Biblical Theology*, "Faithfulness," pp. 239–40.
The verb *to put in charge of* (καθίστημι) occurs 4 times in Matt. (24:45, 47; 25:21, 23).

46 Blessed is that servant, whom his lord when he cometh shall find so doing.
47 Verily I say unto you, That he shall make him ruler over all his goods.
48 But and if that evil servant shall say in his heart, My lord delayeth his coming;
49 And shall begin to smite his fellowservants, and to eat and drink with the drunken;
50 The lord of that servant shall come in a day when he looketh not for him, and in an hour that he is not aware of,
51 And shall cut him asunder, and appoint him his portion with the hypocrites: there shall be weeping and gnashing of teeth.

"Blessed is that slave, whom, when his lord comes, shall find him so doing" (v. 46). He was often rewarded financially and given greater authority.

"Truly I say to you that he shall put him in charge of all of his possessions" (v. 47). That was a remarkable vote of confidence. Joseph is the great example of such a faithful slave (Gen. 39:1–6).

"But if the evil slave shall say in his heart, My lord delays his coming, and shall begin to beat his fellow slaves, and to eat and drink with the drunken" (vv. 48–49). Sin always begins in the heart, and that leads to external acts of wrongdoing (Matt. 15:19).

"The lord of that slave shall come in a day in which he shall not expect and in an hour which he knows not" (v. 50). They will be engrossed in their sin and totally unaware of the will of the Lord.

"And he shall cut him in pieces and appoint him his portion with the hypocrites; there shall be weeping and grinding of teeth" (v. 51). The wicked try to appear better than they are, but God knows their hearts and shall give them exactly what they deserve. The weeping and grinding of teeth manifest their despair at realizing that they shall never get out of hell.

24:48. The verb *to delay* (χρονίζω) occurs twice in Matt. (24:48; 25:5).
For the word *heart* see Matt. 5:8 note.
24:49. The verb *to beat* (τύπτω) occurs twice in Matt. (24:49; 27:30).
The verb *to be drunk* (μεθύω) occurs only here in Matt.
24:50. For the verb *to expect, wait for*, see Matt. 11:3 note.
24:51. The verb *to cut in pieces* (διχοτομέω) occurs only here in Matt.
For the word *hypocrite* see Matt. 6:2 note.
For the word *appoint, put*, see Matt. 5:15 note.
For the word *weeping* see Matt. 2:18 note.
For *grinding of teeth* see Matt. 8:12 note.

Practical Applications from Matthew 24

1. Asking the Lord for help in understanding Scripture always brings an answer (v. 3). The psalmist prayed, "Open thou mine eyes, that I may behold wondrous things out of thy law" (Ps. 119:18). He could also say, "Thy word is a lamp unto my feet, and a light unto my path" (Ps. 119:105).

2. Believers must be on their guard against false teachers (vv. 4–5). "Beloved, believe not every spirit, but keep on testing the spirits whether they are of God, because many false prophets have gone out into the world" (I John 4:1).

3. Wars and disasters shall arise again and again; they are not signs of the end (vv. 6–7). "In the world you shall have tribulation: but be of a good cheer; I have overcome the world" (John 16:33b).

4. Worldwide evangelism is the will of God (v. 14). Believers need to be witnesses for Christ (Acts 1:8).

5. Flight from persecution is proper for believers (v. 16). The apostles fled when they were persecuted (Acts 14:5–7).

6. People should not listen when men claim to have found Christ on earth (v. 23). When He returns in glory, all will know it (v. 27). Until then no one on earth can see Him (I Tim. 6:15–16).

7. No one should try to guess the time of Christ's return (v. 36). God the Father alone decides that (Acts 1:7).

8. Believers should always be watching and ready for the Lord's return (v. 42). The Rapture may occur at any moment (I Thess. 4:16–18).

9. A faithful and wise servant should be busy in his work and ready for an any-moment return of his lord (vv. 45–46). "Be patient therefore, brethren, unto the coming of the Lord" (James 5:7a).

Prayer

Lord Jesus, thank You for Your promise to come again in victory. Keep us faithful until we see You face to face. Help us to serve You from the heart until You take us to Yourself. Amen.

MATTHEW 25

VIRGINS AND TALENTS

Persons
Jesus

Persons referred to

Ten virgins

The Bridegroom

Foolish virgins

Wise virgins

Those that sell

The Son of Man

A man who travels

His servants

Moneychangers

Holy angels

All nations

The blessed on His right

The cursed on His left

The righteous

My brethren

The Devil

Angels

Places mentioned

A place of marriage

A place of merchandise

A far country

The earth

Outer darkness

Everlasting fire

Prison

Doctrines taught

The kingdom of heaven

Wisdom

Foolishness

Watchfulness

The coming of the Lord

Stewardship

Faithfulness

Joy

Coming of Christ

Judgment of the nations

Righteousness

The curse

Everlasting fire

Life eternal

1 Then shall the kingdom of heaven be likened unto ten virgins, which took their lamps, and went forth to meet the bridegroom.
2 And five of them were wise, and five were foolish.
3 They that were foolish took their lamps, and took no oil with them:
4 But the wise took oil in their vessels with their lamps.

Matthew 25 Exposition

I. The Ten Virgins. vv. 1–13.

"Then the kingdom of the heavens shall be like ten virgins, who took their torches and went forth to meet the bridegroom" (v. 1). The Lord Jesus is emphasizing the need for spiritual watchfulness in the light of His any moment return. The scene of the parable is plainly a torch-light procession in the evening. This custom is still practiced in places in the Middle East. The two families met at the house of the bride to determine the dowry and other marriage details, and when all things were settled, they went in a torch-light procession from the house of the bride to the house of the groom, where the marriage would be performed and the banquet was waiting. Along the way, friends of the families would join the procession.

"But five of them were foolish and five were wise" (v. 2). The word *foolish* does not mean merely *empty-headed*, but *wrong-headed*. "Fools hate knowledge" (Prov. 1:22*b*). "The fool hath said in his heart, There is no God" (Ps. 14:1). The Lord Jesus has already characterized the Pharisees as fools (Matt. 23:16–22). He charged them with willful rebellion, not mere stupidity. "In Scripture the 'fool' primarily is the person who casts off the fear of God and thinks and acts as if he could safely disregard the eternal

---

25:1. For the word *virgin* see Matt. 1:23 note.

The word *torch* (λαμπάς) occurs 5 times in this context only in Matt. (vv. 1, 3, 4, 7, 8). For background see ZPEB, "Torch," V, p. 780; ISBE (1988), "Torch," IV, pp. 879–80; Morris, *Matt.*, p. 620, note 5. Moulton and Milligan, *Vocabulary*, pp. 369–70, gives an example of the word used in reference to a torch race. See also Joachim Jeremias, "*Lampades* in Matt. 25:1–13," in J. McDowell Richards, ed., *Soli Deo Gloria*, pp. 83–87. Although we get the English word *lamp* from this Greek word, it is not its primary meaning.

25:2. For the word *foolish* see Matt. 5:22 note.

For the word *wise, thoughtful*, see Matt. 7:24 note and Matt. 11:19 note.

25:3. The word *oil* (ἔλαιον) occurs 3 times in this context only in Matt. (25:3, 4, 8). It refers to olive oil. For further discussion see Walvoord, *The Holy Spirit*, p. 20; ZPEB, "Oil," IV, pp. 513–15; ISBE (1986), "Oil," III, pp. 585–86; Butler, ed., *Holman Bible Dictionary*, "Oil," p. 1043.

5 *While the bridegroom tarried, they all slumbered and slept.*
6 *And at midnight there was a cry made, Behold, the bridegroom cometh; go ye out to meet him.*
7 *Then all those virgins arose, and trimmed their lamps.*
8 *And the foolish said unto the wise, Give us of your oil; for our lamps are gone out.*

principles of God's righteousness' (Harrison, ed., *New Unger's Bible Dictionary*, p. 438).

"For the foolish ones took no oil with them" (v. 3). Small vessels for oil no bigger than a golf ball have been found.

"But the wise ones took oil in the vessels with their torches" (v. 4). They were making adequate preparation for what they knew they would need.

"But while the bridegroom delayed, they all grew drowsy and were sleeping" (v. 5). No doubt the families were haggling over the terms of the dowry!

"But at midnight the cry came, Behold the bridegroom! Go out to meet him" (v. 6). Now the festivities can begin.

"Then all the virgins arose and set their torches in order" (v. 7). Lighting them would set them in order. We must picture them using flint and iron to light them by sparks. Dry cloth on a torch does not catch fire easily. But those who were thoughtful put olive oil on the cloth so that the torch would catch fire quickly. They were soon ready to go. See the description in Jeremias's article in *Soli Deo Gloria*, p. 84.

"But the foolish ones said to the wise ones: Give us of your oil because our torches are being quenched" (v. 8). The picture is of the virgins whacking the flint and iron so that sparks hit the torch, but the torches glow for a moment and then go out. As every Boy Scout knows, you can grow old and die while waiting for a fire to catch that way.

25:4. The word *vessel* (ἀγγεῖον) occurs only here in Matt. See Matt. 13:48 for a cognate.
25:5. For the word *bridegroom* see Matt. 9:15 note.
The verb *to grow drowsy* (νυστάζω) occurs only here in Matt.
For the verb *to sleep* see Matt. 8:24 note.
25:6. The word *cry, shout* (κραυγή) occurs only here in Matt.
The word *meeting* (ἀπάντησις) occurs only here in Matt.
25:7. For the verb *to set in order* see Matt. 12:44.

9 But the wise answered, saying, Not so; lest there be not enough for us and you: but go ye rather to them that sell, and buy for yourselves.
10 And while they went to buy, the bridegroom came; and they that were ready went in with him to the marriage: and the door was shut.
11 Afterward came also the other virgins, saying, Lord, Lord, open to us.
12 But he answered and said, Verily I say unto you, I know you not.

"But the wise answer and say: No, lest there be not sufficient for us and you; rather go to the merchant and buy for yourselves" (v. 9). The wise virgins declare plainly that they will not sacrifice their opportunity to be in the procession just because the foolish ones did not make adequate preparation. At that time of night the merchant would not be happy to see them (Luke 11:8).

"But while they went to buy, the bridegroom came, and the ones who were ready went in with him into the wedding, and the door was locked" (v. 10). This is strong emphasis on the necessity of being ready for the coming of the Lord. There will be no second chance. James warns, "Behold, the judge stands before the door" (James 5:9b). This plainly can be applied both to the Rapture (I Thess. 4:16–18) and to the revelation in glory (Rev. 19:11–15).

"But afterwards the remaining virgins come, saying: Lord, lord, open to us" (v. 11). When the willful and the wicked deign to think of getting right with God, it will be too late. The parable remains a convicting reminder that the sinner must come to God when he is invited, not when he pleases. When the prophet cries, "Ho, every one that thirsteth, come ye to the waters," he also adds, "Seek ye the Lord while he may be found; call ye upon him while he is near" (Isa. 55:1, 6).

"But he answered and said: Truly I say to you, I know you not" (v. 12). The master of the house does not open to strangers. The Lord of the universe will open His door only to those who submit to His dear Son. "The Lord knoweth the thoughts of man, that they are vanity" (Ps. 94:11).

25:9. The verb *to be sufficient* (ἀρκέω) occurs only here in Matt.

For the verb *to be a merchant, sell*, see Matt. 10:29 note.

25:10. For the word *ready* see Matt. 22:4 note.

For the word *wedding* see Matt. 22:2 note. The author has been an observer of weddings in the Middle East. They are still held at night, and the eating, singing, and dancing go on into the night.

For the verb *to shut, lock*, see Matt. 6:6 note.

13 Watch therefore, for ye know neither the day nor the hour wherein the Son of man cometh.
14 For the kingdom of heaven is as a man travelling into a far country, who called his own servants, and delivered unto them his goods.
15 And unto one he gave five talents, to another two, and to another one; to every man according to his several ability; and straightway took his journey.
16 Then he that had received the five talents went and traded with the same, and made them other five talents.
17 And likewise he that had received two, he also gained other two.

"Be watching therefore, because you know not the day nor the hour" (v. 13). The present tense emphasizes the constant need for vigilant watchfulness. The believer cannot know the future, but the Lord does. The apostle Paul urges, "Therefore then let us not be sleeping as the rest, but let us be watching and be sober" (I Thess. 5:6).

II. The Talents. vv. 14–30.

"For even as a man who is leaving the country called his own slaves and delivered to them his own possessions" (v. 14). He trusts them to care for his goods in his absence.

"And to one he gave five talents, but to another two, but to another one, each one according to his ability, and departed" (v. 15). In his absence the slaves had considerable freedom, but only as custodians of their lord's possessions.

"Immediately the one who had received five talents went and worked with them and gained five other talents" (v. 16). He lost no time in using his lord's talents to gain good profit for him.

"Likewise the one who received the two gained other two" (v. 17). This passage is one of the most encouraging in all of Scripture for Christian service. The important thing for believers is not the quantity of the gifts, but the faithfulness in using them for the Lord.

25:11. For the verb *to open* see Matt. 2:11 note.

25:13. For the verb *to watch* see Matt. 24:42 note.

25:14. For the verb *to depart, leave the country*, see Matt. 21:33 note.

25:15. For the word *talent* see Matt. 18:24 note.

25:16. For the verb *to work* see Matt. 7:23 note.

For the verb *to gain* see Matt. 16:26 note.

18 But he that had received one went and digged in the earth, and hid his lord's money.
19 After a long time the lord of those servants cometh, and reckoneth with them.
20 And so he that had received five talents came and brought other five talents, saying, Lord, thou deliveredst unto me five talents: behold, I have gained beside them five talents more.
21 His lord said unto him, Well done, thou good and faithful servant: thou hast been faithful over a few things, I will make thee ruler over many things: enter thou into the joy of thy lord.

"But he who had received the one went and dug in the earth and hid his lord's silver" (v. 18). Instead of thinking of his lord's benefit as the other two did, he thinks only of self-protection and his own ease. There are many people who never have a thought of how God can be benefited by their life and service.

"But after a long time the lord of those slaves comes and settles the account with them" (v. 19). There will be an account given by every human being. Paul calls the judgment for believers "the judgment seat of Christ" (II Cor. 5:10). The judgment for the lost is the Great White Throne judgment (Rev. 20:11–15).

"And the one who had received the five talents came and brought five other talents, saying, Lord, you entrusted five talents to me; behold, I gained five other talents" (v. 20). He had worked faithfully and had managed to double his lord's investment.

"His lord said to him: Well done, good and faithful slave; you were faithful over a few things; I shall make you ruler over many things: enter into the joy of your lord" (v. 21). What a privilege to be able to bring joy to the Lord, and to be able to share in it! He also opens up the vista of even larger service in the future.

25:18. For the verb *to dig* see Matt. 21:33 note.

For the verb *to hide* see Matt. 5:14 note.

The word *silver* (ἀργύριον) occurs 9 times in Matt. (25:18, 27; 26:15; 27:3, 5, 6, 9; 28:12, 15). For background see ISBE (1988), "Silver," IV, pp. 512–13; ZPEB, "Silver," V, pp. 437–38; Ryken, Wilhoit, and Longman, *Dictionary of Biblical Imagery*, "Silver," pp.791–92; Frederick Pough, *A Field Guide to Rocks and Minerals*, p. 82; Charles Chesterman, *Audubon Society Field Guide to North American Rocks and Minerals*, p. 347–48.

25:19. For the verb *to settle* see Matt. 18:23 note.

25:20. For the verb *to bring to* see Matt. 2:11 note.

25:21. For the word *faithful* see Matt. 24:45 note.

22 He also that had received two talents came and said, Lord, thou deliveredst unto me two talents: behold, I have gained two other talents beside them.
23 His lord said unto him, Well done, good and faithful servant; thou hast been faithful over a few things, I will make thee ruler over many things: enter thou into the joy of thy lord.
24 Then he which had received the one talent came and said, Lord, I knew thee that thou art an hard man, reaping where thou hast not sown, and gathering where thou hast not strawed:
25 And I was afraid, and went and hid thy talent in the earth: lo, there thou hast that is thine.

"But the one who had received the two talents came and said: Lord, you entrusted two talents to me; behold I gained two other talents" (v. 22). He had fewer gifts, but he was equally faithful with his trust.

"His lord said to him: Well done, good and faithful slave; you were faithful in a few things; I shall make you ruler over many things; enter into the joy of your lord" (v. 23). He gets the very same commendation that the other slave got. He was equally faithful to his trust. The main thing in all Christian service is not the quantity of the gifts but the faithfulness of the servant. The apostle Paul exhorts, "Let a man thus account us as ministers of Christ and stewards of the mysteries of God. Moreover, it is required in stewards that a man be found faithful" (I Cor. 4:1–2).

"But the one also who had received the one talent came and said: Lord, I knew you that you are a hard man, reaping where you did not sow and gathering where you did not scatter" (v. 24). These words show that he completely misunderstood the nature of God. David expressed it well, "The Lord is merciful and gracious, slow to anger, and plenteous in mercy" (Ps. 103:8).

"And I was afraid and went and hid your talent in the earth; behold, you have what is yours" (v. 25). Every master expected to receive a profit from an investment, but here the slave saw to it that there was no profit at all, just the original sum returned. Most of mankind treats God in just that way.

25:24. The word *hard, harsh* (σκληρός) occurs only here in Matt. Trench notes that it expresses *roughness* and *intractability* such as Nabal manifested (*Synonyms*, p. 47).
The verb *to scatter* (διασκορπίζω) occurs 3 times in Matt. (25:24, 26; 26:31).
25:25. For the verb *to be afraid* see Matt. 1:20 note.

26 His lord answered and said unto him, Thou wicked and slothful servant, thou knewest that I reap where I sowed not, and gather where I have not strawed:
27 Thou oughtest therefore to have put my money to the exchangers, and then at my coming I should have received mine own with usury.
28 Take therefore the talent from him, and give it unto him which hath ten talents.
29 For unto every one that hath shall be given, and he shall have abundance: but from him that hath not shall be taken away even that which he hath.

"But his lord answered and said to him: Evil and lazy slave, you knew that I harvested where I did not sow, and gathered where I did not scatter" (v. 26). The lord snares the evil slave in his own words. The slave had not acted on his wrong belief. Paul urges believers to be diligent rather than *lazy* (Rom. 12:11a).

"It was necessary for you, therefore, to give my silver to the bankers, and when I came I would receive my own with interest" (v. 27). The *bankers* were the ancient equivalent of loan sharks (there was no cap on interest rates). The evil slave could have gotten much interest for his lord, but he did not care to do so.

"Take therefore the talent from him and give it to the one who has the ten talents" (v. 28). This is what actually happens. No matter how fiercely the lost clutch their worldly goods and possessions, they leave them all behind when they leave this world. But God promises His people, "He that overcomes shall inherit all things" (Rev. 21:7a).

"For to everyone who has it shall be given and he shall have more than enough, but to the one who does not have, even what he does have shall be taken away from him" (v. 29). Everyone who has spiritual blessings from God will get more and more, but whoever does not have God's blessing will lose all he now has (material goods and possessions). There are no pockets in shrouds.

25:26. For the word *evil* see Matt. 5:37 note.

The word *lazy* (ὀκνηρός) occurs only here in Matt.

25:27. The word *banker, moneychanger* (τραπεζίτης) occurs only here in the NT.

Moneychangers operated from tables (Matt. 21:12). The word *table* (τράπεζα) is still the modern Greek word for *bank*. Matthew knew them from people who used their services to pay their taxes.

25:29. For the verb *to have more than enough, abundance* (περισσεύω) see Matt. 5:20 note.

*30 And cast ye the unprofitable servant into outer darkness: there shall be
weeping and gnashing of teeth.*
*31 When the Son of man shall come in his glory, and all the holy angels with
him, then shall he sit upon the throne of his glory:*
*32 And before him shall be gathered all nations: and he shall separate them one
from another, as a shepherd divideth his sheep from the goats:*

"And cast the worthless slave into outer darkness; there shall be weeping and grinding of teeth" (v. 30). The Lord warned of the deep darkness
within the evil servant (Matt. 6:23). His surroundings will one day match
the darkness within. The glory of Christian service is to be useful in meeting the needs of the church (Acts 6:3).

III. The Second Coming and the Judgment of the Nations. vv. 31–46.

"But whenever the Son of man shall come in his glory and all the angels
with him, then shall he sit upon the throne of his glory" (v. 31). At the
conclusion of the seven-year tribulation period, the Lord Jesus will return to judge the nations. The judgment of Israel is treated more fully in
Ezekiel 20:34–38. Here the emphasis falls on the Gentile nations. John
describes the whole scene in detail (Rev. 19:11–21).

"And before him shall be gathered all nations, and he shall separate
them one from another, even as the shepherd separates the sheep from
the goats" (v. 32). This judgment will settle the question of who will
enter the great millennial reign. The Great Shepherd calls His sheep and
they come. This judgment should not be confused with the Great White
Throne judgment, which occurs a thousand years later (Rev. 20:7–15).

25:30. The word *worthless, unprofitable* (ἀχρεῖος) occurs only here in Matt.
For the word *darkness* see Matt. 4:16 note.

25:31. For the word *glory* see Matt. 4:8 note.

For the word *throne* see Matt. 5:34 note.

25:32. For the word *Gentile, nation,* see Matt. 4:15 note.

For the verb *to separate* see Matt. 13:49 note.

For the word *shepherd* see Matt. 9:36 note.

For the word *sheep* see Matt. 7:15 note.

The word *goat* (ἔριφος) occurs only here in Matt. For discussion see *Fauna and Flora of
the Bible,* United Bible Societies, "Goat," pp. 36–38; ZPEB, "Goat," II, pp. 739–41; ISBE
(1982), "Goat," II, pp. 491–92; Ryken, Wilhoit, and Longman, *Dictionary of Biblical
Imagery,* "Goat," pp. 331–32.

33 And he shall set the sheep on his right hand, but the goats on the left.
34 Then shall the King say unto them on his right hand, Come, ye blessed of
my Father, inherit the kingdom prepared for you from the foundation of the
world:
35 For I was an hungred, and ye gave me meat: I was thirsty, and ye gave me
drink: I was a stranger, and ye took me in:
36 Naked, and ye clothed me: I was sick, and ye visited me: I was in prison,
and ye came unto me.

"And he shall set the sheep on his right hand, but the little goats on his left" (v. 33). Does the diminutive imply that these wicked people who strutted so proudly on earth are no more than "little goats" before him?

"Then the king shall say to the ones on his right hand: Come, you who are blessed of my Father, inherit the kingdom that has been prepared for you from the foundation of the world" (v. 34). The blessing of God is a powerful thing. God has the kingdom prepared and waiting for His people.

"For I was hungry and you gave me to eat; I was thirsty and you gave me to drink; I was a stranger and you took me in; naked and you clothed me; I was sick and you visited me; I was in prison and you came to me" (vv. 35–36). In the ancient world it took some degree of courage as well as compassion to visit someone in prison. It was a harsh place of suffering. The redeemed saints are stunned to hear this praise from the Lord. They have no memory of such deeds.

25:33. The word *little goat* (ἐρίφιον) occurs only here in the NT. Vincent declares that the diminutive expresses contempt (*Word Studies*, I, p. 135).

25:34. For the verb *to bless* see Matt. 14:19 note.

For the verb *to inherit* see Matt. 5:5 note.

For the word *kingdom* see Matt. 3:2 note.

For the word *prepare* see Matt. 3:3 note.

25:35. For the verb *to be hungry* see Matt. 4:2 note.

For the verb *to eat* see Matt. 6:25 note.

For the verb *to be thirsty* see Matt. 5:6 note.

For the verb *to give to drink* see Matt. 10:42 note.

The word *stranger* (ξένος) occurs 5 times in Matt. (25:35, 38, 43, 44; 27:7).

For the verb *to take in, gather*, see Matt. 2:4 note.

25:36. The word *naked* (γυμνός) occurs 4 times in Matt. (25:36, 38, 43, 44).

For the verb *to be sick* see Matt. 10:8 note.

For the word *prison* see Matt. 5:25 note.

37 Then shall the righteous answer him, saying, Lord, when saw we thee an hungred, and fed thee? or thirsty, and gave thee drink?
38 When saw we thee a stranger, and took thee in? or naked, and clothed thee?
39 Or when saw we thee sick, or in prison, and came unto thee?
40 And the King shall answer and say unto them, Verily I say unto you, Inasmuch as ye have done it unto one of the least of these my brethren, ye have done it unto me.
41 Then shall he say also unto them on the left hand, Depart from me, ye cursed, into everlasting fire, prepared for the devil and his angels:

"Then the righteous shall answer him, saying, Lord, when did we see you hungry and fed you, or thirsty and gave you drink?" (v. 37). They could not imagine supplying anything to such a glorious Lord.

"But when did we see you a stranger and took you in, or naked and clothed you? But when did we see you sick or in prison and came to you?" (vv. 38–39). The Lord is beyond the need for help by any human being.

"And the King shall say to them: Truly I say to you, inasmuch as you did it for one of the least of these my brothers, you did it for me" (v. 40). The King takes all that they have done for the benefit of His people as done for Him. This is grace beyond all expectation.

"Then shall he say to the ones on his left hand: Depart from me, you cursed ones, into the eternal fire that has been prepared for the devil and his angels" (v. 41). God has prepared the gehenna of fire for the Devil and his demons, but all people who share in his sinful rebellion against God will also share in his punishment. Lost people often do not understand the seriousness of their rebellion against God. Every sin is ultimately directed against God. He wills what is right and good.

25:37. For the verb *to feed* (τρέφω) see Matt. 6:26 note.

25:40. For the word *least* see Matt. 2:6 note.

For the word *brother* see Matt. 1:2 note.

25:41. The verb *to curse* (καταράομαι) occurs only here in Matt. A curse was a visitation of divine judgment. The first curse in the Bible was upon the serpent (Gen. 3:14–15). The law pronounced curses upon the wicked (Deut. 27:15–26). For discussion see ISBE (1979), "Curse," I, pp. 837–38; ZPEB, "Curse," I, pp. 1045–46; Elwell, ed., *Evangelical Dictionary of Biblical Theology*, "Curse," p. 139; Ryken, Wilhoit, and Longman, *Dictionary of Biblical Imagery*, "Curse," pp. 186–87.

For the word *fire* see Matt. 3:10 note.

For the word *devil* see Matt. 4:1 note.

42 For I was an hungred, and ye gave me no meat: I was thirsty, and ye gave
me no drink:
43 I was a stranger, and ye took me not in: naked, and ye clothed me not:
sick, and in prison, and ye visited me not.
44 Then shall they also answer him, saying, Lord, when saw we thee an
hungred, or athirst, or a stranger, or naked, or sick, or in prison, and did not
minister unto thee?
45 Then shall he answer them, saying, Verily I say unto you, Inasmuch as ye
did it not to one of the least of these, ye did it not to me.
46 And these shall go away into everlasting punishment: but the righteous into
life eternal.

"For I was hungry and you did not give me to eat; I was thirsty and you
did not give me to drink; I was a stranger and you did not take me in;
naked and you did not clothe me; sick and in prison, and you did not visit
me" (vv. 42–43). God is opposed to all unjust or unethical situations.
Things that are done against helpless people He takes as done against
Himself.

"Then they themselves shall also answer, saying, Lord, when did we see
you hungry, or thirsty, or a stranger, or naked, or sick, or in prison and did
not minister to you?" (v. 44). They had no genuine relationship with God
at all. They would have been glad to curry favor with Him if they had
thought it would help.

"Then he shall answer to them, saying: Truly I say to you, For as much as
you did it not to one of the least of these, you did it not to me" (v. 45).
God is merciful toward needy people and seeks to help them, but these
wicked people never thought of kindness to the needy.

"And these shall go away into eternal punishment, but the righteous into
eternal life" (v. 46). Wicked people often hope that when they die, Poof!
They are gone. Once created, however, existence for a human being is
unending. The wicked have everlasting punishment awaiting; the righteous, everlasting life. Every human being must live somewhere forever.

25:43. The word *sick* (ἀσθενής) occurs 3 times in Matt. (25:43, 44; 26:41).

25:44. For the verb *to serve, minister to*, see Matt. 4:11 note.

25:46. The word *punishment* (κόλασις) occurs only here in Matt. The eternal punishment
of wicked people is a divinely revealed truth. For discussion see ZPEB, "Punishment,
Everlasting," IV, pp. 954–57; Shedd, *The Doctrine of Endless Punishment*; ISBE (1986),
"Punish," III, pp. 1051–54; Elwell, ed., *Evangelical Dictionary of Biblical Theology*,
"Punishment," pp. 659–60; Ryken, Wilhoit, and Longman, *Dictionary of Biblical Imagery*,
"Crime and Punishment," pp. 182–83.

For the word *life* see Matt. 7:14 note.

John saw that final scene: "And the devil that deceived them was cast into the lake of fire and sulfur . . . and whosoever was not found written in the book of life was cast into the lake of fire" (Rev. 20:10, 15).

Practical Applications from Matthew 25

1. Every true believer needs wisdom from God (v. 2). If anyone lacks wisdom, he should ask God for it (James 1:5).
2. Oil was a symbol of the Holy Spirit (v. 4). The tabernacle and the priests were anointed with oil (Exod. 40:9–16).
3. The Lord Jesus will return unexpectedly (v. 6). "The coming of the Lord draws near" (James 5:8b).
4. People must be ready for Him when He comes (v. 10). "For the Lord himself shall descend from heaven with a shout. . . . then we who are alive and remain shall be caught up together . . . to meet the Lord in the air" (I Thess. 4:16a–17a).
5. No one gets into heaven a little late (vv. 11–12). Jesus invites men to come to Him, but they must come when He calls (Matt. 11:28).
6. Believers should maintain a watchful attitude, waiting for the coming of the Lord (v. 13). "Therefore let us not sleep as the rest, but let us keep watching and be sober" (I Thess. 5:6).
7. Different servants have different abilities, but all can be equally faithful (v. 15). "And the things that you heard from me through many witnesses, these things commit to faithful men, who shall be able to teach others also" (II Tim. 2:2).
8. Burying the Lord's gift is a way of being ungrateful (v. 18). "O man of God . . . follow after righteousness, godliness, faith, love, patience, meekness" (II Tim. 6:11b).
9. At the end, all mankind shall be divided into sheep, who belong to the Lord, and goats, who do not (vv. 31–32). Sheep follow their shepherd; goats go their own way. "My sheep hear my voice, and I know them, and they follow me: and I give unto them eternal life" (John 10:27–28a).
10. When the believer helps fellow saints, the Lord takes it as done to Him (vv. 37–40). "For not he that commends himself is approved, but whom the Lord commends" (II Cor. 10:18).

Prayer

Lord Jesus, help us to live for You and to serve You faithfully so that we may be ready to meet You at Your coming. Make us good stewards that we may be among Your sheep in the world to come. Amen.

MATTHEW 26

ARREST AND TRIAL

Persons

Jesus

His disciples

Chief priests

Scribes

Elders

Caiaphas

A woman with ointment

Judas Iscariot

Peter

Two sons of Zebedee

A multitude with swords

A servant of the high priest

Two false witnesses

A damsel

Another maid

They that stood by

Persons referred to

Simon the leper

The poor

The man of the Passover house

The Father

Sinners

Twelve legions of angels

The prophets

The servants

False witnesses

Places mentioned

Palace of the high priest

Bethany

House of Simon the leper

The whole world

The house of the supper

Mount of Olives

Galilee

Gethsemane

The house of Caiaphas

The temple

1 And it came to pass, when Jesus had finished all these sayings, he said unto his disciples,
2 Ye know that after two days is the feast of the passover, and the Son of man is betrayed to be crucified.
3 Then assembled together the chief priests, and the scribes, and the elders of the people, unto the palace of the high priest, who was called Caiaphas,
4 And consulted that they might take Jesus by subtilty, and kill him.

Matthew 26 Exposition

I. The Plot Against Jesus. vv. 1–5 [Mark 14:1–2; Luke 22:1–2].

"And it came to pass when Jesus had ended all these words, he said to his disciples, Know that after two days is the Passover, and the Son of man is betrayed to be crucified" (vv. 1–2). This was a very clear announcement and warning of the coming betrayal. The Lord had warned them before of what was going to happen (Matt. 20:17–19). But the disciples had seen Him get out of all other traps. They could not imagine the Lord's failing to bring in the kingdom. Nor could they imagine that His death was going to be the source of life to all who will believe.

"Then the chief priests and the elders of the people gathered together in the courtyard of the high priest, who was called Caiaphas" (v. 3). The courtyard, or atrium, was large enough to assemble a sizeable group.

"And they took counsel together in order that they might seize Jesus by deceit, and kill him" (v. 4). They feared to do anything in public because the people held Him to be a prophet and a healer. But by deceit and

---

26:1. For the verb *to end, finish*, see Matt. 7:28 note. The Great Teacher had brought His instruction to an end.

Does the phrase *all these words* refer to the conclusion of the Olivet Discourse or to the end of Jesus' teaching ministry? The 2 ideas coincide here.

26:2. The word *Passover* (πάσχα) occurs 4 times in Matt. (26:2, 17, 18, 19). It was the most important festival for the Jew and is filled with meaning for Christians because of Christ's death during this season. For discussion see ZPEB, "Passover," IV, pp. 604–11; ISBE (1988), "Passover," IV, pp. 675–79; Ryken, Wilhoit, and Longman, *Dictionary of Biblical Imagery*, "Passover," pp. 629–30.

This is the chapter of betrayal; the verb *to betray* occurs ten times in this chapter (vv. 2, 15, 16, 21, 23, 24, 25, 45, 46, 48). See Matt. 4:12 note.

26:3. The word *courtyard* (αὐλή) occurs only 3 times in Matt. (26:3, 58, 69).

Caiaphas is mentioned twice in Matt. (26:3, 57). He was the son-in-law of Annas (John 18:13). For background see ZPEB, "Caiaphas," I, pp. 683–85; ISBE (1979), "Caiaphas," I, pp. 570–71; *Who's Who in the Bible*, "Caiaphas," p. 61.

26:4. The verb *to take counsel together* (συμβουλεύω) occurs only here in Matt. They laid their plans carefully.

5 *But they said, Not on the feast day, lest there be an uproar among the people.*
6 *Now when Jesus was in Bethany, in the house of Simon the leper,*
7 *There came unto him a woman having an alabaster box of very precious ointment, and poured it on his head, as he sat at meat.*
8 *But when his disciples saw it, they had indignation, saying, To what purpose is this waste?*
9 *For this ointment might have been sold for much, and given to the poor.*

trickery they were determined to get rid of Him. Morris characterizes it as working "craftily" (*Matt.*, p. 645).

"But they were saying: Not on the feast day, that there not be a tumult among the people" (v. 5). They feared a riot by the people more than anything else. The Roman reprisals could cost them their positions.

II. The Anointing at Bethany. vv. 6–13 [Mark 14:3–9; John 12:2–8].

"But when Jesus was in Bethany in the house of Simon the leper, a woman having an alabaster vessel of ointment, very costly, came to him and poured it out upon his head while he was reclining" (vv. 6–7). John identifies her as Mary of Bethany (John 12:3). Simon was obviously no longer a leper, thanks to the power of the Lord Jesus.

"But when the disciples saw it, they were indignant, saying, For what is this waste? For it might have been sold for much, and given to the poor?" (vv. 8–9). John tells us that it was Judas Iscariot, Simon's son, who voiced this complaint (John 12:4–5). The disciples were used to living in rigid

---

For the verb *to seize, grasp,* see Matt. 9:25 note.

The word *deceit* (δόλος) occurs only here in Matt.

For the verb *to kill* see Matt. 10:28 note.

26:5. The word *feast day* (ἑορτή) occurs twice in Matt. (26:5; 27:15).

The word *tumult, uproar* (θόρυβος) occurs twice in Matt. (26:5; 27:24).

26:7. The word *alabaster* (ἀλάβαστρος) occurs only here in Matt.

The word *ointment, perfume* (μύρον) occurs twice in Matt. (26:7, 12).

The word *very expensive* (βαρύτιμος) occurs only here in the NT.

For the verb *to recline at table* see Matt. 9:10 note.

26:8. For the verb *to be indignant* see Matt. 20:24 note.

The word *waste* is literally *destruction*; see Matt. 7:13 note. To pour out the ointment, Mary probably had to break the vial in which it was sealed.

26:9. For the verb *to sell* see Matt. 13:46 note.

For the word *poor* see Matt. 5:3 note.

10 When Jesus understood it, he said unto them, Why trouble ye the woman? for she hath wrought a good work upon me.
11 For ye have the poor always with you; but me ye have not always.
12 For in that she hath poured this ointment on my body, she did it for my burial.
13 Verily I say unto you, Wheresoever this gospel shall be preached in the whole world, there shall also this, that this woman hath done, be told for a memorial of her.
14 Then one of the twelve, called Judas Iscariot, went unto the chief priests,

self-denial. The idea of giving something precious to Jesus did not come easily to Judas's mind.

"But when Jesus knew, he said to them: Why are you troubling the woman? For she worked a good work for me" (v. 10). The Lord Jesus recognized the gift of a loving heart and treasured it.

"For you are always having the poor with you, but me you are not always having" (v. 11). The public ministry was just three and a half years. The poor are always with us.

"For she poured this ointment upon my body in order to make it ready for my burial" (v. 12). The Lord knew that the time of His death and burial was very near. The disciples would not consider the possibility.

"Truly I say to you, wherever this gospel should be preached in the whole world, that which she did shall be spoken of for her memorial" (v. 13). The Lord gave her deed a place in the Gospel record. Was that ointment Mary's dowry? Was this act of self-sacrifice the giving up of all hope of marriage? Only the Lord knew, but He gave her act the significance of His own coming sacrificial death. (See A. B. Bruce, *The Training of the Twelve,* "The Anointing in Bethany," pp. 297ff.)

III. The Price of Judas's Betrayal. vv. 14–16 [Mark 14:10–11; Luke 22:3–6].

"Then one of the twelve, the one called Judas Iscariot, went to the chief priests and said: What will you give me, and I shall deliver him to you?

26:10. The word *trouble* (κόπος) occurs only here in Matt.

For the verb *to work* see Matt. 7:23 note.

26:12. The verb *to prepare for burial* (ἐνταφιάζω) occurs only here in Matt.

26:13. For the word *gospel* see Matt. 4:23 note.

The word *memorial* (μνημόσυνον) occurs only here in Matt.

26:14. For *Judas Iscariot* see Matt. 10:4 note.

15 And said unto them, What will ye give me, and I will deliver him unto you? And they covenanted with him for thirty pieces of silver.
16 And from that time he sought opportunity to betray him.
17 Now the first day of the feast of unleavened bread the disciples came to Jesus, saying unto him, Where wilt thou that we prepare for thee to eat the passover?
18 And he said, Go into the city to such a man, and say unto him, The Master saith, My time is at hand; I will keep the passover at thy house with my disciples.

And they set for him thirty pieces of silver" (vv. 14–15). Now the plotting of the chief priests receives an unexpected help. A traitor volunteers to betray the Lord. Morris notes that the word *set* does not determine whether they *set* the coins before him or *set* the agreement to pay (*Matt.*, p. 652, note 30). But one way or another, the bargain with hell was agreed. Now all Judas had to do was to find the right time and place for an unexpected arrest.

"And from then on he was seeking an opportune time in order to betray him" (v. 16). The imperfect tense *was seeking* implies continuing vigilance to find a time when the crowds were not present to protest.

IV. The Last Supper. vv. 17–30 [Mark 14:12ff.; Luke 22:7ff.].

"But on the first day of the unleavened bread the disciples came to Jesus, saying, Where do you wish that we prepare for you to eat the passover?" (v. 17). The Lord always observed the religious festivals, but this one was especially important.

"And he said, Go into the city to such a man and say to him: The teacher says: My time is near; with you I will make the Passover with my disciples" (v. 18). The man plainly knew *the Teacher* and gave permission.

26:15. For the verb *to deliver up, betray*, see Matt. 4:12 note.
   1. Judas took advantage of his close relation with Jesus to give Him to enemies.
   2. He did it stealthily by night.
   3. He did it by a kiss, an act that professed affection.
   4. He did it for money.
   5. He knew that Jesus was innocent (Matt. 27:4). See ISBE, "Betray," I, p. 480.
For the verb *to set, stand*, see Matt. 2:9 note.
For the word *silver* see Matt. 25:18 note. For illustrations of the silver tetradrachm of Tyre see V. Gilbert Beers, *The Victor Handbook of Bible Knowledge*, pp. 488–89.
26:16. The word *opportune time* (εὐκαιρία) occurs only here in Matt.
26:17. The word *unleavened, without yeast* (ἄζυμος) occurs only here in Matt.

19 And the disciples did as Jesus had appointed them; and they made ready the passover.

20 Now when the even was come, he sat down with the twelve.

21 And as they did eat, he said, Verily I say unto you, that one of you shall betray me.

22 And they were exceeding sorrowful, and began every one of them to say unto him, Lord, is it I?

23 And he answered and said, He that dippeth his hand with me in the dish, the same shall betray me.

"And the disciples did as Jesus had commanded and prepared the Passover" (v. 19). They secured the lamb, unleavened bread, bitter herbs, and other things for the supper.

"And when evening had come, he reclined at the table with the twelve" (v. 20). The Jews regard this as a very precious time of fellowship with family and friends.

"And while they were eating, he said: Truly I say to you that one of you shall betray me" (v. 21). This was a startling prophecy to the disciples.

"And they were exceedingly grieved, and each one began to be saying to him, Surely it is not I, Lord, is it?" (v. 22). The negative (μή) expresses great doubt that it could be.

"But he answered and said: The one who dips his hand with me in the serving dish, this one shall betray me" (v. 23). Of course all the disciples were dipping their hands into the dish to get their portion of the lamb.

"The Son of man indeed goes even as it has been written concerning him, but Woe to that man through whom the Son of man is betrayed; it would have been good if that man had not been born" (v. 24). The Lord is referring to those major passages that prophesied of His death (Ps. 22:1–18;

26:18. The word such a man (δεῖνα) occurs only here in the NT. It was intended to deliberately veil the identity of the man. His house was not to become a shrine for the Last Supper.

26:19. For illustrations of the Passover celebration see The Reader's Digest Association, Great People of the Bible and How They Lived, pp. 376–77; Joan Comay, The Jerusalem I Love, pp. 96–97.

26:20. For the verb to recline see Matt. 9:10 note.

26:21. For the verb to betray see Matt. 4:12 note.

26:22. For the verb to be grieved see Matt. 14:9 note.

26:23. The word serving dish, bowl (τρύβλιον) occurs only here in Matt. The roast lamb was on this platter.

24 The Son of man goeth as it is written of him: but woe unto that man by whom the Son of man is betrayed! it had been good for that man if he had not been born.
25 Then Judas, which betrayed him, answered and said, Master, is it I? He said unto him, Thou hast said.
26 And as they were eating, Jesus took bread, and blessed it, and brake it, and gave it to the disciples, and said, Take, eat; this is my body.
27 And he took the cup, and gave thanks, and gave it to them, saying, Drink ye all of it;

69:19–21; Isa. 53:1–12). Everyone in the universe will know that Judas was the betrayer. It was a terrible judgment for the Lord to say that it would have been good if the traitor had not been born.

"But Judas, the one who betrayed him, answered and said: Surely it is not I, is it, rabbi? He says to him: You said it" (v. 25). Judas also expresses extreme doubt with the negative (μή). Jesus' words show that He is not in doubt. It is clear that Judas chose to call Jesus "my teacher," not "my Lord" (v. 22).

"But while they were eating, Jesus took bread and having blessed it, he broke it, and having given it to his disciples, he said: Take, eat, this is my body" (v. 26). The Lord Jesus instituted the Lord's Supper in the midst of a meal instead of as a separate act. The unleavened bread was like a big cracker, which He broke into pieces and gave to each disciple. Since His body was in plain view, He was speaking symbolically of the meaning of this ordinance for future times. Denominational wars have been fought over the interpretation of this phrase, but the basic meaning is simple. The most important thing for His people to remember about Him is not His spectacular miracles but His death in their behalf.

"And having taken a cup and having blessed it, he gave it to them, saying: All of you drink of it, for this is my blood of the covenant which has

---

26:24. For the perfect passive form, *it has been written*, see Matt. 2:5 note.

26:25. For the word *rabbi* see Matt. 23:7 note.

26:26. Theological wars have been fought over almost every detail of this account. For a survey of the details see ZPEB, "Lord's Supper," III, pp. 978–86; ISBE (1986), "Lord's Supper," III, pp. 164–70; Elwell, ed., *Evangelical Dictionary of Biblical Theology*, "Lord's Supper, the," pp. 491–94; J. Jeremias, *The Eucharistic Words of Jesus*; I. H. Marshall, *Last Supper and Lord's Supper*; Ryken, Wilhoit, and Longman, *Dictionary of Biblical Imagery*, "Supper," pp. 828–29.

26:27. For the word *cup* see Matt. 10:42 note.

28 For this is my blood of the new testament, which is shed for many for the remission of sins.
29 But I say unto you, I will not drink henceforth of this fruit of the vine, until that day when I drink it new with you in my Father's kingdom.
30 And when they had sung an hymn, they went out into the mount of Olives.

been shed for many unto forgiveness of sins" (vv. 27–28). This command makes the denial of the cup to any believer a sin. But the cup did no good to one like Judas. "The Old Testament was a type of the things to come. He is the truth of those things" (Chrysostom, *Matt.*, Homily 82.1). It is the power of Christ's sacrifice, not the drinking of a sacramental cup, that produces forgiveness of sins.

"But I say to you, I will not drink again from this fruit of the vine until that day when I drink it with you new in the kingdom of my Father" (v. 29). He will not celebrate such a ceremony until He has gathered all His people together for the great kingdom reign. Isaiah describes that festival time: "And in this mountain shall the Lord of hosts make unto all people a feast of fat things, a feast of wines on the lees, of fat things full of marrow, of wines on the lees well refined. And he will destroy in this mountain the face of the covering cast over all people, and the vail that is spread over all nations. He will swallow up death in victory; and the Lord God will wipe away tears from off all faces; and the rebuke of his people shall he take away from off all the earth: for the Lord hath spoken it" (Isa. 25:6–8). It is clear that this description comes after the Great Tribulation period (Isa. 24:1–22).

"And when they had sung a hymn, they went out into the mount of Olives" (v. 30). It is significant that there was singing, even on this moment of sad separation that loomed before them. The psalms sung at this season were certainly from the *Hallel* (Ps. 113–118). God was going to be glorified through all the suffering that was to follow.

26:28. The word *covenant, testament* (διαθήκη) occurs only here in Matt. The writer to the Hebrews will expand this term greatly (7:22; 8:6–10; 9:4, 15–17, 20; 10:16, 29; 12:24; 13:20). For further discussion see Westcott, *Heb.*, pp. 298–302; ZPEB, "Covenant in the NT," I, pp. 995–1000; ISBE (1979), "Covenant (NT)," I, p. 793; Elwell, ed., *Evangelical Dictionary of Biblical Theology*, "New Covenant," pp. 131–32.

The word *forgiveness* (ἄφεσις) occurs only here in Matt. The apostle Paul emphasizes the forgiveness of sins that believers have in Christ (Eph. 1:7; Col. 1:14).

26:29. This is the last time that the word *kingdom* occurs in Matt. See Matt. 3:2 note.

31 Then saith Jesus unto them, All ye shall be offended because of me this night: for it is written, I will smite the shepherd, and the sheep of the flock shall be scattered abroad.
32 But after I am risen again, I will go before you into Galilee.
33 Peter answered and said unto him, Though all men shall be offended because of thee, yet will I never be offended.
34 Jesus said unto him, Verily I say unto thee, That this night, before the cock crow, thou shalt deny me thrice.
V. Peter's Denial Prophesied. vv. 31–35 [Mark 14:27–31; Luke 22:31–38; John 13:36–38].

"Then Jesus says to them: All you shall be offended in me in this night, for it has been written:

I will smite the shepherd,

And the sheep of the flock shall be scattered" (v. 31; Zech. 13:7).

The OT had clearly foretold the events that were now happening. Nothing was an accident.

"But after I am risen, I will go before you into Galilee" (v. 32). The Lord prophesies His resurrection and the important ministry in Galilee (Matt. 28:16–20).

"But Peter answered and said to him: Though all be caused to stumble in you, yet I will never be caused to stumble" (v. 33). Peter meant well, but spiritual self-confidence is always a disaster for the believer. No believer really understands how weak he is apart from the grace of God. We all need to follow Paul's faith: "I can do all things through Christ who strengthens me" (Phil. 4:13).

"Jesus said to him: Truly I say to you that in this night before the rooster crows, you shall deny me three times" (v. 34). The Lord knew all that would happen that night. None of the disciples would have any grounds for pride.

26:30. The *Hallel* was the term for psalms of praise to Jehovah. There were several groups of "Halleluiah Psalms." Ps. 113–118 were (and are) regularly sung at festivals such as the Passover, but Ps. 135–136 and Ps. 146–150 were regularly sung in synagogue services. For further discussion see ISBE (1982), "Hallel," II, p. 600; ZPEB, "Hallel," III, p. 19.

26:31. For the word *shepherd* see Matt. 9:36 note.

The word *flock* (ποίμνη) occurs only here in Matt.

For the verb *to scatter* see Matt. 25:24 note.

26:32. For the verb *to raise* see Matt. 1:24 note.

26:33. For the verb *to cause to stumble* see Matt. 5:29 note.

35 Peter said unto him, Though I should die with thee, yet will I not deny thee. Likewise also said all the disciples.

36 Then cometh Jesus with them unto a place called Gethsemane, and saith unto the disciples, Sit ye here, while I go and pray yonder.

37 And he took with him Peter and the two sons of Zebedee, and began to be sorrowful and very heavy.

38 Then saith he unto them, My soul is exceeding sorrowful, even unto death: tarry ye here, and watch with me.

"Peter says to him: Though it be necessary for me to die with you, I will never deny you. And all the disciples said likewise" (v. 35). They all had good intentions, but when the time came, they all failed. We all need the grace of God. Peter writes earnestly, "Be clothed with humility: for God resists the proud, but gives grace to the humble" (I Pet. 5:5b).

VI. The Prayers in Gethsemane. vv. 36–46 [Mark 14:32–42; Luke 22:39–46].

"Then Jesus comes with them to a place called Gethsemane, and he says to the disciples: Sit here while I go and pray there" (v. 36). The Lord shows us here that the best resource in a crisis is prayer. He could have fellowship with His Father while He awaited the betrayal of men. Friedrich Tholuck has an eloquent sermon on "Jesus in Gethsemane" (*Light from the Cross*, pp. 115–27).

"And he took along Peter and the two sons of Zebedee, and began to be sorrowful and troubled" (v. 37). The Lord understood the enormity of taking upon himself the sins of the world and being forsaken by His Father. J. Oswald Sanders notes that the Lord did not ask the disciples to pray for Him, but for themselves, that they not fall into temptation (*The Incomparable Christ*, p. 14).

"Then he says to them: My soul is very grieved, unto death: remain here and keep on watching with me" (v. 38). Morris notes, "He wanted them

26:34. The word *rooster* (ἀλέκτωρ) occurs 3 times in Matt. (26:34, 74, 75). They lived in an agricultural community.

For the verb *to deny, disown* see Matt. 16:24 note.

26:36. *Gethsemane* is mentioned only here in Matt. For background see ZPEB, "Gethsemane," II, pp. 706–7; ISBE (1982), "Gethsemane," II, pp. 457–58; Pfeiffer and Vos, *The Wycliffe Historical Geography of Bible Lands*, pp. 158–59. For color photographs see Custer, *Stones of Witness*, pp. 88–89.

For the verb *to pray* see Matt. 5:44 note.

26:37. For the verb *to be sorrowful* see Matt. 14:9 note.

The verb *to be troubled* (ἀδημονέω) occurs here only in Matt. Paul mentioned that Epaphroditus was troubled (Phil. 2:26).

39 And he went a little farther, and fell on his face, and prayed, saying, O my Father, if it be possible, let this cup pass from me: nevertheless not as I will, but as thou wilt.
40 And he cometh unto the disciples, and findeth them asleep, and saith unto Peter, What, could ye not watch with me one hour?
41 Watch and pray, that ye enter not into temptation: the spirit indeed is willing, but the flesh is weak.
42 He went away again the second time, and prayed, saying, O my Father, if this cup may not pass away from me, except I drink it, thy will be done.

to share with Him as He prayed through His hour of agony" (*The Cross in the New Testament*, p. 26).

"And having gone forward a little, he fell upon his face, praying and saying: My Father, if it is possible, let this cup pass from me; nevertheless not as I will, but as you will" (v. 39). He understood fully the horror of the coming suffering, but He placed Himself firmly in the center of His Father's will. In this He is the perfect example for all believers.

"And he comes to the disciples and finds them sleeping, and says to Peter: Thus were you not strong enough to watch with me one hour?" (v. 40). Peter had good intentions, but he could not follow through.

"Keep on watching and keep on praying, in order that you may not enter into temptation; the spirit on the one hand is willing, but on the other hand the flesh is weak" (v. 41). The present tense verbs urge constant prayer. We do not use this resource as we should. Our old nature, the flesh, will constantly betray us. Paul warns, "For I know that in me, that is in my flesh, dwells no good thing" (Rom. 7:18a).

"Again the second time he went away and prayed, saying: My Father, if it is not possible for this to pass away except I drink it, let your will come to pass" (v. 42). This petition expresses the Lord's perfect submission to His

26:38. The word *very grieved* (περίλυπος) occurs only here in Matt.
For the verb *to watch* see Matt. 24:42 note. See also Custer, *A Treasury of New Testament Synonyms*, p. 132.
26:39. For the word *cup* see Matt. 10:42 note.
26:40. For the verb *to sleep* see Matt. 8:24 note.
For the verb *to be strong* see Matt. 5:13 note.
26:41. For the word *temptation* see Matt. 6:13 note. See also *to tempt*, Matt. 4:1 note.
The word *willing* (πρόθυμος) occurs only here in Matt.
For the word *weak* see Matt. 25:43 note.

43 And he came and found them asleep again: for their eyes were heavy.
44 And he left them, and went away again, and prayed the third time, saying the same words.
45 Then cometh he to his disciples, and saith unto them, Sleep on now, and take your rest: behold, the hour is at hand, and the Son of man is betrayed into the hands of sinners.
46 Rise, let us be going: behold, he is at hand that doth betray me.
47 And while he yet spake, lo, Judas, one of the twelve, came, and with him a great multitude with swords and staves, from the chief priests and elders of the people.

Father. He understood the terrible suffering ahead, but He gave Himself to His Father's will without reservation.

"And he came again and found them sleeping, for their eyes were heavy" (v. 43). It was sheer exhaustion after a long day and a long night.

"And he left them and went away again and prayed the third time, saying the same words again" (v. 44). He was concentrating all his attention on the will of His Father and the redemption of His people. There does not seem to be a danger in repeating a devout prayer. The danger comes in repeating words without meaning them. Compare "Have mercy" in the psalms (4:1; 6:2; 9:13; 25:16; 27:7; 30:10; 31:9; 51:1; 86:16; 123:2, 3).

"Then he comes to the disciples and says to them: Continue sleeping for the remainder and take your rest; behold the hour has drawn near, and the Son of man is betrayed into the hands of sinners" (v. 45). Now was the moment of betrayal; it would all happen quickly.

"Arise, let us be going; behold, the one who betrays me has drawn near" (v. 46). The Lord knew exactly what was happening and who was doing it.

VII. The Betrayal and Arrest. vv. 47–56 [Mark 14:43–52; Luke 22:47–53; John 18:2–12].

"And while he was speaking, behold, Judas, one of the twelve, came, and with him a great crowd with swords and staves, from the chief priests and elders of the people" (v. 47). The phrase *one of the twelve* emphasizes the fact that the

---

26:42. For the word *will* see Matt. 6:10 note.

26:43. The verb *to be heavy, burdened* (βαρέω) occurs only here in Matt.

26:45. For the word *sinner* see Matt. 9:10 note.

26:47. For the word *sword* see Matt. 10:34 note.

48 Now he that betrayed him gave them a sign, saying, Whomsoever I shall kiss, that same is he: hold him fast.
49 And forthwith he came to Jesus, and said, Hail, master; and kissed him.
50 And Jesus said unto him, Friend, wherefore art thou come? Then came they, and laid hands on Jesus and took him.
51 And, behold, one of them which were with Jesus stretched out his hand, and drew his sword, and struck a servant of the high priest's, and smote off his ear.

betrayer had sweet fellowship with the Lord and the disciples for years. It was a large crowd, well armed, able to deal with resistance if it arose.

"But the betrayer had given to them a sign, saying: Whomever I kiss is he; seize him" (v. 48). So with a false sign of Christian love Judas betrays the Lord of the universe.

"And immediately he went to Jesus and said: Hail, rabbi, and kissed him" (v. 49). He was never more than "my teacher" to Judas. The kiss was a hypocritical veil for his treachery. It was in the same category as Joab's kiss of Amasa before he slew him with the sword (II Sam. 20:9–10).

"But Jesus said to him: Friend, Why have you come? Then they came and laid hands on Jesus and seized him" (v. 50). That question must have pierced the very soul of Judas, but the deed was done now. The Lord knows the heart motive of every person.

"And behold, one of those who were with Jesus reached out his hand and drew his sword and struck the slave of the high priest and cut off his ear" (v. 51). John tells us that it was Simon Peter who struck with the sword (John 18:10ff.). He was aiming for more than an ear! He was attempting to stop this injustice, but the Lord rebuked him.

26:48. For the word *sign* see Matt. 12:38 note.

26:49. For the word *rabbi* see Matt. 23:7 note.

The verb *to kiss* (καταφιλέω) occurs only here in Matt. It was an outward sign of affection, greeting, or reverence. Vincent observes, "The compound verb has the force of an emphatic, ostentatious salute" (*Word Studies*, I, p. 141). For discussion see ZPEB, "Kiss," III, pp. 831–32; ISBE (1986), "Kiss," III, pp. 43–44; Ryken, Wilhoit, and Longman, *Dictionary of Biblical Imagery*, "Kiss," pp. 482–83.

26:50. For the word *friend* see Matt. 20:13 note.

The verb *to come, be present* (πάρειμι) occurs only here in Matt.

26:51. For the word *sword* see Matt. 10:34 note.

The verb *to take off, away* (ἀφαιρέω) occurs only here in Matt.

The word *ear* (ὠτίον) occurs only here in Matt.; for his usual word see Matt. 10:27 note.

379

*52 Then said Jesus unto him, Put up again thy sword into his place: for all
they that take the sword shall perish with the sword.
53 Thinkest thou that I cannot now pray to my Father, and he shall presently
give me more than twelve legions of angels?
54 But how then shall the scriptures be fulfilled, that thus it must be?
55 In that same hour said Jesus to the multitudes, Are ye come out as against
a thief with swords and staves for to take me? I sat daily with you teaching in
the temple, and ye laid no hold on me.*

"Then Jesus says to him: Put away your sword into its place; for all the
ones who take the sword shall perish with the sword" (v. 52). Human violence causes only more violence.

"Or do you think that I am not able to call upon my Father and he shall
supply to me more than twelve legions of angels?" (v. 53). Prayer is the
answer to all persecution, but the Lord will not pray for deliverance. One
angel could overwhelm the country, not just the palace guard (II Kings
19:35). But the Lord goes humbly to His death because He knows the
salvation it will bring to His people.

"How, therefore, shall the scriptures be fulfilled that thus it is necessary to
come to pass?" (v. 54). The Lord Jesus thus teaches that all the prophetic
Scriptures shall come to pass. His teaching is the foundation for all faith
in the inspiration of Scripture. Psalm 22 prophesied His very cry from the
cross (v. 1); and that He would be an object of scorn and mockery (vv.
7–8); His bones would be out of joint (v. 14); His heart would be hurt
(v. 14); He would have weakness and terrible thirst (v. 15); His hands and
feet would be pierced (v. 16); His clothes would be taken from Him (vv.
17–18); and even that they would cast lots for His robe (v. 18). Psalm
41 prophesied that a familiar friend would betray Him (v. 9). Psalm 69
prophesied that they would give Him gall and vinegar to drink (v. 21).
Isaiah 53 prophesied that He would be wounded for our transgressions
(v. 5); that the Lord would lay on Him the iniquity of us all (v. 6); that

---

26:52. For the verb *turn away, put away,* see Matt. 5:42 note.

For the verb *to perish, destroy,* see Matt. 2:13 note.

26:53. The word *legion* (λεγιών) occurs only here in Matt. There were normally 6,000
troops in a Roman legion.

26:54. For *the Scriptures* see Matt. 21:42 note.

26:55. For the word *bandit, robber,* see Matt. 21:13 note.

For the word *sword* see Matt. 10:34 note.

56 But all this was done, that the scriptures of the prophets might be fulfilled. Then all the disciples forsook him, and fled.
57 And they that had laid hold on Jesus led him away to Caiaphas the high priest, where the scribes and the elders were assembled.
58 But Peter followed him afar off unto the high priest's palace, and went in, and sat with the servants, to see the end.

He would suffer as a lamb brought to the slaughter (v. 7); that He would make His grave with the wicked and the rich (v. 9); that He would be an offering for sin (v. 10). F. W. Krummacher has a reverent exposition of these themes (*The Suffering Saviour*, pp. 134ff.).

"In that hour Jesus said to the crowds: Did you come out as against a bandit with swords and staves to seize me? Every day I was sitting teaching and you did not seize me" (v. 55). They came against Him as though He were a dangerous criminal, but He had been sitting in their midst, teaching the people daily without offense.

"But all this came to pass in order that the scriptures of the prophets might be fulfilled. Then all the disciples left him and fled" (v. 56). Again Matthew notes the necessity of the fulfillment of all Scripture (v. 54). Campbell Morgan emphasizes the utter loneliness with which the Lord faced His passion. "No man could help, no man could sympathize, no man could understand" (*The Crises of the Christ*, p. 293).

VIII. The Trial. vv. 57–68 [Mark 14:53–65; Luke 22:54, 63–65; John 18:24].

"But the ones who seized Jesus led him away to Caiaphas, the high priest, where the scribes and elders were gathered" (v. 57). The kangaroo court was already set and waiting. Edersheim notes that the whole trial was against rabbinic law (*Life and Times*, II, p. 553). It was clearly a violation of "that holy Passover night." Men of conscience, such as Gamaliel (Acts 5:34–35) and Nicodemus (John 7:50–51), were simply not invited.

"But Peter was following him afar off into the courtyard of the high priest, and having entered in, he was sitting with the officers to see the end" (v. 58). Peter was trying to maintain a low profile, but he just had to be there.

26:56. For the verb *to flee* see Matt. 2:13 note.
26:57. For *Caiaphas* see Matt. 26:3 note.
For the word *high priest* see Matt. 2:4 note.
26:58. For the word *officer* see Matt. 5:25 note.

59 *Now the chief priests, and elders, and all the council, sought false witness against Jesus, to put him to death;*
60 *But found none: yea, though many false witnesses came, yet found they none. At the last came two false witnesses,*
61 *And said, This fellow said, I am able to destroy the temple of God, and to build it in three days.*
62 *And the high priest arose, and said unto him, Answerest thou nothing? what is it which these witness against thee?*
63 *But Jesus held his peace, And the high priest answered and said unto him,*

"But the chief priests and the whole Sanhedrin were seeking false testimony against Jesus in order that they might put him to death" (v. 59). They were looking for anything with which to accuse Him.

"And although many false witnesses came forward, they found none, but at the last two came forward and said: This man said: I am able to destroy the sanctuary of God and in three days to build it up" (vv. 60–61). This testimony was a failure to understand the teaching of the Lord on the resurrection of His body after three days. But it was the only agreed-upon testimony they had.

"And the high priest arose and said to him: Are you answering nothing? What are these testifying against you?" (v. 62). He was trying to get anything out of Him to use against Him. Tholuck has a sermon on "The Silence of Jesus" (*Light from the Cross*, pp. 139–49).

"But Jesus was silent. And the high priest said to him: I put you under oath before the living God that you tell us whether you are the Christ, the Son of God" (v. 63). The high priest did not care about the truth; all he wanted was something he could pounce upon in court. Peter had confessed that Jesus was "the Christ, the Son of the living God" (Matt. 16:16), and the Lord had said that His Father had revealed it to him (Matt. 16:17). Here Caiaphas has nothing in his heart but bitter hatred for One Who has revealed his sin.

26:59. For the word *Sanhedrin* see Matt. 5:22 note.

For the word *false testimony* see Matt. 15:19 note.

26:60. The word *false witness* (ψευδόμαρτυς) occurs only here in Matt.

26:61. For the word *sanctuary* see Matt. 23:16 note.

26:62. The verb *to testify against* (καταμαρτυρέω) occurs twice in Matt. (26:62; 27:13).

26:63. For the verb *to be silent* see Matt. 20:31 note.

The verb *to put under oath* (ἐξορκίζω) occurs only here in the NT.

I adjure thee by the living God, that thou tell us whether thou be the Christ, the Son of God.
64 Jesus saith unto him, Thou hast said: nevertheless I say unto you, Hereafter shall ye see the Son of man sitting on the right hand of power, and coming in the clouds of heaven.
65 Then the high priest rent his clothes, saying, He hath spoken blasphemy; what further need have we of witnesses? behold, now ye have heard his blasphemy.
66 What think ye? They answered and said, He is guilty of death.
67 Then did they spit in his face, and buffeted him; and others smote him with the palms of their hands,
68 Saying, Prophesy unto us, thou Christ, Who is he that smote thee?

"Jesus said to him: You said it; nevertheless I say to you, After this you shall see the Son of man sitting at the right hand of power and coming upon the clouds of heaven" (v. 64; Dan. 7:13, LXX). The Lord Jesus claimed to belong at the right hand of Almighty God and will come again in glory to rule the world. It is significant that the Lord Jesus claims that He will come *upon* the clouds of heaven. Others may come *with* clouds, but it is Jehovah God "who rideth *upon* a swift cloud" (Isa. 19:1). It is Jehovah Who "makes the clouds his chariot" (Ps. 104:3). It was sober truth, but it was also exactly what Caiaphas wanted to hear. He did not believe a word of it.

"Then the high priest rent his garments saying: He blasphemed; What need have we of further witness? Behold, now you heard the blasphemy" (v. 65). Caiaphas refused the light of divine revelation and now urges his colleagues into the darkness.

"What do you think? But they answered and said, He is guilty of death" (v. 66). They wish to silence the truth and darken the light. They were pronouncing their own eternal sentence. Isaiah cries out, "Woe unto them that call evil good, and good evil" (Isa. 5:20a). Now the real depravity within their hearts comes forth.

"Then they spit in his face and beat him, and the ones who hit him were saying: Prophesy to us, Christ, who is the one who hit you?" (vv. 67–68). They threw off the facade of judicial impartiality and manifested the real

26:64. For the word *power* see Matt. 7:22 note. Here it is a synonym for God.
26:65. For the verb *to blaspheme* see Matt. 9:3 note.
For the noun *blasphemy* see Matt. 12:31 note.

69 Now Peter sat without in the palace: and a damsel came unto him, saying, Thou also wast with Jesus of Galilee.
70 But he denied before them all, saying, I know not what thou sayest.
71 And when he was gone out into the porch, another maid saw him, and said unto them that were there, This fellow was also with Jesus of Nazareth.
72 And again he denied with an oath, I do not know the man.
73 And after a while came unto him they that stood by, and said to Peter, Surely thou also art one of them; for thy speech bewrayeth thee.

hatred within their hearts. They thought that because they had not met Him He would not know who they were. But one day they will stand before that great white throne and see Him again (Rev. 20:11–12).

IX. *Peter's Denial. vv. 69–75 [Mark 14:66–72; Luke 22:54–62; John 18:15–18, 25–27].*

"But Peter was sitting outside in the courtyard, and one female slave came to him, saying: You also were with Jesus of Galilee" (v. 69). She had sharp eyes and a good memory. The *one* implies that there were others also watching the door.

"But he denied before them all, saying: I know not what you are saying" (v. 70). Peter, the boldest of the disciples, had his courage fail him. All believers need to pray for grace to be good witnesses for Christ.

"And when he went out into the gate, another maid saw him and says to those who were there: This one was with Jesus the Nazarene" (v. 71). The test continued to Peter's dismay. Although the maid had no legal authority, the implication was that Peter ought to be arrested and tried along with the Lord.

"And again he denied with an oath: I know not the man" (v. 72). He is getting more emphatic and more alienated.

"But after a short time, the ones who stood there came and said to Peter: Truly you also are one of them, for your speech betrays you" (v. 73). Peter

26:66. For the verb *to think* see Matt. 3:9 note.

For the word *guilty, liable,* see Matt. 5:21 note.

26:67. The verb *to spit on* (ἐμπτύω) occurs twice in Matt. (26:67; 27:30).

The verb *to beat* (κολαφίζω) occurs only here in Matt.

For the verb *to hit* see Matt. 5:39 note.

26:68. For the verb *to prophesy* see Matt. 7:22 note.

26:69. The word *maid, slave girl* (παιδίσκη) occurs only here in Matt. The doorkeeper in the ancient world was regularly a female slave (John 18:17; Acts 12:13).

74 Then began he to curse and to swear, saying, I know not the man. And immediately the cock crew.
75 And Peter remembered the word of Jesus, which said unto him, Before the cock crow, thou shalt deny me thrice. And he went out, and wept bitterly.

unquestionably had a Galilean dialect that was easy to recognize. Today the *lingua franca* of the Middle East is Arabic, but people can tell at once whether the person is from Egypt or Syria or Saudi Arabia, just by the dialect.

"Then he began to curse and swear: I know not the man. And immediately the cock crew" (v. 74). The night was over and the Lord's prophecy was fulfilled (Matt. 26:34).

"And Peter remembered the word of Jesus which he said: Before the cock crow, you shall deny me three times. And he went outside and wept bitterly" (v. 75). Every saint can confess that he has not been what he should have been. We all need more grace. The apostle Paul could say, "But by the grace of God I am what I am" (I Cor. 15:10*a*).

Practical Applications from Matthew 26

1. The Lord Jesus prepared the disciples for the disastrous events that were to follow (vv. 1–2). "The preparation of the heart in man, and the answer of the tongue, is from the Lord" (Prov. 16:1).
2. The Lord is pleased by the heartfelt love of His people (vv. 7, 10). The churches of Macedonia "first gave their own selves to the Lord" (II Cor. 8:5*b*).

26:70. For the verb *to deny* see Matt. 10:33 note.

26:71. The word *gate, gateway* (πυλών) occurs only here in Matt. Large buildings, palaces, often had a gateway that led to the courtyard.

26:72. For the word *oath* see Matt. 5:33 note.

For this verb *to know* see Matt. 6:8 note.

26:73. The word *speech* (λαλιά) occurs only here in Matt.

The word *evident, clear* (δῆλος) occurs only here in Matt.

26:74. The verb *to curse* (καταθεματίζω) occurs only here in the NT.

For the verb *to swear* see Matt. 5:34 note.

26:75. For this verb *to remember* see Matt. 5:23 note.

The adverb *bitterly* (πικρῶς) occurs only here in Matt.

3. Even in emergency conditions the Lord Jesus observed religious holidays (vv. 18–19). "Exalt the Lord our God, and worship at his holy hill; for the Lord our God is holy" (Ps. 99:9).

4. The Lord and the disciples took time to sing praises to God (v. 30). David vowed, "But I will sing of thy power; yea, I will sing aloud of thy mercy in the morning. . . . Unto thee, O my strength, will I sing" (Ps. 59:16–17a).

5. Self-confidence is always dangerous (v. 33). "Trust in the Lord with all thine heart; and lean not unto thine own understanding. In all thy ways acknowledge him, and he shall direct thy paths" (Prov. 3:5–6).

6. The Lord "began to be sorrowful and very heavy" (v. 37b). "Surely he hath borne our griefs, and carried our sorrows" (Isa. 53:4a). "You shall weep and lament . . . but your sorrow shall be turned into joy" (John 16:20b).

7. The Lord Jesus accepted suffering as the Father's will (v. 42). "But and if ye suffer for righteousness' sake, happy are ye. . . . but sanctify the Lord God in your hearts" (I Pet. 3:14–15a).

8. There are people who salute Jesus in hypocrisy (v. 49). "You have obeyed from the heart that type of teaching which was delivered to you" (Rom. 6:17b). "Let us draw near with a true heart in full assurance of faith" (Heb. 10:22a).

9. Believers should fight for the Lord not with weapons, but with prayer (vv. 52–53). "For this shall every one who is godly pray unto thee. . . . Thou art my hiding place; thou shalt preserve me from trouble" (Ps. 32:6a, 7a).

10. The Lord Jesus testified under oath to God (vv. 63–64). The apostle John testified, "And we have seen and do testify that the Father sent the Son to be the Savior of the world" (I John 4:14).

11. The world can provoke a good man to sin (vv. 69–75). "O Lord: let thy lovingkindness and thy truth continually preserve me" (Ps. 40:11b). "And the Lord shall deliver me from every evil work, and will preserve me unto his heavenly kingdom: to whom be glory for ever and ever. Amen" (II Tim. 4:18).

Prayer

Lord Jesus, keep us mindful of Your great love and willingness to suffer for our sakes. Grant us the grace to live for You and willingness to bear our suffering with faith and trust in Your keeping power. Amen.

MATTHEW 27

TRIAL BEFORE PILATE

Persons

Jesus

Chief priests

Elders

Pontius Pilate

Judas Iscariot

Barabbas

Pilate's wife

The multitude

Soldiers

Simon of Cyrene

Two thieves

Persons referred to

Strangers

Jeremiah

The potter

Elijah

Places mentioned

The temple

The potter's field

The judgment seat

The common hall

Golgotha

Doctrines taught

Sin

The blood of Christ

Faith in Christ

They that passed by

Scribes

They that stood there

Saints who slept

A centurion

Women from Galilee

Mary Magdalene

Mary, mother of Zebedee's children

Joseph of Arimathaea

Pharisees

The watch

All the land

Graves

The Holy City

The sepulcher

The resurrection of Christ

Christ, Son of God

Rising from the dead

1 When the morning was come, all the chief priests and elders of the people took counsel against Jesus to put him to death:
2 And when they had bound him, they led him away, and delivered him to Pontius Pilate the governor.
3 Then Judas, which had betrayed him, when he saw that he was condemned, repented himself, and brought again the thirty pieces of silver to the chief priests and elders,

Matthew 27 Exposition

I. The Death of Judas. vv. 1–10 [Acts 1:18–19].

"But when the morning came, all the chief priests and the elders of the people took counsel together against Jesus in order to put him to death" (v. 1). "The pale grey light had passed into that of early morning, when the Sanhedrists once more assembled in the Palace of Caiaphas" (Edersheim, *Life and Times*, II, p. 565). When it became daylight, they called an official meeting of the Sanhedrin, but not in the usual council chamber. All that had taken place during the night was contrary to proper Jewish procedure. The Jewish rulers did not have the legal authority to execute people, so they had to appeal to Pilate.

"And they bound him and led him off and delivered him to Pilate the governor" (v. 2). They turned Him over to Pilate because he was the only one who had the authority to pronounce a death penalty. They intended to pressure the governor to execute Him.

"Then when Judas, the one who betrayed him, saw that he was condemned, it was a care to him afterwards, and he returned the thirty pieces

---

27:1. For the word *counsel* see Matt. 12:14 note.

For the word *to kill, put to death*, see Matt. 10:21 note.

27:2. For the verb *to bind* see Matt. 12:29 note.

For the verb *to deliver over, betray*, see Matt. 4:12 note.

The name *Pilate* (Πιλᾶτος) occurs 9 times in this chapter only in Matt. (27:2, 13, 17, 22, 24, 58 [twice], 62, 65). Pilate was a cruel and ruthless ruler, but he knew what Roman justice was and had some contempt for Jews who did not. For background see ZPEB, "Pilate, Pontius," IV, pp. 790–93; ISBE (1986), "Pilate, Pontius," III, pp. 867–69; *Who's Who in the Bible*, "Pilate," pp. 358–60.

For the word *governor* see Matt. 2:6 note. Pilate was a Roman procurator, who was under the authority of the legate of Syria, a higher office. Procurators had a permanent army to keep the province under control. Palestine was a problem for Rome. For distinctions see ZPEB, "Governor," II, pp. 798–99; ISBE (1982), "Governor," II, pp. 546–47.

27:3. The verb *to have a care afterwards, regret* (μεταμέλομαι) must be distinguished from the word for *having true repentance* (μετανοέω). See Trench, *Synonyms*, pp. 255–61.

4 Saying, I have sinned in that I have betrayed the innocent blood. And they said, What is that to us? see thou to that.
5 And he cast down the pieces of silver in the temple, and departed, and went and hanged himself.
6 And the chief priests took the silver pieces, and said, It is not lawful for to put them into the treasury, because it is the price of blood.
7 And they took counsel, and bought with them the potter's field, to bury strangers in.
8 Wherefore that field was called, The field of blood, unto this day.

of silver to the chief priests and elders" (v. 3). Regrets gnawed at him until he brought the money back.

"Saying: I sinned, having betrayed innocent blood. But they said: What is that to us? You shall see" (v. 4). They had no sympathy for him at all. But they, too, stand guilty.

"And he hurled the silver into the sanctuary and departed, and went away and hanged himself" (v. 5). In a rage he threw the coins into the most holy place, where the priests would have to go in to remove them, becoming ceremonially unclean from the "blood money." He had a guilty conscience but no change of heart. He will always be known as the betrayer of the Lord of the universe. Morris observes, with a fine turn of phrase, "Judas was remorseful rather than repentant" (*Matt.*, p. 695).

"But the chief priests took the silver coins and said: It is not lawful to put them into the temple treasury, since it is the price of blood" (v. 6). Putting them into the treasury would defile the treasury. But they did not want to throw the money away.

"But they took counsel and bought with them the potter's field in order to bury strangers" (v. 7). The ground had clay in it so it was not useful for growing plants. But it could be useful for burying unclaimed bodies.

"Wherefore that field was called the field of blood unto this day" (v. 8). Matthew refers to the day of his writing of the Gospel.

27:4. The word *innocent, guiltless* (ἀθῷος) occurs only twice in the NT (27:4, 24).

27:5. For the word *sanctuary* see Matt. 23:16 note.

The verb *to hang oneself* (ἀπάγχω) occurs only here in the NT.

27:6. The word *temple treasury* (κορβανᾶς) occurs only here in the NT.

27:7. The word *potter* (κεραμεύς) occurs only twice in Matt. (27:7, 10).

27:8. For the word *blood* see Matt. 16:17 note.

9 *Then was fulfilled that which was spoken by Jeremy the prophet, saying,*
And they took the thirty pieces of silver, the price of him that was valued, whom
they of the children of Israel did value;
10 *And gave them for the potter's field, as the Lord appointed me.*
11 *And Jesus stood before the governor: and the governor asked him, saying,*
Art thou the King of the Jews? And Jesus said unto him, Thou sayest.
12 *And when he was accused of the chief priests and elders, he answered noth-*
ing.
13 *Then said Pilate unto him, Hearest thou not how many things they witness*
against thee?

"Then was fulfilled that which was spoken through Jeremiah the prophet,
saying: And I took the thirty pieces of silver, the price of the one who
was valued by the sons of Israel, and gave them for the potter's field, even
as the Lord appointed me" (vv. 9–10; Zech. 11:12–13; Jer. 18:1–4). Matthew conflates words from Zechariah and Jeremiah but gives Jeremiah
as a reference. He once again shows that the Lord foreknew the deeds of
the future. But He did not make it clear enough for people to avoid doing
what they wished to. See the fulfillment formulas in the Theology of Matthew, pp. xxxvii–xxxix.

II. *The Trial Before Pilate.* vv. 11–26 [Mark 15:1–15; Luke 23:1–5, 13–25;
John 18:28–38].

"But Jesus stood before the governor; and the governor asked him, saying:
Are you the king of the Jews? But Jesus said: You say it" (v. 11). Pilate's
main concern was that Jesus might be a rival king who could threaten the
authority of Rome. There must be some grounds for asking a person that
question.

"And while he was being accused by the chief priests and elders, he answered nothing" (v. 12). There were only lies and false accusations.

"Then Pilate says to him: Are you not hearing how many things they
are witnessing against you?" (v. 13). He expected to hear arguments and
denials from the Lord.

"But he answered him not even one word, so that the governor was
marveling greatly" (v. 14). The Lord Jesus is the true Judge of all nations

27:9. For *Jeremiah* see Matt. 2:17 note.

27:10. For the verb *to appoint, direct,* see Matt. 21:6 note.

27:12. For the verb *to accuse* see Matt. 12:10 note.

27:13. For the verb *to witness against* see Matt. 26:62 note.

14 And he answered him to never a word; insomuch that the governor mar-
velled greatly.
15 Now at that feast the governor was wont to release unto the people a pris-
oner, whom they would.
16 And they had then a notable prisoner, called Barabbas.
17 Therefore when they were gathered together, Pilate said unto them, Whom
will ye that I release unto you? Barabbas, or Jesus which is called Christ?
18 For he knew that for envy they had delivered him.

(Matt. 25:31–33). He will return with the proper reward for every man
(Rev. 22:11–12). Pilate saw that Jesus was "certainly in no political sense
a rival of Caesar" (Robertson, *Word Pictures*, I, p. 225).

"But at the festival the governor was accustomed to release to the crowd
one prisoner whom they wished" (v. 15). The Passover festival was a good
time to try to win the favor of the Jews by some act of mercy. The rest of
the year they saw little mercy.

"But they were having then a notorious prisoner, who was called Barabbas" (v. 16). We learn from Mark that Barabbas was wanted for murder
and revolution (Mark 15:7). John calls him a robber (John 18:40). In
the eyes of some Jews he may have been regarded as a "freedom fighter."
There is no sharper contrast than that of a hardened criminal and killer
and the gentle and kindly teacher of peace and good will.

"Therefore when they were gathered together, Pilate said to them: Whom
are you wishing me to release to you, Barabbas or Jesus, the one who
is called Christ? For he knew that it was on account of envy that they
betrayed him" (vv. 17–18). He could plainly see the hatred that they had
toward Jesus.

27:14. For the word *word* see Matt 4:4 note.

For the verb *to marvel* see Matt. 8:10 note.

27:15. The verb *to be accustomed* (εἴωθα) is here a past perfect form of the obsolete verb
ἔθω. It occurs only here in Matt.

27:16. The word *famous, notorious* (ἐπίσημος) occurs only here in Matt.

Barabbas is named 5 times in this chapter only in Matt. (vv. 16, 17, 20, 21, 26). For
further study see ZPEB, "Barabbas," I, pp. 471–72; ISBE (1979), "Barabbas," I, p. 429;
Harrison, ed., *The New Unger's Bible Dictionary*, "Barabbas," p. 145; *Who's Who in the Bible*,
"Barabbas," pp. 53–54.

27:18. The word *envy* (φθόνος) occurs only here in Matt. For discussion see ZPEB,
"Envy," II, p. 314; ISBE (1982), "Envy," II, p. 108. Lightfoot calls envy "the desire to
deprive another of what he has" (*Gal.*, p. 212).

19 When he was set down on the judgment seat, his wife sent unto him, saying, Have thou nothing to do with that just man: for I have suffered many things this day in a dream because of him.
20 But the chief priests and elders persuaded the multitude that they should ask Barabbas, and destroy Jesus.
21 The governor answered and said unto them, Whether of the twain will ye that I release unto you? They said, Barabbas.
22 Pilate saith unto them, What shall I do then with Jesus which is called Christ? They all say unto him, Let him be crucified.

"But while he was sitting upon the judgment seat, his wife sent to him, saying, Have nothing to do with that just man, for I suffered many things today in a dream on account of him" (v. 19). That terrifying dream imparted the information to her that Jesus was a righteous man and harming Him would have dreadful consequences. Whatever the source of the dream, the warning was true. The day will come, however, when the Lord Jesus Christ will sit on the judgment seat of the universe (II Cor. 5:10; Rev. 20:11–15; different judgments, but the same authority), for the Father has committed all judgment to the Son (John 5:22). Pilate will face Him again.

"But the chief priests and the elders persuaded the crowds that they should ask for Barabbas, but destroy Jesus" (v. 20). It was the purpose of evil men from the beginning to destroy Jesus (Matt. 2:13). The word *destroy* emphasizes the malignity of their purpose. They were not content to merely oppose Him.

"But the governor answered and said to them: Which of the two are you wishing that I release to you? And they said, Barabbas" (v. 21). The popular choice was the murderer and revolutionary, Barabbas. To this day the popular choice has often been the basest of men, from rock stars to dictators.

"Pilate says to them: What therefore shall I do with Jesus, the one called Christ? They all say: Let him be crucified" (v. 22). This is a striking example of the cruelty of the "mob."

27:19. The word *judgment seat* (βῆμα) occurs only here in Matt.
For the word *dream* see Matt. 1:20 note.
27:20. The verb *to persuade* (πείθω) occurs 3 times in Matt. (27:20, 43; 28:14).
For the verb *to destroy* see Matt. 2:13 note.
27:22. For the verb *to crucify* see Matt. 20:19 note.

23 And the governor said, Why, what evil hath he done? But they cried out the more, saying, Let him be crucified.

24 When Pilate saw that he could prevail nothing, but that rather a tumult was made, he took water, and washed his hands before the multitude, saying, I am innocent of the blood of this just person: see ye to it.

25 Then answered all the people, and said, His blood be on us, and on our children.

26 Then released he Barabbas unto them: and when he had scourged Jesus, he delivered him to be crucified.

"But he said: For what evil did he do? But they were crying out more vigorously: Let him be crucified" (v. 23). Pilate only agitated the mob into screaming louder.

"But when Pilate saw that he profited nothing, but rather a tumult arose, he took water and washed off his hands before the crowd, saying, I am innocent from the blood of this man; you shall see to it" (v. 24). He was trying to escape what he knew was a miscarriage of justice, but it is not so easy to avoid responsibility. The Pharisees would have been especially sensitive to his action. The washing would denote a ceremonial cleansing from pollution.

"And all the people answered and said: His blood be upon us and upon our children" (v. 25). This was a careless acceptance of responsibility that has consequences. In fact, they were concerned about it later (Acts 5:28).

"Then he released Barabbas to them, but having scourged Jesus, he delivered him to be crucified" (v. 26). In Pilate's eyes the scourging may have been an act of mercy since it was supposed to bring a quicker death, but every part of the process was cruel.

27:23. For the word *evil, bad* see Matt, 21:41 note.

27:24. This verb *to wash off* (ἀπονίπτω) occurs only here in the NT. See also Matt. 15:2 note.

27:25. For the word *blood* see Matt. 16:17 note.

27:26. The verb *to strike with a whip, scourge* (φραγελλόω) occurs only here in Matt. The scourge was made out of strips of leather with pieces of metal or bone embedded in them. The effect was terrible gashes. See ISBE (1988), "Scourge," IV, pp. 358–59; ZPEB, "Scourge," V, pp. 297–98.

*27 Then the soldiers of the governor took Jesus into the common hall, and
gathered unto him the whole band of soldiers.*
28 And they stripped him, and put on him a scarlet robe.
*29 And when they had platted a crown of thorns, they put it upon his head,
and a reed in his right hand: and they bowed the knee before him, and mocked
him, saying, Hail, King of the Jews!*

III. *The Mocking and the Crucifixion. vv. 27–44 [Mark 15:20–32; Luke
23:26–37; John 19:16–27].*

"Then the soldiers of the governor took Jesus into the praetorium hall
and gathered together to him the whole cohort" (v. 27). Matthew provides a very calm and sober account of the suffering and death of the
Lord Jesus. The praetorium was the hall, or fortress, where the guard was
stationed. The *cohort* was a tenth of the legion, six hundred men, the
equivalent of a battalion. For a chronological order of events at the Crucifixion see *The Scofield Study Bible* (Matt. 27:33, p. 1041, note).

"And they took off his clothing and put on him a scarlet robe" (v. 28).
The Messianic Psalms prophesy His cruel treatment. "Thou hast known
my reproach, and my shame, and my dishonor: mine adversaries are
all before thee" (Ps. 69:19). When the soldiers saw that Jesus was condemned to death, they decided to have some cruel "fun" at His expense.
If the political authorities could bend the law, the soldiers felt safe in
abusing such a prisoner. They never imagined that one day they would
have to stand before Him to give an account. God declared, "I have
sworn by myself . . . that unto me every knee shall bow" (Isa. 45:23*a, c*).
"The Father . . . has committed all judgment to the Son" (John 5:22*b*).

"And when they had woven a crown of thorns, they put it upon his head,
and a reed in his right hand, and they bowed the knee before him, and
mocked him, saying: Hail, king of the Jews" (v. 29). Acanthus thorns are

27:27. The word *praetorium* occurs only here in Matt. It was a Latin loan word in Greek.
The word denoted a Roman commander's tent or residence in an encampment, and
later a Roman governor's residence as in Jerusalem or Caesarea. It always had a sizeable
contingent of troops and cavalry. Paul was imprisoned in the Praetorium of Herod (Acts
23:35). For background see ISBE (1986), "Praetorium," III, p. 929; ZPEB "Praetorium," IV,
pp. 833–34.

The word *cohort, battalion* (σπεῖρα) occurs only here in Matt. It was a Latin loan word
in Greek. For the structure of the Roman legions see John Warry, *Warfare in the Classical
World*, pp. 173, 187; for the structure of a legionary fortress see Graham Webster, *The
Roman Imperial Army*, pp. 184–85.

27:28. The verb *to take off* (ἐκδύω) occurs only twice in Matt. (27:28, 31).

30 And they spit upon him, and took the reed, and smote him on the head.
31 And after that they had mocked him, they took the robe off from him, and
put his own raiment on him, and led him away to crucify him.
32 And as they came out, they found a man of Cyrene, Simon by name: him
they compelled to bear his cross.
33 And when they were come unto a place called Golgotha, that is to say, a
place of a skull,

long and very sharp. Such a "crown" would pierce the skin and be agony
to wear.

"And they spit on him, and took the reed and were beating him on his
head" (v. 30). The imperfect tense *were beating* implies continuing action,
every blow driving the thorns deeper.

"And when they had mocked him, they took the robe off him and
clothed him in his garments and led him away in order to crucify him"
(v. 31). By now His clothes were bloodstained indeed. James Kelso observes, "Remember that Jesus, the boy who worked in wood, must die as a
man on a 'tree'" (*An Archaeologist Looks at the Gospels*, p. 39).

"But while they were going out, they found a man of Cyrene, Simon by
name; this one they compelled to carry his cross" (v. 32). By now the Lord
was unable to carry the heavy crossbeam. The upright stake was usually left
in place. This man Simon had the marvelous privilege of helping the Lord
to Calvary. Mark notes that he was the father of Alexander and Rufus, who
were obviously well-known believers in the church (Mark 15:21).

"And when they came into a place called Golgotha, which is called a
place of a skull, they gave him wine having been mixed with gall, and

---

27:29. The verb *to weave* (πλέκω) occurs only here in Matt.

The word *crown* (στέφανος) occurs only here in Matt.

For the word *thorn* see Matt. 7:16 note. Zohary, *Plants of the Bible*, favors the "Thorny
Burnet," or the "Christ Thorn," pp. 154–56.

For the verb *to kneel* see Matt. 17:14 note.

27:30. For the verb *to spit on* see Matt. 26:67 note.

For the verb *to beat* see Matt. 24:49 note.

27:31. For the verb *to lead away* see Matt. 7:13 note.

27:32. Simon of Cyrene was from North Africa, but many Jews came from such places for
festivals such as Passover and Pentecost (Acts 2:10). For background see ISBE (1988),
"Simon," 7, IV, p. 516; ZPEB, "Simon," 6, V, p. 441; *Who's Who in the Bible*, "Simon," 6, p. 403.

For the word *cross* see Matt. 10:38 note. See also *to crucify*, Matt. 20:19 note.

34 *They gave him vinegar to drink mingled with gall: and when he had tasted thereof, he would not drink.*
35 *And they crucified him, and parted his garments, casting lots: that it might be fulfilled which was spoken by the prophet, They parted my garments among them, and upon my vesture did they cast lots.*
36 *And sitting down they watched him there;*
37 *And set up over his head his accusation written, THIS IS JESUS THE KING OF THE JEWS.*

when he had tasted it, he did not wish to drink" (vv. 33–34). He would take nothing that could diminish His suffering. It was infinite.

"And they crucified him and divided his garments, casting lots, and sitting down they were watching him there" (vv. 35–36). The imperfect tense *were watching* implies continued action. They kept watching until He died. It was prophesied that His bones would be stretched out of joint (Ps. 22:14).

"And they set up over his head his charge, having been written:

This is Jesus the King of the Jews" (v. 37).

Pilate took his revenge on those who had pressured him to kill Jesus by making the charge—not that He had claimed to be, but "This *is* the King of the Jews."

"Then two robbers were crucified with him, one on the right hand and one on the left" (v. 38). They were trying to make it look as though Jesus belonged among dangerous criminals.

27:33. The word *Golgotha* (Γολγοθᾶ) occurs only here in Matt. It is a modified spelling of the Hebrew and Aramaic words for *skull*. See Arndt and Gingrich, *Lexicon*, p. 164. For background see ZPEB, "Golgotha," I, pp. 772–74; ISBE (1982), "Golgotha," II, pp. 523–24. The two suggested sites are Gordon's Calvary and within the Church of the Holy Sepulchre. For color photographs see Custer, *Stones of Witness*, pp. 111, 124–25. The word *skull* (κρανίον) occurs only here in Matt.

27:34. For the word *wine* see Matt. 9:17 note.

27:35. The fulfillment of Ps. 22:18 is recorded by John (19:24), but it is not in the oldest manuscripts of Matt. For discussion see Metzger, *A Textual Commentary on the Greek New Testament*, p. 69.

27:36. For the verb *to watch, keep*, see Matt. 19:17 note.

27:37. For the word *charge, accusation*, see Matt. 19:3 note. For a comparison of words see ISBE (1979), "Charge," I, p. 634. Scofield provides a conflation of the wording to give the whole inscription: "This is [Matthew, Luke] Jesus [Matthew, John] of Nazareth [John] the King of the Jews" [all], (*Scofield Study Bible*, p. 1042). John mentions that the inscription was written in Hebrew, Greek, and Latin (John 19:20). Human religion, culture, and law all condemned the Lord.

38 *Then were there two thieves crucified with him, one on the right hand, and another on the left.*
39 *And they that passed by reviled him, wagging their heads,*
40 *And saying, Thou that destroyest the temple, and buildest it in three days, save thyself. If thou be the Son of God, come down from the cross.*
41 *Likewise also the chief priests mocking him, with the scribes and elders, said,*
42 *He saved others; himself he cannot save. If he be the King of Israel, let him now come down from the cross, and we will believe him.*
43 *He trusted in God; let him deliver him now, if he will have him: for he said, I am the Son of God.*

"And the ones who were passing by were blaspheming him, wagging their heads and saying: The one who destroys the sanctuary and in three days builds it, save yourself, if you are the Son of God, and come down from the cross" (vv. 39–40). They were taunting Him in His agony and repeating part of His teaching that they did not understand. He could indeed have come down from the cross, but then all mankind would perish in their sins.

"Likewise also the chief priests were mocking with the scribes and elders and were saying: He saved others, himself he is not able to save; he is king of Israel, let him now come down from the cross and we will believe on him" (vv. 41–42). The religious leaders made it a point to come by and jeer at Him. They had no intention of believing on Him for any reason. It was prophesied that people would mock and scorn Him (Ps. 22:6–8).

"He has trusted upon God; let him rescue him now, if he will have him; for he said, I am the Son of God" (v. 43). They taunted Him in His sufferings that God had forsaken Him. The thought occurred in the Messianic Psalms: "My God, my God, why hast thou forsaken me? why art thou so far from helping me, and from the words of my roaring?" (Ps. 22:1). But Paul gave the answer: Christ "gave himself for our sins that he might deliver us from this present evil world" (Gal. 1:4).

27:38. For the word *robber* see Matt. 21:13 note. The KJV *thieves* is too mild a term for these men. They were not sneak thieves; they were armed and dangerous revolutionaries.

27:39. For the verb *to blaspheme* see Matt. 9:3 note.

For the verb *to shake, move,* see Matt. 23:4 note.

27:40. For the verb *to destroy* see Matt. 5:17 note.

For the verb *to save* see Matt. 1:21 note.

27:41. For the verb *to mock, ridicule,* see Matt. 2:16 note.

27:42. For the verb *to believe* see Matt. 8:13 note.

44 The thieves also, which were crucified with him, cast the same in his teeth.
45 Now from the sixth hour there was darkness over all the land unto the ninth hour.
46 And about the ninth hour Jesus cried with a loud voice, saying, Eli, Eli, lama sabachthani? that is to say, My God, my God, why hast thou forsaken me?

"And the robbers who were crucified with him were reproaching him the same way" (v. 44). These hardened criminals joined in the taunting. Luke records that one of them later repented and asked for forgiveness (Luke 23:39–43).

IV. The Death of Jesus. vv. 45–56 [Mark 15:33–41; Luke 23:44–49].

"And from the sixth hour there was darkness upon all the land until the ninth hour" (v. 45). From the sixth hour (noon) to the ninth hour (3 p.m.) there was supernatural darkness over the land of Palestine. The naturalistic explanations (a sandstorm and so forth) do not fit the descriptions. An eclipse of the sun is not possible when there is a full moon (at the Passover). Periods of light and darkness were prophesied (Ps. 22:2).

"But about the ninth hour Jesus cried with a loud voice, saying:

Eli, Eli, lema sabachthani (Ps. 22:2 Hebrew).

That is: My God, my God, why have you forsaken me?" (v. 46; Ps. 21:2 LXX; Ps. 22:1 KJV). The cry *My God* was in Hebrew; the rest of the cry was in the Palestinian dialect of Aramaic. The theological answer to the Lord's question is that the only way that God could be just in forgiving sinners and bringing them into His presence was to have their judgment fall on His Son. God made Jesus a propitiatory sacrifice for sin "that he might be just, and the Justifier of the one who believes in Jesus" (Rom. 3:26b). It is noteworthy that at this moment of His greatest suffering and despair Jesus was claiming God as His own God. His trust in His Father never wavered. Tholuck has a powerful sermon on "Why Hast Thou For-

---

27:43. For the verb *to persuade, believe*, see Matt. 27:20 note. The second perfect form has the meaning of *having been persuaded*, i.e., *believe, trust.*

For the verb *to rescue, deliver*, see Matt. 6:13 note.

27:44. For the verb *to reproach* see Matt. 5:11 note.

27:45. For the word *darkness* see Matt. 4:16 note.

27:46. The verb *to cry out* (ἀναβοάω) occurs only here in the NT.

The verb *to forsake* (ἐγκαταλείπω) occurs only here in Matt. Paul uses the word of Demas forsaking him (II Tim. 4:10).

47 Some of them that stood there, when they heard that, said, This man calleth for Elias.
48 And straightway one of them ran, and took a spunge, and filled it with vinegar, and put it on a reed, and gave him to drink.
49 The rest said, Let be, let us see whether Elias will come to save him.
50 Jesus, when he had cried again with a loud voice, yielded up the ghost.

saken Me?" (*Light from the Cross*, pp. 239–50). Campbell Morgan raises the question, For whose sin was the Lord forsaken? The answer for each person must be "my sin" (*The Crises of the Christ*, p. 299).

"But some of the ones who stood there, when they heard, were saying, This man is calling Elijah" (v. 47). The Lord was not; He was calling on the God Elijah was named for. *Elijah* means "My God is Jehovah."

"And immediately one of them ran and took a sponge, having filled it with sour wine and put it on a reed and gave him to drink" (v. 48). This too was prophesied, "They gave me also gall for my meat; and in my thirst they gave me vinegar to drink" (Ps. 69:21). The person was trying to do something merciful.

"But the rest were saying: Let it be; we shall see whether Elijah comes to save him" (v. 49). Vincent paraphrases it: "Stop! Do not give him the drink. Let us see if Elijah will come to his aid" (*Word Studies*, I, p. 145). There is a superstitious regard for Elijah in Jewish tradition (Dagobert D. Runes, *The Talmud of Jerusalem*, pp. 116–19).

"But Jesus having cried again with a loud voice, released his spirit" (v. 50). John recorded the cry, "It has been finished!" (John 19:30). The Lord Jesus, having fulfilled the will of His Father in providing the atoning sacrifice for the sins of the world, released His spirit from this life. No one but the divine Son of God had such power. The apostle Paul argues concerning Christ, "in whom we have redemption through his blood, the forgiveness of sins" (Eph. 1:7a).

27:47. For *Elijah* see Matt. 11:14 note.
27:48. The verb *to run* (τρέχω) occurs only twice in Matt. (27:48; 28:8).
The word *sponge* (σπόγγος) occurs only here in Matt.
The word *sour wine* (ὄξος) occurs only here in Matt.
27:49. For the verb *let it be, permit it* see Matt. 3:15 note.
27:50. For the verb *to release* see Matt. 3:15 note.

51 And, behold, the veil of the temple was rent in twain from the top to the bottom; and the earth did quake, and the rocks rent;
52 And the graves were opened; and many bodies of the saints which slept arose,
53 And came out of the graves after his resurrection, and went into the holy city, and appeared unto many.
54 Now when the centurion, and they that were with him, watching Jesus, saw the earthquake, and those things that were done, they feared greatly, saying, Truly this was the Son of God.
55 And many women were there beholding afar off, which followed Jesus from Galilee, ministering unto him:

"And behold the veil of the sanctuary was rent in two from the top to the bottom; and the earth was shaken and the rocks were split" (v. 51). "The way into the holiest" was not open to all in the old dispensation (Heb. 9:8), but now we have "boldness to enter into the holiest by the blood of Jesus, by a new and living way" (Heb. 10:19b–20a). His death brought the people of God into the presence of God. These miraculous events showed the mighty power released by the death of the Son of God.

"And the graves were opened, and many bodies of the saints who had slept were raised and came out of the graves after his resurrection and entered into the holy city and appeared to many" (vv. 52–53). The power of His resurrection was so great that many saints were restored to life and appeared to many after His resurrection. Matthew is the only Gospel writer to mention these startling events. These saints who were raised were a foretaste of the many who shall be raised up when He returns at the Rapture (I Thess. 4:16–17).

"But when the centurion and the ones who were guarding Jesus with him saw the earthquake and the things that happened, they were exceedingly afraid, saying, Truly this man was the Son of God" (v. 54). They knew that these supernatural events could not all be accidental. The Man they had executed was much more than a mere human being.

"But many women were there, beholding from a distance, who had followed Jesus from Galilee in order to minister to him" (v. 55). There was nothing they could do for Him, but they held their vigil from a distance.

27:51. The word *veil* (κατατέτασμα) occurs only here in Matt.

27:52. For the word *grave, tomb*, see Matt. 8:28 note.

27:53. This word *resurrection* (ἔγερσις) occurs only here in the NT.

27:54. For the word *centurion* see Matt. 8:5 note.

For the word *earthquake* see Matt. 8:24 note.

56 Among which was Mary Magdalene, and Mary the mother of James and Joses, and the mother of Zebedee's children.
57 When the even was come, there came a rich man of Arimathaea, named Joseph, who also himself was Jesus' disciple:
58 He went to Pilate, and begged the body of Jesus. Then Pilate commanded the body to be delivered.
59 And when Joseph had taken the body, he wrapped it in a clean linen cloth,
60 And laid it in his own new tomb, which he had hewn out in the rock: and he rolled a great stone to the door of the sepulchre, and departed.

"Among whom was Mary Magdalene and Mary the mother of James and Joseph and the mother of the sons of Zebedee" (v. 56).

V. The Burial of Jesus. vv. 57–66 [Mark 15:42–47; Luke 23:50–56; John 19:31–42].

"But when evening came to pass, a rich man from Arimathaea came, by name Joseph, who himself was also a disciple to Jesus" (v. 57). This shows again that there were important people who were devout followers of Jesus, but their voice was being ignored.

"He went to Pilate and asked for the body of Jesus. Then Pilate commanded that it be given" (v. 58). He was probably surprised that a counselor asked for it rather than one of the "little people." John tells us that Nicodemus, another counselor, helped in the burial (John 19:38–40).

"And Joseph took the body and wrapped it in a clean linen cloth, and laid it in his own new tomb, which he had carved in the rock, and having rolled a great stone to the door of the tomb, he departed" (vv. 59–60).

27:55. The verb *to behold* (θεωρέω) occurs only twice in Matt. (27:55; 28:1). For the verb *to minister to* see Matt. 4:11 note.

27:56. Mary Magdalene is named 3 times in Matt. (27:56, 61; 28:1). For background see ZPEB, "Mary," 6; "Mary Magdalene," IV, pp. 105–6; ISBE (1986), "Mary," 1, "Mary Magdalene," III, p. 268; *Who's Who in the Bible*, "Mary Magdalene," pp. 287–88.

27:57. Joseph of Arimathea is named twice in Matt. (27:57, 59). He was a member of the Sanhedrin, but he did not consent to their condemnation of Jesus (Luke 23:50–51). For background see ISBE (1982), "Joseph of Arimathea," II, pp. 1131–32; Harrison, ed., *The New Unger's Bible Dictionary*, "Joseph," 9, of Arimathea, p. 710; Butler, ed., *Holman Bible Dictionary*, "Joseph," 7, p. 815; *Who's Who in the Bible*, "Joseph of Arimathea," pp. 248–49. For the verb *to be a disciple* see Matt. 13:52 note.

27:58. For the verb *to command, order,* see Matt. 8:18 note.

27:59. The verb *to wrap* (ἐντυλίσσω) occurs only here in Matt. The word *linen cloth* (σινδών) occurs only here in Matt.

61 And there was Mary Magdalene, and the other Mary, sitting over against the sepulchre.
62 Now the next day, that followed the day of the preparation, the chief priests and Pharisees came together unto Pilate,
63 Saying, Sir, we remember that that deceiver said, while he was yet alive, After three days I will rise again.

In the first century, Jews wrapped a dead body like an Egyptian mummy, starting from the foot to the neck. The head was not wrapped; instead a cloth was wrapped around the top of the head. The face was left exposed. The great round stone had a flat side on the round edge so that, once in place, it would be very hard to move.

"And there was Mary Magdalene, and the other Mary, sitting opposite the tomb" (v. 61). The other Mary he has just mentioned was Mary the mother of James and Joseph (v. 56). They stayed to keep a vigil of mourning.

"But on the next day, which was after the day of preparation, the chief priests and the Pharisees came together to Pilate, saying: Lord, we remember that that deceiver said while he was yet living: After three days, I will rise" (vv. 62–63). They were worried that His influence would somehow continue. But in reality He was the truth, as Jesus had said to Thomas, "I am the way, the truth, and the life: no man comes to the Father, but by me" (John 14:6). The apostle Paul characterized such people as "they received not the love of the truth, that they might be saved" (II Thess. 2:10b). The guards at the death of Christ had to testify, "Truly this was the Son of God" (Matt. 27:54b).

"Therefore command that the tomb be made secure until the third day, lest his disciples come and steal him and say to the people: He was risen from the dead, and the last error shall be worse than the first" (v. 64). Their worries continue and they must keep trying to get rid of the influence of Jesus. If someone stole the body, there would be continuing trouble.

27:60. The verb *to carve, cut* (λατομέω) occurs only here in Matt.

The verb *to roll toward* (προσκυλίω) occurs only here in Matt.

27:62. The word *day of preparation* (παρασκευή) occurs only here in Matt. It denotes the day before the Passover.

27:63. For the verb *to remember* see Matt. 5:23 note.

The word *deceiver, deceitful* (πλάνος) occurs only here in Matt.

For the verb *to raise* see Matt. 1:24 note.

64 *Command therefore that the sepulchre be made sure until the third day, lest his disciples come by night, and steal him away, and say unto the people, He is risen from the dead: so the last error shall be worse than the first.*
65 *Pilate said unto them, Ye have a watch: go your way, make it as sure as ye can.*
66 *So they went, and made the sepulchre sure, sealing the stone, and setting a watch.*

"Pilate said to them: You have a guard; go, make it as sure as you know how" (v. 65). Pilate was not going to help their concerns.

"And they went and made the tomb secure, having sealed the stone and with the guard" (v. 66). They thought that the armed guards would be enough to keep the followers away. The appearance of an angel never crossed their minds.

Practical Applications from Matthew 27

1. Evil people often try to use others to accomplish their wicked purposes (v. 2). Adonijah tried to use Bathsheba to his advantage (I Kings 2:17–22).
2. The wicked may have regrets over their evil deeds, but it does not mean true repentance (v. 3). Pharaoh regretted the plagues that came on Egypt, but he still refused to let the Israelites go free (Exod. 8:28–32).
3. A person may be convicted of sin without ever asking God for forgiveness (v. 4). "But after thy hardness and impenitent heart treasurest up unto thyself wrath against the day of wrath and revelation of the righteous judgment of God" (Rom. 2:5).
4. Washing one's hands cannot cleanse the heart (v. 24). Penitent David prayed, "Wash me thoroughly from mine iniquity, and cleanse me from my sin" (Ps. 51:2).
5. The soldiers mocked Jesus as king of the Jews (v. 29). But the Lord is "higher than the kings of the earth" (Ps. 89:27b). He is "KING OF KINGS, AND LORD OF LORDS" (Rev. 19:16b).

27:64. The verb *to make secure* (ἀσφαλίζω) occurs 3 times in Matt. (27:64, 65, 66).

27:65. The word *guard* (κουστωδία) occurs 3 times in Matt. (27:65, 66; 28:11).

27:66. The verb *to seal* (σφραγίζω) occurs only here in Matt.

6. The Lord Jesus prayed to His Father in the time of His suffering (v. 46). "Is any among you afflicted? Let him pray" (James 5:13a).

7. Joseph of Arimathaea donated his own tomb to the use of the Lord Jesus (vv. 57–59). "For I reckon that the sufferings of this present time are not worthy to be compared with the glory which shall be revealed in us" (Rom. 8:18).

8. His enemies called the Lord "that deceiver" (v. 63b). But He was "the truth" (John 14:6b). "Thou therefore endure hardness, as a good soldier of Jesus Christ" (II Tim. 2:3).

9. They sealed the tomb to make sure no one got in to steal the body (v. 66). They never considered that Christ could rise through the stone and none could hinder Him. He said, "Because I live, ye shall live also" (John 14:19b).

Prayer

Thank You, Lord Jesus, for laying down Your life on our behalf that we might live with You forever. Thank You for bearing the penalty for our sins that we might be saved by Your grace. Make us devout believers. Amen.

MATTHEW 28

THE RESURRECTION

Persons

Mary Magdalene

The other Mary [mother of James and Joses]

An angel of the Lord

The guards

Jesus

The chief priests

The elders

The eleven disciples

All nations

Persons referred to

His disciples

The dead

Jesus' brethren

The governor

The Jews

The Father

The Son

The Holy Spirit

Places mentioned

The sepulcher

Galilee

The city

A mountain in Galilee

Heaven

Earth

All nations

Doctrines taught

The Crucifixion

The Resurrection

The empty tomb

Joy

Worshiping Christ

All authority is Christ's

The Trinity

Obedience to Christ's command

The consummation of the age

1 In the end of the sabbath, as it began to dawn toward the first day of the week, came Mary Magdalene and the other Mary to see the sepulchre.
2 And, behold, there was a great earthquake: for the angel of the Lord descended from heaven, and came and rolled back the stone from the door, and sat upon it.
3 His countenance was like lightning, and his raiment white as snow:
4 And for fear of him the keepers did shake, and became as dead men.

Matthew 28 Exposition

I. The Women at the Tomb. vv. 1–10 [Mark 16:1–8; Luke 24:1–8; John 20:1].

"But in the end of the Sabbaths, in the dawning of the first of the week, Mary Magdalene came, and the other Mary, to behold the tomb" (v. 1). They came for the purpose of beholding the tomb. All their hopes rested on the Lord's ability to conquer death as He had promised (Matt. 20:18–19). Mark adds that they brought spices to the tomb (Mark 16:1). In the ancient world people brought spices the way people in our time bring flowers to a funeral.

"And behold there was a great earthquake: for an angel of the Lord came down from heaven and came and rolled away the stone and sat upon it" (v. 2). There was an earthquake when the Lord died (Matt. 27:54), so here there is an earthquake to manifest that He was alive. Since the stone was about shoulder high, the stature of the angel probably appeared twice the height of a man. The stone was so large and heavy that it would take a group of men with levers to move it from the tomb, but the angel rolled it away with no effort at all. He was an immensely powerful being. He did not roll away the stone to let the Lord out; the Lord was already risen. He removed the stone to show the women, and later the disciples, that the tomb was empty.

28:1. The verb *to dawn* (ἐπιφώσκω) occurs only here in Matt.
For the verb *to behold* see Matt. 27:55 note.
28:2. For the word *earthquake* see Matt. 8:24 note.
The verb *to roll away* (ἀποκυλίω) occurs only here in Matt.

5 And the angel answered and said unto the women, Fear not ye: for I know that ye seek Jesus, which was crucified.
6 He is not here: for he is risen, as he said. Come, see the place where the Lord lay.
7 And go quickly, and tell his disciples that he is risen from the dead; and, behold, he goeth before you into Galilee; there shall ye see him: lo, I have told you.

"But his appearance was as lightning and his clothing was white as snow" (v. 3). Lightning is glittering power that makes any person feel uneasy.

"But from fear of him the guards were shaken and became as dead men" (v. 4). They were rough-and-ready men, but the angel was a being of such power that they were paralyzed with fear. If he wished them ill, they were dead, and they knew it. When Daniel saw the angel, he fell upon his face to the ground (Dan. 10:9).

"And the angel answered and said to the women: You stop fearing, for I know that you are seeking Jesus, who has been crucified" (v. 5). He does not tell the guards to stop fearing! He knows that these women are devoted followers of Jesus. There is no deception possible in the spiritual realm. He *answered* the mental questions that the women had. It is significant that the first revelation of Christ's resurrection came to these women, who cared so much that they came first to the tomb. There are times when lay people have more spiritual zeal for the Lord than their pastors do!

"He is not here, for he was raised even as he said; Come, see the place where he was laid" (v. 6). The angel invites them to look in the tomb to see that the body is gone.

"And go quickly and tell his disciples that he was raised from the dead, and, behold, he goes before you into Galilee; there you shall see him; Behold, I

28:3. The word *appearance* (εἰδέα) occurs only here in the NT.

For the word *lightning* see Matt. 24:27 note.

For the word *clothing* see Matt. 3:4 note.

The word *snow* (χιών) occurs only here in Matt.

28:4. For the verb *to shake* see Matt. 21:10 note.

28:5. For the verb *to fear* see Matt. 1:20 note.

For the verb *to seek* see Matt. 2:13 note.

28:6. For the verb *to raise* see Matt. 1:24 note.

For discussion on the resurrection of Jesus see Westcott, *The Revelation of the Risen Lord*; *The Gospel of the Resurrection*; Tenney, *The Reality of the Resurrection*; R. Candlish, *Life in a*

8 *And they departed quickly from the sepulchre with fear and great joy; and did run to bring his disciples word.*
9 *And as they went to tell his disciples, behold, Jesus met them, saying, All hail. And they came and held him by the feet, and worshipped him.*
10 *Then said Jesus unto them, Be not afraid: go tell my brethren that they go into Galilee, and there shall they see me.*

told you" (v. 7). The angel was fulfilling a charge to make known to them the reality of the resurrection of the Lord Jesus. They needed to inform the disciples that the Lord had conquered death. He was also revealing to them that the disciples needed to go back to Galilee in order to receive an important revelation.

"And they departed quickly from the tomb with fear and great joy and ran to announce to his disciples" (v. 8). They had mixed emotions: fear because of the power of the angel, but great joy because of the reality of the Resurrection. The world often devalues the service of women, but God here gives great privilege and honor to these women. They become the first to see the risen Lord.

"And behold, Jesus met them, saying: Rejoice. But they came to him and grasped his feet and worshiped him" (v. 9). It was not just a vision; they were able to grasp His feet. They were filled with joy to see Him, but they knew that He was the divine Son of God and that worship was the only proper attitude. Spurgeon comments, "The Lord Jesus often meets with His people in the way of holy service" ("All Hail," Sermon 2628, C. H. *Spurgeon Collection*, Ages Digital Library).

"Then Jesus says to them: Stop fearing; Go, announce to my brothers that they go into Galilee, and there they shall see me" (v. 10). The Lord also announces that there will be an important revelation in Galilee that the apostles need to receive.

II. The Guard and the Lie. vv. 11–15.

"But while they were going, behold, some of the guard came into the city and reported to the chief priests all the things that had happened"

Risen Saviour; Henry Latham, *The Risen Master*; F. Morison, *Who Moved the Stone?* ZPEB, "Resurrection of Jesus Christ," V, pp. 75–83; ISBE (1988), "Resurrection of Jesus Christ," IV, pp. 150–54; Elwell, ed., *Evangelical Dictionary of Biblical Theology*, "Resurrection," pp. 676–79; Ryken, Wilhoit, and Longman, *Dictionary of Biblical Imagery*, "Resurrection," pp. 713–14.

28:7. For the verb *to go before* see Matt. 2:9 note.

11 Now when they were going, behold, some of the watch came into the city, and shewed unto the chief priests all the things that were done.
12 And when they were assembled with the elders, and had taken counsel, they gave large money unto the soldiers,
13 Saying, Say ye, His disciples came by night, and stole him away while we slept.
14 And if this come to the governor's ears, we will persuade him, and secure you.
15 So they took the money, and did as they were taught: and this saying is commonly reported among the Jews until this day.
16 Then the eleven disciples went away into Galilee, into a mountain where Jesus had appointed them.

(v. 11). The word *some* indicates that there were others who fled rather than face a charge of dereliction of duty. The chief priests took the report very seriously but did not repent of their crime.

"And when they had gathered together with the elders and had taken counsel, they gave sufficient silver to the soldiers, saying: Say that his disciples came by night and stole him while we were sleeping" (vv. 12–13). Although they recognize the supernatural nature of what had happened, they bribe the guards to lie. In full knowledge of a miracle they oppose the divine will at all costs. *Sufficient silver* meant a great deal of money changed hands because dereliction of duty by guards regularly meant execution by the Romans.

"And if this should be heard by the governor, we will persuade him and make you free from anxiety" (v. 14). They guarantee protection to the guards if they stick to their story.

"And they took the silver and did as they were taught. And this word was spread abroad among the Jews unto this day" (v. 15). The guards became coconspirators with the Jews in spreading a lie. The phrase *unto this day* implies a date before A.D. 70, when the assumptions and practices of the Jews were seriously curtailed.

III. The Great Commission. vv. 16–20 [Mark 16:15–18; cf. I Cor. 15:6].

"And the eleven disciples went to Galilee to the mountain which Jesus had appointed them" (v. 16). The Lord directed them to a specific mountain,

---

28:8. For the verb *to run* see Matt. 27:48 note.

For the verb *to announce, declare* see Matt. 2:8 note.

For the word *joy* see Matt. 2:10 note.

28:9. For the verb *to grasp, hold* see Matt. 9:25 note. This action demands physical reality.

17 And when they saw him, they worshipped him: but some doubted.
18 And Jesus came and spake unto them, saying, All power is given unto me in heaven and in earth.
19 Go ye therefore, and teach all nations, baptizing them in the name of the Father, and of the Son, and of the Holy Ghost:

but Matthew does not identify it. The Lord Jesus began his ministry in Galilee (Matt. 4:12–17); now He brings it to a close in Galilee.

"And when they saw him, they worshiped, but some doubted" (v. 17). Some of the apostles had lingering doubts, but now the Lord gives them a revelation that removes every doubt. "All doubt vanished when Jesus approached and spoke to them . . . never had human lips, even the lips of the Son of Man, spoken thus before" (H. B. Swete, *The Appearances of Our Lord After the Passion*, p. 69).

"And Jesus came and spoke to them, saying: All authority is given to me in heaven and upon the earth" (v. 18). John recorded that Jesus had taught this earlier: "For the Father judges no one, but has given all judgment to the Son, that all men should honor the Son even as they honor the Father" (John 5:22–23a). But now in the presence of the risen Lord all the apostles understood what it meant. He does not say this merely to put a distance between Himself and the disciples, "but to cheer them on their way through the world as the messengers of the kingdom; to make them feel that the task assigned them was not, as it might well seem, an impossible one" (A. B. Bruce, *The Training of the Twelve*, p. 534).

"Having gone therefore, make disciples of all nations, baptizing them into the name of the Father, and of the Son, and of the Holy Spirit" (v. 19). This command is "the Great Commission," which remains the marching orders of the church to the end of the age. The participle *having gone as-*

For the verb *to worship* see Matt. 2:2 note.

28:10. For the verb *to fear* see Matt. 1:20 note.

28:14. The word *free from anxiety* (ἀμέριμνος) occurs only here in Matt.

28:15. For the word *silver* see Matt. 25:18 note.

For the verb *to spread abroad* see Matt. 9:31 note.

28:16. The number 11 occurs only here in Matt. See Introduction, "Numbers," p. xxii.

For *Galilee* see Matt. 2:22 note.

The verb *to appoint* (τάσσω) occurs only here in Matt.

28:17. For the verb *to worship* see Matt. 2:2 note.

For the verb *to doubt* see Matt. 14:31 note.

20 Teaching them to observe all things whatsoever I have commanded you: and, lo, I am with you always, even unto the end of the world. Amen.

sumes that they will go as far as they know anyone exists. It is regularly interpreted as an imperative. The main verb *to make disciples* is an imperative and means more than merely *teach*; it means *to make committed followers* of the Lord. The field is the world (Matt. 13:38). The converts should be baptized in the name of the one true God, the Holy Trinity, Father, Son, and Holy Spirit. Both Peter and Paul were divinely called to this ministry (Acts 10:9–48; 13:1–4; 28:30–31). "The baptized person is not only brought into union with the Three, but he is devoted to Their service, living thenceforth a consecrated life" (H. B. Swete, *The Holy Spirit in the New Testament*, p. 125).

The apostle Paul fully understood the meaning of this commission. He declared, "I am a debtor both to the Greeks, and to the Barbarians; both to the wise, and to the unwise. So, as much as in me is, I am ready to preach the gospel to you that are at Rome also. For I am not ashamed of the gospel of Christ: for it is the power of God unto salvation to every one that believeth; to the Jew first, and also to the Greek" (Rom. 1:14–16). The believer does not need anyone beyond the Lord Jesus Christ, the

---

28:18. For the word *authority* see Matt. 7:29 note.

28:19. The verb *to go* here reverses the command during the public ministry to go only to Jews (Matt. 10:6).

For the verb *to make a disciple of* see Matt. 13:52 note.

For further discussion on the Great Commission see Donald Guthrie, *New Testament Theology*, pp. 715–16; ZPEB, "Commission, the Great," I, pp. 927–28; Elwell, ed., *Evangelical Dictionary of Biblical Theology*, "Great Commission, the," p. 317.

Nigel Turner argues that "in Mt, the epistles, and Rev we can always presume that εἰς has its full sense even where one might suspect that it stood for ἐν (e.g. Mt 28:19 baptism *into* the name, i.e. a relationship as the goal of baptism)" (Moulton, III, *Syntax*, Turner, p. 255).

Vincent notes, "The *name*, as in the Lord's Prayer ("Hallowed be thy name"), is the expression of the sum total of the divine Being" (*Word Studies*, I, p. 150).

For the doctrine of the Trinity see B. B. Warfield, "The Biblical Doctrine of the Trinity," in *Biblical and Theological Studies*, pp. 22–59; L. Berkhof, *Systematic Theology*, "The Holy Trinity," pp. 82–99; ISBE (1988), "Trinity," IV, pp. 914–21; ZPEB, "Trinity," V, pp. 822–24; H. B. Swete, *The Holy Spirit in the New Testament*, pp. 123–26; R. Morey, *The Trinity: Evidence and Issues*; H. Bavinck, *The Doctrine of God*, Inter-Personal Relations, pp. 304–13.

See also *Fatherhood of God*, Matt. 5:16 note; Christ the *Son of God*, Matt. 4:3 note; the *Holy Spirit*, Matt. 1:18 note.

28:20. For the verb *to teach* see Matt. 4:23 note.

great King. "For in him dwells all the fullness of deity bodily, and you are complete in him, who is the head of all rule and authority" (Col. 2:9–10).

"Teaching them to keep all things as many as I commanded you; and behold, I am with you all the days, unto the consummation of the age" (v. 20). Believers are not to pick and choose among the Lord's teachings. All that He taught is the will of God for His people. The Lord Jesus has defeated all the attacks of His foes. Now His power will reach out to the evangelization of the world, as the book of Acts will show. The promise of His abiding presence with His people is our great comfort. John recorded His promise, "I will not leave you orphans" (John 14:18a). All the authority for the commission rests in the Son, Jesus Christ. A. M. Hunter relates the old Latin motto to the Lord. "Vexilla Regis prodeunt! The standard of the King goes forward!" (*Introducing New Testament Theology*, p. 61). All who witness and preach are simply messengers of *the King*.

Practical Applications from Matthew 28

1. The ministry of angels is powerful but rarely seen (v. 2). "For he shall give his angels charge over thee, to keep thee in all thy ways" (Ps. 91:11).
2. The wicked often have no idea of the danger they are in from angels (v. 4). "And God's anger was kindled because he went: and the angel of the Lord stood in the way for an adversary against him" (Num. 22:22a).

For the verb *to command* see Matt. 4:6 note.

For the word *consummation, end*, see Matt. 13:39 note. This last promise of Matthew anticipates the glories of the conclusion of the book of Revelation. It sets forth a consummation vastly greater than any man can imagine (Rev. 21–22). See Custer, *From Patmos to Paradise*, pp. 236ff.

Every point in the Lord's last words to His disciples has been obeyed, taught, and treasured by His people.

1. The authority of Christ. Rom. 9:5; I Cor. 15:25; II Cor. 5:10; Eph. 1:20–23.
2. The command to go to others. Acts 13:6; 15:41; 16:6.
3. To make disciples. Acts 14:21; Col. 1:20–22.
4. To observe ordinances. Acts 2:38, 41; 8:12; 9:18; 16:15; I Cor. 12:13.
5. The doctrine of the Trinity. II Cor. 13:14; Gal. 4:6; Eph. 4:4–6; I Pet. 1:2.
6. The teaching ministry. Acts 5:21, 25, 42; 11:26; I Cor. 4:17.
7. To obey His commands. Rom. 6:16–17; Gal. 3:1; 5:7.
8. To teach the constant presence of Christ. Col. 1:27; Heb. 13:5–6.
9. The final and total victory. I Cor. 15:24–25; II Pet. 3:10–13; Rev. 21:1–5.

3. Believers have no reason to fear God's angels (v. 5). "Some have entertained angels unawares" (Heb. 13:2*b*).
4. Knowledge of the Resurrection brought the believers both godly reverence and great joy (v. 8). "Now the God of hope fill you with all joy and peace in believing" (Rom. 15:13*a*).
5. Worshiping Jesus is proper (v. 17). "The grace of the Lord Jesus Christ, and the love of God, and the communion of the Holy Ghost, be with you all. Amen." (II Cor. 13:14).
6. The age-long responsibility of all believers is to make disciples of all nations (v. 19). "God our Savior, who will have all men to be saved, and to come to the knowledge of the truth" (I Tim. 2:3*b*–4).
7. The Lord is with His people to the end of the age (v. 20). "For he has said, I will never leave you nor forsake you" (Heb. 13:5*b*).

Prayer

Thank You, Lord Jesus, for conquering death and rising again from the tomb that we might have eternal life with You. Give us the grace to make disciples of all nations that we might together live with You forever. May Your grace transform us into eternal servants to Your glory. Amen.

Epilogue

"And behold, I am with you all the days,
unto the consummation of the age" (Matt. 28:20).

"*I*, in the fullest sense: not the *Divine Presence, as distinguished from the Humanity* of Christ. His Humanity is with us likewise. The vine lives in the branches. The contrast between this 'I am with you,' and the view of Nicodemus (John 3:2) 'no man can do these miracles—except *God be with him*.' *With you* mainly by the promise of the Father (Luke 24:49) which he has poured out on His church. But the presence of the Spirit is the effect of the presence of Christ—and the presence of Christ is part of the 'was given' above—the effect of the well-pleasing of the Father. So that the mystery of His name Emmanuel (with which this Gospel begins and ends) is fulfilled—God is *with us*. And all the appointed days—for they are numbered by the Father, though by none but Him. . . . To understand the *with you* only of the Apostles and their [?] successors, is to destroy the whole force of these most weighty words. . . . The command is to the UNIVERSAL CHURCH—to be performed, in the nature of things, by her *ministers* and *teachers*, the manner of appointing which is not here prescribed, but to be learnt in the unfoldings of Providence recorded in the Acts of the Apostles, who by His special ordinance were the founders and first builders of that Church. . . . The narrative here is suddenly brought to a termination; that in John ends with an express declaration of its incompleteness" (Henry Alford, *Greek Testament*, IV, p. 308).

Though not exhaustive, this bibliography is a fair sampling of the commentaries on Matthew of genuine value to the expositor. Those which, in the opinion of the author, are the finest and most helpful for the pastor have been marked with an asterisk (*). Commentaries are classified as Conservative and Critical rather than Liberal, because some authors in the Critical group, though expressing skepticism about significant portions of Scripture, are theological conservatives.

Conservative Commentaries

Alford, Henry. *Matthew* in Vol. I of *The Greek Testament*. 4 vols. London: Rivingtons, 1874; rpt. in 2 vols., Moody Press. 308 pp.

> Concise comments on the Greek text. He defends the Virgin Birth (p. 5), miracles (p. 76), the reality of demons (pp. 86–87). He applies the "salt" and "light" to all believers (p. 42), gives the parable of the leaven a good sense (p. 145), and applies Matt. 24–25 partly to the present age, including A.D. 70, and partly to the eschatological end (pp. 235ff.).

Bengel, John Albert. Matthew. Vol. I of *Gnomon of the New Testament*. Edinburgh: T. and T. Clark, 1863. 490 pp.

> Old, but very perceptive comments on the Greek text of Matthew.

*Blomberg, Craig L. Matthew in *The New American Commentary*. Nashville: Broadman Press, 1992. 464 pp.

> A conservative commentary based on the NIV. He notes the significance of some of the titles applied to Christ (pp. 27–29); holds that "Matthew remains the most plausible choice for author" (p. 44); defends the Virgin Birth (p. 60); argues for a baptistic interpretation of the mode of baptism (p. 76); notes that Jesus refers to no human authorities or traditions in the Sermon on the Mount (p. 134); notes the rarity of miracles over nature (p. 150); holds that the parables are limited allegories (p. 211); but fails to see that the church is to be called out, separate from the world (p. 253); stresses that all true believers are equal in God's eyes (p. 304); holds to a preterist-futurist view on the Olivet Discourse (p. 352, note 34); argues that "there

must be a balance between evangelistic proclamation and relevant exposition of all parts of God's word" (p. 433).

Boice, James Montgomery. *The Gospel of Matthew.* 2 vols. Grand Rapids: Baker Books, 2001. 363 pp.

A series of sermons on Matthew. He defends the Virgin Birth (p. 22), the supernaturalness of the star at Bethlehem (p. 30); attacks dispensational interpretations (pp. 48, 73); stresses that Jesus was attacked from the outside by Satan (p. 55); defends the verbal inerrancy of Scripture (p. 82); warns that all roads do not lead to heaven (p. 111); notes that the demons recognize the authority of Jesus and the reality of hell (p. 142); warns against coming judgment (pp. 197f.); argues that the Lord was in the tomb three actual days and nights (pp. 222f.); holds that Jesus is the Rock of Peter's confession (pp. 305f.).

*Broadus, John A. *A Commentary on the Gospel of Matthew.* Philadelphia: American Baptist Publication Society, 1886. 661 pp.

The most helpful of the older expositions of Matthew. Although one will not agree with every interpretation, one can turn to almost any random verse and find more practical help in understanding it than in any other work. He defends the Virgin Birth (p. 8), miracles (pp. 80–81). His explanations of some hard passages are impressive: "Resist not evil" (pp. 118ff.), "The Kingdom of heaven suffereth violence" (pp. 241ff.). He gives an amillennial interpretation of Matt. 24–25.

Bruce, William. *Commentary on the Gospel According to St. Matthew.* London: James Speirs, 1866. 682 pp.

A devout, practical exposition. Although some of his comments sound archaic, this is still a rich Puritan exhortation. He avoids mentioning many difficulties; some of his interpretations are allegorical.

Carson, D. A. *When Jesus Confronts the World.* Grand Rapids: Baker Book House, 1987. 154 pp.

An exposition of Matthew 8–10. He gives a thoughtful exposition of Jesus' authority (pp. 11–36); lists some characteristics of the authentic Jesus (pp. 41ff.).

Chrysostom. *Homilies on the Gospel of Saint Matthew.* Vol. 10 of *The Nicene and Post-Nicene Fathers,* ed. Philip Schaff. Grand Rapids: Wm. B. Eerdmans Publishing Company, 1956. 573 pp.

Remarkably sensible and helpful messages. Some statements sound archaic (as one would expect from the fourth century), but much of his
reasoning is close to the meaning of the Greek text. His expositions
of the Beatitudes (pp. 91–102) and fulfilling the law (pp. 103–15) are
especially instructive.

English, Eugene Schuyler. *Studies in the Gospel According to Matthew.* New
York: Fleming H. Revell Company, 1935. 226 pp.

Extremely dispensational comments on this Gospel. Matthew is a
Jewish book (p. 17); church is heavenly; Sermon on the Mount "is
to a great extent earthly in its application" (p. 46); "Christians can
never pray, 'Forgive us our debts, as we forgive our debtors'" (p. 53);
between A.D. 30 and 70 the apostles did not preach the gospel of the
kingdom at all, but the gospel of grace (p. 171); Matt. 24 deals with
the Tribulation period. These comments were originally Sunday
school lessons and still are.

Erdman, Charles R. *The Gospel of Matthew.* Philadelphia: Westminster
Press, 1920. 224 pp.

Brief conservative exposition. He defends the Virgin Birth and miracles; he gives a moving explanation of the Sermon on the Mount and
a premillennial view of the Olivet Discourse. Always kind and tem-
perate in his comments.

*Franzmann, Martin H. *Follow Me: Discipleship According to Saint
Matthew.* St. Louis: Concordia Publishing House, 1961. 249 pp.

A reverent exposition of Matthew, with the purpose of showing how
the Lord molded the disciples for their future service. Not a verse-
by-verse commentary but a careful portrayal of the thought of every
part of Matthew. His Lutheran background is seen most clearly in his
treatment of the sacraments. He holds strongly to the Virgin Birth,
miracles, etc. "The embarrassed fumbling with the miraculous which
is characteristic of so much present-day theology is but one of a
number of indications that the church's teaching and preaching has
become sicklied o'er by the pale cast of thought and can deal only in-
adequately with the bright and plastic world of divine revelation" (p.
68). He has a marvelous passage on the failure of the disciples so that
Jesus went alone where only "The Son of God" could go "under the

judgment of the God who smites the Shepherd and lays on One the iniquity of all" (pp. 206–7).

Gaebelein, Arno Clemens. *The Gospel of Matthew*. New York: Loizeaux Brothers, rpt., 1910. 624 pp.

A thoroughly dispensational exposition of Matthew. He holds that Matthew is "the Jewish Gospel" (p. 5), kingdom of David was offered to the Jews, rejected, postponed (pp. 60–61), Lord's Prayer is for Jewish believers (p. 140), Great Commission is for the Jewish remnant (p. 622). He puts dispensational meaning into many purely historical events (Matt. 8); leper signifies Israel (p. 170), centurion's servant signifies Gentiles, etc. He is at his best on genuinely prophetic subjects such as Matt. 24–25, which he relates to the Jews, the professing church, and the nations. Sometimes he chooses a poor text (p. 126). He distinguishes between the gospel of grace and the gospel of the kingdom (p. 488).

Gibson, John Monro. *Matthew* in The Expositor's Bible. London: Hodder and Stoughton, 1896; rpt. Eerdmans. 458 pp.

Brief conservative expositions. He holds to the Virgin Birth (p. 8), the reality of the miracles (pp. 107–8) and of demons (p. 118). There is not much help on individual verses: he dispatches all seven parables of Matt. 13 in four pages (pp. 182–85).

*Glasscock, Ed. *Matthew: Moody Gospel Commentary*. Chicago: Moody Press, 1997. 635 pp.

A careful, conservative premillennial exposition. He defends Matthew as author (pp. 23ff.); dates it c. A.D. 65 (p. 28); argues that the word *Father* evokes the image of one who protects and provides for His people (p. 146); gives a brief outline of the Sermon on the Mount (p. 178); holds that the image of the barn portrays the gathering of the souls of the elect into God's presence (p. 291); notes a chiastic parallelism (p. 293); warns that the term *kingdom* is a broader one than *church* (p. 301); notes the woman's argument: what falls from the table the dogs can eat (p. 327); holds that the Pharisees were sincere (?) hypocrites (p. 330); holds that a Christian today ought not object to a person's style in music or clothing (p. 373); stresses that the twelve apostles will rule the twelve tribes during the Millennium

(p. 394); notes the aggressive behavior of the Lord in throwing out the profiteers from the temple (p. 414); warns believers today not to react to the sins of today like Pharisees instead of evangelists (p. 425); gives a dispensational interpretation of the Olivet Discourse (pp. 463ff.); argues for the unique nature of the Great Tribulation (pp. 470ff.); points out the violations of Jewish law in Jesus' trial (pp. 513f.).

Glover, Richard. *A Teacher's Commentary on the Gospel of Matthew.* Grand Rapids: Zondervan, rpt. 1956. 238 pp.

Holds Matthean authorship (p. 5); defends Virgin Birth (p. 11); says chapters 5–7 are "the greatest utterance in human language" (p. 39); defends the miracles (p. 79); says mustard and leaven refer to the church (pp. 149–50), Matt. 24:15 is parallel to Luke 21:20 "armies" (p. 272) but vv. 29ff. seem to refer to eschatological judgment (p. 272), 24:40–41 means taken away to blessedness, 25:31ff. refers to final judgment (p. 285). He has a number of epigrammatic comments: "Beware of negative lives" (pp. 288–89). Devotional and practical but often inadequate.

Henry, Matthew. Matthew in *An Exposition of the Old and New Testament.* Vol. V. New York: Fleming H. Revell, n.d.

Warm-hearted devotional comments by a master expositor.

Hobbs, Herschel H. *An Exposition of the Gospel of Matthew.* Grand Rapids: Baker Book House, 1965. 422 pp.

Expository comments (not verse-by-verse) echoing the thoughts of Broadus, A. T. Robertson, and other Baptist writers. He advocates Scofield's view of the parables of treasure and pearl but picks Broadus's view of the leaven and mustard seed. He also holds to Broadus's amillennial explanation of Matt. 24–25. He strongly defends the Virgin Birth, dates Matthew after Mark.

Howard, Fred D. *The Gospel of Matthew.* Shield Bible Study Series. Grand Rapids: Baker Book House, 1961. 98 pp.

Brief survey of Matthew, giving the main argument. He defends the Virgin Birth (p. 19), immersion (p. 24), Christ's resurrection (p. 98); gives an amillennial interpretation of Matt. 24–25 (pp. 78ff.), misinterpreting, however, the premillennial view (p. 81).

Lange, John Peter. *Matthew* in *Commentary on the Holy Scriptures.* Grand Rapids: Zondervan Publishing House, rpt. 1857. 568 pp.

Conservative Lutheran exposition. He holds to Matthean authorship (pp. 41–42), dates it A.D. 67–69 (p. 42), defends the Virgin Birth (p. 53), defends the miracles (p. 153), classifies them (p. 154), gives a variety of views and notes on Peter's confession (pp. 296–99), defends the Resurrection (pp. 541–42), gives the Lutheran view of baptism (p. 557).

Lenski, Richard Charles Henry. *The Interpretation of St. Matthew's Gospel.* Columbus, Ohio: The Wartburg Press, 1943. 1181 pp.

Very thorough, strongly Lutheran interpretation of Matthew. He holds to Matthean authorship and an early date (p. 19); militantly defends the Virgin Birth (pp. 38ff.), the miracles (pp. 320, 350), the Resurrection (p. 1153). He has a great amount of material on Peter's confession and Christ's words following it (pp. 618–33). He attacks the idea that the Sermon on the Mount is nothing but law (pp. 179–80).

Maclaren, Alexander. *Matthew.* Vols. 6 and 7 of *Expositions of Holy Scripture.* Grand Rapids: Wm. B. Eerdmans Publishing Company, 1944. 1208 pp.

Warm expository messages on selected texts from Matthew, not a verse-by-verse commentary. He has remarkable messages on "The New Sinai," the Beatitudes (6:97–108), and "The Obscure Apostles" (7:55–67).

Marshall, F. *The School and College St. Matthew.* London: George Gill and Sons, n.d. 239 pp.

Very brief conservative notes on Matthew. He holds to Matthean authorship (p. vii). The seventy-four-page introduction to Matthew is valuable; he has articles on the characteristics and peculiarities of Matthew: parables, miracles, kingdom of heaven, teaching of the Lord, use of the OT, demon possession, titles of Christ, etc.

*Morgan, G. Campbell. *The Gospel According to Matthew.* New York: Fleming H. Revell Company, 1929. 321 pp.

Seventy-three expository messages, which amount to a verse-by-verse commentary on Matthew. He strongly defends the Virgin Birth (pp. 10ff.), the miracles (pp. 81ff.); gives the usual premillennial interpretation of the parables of Matt. 13; divides up the Olivet Discourse so that Matt. 24:1–44 refers to Jews, 24:45–25:30 refers to the church, and 25:31–46 refers to the judgment of the nations (pp. 280–95). On the whole he gives remarkably practical explanations. Very helpful on the Sermon on the Mount.

*Morris, Leon. *The Gospel According to Matthew*. Grand Rapids: Eerdmans, 1992. 781 pp.

A detailed and reverent commentary on Matthew. He notes the distinctive characteristics of Matthew (Jewishness, fulfillment theme, etc., pp. 2ff.); prefers Matthew as author (p. 15); defends the Virgin Birth (p. 31); notes that Matthew refers to the worship of Christ 10 times (Matt. 2:2, 8, 11; 8:2; 9:18; 14:33; 15:25; 20:20; 28:9, 17, p. 37); argues that the Devil's temptations proceed from the fact that He is the Son of God (p. 70); comments on the Sermon on the Mount, "No matter how far we have come along the Christian road the sermon tells us that there is more ahead of us" (p. 92); "pray is a command; prayer is not simply desirable but necessary" (p. 141); he holds that commitment to Jesus is the prerequisite for a true understanding of His parabolic teaching (p. 339); refers to the renewal of all things in the messianic age (p. 495); argues that part of the Olivet Discourse refers to the destruction of A.D. 70 and part to the judgment at the end of the age (p. 593).

Plumptre, E. H. *The Gospel According to Matthew* in *The Layman's Handy Commentary*, ed. Charles J. Ellicott. Grand Rapids: Zondervan Publishing House, 1903. 460 pp.

Popular exposition. He holds to Matthean authorship; defends the Virgin Birth, most miracles; but in an excursus he leaves open whether the Lord accommodated His teaching on demons to popular superstition or whether He put His seal of approval on such teaching (pp. 430–33). He interprets Matt. 24:1–28 as happening in A.D. 70, giving an amillennial view.

Rice, John R. *The King of the Jews*. Wheaton, Ill.: Sword of the Lord Publishers, 1955. 504 pp.

Baptist Bible study lessons expanded into a commentary. He, of course, strongly defends the verbal inspiration of the original manuscripts (p. 12), the Virgin Birth (pp. 31–38), etc. In reading the words one can almost hear the solemn tones of this famous preacher. He attacks extreme dispensationalism (p. 504), but he also gives some idiosyncratic interpretations (attacking life insurance, p. 110; attributing continuous action to the future tense, p. 244; etc.). He is at his best preaching on prayer (pp. 228–30).

Robertson, Archibald Thomas. *Commentary on the Gospel According to Matthew*. New York: The Macmillan Company, 1911. 307 pp.

Conservative comments on Matthew. He has a thorough introduction (50 pp.) in which he evaluates many liberal theories ("Q," etc.), usually showing that they are not settled by the evidence. He defends the Virgin Birth (p. 57), the miracles (p. 120), the Resurrection (pp. 281–82), and has an interesting exposition of Peter's confession (pp. 190–92).

———. "Matthew," in Vol. 1 of *Word Pictures in the New Testament*. Nashville: Broadman Press, 1930. Pp. 1–246.

Grammatical and interpretative explanations of Matthew.

Simcox, Carroll E. *The First Gospel*. Greenwich, Conn.: Seabury Press, 1963. 319 pp.

Devotional and practical meditations from an Anglican background. He defends the Virgin Birth (pp. 8–9), the miracles (p. 87), reality of demons (p. 134); holds to the Anglican interpretation of baptismal regeneration (p. 311). Weak on the doctrine of inspiration (p. 144).

Spurgeon, Charles Haddon. *The Gospel of the Kingdom*. London: Passmore and Alabaster, 1893. 270 pp.

A devotional exposition of Matthew, fervent and practical, the last labor of the "prince of preachers." It is filled with prayer and the very fragrance of the home to which he shortly went. He defended all the major doctrines of the faith and held to the imminency of the Second Coming (p. 219).

Tasker, R. V. G. *The Gospel According to St. Matthew* in *Tyndale Commentaries*. Grand Rapids: Wm. B. Eerdmans Publishing Company, 1961. 285 pp.

Questions Matthean authorship "though it contains material which was originally recorded in Aramaic by the apostle Matthew" (p. 17).

Defends the Virgin Birth (pp. 33ff.); holds that Matthew assembled
sayings uttered at various times into one discourse, Sermon on the
Mount (p. 59); Sermon on the Mount was written against a legalistic
attitude; we can't keep it now (p. 60); Matt. 24:1–36 refers to A.D. 70
(pp. 226ff.). On the whole, an inferior commentary. He is lavish in
his praise of the New English Bible (pp. 278–85).

Thomas, David. *The Gospel of St. Matthew.* 1873; rpt. Grand Rapids:
Baker Book House, 1956. 576 pp.

Homiletical and practical exposition, divides Matthew into preaching
sections, gives outlines and exhortations for each in a Puritan style. It
overlooks many difficulties but is helpful for the preacher.

Thomas W. H. Griffith. *Outline Studies in the Gospel of Matthew.* Grand
Rapids: Wm. B. Eerdmans Publishing Co., 1961. 476 pp.

Homiletical and expository outlines, conservative and thought-
provoking. This work lacks the unity of his other books because it was
compiled after his death from notes that he left. He gives a dispensational interpretation of Matt. 24–25.

*Toussaint, Stanley D. *Behold the King.* Portland, Ore.: Multnomah Press.
1980. 399 pp.

A conservative, dispensational commentary on Matthew. He stresses
the Jewish character of the book (p. 15f.); provides a thorough outline
(pp. 25–32); quotes liberals such as Eduard Schweizer and conservatives such as Merrill Tenney (p. 36); gives the prophecy in Isa. 7:14
a double fulfillment (p. 46); emphasizes that the kingdom and the
church are not to be confused (p. 68); concludes that the King is
qualified legally, scripturally, and morally (p. 78); commends Albert
Schweitzer's interim ethic interpretation (p. 91); shows that the King
presents Himself as Savior and Judge (p. 117); interprets the struggle
in Matt. 11:12 as against the kingdom (p. 152); discusses parabolic
interpretation (pp. 168ff.); holds that the "rock" is the truth of Peter's
confession (p. 202); holds that the Triumphal Entry was "the final and
official presentation of Jesus to Israel as its Messiah" (p. 241); gives a
dispensational interpretation of Matt. 24–25 (pp. 266ff.).

Van Ryn, August. *Meditations in Matthew.* New York: Loizeaux Brothers,
1958. 319 pp.

Brief devotional thoughts from a strongly dispensational view. Some of his dispensational teaching comes from strange passages: the order of the historical events in Matt. 8 and 9 (pp. 57–60). Few expositors will agree that the holy family was "undoubtedly" living in Nazareth when the wise men came (p. 33). The thoughts are very warmhearted but not always appropriate.

Walvoord, John F. *Matthew: Thy Kingdom Come.* Chicago: Moody Press, 1974. 259 pp.

A popular exposition from a premillennial viewpoint. He defends Matthean authorship (p. 9), the Virgin Birth (p. 20), the supernatural nature of the star at Bethlehem (p. 23); notes that the phrase *kingdom of heaven* has an antecedent in Dan. 2:44 (p. 30); holds that the Sermon on the Mount presents Christ as the King of the predicted earthly kingdom (p. 45); thinks that Matt. 8–9 show the mighty power of the King (p. 63); stresses Jesus' power to forgive sin (p. 68); admits that the postponement of the kingdom is from the human side only (p. 96); stresses the compassion of the rejected King (pp. 111ff.); thinks that a future appearance of Elijah is debatable (p. 131); holds that the Olivet Discourse is one of the four major discourses of Christ (p. 179) and should be interpreted literally (p. 181); stresses that the future tribulation is identified with Daniel's abomination of desolation (p. 185); identifies the Great Tribulation as "a specific period of time beginning with the abomination of desolation and closing with the second coming of Christ" (p. 188); holds that 25:1–13 may apply to either the Rapture or the Second Coming (p. 197).

Wiersbe, Warren W. *Be Loyal.* Wheaton, Ill.: Victor Books, 1980. 216 pp.

An expository survey of Matthew. Matthew is the bridge that leads from the OT to the NT (p. 9); he divides the book into ten sections that alternate "doing" and "teaching" (p. 11); defends the Virgin Birth (p. 17); stresses that it is important for believers to read all of Scripture (p. 27); gives *true righteousness* as the theme of the Sermon on the Mount (p. 32); stresses plural pronouns in the Lord's Prayer (p. 43); notes that the Lord's claim of being "Lord of the Sabbath" affirmed equality with God (p. 77); holds that the Lord's "exodus" would be deliverance for His people (p. 118); holds that Matt. 24 deals with the Tribulation period (p. 173).

BIBLIOGRAPHY

Williams, A. Lukyn, and B. C. Caffin. *Matthew* in Vol.15 of *The Pulpit Commentary*, ed. H. D. M. Spence and J. S. Exell. Grand Rapids: Wm. B. Eerdmans Publishing Company, rpt. 1950. 1246 pp.

A massive quantity of homiletical material, some of it platitudinous, some genuinely helpful. They hold to Matthean authorship (p. xii), the reality of the Virgin Birth (1:6) and the miracles (2:328–329); they give a postmillennial view of the leaven (2:21), refer Matt. 24:15 solely to the destruction of Jerusalem (2:448).

Critical Commentaries

Albright, William F., and C. S. Mann. *Matthew* in *The Anchor Bible*. Garden City, N.Y.: Doubleday, 1971. 564 pp.

A critical commentary urging a reverent attitude toward Scripture without the faith of the Fundamentalist. The authors have formed critical presuppositions (p. XXVI) and discuss the "Synoptic Problem," oral tradition, and "Q" (pp. XXXVIIff.); attack the idea that miracles cannot happen (p. CXXVI); recommend a variety of Matthean authorship (pp. CLXXXIIIf.); argue for authentic traditions with inconsistencies in the genealogies (pp. 5–6); discuss the Hebrew words behind the Greek (p. 46); hold that the Sermon on the Mount is not a new law but should be linked to the Pauline letters (pp. 51–53); suggest that an editor added verses (p. 62); hold that the Greek of 6:18 is impossible (p. 78); attack the old liberal idea of the fatherhood of God (p. 121); treat the exceptive clause as an interpolation (p. 226); claim that blocks of oral tradition are pieced together in Matt. (p. 238); refer to Second Isaiah (p. 244); think that the figure of sheep and goats counts against the scene being the final judgment in Matt. 25 (p. 310); hold that much of the debate about the NT comes from "an *a priori* assumption that all our sources are late and unreliable" (p. 336).

Allen, Willoughby C. *The Gospel According to St. Matthew* in *International Critical Commentary*. Edinburgh: T. and T. Clark, 1907. 448 pp.

Liberal commentary on Greek text of Matthew. He has a thorough critical introduction (96 pp.) with a helpful section on the theology of Matthew (pp. lxvi–lxxix); he denies Matthean authorship

427

(p. lxxx), dates the book soon after A.D. 70, holds to the Virgin Birth
(p. 10), but has a poor doctrine of inspiration (pp. 45, 70, etc.). He
often says that Matthew changed Mark (pp. 83, 253, etc.) or inserted
into Mark's account (p. 162).

Argyle, Aubrey William. *The Gospel According to Matthew*. Cambridge:
The University Press, 1963. 228 pp.

A commentary on the NEB by a British liberal. He confesses Christ
as human and divine (pp. 6–7); commends form critical ideas (pp.
14–15); rejects Matthean authorship (p. 16); claims that there "is no
adequate reason to doubt that the virgin birth is historical" (p. 27);
thinks that Matthew gathered different teachings to manufacture the
Sermon on the Mount (p. 44); suggests that Matthew reversed the
meaning of the parables (p. 102) and has abridged Mark's account of
the same events (p. 112); sees contradictions between Matthew and
Mark (p. 145); thinks Matthew misunderstood Zech. (p. 156); can see
nothing prophetic about the abomination of desolation (p. 182); holds
that there are some genuine utterances of Jesus in Matt. 24–25 (p.
186); doubts that the whole Sanhedrin was assembled at night (p. 206);
claims that the early church invented details of the burial (p. 219).

Beare, Francis Wright. *The Gospel According to Matthew*. San Francisco:
Harper and Row, 1981. 550 pp.

A critically unbelieving exposition. He rejects Matthean authorship
(p. 7); holds that the author was primarily concerned with the life
and faith of the church of his own time (p. 13); thinks that Matthew
added "further fictional details" to Mark's record (pp. 15–17); calls
the genealogy "artificial" (p. 62); classes the visit of the Magi in a "cy-
cle of infancy legends" (p. 72); terms the temptation story "myth" (p.
104); holds that the Sermon on the Mount was not really a sermon,
but a compilation of "sayings" (p. 124) followed by a compilation of
miracle "stories" from different sources (p. 201); calls 11:27 a theological composition "from the hand of an unknown mystic" (p. 266);
thinks that Matthew composed allegorical interpretations to the
parables (p. 287); terms the feeding of the five thousand "preposter-
ous" (p. 326), the messianic utterances of Jesus not genuine (p. 353),
the Transfiguration "a creation of mythopoetic imagination" (p. 361),
the cursing of the fig tree "not an actual incident" (p. 419), the death

of Judas "legendary embroidery" (p. 499), and the Great Commission "a relatively late formulation" (p. 545).

Bruce, Alexander Balmain. *Matthew* in Vol. 1 of *The Expositor's Greek Testament*. Grand Rapids: Wm. B. Eerdmans Publishing Company, rpt. 1907. 280 pp.

A critical commentary on the Greek text. He leaves authorship un-settled with a date after A.D. 70 (p. 43); holds that the Sermon on the Mount is "a skillful combination of originally distinct lessons" (p. 95); gives a rationalistic denial of the "oft-told tale" of the Gadarene demoniac (p. 147); holds that the Transfiguration was a vision (Moses and Elijah were not necessarily there, p. 229); on Matt. 24:15 holds that the "abomination of desolation" was the Roman army (p. 292) and that the post-resurrection meeting in Galilee is "so brief and vague" that it may not be a particular occurrence (p. 339); Great Commission perhaps "is not to be taken as an exact report of what Jesus said to His disciples at a certain time and place" (p. 340).

Buttrick, George A., and Sherman E. Johnson. *The Gospel According to St. Matthew* in Vol. 7 of *The Interpreter's Bible*. New York: Abingdon-Cokesbury Press, 1951. Pp. 229–625.

A liberal interpretation. They date Matthew "not far from the year 100" (p. 241), deny Matthean authorship (p. 242), state that the Vir-gin Birth "arises out of pious speculation" (p. 254), manifest consis-tent unbelief by distinguishing between their view and what Scripture says: the early Christians took the stilling of the storm "as an actual occurrence" (p. 346); the appearance of the angel at the Resurrection "may be the evangelist's free composition" (p. 615).

Cox, George Ernest Pritchard. *The Gospel According to St. Matthew*. London: SCM Press Ltd., 1952. 168 pp.

Neo-orthodox commentary. Doubts the Matthean authorship, ad-vocates "Q"; holds to five books of Matthew plus the birth and the passion as prologue and epilogue; holds to the Virgin Birth, some miracles; on demons he questions the supernatural causes of insanity (p. 69); holds to the Resurrection but says that Matthew embellished the account (p. 166).

Ellis, Peter F. *Matthew: His Mind and His Message.* Collegeville, Minn.: The Liturgical Press (St. Benedict), 1974. 179 pp.

A critical Roman Catholic study. He holds that Matthew was a con-verted rabbi (p. 3) who regarded Pharisees as enemies (p. 4); dates it A.D. 85 (p. 5); holds that Matthew used Mark and "Q" (p. 7); admits that Matthew is well structured and highly articulated (p. 8); thinks that Matthew represents Jesus as saying in a discourse what He said on different occasions and places (p. 14); stresses the primacy of St. Peter (pp. 64, 66); thinks that Matt. 24 is a farewell address (p. 83); holds that it is difficult to prove that the title *Son of God* means a unique sense of divinity and equality with the Father (p. 104), but admits that "for Matthew, Jesus is more than the Messiah and more than the Son of Man. He is the Son of God and one with the Father" (p. 111); thinks that Matthew changed the chronology and context of some material (p. 159); does not teach "strict historicity" but "trustworthiness" (p. 161).

Fenton, J. C. *Saint Matthew.* Philadelphia: Westminster Press, 1963. 487 pp.

He holds that the reader who comes to Matthew expecting to find "an accurate historical account of the life of Jesus" will be "disap-pointed" (p. 9). He thinks it was written between A.D. 85 and 105 (p. 11); holds that Matthew drew from Mark and "Q" (p. 14); thinks that Matthew was mistaken in thinking that the OT was fulfilled in the NT (p. 18); holds that Matthew composed chap. 2 himself (p. 44) but borrowed the account of the baptism from Mark (p. 60); holds that the Sermon on the Mount "has almost certainly been contrived by the Evangelist himself" (p. 78).

Filson, Floyd V. *The Gospel According to St. Matthew.* New York: Harper and Brothers, 1960. 306 pp.

Denies Matthew's authorship (pp. 16–20); has a good treatment of Matthean theology in "Prominent Themes" (pp. 25–44); discusses titles of Jesus, Moses and Law, the kingdom (pp. 32–35), miracles, cross and resurrection, and the church (pp. 41–44).

Gardner, Richard B. *Matthew: Believers Church Bible Commentary.* Scottdale, Pa.: Herald Press, 1991. 446 pp.

He maintains that the author was not the apostle but an unknown Jewish Christian, a second or third generation leader who built on the work of his predecessors (p. 21); holds that the stories of Jesus' infancy are modeled after those of Moses' infancy (p. 26); suggests that the stories about Jesus' birth may have been invented to explain the meaning of His birth (p. 37); thinks that the Christmas story came from Balaam (p. 44); holds that Matthew borrowed from Mark and "Q" (but will not call it that, p. 59); quotes from Roman Catholic writers (p. 71) and from liberals such as Bonhoeffer (p. 101), Eduard Schweizer (p. 120); suggests that the Lord's Prayer in Luke may be an earlier version (p. 118); holds that the centurion was not really an officer (p. 146); suggests that Matthew and Levi were two different persons (p. 155).

Gundry, Robert Horton. *Matthew: A Commentary on His Literary and Theological Art.* Grand Rapids: Eerdmans, 1982. 652 pp.

Not a normal commentary but a redaction criticism that minimizes interpretation to give overwhelming concentration on the mechanics of how Matthew composed and edited his Gospel. He discusses Matthew's theology (pp. 5–10) and warns against imposing an outline on Matthew (p. 10); applies prophecies to Matthew's own time (pp. 6ff.); claims that "the genealogy has become a large figure of speech for Jesus' messianic kingship" (p. 154); likes the "history" of Luke better than the "history" of Matthew (p. 628); claims that "Matthew has transformed the praiseful return of the shepherds (Luke 2:20) into the Magi's flight from persecution" (p. 32); does declare that "Mary bore a divine child as a result of generation by the Holy Spirit" (p. 20).

M'Neile, Alan Hugh. *The Gospel According to St. Matthew.* London: Macmillan and Co., 1915. 483 pp.

Critical commentary on the Greek text. Date: A.D. 80–100 (p. xxiii); denies Matthean authorship (p. xxiii); he does not deny miracles as such, nor does he deny the legendary; each miracle must be evaluated on its own merits (p. xv); does not deny the Virgin Birth, even though admitting that the narrative contains an "imaginative element" (p. xiv); maniac frightened the swine into a panic (p. 114); suggests that feeding of four thousand is duplicate of five thousand

(p. 233); condemns confession in 14:33 on literary grounds (p. 240); very thorough; once in a while helpful.

Meyer, Heinrich August Wilhelm. *The Gospel of Matthew*. New York: Funk and Wagnalls, 1884. 591 pp.

Technical and critical commentary. He holds that the present Matthew is a Greek translation from a Hebrew original that had the authority of Matthew (pp. 2–3), dates the translation just before A.D. 70 (p. 18), admits the Virgin Birth (p. 48), but believes that the temptation of Christ (p. 108) and demonic possession (pp. 190–91) were legends. He would limit Matt. 24:15 to the Zealots before the Roman war (p. 414).

Micklem, Philip A. *St. Matthew* in *Westminster Commentaries*. London: Methuen and Co., 1917. 340 pp.

A liberal exposition of Matthew. He dates it shortly after A.D. 70 (p. ix), denies the Matthean authorship (p. xix), does not deny the Virgin Birth (p. 8), but implicitly denies the reality of demons (p. 81), has a poor understanding of inspiration (p. 31, etc.), limits the fulfillment of 24:15 to A.D. 70.

Newman, Barclay M. and Philip C. Stein. *A Handbook on the Gospel of Matthew*. New York: United Bible Societies, 1988. 911 pp.

A critical commentary designed to provide help for translators; often use "a dynamic restructuring" of verses (pp. 16, 29, 48–49, 64, etc.).

Nicholson, Edward Bryon. *The Gospel According to Matthew*. London: C. Kegan Paul and Company, 1881. 298 pp.

A commentary that professes complete neutrality on all theological issues. Since the author will not take a stand on the authenticity of any passage, the book amounts to a collection of critical problems without solutions and some background information from Jewish literature.

*Plummer, Alfred. *The Gospel According to St. Matthew*. Grand Rapids: Wm. B. Eerdmans Publishing Company, rpt. 1956. 497 pp.

The most helpful technical and critical commentary on Matthew. He denies Matthean authorship (p. x), holds to a date a little after A.D. 70 (p. xxxii), has an interesting section on the plan of the Gospel (pp. xviii–xxv). He defends the Virgin Birth (pp. 3–11), the reality of the miracles (pp. 51–53, 122), demonic possession (pp. 134ff.); but he has a wretched doctrine of inspiration, wishing to remove the Lord's Prayer from the Sermon on the Mount (p. 93), admitting inaccuracies in Scripture (pp. 132–33), etc.

Robinson, Theodore H. *The Gospel of Matthew.* Moffatt Commentary. New York: Harper and Brothers, 1927. 257 pp.

Old-line liberal commentary. Holds to a date after A.D. 70 (p. 198); denies Matthean authorship (p. xiii); denies the Virgin Birth, translates 1:16 according to Syriac: "Joseph the father of Jesus" (pp. 2–3). Matthew united the Sermon on the Mount into one passage (p. 26); the demoniac needs to be understood in light of the first century: "Men believed themselves to live in a world peopled by spiritual beings" (p. 76); swine dying was a coincidence (p. 77); "The miracle of the stilling of the storm may have been a complete change in the minds of the disciples rather than in the actual state of the weather" (p. 85).

Works on the Gospels

Burton, Ernest De Witt, and Edgar Johnson Goodspeed. *A Harmony of the Synoptic Gospels in Greek.* Chicago: The University of Chicago Press, 1920. 316 pp.

A critical harmony on the Greek text.

Godet, Frederic. *Studies on the New Testament.* New York: E. P. Dutton and Co., 1873. 398 pp.

In his essay "The Origin of the Four Gospels" (pp. 1–83), he notes Matthew's opening words, "The book of the generation of Jesus Christ, the son of David, the son of Abraham," and concludes, "He is, then, the expected Messiah, the King of Israel, and consequently also the Saviour of the world" (p. 10); he sees five major discourses in Matthew (pp. 12ff.); holds that the Gospel of Matthew was the ultimatum of Jehovah to the Jewish people: "Recognize Jesus as the Messiah, or await Him as your Judge!" (p. 23).

Greenleaf, Simon. *The Testimony of the Evangelists.* Grand Rapids: Baker Book House, 1874, rpt. 1965. 613 pp.

An examination of the trustworthy nature of the Gospel records by a famous lawyer.

Hastings, James. *Dictionary of Christ and the Gospels*. 2 vols. Grand Rapids: Baker Book House, 1906–8, rpt.1973. 936, 912 pp.

A thorough discussion of topics in the Gospels, such as "Adultery," pp. 29–32; "Authority of Christ," pp. 146–53; "Character of Christ," pp. 281–97; "Ethics," pp. 543–47; "Kingdom of God," pp. 932–35; "Lord's Prayer," II, pp. 57–63; "Matthew, Gospel According to," pp. 143–50; "Names and Titles of Christ," pp. 219–25; "Preaching Christ," pp. 393–403; "Redemption," pp. 435–84; "Sin," pp. 630–35; "Trinity," pp. 759–66.

Kistemaker, Simon J. *The Gospels in Current Study*. Grand Rapids: Baker Book House, 1972, 1980. 181 pp.

He discusses different types of criticism (source, form, redaction, audience, pp. 35ff.); the historical Jesus (pp. 63ff.); the new hermeneutic (pp. 71ff.); the nature of the gospel (pp. 79ff.); the four Gospels (pp. 97ff.); and the theology of the Gospels (pp. 131ff.); recommends the study of the structure of the historical Gospels (pp. 161ff.). He argues that the church did not have to formulate the sayings of Jesus; they treasured the authentic sayings (pp. 81f.).

Latham, H. G. D. *The Gospel According to the Four*. London: The Religious Tract Society, 1914. 239 pp.

An examination of the differences as well as the agreements among the four Gospels.

Robertson, A. T. *A Harmony of the Gospels*. Nashville: Broadman Press, 1922, 1950. 305 pp.

A standard harmony.

Scroggie, W. Graham. *A Guide to the Gospels*. London: Pickering and Inglis, 1948. 664 pp.

Provides synthetic studies (pp. 35ff.); analytical studies in Mark (pp. 164ff.); analytical studies in Matthew, including reading plans (pp. 242ff.), date and place of writing (pp. 248ff.), Matthew's plan (pp. 255ff.), omissions (pp 258f.), the OT in Matthew (pp. 267ff.), parables in Matthew (pp. 278ff.), miracles (pp. 286ff.), discourses (pp.

291ff.), and an analysis of Matthew's gospel (pp. 317ff.); he also covers Luke (pp. 332ff.), and John (pp. 396ff.).

Stegner, William Richard. *Narrative Theology in Early Jewish Christianity.* Louisville: Westminster/John Knox Press, 1989. 141 pp.

A study of the faith of the church before A.D. 70. He argues that the Jews often depict their theology through stories (p. 3). He seeks to enlarge Gerhardsson's methods of analysis (pp. 6–8). He shows parallels between the baptism of Jesus and the binding of Isaac (pp. 13–31); holds that Jesus' sonship is the central focus of the temptation account (p. 49); sees parallels to the manna in the feeding of the five thousand (p. 77); argues that the command "Hear him," in the Transfiguration account means obey the eschatological vision (p. 101); suggests that the title "Son of God" was the contribution of Jewish Christianity to the church (p. 111).

Vos, Geerhardus. *The Self-Disclosure of Jesus.* Grand Rapids: Eerdmans, 1926, 1954. 311 pp.

A theological investigation of the messianic consciousness of Jesus. He surveys the agnostic denials (pp. 37ff.); discusses the titles "Christ" (pp. 105ff.), "Lord" (pp. 118ff.), "Son of God" (pp. 141ff.), "Saviour" (pp. 255ff.); concludes that the messianic death of Christ was the atonement for sin (pp. 273ff.).

Works on the Sermon on the Mount

Augustin, Saint. *Sermon on the Mount* in Vol. 6 of *The Nicene and Post-Nicene Fathers*, ed. Philip Schaff. Grand Rapids: Wm. B. Eerdmans Publishing Company, 1956. pp. 1–63.

Practical explanations of the Sermon on the Mount, sometimes helpful, sometimes archaic. He holds that the Sermon on the Mount is "a perfect standard of the Christian life" (p. 3). There are tinges of approval for celibacy (p. 18). He treats fornication (on Matt. 5:32) in an allegorical as well as a literal manner.

Bauman, Clarence. *The Sermon on the Mount.* Macon, Ga.: Mercer University Press, 1985, 1990. 440 pp.

A grand survey of possible interpretations. He covers Tolstoy (pp. 11ff.), Herrmann (pp. 37ff.), Ragaz (pp. 53ff.), Naumann (pp. 75ff.),

Johannes Weiss (pp. 95ff.), Schweitzer (pp. 111ff.), Muller (pp. 129ff.), Baumgarten (pp. 139ff.), Bornhauser (pp. 153ff.), Wunsch (pp. 163ff.), Stange (pp. 177ff.), Kittel (pp. 187ff.), Bultmann (pp. 197ff.), Windisch (pp. 209ff.), Dibelius (pp. 229ff.), Bonhoeffer (pp. 249ff.), Thurneysen (pp. 275ff.), Jeremias (pp. 291ff.), Stadeli (pp. 299ff.); discusses the current state of inquiry (pp. 331ff.).

Boice, James Montgomery. *The Sermon on the Mount.* Grand Rapids: Zondervan, 1972, 328 pp.

A New Evangelical exposition of Matt. 5–7. He quotes Billy Graham with approval (pp. 17, 66, 131–32); often quotes Donald Barnhouse (pp. 20, 51, 54, 120, 142, 229, etc.); emphasizes that the law cannot make man righteous (p. 25); argues for the absolute authority of Scripture (pp. 84ff.); gives various grounds for divorce (pp. 139–40); stresses that God is our "Daddy" (p. 196); refers to the liberal William Barclay as "the great British devotional commentator" (p. 270); quotes Dietrich Bonhoeffer with approval (pp. 299–300); recounts William Borden's famous dying note, "No reserve, no retreat, and no regrets" (p. 311).

Bowman, John Wick (assisted by R. W. Tapp). *The Gospel from the Mount.* Philadelphia: Westminster Press, 1957. 189 pp.

Liberal interpretation and very free paraphrase of Sermon on the Mount. He doubts Matthean authorship (p. 10); holds that Sermon on the Mount is poetry (pp. 11ff.); holds that introduction starts in Matt. 4:23, that this is a sample of the gospel of the kingdom (pp. 19ff.); denies that this is "interim Ethik" (p. 36); is always quoting T. W. Manson, V. Taylor, Dodd, Barth, etc.

Carson, D. A. *The Sermon on the Mount.* Grand Rapids: Baker, 1978. 157 pp.

A brief evangelical exposition. He gives a careful outline (pp. 7–8); corrects the KJV (p. 26); disparages divorce (pp. 45–46); compares the Sermon on the Mount with Paul's teaching (pp. 115f.); teaches the reality of hell (p. 134); includes an appendix dealing with critical questions (pp. 139ff.); in another appendix attacks dispensationalism (pp. 155–57).

Chappell, Clovis G. *The Sermon on the Mount.* Nashville: Cokesbury Press, 1930. 227 pp.

Messages by a well-known preacher; they are somewhat dated but still interesting. He had a knack for titles and phrases: "A Good Appetite" (hungering and thirsting for righteousness), "Drastic Operations" (If thine . . . offend), etc.

Davis, W. D. *The Setting of the Sermon on the Mount*. Cambridge: Cambridge University Press, 1964. 547 pp.

Although he speaks of the "plague of source criticism" and the "nightmare of form-criticism," he uses both (p. 3). He gives the "Pentateuchal form" of Matthew (p. 15), but he rejects it (p. 25). He gives ideas of "New Moses on New Sinai giving New Torah to New Israel" (pp. 25ff.), but they are implied, not stated (p. 108). He surveys Jewish messianic expectation in OT, Apocrypha, pseudepigraphic, Dead Sea, and rabbinic sources; surveys Gnosticism, Qumran, Jamnia, anti-Paulinism, "Q," etc. "Sermon on the Mount in its setting spans the arch of Grace and Law," links together James and Paul (p. 440), man's need and grandeur.

Hargrove, Hubbard Hoyd. *At the Master's Feet*. Grand Rapids: Baker Book House, 1963. 211 pp.

Conservative passages on the Sermon on the Mount. He strongly advocates the need for the new birth (p. 182). Although there are errors in fact ("synagogue" for "temple," p. 82), there are many helpful comments.

Hunter, Archibald M. *A Pattern for Life*. Philadelphia: Westminster Press, 1953. 124 pp.

Liberal explanation of the Sermon on the Mount. Advocates documentary sources: Q, Mk., M (pp. 11–14); holds that style is poetical, pictorial, and proverbial (pp. 15–20); outline (p. 28); in exegesis he uses methods of hyperbole (p. 56), principles-not-acts (pp. 29–92); throws out 5:18–20 (jot, p. 43) and 5:32 (exceptive clause, p. 50); 5:39 (cheek) means "non-retaliation in cases of personal wrong" (p. 53), not a nonresistance; surveys six different methods of interpretation (pp. 95–99). "It is an unattainable ethic which, as Christians, we must nevertheless try to attain" (p. 106).

*Lloyd-Jones, D. Martyn. *Studies in the Sermon on the Mount.* 2 vols. Grand Rapids: Wm. B. Eerdmans Publishing Company, 1959, 1960. 320, 337 pp.

Careful and thorough expository messages, which still retain their original sermonic form. He manifests good common sense and a warm heart. He stresses principles, not just actions (p. 220); often harmonizes the Sermon on the Mount with Paul's teaching (p. 207); holds that Christ was giving the proper interpretation of the Mosaic law (pp. 213–14). Although the style is certainly British, it is a most helpful work.

Luther, Martin. *The Sermon on the Mount* in Vol. 21 of *Luther's Works,* ed. Jaroslav Pelikan. St. Louis: Concordia Publishing House, 1956. 294 pp.

Pungent sermons. The fury of the battle he was waging is apparent in phrases like "that jackass of a pope" (p. 3). Although he has much common sense, his doctrine of the two realms (life divided into the secular and the sacred) is dangerous (p. 105); he applies the Sermon on the Mount only to the sacred (p. 114). He has an interesting point on the "salt." Salt bites (pp. 55–57); therefore, Christians should be stinging the world for its sin; other warnings he calls "a pinch of salt" (p. 84). His confidence in Christ is moving (p. 47).

McArthur, Harvey K. *Understanding the Sermon on the Mount.* New York: Harper and Brothers, 1960. 192 pp.

Careful discussion of four main topics: the Sermon on the Mount and Mosaic law; Sermon on the Mount and Paul's teaching; Sermon on the Mount and eschatology; Sermon on the Mount and ethics. Although liberal in his presuppositions, he gives a very helpful survey and evaluation of twelve different methods of interpreting the Sermon on the Mount (pp. 106–27). He gives illustrations of all his points by quoting everyone from the early fathers to modern liberals and dispensationalists.

Meyer, Frederick Brotherton. *The Directory of the Devout Life.* Grand Rapids: Baker Book House, rpt. 1954. 191 pp.

Warmly devotional meditations on the Sermon on the Mount. He warns against taking certain statements ("resist not evil") too literally (pp. 78–81), has a good section on the Lord's Prayer (pp. 110–33).

Some of his statements sound a little Victorian (on Matt. 5:28, pp. 60–66).

Morgan, Edward J. *No Thought for Tomorrow*. Grand Rapids: Wm. B. Eerdmans Publishing Co., 1961. 123 pp.

A psychological interpretation of the Sermon on the Mount by a skilled counselor, pointing out principles that can stabilize character. The author strongly emphasizes the deity of Christ (p. 122), and although the reader would not accept every interpretation, there is much here to help a disturbed personality.

Pink, Arthur. *An Exposition on the Sermon on the Mount*. Grand Rapids: Baker Book House, 1951. 442 pp.

A very thorough, phrase-by-phrase exposition. There is much that is genuinely helpful here; he is particularly good on "Resist not evil" (pp. 109–20), but the work is seriously marred by many "Pinkian peculiarities." He limits the "salt" and "light" to ministers only (pp. 43ff.), advocates strict Sabbatarianism (p. 59); is an avowed foe of the Scofield Reference Bible (p. 266) and of premillennialists in general (p. 81); uses the phrase "Give not that which is holy unto the dogs" to launch an attack on the literal four-footed animals (p. 294)! Matthew, being the fortieth book in the canon, marks probation (p. 9).

Ridderbos, Herman N. *When the Time Had Fully Come*. Grand Rapids: Eerdmans, 1957. 104 pp.

Chapter two, "The Significance of the Sermon on the Mount" (pp. 26–43) is a perceptive evaluation of the meaning of the Sermon on the Mount.

Stott, John R. W. *The Message of the Sermon on the Mount*. Downers Grove, Ill.: Inter-Varsity Press, 1978. 222 pp.

He seeks to offer an authentic Christian counterculture (p. 10); takes the key text of the sermon as "Do not be like them" (Matt. 6:8, p. 18); agrees with A. B. Bruce that the content of Matt. 5–7 is not a single sermon but a period of instruction (pp. 23f.); holds that the new birth is the only thing that keeps one from "reading the Sermon on the Mount with either foolish optimism or hopeless despair" (p. 29); characterizes the second beatitude as "Happy are the unhappy" (p. 40); quotes Bonhoeffer with approval (p. 53); warns against merely external conformity to God's Word (p. 75); holds that "authentic Christian non-resistance is non-retaliation" (p. 108); argues that the basic difference between non-Christian and Christian praying is "the kind of God we pray to" (p. 145).

Thielicke, Helmut. *Life Can Begin Again*. Philadelphia: Fortress Press, 1963 (German ed., 1956). 230 pp.

Rather philosophical messages on the Sermon on the Mount. He has a curious blend of liberal and conservative ideas; very catchy sermon titles: "Journey Without Luggage," "Every Word an Oath," etc. He endured persecution under Hitler; consequently, some of his messages are deeply moving. He stresses that the key to the Sermon on the Mount is the One Who delivered it.

Tholuck, A. *Commentary on the Sermon on the Mount*. Edinburgh: T. and T. Clark, 1869. 451 pp.

An exhaustive exposition of the Sermon on the Mount. Although he is conservative, he spends much time citing nineteenth-century liberals such as Bauer, De Wette, etc. He holds that the Sermon on the Mount is identical with the message in Luke 6. He has a fine survey of the older literature on the Sermon on the Mount (pp. 41–49).

Windisch, Hans. *The Meaning of the Sermon on the Mount*. Philadelphia: Westminster Press, 1951 (German ed., 1937). 224 pp.

Liberal view of the Sermon on the Mount; agrees and disagrees with Johannes Weiss, A. Schweitzer, Bultmann, etc.; holds that the Sermon on the Mount must be interpreted apart from Pauline views and therefore contradicts Rom. 7, 3, 8, etc.; salvation should come through keeping these commands. This at least was Matthew's view; he may decide to side with Paul! He believes that the Sermon on the Mount was not a theological unity; some sayings are not genuine, etc.

Works on the Beatitudes

Baker, Eric. *The Neglected Factor*. New York: Abingdon Press, 1963. 109 pp.

Liberal Methodist exposition of the Beatitudes. He intends to show that religion and morality are inseparable. Although he clearly commits himself to the deity of Christ (p. 10), there are a number of liberal statements, such as "It is recognized that there is probably no single extant saying which can be attributed to our Lord with absolute certainty" (p. 90). He loves the New English Bible (pp. 25, 30, 55, etc.).

Boreham, Frank William. *The Heavenly Octave*. New York: The Abingdon Press, 1936. 115 pp.

Eight powerful messages on the Beatitudes, filled with Boreham's characteristically eloquent rhetoric. The very titles are an indication of his gift for the catching phrase: "The Princely Poor," "The Happy Mourner," "The Delicious Hunger," etc.

*Fitch, William. *The Beatitudes of Jesus*. Grand Rapids: Wm. B. Eerdmans Publishing Company, 1961. 132 pp.

A warmly devotional exposition of the Beatitudes. Probably the best book on the Beatitudes. The author has a fine sense of the right hymn or poem to illustrate his points. He takes strong exception to the extreme dispensational interpretation that would remove the Sermon on the Mount from present concern (p. 6).

Maclaren, Alexander. *A Garland of Gladness*. Grand Rapids: Wm. B. Eerdmans Publishing Company, rpt.1945. 132 pp.

Rich devotional messages on the Beatitudes by the "prince of expositors." The first message surveys all the Beatitudes; the other eight take one at a time. He hits hard at the sinfulness of man (pp. 32ff, 44, etc.). He is especially good on "Divine Discontent" (hungering after righteousness, pp. 67ff.).

Wiersbe, Warren W. *Live Like a King*. Chicago: Moody Press, 1976. 159 pp.

A devotional book that sets forth the idea that Jesus was born a King; we are to be like Him; the Beatitudes show us how (pp. 11ff.). He holds that true humility looks to God for everything needed (p. 37); a godly sorrow changes the life (p. 51); he defines meekness as power under control (p. 63); hunger for God will be satisfied (p. 82).

Wirt, Sherwood Eliot. *Magnificent Promise*. Chicago: Moody Press, 1959. 129 pp.

Eight messages on the Beatitudes. They are mostly practical applications and illustrations. The author speaks glowingly of Billy Graham and Albert Schweitzer in the same breath (p. 39). He denies any future fulfillment of the beatitude promises in the life hereafter (pp. 91–92).

Zodhiates, Spiros. *The Pursuit of Happiness*. Grand Rapids: Wm. B. Eerdmans Publishing Company, 1966. 681 pp.

> An exhaustive (and sometimes exhausting) exposition of the Beatitudes. He is conservative, knows the Greek very well, and sometimes gives excellent differentiation between Greek words (p. 58), but once in a while his imagination goes beyond what Scripture says (pp. 200–201). In any work of this length on so few verses there will be much repetition, digression, and illustration.

Works on the Lord's Prayer

Allen, Charles L. *The Lord's Prayer*. Westwood, New Jersey: Fleming H. Revell Company, 1963. 64 pp.

> Warmly devotional meditations on the Lord's Prayer. This book provokes both thought and prayer. There are unusual drawings to illustrate the text.

Dods, Marcus. *The Prayer That Teaches to Pray*. Cincinnati: Cranston and Curts, 1893. 176 pp.

> A fervent, eloquent, and powerful exposition of the Lord's Prayer. Although the reader may not agree with everything here, he will be struck with more devotional and inspirational thoughts per page than he would think possible.

Hoeksema, Herman. *The Perfect Prayer*. Grand Rapids: Wm. B. Eerdmans Publishing Company, 1956. 224 pp.

> A conservative exposition of the Heidelburg Catechism questions dealing with the Lord's Prayer. He speaks out against modernism (p. 48). He goes out of his way to attack the view that James's "prayer of faith" has anything to do with physical healing (pp. 135–39).

Kuiper, Henry J., ed. *Sermons on the Lord's Prayer*. Grand Rapids: Zondervan Publishing House, 1956. 138 pp.

> Sermons by Reformed pastors. Six of the eight sermons repeatedly cite the Heidelburg Catechism for evidence. The sermon "Thy Kingdom Come" attacks the views of the Scofield Reference Bible (p. 62). Perhaps the best sermon is by Martin M. Monsma.

Lohmeyer, Ernest. *"Our Father."* New York: Harper and Row, 1965 (German ed., 1952). 320 pp.

A most thorough liberal exposition of the Lord's Prayer. Although one will not agree with everything found here, the exposition is most careful and a help. His treatments of "Father" (pp. 41–56), "will of God" (p. 115–23), the "evil one" (pp. 214–25) are memorable. On temptation: "The person who is tempted does not have a choice between two ways on which he could go; he has the unconditional duty to go the one way prescribed for him. The other way which temptingly attracts him is only apparently a way; in reality, it is a fall into the abyss" (p. 200).

Lowe, John. *The Lord's Prayer.* Oxford: The Clarendon Press, 1962. 77 pp.

Brief liberal comments on the Lord's Prayer. He has a few interesting thoughts, but mostly he evaluates the opinions of other liberals (p. 16) or discusses critical problems (p. 34). He is indebted to Lohmeyer.

Macartney, Clarence Edward. *The Lord's Prayer.* New York: Fleming H. Revell Company, 1942. 87 pp.

An exposition of each of the clauses of the Lord's Prayer by a famous preacher. Popularly written, helpful, good illustrations.

Macaulay, Joseph Cordner. *After This Manner.* Grand Rapids: Wm. B. Eerdmans Publishing Company, 1952. 86 pp.

Brief devotional meditations on the Lord's Prayer. He uses a careful outline, good illustrations. The chapters were originally sermons.

Saphir, Adolph. *The Lord's Prayer.* James Nisbet and Company, 1870. 428 pp.

Devotional and inspirational messages on the Lord's Prayer. These fervent messages contain much more than an exposition of the text, but they do contain that. He gives a strongly premillennial exposition of "Thy Kingdom Come." A typical outline is "The Daily Gift": I. The Giver: Our Father in Heaven. II. The Gift: Bread. III. The Expansion of the Gift: Our Bread. IV. The Limit of the Gift: Today. (p. 252).

Thielicke, Helmut. *Our Heavenly Father*, trans. John W. Doberstein. New York: Harper and Brothers, 1960 (German ed., 1953). 157 pp.

A series of sermons on the Lord's Prayer preached in Stuttgart during 1944 while the destruction and chaos of advancing armies swept across Germany. This setting gives these messages more than ordinary force. Thielicke defies classification: his thoughts range from the out-and-out liberal (p. 81) to the conservative (pp. 132–34).

Thompson, James G. S. S. *The Praying Christ.* Grand Rapids: Wm. B. Eerdmans Publishing Company, 1959. Pp. 79–103.

A survey of the teaching and practice of our Lord on prayer, including an exposition of John 17, the Lord's Prayer, Christ as a High Priest, and waiting on the Lord. The chapter on the Lord's Prayer is brief but extremely helpful.

Watson, Thomas. *The Lord's Prayer.* London: Banner of Truth Trust, rpt. 1960. 241 pp.

A lengthy Puritan exposition of the Lord's Prayer. Although parts sound archaic (the debtor's prison, p. 152), there is much fervent and practical exhortation in this work. He can get a great amount of theology out of a small text (27 pp. of exposition on "Our Father").

Other Works on Matthew

Armerding, Carl. *The Olivet Discourse.* Findlay, Ohio: Dunham Publishing Company, 1955. 95 pp.

A strictly dispensational interpretation of Matt. 24–25. He holds that the discourse deals with the Tribulation period only (p. 5), identifies the "desolation" of Matt. 24:15 with the "beast" of Rev. 13 (p. 23), and believes that the "one taken" (Matt. 24:40–41) is taken away in judgment, not in the Rapture (pp. 48–49).

Barker, William P. *As Matthew Saw the Master.* Westwood, New Jersey: Fleming H. Revell Company, 1964. 154 pp.

Conservative messages from select passages of Matthew. He holds to the two natures of Christ (pp. 18ff.), the reality of miracles (p. 34). There is an endless procession of apt illustrations.

Bingham, Rowland Victor. *Matthew the Publican and His Gospel.* Toronto: Evangelical Publishers, n.d. 126 pp.

A stirring indictment of the extreme dispensational view that would relegate the Gospel of Matthew and the Sermon on the Mount in particular to the limbo of OT legalism. Although he overstates his case (p. 124), it is refreshing to find one who urges the Great Commission on the church and not on the Jews in the Tribulation period.

Blair, Edward P. *Jesus in the Gospel of Matthew.* New York: Abingdon Press, 1960. 176 pp.

A liberal survey of the Christology of Matthew. He holds that it was written by "a Jewish Christian" (p. 42) between A.D. 70 and 100 (p. 43). He discusses Jesus' authority, as Matthew portrays it (pp. 45ff.) and His authority in the realms of knowledge and conduct. His summary of Matthew's teaching on Christ is very helpful (pp. 139ff.). He draws strong parallels between Matthew's teaching and that of Stephen and the Qumran community (pp. 145ff.). The centurion's phrase, "a Son of God," should be "the Son of God." "God" made it definite. Cf. Matt. 14:33 (p. 61).

Ford, W. Herschel. *Simple Sermons from the Gospel of Matthew.* Grand Rapids: Zondervan, 1963. 242 pp.

Chapter studies, with more detail on the Sermon on the Mount. He defends the Virgin Birth (pp. 15f.); holds that the Beatitudes picture the character of the children of God (p. 41); warns against merely external religion (p. 55); uses numerous illustrations (pp. 140, 155, 158, etc.); refers to Billy Graham (pp. 162), the Duke of Windsor (p. 175), etc.

Gerhardsson, Birger. *The Mighty Acts of Jesus According to Matthew.* Lund, Sweden: The Royal Society of Letters, Gleerup, 1979. 94 pp.

He defines the Greek words used (pp. 11ff.); summarizes the accounts of therapeutic miracles (pp. 20ff.); discusses the paragraphs (pp. 38ff.); discusses the nontherapeutic miracles (pp. 52ff.); notes the resistance and controversies (pp. 68ff.) and the titles applied to Christ in context (pp. 82ff.). He concludes that Jesus is the Messiah, the Son of the living God (p. 94).

Govett, Robert. *The Prophecy on Olivet.* Miami Springs, Fla.: Conley and Schoettle Publishing Co., Inc., rpt, 1985. 126 pp.

He notes the differences between the prophesied destruction of Jerusalem and what happened in A.D. 70 (pp. 3ff.); divides the Olivet Discourse into two groups of seven sections each (p. 7); argues that for the prophesy to be fulfilled, the temple must be rebuilt, sacrifices restored, and the Sabbath observed (pp. 17f.); holds that believers will again be persecuted and killed (p. 22) and that the Antichrist will compel the Jews to forsake the holy covenant (p. 29) and worship an idol, the image of himself (p. 41); thinks that the two witnesses will be Enoch and Elijah (p. 45); warns against coming false messiahs (pp. 55f.); holds that the sign will be a cross that appears in heaven (pp. 66f.) and that there will be national mourning by the remnant (pp. 70f.); holds that the time of the Lord's coming is wholly unknown (p. 93).

Johnson, Sherman. *The Theology of the Gospels.* London: Gerald Duckworth and Company, Ltd., 1966. 207 pp.

A liberal survey of doctrinal teaching in the Gospels. He regards the preexistence of Christ as "myth" (p. 16) and most of Christian revelation as lying between "myth" and history. The section on Matthew's theology has some helpful things (pp. 50–64). There are also interesting chapters on "The Reign of God," "God the Father," etc. One must pick among the bones of unbelief, but there are helpful ideas.

Ohm, Arnold T. *The Gospel and The Sermon on the Mount.* New York: Fleming H. Revell Company, 1948. 109 pp.

An attempt to correct misconceptions about the Gospel. He attacks the dispensational idea that the Sermon on the Mount is law, as well as the Lutheran distinction between law and gospel. To the believer Christ and His words are only gospel (p. 55); all of Christ's words are blessings, not demands (pp. 62–63). To the unbelievers they are law and demands.

Price, Walter K. *Jesus' Prophetic Sermon.* Chicago: Moody Press, 1972. 160 pp.

Warm-hearted expositions on the Olivet Discourse. He sees Israel set aside in unbelief (pp. 16ff.) and the church now occupying the central position until the Rapture (pp. 26ff.); holds that the Lord left Jerusalem the same direction that the glory of the Lord left it (Ezek. 11:23, p. 37); notes events of the Great Tribulation (p. 48), which will not occur until after the church age (p. 60).

Przybylski, Benno. *Righteousness in Matthew and His World of Thought.* Cambridge: Cambridge University Press, 1980. 184 pp.

A study of Matthew's concept of righteousness in comparison with that of the OT (pp. 8ff.), the Dead Sea Scrolls (pp. 13ff.), and the Tannaitic literature (pp. 39ff.). He discusses specific passages in detail: Matt. 5:6, 10, 20; 6:1, 33 (pp. 80ff.). The work is filled with form-critical discussions.

Ridderbos, Herman. *Matthew's Witness to Jesus Christ*. London: Lutterworth Press, 1958. 91 pp.

He holds that Matthew wrote to prove that Jesus is the Christ, the Son of God (pp. 7–8) and that the leading principle of the Gospel of Matthew is "the coming of the Kingdom of Heaven" (p. 15). He shows that Jesus was born King of the Jews (pp. 16ff.); the Devil tested Him and failed (pp. 24f.). He holds that the Sermon on the Mount is the law of love, but at the end the King is also the Judge (pp. 27–33).

Stonehouse, Ned Bernard. *The Witness of Matthew and Mark to Christ*. Grand Rapids: Wm. B. Eerdmans Publishing Company, 1944, rev. 1958. 285 pp.

Brief evaluation of critical theories about Mark and Matthew. He holds that the evidence cannot decide which is first (p. ix). Both show a relative indifference to locality and chronology; both present an exalted Christ Who cannot be a mere man. He discusses Jesus' use of the OT in Matthew and the kingdom and the Son of Man.

Zahn, Theodor. *Introduction to the New Testament*. 3 vols. Grand Rapids: Kregel Publications, rpt. 1953. II, pp. 506–601.

Conservative introduction. He surveys the tradition concerning Matthew (pp. 506–30), gives a brief summary of the contents of the Gospel (pp. 531–70). Some of his views are interesting, for example, on the purpose of the genealogy (p. 534). He holds to Matthean authorship and a date between A.D. 61 and 66 (p. 573).

Works on Jesus Christ

Barclay, William. *The Mind of Jesus*. New York: Harper and Brothers, 1960. 350 pp.

A liberal theological study of the person and work of Jesus as revealed in His thinking. He holds that Jesus discovered God's purpose for

THE GOSPEL OF THE KING

Himself at the age of twelve (p. 7); defends some of the miracles, but denies the raising of Lazarus (p. 86); has a good chapter on "The Master Teacher" (pp. 89–97); defends the Resurrection (pp. 287–314) but leaves open what kind of body Jesus had (p. 301).

Candlish, R. *Life in a Risen Saviour.* Grand Rapids: Kregel, 1863, rpt. 1989. 437 pp.

Studies in the resurrection of Christ in I Cor. 15.

Denney, James. *Jesus and the Gospel.* Philadelphia: Westminster Press, 1909. 384 pp.

In part I he shows what the NT actually taught about Christ (pp. 9–93); in part II he discusses Jesus' resurrection and self-revelation. He concludes that no one can correctly water down the NT portrait of Jesus.

Erickson, Millard. *The Word Became Flesh.* Grand Rapids: Baker, 1991. 663 pp.

A formal defense of the incarnate nature of Christ. He surveys the biblical picture of Christ (pp. 17–39) and the history of the doctrine (pp. 41–86). He then presents the problems: critical Christology (pp. 89ff.), existential Christology (pp. 111ff.), liberation Christology (Sobrino, pp. 135ff.), black Christology (Cone, pp. 163ff.), feminist Christology (Daly, pp. 187ff.), functional Christology (James Barr, pp. 215ff.), process Christology (Cobb, pp. 243ff.), postmodern Christology (Taylor, pp. 305ff.). He constructs a contemporary incarnational Christology (pp. 383ff.); covers the reliability of the evidence, Jesus' testimony (pp. 431ff.), the NT witness (pp. 455ff.), His resurrection (pp. 481ff.), the logic of the Incarnation (pp. 531ff.); and defends at length Jesus' care for women (pp. 577–93).

Findlay, J. Alexander. *Jesus in the First Gospel.* London: Hodder and Stoughton, n.d. 317 pp.

Not a formal commentary, but a study in the structure and teaching of Matthew. He argues that Jesus was greater than Moses, greater than Joshua, greater than Solomon, and shows that the structure of Matthew proves the thesis.

Goodman, George. *Seventy Lessons in Teaching and Preaching Christ.* Grand Rapids: Kregel Publications, 1939, rpt. 1965. 402 pp.

Practical homiletical notes for seventy sermons on the person of Christ. He covers the preexistence of Christ; His glory; the wonder of His words, works, walk; His parables, promises, warnings, invitations; the "I am's," types, titles, etc.

Gray, James M. *My Faith in Jesus Christ*. New York: Revell, 1927. 186 pp.

A formal defense of the Trinity (pp. 11ff.), the divine-human personality (pp. 24ff.), the Virgin Birth (pp. 35ff.), the Atonement (pp. 66ff.), the bodily resurrection (pp. 81ff.), the Second Coming (pp. 121ff.). He includes his personal testimony of how he was saved (pp. 82–84).

Headlam, Arthur C. *Jesus Christ in History and Faith*. London: John Murray, 1925.

He defends the authenticity of Jesus' teaching on the Jewish law in the Sermon on the Mount (p. 88) but thinks that the form of the sermon is due to Matthew alone (p. 87). He defends the bodily resurrection of Jesus (pp. 159–69) and the Virgin Birth (pp. 169–80), and concludes that they form a harmonious part of the narrative of Jesus (p. 180).

Henry, Carl F. H. *Jesus of Nazareth: Saviour and Lord*. Grand Rapids: Eerdmans, 1966. 285 pp.

An anthology of New Evangelical theology from around the world, including articles by Birger Gerhardsson (pp. 47ff.), Adolf Koberle, "Jesus Christ, the Center of History" (pp. 61ff.), F. F. Bruce, "History and the Gospel" (pp. 87ff.), Paul Althaus, Kenneth Kantzer, and others.

Henry, Philip. *Christ All in All*. 1691; rpt. Swengel, Pa.: Reiner Publications, 1970. 380 pp.

Christ is made to the believer foundation (p. 1), food (p. 12), the root (p. 22), the raiment (p. 32), the head (p. 41), our hope (p. 54), our refuge (p. 62), our righteousness (p. 71), our light (p. 81), our life (p. 91), our peace (p. 99), etc.

Horton, T. C. *The Wonderful Names of Our Wonderful Lord*. Los Angeles: Grant Publishing House, 1925.

Devotional meditations on 365 names of Christ in the OT and NT.

Kähler, Martin. *The So-Called Historical Jesus and the Historic, Biblical Christ*. Philadelphia: Fortress Press, 1964. 153 pp.

Carl Braaten gives a biographical sketch of Kähler; Kähler centered his thought on justification by faith (p. 8); would not separate the historical Jesus from the biblical Christ (p. 14); did not hold to biblical inerrancy because he thought it violated justification by faith alone (p. 17); charged liberal theology with idolatry: worshipping a hero, not Christ, the divine Savior (pp. 24–25); held that the Scriptures were given to awaken faith in Jesus: "when measured by this purpose, I regard them as completely perfect" (p. 127).

Kinney, LeBaron W. *"He Is Thy Lord and Worship Thou Him."* New York: Loizeaux, 1945. 247 pp.

Devotional meditations on the Lord Jesus and His worship. He deals with how great is His beauty, His deity, "I am the Way," worship of the Son, and other subjects.

Krummacher, Friedrich W. *The Suffering Saviour.* 1854; rpt. Chicago: Moody Press, 1948. 444 pp.

Powerful, reverent meditations on the last days of the Lord. He divides the messages into "The Outer Court," from the announcement to the walk to Gethsemane (pp. 3–92); "The Holy Place," from Gethsemane to the daughters of Jerusalem (pp. 95–321); "The Most Holy Place," from the Crucifixion to the interment (pp. 325–440). "Jesus carries His cross. When did He ever show so plainly in His outward circumstances that He bore the curse, as now?" (p. 307).

Large, James. *Two Hundred and Eighty Titles and Symbols of Christ.* Grand Rapids: Baker Book House, 1888, rpt. 1959. 486 pp.

Latham, Henry. *The Risen Master.* Cambridge: Deighton Bell, 1901. 488 pp.

Devotional studies on our Lord's resurrection. He explains the empty tomb and the witness of the grave clothes, arguing that the grave clothes were undisturbed, but fallen flat after Jesus rose through them (p. 3); notes that Peter was struck by the sight of the clothes lying flat (p. 41); thinks that the head cloth was "wrapped around" and not folded (p. 43); argues that Peter and John realized that nothing could be done, which would not have been their attitude if they had thought the body had been stolen (p. 48).

Liddon, Henry P. *The Birth of Christ.* A reprint of Liddon's *The Magnificat,* 1891. Minneapolis, Minn.: Klock and Klock, n.d.

A series of sermons preached in St. Paul's in August, 1889. It contains a thorough treatment of the Incarnation (pp. 86ff.).

————. *The Divinity of Our Lord and Saviour Jesus Christ.* London: Longmans, Green, and Co., 1892. 585 pp.

A fervent, but scholarly, defense of the deity of the Lord Jesus. He notes that the Lord Himself raised the question (p. 3); discusses the OT theophanies (pp. 52ff.); the Lord's plan (pp. 100ff.); His divinity witnessed to by His consciousness (pp. 154ff.), His divinity in the writings of John (pp. 209ff.), His divinity in the writings of James, Peter, and Paul (pp. 279ff.). He concludes with "Brethren, you shall not repent it, if, when life's burdens press heavily, and especially at that solemn hour when human help must fail, you are able to lean with strong confidence on the arm of an Almighty Saviour" (p. 509).

Macartney, Clarence E. *Twelve Great Questions About Christ.* Grand Rapids: Baker Book House, 1956. 221 pp.

He asks questions that settle the nature of Christ: Was He born of a virgin? Did He fulfill prophecy? Did He work miracles? Was He the Son of God? Did He die for our sins? Did He rise from the dead? Did He ascend into heaven? Will He come again?

McDowell, Josh. *More Than a Carpenter.* Wheaton, Ill.: Tyndale, 1977. 128 pp.

A formal defense of a strong Christology. He poses three choices: that Christ is Lord, liar, or lunatic (pp. 25ff.); argues for the accuracy of the biblical records (pp. 41ff.), and from the conversion of Saul (pp. 78ff.).

Morgan, G. Campbell. *The Crises of the Christ.* New York: Revell, 1903, 1936. 477 pp.

A study of the great high points in the life of Christ: the birth (pp. 67ff.), the baptism (pp. 107ff.), the temptation (pp. 153ff.), the Transfiguration (pp. 215ff.), the Crucifixion (pp. 275ff.), the Resurrection (pp. 350ff.), the Ascension (pp. 389ff.); the goal was always man's redemption (pp. 421ff.).

Morison, Frank. *Who Moved the Stone?* Grand Rapids: Zondervan, 1987. 192 pp.

A formal defense of the resurrection of Christ by an English journalist who was converted by studying the evidence.

Morris, Leon. *The Lord from Heaven*. Grand Rapids: Eerdmans, 1958. 112 pp.

A summary of the NT teaching on the deity and humanity of Jesus Christ. He proves the Lord's sinlessness (pp. 21ff.); argues that the title *Son of man* means deity (p. 28); notes the Lord's emphatic use of "I" (pp. 39f.); defends the virgin conception (p. 44); holds that "a prince and a Savior" characterizes the testimony of Acts (pp. 53ff.); "The Lord of glory" gives Paul's view of Christ (pp. 66ff.); "God the Word" gives the Johannine view (pp. 93ff.).

Pax, Wolfgang E. *In the Footsteps of Jesus*. New York: Putnam, 1970. 231 pp.

Beautiful color photographs of the Holy Land.

Rimmer, Harry. *The Magnificence of Jesus*. Grand Rapids: Eerdmans, 1944. 200 pp.

A formal defence of the deity of Jesus (pp. 11ff.), His preexistence (pp. 53ff.), the attributes of God seen in Jesus (pp. 68ff.), the Incarnation (pp. 90ff.), the psychology of the Virgin Birth (pp. 113ff.), His offices of prophet, priest, and king. He gives an apt illustration of Will Snow (an Indian) and the ocean (pp. 54ff.).

Rowdon, Harold H., ed. *Christ the Lord*. Downers Grove, Ill.: InterVarsity, 1982. 344 pp.

Studies in Christology presented to Donald Guthrie. I. H. Marshall contributes "Incarnational Christology in the N.T." and claims that "Jesus Christ is the Son of God made flesh" (p. 13); France discusses "Worship of Jesus" and warns that it was not easy for pious Jews to worship a carpenter (p. 35); R. P. Martin writes on "Reflections on N.T. Hymns" and notes that they show both His deity and His humanity (p. 49); F. F. Bruce writes on the "Son of Man Sayings" (pp. 50–70); D. A. Carson writes on "Christological Ambiguities in Matthew"; Klaas Runia writes on Karl Barth's Christology and agrees with it; Richard Sturch writes on "Can One Say 'Jesus Is God'?" and concludes that we can, and it makes sense (p. 340).

Schaff, Philip. *The Person of Christ*. New York: Scribners, 1965. 375 pp.

He claims that the person of Christ is the miracle of history. He describes the perfection of Christ's humanity (p. 16), His accomplishments (pp. 48ff.), His sinlessness (pp. 51ff.); holds that He is the harmony of all graces and virtues (pp. 84ff.); claims His character is the greatest moral miracle in history (p. 104); gives Jesus' teaching about Himself (pp. 113–28).

Smith, Wilbur M. *The Supernaturalness of Christ*. Boston: W. A. Wilde Company, 1944. 235 pp.

A defense of the divine nature of Christ. He deals with the denial of the supernatural Christ (pp. 3ff.); "The Historical Trustworthiness of the Gospel Records" (pp. 33ff.); "The Supernatural Elements in the Birth of Our Lord" (pp. 73ff.); "The Miraculous Works of Christ" (pp. 109ff.); "The Unique Transfiguration of Christ" (pp. 165ff.); and Christ's resurrection (pp. 189ff.).

Stalker, James. *Imago Christi: The Example of Christ*. 1889; rpt. BJU Press 2002. 230 pp.

An attempt to improve on *The Imitation of Christ* by Thomas à Kempis (p. 3); he covers Christ in the home (pp. 15ff.), in the state (pp. 29ff.), as a friend (pp. 55ff.), in society (pp. 69ff.), as a man of prayer (pp. 81ff.), as a student of Scripture (pp. 95ff.), as a winner of souls (pp. 147ff.), as a preacher (pp. 161ff.), as a teacher (pp. 175ff.), as a controversialist (pp. 189ff.), as a man of feeling (pp. 201ff.). In the chapter "Christ in Society" he notes that the Lord often came to feasts (p. 73), did not neglect the courtesies of life (p. 74), and used hospitality to speak words of eternal life (p. 76).

Swete, Henry Barclay. *The Appearances of Our Lord After the Passion*. London: Macmillan, 1912. 151 pp.

A reverent portrayal of the resurrection appearances to the women at the tomb, to Peter, to Cleopas, to Thomas, and others.

Tholuck, Friedrich August. *Light from the Cross*. Chicago: Moody, 1857, rpt. 1952. 293 pp.

Part I, devotional messages on the cross, a revealer of the hearts of men. It shows what was in the heart of Caiaphas (pp. 33ff.), Judas (pp. 48ff.), Pilate (pp. 61ff.), Peter (pp. 73ff.), Mary (pp. 86ff.),

Thomas (pp. 99ff.). Part II covers the sufferings and death of Christ, Gethsemane (pp. 115ff.), the silence of Jesus (pp. 139ff.), the seven last words (pp. 201ff.); His death and its effects (pp. 282ff.).

Torrey, Reuben Archer. *The Real Christ*. Grand Rapids: Zondervan, rpt. 1966. 157 pp.

He argues that the real Christ is the biblical Christ, not the Christ of Buddhism, spiritualism, Roman Catholicism (pp. 14f.). He covers His love to the Father, to men, for souls; His compassion (pp. 72ff.), His meekness (pp. 88ff.), His humility (pp. 101ff.), His manliness (pp. 113ff.), His imperturbable peace, constant joyfulness, unconquerable optimism, prayerfulness, and so forth.

Van Bruggen, Jacob. *Jesus the Son of God*. Grand Rapids: Baker Books, 1999. 307 pp.

A defense of the Gospel narratives as teaching content. He shows that Jesus was sent by God (pp. 58ff.); that Jesus used special terms to set forth His authority (pp. 93ff.); that He is the Son of God (pp. 114ff.; p. 142ff.); that He is the Lamb of God (p. 163); concludes with an appendix on the Pharisees (pp. 236ff.).

Vos, Geerhardus. *The Self-Disclosure of Jesus*. New York: George H. Doran Company, 1926. 305 pp.

A study of the messianic consciousness of Jesus. He attacks the liberal views of Wrede (pp. 65ff.), Harnack (p. 97), Bousset (pp. 136–39); discusses some of the titles of Jesus: Christ, the Lord, Son of God, Son of Man, Savior; in the Synoptic accounts of the baptism he makes "chosen" to mean "beloved" (p. 186); holds that "only begotten" cannot be limited to the Incarnation to mean "only" or "unique," but it must refer to the preincarnate state (pp. 213–27).

Walvoord, John F. *Jesus Christ Our Lord*. Chicago: Moody Press, 1969. 318 pp.

A conservative Christology organized on major topics. He treats Christ in contemporary theology, in eternity past, in OT history, typology, prophecy; His incarnation, person, life, suffering, death, resurrection, present and future work; holds that Christ was impeccable (p. 152); seems to have a weak definition of propitiation (pp. 155, 171).

A special study of the names and titles of the Lord Jesus, emphasizing references to His deity. He shows that the designations in Matthew prove His deity. He covers the entire NT.

————. *The Person and Work of Christ*. Philadelphia: Presbyterian and Reformed, rpt. 1970. 575 pp.

A collection of articles on "The Historical Christ" (pp. 5ff.), "The Christ That Paul Preached" (pp. 73ff.), "The Emotional Life of Our Lord" (pp. 93ff.), "The Humanitarian Christ" (pp. 189ff.), "Redeemer and Redemption" (pp. 325ff.), "Chief Theories of the Atonement" (pp. 351ff.), "Christ Our Sacrifice" (pp. 391ff.), and others.

Westcott, Brooke Foss. *The Revelation of the Risen Lord*. London: Macmillan and Company, 1882. 199 pp.

He defends the resurrection appearances to Mary Magdalene (p. 33); to the disciples (pp. 43f.); the Great Commission (pp. 80ff.).

————. *The Gospel of the Resurrection*. London: Macmillan and Company, 1891. 307 pp.

Whyte, Alexander. *The Walk, Conversation and Character of Jesus Christ Our Lord*. New York: Revell, 1905. 340 pp.

Devotional meditations on Christ: "The Express Image of His Person" (pp. 11ff.); "That Holy Thing" (pp. 19ff.); "About His Father's Business" (pp. 59ff.); "Our Lord's First Text" (pp. 115ff.); "His Meat" (pp. 193ff.); "Our Lord and the Bible" (pp. 280ff.); "Our Lord's Favourite Graces, Meekness and Lowliness of Heart" (pp. 316ff.).

Wiersby, Warren W. *Classic Sermons on the Cross of Christ*. Grand Rapids: Kregel, 1990. 157 pp.

An anthology of powerful messages. He gives sermons by Spurgeon, "The Death of Christ"; J. H. Jowett, "The Power of the Cross"; George H. Morrison, "The Offense of the Cross"; Maclaren, "The Cross: The Proof of the Love of God"; R. A. Torrey, "The Uplifted Christ"; Biederwolf, "The Logic of the Cross"; and others.

Encyclopedia Articles and Periodicals

Bailey, Mark L. "Guidelines for Interpreting Jesus' Parables." *Bibliotheca Sacra*, vol 155, no. 617 (Jan.–Mar., 1998): 29–38.

He urges noting the parable's historical setting, cultural setting, ana-lyzing the structure and details, stating the central truth of the par-able and its relationship to the kingdom.

—————. "The Parable of the Sower and the Soils." *Bibliotheca Sacra*, vol. 155, no. 618 (Apr.–Jun, 1998): 172–88.

—————. "The Parable of the Tares." *Bibliotheca Sacra*, vol. 155, no. 619 (July–Sept., 1998): 266–79.

He holds that the central truth is the reality of coming judgment (p. 276).

—————. "The Parable of the Mustard Seed." *Bibliotheca Sacra*, vol. 155, no. 620 (Oct.–Dec., 1998): 449–59.

He terms it the parable of encouragement, from a small beginning to worldwide growth.

—————. "The Parable of the Leavening Process." *Bibliotheca Sacra*, vol. 156, no. 621 (Jan.–Mar., 1999): 61–71.

The parable manifests subtle power in spreading itself through society and transforming it.

—————. "The Parables of the Hidden Treasure and the Pearl Merchant." *Bibliotheca Sacra*, vol. 156, no. 622 (Apr.–Jun., 1999): 175–89.

He emphasizes the reward of the righteous and the great value of the kingdom.

—————. "The Parable of the Dragnet and of the Householder." *Bibliotheca Sacra*, vol. 156, no. 623 (July–Sept., 1999): 282–96.

He stresses the believer's responsibility of catching the fish and the certainty of final judgment.

—————. "The Doctrine of the Kingdom in Matthew 13." *Bibliotheca Sacra*, vol. 156, no. 624 (Oct.–Dec., 1999): 453–51.

He concludes that the reception of the Word is God's goal for every hearer, that the great conflict is between the Son of man and Satan, that God alone is the Judge, and that Jesus is the coming King.

Biblical Viewpoint. vol. I, no. 2 (Nov. 1967).

Focus on Matthew. "Destroying the Works of the Devil (Matt. 4)" by Daniel Krusich (pp. 80ff.); "The Sermon on the Mount (Matt. 5–7)" by Stewart Custer (pp. 85ff.); "Rewards in God's Kingdom (Matt.

19:26–20:6)" by Marshall Neal (pp. 92ff.); "The Olivet Discourse (Matt. 24–25)" by Ernest Pickering (pp. 98ff.); "Matthew's View of the Old Testament" by Anthony D. York (pp. 104ff.); "Our Lord's View of the Old Testament According to Matthew" by Robert L. Reymond (pp. 111ff.); "The Theology of Matthew" by Stewart Custer (pp. 123ff.).

Biblical Viewpoint. vol. XXIII, no. 1 (April, 1989).

Focus on Matthew. "The Legacy of the First Gospel" by Edward M. Panosian (pp. 7ff.); "The Message Matthew Communicates Through His Service" by Mark Minnick (pp. 13ff.); "The Principles of the Kingdom (Matt. 5)" by Stewart Custer (pp. 29ff.); "True Religion (Matt. 6)" by Earl Nutz (pp. 35ff.); "The Sending of the Twelve (Matt. 9:35–10:42)" by James Frederick Creason Jr. (pp. 41ff.); "Christ Teaches Concerning the Kingdom (Matt. 19)" by Marshall Neal (pp. 53ff.); "The Teacher's Truths (Matt. 22)" by Ward Andersen (pp. 61ff.).

Brown, Colin, ed. "Spirit, Holy Spirit." *The New International Dictionary of New Testament Theology,* vol. III, pp. 689–709. Grand Rapids: Zondervan, 1978.

Jesus' conception "was effected by the power of the Spirit without the agency of a human father: Matt. 1:18–25—so that Jesus fulfills the Emmanuel prophecy (Isa. 7:14)" (p. 697).

Butler, Trent C. gen. ed. *Holman Bible Dictionary.* Nashville: Holman Bible Publishers, 1991. 1450 pp. and maps.

Charlesworth, J. H. "The Jewish Roots of Christology: The Discovery of the Hypostatic Voice." *Scottish Journal of Theology,* vol. 39, no. 1: 19ff.

He discusses the "Bath Kol" and the uses in the NT of the divine "voice."

Douglas, J. D., and Merrill C. Tenney, eds. *The New International Dictionary of the Bible.* Grand Rapids: Zondervan, 1963, 1987. 1162 pp. and maps.

Elwell, Walter A., ed. "Jesus Christ," *Evangelical Dictionary of Biblical Theology,* pp. 396–406. Grand Rapids: Baker Books, 1996.

Gardner-Smith, Percival. "Christology." *Hastings Dictionary of the Bible*. Rev. ed. F. C. Grant and H. H. Rowley. New York: Scribner's Sons, 1963. 1080 pp.

He has 26 columns of discussion in the biblical theological order: Synoptic Gospels, Paul, Hebrews, I Peter, Apocalypse, other books. He covers the great titles, "Son of Man," "Son of God," Peter's confession, and other subjects. He admits the possibility of legendary material in with generally reliable information in the NT.

Guelich, R. A. "Interpreting the Sermon on the Mount." *Interpretation*, vol. XLI, no. 1 (Jan. 1987): 117–30.

He gives a concise history of interpretation of the sermon; concludes that the sermon is a literary product, not a transcription of Jesus' teaching (p. 130).

Guthrie, Donald. "Jesus Christ." *Zondervan Pictorial Encyclopedia of the Bible*, vol. III, pp. 497–583. Grand Rapids: Zondervan Publishing House, 1975.

Hagner, D. A. "Matthew, Gospel According to." *International Standard Bible Encyclopedia*, vol. III, pp. 280–88. Grand Rapids: W. B. Eerdmans, 1986.

———. "Matthew." *New Dictionary of Biblical Theology*. Alexander, pp. 262–67. Rosner, Carson, and Goldworthy, eds. Downers Grove, Ill.: InterVarsity Press, 2000.

Harrison, R. K., ed. *The New Unger's Bible Dictionary*. Chicago: Moody Press, 1957, 1988. 1400 pp. and maps.

Hastings, James. *Dictionary of Christ and the Gospels*. 2 vols. New York: Scribners, 1908, 1924.

Individual articles on Christ's divinity, humanity, the Incarnation, titles such as "Son of God," "Son of Man," etc.

Holman Bible Dictionary. Trent C. Butler, gen. ed. Nashville: Holman Bible Publishers, 1991. 1450 pp. and maps.

Hutchison, John C. "Women, Gentiles, and the Messianic Mission in Matthew's Genealogy." *Bibliotheca Sacra*, vol. 158, no. 630 (April–June, 2001): 152–64.

He holds that they demonstrate God's providence in preserving the messianic line; God's heart for godly Gentiles; the importance of the Abrahamic and Davidic covenants and they call Matthew's readers to repentance and humility.

Huxley, Anthony. *Standard Encyclopedia of the World's Mountains.* New York: G. P. Putnam's Sons, 1962. 383 pp.

It includes geographical information on biblical mountains as well.

Knowling, Richard John. "Birth of Christ," Hastings, gen. ed. *Dictionary of Christ and the Gospels,* vol. I, pp. 202–8. Grand Rapids: Baker Book House, 1973.

Ladd, G. E. "The Kingdom of God," Harrison, Bromily, and Henry, *Baker's Dictionary of Theology,* pp. 309–14. Grand Rapids: Baker Book House, 1960.

Marshall, I. H. "Jesus Christ." *New Dictionary of Biblical Theology,* Alexander, Rosner, Carson, and Goldsworthy, eds., pp. 592–602. Downers Grove, Ill.: InterVarsity Press, 2000.

Martin, R. P. "Jesus Christ." *International Standard Bible Encyclopedia,* vol. II, pp. 1034–49. Grand Rapids: Eerdmans, 1982.

Orr, James. "Jesus Christ." *International Standard Bible Encyclopedia,* vol. III, pp. 1624–68. Grand Rapids: Eerdmans, 1952.

Pagankemper, Karl E. "Rejection Imagery in the Synoptic Parables." *Bibliotheca Sacra,* vol. 153, no. 610 (Apr.–Jun, 1996): 179–98.

He examines the theme of judgment in the parables under the image of rejection (goats, bad fish).

Petersen, L. M. "Matthew, Gospel of." *Zondervan Pictorial Encyclopedia of the Bible,* vol. IV, pp.120–38. Grand Rapids: Zondervan Publishing House, 1975.

Pond, Eugene W. "Who Are the Sheep and the Goats in Matt. 25:31–46." *Bibliotheca Sacra,* vol. 159, no. 636 (July–Sept., 2002): 288–301.

———. "Who Are 'the Least' of Jesus' Brothers in Matt. 25:40." *Bibliotheca Sacra,* vol. 159, no 636 (Oct.– Dec. 2002): 436–48.

The usual answer is Jews in the Tribulation period (Scofield, Gaebelein, Walvoord). He holds that "the least" are believers slain for their faith during the Tribulation period, perhaps including Jews and Gentile martyrs.

Ryken, Leland, James Wilhoit, and Tremper Longman III, eds. *Dictionary of Biblical Imagery*, "Jesus, Images of," pp. 437–51. Downers Grove, Ill.: InterVarsity, 1998.

Saucy, Mark R. "Miracles and Jesus' Proclamation of the Kingdom of God." *Bibliotheca Sacra*, vol. 153, no. 611 (Jul.–Sept., 1996): 281–307.

He gives a formal defense of the authenticity of Jesus' miracles and shows their relation to the kingdom of God.

———. "The Kingdom-of-God Sayings in Matthew." *Bibliotheca Sacra*, vol. 151 (Apr.–Jun., 1994): 175–97.

He argues that Jesus' teaching of the kingdom of God changed after the rejection in Matt. 11–12. The kingdom sayings in Matt. 13 show that the kingdom is awaiting a final action of Christ, and the church is soon introduced (Matt. 16).

Turner, David L. "Matthew 21:43 and the Fathers of Israel," *Bibliotheca Sacra*, vol. 159, no. 633 (Jan.–Mar., 2002): 46–51.

He sees parallels with Isa. 5:1–2; holds that the judgment is not pronounced on Israel as a nation but on the religious leaders (pp. 60–61).

Van der Toorn, Karel, Bob Becking, and Pieter W. van der Horst, eds. *Dictionary of Deities and Demons in the Bible*. Grand Rapids: Eerdmans, 1999. 960 pp.

Technical articles on "Satan" (pp. 726–32), "Devil" (pp. 244–49).

Wachsmann, Shelley. "The Galilee Boat," *Biblical Archaeology Review*, vol. XIV, no. 5 (Sept./Oct., 1988): 18–33.

He provides a description of its discovery and preservation at the Yigal Allon Museum at the Nof Ginnosar Kibbutz, with color photos.

Electronic Media

Allon Museum. *The Galilee Boat*. Video.

Awwad, Sami. *The Homeland of Jesus*. Mount Scopus Hotel, Jerusalem. Video.

———. *The Land of the Bible*. Mount Scopus Hotel, Jerusalem. Video.

Israel. Steimatzky, Ltd. Video.

Israel. Video Visits. International Video Network, 1988. Video.

Israel: Land of Milk and Honey. Israel Music. Newe-Monoson. Video.

The C. H. Spurgeon Collection. The Metropolitan Tabernacle Pulpit. Ages Digital Library.

The Theological Journal Library, Version 2. *Bibliotheca Sacra.*

Bibles and Testaments

Aland, Barbara and Kurt, Johannes Karavidopoulos, Carlo Martini, and Bruce Metzger. *The Greek New Testament.* 4th revised edition. Stuttgart: Deutsche Bibelgesellschaft, 1966, 1993. 918 pp.

The Holy Bible: English Standard Version. Wheaton, Ill.: Crossway Bibles, 2002. 1328 pp.

The International Inductive Study Bible. NAS. Eugene, Ore.: Harvest House Publishers, 1977. 2206 pp.

Kittel, Rudolf. *Biblia Hebraica.* Stuttgart: Privileg. Wurtt. Bibelanstalt, 1937, 1954. 1434 pp.

Nestle, Eberhard, and Kurt Aland. *Novum Testamentum Graece.* 26th ed. Stuttgart: Deutsche Bibelstiftung, 1898, 1979. 779, 78 (intro.) pp.

Rahlfs, Alfred. *Septuaginta.* [The OT in Greek.] Stuttgart: Privilegierte Wurttembergische Bibelanstalt, 1935. 2 vols. 1184, 941 pp.

Rotherham, Joseph Bryant. *The Emphasized Bible.* Grand Rapids: Kregel Publications, rpt. 1959. 920, 272 (intro.) pp.

Ryrie, Charles Caldwell. *The Ryrie Study Bible.* Chicago: Moody Press, 1976. 2006 pp.

Scofield, C. I. *The Scofield Study Bible.* New York: Oxford University Press, 1909, 1945. 1362 pp.

Other Works Cited

Alden, Peter C. *National Audubon Society Field Guide to African Wildlife.* New York: Alfred A. Knopf, 1995. 988 pp.

There is much wildlife that is found on both African and Asian sides of the Red Sea and the Mediterranean.

Alexander, David. *The Lion Photoguide to the Bible.* Tring, Herts, England: Lion Publishing, 1981, 1983. 287 pp.

Alexander, T. Desmond, and Brian S. Rosner, eds. *New Dictionary of Biblical Theology.* Downers Grove, Ill.: InterVarsity Press, 2000. 866 pp.

A New Evangelical study of biblical theology (pp. 3ff.) with a brief analysis of the themes in Matthew (pp. 262–67) and articles on "Atonement" (pp. 388ff.), "Baptism," (pp. 395ff.) and other subjects.

Alon, Azaria. *The Natural History of the Land of the Bible.* New York: Paul Hamlyn, 1969. 276 pp.

A survey of the plants and animals of the Holy Land. Color and black and white photos with biblical references.

Arav, Rami, and Richard Freund. *Bethsaida.* Kirksville, Missouri: Truman State University Press, 1999. 463 pp.

A preliminary report on excavations from 1994–96. Gloria London and Robert Schuster write on "Bethsaida Iron Age Ceramics" (p. 175ff.); Arie Kindler reports on "Coins of the Tetrarch Philip and Bethsaida" (pp. 245ff.).

Arndt, William, and Wilbur Gingrich. *A Greek-English Lexicon of the New Testament.* Chicago: University of Chicago Press, 1957. 909 pp.

This is the most helpful Greek-English lexicon.

Augustine, Saint. *On the Trinity* in Vol. II of *The Basic Writings of Saint Augustine,* New York: Random House, 1948. 2 vols. Pp. 667ff.

Profound meditations on the nature of the one true God.

Backhouse, Robert. *The Kregel Pictorial Guide to the Temple.* Grand Rapids: Kregel Publications, 1996. 32 pp.

Color illustrations of Herod's temple based on an accurate scale model of the building and area.

Bahat, Dan. *Jerusalem.* Jerusalem: Ariel Publishing House, 1969, 1980. 128 pp.

Architectural drawings of famous buildings and places in Jerusalem.

Ball, Barbara. *The River Jordan: An Illustrated Guide from Bible Days to the Present,* Carta, 1998. Distributed by Kregel. 48 pp.

Bavinck, Herman. *The Doctrine of God.* Grand Rapids: Eerdmans, 1951. 407 pp.

A technical, Reformed study. He covers God's incomprehensibility (pp. 13ff.), God's incommunicable attributes (pp. 113ff.), communicable attributes (pp. 175ff.); the holy Trinity (pp. 255ff.).

Beers, V. Gilbert. *The Victor Handbook of Bible Knowledge.* Wheaton, Ill.: Victor Books, 1981. 640 pp.

An illustrated Bible dictionary arranged in the order of Bible books.

Berkhof, Louis. *Systematic Theology.* Grand Rapids: Eerdmans, 1949. 784 pp.

Orthodox Reformed theology. He has a precise section on the holy Trinity (pp. 82–99).

Blanchard, John. *Whatever Happened to Hell?* Darlington, Co.: Evangelical Press, 1993. 336 pp.

A formal defense of the biblical doctrine of hell. He defends the biblical teaching (pp. 19ff.); discusses the words *hades*, *gehenna*, and so forth (pp. 33–43; 130–42); defends the idea of life after death (pp. 63ff.) and the idea of a day of judgment (pp. 98ff.); attacks conditional immortality (pp. 210ff.); explains how to avoid hell (pp. 267ff.).

Blomberg, Craig L. *Interpreting the Parables.* Downers Grove, Ill.: InterVarsity Press, 1990. 333 pp.

He disassociates himself from the majority of liberal interpretations (pp. 19ff.) and argues that "one may actually view the parables of Jesus as both allegorical and authentic" (p. 23); he provides perhaps the single most helpful discussion of parable, allegory, and symbolism in the literature (pp. 29–69); thinks that Jesus' followers did memorize Jesus' teachings (p. 98); discusses three-point parables (pp. 171–253), two-point and one-point parables (pp. 255–88), and the theology of the parables: the kingdom and the Christ (pp. 289–324).

Bounds, E. M. *The Necessity of Prayer.* Grand Rapids: Baker, rpt. 1976. 144 pp.

Fervent exhortations to pray by a praying saint.

Bourbon, Fabio, and Enrico Lavagno, *The Holy Land.* New York: Barnes and Noble, 2001. 228 pp.

A guide to the archaeological sites and historical monuments. It is lavishly illustrated with color photographs and includes architectural diagrams.

Branigan, Keith, and Michael Vickers. *Hellas*. New York: McGraw-Hill Book Company, 1980. 224 pp.

A lavishly illustrated survey of Greek civilization.

Browne, A. Gondrexon-Ives. *Guide to the Dogs of the World*. London: Treasure Press, 1974, 1987. 256 pp.

The Canaan dog (pp. 82–83); Pharaoh hound (pp. 180–81).

Bruce, Alexander Balmain. *The Training of the Twelve*. New York: Richard R. Smith, Inc., 1930. 552 pp.

Devotional studies in the Lord's instructions to the apostles. Note especially Chapter III, "Matthew the Publican" (pp. 19–28).

Bruce, Frederick Fyvie. *Peter, Stephen, James, and John: Studies in Early Non-Pauline Christianity*. Grand Rapids: Eerdmans, 1980.

Bultmann, Rudolf. *Faith and Understanding*. New York: Harper, 1969.

A bitter attack on the faith of Christians by a form critic who denies the authenticity of the entire NT.

Chafer, Louis Sperry. *Satan*. Chicago: Moody, 1919. 180 pp.

He covers the career of Satan, the satanic system, the satanic host, Satan's motives and methods, the man of sin, modern devices, etc.

Chesterman, Charles W. *The Audubon Society Field Guide to North American Rocks and Minerals*. New York: Alfred A. Knopf, 1978. 850 pp.

A standard guide to mineral identification.

Comay, Joan. *The Jerusalem I Love*. Tel Aviv, Israel: Leon Amiel Publisher, 1976. 158 pp.

Beautiful color photographs of the Dome of the Rock in snow (pp. 18–19), the bazaars (pp. 36–37), the Church of All Nations (pp. 54–55), the pool of Siloam (p. 60), a Passover meal (pp. 96–97), the Chagall windows (p. 134).

Couch, Mal, ed. *Dictionary of Premillennial Theology*. Grand Rapids: Kregel, 1996. 442 pp.

Helpful articles on the Olivet Discourse (pp. 286–89); various judgments (pp. 225ff.); Millennium (pp. 259ff.); and many other topics.

Custer, Stewart. *Does Inspiration Demand Inerrancy?* Nutley, N.J.: Craig Press, 1977. 120 pp.

The thesis of the author is that the teaching of the Bible does demand the doctrine of inerrancy. He provides answers to the "alleged errors" (pp. 93ff.).

———. *The Stars Speak.* 2 ed. Greenville, S.C. : BJU Press, 2002. 212 pp.

Devotional studies in the biblical references to the sun, moon, stars, planets, and other heavenly bodies. Illustrated by color photographs from the Hubble Space Telescope.

———. *Stones of Witness.* Greenville, S.C.: BJU Press, 2002. 236 pp.

Images of the Holy Land from Dan to Beersheba and on to the Red Sea. There is an accompanying interactive CD-ROM with 635 color photos of the Holy Land.

———. *Tools for Preaching and Teaching the Bible.* 2 ed. Greenville, S.C.: BJU Press, 1979, 1998. 400 pp.

Recommended books for the pastor: concordances, atlases, commentaries, books on prophecy, cults, ethics, and so forth.

———. *Treasury of New Testament Synonyms.* Greenville, S.C.: BJU Press, 1975. 143 pp.

An investigation of thirty-two different groups of Greek synonyms to bring out distinctions in meaning. It covers such words as *burden, devil, power, righteousness, soul, trickery.*

Dana, H. E. *The New Testament World.* Nashville: Broadman Press, 1937, 1951. 267 pp.

A brief sketch of the historical background of the NT.

Deissmann, Adolf. *Light from the Ancient East.* New York: Harper, 1908, 1922. 535 pp.

The NT background from the papyri and Greek inscriptions.

Dorling Kindersley Travel Guide. *Jerusalem and the Holy Land.* London: Dorling Kindersley Publishing, Inc., 2000. 304 pp.

A very helpful guide that covers the land region by region with maps, color photos, and advice concerning food, museums, hotels, and so forth.

Douma, J. *The Ten Commandments*. Phillipsburg, N.J.: P and R Publishing, 1992, 1996. 410 pp.

A conservative Reformed exposition of the Mosaic code.

Engelder, T. E. *Scripture Cannot Be Broken*. St. Louis: Concordia Publishing House, 1944.

A strong defense of the verbal inspiration of Scripture.

Euripides. Alcest. Loeb Classical Library. Trans. A. S. Way.

Feinberg, Charles L. *The Fundamentals for Today*. 2 vols. Grand Rapids: Kregel Publications, 1909, 1958.

A great anthology in defense of the faith. James M. Gray defended the inspiration of the Bible (I, pp. 125ff.); A. C. Gaebelein wrote on fulfilled prophecy (I, pp. 185ff.); Philip Mauro wrote on life in the Word (I, pp. 191ff.).

Foure, Catherine, ed. *The Holy Land*. New York: Alfred A. Knopf, Inc., 1995. 480 pp.

The Knopf guide to the Holy Land, well illustrated, with much information for the traveler as well as the student.

Frederick, Kenneth. *The Making of a Disciple*. Greenville, S.C.: BJU Press, 2001.

A study in the Lord's transformation of Peter into a disciple.

Geldenhuys, J. Norval. *Supreme Authority*. Grand Rapids: Eerdmans, 1953. 128 pp.

He holds that the Lord Jesus is the supreme authority; the authority of the apostles was derived from the Lord.

Gilbert, Martin. *Jerusalem in the Twentieth Century*. John Wiley and Sons, 1996. 412 pp.

He covers early conflicts, the British conquest in 1917; British Mandate; the Second World War; May, 1948; the Six-Day War; the intifada.

Girdlestone, Robert B. *The Grammar of Prophecy*. Grand Rapids: Kregel, 1955, rpt. 192 pp.

He covers early conflicts, the British conquest in 1917; British Mandate; the Second World War; May, 1948; the Six-Day War; the intifada.

Girdlestone, Robert B. *The Grammar of Prophecy*. Grand Rapids: Kregel, 1955, rpt. 192 pp.

He explains prophetic forms of thought, prophetic formulae, methods of studying prophecy; defends the Millennium (pp. 141ff.).

————. *Synonyms of the Old Testament*. Grand Rapids: Eerdmans, 1897, 1956. 346 pp.

He discusses the names of God (pp. 18ff.), words for man (pp. 45ff.), soul and spirit (pp. 55ff.), heart (pp. 64ff.), sin (pp. 76ff.), repentance (pp. 87ff.), and others.

Govett, Robert. *Eternal Suffering of the Wicked, and Hades*. 1871, rpt. Miami Springs, Fla.: Schoettle Publishing Co., 1989. 181, 22 pp.

He defends the doctrine from the Scriptures, distinguishing the judgment of the nations from the Great White Throne judgment (pp. 3ff.); traces the words *eternal, punishment,* and so forth through Scripture (pp. 6ff.); argues that punishment is a process (pp. 15ff.) and that eternal punishment does not mean instant annihilation (pp. 20ff.); stresses that the wrath of God abides on the wicked (pp. 38ff.).

Guthrie, Donald. *New Testament Theology*. Downers Grove, Ill.: InterVarsity Press, 1981. 1064 pp.

Reverent studies on God (pp. 75ff.); man (pp. 116ff.); Christology (pp. 219ff.); the mission of Christ (pp. 408ff.); the Holy Spirit (pp. 510ff.); the Christian life (pp. 573ff.); the church (pp. 701ff.); the future (pp. 790ff.); ethics (pp. 893ff.); and Scripture (pp. 953ff.).

Hall, H. R. *The Ancient History of the Near East*. London: Methuen and Co. Ltd. 1952. 620 pp.

History of Egypt, Babylon, Hittites, Assyrian empire, Medes and Persians, and Greece to the battle of Salamis.

Henry, Matthew. *The Quest for Communion with God*. Grand Rapids: Eerdmans, 1712, 1954. 110 pp.

He urges beginning every day with prayer (pp. 9ff.), spending the day with God (pp. 39ff.), closing the day with God (pp. 72ff.).

Herzog, Chaim, and Mordechai Gichon. *Battles of the Bible*. London: Greenhill Books, 1997. 320 pp.

A military history from the campaigns of Joshua to the fall of Judah. There are many maps with battle plans (Gibeah, Michmash, pp. 69, 71); the Assyrian conquest (p. 144).

Hiebert, D. Edmond. *Working with God Through Prayer*. Greenville, S.C.: BJU Press, 1991. 129 pp.

He includes working by prayer (pp. 1ff.), the power of prayer (pp. 9ff.), prayer-sent laborers (pp. 25ff.), the prayer ministry of the church (pp. 35ff.), and others.

Hort, Fenton John Anthony. *The Christian Ecclesia*. London: Macmillan, 1898. 306 pp.

He surveys the early history of the church, and treats "The One Universal Ecclesia in the Epistles of the First Roman Captivity" (pp. 135ff.); gives 11 different meanings of *ecclesia* in Acts and the Epistles (pp. 115f.); stresses that all believers have a direct relation to the universal ecclesia (p. 168).

Hughes, Philip. *The Theology of the English Reformers*. Grand Rapids: Eerdmans, 1965. 283 pp.

A study of the English reformers and their views on Scripture, justification, sanctification, worship, and other subjects.

Hunter, Archibald M. *Introducing New Testament Theology*. Philadelphia: Westminster Press, 1957. 160 pp.

A short, reverent introduction from the history of salvation school.

————. *The Parables Then and Now*. Philadelphia: Westminster Press, 1971. 128 pp.

He defends their authenticity, "the background is authentically Palestinian" (p. 14); he notes the crisis of the kingdom (the great supper, p. 21), the coming of the kingdom (pp. 35ff.), the grace of the kingdom (pp. 52ff.), the men of the kingdom (pp. 74ff.).

Huxley, Anthony, ed. *Standard Encyclopedia of the World's Mountains*. New York: G. P. Putnam's Sons, 1962. 383 pp.

"Mount Hermon impresses by its bulk and isolation rather than by the more usual and dramatic features of precipices and pointed peaks" (p. 167).

Jeremias, Joachim. "*Lampades* in Matt. 25:1–13." *Soli Deo Gloria*, J. McDowell Richards, ed. Richmond, Va.: John Knox Press, 1968. Pp. 83–87.

He defends the thesis that the word means *torch*, not *lamp*.

————. *The Eucharistic Words of Jesus*. New York: Charles Scribner's Sons, 1966. 278 pp.

An exhaustive analysis of all the details of the Last Supper. He concludes that the Last Supper was a Passover meal (p. 84); holds that "I Cor. 11:23–25 is from a literary point of view the oldest account. Paul wrote it probably in the spring of 54" (p. 138).

Josephus, Flavius. *The Life and Works of Flavius Josephus*. Philadelphia: John C. Winston Company, 1957.

It includes *The Antiquities of the Jews* (pp. 32–603) and the *Wars of the Jews* (pp. 603–857).

Kelso, James L. *An Archaeologist Looks at the Gospels*. Waco, Tex.: Word Books, 1969. 142 pp.

He provides archaeological insights to the biblical record.

Kern, Paul Bentley. *Ancient Siege Warfare*. Bloomington, Ind.: Indiana University Press, 1999. 419 pp.

Begins by noting that Jericho was a heavily fortified city in neolithic times. The city wall at that time was ten feet thick (p. 9).

Kistemaker, Simon J. *The Parables of Jesus*. Grand Rapids: Baker Book House, 1980. 301 pp.

A Reformed exposition of forty parables. He stresses the historical settings of the parables (p. xxiii).

Lang, G. H. *The Parabolic Teaching of Scripture*. Grand Rapids: Eerdmans, 1956. 400 pp.

He emphasizes the mysteries of the kingdom (Matt. 13, pp. 63ff.) and the Olivet parables (Matt. 24–25, pp. 311ff.).

Lehman, Chester K. *Biblical Theology: Vol. 2, New Testament*. Scottdale, Pa.: Herald Press, 1974. 566 pp.

THE GOSPEL OF THE KING

A conservative Arminian study. He "maintains that each Gospel stands in its own right as a literary whole in which each writer presented the life and teachings of Jesus in such a manner as to set forth his own respective purpose in writing his Gospel" (p. 35).

Lightfoot, Joseph Barber. *The Epistle of St. Paul to the Galatians*. 1865. rpt. Grand Rapids: Zondervan, n.d. 384 pp.

The best older commentary on the Greek text.

Lightner, Robert P. *The Saviour and the Scriptures*. Philadelphia: Presbyterian and Reformed Publishing Company, 1966.

He proves the doctrine of verbal inspiration from the words of the Lord Jesus.

Machen, J. Gresham. *The Christian View of Man*. Carlisle, Pa.: Banner of Truth Trust, 1984.

An orthodox portrait.

McClain, Alva J. *The Greatness of the Kingdom*. Grand Rapids: Zondervan, 1959, 1974. 556 pp.

A defense of the premillennial interpretation of the kingdom.

McRay, John. *Archaeology and the New Testament*. Grand Rapids: Baker Book House, 1991. 432 pp.

The chapter "Herodian Jerusalem" (pp. 91–127) discusses the temple mount, the judgment pavement of Pilate, the water supply, the theater, and other excavations.

Magi, Giovanna. *The Holy Land*. Florence, Italy: Bonechi, Steimatzky, 1992. 128 pp.

Full-color photographs of Jerusalem (pp. 3ff.), Bethlehem (pp. 58ff.), Sea of Galilee (pp. 101ff.), Capernaum (pp. 104ff.), and others.

Marshall, I. Howard. *Last Supper and Lord's Supper*. Grand Rapids: Eerdmans Publishing Company, 1980. 191 pp.

He surveys the details of the last week and argues "that Jesus held a Passover meal earlier than the official Jewish date, and that he was able to do so as the result of calendar differences among the Jews" (p. 75).

Maston, Thomas Bufford. *Biblical Ethics*. Waco, Texas: Word Books, Publishers, 1967, 1977. 300 pp.

A technical explanation for the choices made in the editing of the United Bible Societies' Greek NT.

Minear, Paul. *Images of the Church in the New Testament*. Philadelphia: Westminster Press, 1960. 294 pp.

He records minor images (salt, fish, the boat, the ark, altar, vine, virgins, and so forth); images on the people of God (remnant, little flock, Israel), the new creation (Son of man, light, life, the last Adam), the fellowship in faith (the faithful, disciples, friends), the body of Christ (one body, spiritual body, growth of the body).

Minnick, Mark. *The Doctrine of Eternal Punishment*. Woodridge, Ill.: Preach the Word Ministries, Inc., 1996. 41 pp.

A formal defense of the biblical teaching on hell. He notes that a denial of the doctrine attacks the deity of Christ (p. 5); distinguishes between hades and gehenna (pp. 10f.); defines the characteristics of brimstone, sulfur (p. 21); defends the eternality of hell (pp. 31ff.).

Moldenke, Harold N., and Alma L. Moldenke. *Plants of the Bible*. Waltham, Mass.: Chronica Botanica Company, 1952. 328 pp. and plates.

A technical classification of plants found in Bible lands.

Moore, David George. *The Battle for Hell*. New York: University Press of America, Inc., 1995. 102 pp.

He notes the current disappearance of belief in hell (p. 3), the opinions of evangelicals like Clark Pinnock, who hold to annihilationism (p. 5); evaluates the objections to the doctrine of hell (pp. 18ff.); argues that God would be unjust to annihilate Himmler in view of the sufferings of the Jews at Auschwitz (pp. 28f.); charges that the rejection of hell is an emotional reaction rather than biblical faith (pp. 45ff.); warns against the self-centeredness of modern Christianity (pp. 63ff.).

Morey, Robert. *The Trinity*. Grand Rapids: World Publishing, 1996. 587 pp.

A conservative discussion of the evidence and modern issues.

Morris, Leon. *The Cross in the New Testament*. Grand Rapids: Eerdmans, 1965. 454 pp.

Probably the finest single work on soteriology. He traces the doctrine of the Cross through the Gospels (pp. 13ff.), the Pauline Epistles (pp. 180ff.), Hebrews (pp. 270ff.), and the Catholic Epistles and Revelation (pp. 309ff.). He refutes C. H. Dodd's arguments against *propitiation* (pp. 225–27).

Moulton, James Hope in *A Grammar of New Testament Greek*. Vol. III of *Syntax* by Nigel Turner. Edinburgh: T. and T. Clark, 1963. 417 pp.

The most thorough study of Greek syntax.

Moulton, James Hope, and George Milligan. *The Vocabulary of the Greek New Testament*. Grand Rapids: Eerdmans, 1963. 705 pp.

A thorough listing of the words of the Greek NT that are also found in the papyri. They provide helpful background.

Murray, Andrew. *Abide in Christ*. New York: Grosset and Dunlap, n.d. 223 pp.

Meditations on fellowship with Christ, as the branch in the vine (pp. 30ff.), every moment (pp. 92ff.), at this moment (pp. 106ff.).

———. *The Ministry of Intercession*. London: James Nisbet and Co., 1898. 205 pp.

Exhortations to serve God through intercessory prayer.

———. *With Christ in the School of Prayer*. New York: Revell, 1886, rpt.

He covers subjects such as the only Teacher (pp. 1ff.), the model prayer (pp. 24ff.), "How much more" (pp. 39ff.), "What wilt thou?" (pp. 71ff.).

Ogden, Schubert Miles. *Christ Without Myth*. New York: Harper, 1961. 189 pp.

A radical form critic who thought that Bultmann did not go far enough. Bultmann held that there actually was a man named Jesus, but nothing written about Him is correct. Ogden holds that there never was such a person. To him all of Christianity is a myth.

Packer, J. I. *Knowing God*. Downers Grove, Ill.: InterVarsity Press, 1973. 256 pp.

Devotional studies in the nature of God. He covers God incarnate (pp. 45ff.), God's majesty (pp. 73ff.), His wisdom (pp. 89ff.), His love (pp. 106ff.), His grace (pp. 116ff.), His wrath (pp. 134ff.), and other studies.

Pax, Wolfgang E. *In the Footsteps of Jesus.* Tel Aviv, Israel: Leon Amiel Publisher, 1975. 224 pp.

Beautiful photographs of the Holy Land.

Pentecost, J. Dwight. *Things to Come.* Findley, Ohio: Dunham Publishing Company, 1958. 633 pp.

A thorough presentation of biblical eschatology from a premillennial viewpoint. He discusses methods of interpretation, the covenants, rapture views, the Tribulation period, the Second Advent, the Millennium, the eternal state.

Peters, George N. H. *The Theocratic Kingdom.* 3 vols. Grand Rapids: Kregel Publications, 1883, rpt. 1957. 701, 780, 694 pp.

An exhaustive defense of the premillennial interpretation of Scripture.

Pfeiffer, Charles F. *The Biblical World.* Grand Rapids: Baker Book House, 1966. 612 pp.

A dictionary of biblical archaeology throughout the Near East.

Pfeiffer, Charles F., and Howard F. Vos. *The Wycliffe Historical Geography of Bible Lands.* Chicago: Moody Press, 1967. 588 pp. and color maps.

They cover Mesopotamia, Egypt, Palestine, Phoenicia, Syria, biblical Iran, Cyprus, Asia Minor, Greece, and Italy.

Porter, J. R. *The Illustrated Guide to the Bible.* New York: Oxford University Press, 1995. 288 pp.

A liberal survey of the biblical narratives in their "historical, social, archaeological, and mythological contexts."

Porter, R. F., S. Christensen, and P. Schiermacker-Hansen. *Field Guide to the Birds of the Middle East.* London: T and AD Poyser, 1996. 460 pp. (U.S. ed., San Diego: Academic Press, Inc., n.d.).

Sparrows (pp. 202–5).

Pough, Frederick H. *A Field Guide to Rocks and Minerals.* Boston: Houghton Mifflin Company, 1960. 349 pp.

A standard guide to mineral identification.

Reader's Digest Association, G. Ernest Wright, ed. consultant. *Great People of the Bible and How They Lived*. Pleasantville, N.Y.: Reader's Digest Association, 1974. 432 pp.

A popular description of biblical history and culture.

Reader's Digest Association, David Noel Freedman, ed. consultant. *Who's Who in the Bible*. Pleasantville, N.Y.: Reader's Digest Association, 1994. 480 pp.

Brief biographical sketches of Aaron to Zophar.

Richards, J. McDowell. *Soli Deo Gloria*. Richmond, Va.: John Knox Press, 1968. 160 pp.

An anthology in honor of William Childs Robinson, including "Jesus Is Lord" by F. F. Bruce; "Theological Persuasion" by Torrance; and others.

Rosten, Leo. *Treasury of Jewish Quotations*. New York: Bantam Books, 1980. 654 pp.

A collection of quotations such as, "If you want people to think you wise, just agree with them" (p. 140); "Plan for this world as if you expect to live forever; but plan for the hereafter as if you expect to die tomorrow" (p. 208).

Runes, Dagobert D. *The Talmud of Jerusalem*. New York: Philosophical Library, 1956. 160 pp.

An anthology of selections.

Ryle, J. C. *Holiness*. Durham, England: Evangelical Press, 1879, rpt. 1995. 324 pp.

"The Church Which Christ Builds" (Matt. 16:18; pp. 210ff.). Warm-hearted sermons.

Saphir, Adolph. *The Divine Unity of Scripture*. London: Hodder and Stoughton, 1892. 361 pp.

A warm-hearted defense of the power and unity of the Scriptures.

Schweizer, Eduard. *Lordship and Discipleship*. Naperville, Ill.: Alec R. Allenson, Inc., 1960. 136 pp.

A form critical study of the word *follow*. He admits that the old liberal idea of following Jesus' example is not a NT teaching (p. 99).

Scudder. Henry. *The Christian's Daily Walk*. Sprinkle Publications, rpt. 1984.

A Puritan devotional work.

Smith, Jerome H. *The New Treasury of Scripture Knowledge*. Nashville: Thomas Nelson, 1992. 1660 pp.

The most complete system of Bible cross-references in existence. There is no text; just cross references and helps.

Smith, Marsha A. Ellis. *Holman Book of Biblical Charts, Maps, and Reconstructions*. Nashville: Broadman and Holman Publishers, 1993. 176 pp.

She provides a reconstruction and ground plan of Herod's temple in Jerusalem (pp. 153–55).

Smith, Wilbur M. *Therefore Stand*. Boston: W. A. Wilds Co., 1945. 614 pp.

An apologetic for a vigorous defense of the Christian faith.

———. *The Biblical Doctrine of Heaven*. Chicago: Moody Press, 1968. 317 pp.

An investigation of the doctrine. He discusses liberal objections, heaven as the abode of God, the angels, the redeemed; "Occupations of the Redeemed in Heaven" (pp. 190–201). He provides appendixes on great hymns about heaven.

Stein, Robert H. *An Introduction to the Parables of Jesus*. Philadelphia: Westminster Press, 1981. 180 pp.

Preliminary studies on parables, covering why Jesus taught in parables (pp. 33f.), the authenticity of the parables (pp. 38f.), their interpretation (pp. 53ff.); emphasizes the kingdom as a present reality (pp. 82ff.), the kingdom as demand (pp. 98ff.), the God of the parables (pp. 115ff.), and the final judgment (pp. 130ff.).

Steveson, Peter. A. *Isaiah*. Greenville, S.C.: BJU Press, 2003. 574 pp.

A conservative exposition from a premillennial viewpoint.

Stonehouse, Ned. B. *The Infallible Word*. Philadelphia: Presbyterian and Reformed Publishing Company, 1968.

A defense of verbal inspiration.

Swete, Henry Barclay. *The Holy Spirit in the New Testament*. Grand Rapids: Baker, 1910, rpt. 1964. 417 pp.

A thought-provoking survey of the NT teaching about the Holy Spirit. He holds that the seven spirits of God refer to the one Holy Spirit of God (p. 274).

Tasker, R. V. G. *The Biblical Doctrine of the Wrath of God.* London: Tyndale Press, 1951. 48 pp.

He argues that all mankind stands under the wrath of God (p. 16); that God must visit wrath upon sin (p. 24); that the sacrifice of Christ alone can deliver from wrath (pp. 36–37); and that there will be a final day of wrath in which God's judgment will be poured out on the wicked (pp. 46–48).

Tenney, Merrill C. *The Reality of the Resurrection.* New York: Harper and Row, 1963. 221 pp.

A defense of the doctrine of the Resurrection based on the triumph of Christ over the grave. He notes the proclamation of the Resurrection in Acts and the Gospels (pp. 47ff.); shows the developing theology in Paul's Epistles, Hebrews, and John's writings (pp. 67ff.); goes on to show the emerging creed (pp. 91ff.).

Thomson, W. M. *The Land and the Book.* London: T. Nelson and Sons, 1888.

First-hand descriptions of customs and people in the Holy Land.

Thubron, Colin. *Jerusalem.* Amsterdam: Time-Life Books, 1976. 200 pp.

Text and photographs of porters (pp. 26–27), the Wailing Wall (pp. 46–47, 52), shepherd and sheep (pp. 64–65), the Armenian church of St. James (pp. 110–11), Dome of the Rock (pp. 126–35), Mea Shearim (pp. 164–71).

Torrey, Reuban Archer. *What the Bible Teaches.* New York: Revell, 1898, 1933. 539 pp.

A thorough presentation of what the Bible teaches in propositions about God (pp. 13ff.), Christ (pp. 68ff.), the Holy Spirit (pp. 225ff.), man (pp. 293ff.), angels (pp. 501ff.), the Devil (pp. 513ff.).

Tozer, A. W. *The Pursuit of God.* Harrisburg, Pa.: Christian Publications, 1948. 128 pp.

A warm-hearted book that encourages believers to follow hard after God.

Trench, Richard Chenevix. *Synonyms of the New Testament*. Grand Rapids: Eerdmans, 1880, rpt. 1953. 405 pp.

A study of more than a hundred groups of synonyms, with careful distinctions among them.

————. *The Parables of Our Lord*. Grand Rapids: Baker, 1861, 1948. 211 pp.

Old, but reverent studies.

Tyndale, William. *The Parable of the Wicked Mammon*. See Philip Hughes, *The Theology of the English Reformers*.

Unger, Merrill. *Biblical Demonology*. Wheaton, Ill.: Van Kampen Press, 1952. 250 pp.

He defends the reality of demons (pp. 35ff.), demon possession (pp. 77ff.), magic (pp. 107ff.), divination (pp. 119ff.), necromancy (pp. 143ff.), and so forth.

United Bible Societies. *Fauna and Flora of the Bible*. United Bible Societies, 1972. 207 pp.

Helps for translators, vol. XI.

Van der Toorn, Karel, Bob Becking, and Pieter van der Horst, eds. *Dictionary of Deities and Demons in the Bible*, 2 ed. Leiden: Brill, 1999. 960 pp.

A list of supernatural beings mentioned in the Bible. Although there is strong liberal bias in the work, the article on "Satan" (pp. 726–32) provides valuable historical information.

Vincent, Marvin R. *Word Studies in the New Testament*. 4 vols. Grand Rapids: Eerdmans, 1887, rpt. 1946.

He covers Matthew in vol. I, pp. 9–152. He distinguishes between *sickness, disease, torments*, and other terms (pp. 31–32); explains the place of tolls (p. 55).

Walvoord, John F. *Major Bible Prophecies*. Grand Rapids: Zondervan, 1991. 450 pp.

Studies in 37 crucial prophetic passages. He covers the Sermon on the Mount (pp. 192ff.), the mysteries of the kingdom of heaven (pp. 205ff.).

————. *The Holy Spirit*. Wheaton, Ill.: Van Kampen Press, 1954. 275 pp.

A study in the person and work of the Holy Spirit.

Warfield, Benjamin B. *The Inspiration and Authority of the Bible.* Philadelphia: Presbyterian and Reformed Publishing Company, 1948. 442 pp.

A formal defense of the verbal inspiration of Scripture.

Warry, John. *Warfare in the Classical World.* New York: Barnes and Noble, 1993. 224 pp.

A popular study of warfare from Homer to imperial Rome. The drawings of the soldiers and the diagrams of the structure of the legions are helpful (pp. 186–87).

Webster, Graham. *The Roman Imperial Army.* New York: Barnes and Noble, 1969, 1979. 334 pp.

A thorough discussion of the Roman legions, their camps and fortresses, and their deployment throughout the empire.

Wenham, David. *The Parables of Jesus.* Downers Grove, Ill.: InterVarsity Press, 1989. 256 pp.

He stresses studying the context (pp. 14ff.); includes parabolic teaching from John's Gospel as well (p. 19); shows that some parables teach the revolutionary nature of Jesus' teaching (pp. 28ff.); stresses that the parables are about the kingdom of God (pp. 43ff.); in Appendix 1 he defends the authenticity of the parables (pp. 213ff.).

Westcott, Brooke Foss. *The Epistle to the Hebrews.* Grand Rapids: Eerdmans, 1955. 588 pp.

A thorough commentary on the Greek text of Hebrews, with notes on special subjects such as blessing (pp. 203–6).

Whyte, Alexander. *Bible Characters.* 6 vols. London: Oliphants, n.d.

Memorable sermons by a famous Scottish preacher. Vol. 4 covers "Joseph and Mary to James, the Lord's Brother."

———. *Lancelot Andrews and His Private Devotions.* Edinburgh: Oliphants, Anderson and Ferrier, 1896. 232 pp.

Powerful, moving prayers by a translator of the KJV.

Wilkinson, John. *Jerusalem as Jesus Knew It.* London: Thames and Hudson, 1978. 208 pp.

A study of the places that Jesus walked that are still visible amid the ruins of today's city. There are photos of the Phasael Tower (p. 55), the Pool of Bethesda (p. 60), the steps by the Church of St. Peter in Gallicantu (p. 62), and others.

Young, Edward J. *My Servants the Prophets*. Grand Rapids: Eerdmans, 1952. 231 pp.

He surveys their divine origin, the terminology for them, the schools of the prophets, the NT references.

Young, Edward J. *Thy Word Is Truth*. Grand Rapids: William B. Eerdmans Publishing Company, 1957.

A readable yet scholarly defense of the verbal inspiration of Scripture.

Zahn, Theodor. *Introduction to the New Testament*. 3 vols. Grand Rapids: Kregel Publications, 1953. 564, 617, 539 pp.

He defends the traditional authorship of Matthew (II, pp. 386ff.).

Zohary, Michael. *Plants of the Bible*. Cambridge: Cambridge University Press, 1982. 223 pp.

Beautiful color photographs of every plant mentioned. He covers the olive, carob, almond, watermelon, muskmelon, acanthus, mandrake, and many others.

SCRIPTURE INDEX

Topical Summary Index